Handbook on Animal-Assisted Therapy

Handbook on Animal-Assisted Therapy

THEORETICAL FOUNDATIONS AND GUIDELINES FOR PRACTICE

Edited by

Aubrey H. Fine

School of Education and Integrative Studies
California State Polytechnic University
Pomona, California

ACADEMIC PRESS
A Harcourt Science and Technology Company

San Diego   San Francisco   New York   Boston   London   Sydney   Tokyo

This book is printed on acid-free paper.

Academic Press
a division of Harcourt Brace & Company
525 B Street, Suite 1900, San Diego, California 92101-4495, USA
http://www.apnet.com

Academic Press
24-28 Oval Road, London NW1 7DX, UK
http://www.hbuk.co.uk/ap/

Library of Congress Catalog Card Number: 99-62845

International Standard Book Number: 0-12-256475-8

PRINTED IN THE UNITED STATES OF AMERICA
99 00 01 02 03 04 ML 9 8 7 6 5 4 3 2 1

To Puppy, Hart, and Snowflake,
who have been inspirational in extending my abilities
to work with others,

and to my son,
Corey.
Our love and work with animals have strengthened
our relationship.
You are the sparkle in my eyes.

CONTENTS

SECTION **I**

The Conceptualization of the Animal–Human Bond: The Foundation for Understanding Animal-Assisted Therapy

SECTION II

Animal-Assisted Therapy: Conceptual Model and Guidelines for Quality Assurance

5 Methods, Standards, Guidelines, and Considerations in Selecting Animals for Animal-Assisted Therapy

PART A

Understanding Animal Behavior, Species, and Temperament as Applied to Interactions with Specific Populations

Lynette A. Hart

PART **B**

Guidelines and Standards for Animal Selection in Animal-Assisted
Activity and Therapy Programs

Maureen Fredrickson and Ann R. Howie

6 Designing and Implementing Animal-Assisted
Therapy Programs in Health and Mental
Health Organizations

Gerald P. Mallon, Samuel B. Ross, Jr., and Lisa Ross

7 Program Evaluation and Quality Assurance in Animal-Assisted Therapy

Mary R. Burch

SECTION **III**

Best Practices in Animal-Assisted Therapy:
Guidelines for Use of AAT
with Special Populations

8 **The Centaur's Lessons: Therapeutic Education**
   through Care of Animals and Nature Study
   Aaron Honori Katcher and Gregory G. Wilkins

9 **Animals and Therapists: Incorporating Animals in**
   Outpatient Psychotherapy
   Aubrey H. Fine

10 Animal-Assisted Therapy in Specialized Settings

Ben P. Granger and Lori Kogan

11 The Role Animals Play in Enhancing Quality of Life for the Elderly

Mara M. Baun and Barbara W. McCabe

12 History, Theory, and Development of Human–Animal Support Services for People with AIDS and Other Chronic/Terminal Illnesses

Kenneth Gorczyca, Aubrey H. Fine, and C. Victor Spain

13 Service Animals and Their Roles in Enhancing Independence, Quality of Life, and Employment for People with Disabilities

Susan L. Duncan and Karen Allen

14 Animal Abuse and Developmental Psychopathology: Recent Research, Programmatic, and Therapeutic Issues and Challenges for the Future

Frank R. Ascione, Michael E. Kaufmann, and Susan M. Brooks

SECTION **IV**

Special Topics and Concerns in
Animal-Assisted Therapy

15 The Companion Animal within the Family System: The Manner in Which Animals Enhance Life within the Home

Sandra Lookabaugh Triebenbacher

16 Companion Animals and the Development of Children: Implications of the Biophilia Hypothesis

Gail F. Melson

17 Nature Therapy

Linda Nebbe

18 The Welfare of Assistance and Therapy Animals: An Ethical Comment

James Serpell, Raymond Coppinger, and Aubrey H. Fine

19 Synergy and Symbiosis in Animal-Assisted Therapy: Interdisciplinary Collaborations

Phil Arkow

20 **The Future of Education and Research on the Animal–Human Bond and Animal-Assisted Therapy**

PART **A**

The Role of Ethology in the Field of Human–Animal Relations and Animal-Assisted Therapy

Dennis C. Turner

PART **B**

Animal-Assisted Therapy and the Study of Human–Animal Relationships: Discipline or Bondage? Context or Transitional Object?

Aaron Honori Katcher

CONTRIBUTORS

Numbers in parentheses indicate the pages on which the authors' contributions begin.

KAREN ALLEN (303), School of Medicine, State University of New York at Buffalo, Buffalo, New York 14214

PHIL ARKOW (433), Chair, Family Violence Prevention Project The Latham Foundation, Stratford, New Jersey 08084

FRANK R. ASCIONE (325), Department of Psychology, Utah State University, Logan, Utah 84322

MARA M. BAUN (237), College of Nursing, University of Nebraska Medical Center, Omaha, Nebraska 68198

ALAN M. BECK (21), Center for the Human–Animal Bond, School of Veterinary Medicine, Purdue University, West Lafayette, Indiana 47907

SUSAN M. BROOKS (325), Green Chimneys, Brewster, New York 10509

MARY R. BURCH (129), Behavior Management Consultants, Inc., Tallahassee, Florida 32308

RAYMOND COPPINGER (415), Department of Clinical Studies, Center for the Interaction of Animals and Society, University of Pennsylvania School of Veterinary Medicine, Philadelphia, Pennsylvania 19104

SUSAN L. DUNCAN (303), Delta Society National Service Dog Center, Renton, Washington 98055

AUBREY H. FINE (179, 253, 415), School of Education and Integrative Studies, California State Polytechnic University, Pomona, California 91768

MAUREEN FREDRICKSON (99), Delta Society, Renton, Washington 98055

ERIKA FRIEDMANN (41), Department of Health and Nutrition Sciences, Brooklyn College of CUNY, Brooklyn, New York 11210

KENNETH GORCZYCA (253), Pets Are Wonderful Support, San Francisco, California 94114

BEN P. GRANGER (213), Department of Social Work, Colorado State University, Fort Collins, Colorado 80523

LYNETTE A. HART (59, 81), Center for Animals in Society, School of Veterinary Medicine, University of California, Davis, California 95616

ANN R. HOWIE (99), Delta Society, Renton, Washington 98055

AARON HONORI KATCHER (153, 461), The Devereux Foundation, Villanova, Pennsylvania 19085 and University of Pennsylvania, Philadelphia, Pennsylvania 19103

MICHAEL E. KAUFMANN (325), American Humane Association, Englewood, Colorado 80112

LORI KOGAN (213), Department of Psychology, Colorado State University, Fort Collins, Colorado 80523

GERALD P. MALLON (115), Hunter College School of Social Work, City University of New York, New York, New York 10021

BARBARA W. McCABE (237), College of Nursing, University of Nebraska Medical Center, Omaha, Nebraska 68198

GAIL F. MELSON (375), Purdue University, West Lafayette, Indiana 47907

LINDA NEBBE (385), Department of Education: Counselor Education, Drake University, Des Moines, Iowa 50311

LISA ROSS (115), Green Chimneys Children's Services, Brewster, New York 10509

SAMUEL B. ROSS, JR. (115), Green Chimneys Children's Services, Brewster, New York 10509

JAMES A. SERPELL (3, 415), Center for the Interaction of Animals and Society, Department of Clinical Studies, School of Veterinary Medicine, University of Pennsylvania, Philadelphia, Pennsylvania 19104

C. VICTOR SPAIN (253), College of Veterinary Medicine, Cornell University, Ithaca, New York 14853

SANDRA LOOKABAUGH TRIEBENBACHER (357), Department of Child Development and Family Relations, East Carolina University, Greenville, North Carolina 27858

DENNIS C. TURNER (449), Institute for applied Ethology and Animal Psychology, Hirzel, and Zoology Institute, University of Zurich–Irchel, 8816 Hirzel, Switzerland

GREGORY G. WILKINS (153), William Penn School District, Lansdowne, Pennsylvania 19050

FOREWORD

I. INTRODUCTION

This foreword has developed in rather atypical ways. In 1981, Boris Levinson set out some challenges for those working on human–animal interactions, and one of us (ANR) responded to this challenge by developing some observations that reviewed what had been done in the field since 1981. It also seemed appropriate to provide some historical context for Levinson's comments. Finally, a foreword should comment on the contents of the book it introduces, and so we include some remarks on the various chapters and how they might be perceived in light of Levinson's challenge.

II. HISTORICAL CONTEXT

Most people date the beginning of the modern interest in human–animal interactions research to Boris Levinson's first paper on the subject published in *Mental Hygiene* (Levinson, 1962) entitled "The Dog as a 'Co-Therapist.'" However, an earlier paper published in *Mental Hygiene* in 1944 by James H. S. Bossard also addressed the therapeutic value of dog ownership. He discussed the important role that domestic animals play "in family life and in the mental health of its members, with particular reference to the children in the family" (p. 408) from a sociological as well as a layperson's perspective. Based on personal observation and case studies, Bossard listed a number of "roles" that the family pet may play. He described the animal as a source of unconditional love; as an outlet for people's desire to express love; as fulfilling a human's desire for exercising power; as a "teacher" of children on topics such as toilet training, sex education, and responsibility; as social lubricants; and as companions.

In 1950, Bossard published a follow-up article in *Mental Hygiene* entitled "I Wrote About Dogs." The original article had caught the eye of a New York *Sun* editor, who reprinted it. It was reprinted by a number of major newspapers, veterinary journals, and animal welfare publications. The National Committee for Mental Hygiene sold more than 1500 reprints. Over a 5-year period, Bossard received 1033 letters asking for reprints or referring to his original article. The author notes that "[a]lthough I contributed more than a hundred articles to a variety of journals, many of them dealing with controversial issues and all of them confined to the field of human relations, no other article has brought forth such a flood of letters. The nearest approach was an article on family table talk, which yielded exactly twenty-five letters from readers" (Bossard, 1950, p. 387).

Bossard (1950) concludes in his second article:

> The responses to the original publication of the article were so frank, so spontaneous, and from such a large segment of the population, representing such a wide range of social strata, as to leave no doubt that the love of animals by humans is one of the universals in the existence of both. Household pets are an integral part of family life; they must be considered as a basic implement in mental hygiene.

There is no evidence that the public fondness for companion animals has diminished since the late 1940s.

Levinson (1962), a child psychologist, extended Bossard's idea of the health value of an animal from the household to a therapeutic setting. However, his promotion of "pet-therapy" or "pet-oriented child psychotherapy" or "human/companion animal therapy" (all terms that he coined for his work) was met with cynicism and disdain by many colleagues. It was reported that one member of a professional audience to which Levinson presented his thesis asked: "Do you share your fee with the dog?" (Beck & Katcher, 1983, p. 166). The situation has not changed that much since the mid-1970s, despite much more research and some supporting data.

In one analysis of citations to landmark papers in the field of animal-assisted therapy (AAT), it was shown that very few citations came from public health or medical professionals outside the immediate narrow confines of the field itself (Rowan, 1995). Mostly, the people who cite papers are drawn from the same group of researchers who have long been interested in the issue. In other words, citation records tend to be circular and internal to the group. In addition, most studies are performed on small sample sizes or are relatively superficial, reflecting the fact that there is very little funding support for studies in the field. Most of the significant literature in the field has come from studies that are piggy-backed on existing projects (e.g., Anderson *et al.*, 1992) or are supported by foundations or individuals that develop an interest in the field (e.g., the papers coming from Lago *et al.*, 1983, at Pennsylvania State University, or the paper on service dogs by Allen & Blascovich, 1996).

There have been several significant reviews of the field. In 1984, Alan Beck and Aaron Katcher published a critical review in which they conclude that the available literature on pet therapy consisted almost exclusively of descriptive or hypothesis-generating studies. The contribution by Levinson and those of other pioneers were based on observations and case studies rather than on designed experiments. "Their work provides evidence justifying serious scientific exploration of the ability of pets to facilitate more conventional therapy, not evidence demonstrating a therapeutic effect of animals" (Beck & Katcher, 1984, p. 415). The article cites a number of anecdotal and/or undocumented accounts of the remarkable results of introducing animals to individuals with specific emotional or physical impairments.

Beck and Katcher report that they were only able to find six experimental studies of the therapeutic value of pets in which control groups were used. Of the six studies, only one showed a measurable benefit of pets—the Mugford and M'Comisky trial placement study (1975). However, the number of subjects in the study sample was too small to claim a statistically significant finding. (It is interesting to note that this study continues to be cited as a landmark example of the benefits of pets, despite the shortcomings of the statistical analysis.) The other five studies showed insignificant or no positive results from the presence of animals.

In their same article, Beck and Katcher move on to review the literature on the association between pet ownership and health, concluding that the key studies were not entirely convincing. County surveys of older women in Maryland (Ory & Goldberg, 1983) and families in California (Franti et al., 1980) found income to be the determining factor in the measured degree of good health, as opposed to the presence or absence of pets. Surveys conducted by Akiyima et al. (1986), Lago et al. (1983), and Robb and Stegman (1983) also did not report support for the claim that pet ownership is a factor in promoting good health.

The most cited of the longitudinal studies, a means of measuring lasting effects, is the 1980 Friedmann et al. study, which looked at the survival rate of coronary patients 1 year after discharge. Beck and Katcher (a co-author on Friedmann's study) note a critique by Wright and Moore, who argue that personality type studies have shown "personality type A" to be a significant indicator of heart disease. However, it was later reported that there was no health outcome difference between pet owners and non–pet owners among personality type A subjects (Collis & McNicholas, 1998).

Beck and Katcher concluded in the 1984 review that no other longitudinal studies have proved pet ownership to improve health and well-being. In the blood pressure studies, it has been demonstrated that although blood pressure drops by a small but consistent and measurable amount while a subject is in the presence of an animal, "[n]o study has shown sustained reductions in blood pressure as the result of pet ownership" (1984, p. 418). In their conclusion, Beck and Katcher note that a "clear distinction should be made between emotional response to animals, that is, their recreational use, and therapy. It should not be concluded that any event that is enjoyed by the patients is a kind of therapy" (1984, p. 419).

Levinson was aware of the problems and many unanswered questions surrounding animal-facilitated therapy at the second international HAB conference in 1981 at the University of Pennsylvania. In his talk on the future needs in the field, he outlined the following four areas of research that needed more attention:

1. The role of animals in various human cultures and ethnic groups over the centuries
2. The effect of association with animals on human personality development
3. Human–animal communication
4. The therapeutic use of animals in formal psychotherapy, institutional settings, and residential arrangements for handicapped and aged populations (Levinson, 1983, p. 283).

III. LEVINSON'S CHALLENGE AND RESULTS SINCE 1981

A. THE ROLE OF ANIMALS IN VARIOUS HUMAN CULTURES AND ETHNIC GROUPS OVER THE CENTURIES

Animals have appeared in structural–functional anthropological analyses such as those by Claude Levi-Strauss (1992, animals are good to think) and Edward Leach (1964, animal terms as words of abuse). In recent years, however, there has been an explosion of anthropological and sociological interest in the roles played by animals in human society and culture. Over the past few decades, researchers have tended to explore the human–animal relationship from more metaphorical and psychosocial perspectives than either Levi-Strauss or Leach.

For example, there have been studies of the symbolism of animals in recreation such as bullfights (e.g., Marvin, 1987) and the rodeo (a masterful study by Lawrence, 1984). Each author theorizes how the animal represents an extension of the human group engaged in the activity. The machismo of the matador is emphasized by his being able to overcome the powerful, male figure of the bull even as he (the matador) is arrayed in a very feminine and dandified costume. In rodeo, the bucking bronco represents the wild animal that must be brought under the control of the intrepid cowboy. Paradoxically, the cowboy admires and respects the wild animal, yet is bent on taming it and changing nature to a more domesticated (and, to the cowboy, less admirable) form.

Other studies have explored the role of animals in modern human society. Arnold Arluke published a fascinating set of articles that explore the ethnography of animal research. He concludes that the use of animals in laboratories leads to significant psychological tension among those who care for and use the animals in their studies.

Another intriguing analysis is the Arluke and Sax (1992) exploration of Nazis and their relationship to animals. The authors examine the advocacy of animal welfare by the Nazi regime and the apparent contrast of the Nazis' treatment of various categories of humans. Arluke and Sax conclude that the Nazis had no internally consistent cosmology, but they tended to include animals (or some animals) in a hierarchy of categories for both animals and people in which "racial purity" was a primary factor. Thus, animals such as wolves that represent "pure" wildness are ranked higher than peoples such as Jews, gypsies, and the handicapped, who were considered to be impure or defective in some way.

There have been a number of interesting studies of animal roles and images in literature, television, advertising, and cartoons, and animal characters appear to be playing more central roles in fiction (and not just fiction aimed at children). Elizabeth Lawrence (1986) discusses the neotenization of animal imagery as a means of dominion as exemplified by such major cultural icons as Mickey Mouse. Mickey and his cohorts are juvenilized in appearance to evoke a sense of maternalistic love as opposed to equal respect. Daniel Quinn's (1995) *Ishmael* is a direct contrast to this neotenization and has developed a significant following on campuses. The story has a gorilla in the role of teacher and a human in the role of student.

Sociologically, one of the most important studies since the late 1970s is Stephen Kellert's (1980) survey of American attitudes toward animals. Using his survey data, he developed 10 different typologies of attitudes toward animals that appear in American society (and that can seemingly also be found in many other cultures). At the time of his survey, he reported that the two most prevalent attitudes in American society were (1) "humanistic"—associated with pets, wildlife tourism, and casual zoo visitation and (2) "neutralistic"—associated with the avoidance of animals. Each typology could be identified in about 35% of the American population. However, he also reported that attitude frequencies do change with time and there may be considerable overlap between different typologies.

In recent historical studies, authors such as Salisbury (1994), Ritvo (1987), and Thomas (1983) trace a steady increase in human sensibility to animal pain and suffering from the classical era through the medieval period and into modern times. From another perspective, Darnton (1985) analyzes a cat massacre in 18th-century Paris. Darnton argues that the cats are slaughtered as a ruse and he uses the incident as a means to explore human–human interactions. The analysis also illuminates attitudes about animals and the symbolic roles they play. Echoing themes raised by Levi-Strauss and Leach, Darnton notes that "[c]ertain animals are good for swearing, just as they are 'good for thinking' . . . " (1985, p. 11). Darnton's analysis also indicates how cats have shifted from mysterious, sinister, and taboo creatures to icons of cute and comfortable domesticity.

Numerous other academic disciplines could be highlighted. Philosophically, more has been written on the moral status of animals since the late 1960s than in the previous 2000 years. Domestication is another major topic that has been slighted in this brief overview. In sociology, Arluke and Sanders (1997) repeated the call for more attention from sociologists, who continue a tendency to define animals as being outside human society and culture. Robert Garner and other authors discuss the political science of animal issues and the animal protection movement, and legal scholars have written about the jurisprudence of animals and animal law.

B. The Effect of Association with Animals on Human Personality Development

Boris Levinson (1970, p. 1759) advocated that companion animals might serve not only as a means of reaching out therapeutically to emotionally disturbed children, but also as assisting in the healthy development of a child:

> Pets decrease alienation by providing communication with nature—contact, comfort, and companionship. Pets may play a crucial role in a child's emotional development and abort mental illness, particularly in homes devoid of affection and emotional security. The pet may thus become the touchstone with which the child approaches himself and reality. Love for the pet creates a relationship of mutual trust and confidence while building a bridge to the future and to greater self-awareness.

In many of Levinson's papers, he continues to note the value of pets in one's ego development.

Measuring the effect of personality development is probably even harder than measuring the effect of a companion animal's emotional or physiological impact, and funding for such work has been rather limited. Therefore, this type of research has not been developed to a great degree since Levinson's 1981 challenge. Aline and Robert Kidd published a number of studies of the effect of companion animals on children as well as children's attitudes toward animals. Kidd and Kidd (1996) investigated children's development of attitudes toward wildlife compared to domestic animals, hypothesizing that children move through the same Piagetian stages for both categories of animals. Through interviews and observations of 102 parents and 102 children (3–12 years old), the researchers found that a similar developmental staging does occur. Kidd and Kidd also attempt to study the differences in attitudes toward animals in different age groups, and whether and how pet ownership has affected them (cf. Hart, 1993).

Others who have also studied the impact of companion animals on the development of children include Gail Melson, Brenda Bryant, and Robert Poresky. Ascione and Weber (1996), studying a group of children who attended a year-long school-based humane education program, found a higher mean for humane attitudes than for a control group, even a year after the program ended. Furthermore, the enhanced "attitudes toward animals generalized to human-directed empathy—especially when the quality of the children's relations with their pets was considered as a covariate" (p. 188).

Paul and Serpell (1996) attempted to determine the effects of a new pet dog on children in middle childhood and their families. However, the study focused more on impacts such as family interaction and association with friends—which might likely have a bearing on personality development—rather than actual development in and of itself. Gene Myers (1998) completed an ethnographic study of children in a nursery school and their relationship with pet animals in the classroom. In his observations, he notes that the children displayed a special relationship and understanding of animals through pretend play and in preverbal as well as verbal experience.

Using attitudes toward animals as a personality indicator, Kidd and Kidd (1980) attempt to measure personality differences between pet cat and dog owners. They found cat lovers scored lower on nurturance and dog lovers scored higher on aggression and dominance than those in other groups. Selby and Rhoades (1981) also found age and gender factors in attitudes toward pet dogs and cats.

Frank Ascione, Randy Lockwood, Arnold Arluke, and Steven Kellert have all published important papers on a darker side of human–animal interaction—namely, the links between abuse of animals and abuse of humans. One publication edited by Randy Lockwood and Frank Ascione (1998) contains reprints of all the major papers in the field.

C. Human–Animal Communication

The field of human–animal communication may be divided into nonverbal forms of communication as well as more ambitious attempts to communicate with animals using symbols or specialized forms of human speech. In the first category, John Bradshaw and his group at the Anthrozoology Institute in Southampton, Dennis Turner in Switzerland, and Montagner and Filiatre in France have all studied human–companion animal interactions. These studies consist mostly of careful ethological projects and observations.

At the other end of the spectrum, the ape language studies of the Gardners, the Rumbaughs, and others challenge our ideas about animal cognition and the meaning of language. Although some theorists believe the capacity to use language is a distinctive divide between humans and the rest of the animal kingdom, language acquisition studies in apes have threatened that contention. These studies tend to support Charles Darwin's belief that the behavior of humans differs from the behavior of other animals in degree, not in kind.

The most rigorous studies of ape language have been conducted by Sue Savage-Rumbaugh. In 1981, Savage-Rumbaugh began to train a wild-caught female pygmy chimpanzee (*Pan paniscus*) using a lexigram system of symbols to express words and word sequences. Although the targeted chimp, Matata, never quite caught on, it was soon discovered that her adopted son, Kanzi, had been observing the lessons and learned many symbols. Kanzi subsequently showed an ability to understand not only lexigram symbols, but also verbalized English and the syntactical structure of sentences (Savage-Rumbaugh & Lewin, 1994).

Irene Pepperberg (1990) studied language development in gray parrots, who have the ability to mimic spoken human language. She has shown that a level of cognitive understanding of language exists. There are also studies of course on intraspecies communication between many species such as primates, whales, dolphins, elephants, wolves, ants, and bees, to name just a few. Donald Griffin is well known for his vanguard role in cognitive ethology, focusing in particular on the complex communication system of bees.

Many ordinary people, of course, claim first-hand experience in human–animal communication. Pet owners claim that their companion animal can understand them, and anecdotes abound of pet owners claiming that their pet knows when they are about to arrive home, or even more remarkable abilities. Animal trainers often display a special two-way communication system with their animal "co-workers." Sociologists Arnold Arluke and Clinton Sanders (1997) make a strong case for the importance of continuing to delve into the study of human–animal communication. They argue that it goes beyond "enlarging the corpus of sociological theory and method" and allows for a significant expansion of understanding how the mind works.

D. THE USE OF ANIMALS TO PROMOTE HUMAN HEALTH

As noted earlier, Beck and Katcher concluded in 1984 that, although animals may provide recreational benefits, there was little data supporting claims that pets induce long-term therapeutic benefits for improved emotional and physical well-being. Since their review, many other studies that attempt to measure the benefits gained by humans interacting with animals have been published. In general, such uses may be classified in one of two ways: (1) as providing specific therapy or (2) as promoting human health.

1. Animal-Assisted Therapy

In terms of the therapeutic benefits of animals, there is still relatively little strong evidence of a positive effect outside of the use of animals as icebreakers in psychotherapy (the way Levinson used his own dog) and the use of animal helpers for persons with physical disabilities (Allen & Blascovich, 1996). There are many anecdotes describing how an institutionalized individual responded positively to a therapy animal, but studies involving groups of patients have usually given disappointing results.

The Delta Society estimates that there are about 2000 AAT programs in the United States, with psychotherapy and physical rehabilitation using dogs being the most common. Holcomb and Meacham (1989) found the presence of animals in group activities in inpatient psychiatric units drew the highest percentage of voluntary attendance of solitary inpatients. Although their study acknowledged that attendance does not prove therapeutic effectiveness, it was found to be a successful means of drawing isolated individuals to group settings where they could be better evaluated. Perelle and Granville (1993) measured an increase in social behaviors of residents of a nursing home during a pet visitation program.

Crowley-Robinson et al. (1996) conducted a long-term, controlled study to evaluate the role of pets in a nursing home setting. Ninety-five elderly residents from three different nursing home environments (resident pet vs visiting pet vs no pet) were compared for dimensions of tension, depression, vigor, confusion, anger, and fatigue. The study commenced 4 months before a dog resided in/visited the nursing home, continued for 15 months with a dog's presence, and terminated 3 months following the removal of the dog. Reduced tension and confusion were most strongly associated with a resident dog, although a visiting dog or person also produced a similar response but to a lesser degree. Depression, vigor, and fatigue dropped for all three groups to some degree, which, the authors argue, signifies the benefit of a resident pet or a visiting pet or person.

Perhaps the results with the greatest potential impact are those reported by Allen and Blascovich (1996), who studied the effects of service-dog ownership for people with severe ambulatory disabilities. The researchers reported significant positive changes in psychological well-being, social interaction, and school attendance and/or part-time employment. Of particular interest to those who pay for the care of wheelchair-bound individuals is the authors report of a decline in both paid and unpaid assistance hours equivalent to a savings of about $55,000 over the working life of the dog.

Therapeutic riding programs and dolphin-assisted therapy are also being implemented. Nathanson (1998) studied the effects of the Dolphin Human Therapy program. He compared children with severe disabilities with many etiologies, from eight countries, after they had received either 1 or 2 weeks of therapy in the multidisciplinary behavior modification program. Nathanson found that:

1. Children maintained or improved the skills acquired in therapy about 50% of the time, even after 12 months away from therapy
2. There was no difference in long-term effects as a function of differences in categories of etiologies
3. About 2 weeks of therapy produced significantly better long-term results than did 1 week of therapy

In 1993, Nathanson and de Faria conducted a control study comparing responses of children with mental disabilities interacting in water with dolphins and interacting in water with favorite toys. The researchers found a significant improvement in hierarchical cognitive responses when the interaction involved a dolphin as compared to a favorite toy.

2. The Role of Companion Animals in Health Promotion

The keeping of companion animals is relatively expensive in terms of both time and financial commitments. Therefore, it is likely that there are some benefits to the keeping of companion animals that offset the costs. The question to be answered is: Do the benefits outweigh the costs and, if so, what are the benefits? We are still at a relatively early stage in determining benefits and understanding the mechanisms underlying these benefits. It might be suggested that animals may protect against stress (providing tactile affection), may promote socialization (through a social lubrication effect), may provide social support in themselves, or may diminish anxiety through some atavistic mechanism in which a calm animal is a signal of a safe environment. Various descriptive and experimental studies since the late 1970s have addressed one or more of these options.

Experimental studies have been designed to measure the social lubrication presence of animals. Given a basic tenet that, in most cases, people who have more interaction with other people have better emotional health, the interaction between people with pets and strangers is of interest. Sanders and Robins (1991) conducted a participant–observation study to determine the effect of the presence of a dog between unacquainted strangers. The authors concluded that, in public places, dogs expose their human companions to encounters with strangers, facilitate interaction among previously unacquainted persons, and help establish trust among the newly acquainted persons.

Hart *et al.* (1987) found similar results for people in wheelchairs who have service dogs. Steffens and Bergler (1998) conducted an empirical study of the effects of seeing-eye dogs. A cohort of 80 blind subjects revealed that both dog owners and nonowners found that seeing-eye dogs exceeded their expectations and were preferred over the use of canes or human chaperones (in Wilson & Turner, 1998). A complementary study by Hart *et al.* (1996) retrospectively studied the effects of hearing-dog ownership. Owners found a heightened sense of security, a lessened sense of loneliness, and increased social interaction with the hearing community.

A number of studies have examined targeted population groups as a means of understanding the value of pets for particular groups of individuals, especially individuals who may be isolated or disenfranchised in some way. For instance, Kidd and Kidd (1994) found that many homeless people had pets to which they felt great attachment. However, providing food and veterinary care was especially difficult. Batson *et al.* (1998) found "[t]he presence of [a] therapy dog enhanced nonverbal communication as shown by increases in looks, smiles, tactile contact, and physical warmth" in Alzheimer's patients (Wilson & Turner, 1998, p. 211). However, these behaviors declined 4 weeks posttest.

Zasloff and Kidd (1994) concluded that pet ownership is a means of diminishing feelings of loneliness, based on a study of adult female students, both pet owners and nonowners. This feeling of diminished loneliness may not correlate with increased organic health, however. Garrity *et al.* (1988) found that pet ownership alone did not correlate with either emotional or physical health status in a national sample group of elderly persons, although strong attachment to a pet was associated with less depression. This contrasted with findings by Miller and Lago (1990), who reported that pet ownership and attachment had little affect on the measured psychological or physical well-being among a group of elderly women.

A number of studies have followed up on the Friedmann *et al.* (1980) findings on the cardiovascular impact of pet ownership. Katcher *et al.* (1989) conducted an evaluation of a pet program in a prison and noted that the blood pressure of prisoners was lower when they were interacting with pets than when they were talking to experimenters. Grossberg *et al.* (1988) attempted to discern the specific activities associated with pets that caused lowered blood pressure. They reported that touching a dog lowered blood pressure more than talking to a dog. Allen *et al.* (1991) found that female subjects exhibited less physiological reactivity when performing a stressful task (arithmetic problems) in the presence of their pet dog than when alone in the presence of an experimenter or accompanied by a human friend.

One of the most significant studies to date of the evaluation of the affect of pet ownership on cardiovascular health was conducted by a group of Australian cardiologists (Anderson *et al.*, 1992). Data on more than 5000 clients who had signed up for a "healthy heart" project were analyzed over a 3-year period. Distinct differences were found between pet owners and nonowners. Pet-owning women older than 40 and male pet owners of all ages had lower blood pressures and 20% lower plasma triglyceride levels than did nonowners. Male pet owners between the ages of 30 and 60 had lower cholesterol levels than did nonowners. The researchers found no difference in exercise levels, body mass, or eating habits between the two groups.

General health surveys have been conducted to determine if pet ownership is associated with an increased level of well-being. Serpell (1991) conducted a prospective study in the changes of behavior of 71 adults following their acquisition of a pet (dog or cat) as compared to a nonmatching control group of 26 adults. Both the dog and cat owners reported a reduction in minor health problems (of the order of 50%) during the first month following acquisition. In dog owners, the health effects were maintained for the full 10-month period of the study. Both pet owner groups also demonstrated improvements in psychological well-being after the first 6 months. These improvements persisted in dog owners for the full 10 months. The dog owners fared better overall than the cat owners, who fared better than the control group.

Siegel (1990) reviewed a group of 938 elderly Medicare enrollees. Controlling for demographic characteristics and health status at baseline, Siegel found that pet owners reported fewer doctor contacts over a 1-year period than did nonowners. Siegel notes that there are similarities in the findings of pet ownership studies and human social support studies. She also noted that it is not clear whether the observed results are due to the promotion of general well-being because of the pet presence as opposed to a protective impact of the pet's presence during critical periods of stress.

It is open to question whether people who choose to interact with pets are healthier to begin with. Tucker *et al.* (1995) explored this question by studying a group of older noninstitutionalized individuals, comparing a number of health-related characteristics between those who choose to play with pets and those who choose not to. The researchers found no association between health status and choice of pet interaction, thus increasing confidence that "association between human–pet interaction and health is due to the human–pet interaction itself, rather than to a self-selection bias" (p. 6).

One review of the literature in the 1990s has been published (Garrity & Stallones, 1998) and, although this review was somewhat different from the Beck and Katcher (1984) paper, the authors found similar patterns. The authors were interested in the impact of animals on human quality of life, and in particular on how social support concepts (direct impact vs a buffering of life stress) have been used. They identified more than 100 papers examining the effects of animals on human health published between 1990 and 1995 and excluded all papers dealing with child development, the use of animals as therapeutic adjuncts, and bereavement issues. Twenty-five published papers met their criteria (Table I).

Garrity and Stallones (1998) conclude that this collection of papers does not represent an overwhelming endorsement of the notion that companion animals provide important health benefits given the tendency to publish papers reporting positive outcomes. Nonetheless, they believe that the studies were broadly consistent with findings on the impact of social support in the human literature. The findings indicated that the benefits of companion animals were apparent in specific circumstances and suggest that companion animal association probably benefits a person both directly and through a buffering mechanism. They concluded that future research should be directed at identifying the special moderating factors that influence when companion animals play a beneficial role.

In summary, there have been a few studies that reported interesting associations between companion animal ownership and human health. The main problem has been a lack of significant research funding to support the further exploration of such findings. However, on a more positive note, the Midland Life Insurance Company, headquartered in Columbus, Ohio, announced that it is including living with a companion animal as one of the factors seniors can list as part of a healthy lifestyle. This provides policyholders with the potential to reduce their rates (Anonymous, 1998).

3. How Does This Book Address Levinson's Challenge?

For the most part, this book focuses mainly on the therapeutic use of animals. In fact, it would be unfair to expect any single book to provide a comprehensive response to Levinson. A detailed discussion of the research since 1981 on the

TABLE I   Characteristics of Papers ($n = 25$) Assessing the Impact of Animal Companionship on Human Quality of Life, 1990–1995[a]

Type of paper	Type of well-being studied	Outcome[b]
4—Descriptive	11—Psychological	16 +ve
16—Correlational	6—Behavioral	11 −ve
5—Experimental	7—Physical/physiological	
	2—Social	

[a] From Garrity & Stallones, 1998.
[b] Some papers reported both +ve and −ve.

cultural and symbolic roles of animals in human society would fill numerous volumes by itself. However, there are chapters that touch on some of these issues in interesting ways. For example, Serpell explores the role animals play in health and disease in different cultures and over different periods. These include animistic and shamanistic cultures and how some modern superstitions and attitudes may be derived from shamanistic beliefs. He is, however, the only one to discuss cultural issues in any detail.

Levinson's second category deals with the role animals play in the development of human personality, and several of the chapters deal directly or indirectly with this issue. Melson, Serpell, Triebenbacher, and Ascione, Kaufman, and Brooks all address this topic from slightly different perspectives. Melson use biophilia as a theoretical framework, whereas Serpell discusses the social support impact of animals. Triebenbacher uses a family life stage approach, whereas Ascione and coauthors discuss the links between violence toward animals and violence toward people.

Only one paper, that by Turner, discusses human–animal communication. Turner has long used ethological methods to examine human–cat interactions, and he provides a summary of findings from this corpus of research and suggest that there is much more that could be learned from extensions of ethological study of human–animal interactions.

With the exception of Nebbe, whose chapter deals with nature therapy, the remaining papers all deal with Levinson's final category—namely, the use of animals in therapeutic settings or in the promotion of human health. Serpell provides one theoretical approach at the beginning of the book (animals as providers of social support), whereas Katcher provides another possible theoretical approach at the end of the book. Katcher, like Melson, uses the concept of biophilia and an idea about transitional objects to make some observations and predictions about AAT.

The majority of the chapters concerned with AAT consist of descriptive or prescriptive (how-to) material rather than critical reviews of what we know about AAT. Beck, who co-authored with Katcher the important 1984 review of AAT studies, devotes major sections of his review to ethical issues. Friedmann provides a critical overview of long- and short-term cardiovascular health impacts and Serpell discusses data from studies dealing with social support. The chapters on elderly patients (Baun and McCabe), on patients with chronic illnesses (Gorczyca, Fine, and Spain), and on service animals (Duncan and Allen) include sections reviewing earlier studies, including the important study on the impact of service animals by Allen and Blascovich, but most of these three chapters are prescriptive and descriptive.

The chapters by Granger and Kogan (AAT in Specialized Settings), Hart, Frederickson, and Howie (AAT Activity and Guidelines), Mallon, Ross, and Ross (AAT at Green Chimneys), and Burch (AAT and Program Evaluation) are mainly descriptive and prescriptive. We strongly agree with Burch's call for more program evaluation but, after years of such urging, we suspect that most of the current AAT programs will continue without any serious attempt to evaluate outcomes. For most, the immediate responses obtained from institutional residents or staff are sufficiently rewarding that further evaluation is deemed unnecessary. However, I (ANR) was delighted to see several case studies of AAT presented in this book (e.g., those described by Fine and by Ascione, Kaufman, and Brooks) and I suspect that this book will virtually double the number of case studies in the published literature.

IV. CONCLUSION

As an added note, Levinson (1983, p. 284) not only highlighted the previously mentioned four areas of scientific investigation, but also promoted the importance of intuitive study:

> On one hand, this discipline [of human/companion animal/environment interrelationships] touches upon problems that might well be investigated by rigorous, scientific experimentation. On the other hand, it involves enquiry [sic] where measurement cannot bring answers and intuition must reign—a path of study used by artists, as well as by generations of ordinary people. Both approaches are, in my opinion, equally valid and equally worthwhile.

Anecdotal, unique, and magical experiences with animals are often the major reason people become involved with animals and in the study of human–animal relations. The very fact that so many people responded so strongly to Bossard's article in 1944 confirms the attraction of the field. We may not know why we are drawn to animals, but we may have some evolutionary knowledge, even if buried in the unconscious, of the true value and advantage of our association with another species (Kellert & Wilson, 1995). Animals not only may be good thinking, but also may be good to spend time with.

In conclusion, we welcome the appearance of this volume and hope that it will provide another benchmark volume of AAT that both scientists and practitioners will find useful in their work and studies.

Andrew N. Rowan
Humane Society of the United States, Washington, DC

Lori Thayer
Department of Anthropology, University of Massachusetts, Amherst, Massachusetts

REFERENCES

Akiyama, H., Holtzman, J. M., & Britz, W. E. (1986). Pet ownership and health status during bereavement. *Omega* 17, 187–193.

Allen, K. M., & Blascovich, J. (1996). The value of service dogs for people with severe ambulatory difficulties. *Journal of the American Medical Association, 275*, 1001–1006.

Allen, K. M., Blascovich, J., Tomaka, J., & Kelsey, R. (1991). Presence of human friends and pet dogs as moderators of autonomic responses to stress in women. *Journal of Personality and Social Psychology, 61*, 582–589.

Anderson, W. P., Reid, C. M., & Jennings, G. L. (1992). Pet ownership and risk factors for cardiovascular disease. *Medical Journal of Australia, 157*, 298–301.

Anonymous (1998). *The Animal Policy Report,* Sept. 1998.

Arluke, A. (1988). Sacrificial symbolism in animal experimentation: Object or pet? *Anthrozoös, 2*, 98–117.

Arluke, A., & Sanders, C. (1997). *Regarding Animals.* Philadelphia: Temple University Press.

Arluke, A., & Sax, B. (1992). Understanding Nazi animal protection and the Holocaust. *Anthrozoös, 5*, 6–31.

Ascione, F., & Weber, C. V. (1996). Children's attitudes about the humane treatment of animals and empathy: One-year follow up of a school-based intervention. *Anthrozoös, 9*, 188–195.

Batson, K., McCabe, B., Baun, M., & Wilson, C. (1998). The effect of a therapy dog on socialization and physiological indicators of stress in persons diagnosed with Alzheimer's disease. In D. Turner & C. Wilson (Eds.), *Companion Animals in Human Health* (pp. 203–215). Thousands Oaks, CA: Sage Publications.

Beck, A. M., & Katcher, A. H. (1983). *Between Pets and People.* New York: Putnam.

Beck, A. M., & Katcher, A. H. (1984). A new look at pet facilitated therapy. *Journal of the American Veterinary Medical Association, 184*, 414–421.

Bossard, J. H. S. (1944). The mental hygiene of owning a dog. *Mental Hygiene, 28*, 408–413.

Bossard, J. H. S. (1950). I wrote about dogs. *Mental Hygiene, 34*, 345–349.

Bryant, C. D. (1979). The zoological connection: Animal related human behavior. *Social Forces, 58*, 399–421.

Collis, G. M., & McNicholas, J. (1998). A theoretical basis for health benefits of pet ownership: Attachment versus psychological support. In C. C. Wilson & D. C. Turner, (Eds.), *Companion Animals in Human Health* (pp. 105–122). Thousand Oaks, CA: Sage Publications.

Crowley-Robinson, P., Fenwick, D. C., & Blackshaw, J. K. (1996). A long-term study of elderly people in nursing homes with visiting and resident dogs. *Applied Animal Behaviour Science, 47*, 137–148.

Darnton, R. (1985). *The Great Cat Massacre and Other Episodes in French Cultural History.* New York: Random House.

Franti, C., Krause, J. F., Borhani, N. O., Johnson, S. L., & Tucker, S. D. (1980). Pet ownership in rural northern California (El Dorado County). *Journal of the American Veterinary Medical Association, 176*, 143–149.

Friedmann, E., Katcher, A. H., Lynch, J. J., & Thomas, S. S. (1980). Animal companions and one-year survival of patients after discharge. *Public Health Reports, 95*, 307–312.

Garrity, T. F., & Stallones, L. (1998). Effects of pet contact on human well-being: Review of recent research. In C. Wilson & D. Turner (Eds.), *Companion Animals in Human Health,* (pp. 3–22). Thousand Oaks, CA: Sage Publications.

Garrity, T. F., Marx, M. B., Stallones, L., & Johnson, T. P. (1988). Demographics of pet ownership among U.S. adults 21 to 64 years of age. *Anthrozoös, 2*, 33–37.

Grossberg, J. M., Alf, E. F., & Vormbrock, J. K. (1988). Does pet dog presence reduce human cardiovascular responses to stress? *Anthrozoös, 2*, 38–44.

Hart, L. A. (1993). Companion animals throughout the human life cycle: The contributions of Aline and Robert Kidd. *Anthrozoös, 6*, 148–153.

Hart, L. A., Hart, B., & Bergin, B. (1987). Socializing effects of service dogs for people with disabilities. *Anthrozoös, 1*, 41–44.

Hart, L. A., Zasloff, R. L., & Benfatto, A. M. (1996). The socializing role of hearing dogs. *Applied Animal Behavior Science*, 47, 7–5.

Holcomb, R., & Meacham, M. (1989). Effectiveness of an animal-assisted therapy program in an inpatient psychiatric unit. *Anthrozoös*, 2, 259–264.

Katcher, A., Beck, A. M., & Levine, D. (1989). Evaluation of a pet program in prison: The PAL Project at Lorton. *Anthrozoös*, 2, 175–180.

Kellert, S. R. (1980). American attitudes towards and knowledge of animals: An update. *International Journal for the Study of Animal Problems*. 1, 87–119.

Kellert, S. R., & Wilson, E. O. (Eds.). (1995). *The Biophilia Hypothesis*. Washington, DC: Island Press.

Kidd, A. H., & Kidd, R. M. (1980). Personality characteristics and preferences in pet ownership. *Psychological Reports*, 46, 939–949.

Kidd, A. H., & Kidd, R. M. (1994). Benefits and liabilities of pets for the homeless. *Psychological Reports*, 74, 715–722.

Kidd, A. H., & Kidd, R. M. (1996). Developmental factors leading to positive attitudes toward wildlife and conservation. *Applied Animal Behaviour Science*, 47, 119–125.

Lago, D., Connell, C. M., & Knight, B. (1983). A companion animal program. In *Mental Health and Aging: Programs and Evaluations*. Beverly Hills, CA: Sage Publications.

Lawrence, E. A. (1984). *Rodeo: An Anthropologist Looks at the Wild and the Tame*. Chicago: University of Chicago Press.

Lawrence, E. A. (1986). Neoteny in American perception of animals. *Journal of Psychoanalytic Anthropology*, 9, 41–54.

Leach, E. (1964). Anthropological aspects of language: Animal categories and verbal abuse. In E. Lennenberg (Ed.), *New Directions in the Study of Language* (pp. 23–53). Cambridge, MA: MIT Press.

Levinson, B. M. (1962). The dog as co-therapist. *Mental Hygiene*, 46, 59–65.

Levinson, B. M. (1970). Pets, child development and mental illness. *Journal of the American Veterinary Medical Association*, 157, 1759–1766.

Levinson, B. M. (1983). In A. Katcher & A. Beck (Eds.), *New Perspectives on our Lives with Companion Animals* (p. 283). Philadelphia: University of Pennsylvania Press.

Levi-Strauss, C. (1992). *Tristes Tropiques*. New York: Penguin.

Lockwood, R., & Ascione, F. R. (Eds.) (1998). Cruelty to animals and interpersonal violence. *Readings in Research and Application*. W. Lafayette, IN: Purdue University Press.

Marvin, G. (1987). *Bullfight*. New York: Basil Blackwell.

Miller, M., & Lago, D. (1990). The well-being of older women: The importance of pet and human relations. *Anthrozoös*, 3, 245–252.

Mugfori, R. A., & M'Comisky, J. G. (1975). Some recent work on the psychotherapeutic value of caged birds with old people. In R. S. Anderson (Ed.), *Pets, Animals and Society* (pp. 54–65). London: Bailliere Tindall.

Myers, G. (1998). *Children and Animals: Social Development and Our Connections to Other Species (Lives in Context)*. Boulder, CO: Westview Press.

Nathanson, D. (1998). Long term effectiveness of dolphin-assisted therapy for children with severe disabilities. *Anthrozoös*, 11, 22–31.

Nathanson, D. E., & de Faria, S. (1993). Cognitive improvement of children in water with and without dolphins. *Anthrozoös*, 6, 17–29.

Ory, M., & Goldberg, E. (1983). Pet possession and life satisfaction in elderly women. In A. Katcher and A. Beck (Eds.), *New Perspectives on our Lives with Companion Animals* (pp. 303–317). Philadelphia: University of Pennsylvania Press.

Paul, E. S., & Serpell, J. A. (1996). Obtaining a new pet dog—effects on middle childhood children and their families. *Applied Animal Behaviour Science*, 47, 17–29.

Pepperberg, I. M. (1990). Some cognitive capacities of an African grey parrot (*Psittacus erithacus*). *Advances in the Study of Behavior,* 19, 357–409.

Perelle, I. B., & Granville, D. A. (1993). Assessment of the effectiveness of a pet facilitated therapy program in a nursing home setting. *Society and Animals,* 1, 91–100.

Quinn, D. (1995). *Ishmael.* New York: Bantam.

Ritvo, H. (1987). *The Animal Estate: The English and Other Creatures in the Victorian Age.* Cambridge: Harvard University Press.

Robb, S. S., & Stegman, C. F. (1983). Companion animals and elderly people: Challenge for evaluators of social support. *The Gerontologist,* 23, 277–282.

Rowan, A. N. (1995). Medical disinterest in human–animal bond research? *Anthrozoös,* 8, 130–131.

Salisbury, J. E. (1994). *The Beast Within: Animals in the Middle Ages.* New York: Routledge.

Sanders, C. R., & Robins, D. M. (1991). Dogs and their people: Pet-facilitated interaction in a public setting. *Journal of Contemporary Ethnography,* 20, 3–25.

Savage-Rumbaugh, E. S., & Lewin, R. (1994). *Kanzi: At the Brink of the Human Mind.* New York: John Wiley & Sons.

Selby, L. A., & Rhoades, J. D. (1981). Attitudes of the public towards dogs and cats as companion animals. *Journal of Small Animal Practice,* 22, 129–137.

Serpell, J. A. (1991). Beneficial effects of pet ownership on some aspects of human health and behaviour. *Journal of the Royal Society of Medicine,* 84, 717–720.

Siegel, J. M. (1990). Stressful life events and use of physician services among the elderly: The moderating role of pet ownership. *Journal of Personality and Social Psychology,* 58, 1081–1086.

Steffens, M. C., & Bergler, R. (1998). Blind people and their dogs: An experimental study on changes in everyday life, in self-experience, and in communication. In C. C. Wilson & D. C. Turner (Eds.), *Companion Animals in Human Health* (pp. 149–157). Thousand Oakes, CA: Sage Publications.

Thomas, K. (1983). *Man and the Natural World: Changing Attitudes in England 1500–1800.* London: Allen Lane.

Tucker, J. S., Friedman, H. S., Tsai, C., & Martin, L. R. (1995). Playing with pets and longevity among older people. *Psychology and Aging,* 10, 3–7.

Wilson, C. C., & Turner, D. C. (Eds.) (1998). *Companion Animals in Human Health.* Thousand Oaks, CA: Sage Publications.

Zasloff, R. L., & Kidd, A. H. (1994). Attachment to feline companions. *Psychological Reports,* 74, 747–752.

PREFACE

Animals have been an integral part of my therapeutic practice as well as my personal life, so I was elated with the opportunity to edit this book. I wanted to develop a book that not only provides a strong theoretical overview, but also provides readers with practical suggestions on how to incorporate animals therapeutically with a variety of clients.

Before I begin to explain the organization and the various components of this book, I thought it would be helpful to define animal-assisted therapy (AAT). I have used the Delta Society's definition for this purpose. The Delta Society is an international, not-for-profit organization whose purpose is to "promote animals helping people improve their health, independence, and quality of life." According to the Delta Society's Standards of Practice for Animal-Assisted Activities and Therapy (1996), AAT "involves a health or human service professional who uses an animal as part of his/her job. . . . AAT is a goal-directed intervention in which an animal meeting specific criteria is an integral part of the treatment process. . . . The process is documented and evaluated." However, the term *animal-assisted activities* (AAA) "involves animals visiting people. The same activity can be repeated with different people, unlike a therapy program that is tailored to a particular person or medical condition. . . . AAA are delivered in a variety of environments by specially trained professional, paraprofessional and/or volunteers in association with animals that meet specific criteria."

The chapters in this book are divided into four major sections. The strength of each section relates to how the chapters are closely interrelated. It will become apparent to the reader that the therapeutic use of animals is an emerging approach that is built on a long history of our association with and curiosity about other living beings. Animal-assisted activities and therapy have qualitatively demonstrated a significant contribution to the overall quality of life.

ıt to point out that leadership in the scholarly investigation ι is built on an interdisciplinary interest bridging the worlds ysical health professionals, with their counterparts in ethology, , and animal welfare. The reader is cautioned that empirical research in this emerging area is limited.

An incentive for the preparation of this book was to encourage a more refined understanding for the incorporation of animals within therapy and provide the reader with a clear perception of its values as well as limitations. It is also hoped that the contents of this book act as an impetus for further empirical investigations into the therapeutic use of animals in clinical practices (serving clients of all ages in order to demonstrate the efficacy of this modality).

Section I concerns the conceptualization of the animal–human bond and consists of four chapters describing an historical exploration of the value of human–animal relationships. James Serpell provides an eloquent overview advocating a more open-minded view of the potential contribution of animals to human well-being. Within his chapter, Dr. Serpell provides an insightful commentary documenting the various belief systems concerning how animals have played a part in the treatment of illness and disease over time. This introductory chapter naturally leads into the following three chapters, in which the benefits (health and wellness and the psychosocial assets) of the animal–human bond are clearly stated. The safe and fair treatment of animals is an underlying concern noted throughout various chapters within this volume. In the second chapter there is some early attention given to the ethical treatment of animals as well as their welfare needs. In the final section of the book, a whole chapter is designated for this purpose.

Section II, on conceptual models of AAT, contains three chapters providing an overview of designing and implementing AAT services. This information is invaluable in understanding how to develop institutionally based AAT programs. The reader also becomes acquainted with methods and standards to consider in selecting certain species of animals with various populations. Chapter 5 also focuses on the factors that affect the performance of various animal species. For those readers interested in designing and implementing AAT programs in health and mental health organizatons, in Chapter 6, Mallon *et al.* provide the reader with a series of concerns that must be addressed for effective program integration. The authors incorporate within their discussion various organizational, staff, and client issues that must be considered. The final chapter in this section provides an overview of program evaluation and quality assurance. Burch suggests a variety of methods to be incorporated as criteria for justifying programs and procedures.

Section III documents the therapeutic efficacy of animal–human relationships with specific populations. Chapters discuss using animals in dealing with children with various behavioral and developmental constraints, elderly persons, and persons with AIDS and other terminal illnesses. Models explain how animals can be strong members of an individual's support system. Chapter 9 explores how animals can be incorporated in traditional psychotherapy for children and adults, including metaphors and images of the lives of animals, toy animals, and real animals. Readers will also find a chapter on animal abuse and appropriate treatment regimes, as well as research on the relationship between animal abuse and interpersonal violence. Finally, there is discussion on the role of service animals in enhancing independence and quality of life for people with disabilities. Duncan and Allen provide a multifaceted argument documenting the potential psychosocial and economic value of service animals. Their chapter is enriched with incorporation of case studies that have personal highlights concerning the value of service dogs.

Section IV of the book, on special topics, consists of five chapters that are more general in nature. Sandra Triebenbacher discusses the value of companion animals within the home. Melson and Nebbe discuss the exploration of biophilia and nature therapy in the context of traditional AAA. Arkow discusses the interdisciplinary nature of AAT and provides insight on the importance of interdisciplinary involvement in this area.

The last three chapters within this section address two very current and important subjects. Serpell, Coppinger, and Fine address the importance of safeguarding the animals' welfare while they are used as therapeutic aides for assisting citizens with disabilities. Clinicians must be aware of the needs of the clients they serve as well as those of the animals they use. Within this chapter and the chapter by Arkow, the authors examine the animal–human partnership and point out numerous concerns and suggestions about how to protect the animal's welfare within this relationship. In the final chapter, Turner and Katcher discuss two very distinct points of view on the future direction of AAT.

I believe the reader will finish this book with an understanding of how animals can become members of a therapeutic team. Although this book has been written at a more theoretical level, I have decided to conclude this preface with the written impressions of my 14-year-old son (written when he was 13). I realize that Corey's comments may not be scholarly, but his sensitivity in understanding deserves some recognition. Although Corey cannot adequately address the elements that make AAT or AAA valuable, he seems to understand why consumers reap the benefits. His experience as a volunteer (visiting elderly persons with his animals) also provides insights into the benefits that some may gain with the support of their animals. I believe his words will perhaps enable the reader to honestly hear how strong the human–animal bond may become (especially for our clients). I have taken the liberty to abstract only a few portions of his lengthy essay.

I have always been in a home with animals. I was raised with them. Their playfulness has made our home a great place to live. However, my life with animals is not limited to being a pet owner. My impression is that children see animals as their friends. When I was younger I played with my dogs and birds. I found them helpful when I felt sad and needed some support. They were always there for me. Over the years, I have noticed how animals can help with your emotions. For example, I have seen people depressed and their animals seem to comfort them. Also I have known some boys and girls who didn't have many friends. Their pets were their closest companions. Sometimes their animals encouraged others to come over and talk to them. . . .

Over the years I have volunteered at nursing homes, rehabilitation centers and at schools for children with disabilities. When I visit, I am always accompanied by several of our family's animals including our dogs, birds and rabbit. These experiences have truly impacted my life. They have taught me compassion as well as educated me on a number of inequities that are experienced by some. . . .

My love of animals helped me realize that I could help others. I started volunteering with my animals about the age of five. My father thought the joy that the animals had given me could be contagious to others. Over the past nine years, this contagiousness has not worn off. When I was five, I thought it would be really fun to bring animals to places and put a smile on the people's faces. I must confess that I was a little ambivalent when I started because I didn't know what to expect. Over the years I have developed more confidence and poise. In some ways I let the animals build the pathways to the relationships. They made it very easy for me to talk and interact. . . .

My animals have given me experiences that money cannot buy. By volunteering, I have learned that giving is important. We must be concerned about the well being of others! The opportunities also allowed me to experience what old age and disabilities are like. I found that many of the people were lonely and didn't have much to do. I realized that although some talked or moved slower, they were still loving and caring people who wanted to be wanted! My community service with my animals is a strong part of who I am. It has helped me grow and learn that I should care about others. Perhaps I learned that lesson from my animals which I helped raise. Volunteering is like giving a piece of your heart, without giving it away. That is an experience that will last forever. The animals gave me a chance to give to others. Without them I probably would have been at a loss for what to do. They just lead me in. In many ways they did the walking and I did the talking. We both shared in giving the hugs. . . .

My life with my animals has been great. They have been an important part of my life. Without my animals, my life wouldn't be as rich and colorful. They helped me learn patience, responsibility and to be caring. My animals have given me joy in life. My animals have enhanced my confidence to go and help others. This has been their greatest gift. When I enrolled as a volunteer for Guide Dogs of America, there was a quote I saw on their brochure. The quote is what Oscar Hammerstein once wrote, "Love in your heart wasn't put there to stay, love isn't love until you give it away." My animals have enabled me to give that love. . . .

Corey's reflections demonstrate the essence of the animal–human bond. It is anticipated throughout this text that the reader will begin to appreciate the vitality of an animal's presence and his/her interaction with humans. Although we are only at the frontier of understanding how to harness this wealth, the future may bring to us a clearer understanding. It is hoped that the contents of this book will become an impetus for further study and investigation. No one can truthfully interpret the future, but my belief is that after more careful research is conducted, we may find this form of intervention more commonly practiced, respected, and applied.

ACKNOWLEDGMENTS

This book could not have been written without the support of all the contributing authors. Their insight into the field of animal-assisted therapy, service animals, and the human–animal bond has made this a wonderful project to edit. I thank Nikki Levy and Barbara Makinster from Academic Press, who were very supportive throughout this project.

I also thank the many individuals who took the time to act as internal chapter reviewers. Their comments and feedback were important contributions to the formation of the final text. I acknowledge each of these individuals. Words cannot express my appreciation.

Karen Allen	Stephanie La Farge
Aaron Beck	Gale Melson
Barbara Boats	Jeff Mio
Ruth Deich	Patti Olson
Richard Denovellis	Mary Lou Randour
Maureen Fredrickson	Carol Raupp
Frank Gibbons	Andrew Rowan
Michael Kauffman	Stephanie Saccomon
Sherry Kerwin	Cindy Wilson

Thanks also to Rochelle Winderman and Jay B. Winderman for their efficient and thorough work on the index.

Finally, I thank my family, my wife, Nya, and my two sons, Sean and Corey, who were very supportive during this entire process. Their encouragement and their shared love of animals also made this project more meaningful.

Aubrey H. Fine

The Conceptualization of the Animal– Human Bond

THE FOUNDATION FOR UNDERSTANDING ANIMAL-ASSISTED THERAPY

Animal Companions and Human Well-Being: An Historical Exploration of the Value of Human– Animal Relationships

JAMES A. SERPELL

Center for the Interaction of Animals and Society, Department of Clinical Studies, School of Veterinary Medicine, University of Pennsylvania, 3850 Spruce Street, Philadelphia, Pennsylvania

I. INTRODUCTION

Historical accounts of people's relationships with animals are, for the most part, sketchy, and the little documentary evidence we have refers primarily to the lives of the rich and famous. Our knowledge of how ordinary people in the past related to animals, or benefited from their company, therefore remains indistinct and largely speculative. Even where the historical evidence is relatively complete, there is a danger of overinterpreting it—of attributing values, attitudes, and sentiments that make sense to us from a modern perspective, but which would not necessarily have had any meaning for our historical predecessors. All of this demands that we treat historical evidence with an appropriate degree of caution. In addition, "well-being" is clearly a multifactorial concept and it would be impossible, within the scope of this brief review, to explore the past impact of animals on all of its different constituents.

With these provisos in mind, the present chapter will confine itself to the theme of human health and the ways in which animals in general, and companion animals in particular, have been perceived as contributing to its maintenance and improvement. While attempting to set this work in historical context, the chapter will not attempt a detailed review of recent studies of animal–human therapeutic interactions, because this material has already been adequately covered elsewhere (see Serpell, 1996; Wilson & Turner, 1998).

II. ANIMAL SOULS AND SPIRITUAL HEALING

In the history of human ideas concerning the origins and treatment of illness and disease, nonhuman animals play a variety of important roles. The precise characteristics of these roles depend, however, not only on the prevailing view of animals, but also on the particular supernatural or "scientific" belief systems in which they are imbedded.

Probably the most archaic of these belief systems, usually referred to as *animism,* involves the concept that all living creatures, as well as other natural objects and phenomena, are imbued with an invisible soul, spirit or "essence" that animates the conscious body, but that is able to move about and act independently of the body when the bearer is either dreaming or otherwise unconscious. According to the typical animist worldview, all manifestations of sickness or misfortune are the direct result of assaults against a person's soul or "essence" by other angry or malevolent spirits encountered during these periods of unconsciousness. In some cases, these spiritual assaults are thought to be retaliatory; the result of some deliberate or inadvertent moral transgression on the part of the person. Alternatively, the person may be the innocent victim of an attack by spirits acting on behalf of a malevolent shaman or witch. Clues to the origins of spiritual assaults are often provided by the content of the dreams or visions that immediately preceded a particular bout of illness, injury, or misfortune (Benedict, 1929; Campbell, 1984; Eliade, 1964; Hallowell, 1926; Martin, 1978; Nelson, 1986; Speck, 1977; Wenzel, 1991).

Animist belief systems are characteristic of all hunting and gathering societies, and among these societies, offended animal spirits are often viewed as the most common source of malign spiritual influences. Many Inuit peoples believe, for example, that the spirits of hunted animals, like the ghosts of murdered humans, are capable of seeking vengeance. To avoid this happening, all animals, whether dead or alive, are treated with great respect. Otherwise, the hunter or his family can expect to suffer some misfortune: The animals will no longer allow themselves to be killed, or they may take their revenge by afflicting someone with disease, physical handicap, or even death (Wenzel, 1991). As an Inuit informant once eloquently expressed it:

> The greatest peril in life lies in the fact that human food consists entirely of souls. All the creatures that we have to kill and eat, all those that we have to strike down and destroy to make clothes for ourselves, have souls, like we have, souls that do not perish with the body, and which must therefore be propitiated lest they

should avenge themselves on us for taking away their bodies. (Rasmussen, 1929, p. 56)

In other hunting and gathering cultures, more specialized sets of moral relations existed between people and the animals they hunted for food. For instance, many Native American and Eurasian peoples believed in the concept of personal "guardian spirits" (Benedict, 1929; Hultzkrantz, 1987). Among the Ojibwa (Chippewa) and their Algonkian neighbors, these spirits were known as *manito* and they were commonly represented as the spiritual prototypes or ancestor figures of wild animals. All of these *manito* were thought of in highly anthropomorphic terms. They were easily offended, capricious, and often bad tempered, but they could also be appeased and, to some extent, cajoled by ritual means. Living animals were regarded as "honored servants" of their respective *manito,* and one such spirit apparently presided over and represented all of the earthly members of its species. At the same time, animals were also viewed as temporary incarnations of each *manito* who sent them out periodically to be killed by favored hunters or fishermen. For this reason, hunters invariably performed deferential rituals upon killing an animal, so that its essence would return to the *manito* with a favorable account of how it was treated.

According to the Ojibwa worldview, the activities of *manito* explained nearly all the circumstances of everyday life. Every natural object, whether animate or inanimate, was charged with spiritual power, and no misfortune, whether illness, injury, death, or failure in hunting or fishing, was considered accidental or free from the personalized intent of one *manito* or another (Landes, 1968). Animal guardian spirits were also believed to vary in terms of power. Some species, especially small and relatively insignificant ones, such as the majority of insects and such things as mice, rats, or squirrels, were believed to possess correspondingly limited spiritual influence, and rarely furnished people with useful guardian spirits. In contrast, more physically impressive species, such as bears, bison, wolves, or eagles, were deemed to possess extraordinary spiritual power and were therefore eagerly sought as patrons (Benedict, 1929; Landes, 1968).

The methods used to obtain the patronage of these kinds of guardian spirits varied from culture to culture, but they almost invariably involved some form of physical ordeal (Benedict, 1929). Among the Ojibwa, young men at puberty were expected to isolate themselves in the forest and endure long periods of fasting, sleeplessness, and eventual delirium in an effort to obtain visions. Those who were successful experienced vivid hallucinations in which their "souls" entered the spirit world and encountered one or more *manito* who offered their future help and protection in return for a variety of ritual obligations. *Manito* advice or assistance could sometimes be discerned through natural portents and coincidences but, more often, guidance came indirectly through the medium of subsequent dreams and visions. At such times the person's soul was believed to reenter the supernatural dimension and confer with its spiritual guardian. The content of dreams was therefore considered of primary importance as a guide to action in daily life (Landes, 1968).

In some societies, it was regarded as virtual suicide to injure, kill, or eat any member of the same species as one's guardian spirit. Like the Ancient Mariner's albatross, it could result in the withdrawal of spiritual patronage, and cause general misfortune, illness, and death. On the other hand, and in an equally large number of cultures, the guardian spirit specifically awarded its protégé the authority to kill members of its own species (Benedict, 1929; Hallowell, 1926).

As in most fields of individual achievement, not all men and women were equally good at obtaining the support of animal guardian spirits. Some never obtained visions and were regarded as "empty, fearful and cowardly" for the rest of their lives. A small minority, on the contrary, displayed extraordinary visionary talents and were henceforth regarded as medicine men, sorcerors, or shamans (Landes, 1968).

III. ANIMAL POWERS AND SHAMANISM

Mircea Eliade refers to shamanism as an "archaic technique of ecstacy" derived from guardian spirit belief. Both represent quests for magico-religious powers, and shamans differ from everyone else only in "their capacity for ecstatic experience, which, for the most part, is equivalent to a vocation" (Eliade, 1964, p. 107). Although shamanic power was derived from the assistance of one or more guardian spirits, the relationship between the shaman and his spiritual "helpers" or "familiars" was both more intimate and more intense than that attained by ordinary persons. In most cases, the shaman not only earned the patronage of guardian spirits but also developed the capacity to control them.

Shamans, typically, could achieve this power at will by entering a state of trance or ecstasy, usually induced by monotonous chanting, drumming, and dancing, and commonly assisted by the consumption of psychoactive drugs. Such states were considered to be analogous to death—the only other time when a person's essence becomes truly detached from the body and capable of independent actions in time and space. According to Eliade (1964), this ecstatic out-of-body experience enables the shaman to divest himself of human form and recover the situation that existed at the beginning of time when no clear distinctions separated humans from animals. As a result, he is able to reestablish friendship with animals, acquire knowledge of their language, and also acquire the ability to transform himself into an animal as and when when occasion demands. The result is a kind of symbiosis in which the person and the guardian spirit fuse to become two aspects of the same individual (Eliade, 1964).

Although they occasionally take human form, the vast majority of shamanic "familiars" are animals of one kind or another. Once he has adopted this disguise, the shaman is able to move about freely, gather information, and perform magical acts at a distance from his body. It is unclear from the various anthropological accounts, however, whether the animal spirit had its own independent existence when not in the shaman's service, or whether it was simply a material form assumed by the shaman when engaging in the practice of magic. Stories and legends concerning shamans provide conflicting evidence in this respect. In some, shamans are said to be able to disappear when attacked or pursued, whereupon all that will be seen is some swift-footed animal or bird departing from the scene. If this animal is injured or killed, the shaman will experience an identical mishap wherever his or her body happens to be. On the other hand, shamans never killed or consumed the flesh of animals belonging to their familiar's species, implying that these spirits existed separately and could easily be mistaken for ordinary animals (Speck, 1918).

Depending on their particular talents, shamans are believed to be able to foretell the future, advise on the whereabouts of game animals, or predict impending catastrophes. Their ability to control the forces of nature can also be employed to manipulate the weather, subdue animals, or bring them close to the hunter. Above all, since all manifestations of ill-health are thought to be caused by angry or malignant spirits, shamans possess a virtual monopoly on the treatment of sickness. Because the shaman is generally the only individual capable of visiting the spirit world at will through the agency of his animal familiars, he provides the only reliable method of discovering and counteracting the spiritual origins of physical and mental illness (Eliade, 1964; Speck, 1918).

IV. ANIMISM IN CLASSICAL AND MEDIEVAL TIMES

Although animist belief systems are particularly characteristic of hunting and gathering peoples, they have also persisted in a variety of forms in many pastoral nomadic and agricultural societies where they often coexist, through a process of synchretic fusion, with more recently imposed religious creeds and practices. An interesting contemporary example still flourishes among Central American indigenous peoples such as the Maya. Although Christianized and agricultural, the Mayan inhabitants of Chamula in the Mexican province of Chiapas believe in the existence of individual "soul animals" or *chanul* that are assigned to each person at birth by the celestial powers, and which share reciprocally every stroke of fortune that their human counterparts experience. All *chanul* are nondomesticated mammals with five digits, and they are physically indistinguishable from actual wild animals. Indeed, a person may only discover the identity of his soul animal through its recurrent appearance in dreams or with the help of a shaman (Gossen, 1996).

The Maya believe that most illness is the result of an injury inflicted on a person's *chanul*. These injuries may be inflicted deliberately via witchcraft, by another person mistaking one's *chanul* for an ordinary animal and hurting or killing it, or it may be "self-inflicted" in the sense that the person may allow him- or herself to experience overly intense emotions, such as intense fear, rage, excitement, or sexual pleasure, that can frighten or upset the *chanul*. The people of Chamula are also extremely reluctant to kill any wild mammal with five digits, since by doing so they believe they might inadvertently kill themselves or a friend or relative.

As far as curative measures are concerned, the only traditional remedy for an illness resulting from damage to one's soul animal is to employ the services of a shaman who will use various rituals, and the influence of his own, more powerful soul animals, to discover the source of the affliction and counteract it. According to Mayan folklore, shamans and witches also possess the ability to adopt the material form of their *chanul* in order to gain access to the supernatural realm (Gossen, 1996).

The purpose of dwelling on this particular example of contemporary Amerindian belief in soul animals is that it illustrates, according to Gossen (1996), the remarkable tenacity of animistic-shamanistic ideas and practices in Central America, despite the coercive influence of nearly five centuries of imported Roman Catholicism. Similarly, in Europe and around the Mediterranean basin, it appears that vestiges of comparable belief systems survived in a number of local and regional healing cults, at least until the early modern period.

In the pre-classical period the connection with animism was particularly obvious. In ancient Egypt, for example, the entire pantheon was dominated by distinctly shamanic images of animal-headed gods and goddesses, including the dog-headed Anubis who guided the souls of the dead on their journey through the underworld, and whose other roles included physician and apothecary to the gods, and guardian of the mysteries of mummification and reincarnation. Dogs and snakes were also the sacred emblems of the Sumerian goddess, Gula the "Great Physician," and of the Babylonian and Chaldean deity, Marduk, another god of healing and reincarnation (Dale-Green, 1966; Schwabe, 1994).

In the classical period the animist associations are somewhat less prominent but still readily discernible. Within the Greek pantheon, the gods were less often represented as animals, but they retained the shamanic ability to transform themselves into animals in order to disguise their true identities. Dogs and serpents also played a central role in the cult of Asklepios (Aesculapius), the son of Apollo, who was known as the God of Medicine and the Divine

Physician. Asklepios's shrine in the sacred grove at Epidaurus functioned as a kind of ancient health resort. Like modern-day Lourdes, it attracted crowds of suppliants seeking relief from a great variety of maladies. As part of the "cure," it provided an early instance of institutional, animal-assisted therapy. Treatment involved various rites of purification and sacrifice followed by periods of (drug-induced?) sleep within the main body of the shrine. During their slumbers the God visited each of his "patients," sometimes in human form but more often in the guise of a snake or a dog that licked them on the relevant injured or ailing portions of their anatomy. It appears that the dogs that lived around the shrine may have been specially trained to lick people. It was believed that these animals actually represented the god and had the power to cure illness with their tongues (Dale-Green, 1966; Toynbee, 1973). Inscribed tablets found within the precincts of the temple at Epidaurus testify to the miraculous powers of the local dogs:

> Thuson of Hermione, a blind boy, had his eyes licked in the daytime by one of the dogs about the temple, and departed cured.

> A dog cured a boy from Aigina. He had a growth on his neck. When he had come to the god, one of the sacred dogs healed him while he was awake with his tongue and made him well.

Although evidently material in form, the healing dogs and snakes at Epidaurus clearly fulfilled much the same function as shamanic spirit helpers. Through their ability to renew themselves periodically by shedding their skins, not to mention their potentially venomous qualities, snakes have always possessed strong associations with healing, death, and reincarnation (Morris & Morris, 1968). Likewise, in mythology, the dog is commonly represented as an intermediary between this world and the next. Some authors have attributed this to the dog's carrion-eating propensities, while others ascribe it to the dog's proverbial watchfulness and alertness to unseen "spiritual" threats, as well as its liminal, ambiguous status as a voluntary occupant of the boundary zone separating human and animal, culture and nature (White, 1991; Serpell, 1995).

During the early centuries of Christianity, traces of ancient shamanic ideas and practices were still prevalent throughout much of Europe. In addition to being healers, most of the early Celtic saints and holy men of Britain and Ireland were distinguished by their special rapport with animals, and many, according to legend, experienced bodily transformations into animal form (Armstrong, 1973; Melia, 1983). St. Francis of Assisi, who appears to have been influenced by Irish monastic traditions, has also been described as a nature mystic. Among other feats, he preached sermons to rapt audiences of birds, and was able to pacify rabid wolves (Armstrong, 1973). One of his followers, St. Anthony of Padua (1195–1231), preached so eloquently to the fishes in the sea that they all lined up along the shoreline to listen to his words of wisdom (Spencer, 1993).

The particular notion that dogs could heal injuries or sores by touching or licking them also persisted well into the Christian era. St. Roch who, like Asklepios, was generally depicted in the company of a dog, seems to have been cured of plague sores by the licking of his canine companion. St. Christopher, St. Bernard, and a number of other saints were also associated with dogs, and many of them had reputations as healers.

A faint ghost of older, shamanistic traditions can also be detected in the curious medieval cult of the greyhound saint, St. Guinefort. Guinefort, so the legend goes, was unjustly slaughtered by his noble master who mistakenly believed that the dog had killed and devoured his child. Soon afterward, however, the babe was found sleeping peacefully beside the remains of a huge, predatory serpent that Guinefort had fought and killed. Overcome with remorse, the knight threw the dog's carcass into a well, covered it with a great pile of stones, and planted a grove of trees around it to commemorate the event. During the 13th century, this grove, about 40 kilometres north of the city of Lyons, became the center of a pagan healing cult. Peasants from miles around brought their sick and ailing children to the shrine where miraculous cures were apparently performed (Schmitt, 1983).

Centuries later, the close companionship of a "Spaniel Gentle or Comforter"—a sort of nondescript, hairy lapdog—was still being recommended to the ladies of Elizabethan England as a remedy for a variety of ills. William Harrison, in his *Description of England* (1577) admitted to some scepticism on the subject: "It is thought by some that it is verie wholesome for a weake stomach to beare such a dog in the bosome, as it is for him that hath the palsie to feele the dailie smell and savour of a fox. But how truelie this is affirmed let the learned judge." The learned Dr. Caius, author of *De Canibus Britannicus* (1570), was less inclined to doubt: "though some suppose that such dogges are fyt for no service, I dare say, by their leaves, they be in a wrong boxe." He was of the opinion that a dog carried on the bosom of a diseased person absorbed the disease (Jesse, 1866).

Thus, over historical time, a kind of progression appears to occur from a strong, archaic belief in the supernatural healing power of certain animals, such as dogs, to increasingly vague and superstitious folk practices in which the special "spiritual" qualities of the animal can no longer be discerned, and all that remains is a sort of "quack" remedy of dubious therapeutic value. In medieval Europe, this trend was associated with the Church's vigorous supression of pre-Christian and unorthodox religious beliefs and practices. In the year 1231 A.D., in an effort to halt the spread of religious dissent in Europe, the office of the Papal Inquisition was created in order to provide the Church with an instrument for identifying and combating heresy. Prior to this time, religious and secular authorities had adopted a relatively lenient attitude to the variety of pagan customs and beliefs that abounded locally throughout Europe. The Inquisition systematically rooted them out and obliterated them. Ancient nature cults and rituals connected with pre-Christian deities or sacred groves, trees, streams, and wells were ruthlessly extirpated. Even the harmless cult of St. Guinefort was the object of persecution. A Dominican friar, Stephen of Bourbon, had the dead dog disinterred, and the sacred grove cut down and burned, along with the remains of the faithful greyhound. An edict was also passed making it a crime for anyone to visit the place in the future (Schmitt, 1983).

Although the picture is greatly distorted by the Inquisition's peculiar methods of obtaining and recording evidence, it appears that the so-called "witch craze" that swept through Europe between the 15th and 17th centuries originated as an attack on local folk healers or cunning folk; the last degenerate practioners of archaic shamanism (Briggs, 1996). According to the establishment view, not only did these medieval witches consort with the Devil in animal form, they also possessed the definitively shamanic ability to transform both themselves and others into animals (Cohn, 1975). In Britain and Scandinavia, witches were also believed to possess supernatural "imps" or familiars, most of which appeared in animal form. In fact, judging from the evidence presented in contemporary pamphlets and trial records, the majority of these familiars belonged to species we nowadays keep as pets: dogs, cats, cage birds, mice, rats, ferrets, and so on (Ewen, 1933; Thomas, 1971). In other words, close association or affinity with animals, once a sign of shamanic power or budding sainthood, became instead a symptom of diabolism. Animal companions still retained a certain "otherworldly" quality in the popular imagination of the Middle Ages and the Renaissance, but mainly as potential instruments of *maleficium*—the power to harm others by supernatural means.

All of these trends also reflected the marked medieval tendency to impose a rigid separation between human and nonhuman animals; a tendency that was reinforced by ideals of human conduct that emphasized self-control, civility, and chastity, while at the same time rejecting what were then viewed as animal-like attributes, such as impulsiveness, coarseness, and licentiousness (Elias, 1978; Salisbury, 1994).

V. ANIMALS AS AGENTS OF SOCIALIZATION

The close of the 17th century, and the dawn of the so-called "Age of Enlightenment," brought with them certain changes in the public perception of animals that have been thoroughly documented by historians of the early modern period (e.g., Maehle, 1994; Thomas, 1983). These changes included a gradual increase in sympathetic attitudes to animals and nature, and a gradual decline in the anthropocentric attitudes that so characterized the medieval and Renaissance periods (Salisbury, 1994). The perception of wild animals and wilderness as threatening to human survival also decreased in prevalence, while the practice of pet-keeping expanded out of the aristocracy and into the newly emergent, urban middle classes. This change in animal-related attitudes and behavior can be plausibly attributed, at least in part, to the steady migration of Europeans out of rural areas and into towns and cities at this time. This rural exodus helped to distance growing sectors of the population from any direct involvement in the consumptive exploitation of animals, and removed the need for value systems designed to legitimize or reinforce such practices (Serpell, 1996; Serpell & Paul, 1994; Thomas, 1983).

The notion that nurturing relationships with animals could serve a socializing function, especially for children, also surfaced at about this time. Writing in 1699, John Locke advocated giving children "dogs, squirrels, birds or any such things" to look after as a means of encouraging them to develop tender feelings and a sense of responsibility for others (Locke, 1699, p. 154). Deriving their authority from the works of John Calvin and Thomas Hobbes, many 18th-century reformers believed that children could learn to reflect on, and control, their own innately beastlike characteristics through the act of caring for and controlling real animals (Myers, 1998). Compassion and concern for animal welfare also became one of the favorite didactic themes of children's literature during the 18th and 19th centuries, where its clear purpose was to inculcate an ethic of kindness and gentility, particularly in male children (Grier, 1999; Ritvo, 1987; Turner, 1980).

In the late 18th century, theories concerning the socializing influence of animal companionship also began to be applied to the treatment of the mentally ill. The earliest well-documented experiment in this area took place in England at the York Retreat, the brainchild of a progressive Quaker called William Tuke. The York Retreat employed treatment methods that were exceptionally enlightened when compared with those that existed in other mental institutions of the day. Inmates were permitted to wear their own clothing, and they were encouraged to engage in handicrafts, to write, and to read books. They were also allowed to wander freely around the retreat's courtyards and gardens, which contained various small domestic animals. In his *Description of the Retreat* (1813, p. 96), Samuel Tuke, the founder's grandson, described how the internal courtyards of the retreat were supplied "with a number of animals; such as rabbits, sea-gulls, hawks, and poultry. These creatures are generally very familiar with the patients: and it is believed they are not only the means of innocent pleasure; but that the intercourse with them, sometimes tends to awaken the social and benevolent feelings."

During the 19th century, pet animals became increasingly common features of mental institutions in England and elsewhere. For example, in a highly critical report on the appalling conditions endured by the inmates of Bethlem Hospital during the 1830s, the British Charity Commissioners suggested that the grounds of lunatic asylums "should be stocked with sheep, hares, a monkey, or some other domestic or social animals" to create a more pleasing and less prison-like atmosphere. Such recommendations were evidently taken seriously. According to an article published in the *Illustrated London News* of 1860, the women's ward at the Bethlem Hospital was by that time "cheerfully lighted, and enlivened with prints and busts, with aviaries and pet animals," while in the men's ward the same fondness was manifested "for pet birds and animals, cats, canaries, squirrels, greyhounds. . . . [Some patients] pace the long gallery incessantly, pouring out their woes to those who listen to them, or, if there be none to listen, to the dogs and cats." (cited in Allderidge, 1991).

The beneficial effects of animal companionship also appear to have been recognized as serving a therapeutic role in the treatment of physical ailments during this period. In her *Notes on Nursing* (1860), for instance, Florence Nightingale observes that a small pet "is often an excellent companion for the sick, for long chronic cases especially."

VI. ANIMALS AND PSYCHOTHERAPY

Despite the apparent success of 19th-century experiments in animal-facilitated institutional care, the advent of scientific medicine virtually eliminated animals from hospital settings by the early decades of the 20th century (Allderidge, 1991). For the following 50 years, virtually the only medical contexts in which animals are mentioned are those concerned with zoonotic disease and public health, or as symbolic referents in psychoanalytic theories concerning the origins of mental illness.

Sigmund Freud's ideas concerning the origins of neurosis tended to reiterate the Hobbesian idea of mankind's inherently beastlike nature (Myers, 1998). According to Freud, infants and young children are essentially similar to animals, insofar as they are ruled by instinctive cravings or impulses organized around basic biological functions such as eating, excreting, sexuality, and self-preservation. Freud referred to this basic, animal aspect of human nature as the *id*. As children mature, their adult caretakers "tame" or socialize them by instilling fear or guilt whenever the child acts too impulsively in response to these inner drives. Children, in turn, respond to this external pressure to conform by repressing these urges from consciousness. Mental illness results, or so Freud maintained, when these bottled-up animal drives find no healthy or creative outlet in later life, and errupt uncontrollably into consciousness (Shafton, 1995).

Freud interpreted the recurrent animal images that surfaced in his patients' dreams and free associations as metaphorical devices by means of which people disguise unacceptable thoughts or feelings. "Wild beasts," he argued "represent passionate impulses of which the dreamer is afraid, whether they are his own or those of other people" (Freud, 1959, p. 410). Because these beastly thoughts and impulses are profoundly threatening to the *Ego,* they are locked away in dark corners of the subconscious where they can be safely ignored—at least during a person's waking hours. To Freud and his followers, the aim of psycho-analysis was to unmask these frightening denizens of the unconscious mind, reveal their true natures, and thus, effectively, to neutralize them.

Freud's concept of the id as a sort of basic, animal essence in human nature bears more than a superficial resemblance to animistic and shamanistic ideas concerning animal souls and guardian spirits, and the "inner" or spiritual origins of ill-health (Serpell, in press). In the works of Carl Jung, particularly his discussions of mythological archetypes in dreams and visions, and his concept of the "collective unconscious," this resemblance becomes more or less explicit (Cook, 1987). It is also echoed in the writings of Boris Levinson, the founder of "pet-facilitated therapy." In his book, *Pets and Human Development,* Levinson states:

> One of the chief reasons for man's present difficulties is his inability to come to terms with his inner self and to harmonize his culture with his membership in the world of nature. Rational man has become alienated from himself by refusing to face his irrational self, his own past as personified by animals. (Levinson, 1972, p. 6)

The solution to this growing sense of alienation was, according to Levinson, to restore a healing connection with our own, unconscious animal natures by establishing positive relationships with real animals, such as dogs, cats, and other pets. He argued that pets represent "a half-way station on the road back to emotional well-being" (Levinson, 1969, p. xiv) and that "we need animals as allies to reinforce our inner selves" (Levinson, 1972, pp. 28–9). Levinson went beyond the Freudian idea that animals were essentially a symbolic disguise for things we are afraid to confront in the flesh to arguing that relations with animals played such a prominent role in human evolution that they have now become integral to our psychological well-being (Levinson, 1972, p. 15).

VII. ANIMALS, RELAXATION, AND SOCIAL SUPPORT

During the last 20 years, and at least partly in response to the skepticism of the medical establishment, the theoretical emphasis has shifted away from these relatively metaphysical ideas about animals as psychospiritual mediators, toward more prosaic, scientifically "respectable" explanations for the apparent therapeutic benefits of animal companionship (Serpell, in press). The primary catalyst for this change of emphasis was a single, ground-breaking study of 92 outpatients from a cardiac care unit who, statistically speaking, were found to live longer if they were pet owners (Friedmann *et al.,* 1980). This finding prompted a whole series of other health-related studies (see Garrity & Stallones, 1998) and also stimulated a lot of discussion concerning the possible mechanism(s) responsible for the apparent salutory effects of pet ownership. Of these, at least two have stood the test of time. According to the first, animals are able to induce an immediate, physiologically de-arousing state of relaxation simply by attracting and holding our attention (Katcher *et al.,* 1983). According to the second, companion animals are capable of providing people with a form of stress-reducing or stress-buffering social support (McNicholas & Collis, 1995; Serpell, 1996; Siegel, 1990).

Although the de-arousing effects of animal contact have been demonstrated by a considerable number of recent studies, little evidence exists at present that these effects are responsible for more than transient or short-term improvements in physiologic parameters, such as heart rate and blood pressure (Friedmann, 1995). In contrast, the concept of pets serving as sources of social support seems to offer a relatively convincing explanation for the more long-term benefits of animal companionship.

Cobb (1976) defined social support as "information leading the subject to believe that he is cared for and loved, esteemed, and a member of a network of mutual obligations." More recent authors, however, have tended to distinguish between "perceived social support" and "social network" characteristics. The former represents a largely qualitative description of a person's level of satisfaction with the support he or she receives from particular social relationships, while the latter is a more quantitative measure incorporating the number, frequency, and type of a person's overall social interactions (Eriksen, 1994). However we choose to define it, the importance of social support to human well-being has been acknowledged implicitly throughout history. Loneliness—the absence of social support—has always been viewed as such a painful and unpleasant sensation that, since time immemorial, societies have used solitary confinement, exile, and social ostracism as methods of punishment.

The autobiographical accounts of religious hermits, castaways, and prisoners of war provide a clear picture of the psychological effects of social isolation. Most describe feelings equivalent to physical torture which increase gradually to a peak before declining, often quite sharply. This decrease in pain is generally associated with the onset of a state of apathy and despair, sometimes so severe that it involves complete catatonic withdrawal (Serpell, 1996).

Within the last 10 years, an extensive medical literature has emerged confirming a strong, positive link between social support and improved human health and survival (see Eriksen, 1994; Esterling *et al.*, 1994; House *et al.*, 1988; Sherbourne *et al.*, 1992; Vilhjalmson, 1993). The precise mechanisms underlying these life-saving effects of social support are still the subject of some debate, but most authorities appear now to agree that the principal benefits arise from the capacity of supportive social relationships to buffer or ameliorate the deleterious health effects of prolonged or chronic life stress (Ader *et al.*, 1995). In theory, this salutory effect of social support should apply to any positive social relationship; any relationship in which a person feels *cared for, loved,* or *esteemed.* As far as the vast majority of medical researchers and practitioners are concerned, however, the only relationships that are assumed to matter are those that exist between closely affiliated persons—friends, marital partners, immediate family members, and so on. Despite the growing evidence of recent anthrozoological research, the notion that animal companions might also contribute socially to human health has still received very limited medical recognition (Serpell, 1996).

VIII. CONCLUSIONS

For most of human history, animals have occupied a central position in theories concerning the ontology and treatment of sickness and disease. Offended animal spirits were often believed to be the source of illness, injury, or misfortune, but, at the same time, the assistance of animal guardian spirits—either one's own or those belonging to a medicine man or shaman—could also be called on to mediate in the process of healing such afflictions.

Although such ideas survived here and there into the modern era, the spread of anthropocentric and monotheistic belief systems during the last 1000 to 2000 years virtually annihilated animist belief in the supernatural power of animals and animal spirits throughout much of the world. In Europe during the Middle Ages, the Christian Church actively persecuted animist believers, branding them as witches and heretics, and identifying their familiar spirits with the devil and his minions in animal form.

During the period of the Enlightenment, the idea that pet animals could serve a socializing function for children and the mentally ill became popular, and by the 19th century the introduction of animals to institutional care facilities was widespread. However, these early and preliminary experiments in animal-assisted therapy were soon displaced by the rise of scientific medicine during the early part of the 20th century. Animals continued to play a somewhat negative symbolic role in the development of psychoanalytic theories concerning the origins of mental illness, but no further medical discussion of their value as therapeutic adjuncts occurred until the late 1960s and 1970s when such ideas resurfaced in the writings of the influential child psychotherapist, Boris Levinson.

Recent interest in the potential medical value of animal companionship was largely initiated by a single study that appeared to demonstrate life-prolonging effects of pet ownership among heart attack sufferers. This study has since prompted many others, most of which have demonstrated either short-term, relaxing effects of animal contact, or long-term health improvements consistent with a view of companion animals as sources of social support. Despite these findings, the positive therapeutic value of animal companionship continues to receive little recognition in mainstream medical literature, and as a field of research it is grossly undersupported by government funding agencies.

Considered in retrospect, it is difficult to escape the conclusion that the current inability or unwillingness of the medical establishment to address this topic seriously is a legacy of the same anthropocentrism that has dominated European and Western thinking since the Middle Ages. Hopefully, with the gradual demise of this old-fashioned and prejudiced mind-set, we can return to a more holistic and open-minded view of the potential contribution of animals to human well-being.

REFERENCES

Ader, R. L., Cohen, N., & Felten, D. (1995). Psychoneuroimmunology: Interactions between the nervous system and the immune system. *The Lancet, 345*, 99–103.

Allderidge, P. H. (1991). A cat, surpassing in beauty, and other therapeutic animals. *Psychiatric Bulletin, 15*, 759–762.

Armstrong, E. A. (1973). *Saint Francis: Nature mystic.* Berkeley, CA: University of California Press.

Benedict, R. F. (1929). The concept of the guardian spirit in North America. *Memoirs of the American Anthropological Association, 29*, 3–93.

Briggs, R. (1996). *Witches and neighbours.* London: Vicking.

Campbell, J. (1984). *The way of the animal powers.* London: Times Books.

Cobb, S. (1976). Social support as a moderator of life stress. *Psychosomatic Medicine, 38*, 300–314.

Cohn, N. (1975). *Europe's inner demons.* New York: Basic Books.

Cook, D. A. G. (1987). Jung, Carl Gustav (1875–1961). In R. Gregory (Ed.), *The Oxford companion to the mind* (pp. 403–405). Oxford: Oxford University Press.

Dale-Green, P. (1966). *Dog.* London: Rupert Hart-Davis.

Eliade, M. (1964). *Shamanism: Archaic techniques of ecstacy,* trans. W. R. Trask. New York & London: Routledge.

Elias, N. (1978). *The Civilizing Process* (trans. E. Jephcott). Oxford: Basil Blackwell.

Eriksen, W. (1994). The role of social support in the pathogenesis of coronary heart disease: A literature review. *Family Practice, 11*, 201–9.

Esterling, B. A., Kiecolt-Glaser, J., Bodnar, J. C., & Glaser, R. (1994). Chronic stress, social support, and persistent alterations in the natural killer cell response to cytokines in older adults. *Health Psychology, 13*, 291–128.

Ewen, C. L.'E. (1933). *Witchcraft and demonianism.* London: Heath Cranton.

Freud, S. (1959). *The interpretation of dreams* (trans. J. Strachey). New York: Basic Books.

Friedmann, E. (1995). The role of pets in enhancing human well-being: Physiological effects. In I. Robinson (Ed.), *The Waltham book of human–animal interaction: Benefits and responsibilities of pet-ownership* (pp. 33–53). Oxford: Pergamon.

Friedmann, E., & Thomas, S. A. (1995). Pet ownership, social support, and one-year survival after acute myocardial infarction in the Cardiac Arrhythmia Suppression Trial (CAST). *American Journal of Cardiology, 76*, 1213–1217.

Friedmann, E., Katcher, A. H., Lynch, J. J., & Thomas, S. A. (1980). Animal companions and one-year survival of patients after discharge from a coronary care unit. *Public Health Reports, 95*, 307–12.

Garrity, T. F., & Stallones, L. (1998). Effects of pet contact on human well-being: Review of recent research. In C. C. Wilson & D. C. Turner (Eds.), *Companion animals in human health* (pp. 3–22). Thousand Oaks, CA: Sage.

Gossen, G. H. (1996). Animal souls, co-essences, and human destiny in Mesoamerica. In A. J. Arnold (Ed.), *Monsters, tricksters, and sacred cows: Animal tales and american identities* (pp. 80–107). Charlottesville, VA: University Press of Virginia.

Grier, K. C. (1999). Childhood socialization and pet keeping in nineteenth-century America. *Society & Animals, 7*, 95–120.

Hallowell, A. I. (1926). Bear ceremonialism in the Northern Hemisphere. *American Anthropologist, 28*, 1–175.

House, J. S., Landis, K. R., & Umberson, D. (1988). Social relationships and health. *Science, 241*, 540–5.

Hultzkrantz, A. (1987). On beliefs in non-shamanic guardian spirits among the Saamis. In T. Ahlbäck (Ed.), *Saami religion* (pp. 110–123). Åbo, Finland: Donner Institute for Research in Religious and Cultural History.

Jesse, G. R. (1866). *Researches into the history of the British dog* (Vols. 1 & 2). London: Robert Hardwicke.

Katcher, A. H., Friedmann, E., Beck, A. M., & Lynch, J. J. (1983). Looking, talking and blood pressure: The physiological consequences of interaction with the living environment. In A. H. Katcher & A. M. Beck (Eds.), *New perspectives on our lives with companion animals* (pp. 351–359). Philadelphia, PA: University of Pennsylvania Press.

Landes, R. (1968). *Ojibwa religion and the Midéwiwin.* Madison, WI: University of Wisconsin Press.

Levinson, B. (1969). *Pet-oriented child psychotherapy.* Springfield, IL: Charles C. Thomas.

Levinson, B. (1972). *Pets and human development.* Springfield, IL: Charles C. Thomas.

Locke, J. (1699). *Some thoughts concerning education.* Reprinted with an introduction by F. W. Garforth (1964). London: Heinemann.

Maehle, A.-H. (1994). Cruelty and kindness to the 'brute creation': Stability and change in the ethics of the man–animal relationship, 1600–1850. In A. Manning & J. A. Serpell (Eds.), *Animals and human society: Changing perspectives* (pp. 81–105). London & New York: Routledge.

Martin, C. (1978). *The keepers of the game.* Berkeley, CA: University of California Press.

McNicholas, J., & Collis, G. M. (1995). The end of a relationship: Coping with pet loss. In I. Robinson (Ed.), *The Waltham book of human–animal interaction: Benefits and responsibilities of pet-ownership* (pp. 127–143). Oxford: Pergamon.

Melia, D. F. (1983). The Irish saint as shaman. *Pacific Coast Philology, 18*, 37–42.

Morris, R., & Morris, D. (1968). *Men and Snakes.* London: Sphere Books.

Myers, O. E. (1998). *Children and animals.* Boulder, CO: Westview Press.

Nelson, R. K. (1986). A conservation ethic and environment: The Koyukon of Alaska. In N. M. Williams & E. S. Hunn (Eds.), *Resource managers: North American and Australian Hunter-gatherers* (pp. 211–228). Canberra, Australia: Institute of Aboriginal Studies.

Nightingale, F. (1860). *Notes on nursing, what it is, and what it is not.* New York: Appleton.

Rasmussen, K. (1929). Intellectual life of the Iglulik Eskimos. *Report of the Fifth Thule Expedition* (Vol. 7, No. 1, p. 56).

Ritvo, H. (1987). *The animal estate: The English and other creatures in the Victorian age.* Cambridge, MA: Harvard University Press.

Salisbury, J. (1994). *The beast within: Animals in the Middle Ages.* London & New York: Routledge.

Schmitt, J.-C. (1983). *The holy greyhound: Guinefort, healer of children since the 13th century* (trans. M. Thom). Cambridge: Cambridge University Press.

Schwabe, C. W. (1994). Animals in the ancient world. In A. Manning & J. A. Serpell (Eds.), *Animals and human society: Changing perspectives* (pp. 36–58). London & New York: Routledge.

Serpell, J. A. (1995). From paragon to pariah: Some reflections on human attitudes to dogs. In J. A. Serpell (Ed.), *The domestic dog: Its evolution, behaviour and interactions with people* (pp. 245–256). Cambridge: Cambridge University Press.

Serpell, J. A. (1996). *In the company of animals* (2nd ed.) Cambridge: Cambridge University Press.

Serpell, J. A. (in press). Creatures of the unconscious: companion animals as mediators. In A. L. Podberscek, E. S. Paul, & J. A. Serpell (Eds.), *Companion animals and us.* Cambridge: Cambridge University Press.

Serpell, J. A., & Paul, E. S. (1994). Pets and the development of positive attitudes to animals. In A. Manning & J.A. Serpell (Eds.), *Animals and human society: Changing perspectives* (pp. 127–144). London & New York: Routledge.

Siegel, J. M. (1980). Stressful life events and use of physician services among the elderly: The moderating role of pet ownership. *Journal of Personality and Social Psychology, 58,* 1081–1086

Shafton, A. (1995). *Dream reader: Contemporary approaches to the understanding of dreams.* Albany, NY: SUNY Press.

Sherbourne, C. D., Meredith, L. S., Rogers, W., & Ware, J. E. (1992). Social support and stressful life events: Age differences in their effects on health-related quality of life among the chronically ill. *Quality of Life Research, 1,* 235–246.

Speck, F. G. (1918). Penobscot shamanism. *Memoirs of the American Anthropological Association, 6,* 238–288.

Speck, F. G. (1977). *Naskapi* (3rd ed.). Norman, OK: University of Oklahoma Press.

Spencer, C. (1993). *The heretic's feast.* London: 4th Estate.

Thomas, K. (1971). *Religion and the decline of magic.* Harmondsworth: Penguin Books.

Thomas, K. (1983). *Man and the natural world: changing attitudes in England, 1500–1800.* London: Allen Lane.

Toynbee, J. M. C. (1973). *Animals in Roman life and art.* London: Thames & Hudson.

Tuke, S. (1813). *Description of the retreat.* Reprinted with an introduction by R. Hunter and I. Macalpine (1964). London: Dawsons.

Turner, J. (1980). *Reckoning with the beast: Animals, pain, and humanity in the Victorian mind.* Baltimore, MD: Johns Hopkins University Press.

Vilhjalmson, R. (1993). Life stress, social support and clinical depression: A reanalysis of the literature. *Social Science Medicine, 37,* 331–342.

Wenzel, G. (1991). *Animal rights, human rights: Ecology, economy and ideology in the Canadian arctic.* London, Belhaven Press.

White, D. G. (1991). *Myths of the dog-man.* Chicago: Chicago University Press.

Wilson, C. C., & Turner, D. C. (Eds.) (1998). *Companion animals in human health.* Thousand Oaks, CA: Sage.

CHAPTER 2

The Use of Animals to Benefit Humans: Animal-Assisted Therapy

ALAN M. BECK

Center for the Human–Animal Bond, School of Veterinary Medicine, Purdue University, West Lafayette, Indiana

Animals have generally played a great role in human ecological adjustment. Just as credible a reason as any for the domestication of animals is their use as pets. In other words, there is much reason to believe that man's psychological needs were the primary cause for domestication of animals as that man needed to use animals for such material purposes as the saving of human labor and the satisfaction of a hunger for food.

Boris M. Levinson (1969)

I. INTRODUCTION

Animals have always been used by human beings, usually for food and then for transportation. When people began to live in villages, more than 15,000 years ago, additional roles included companionship, and the animals began to share the human living space. In all cases, concerns for the ethical treatment

Handbook on Animal-Assisted Therapy: Theoretical Foundations and Guidelines for Practice

for those animals evolved long after the animals had been pressed into service. Only in the last 100 years have laws been codified to protect animals used for draft or companionship, and only in the last 30 years, with the Animal Welfare Act, has protection extended to animals used in research. The use of animals to assist human therapeutic activities has a long history, but extensive, documented, and organized use is relatively new (Beck, 1985; Beck & Katcher 1984, 1996; Beck & Meyers, 1996; Katcher & Beck, 1983).

From the very beginning, animal-facilitated therapy (AFT) has paralleled the use of animals as pets, and many of the therapeutic uses are extensions of the health benefits now recognized for those who own or interact with companion animals. These included the early observations that people interacting with animals experienced a decrease in blood pressure (Katcher *et al.,* 1983) to the more overt behaviors indicating a more relaxed state (Katcher & Beck, 1986; Wilson, 1991).

The first report, in a recognized medical journal, indicating that animal ownership may have actual therapeutic value came nearly two decades ago. Pet owners experienced increased 1-year survival after discharge from a coronary care unit than nonowners (Friedmann *et al.,* 1980). The effect was small but statistically and medically significant.

Evidence that is more recent indicates animal contact not only aids recovery from cardiovascular disease but also may even help prevent it (Anderson *et al.,* 1992). In Australia, pet owners had lower systolic blood pressures and plasma cholesterol and triglyceride values when compared with nonowners and, thus, in theory, had a reduced risk of cardiovascular disease. Although pet owners engaged in more exercise, they also ate more meat and "take-out" foods than nonowners did and the socioeconomic profiles of the two groups were very similar (Anderson *et al.,* 1992). Related studies that are still under way are finding that males who do not own animals have more complaints of angina pain than those who do not (Jennings *et al.,* 1997).

Apparently, pet ownership reduces the risk factors associated with cardiovascular disease, and possibly for reasons that go beyond simply influencing risk behaviors. For example, it has been hypothesized that pet ownership improves survival because it influences psychosocial risk factors that lessen the risk of coronary heart disease (Patronek & Glickman, 1993). Considering the frequency of cardiovascular disease in all populations, any intervention that reduces, even slightly, the frequency of heart-related complaints and disease has significant financial implications for any health care system.

The public health and financial implications of animal ownership may be particularly important to older adults, who may have less social support than younger people because their human companions may have died or live at some distance. One study prospectively evaluated 938 noninstitutionalized elderly Medicare patients. Those people who owned pets appeared to experience less distress and required fewer visits to their physicians than nonowners. While animal ownership generally had value, the most remarkable benefits to health were for those who owned dogs. Medicare patients with dogs experienced fewer physician visits than those without. Most of the people noted that the pets provided them with companionship and a sense of security and the opportunity for fun/play and relaxation (Siegel, 1990). Normal interaction with companion animals may be just one of the things people do that is good for them.

II. THE USE OF ANIMALS AS THERAPEUTIC AGENTS

A small pet animal is often an excellent companion for the sick. . . .

Florence Nightingale (1820–1910),
Notes on Nursing, 1860

Long before there was any evidence that animal contact enhanced physical and mental health, animals were being used in therapeutic settings. Much of the early literature documents nothing more than fortuitous interactions with animals that happen to be present in a therapeutic setting (McCulloch, 1983). The animals were to provide a diversion or the joys traditionally associated with pet care. These expectations may be correct, as often the best "medicines" are appropriate concentrations of what is generally beneficial (Beck & Katcher, 1984). Nevertheless AFT studies are always struggling for acceptance in mainstream medicine, and much effort is directed at attempting to find acceptable methods that can validate the specific role of animal contact. It must be remembered that animal interaction is always just a small part of life of people in therapeutic settings. In addition, just how to assess improvement is also an ongoing problem because improvement can be subtle, transient, or delayed.

Just as the therapeutic value of animals is an extension of our keeping of pets, most of the laws and ethical principles that already address animal welfare for companion animals can be appropriately applied to companion animals in therapeutic settings. Like other uses of animals, AFT must be concerned for the welfare and safety of both people and animals. Experience, tradition, and guidelines have evolved for the various programs that use animals in the therapy of people. The most common kinds of AFT programs are (1) institutionally based programs, (2) noninstitutional programs for older adults, (3) service animals for people with disabilities in the home setting, and (4) horseback riding (equine) programs.

A. INSTITUTIONALLY BASED PROGRAMS

Historically the first AFT approaches were hospital settings for adults, now more common with younger people both in hospital and educational environments (Beck, 1985). The first recorded use of animals in a therapeutic setting was in 1792, when William Tuke used common farm animals in his York Retreat, an asylum run by the Society of Friends, a Quaker group. Pets were part of the treatment for epileptics at Bethel in Bielfeld, West Germany, in 1867. The first well-documented use of animals in the United States involved the rehabilitation of airmen at the Army Air Force Convalescent Center in Pawling, New York, from 1944 to 1945. Sponsored by the American Red Cross, the program used dogs, horses, and farm animals as a diversion from the intense therapeutic programs the airmen underwent. Few records were kept of these and other programs (McCulloch, 1983; Beck & Katcher, 1996).

One of the first studies to evaluate the effects of animals in an institutional setting was conducted by Dr. Samuel and Elizabeth Corson. They recognized the difficulties of finding an appropriate control for an animal intervention, so they chose to work with were patients who had failed to respond to any traditional form of therapy. Since nothing had proven useful, any intervention that did improve the situation could be considered effective. By comparing ineffective therapies with animals, the patients served as their own controls. Common ethical practice demanded that the patients continue to receive the traditional therapies as well. The patients were introduced to dogs (and some cats) in the kennels, on the wards, or at their bedsides, whichever was appropriate for that person. Patient and pet enjoyed many sessions together, and many sessions were videotaped to permit analysis of the patients' interactions with the animals and the human therapists. The analyses showed that most of the patients became less withdrawn, answering a therapist's questions sooner and more fully. Subjectively, the patients appeared happier—the immediate response that makes so many converts to AFT. Only 3 of the 50 patients absolutely failed to respond (Corson *et al.*, 1977).

A totally different experimental design was undertaken by Clark Brickel in a hospital-based nursing care facility in California. Instead of using individual animals on a one-to-one basis with each patient, Brickel introduced a single mascot (a cat) into each ward. He based his findings on observations made by the staff. While some negative aspects were reported, such as concern about fleas and allergies, the overall impression was that the cats improved the patients' responsiveness, offering them pleasure and enhancing the general milieu of the treatment setting (Brickel, 1979). Ward mascots may be easier to integrate into institutions and have many of the same positive effects as individual pets (Beck & Katcher, 1996).

An area of great interest is the Alzheimer's disease client, an ever-growing part of the nursing home population. There is evidence that the presence of a dog, either temporarily or permanently, can increase social behaviors. Behaviors including smiles, laughs, looks, leans, and touches were more normal for many people, and those whose did not appear to benefit from the animal were always the same individuals (Kongable et al., 1989; Batson et al., 1997). There is evidence that older people with Alzheimer's would benefit from contact with animals in their environment (Verderber, 1991).

There are studies that compare subjects exposed to animals and others in similar settings without animal contact. A group of psychiatric inpatients met in a room that had caged birds and a comparative group met in a similar room with no animals. The group in the room with birds was more comfortable talking and participated more than those in the same room without animals present. The effect that animals improve the perceived quality of the environment has many therapeutic implications (Beck et al., 1986).

Although standard clinical methodologies are most usual, AFT scholars should be prepared to look to those of sociology as well. Using ethnographic methods, hospitalized adolescents were perceived to have responded positively to the presence of a dog. The dog was a catalyst for interactions, improved self-esteem, a good distraction, and a sense of safety (Bardill, 1997).

Although small companion animals are used most often in AFT programs, farm animals are employed in some nonurban settings or transported to urban institutions for visitation (Senter et al., 1993).

1. Ethical Considerations with Institutionally Based Programs

Resident animals, often institutional mascots, pose some of the ethical problems that face all owned animals; that is, they must be well maintained with appropriate food, water, shelter, social interaction, and veterinary care. Abuse is a minor issue, especially compared to normal ownership, however, it is important that specific people be responsible for their care to avoid the neglect that sometimes happens because everyone believes the care will come from someone else. In addition, unlike the house pet, institutionalized animals may be on "duty," that is, kept active, much of the day and there is the potential for abuses associated with fatigue and burnout (Iannuzzi & Rowan, 1991). It has been suspected that overt abuse may occur in programs in mental hospitals (Beck et al., 1986) and prisons, though there is little documentation as to the extent of the problem (Katcher et al., 1989). Programs for elderly people must be supervised for covert mishandling because of well-intentioned but inappropriate overfeeding, the "grandparent syndrome." All programs have to be sensitive to poor management due to oversight of care that might occur because the animal is just one of many in need attention from a busy staff. Because the human residents are captive, special attention must be paid to human desires, fears, and choices where animal contact is concerned (Beck & Katcher, 1984). It would be unethical to provide less attention or fewer services to patients who choose not to participate in any animal-related programs.

Dogs especially have to be selected carefully because breeds and individual behaviors differ widely. It has been suggested that medium size dogs might be best, like the retrievers—the Labrador retriever is perceived to be more calm than the golden retriever, and younger dogs may be too energetic in the nursing home setting (Neer et al., 1987). Using animals just because they are available, for instance, a personal pet of a staff member, may be unethically exposing the animals to stress and the residents to health risks. In a like manner, it is the ethical responsibility of those involved in AFT programs to address all the health implications of having animals in a confined human population that may include people who have decreased disease resistance. Although AFT has a good safety record, as programs involve more people the risks increase. Potential exists for zoonotic infectious or parasitic disease, bite injury, accident, or allergy. To reduce human health issues AFT programs should consider (1) selection of the animals, (2) plans to avoid exposing to animal-allergic people to animals, (3) comprehensive infection-control programs in the institutional setting, (4) designing pet policies with the advice from public health veterinarians, and (5) developing a surveillance program and response to problems (Schantz,1990). All problems must be reported and evaluated.

A survey of 150 selected U.S. and 74 Canadian humane societies found that 49 (46%) of the U.S. and 49 (66%) of the Canadian society programs ran animal-assisted therapy (AAT) programs. More than 94% used dog and/or cats, 28% rabbits, 15% small mammals, and 10% birds (excluding poultry) in their programs. More than 48% of U.S. and 43% of Canadian programs consulted health professionals about zoonotic prevention. Nearly 10% of community-based and 74% of hospital-based programs had printed guidelines. Potential problems involve rabies, *Salmonella* and *Campylobacter* infections, allergy, and ringworm (Walter-Toews, 1993).

Special consideration must be given to people with depressed immune responses, such as those in programs oriented toward AIDS, oncology, Lupus, or organ transplant patients. Veterinary screening for salmonellosis, campylobacterosis, listeriosis, toxoplasmosis, chlamydiosis, and external parasites are particularly appropriate (Reeves et al., 1990).

Nevertheless, animals in nursing homes appear to be quite safe. A survey of 284 Minnesota nursing homes with visiting and live-in animals found no cases of animal-related infections in a 1-year period (Stryler-Gordon *et al.*, 1985).

Dolphin swimming programs receive positive media coverage, but keeping dolphins in captivity for a therapy that may have limited application raises some concerns. The value of dolphin programs comes from limited self-selected samples (Nathanson & de Faria, 1993; Nathanson, 1998). Even the so-called "swim with the Dolphins" programs, which keep the animals relatively "free," have not been evaluated as to the ability of the animals to return to the wild. Dolphins do show stress in captivity and often do not show the increase in life span seen with other captive wildlife. It remains to be seen if the risks and expense of using dolphins can be justified if similar therapeutic success can be achieved with dogs or other animals that thrive in captivity and easily interact with humans.

Many institutions do not own their own animals but invite people and their animals to visit for interactions with the patients. Visitation programs have become more common and are especially common for nursing home settings (Bustad, 1980).

Visitation programs often use animals from local humane societies, believing that such programs (1) enhance the status of animals, therefore making ownership more acceptable; (2) enhance the morale of their staff, who are often only involved catching or killing unwanted animals; and (3) provide a positive public image of their organization, which improves public support and public donations. Nevertheless, even the Humane Society of the United States (Lockwood, 1986) questions the use of shelter animals as because it feels (1) AFT takes time, vehicles, and money away from their own mission, which is preventing animal cruelty, aiding injured and stray animals, and finding homes for unwanted dogs and cats; (2) some AFT programs are part of research projects, and the Humane Society questions any research using animals; (3) AFT visits keep animals that might otherwise be adopted out of the shelter; (4) the animals return exhausted from visits; and (5) often there is little known about the behavior or past health history of the animals used. Remember that shelter animals are usually not temperament tested, so puppies and kittens might nip, and often little is known about an animal's vaccination status.

In August 1986, in Canada, a puppy given to a local shelter was used for visitation. The shelter was not told that the dog had come into contact with a fox. The puppy was rabid and exposed 139 people, including 62 local neighbors, 6 veterinary staff, 5 shelter personnel, and 60 at a nursing home. The cost for postexposure treatment ranged from $400–700 per person for a total cost of more than $65,000 (MMWR, 1987).

While zoonoses may be a potential problem, programs appear to have a good safety record. Concerns appear to be greater than found. One staff survey about concerns and expectations for AAT were greater before any actual experience. There were no injuries, some reported improvements, and only some annoyance on the part of residents. Professional staff tended to emphasize benefits and minimize risks of the proposed visitation program, whereas non-professional staff and those with less experience expressed the most concerns. After 4 months, 86% of staff members changed their attitudes to be more positive and 91% after 8 months. Favorable change is more a function of a decrease in expected risk than an increase in expected benefits (Kranz & Schaaf, 1989).

For all of these reasons, the current trend is to use animals known to the handlers, such as the lay volunteers. Volunteer owners enjoy having more time with their animals and most animals appear to enjoy having time with them (Rowan, 1991).

The health precautions that programs take for residential programs are also appropriate for animals that are just visiting institutions.

"Animal assisted therapy differs from animals used as entertainment in that AAT is considered to be an applied science using animals to solve a human problem. It is an interdisciplinary approach using animals as an adjunct to other therapies. It is goal-oriented, using assessment and evaluations procedures" (ref, p. 13). "It is this bonding relationship, used therapeutically, that differentiates AAT from animal entertainment" (ref, p. 13). Animals increase functioning, relationships, activity, and cognitive and spiritual processes (Gammonley & Yates, 1991).

B. Noninstitutional Programs for Older Adults

One common belief is that animal companionship is especially important for older adults and many early AFT programs were in nursing homes. What is often not appreciated is that the vast majority of older people live on their own outside of any institutional setting.

In the United States, about 95% of the elderly live in the community; 30% of those live alone (Harris et al., 1993). This adds significance to the growing evidence that animals play a positive role for elderly persons living alone (Siegel, 1990, 1993) and that there should be support for older adults who want to adopt animals from local humane societies.

Nearly 20 years ago, the first pet intervention study compared elderly people (65 years of age and older) living alone who were given either a plant or a small bird. Television ownership (as a control for a new intervention) was also considered. Having a bird appeared to improve morale and increase visits by friends; the birds served as a "social lubricant" (Mugford & M'Comisky, 1975). Since then, there have been programs to facilitate animal ownership, but there has been no evaluation of the programs to assess the psychological impact on the people or the animal companions.

One study followed 16 homebound clients of a medical services program (65–91, mean 81) who were visited by volunteers alone or with a pet. Vital signs were taken before and after visits. There were no changes when a pet was not included, but both blood pressure and pulse were lower after a pet visit. Interviews with participants showed that the animals were often an important focus of attention and conversation (Harris *et al.*, 1993).

1. Ethical Considerations for Noninstitutional Programs

Although attempts have been made to aid older people in securing animals, little attention has been paid to addressing two major issues facing the senior citizens after they have an animal: (1) Pets are an important determinant to housing choice and (2) many elderly owners have not arranged for the pet if they predecease it (Smith *et al.*, 1992). Being able to keep animals is "very important" to 59% of elderly people and "somewhat important" to another 27% for a total of 86%, yet assisting these people, either legally or financially, to secure an animal companion, is still rare. If indeed, pet keeping is therapeutic, it should be protected and funded as such. What other proven therapeutic modality is denied by landlords? Some people choose to live in suboptimum living quarters because they cannot find appropriate housing that will accept them with their animal companions. Even homeless people, many of whom are elderly, benefit from animal ownership for companionship, friendship, and love, have problems providing food and veterinary care for their pets (Kidd & Kidd, 1994).

The observation that 49.6% of elderly owners have not arranged for the pet if they predecease it raises ethical issues if the person has no one who would take the animal (Smith *et al.*, 1992). Some programs do exist for wealthier people who can donate ahead of time to a university, but the average owner's animal would experience the same fate as any abandoned animal. Perhaps more elderly people would avail themselves of the advantages of pet keeping if people felt animals were more protected while they were alive, and the animal would be more protected afterward. An ethical consideration of any AFT program must address its consequences. At this time, there have been no objective reviews of the animals placed in people's homes.

C. Service Animals for People with Disabilities in the Home Setting

Initially, most people thought of service animals as the dogs that guided the blind in public places. Actually, only about 1400 dogs a year are placed with blind users by the nine institutions belonging to the Council of U.S. Dog Guide Schools. At any given time, about 10,000 dogs are in use in the United States. The numbers of dogs used with blind people is decreasing, but the number is increasing for those with hearing impairments. About 19 hearing dog programs have placed about 3000 dogs as of 1999. All guide dogs typically work 8 to 12 years. Guide dogs for the blind are usually bred for that purpose, while most dogs for persons with hearing impairments come from shelters or are donated (Clifton, 1993). Regardless of the task the service dog is to play, the animal often provides positive psychological benefits, especially for young people (Mader *et al.,* 1989).

The growth, involvement of professionals, and acceptance of animals trained to serve people in their homes has been one of the great successes of the AFT movement. Animals, mostly dogs, now significantly assist people with vision and hearing loss, physical disabilities, and seizures (Edney, 1993). Although there is the possibility the animals can become victims of fatigue, overwork, and burnout, there is little evidence for these events being common. It has been informally reported that dogs used to guide the blind have more skin and intestinal problems than is usual, perhaps indicating stress. In any event, the problem is far less serious than that associated with people with high-stress jobs. There is always the danger that dogs working with people who use wheelchairs and canes are at risk of injury, but it would be ludicrous to consider the risk significant. Perhaps there is a need for more research on the veterinary needs of the animals used in AFT and more training on how to provide appropriate care for working animals. Veterinarians must better understand the demands placed on service animals and the consequences of any intervention to the human partner. Veterinarians must be sensitive to any abuse, regardless of the cause, and be prepared to work with the service animal user to resolve the problem.

There is a need to assess objectively the use of service animals so they can be considered part of the more recognized approach to help people with disabilities. A variation of using patients as their own controls is the use of the waiting list control, that is, assessing the same patient before and after an animal intervention. In a recent study, people with ambulatory motor impairment received a service dog either 1 month *or* 12 months after study began. The delay served as a "waiting list control" allowing people to serve as their own comparison subjects. The subjects were followed for 2 years, with five data mail-back questionnaires. The experimental group fared much better than the non-canine-assisted wait-list control group in measures that assessed self-esteem, internal locus of control, and community integration. The dog group required fewer services, resulting in savings of more than $60,000 per dog (Allen & Blascovich, 1996). Note that some serious questions have been raised about this study. The exact match of groups and the numbers of subjects seemed implausible, and no group was identified that supplied the service dogs. In addition, the funding of the study was unclear (Eames & Eames, 1996; Rowan, 1996).

1. Ethical Considerations of Service Animals

The ethics of keeping a companion animal as a working animal have been questioned, especially in the following three areas: (1) source of the animals, (2) work stress for the animal, and (3) the well-being of the animal after its usefulness is over.

Guide dogs and some other service dogs are bred solely for service; however, only a portion of the total number of dogs bred is usable, meaning there are dogs for which a nonservice home must be found or, at least in theory, the dog must be put to death. Dogs used for more general service, such as helping persons with hearing impairments, can often be found in humane shelters or as donations from owners. The supply side of the industry has received little scholarly attention.

Just as there has been limited study of the animals used in service programs, limited attention has been paid to any humane concerns, which are probably correctable. The lack of critical inquiry is a casualty of the attribution error made about animals—we assume that all is wonderful and never question whether that is indeed true. Nevertheless, the potential for problems exists.

Service dogs are often asked to perform tasks that are physically stressful and not an intuitive part of the animal's behavior. As an example, a harnessed dog pulling a person in a wheelchair often forces the dog to work in an awkward position due to an ill-fitting harness. Pulling a door open can require a great deal of energy. Carrying an additional backpack adds to the dog's heat load. Sometimes the dogs are overweight, thus adding to the physiologic stress of the animal. Many tasks are outside the normal dog repertoire of naturally motivated behaviors, thus requiring verbal rewards. Many of the problems could be lessened if trainers and users had more training on how to work with dogs without causing physical and mental stress (Coppinger et al., 1998). Trainers know dog behavior but do not necessarily understand dog physiology and anatomy. They must recognize that dogs will work for human leaders even beyond their own self-interest.

In general, there is great variation in the training of service dogs, and better communication and networking would benefit both animals and their users (Miura et al., 1998). Some service dog providers insist that a service dog not remain in the home as a pet after its service career is over and it has been replaced with another, younger dog. In addition, the criteria for selection for those eligible for service dogs have to be reviewed; at this time, people with special needs who are younger than age 16 are not elligible, although there is evidence that animals are important to child development (Melson, 1988).

These issues persist because most providers are somewhat secretive about their methods and the reasons for their policies. The sharing of methods and assessment of programs are issues demanding further discussion.

Service simians (monkeys) are also used by people with special needs. To date, only a limited number of monkeys have been placed and few objective reviews have been done. Ethical concerns include the potential for transfer of zoonotic diseases from primates, the use of shock packs for training and backup, and the need for teeth removal to reduce bite injuries to the human users or their visitors (Iannuzzi & Rowan, 1991). The animals do not appear to remain in service for more than a few years. More information is needed to judge the risk/benefit ratio before we can justify the animal welfare and risks issues. Remember that all new programs appear to take risks and are more expensive than when fully established. Perhaps it is time to assess AFT programs as one would any new intervention. Clinical trials are needed to assess effectiveness, cost, safety, and welfare.

It has been suggested that people with special needs, but who have good physical mobility, could be used instead of a service simian. Elderly people or those with slow mental development could easily aid a wheelchair user at less cost than using trained animals. In this way, society would be helping two humans, not one, without risking an animal's welfare.

D. HORSEBACK RIDING (EQUINE) PROGRAMS

Therapeutic riding or equine-assisted psychotherapy activities including riding and vaulting are designed to coordinate with the overall psychotherapeutic treatment of the patient. The goals include improving self-confidence, social competence, and improving the quality of life, but not specifically learning riding skills (Fitzpatrick & Tebay, 1997). Riding is used with a variety of physical disabilities including cerebral palsy (Bertoti, 1988; Campbell, 1990; Copeland 1991; Piper, 1990). Hippotherapy, in contrast to therapeutic riding, is provided by trained physical and occupational therapists to improve neuro-motor function using horses. It is based on the idea of transfer of movement from horse to patient (American Hippotherapy Association, 1995).

Horseback riding programs are different from other AFT programs in that they require the client to visit the horse's facility, not the other way around. Consequently, most concerns address appropriate husbandry at the stable or barn. There is also a concern for overwork, but all programs appear sensitive to the problem and report that no horse is ever used for more than six consecutive sessions or more than 2.5 hours without a rest (Iannuzzi & Rowan,

1991). Usually, therapeutic riding is only a small part of the horse's riding experience. Most riding programs are well planned, and established organizations provide support for therapy protocols, client safety, and insurance (Copeland, 1991).

III. CONSIDERATIONS FOR THE HUMAN PARTNER OF AFT PROGRAMS

Human–animal interaction is assumed to be beneficial to human health, hence its therapeutic potential. The rationale behind AFT is a logical extension of the long-standing belief that animals are good for people, especially for children, the sick, the lonely, and elderly people. It is difficult to deny the value of a therapy that is inexpensive, embodied strongly in the belief system of our society, reinforces the interests of animal lovers, and is apparently free of adverse effects (Beck, 1985). However, the literature describing the use of animals in therapeutic situations has failed to document *conclusively* a significant effect of pets for any *specific* human disease or condition (Beck & Katcher, 1984). Therefore, while there is good reason to believe that animals are beneficial for a vast majority of patients, it is necessary to test whether there is a causal relationship between animal contact and human health in specific, well-defined situations (National Institutes of Health [NIH], 1987). It is not ethical to proselytize the values of AFT for funding and public support without conducting appropriate, objective research on all aspects of it.

The major justification for funding for AFT has been research, not on the animals, but on the humans exposed to the programs. The popular notion that animals are usually beneficial has permitted AFT to flourish remarkably unencumbered by the bureaucracy and precautions usually associated with using human beings for medical research. Nevertheless, it must be recognized that, at least in the United States, there are guidelines for human research subjects. These guidelines require (1) informed consent; (2) confidentiality; (3) right to withdraw at any time, for any reason; (4) assessment of risk; and (5) assessment that the benefits outweigh any risks. Because the long-term effects of most AFT programs have yet to be proven, society has been fairly lenient, permitting most AFT projects to continue. To be sure, AFT has a good safety record, but as programs grow there is a greater possibility of occurrence of low-frequency events. It is society's ethical responsibility not to take advantage of the freedom we have enjoyed and plan programs with appropriate safeguards for the animals, staff, and patients associated with AFT programs. Therefore, it is our obligation to conduct responsible research to validate the therapeutic effects of animals for people in need, while minimizing all risks of discomfort and suffering for both the people and the animals. One way out of the ethical quandary of employing an animal intervention that has not been specifically proven would be to direct research efforts toward why some people appear to thrive without animal contact or do not avail themselves of the pet experience.

IV. CONSIDERATIONS FOR THE ANIMAL PARTNER OF AFT PROGRAMS

Just as there are guidelines to protect human research subjects, there are regulations to protect animal research subjects. Most animals used in AFT are usually owned by the researcher or institution where the animal resides. Researchers should remember that any vertebrate that is owned or maintained by a university can only be used in ways consistent with institutional animal use and care committees. Fortunately, most of the ethical and animal welfare concerns for animals used in therapy have been specifically articulated, and to the credit of most involved in the field, guidelines have been developed and continue to be improved. Green Chimneys Children's Services has published *People and Animals: A Therapeutic Animal-Assisted Activities Manual* for residential programs with attention to space, maintenance, animal health, and even funding (Senter *et al.*, 1993). Most AFT programs use volunteers and there are guidelines for them and the professionals that depend on them (Bernard, 1995).

Most AFT programs involve animals in institutionalized settings, especially with elderly people, and the Delta Society has developed *Guidelines: Animals in Nursing Homes* to address everything from selection of the animals to evaluation of the program (Lee *et al.*, 1983). The most complete guide is Delta's *Handbook for Animal-Assisted Activities and Animal-Assisted Therapy*, which includes guidelines for a wide range of programs. The guide maintains that (1) the programs that employ animals should meet the planned use of the animal, including predictability of behavior and health, controllability in the special setting, and suitability for situation and client population; (2) there should be standards for the treatment plan and evaluation of the animal's role; and (3) there should be an assessment of the facility addressing appropriate management of the animal while in service and not in service (Fredrickson, 1992). The handbook also includes a "Code of Ethics" which reads:

> Code of Ethics for Personnel in Animal-Assisted Activities and Animal-Assisted Therapy. These personnel must: (1) treat people, animals, and nature with respect, dignity, and sensitivity; (2) promote quality of life in their work; (3) abide by the professional ethics of their respective professions and/or organizations; (4) perform duties commensurate with their training and position; and (5) comply with all

applicable Delta Society policies, and local, state, and federal laws relating to their work.

This Delta Society code is an excellent start. In addition, there are general guides for helping grieving clients, clients with physical disabilities, and immunocompromised clients, so veterinarians can better serve the animals of people with special needs (American Veterinary Medical Association [AVMA], 1995).

Nondomesticated animals have been used both in their captive settings and placed with people in their own homes. These programs pose some special ethical dilemmas because these animals—though they may be tamed or trained—find human contact stressful. There is also increased risk to both animals and nonhandlers, especially as the animals age (Iannuzzi & Rowan, 1991). At an earlier time, when AFT needed novelty to attract attention and support, dolphin and monkey programs served the vital roles of consciousness and fund raising. Now that AFT is more widely accepted, it is time to use animals effectively and humanely.

V. GENERAL ETHICAL CONSIDERATIONS

There is now general acceptance that animals are therapeutic, and natural surroundings and contact with of nature is good for people (Ulrich, 1993). Viewing nature in general has therapeutic value. In one early study, mildly stressed subjects viewed colored slides of either common nature scenes (excluding built structures) dominated by green vegetation or urban scenes lacking vegetation. Stressed individuals felt significantly better after viewing natural scenes, experiencing increases in positive affect, including feelings of affection, friendliness, and play (Ulrich, 1979).

In a more realistic study, recovery records from hospital patients aged 20–69 who had undergone a cholecystectomy (surgical removal of gall bladder) without undue complications were studied. Those included had no history of psychological disturbance and all had their operations between May 1 and October 20 (1972–1981) because trees have foliage during those months. The patients were matched by sex, age (within 5 years), smoking history, weight at year of surgery (within 6 years), and hospital floor level. Windows on one side of the hospital wing looked out on either a small stand of deciduous trees or a brown brick wall. The same nurses were assigned on a given floor; rooms were all double occupancy and nearly identical in terms of dimensions, window size, and arrangement of beds and furniture. The placement of the window permitted a view from the bed. The patients with a natural view had shorter postoperative stays, had fewer negative evaluations from nurses, took fewer moderate and strong analgesic doses, and had slightly lower scores for minor postsurgical complications (Ulrich, 1984). Perhaps one of the most important considerations for study is to better understand how companion animals fit into our belief systems about nature and how we can better use all of nature for human health. Almost every AFT study notes that some people do not benefit and perhaps we should be more dedicated to them to see if nature in general has value.

The paramount ethical considerations regarding the animals that are used in therapy are no different from the concerns society has for all animal use—are the animals treated with the respect they deserve? Ethicist Jerrod Tannenbaum (1989) acknowledges the value of AFT but notes ". . . if is often difficult to find in such [AFT] studies mention of what these contacts ultimately do to the animals. One does not always find a concern about their needs or interests, and an appreciation that they are beings that count for something in their own right and not simply tools for making people healthier or happier" (p. 127). A footnote follows that this criticism cannot be made for Dr. Leo Bustad, who has always been concerned with the animals as well. Tannenbaum asks if AFT is a "one-sided bond" Remember, "a bond must be bi-directional, with each party to the bond offering its attention to the other" (Tannenbaum, 1989, p. 124) and the benefit, to each, must be significant. It has been long documented that stroking an animal lowers one's blood pressure, presumably an indication of reduced stress (Katcher & Beck, 1987). Dogs (Lynch & McCarthy, 1969) and horses (Lynch et al., 1974) being petted demonstrate a similar lowering of blood pressure or heart rate, presumably for the same reason, or at least as an indication that the animal enjoys the experience. Studies are beginning to look at behavior and physiological indicators of relaxation in animals as they interact with people. It is known that most domestic animals actively try to be with people, presumably for the same reasons humans want to be with them—the comfort of the family, group, or pack. Remember that one requirement of the new Animal Welfare Act for research dogs is that the dogs have access to exercise and socialization, with people—human-facilitated therapy for institutionalized dogs.

Nevertheless, the animal rights community still questions the utilitarian emphasis of AFT, that is, animals as mere "tools" with respect for their inherent worth. Even the pragmatic philosopher Bernard Rollin has said: ". . . nothing in the PFT movement promotes the intrinsic value of animals" (Lockwood, 1986). While true, I propose that improving the utility of animals has basic value to their existence and therefore to their protection. It is naive to believe that companion and domesticated animals will thrive in a world that had no value for them. But helping people is not enough—their utility to people must not include psychological or physical abuse, and whatever discomfort is absolutely necessary is clearly balanced with benefits that will foster improved health for both the humans and the animals involved.

"Reconciling the risks to the animals with their rehabilitation value is neither simple nor easy unless one follows the dictum that animals absolutely should not be used as means to an end" (Iannuzzi & Rowan, 1991, p. 159). After a therapeutic session has ended, all involved—the recipient of the service, the therapist, and the animal—must have benefited from the experience. In this way, all society will benefit.

At the final presentation of the 1987 NIH Technology Assessment Workshop, Beck and Glickman (1987) proposed that "All future studies of human health should consider the presence or absence of a pet in the home and, perhaps, the nature of this relationship with the pet, as a significant variable. No future study of human health should be considered comprehensive if the animals with which they share their lives are not included."

REFERENCES

Allen, K., & Blascovich, J. (1996). The value of service of dogs for people with severe ambulatory disabilities, a randomized controlled trial. *Journal American Medical Association,* 275, 1001–1006.

American Hippotherapy Association. (1995). *Overview curriculum.* Denver, Co: North American Riding for the Handicapped Association.

American Veterinary Medical Association, Committee on the Human–Animal Bond (1995). AVMA guidelines for responding to clients with special needs. *Journal American Veterinary Medical Association,* 206, 961–976.

Anderson, W. P., Reid, C. M., & Jennings, G. L. (1992). Pet ownership and risk factors for cardiovascular disease. *Medical Journal of Australia,* 157, 298–301.

Bardill N. (1997). Animal-assisted therapy with hospitalized adolescents. *Journal of Child and Adolescent Psychiatric Nursing,* 10(1), 17–24.

Batson, K., McCabe, B., Baun, M. M., & Wilson, C. (1997). The effect of a therapy dog on socialization and physiological indicators of stress in persons diagnosed with Alzheimer's disease. In C. C. Wilson & D. C. Turner (Eds.), *Companion animals in human health* (pp. 203–215). London: Sage Publications.

Beck, A. M. (1985). The therapeutic use of animals. *Veterinary Clinics of North America, Small Animal Practice,* 15(2), 365–375.

Beck, A. M., & Glickman, L. T. (1987, September). Future research on pet facilitated therapy, a plea for comprehension before intervention. Paper presented at Health Benefits of Pets, NIH Technology Assessment Workshop, Washington, DC.

Beck, A. M., & Katcher, A. H. (1984). A new look at pet-facilitated therapy. *Journal American Veterinary Medical Association,* 184, 414–421.

Beck, A. M., & Katcher, A. H. (1996). *Between pets and people: The importance of animal companionship.* West Lafayette, IN: Purdue University Press.

Beck, A. M., & Meyers, N. M. (1996). Health enhancement and companion animal ownership. *Annual Review of Public Health,* 17, 247–257.

Beck, A. M., Seraydarian, L., & Hunter, G. F. (1986). The use of animals in the rehabilitation of psychiatric inpatients. *Psychological Reports,* 8, 63–66.

Bernard, S. (1995). *Animal assisted therapy: A guide for health care professionals and volunteers.* Whitehouse, TX: Therapet L.L.C.

Bertoti, D. B. (1988). Effects of therapeutic horseback riding on posture in children with cerebral palsy. *Physical Therapy, 68*, 1505–1512.

Brickel, C. M. (1979). The therapeutic roles of cat mascots with a hospital-based geriatric population, a staff survey. *The Gerontologist, 19*(4), 368–372.

Bustad, L. K. (1980). *Animals, aging, and the aged.* Minneapolis: University of Minnesota Press.

Campbell, S. K. (1990). Efficacy of physical therapy in improving postural control in cerebral palsy. *Pediatric Physical Therapy, 2*,135–140.

Clifton, M. (1993). Dogs for people who can't live without them. *Animal People, 2*(9), 1,5.

Copeland, J. C. (1991). A challenger to therapeutic riding. *Anthrozoös, 4*, 210–211.

Coppinger, R., Coppinger, L., & Skillings, E. (1998). Observations on assistance dog training and use. *Journal Applied Animal Welfare Science, 1*, 133–144.

Corson, S. A., Corson, E. O., Gwynne, P. H., & Arnold L. E. (1977). Pet dogs as nonverbal communication links in hospital psychiatry. *Comprehensive Psychiatry, 18*(1), 61–72.

Eames, E. & Eames T. (1996). Economic consequences of partnerships with service dogs. *Disability Studies Quarterly, 16*(4), 19–25.

Edney, A. (1993, April). Dogs and human epilepsy. *Veterinary Record, 3*, 337–338.

Fitzpatrick, J. C., & Tebay, J. M. (1997). Hippotherapy and therapeutic riding. In C. C. Wilson & D. C. Turner (Eds.), *Companion animals in human health* (pp. 41–58). London: Sage Publications.

Fredrickson, M. (1992). *Handbook for animal-assisted activities and animal-assisted therapy.* Renton, WA: Delta Society.

Friedmann, E., Katcher, A. H., Lynch, J. J., and Thomas, S. S. (1980). Animal companions and one-year survival of patients after discharge from a coronary care unit. *Public Health Reports, 95*, 307–312.

Gammonley, J., & Yates, J. (1991). Pet projects, animal assisted therapy in nursing homes. *Journal of Gerontological Nursing, 17*(1), 13–15.

Harris, M. D., Rinehart, J. M., & Gerstman, J. (1993). Animal-assisted therapy for the homebound elderly. *Holistic Nurse Practice, 8*(1), 27–37.

Iannuzzi, D., & Rowan, A. N. (1991). Ethical issues in animal-assisted therapy programs. *Anthrozoös, 4*, 154–163.

Jennings, G. L. R., Reid, C. M., Christy, I., Jennings, J., Anderson, W. P., & Dart, A. (1997). In C. C. Wilson & D. C. Turner (Eds.), *Companion animals in human health* (pp. 161–171). London: Sage Publications.

Katcher, A. H., & Beck, A. M. (Eds.). (1983). *New perspectives on our lives with companion animals.* Philadelphia, PA: University of Pennsylvania Press.

Katcher, A. H., & Beck, A. M. (1986). Dialogue with animals. *Transactions & Studies College of Physicians Philadelphia, 8*, 105–112.

Katcher, A. H., & Beck, A. M. (1987). Health and caring for living things. *Anthrozoös, 1*, 175–183.

Katcher, A. H., Friedmann, E., Beck, A. M., & Lynch, J. (1983). Looking, talking, and blood pressure, the physiological consequences of interaction with the living environment. In A. H. Katcher & A. M. Beck (Eds.), *New perspectives on our lives with companion animals* (pp. 351–359). Philadelphia, PA: University of Pennsylvania Press.

Katcher, A. H., Beck, A. M., & Levine, D. (1989). Evaluation of a pet program in prison: The Pal Project at Lorton. *Anthrozoös, 2*, 175–180.

Kidd, A. H., and Kidd, R. M. (1994). Benefits and liabilities of pets for the homeless. *Psychological Reports, 74*, 715–722.

Kongable, J. G., Buckwalter, K. C., & Stolley, J. M. (1989). The effects of pet therapy on the social behavior of institutionalized Alzheimer's clients. *Archives of Psychiatric Nursing, 3*, 191–198.

Kranz, J. M., & Schaaf, S. (1989, July/August). Nursing-home staff attitudes toward a pet visitation program. *Journal American Animal Hospital Association, 25*, 409–417.

Lee, R. L., Zeglen, M. E., Ryan, T, & Hines, L. M. (1983). Guidelines: Animals in nursing homes. *California Veterinarian*, Suppl. 3, 1–42.

Levinson, B. M. (1969). *Pet-oriented child psychotherapy*. Springfield, IL: Charles C. Thomas.

Lockwood, R. (1986, Spring). Pet-facilitated therapy grows up. *Humane Society News*, pp. 4–8.

Lynch, J. J., & McCarthy, J. F. (1969). Social responding in dogs: Heart rate changes to a person. *Psychophysiology*, 5(4), 389–393.

Lynch, J. J., Fregin, G. F., Mackie, J. B., & Monroe, Jr., R. R. (1974). Heart rate changes in the horse to human contact. *Psychophysiology*, 11(4), 472–478.

Mader, B., Hart, L. A., & Bergin, B. (1989). Social acknowledgments for children with disabilities: Effects of service dogs. *Child Development*, 60, 1529–1534.

McCulloch, M. J. (1983). Animal-facilitated therapy, overview and future directions. In A. H. Katcher & A. M. Beck (Eds.), *New perspectives on our lives with companion animals* (pp. 410–430). Philadelphia, PA: University of Pennsylvania Press.

Melson, G. F. (1988). Availability of and involvement with pets by children: Determinants and correlates. *Anthrozoös*, 2, 45–52.

MMWR (1987). 36:3S, Aug. 28.

Miura A., Tanida H., & Bradshaw, J. W. S. (1998). Provision of service dogs for people with mobility disabilities. *Anthrozoös*, 11, 105–108.

Mugford, R. A., & M'Comisky, J. G. (1975). Some recent work on the psychotherapeutic value of cage birds with old people. In R. S. Anderson (Ed.), *Pet animals and society* (pp. 54–65). London: Bailliere Tindall.

Nathanson, D. E. (1998). Long-term effectiveness of dolphin-assisted therapy for children with severe disabilities. *Anthrozoös*, 11, 22–32.

Nathanson, D. E., & de Faria, S. (1993). Cognitive improvement of children in water with and without dolphins. *Anthrozoös*, 4, 17–29.

National Institutes of Health. (1987, September). *The health benefits of pets. Workshop summary*. Bethesda, MD: National Institutes of Health, Office of Medical Applications of Research, Technology Assessment Workshop.

Neer, C. A., Dorn, C., & Grayson, I. (1987). Dog interaction with persons receiving institutional geriatric care. *Journal American Veterinary Medical Association*, 191, 300–304.

Patronek, G. J., & Glickman, L. T. (1993). Pet ownership protects the risks and consequences of coronary heart disease. *Medical Hypotheses*, 40, 245–249.

Piper, M. C. (1990). Efficacy of physical therapy, rate of motor development in children with cerebral palsy. *Pediatric Physical Therapy*, 2, 126–130.

Reeves, D. E., Reid, W. H., Miller, D. M., & Tankersley, T. B. (1990). *The people pet connection, a pet facilitated therapy program*. Athens, GA: University of Georgia College of Agriculture, Cooperative Extension Service.

Rowan, A. N. (1991). Ethical issues (editorial). *Anthrozoös*, 4, 143–144.

Rowan, A. N. (1996). Research and practice (editorial). *Anthrozoös*, 9, 2–3.

Schantz, P. M. (1990). Preventing potential health hazards incidental to the use of pets in therapy. *Anthrozoös*, 4, 14–23.

Senter, S., Ross Jr., S. B., & Mallon, G. (1993). *People and animals: A therapeutic animal-assisted activities manual*. Brewster, NY: Green Chimneys.

Siegel J. M. (1990). Stressful life events and use of physician services among the elderly: The moderating role of pet ownership. *Journal of Personality and Social Psychology*, 58(6), 1081–1086.

Siegel, J. M. (1993). Companion animals: In sickness and in health. *Journal of Social Issues*, 49(1), 157–167.

Smith, D. W., Seibert, C. S., Jackson III, F. W., & Snell, J. (1992). Pet ownership by elderly people: Two new issues. *International Journal of Aging and Human Development*, 34(3), 175–184.

Stryler-Gordon, R., Beall, N., & Anderson, R. K. (1985). Facts & fiction: Health risks associated with pets in nursing homes. *Journal of Delta Society,* 2(1), 73–74.

Tannenbaum, J. (1989). *Veterinary ethics.* Baltimore, MD: Williams & Wilkins.

Ulrich, R. S. (1979). Visual landscapes and psychological well-being. *Landscape Research, (England),* 4(1), 17–23.

Ulrich, R. S. (1984). View through a window may influence recovery from surgery. *Science,* 224, 420–421.

Ulrich, R. S. (1993). Biophilia, biophobia, and natural landscapes. In S. R. Kellert & E. O. Wilson (Eds.), *The biophilia hypothesis* (pp. 73–137). Washington, DC: Island Press.

Verderber, S. (1991). Elderly persons' appraisal of animals in the residential environment. *Anthrozoös, 4,* 164–173.

Walter-Toews, D. (1993). Zoonotic disease concerns in animal assisted therapy and animal visitation programs. *Canadian Veterinary Journal, 34,* 549–551.

Wilson, C. C. (1991). The pet as an anxiolytic intervention. *Journal Nervous and Mental Disease,* 179(8), 482–489.

CHAPTER 3

The Animal–Human Bond: Health and Wellness

ERIKA FRIEDMANN

Department of Health and Nutrition Sciences, Brooklyn College of CUNY, Brooklyn, New York

I. INTRODUCTION

Health is a dynamic process that can be conceptualized as degree of optimum functioning achieved along the continuum possible for the individual. Maximal health and wellness is life lived to its fullest. Rather than being unidimensional, health involves the integration of psychological, physical, social, environmental, and spiritual aspects. Healthy individuals live in harmony with themselves, others, and their environment. Individuals with personal, environmental, or physical limitations can achieve a high degree of health and wellness by living to their maximal capacities in a combination of these spheres.

Animals have direct positive and negative impact on some physical aspects of health. Animals contribute to basic human health needs (Maslow, 1970) by providing food and clothing and by assisting people in their daily lives by acting as beasts of burden, working, and assistance animals. Animals also are used as human surrogates in the development of medical procedures and products and as sources for medical and health care products (Lierman, 1987). In contrast to the ways animals directly impact physical health, animals also have well-documented detrimental health effects including transmitting infectious diseases, causing allergies, and inflicting injuries such as bites and scratches (Schantz, 1990; Plaut *et al.*, 1996; Centers for Disease Control and Prevention, 1997).

The direct impact of animals on some physical aspects of health is easy to document and quantify. For example, it is relatively easy to count the number of injuries caused by dog bites or the number of pounds of chickens consumed per individual in a given year in a specific area. However, it is considerably more difficult to delimit the impact of animals, both positive and negative, on other aspects of physical health as well as on the other components of health.

The integrative aspect of the various components of health is demonstrated by the combined contributions of social, psychological, environmental, and physical factors to chronic diseases. Coronary heart disease was among the first chronic diseases for which the contribution of social and psychological factors was demonstrated (Jenkins, 1976). Pets were conceptualized as a contributor to the social aspect of health; thus the cardiovascular system was a logical starting point for evaluating the possible effects of owning pets on human health (Friedmann *et al.*, 1980).

This chapter will address the evidence for the positive impact of animals on human health. Evidence for long-term health benefits will be presented first. Once long-term benefits for cardiovascular health were established (Friedmann *et al.*, 1980), experimental and quasi-experimental studies were conducted to elucidate possible mechanisms for the long-term benefits already found and to extend the scope of the investigation to other types of health benefits. The evidence for short-term benefits of health from studies conducted using three categories of human–animal interaction is presented. This is followed by a summary of the research findings and a discussion of their implications for future research and for animal-assisted therapy.

II. LONG-TERM HEALTH EFFECTS

A. CARDIOVASCULAR EFFECTS

Several case control studies demonstrate the association of owning a pet with cardiovascular health. In the first study of this type, pet ownership was associated with survival among patients who were hospitalized for heart attacks, myocardial infarctions, or severe chest pain, angina pectoris (Friedmann *et al.*, 1980). Only 5.7% of the 53 pet owners compared with 28.2% of the 39 patients who did not own pets died within 1 year of discharge from a coronary care unit ($p < .05$). The effect of pet ownership on survival was independent of the severity of the cardiovascular disease. That is, among people with equally severe disease, pet owners were less likely to die than nonowners. Owning a pet did not appear to substitute for other forms of social support such as being married or living with others. This study was replicated and extended to a larger number of subjects with improved measures of cardiovascular physiology and psychosocial status (Friedmann & Thomas, 1995). Among 369 patients who had experienced myocardial infarctions and had ventricular arrhythmias (life-threatening irregular heartbeats), both owning pets and having more support from other people tended to predict 1-year survival. As in the previous study the association of pet ownership with survival could not be explained by differences in the severity of the illness, psychological or social status, or demographic characteristics between those patients who owned pets and those who did not.

The possibility that various types of pets might provide distinct benefits to their owners gained limited support from epidemiologic evidence. In Friedmann and Thomas's (1995) study, dog owners were approximately 8.6 times more likely to be alive in 1 year as those who did not own dogs ($p = .02$, $\exp[B] = .1167$). The effect of dog ownership on survival did not depend on the amount of social support or the severity of the cardiovascular disease. No parallel independent effect of cat ownership was observed. In contrast, cat owners were more likely to die ($p = .03$, $\exp[B] = 5.76$) than people who did not own cats. The relationship of cat ownership to survival was confounded by the effect of social support, which was low among cat owners and among those who died, and by the overrepresentation among cat owners of women, who were almost two times as likely to die than men ($p < .01$, $\exp[B] = 1.9$).

A subsequent study of 6-month survival among 454 patients who were admitted to a hospital for myocardial infarctions also suggested that cat ownership might have different health impact than dog ownership (Rajack, 1997). Cat owners were more likely ($p = .027$) to be readmitted for further cardiac problems or angina than people who didn't own pets. However, in contrast to the previous studies, pet ownership was not related to 6-month survival ($p = .24$) or to other indicators of health such as incidence of angina ($p = .84$), changes in psychological health ($p = .80$), readmission to hospital for angina or other cardiovascular causes ($p = .73$) or experience of further cardiac problems ($p = .22$) within 6 months after myocardial infarction. The one difference between dog and cat owners' cardiovascular health must be interpreted cautiously; one significant difference among many comparisons raises the possibility of a random effect.

Pet ownership may protect people from developing coronary heart disease or slow its progression in addition to influencing the survival of individuals who have experienced myocardial infarctions. Two cross-sectional epidemiologic studies address the differences between pet owners and nonowners in physiological and behavioral variables, known as risk factors, which are associated with increased likelihood of developing coronary heart disease (Anderson *et al.*, 1992; Dembicki & Anderson, 1996). Among 5741 people attending a screening clinic in Melbourne, Australia, risk factors for coronary heart disease were significantly greater among the 4957 pet nonowners than among the 784 pet owners. For men, plasma levels of cholesterol ($p < .01$) and triglycerides ($p < .01$) and systolic blood pressure ($p < .01$) were higher among pet nonowners than pet owners. For women, differences in risk factors between pet owners and nonowners occurred only for those women who are most susceptible to coronary heart disease, women in the menopausal and postmenopausal age groups. A study of senior citizens ($n = 127$) also indicated that pet owners have lower serum triglyceride levels ($p < .01$) than nonowners (Dembicki & Anderson, 1996). Both cross-sectional studies indicated that dog owners exercised more than other study participants. While dog owners were more likely to exercise than owners of other pets, there were no systematic differences in other health-related behaviors between pet owners and nonowners or between dog and cat owners.

B. OTHER HEALTH EFFECTS

Owning a pet has been shown to influence other aspects of health and related behavior. Several surveys have attempted to describe relationships of pet ownership to health status of an elderly population (Ory & Goldberg, 1983; Goldmeier, 1986; Garrity *et al.*, 1989; Siegel, 1990). Other surveys have failed to find differences in psychological status between pet owners and those who do not own pets (e.g., Friedmann *et al.*, 1983a; Watson & Weinstein, 1993; Zasloff & Kidd, 1994). Adults who adopt pets also experience decreases in frequency of minor health problems (Serpell, 1991).

Pet owners ($n = 345$) among the 938 Medicare enrollees in an HMO made fewer medical visits including both fewer total doctor contacts ($p < .05$) and fewer patient-initiated medical contacts ($p < .05$) over a 1-year period than nonowners (Siegel, 1990). Analyses of the data further indicated that pet ownership was a significant moderator of the impact of psychological distress on doctor contacts, independent of the effects of health status, depressed mood, and other demographic factors. For individuals who did not own pets, psychosocial distress, as assessed by stressful life events, was directly correlated ($p < .01$) with doctor contacts; the higher the stress level, the more contacts. However, for pet owners increased stress levels did not predict more physician contacts. There was also evidence for differences in the effects of dogs and other pets on health as assessed by health behavior. For individuals who did not own dogs, doctor contacts increased as life events increased ($p < .01$). In contrast, among dog owners, life events were unrelated to respondent-initiated doctor contacts. Among 1585 white married women ages 65 to 75, pet ownership was not related to happiness (Ory & Goldberg, 1983). However, among subgroups of the population, different patterns emerged. Among individuals with high socioeconomic status, pet ownership was associated with greater happiness, whereas among individuals with low socioeconomic status, pet ownership was associated with lower happiness. In the Garrity et al. (1989) survey of 1232 people over the age of 65, there was an association between strong attachment to a pet and lower depression among elderly persons who suffered great distress, not the elderly population as whole. Similarly, pet ownership has been associated with better morale among elderly women living alone, but not those living with others (Goldmeier, 1986).

Adopting a pet was associated with improved health status for people who chose to adopt one (Serpell, 1991). The 71 adults who adopted pets from an animal shelter experienced significant decreases (dog owners: $p < .001$; cat owners: $p < .01$) in minor health problems 1 month after adopting the pet. Minor health problems surveyed included headaches, painful joints, hay fever, difficulty concentrating, difficulty sleeping, palpitations or breathlessness, constipation, trouble with ears, trouble with eyes, worrying over every little thing, a bad back, indigestion or other stomach trouble, nerves, sinus trouble or catarrh, colds and flu, persistent cough, general tiredness, faints or dizziness, kidney or bladder trouble, and trouble with feet. The health of 26 volunteers who did not adopt pets did not change during the same period.

This research also provides evidence that dogs and cats have different impact on their respective owners' health. Dog owners ($n = 47$) maintained a decrease in minor health problems over the 10-month duration of the study ($p < .05$); cat owners ($n = 24$) did not (Serpell, 1991). Dog owners both appeared to walk slightly more at baseline and reported increased frequency and duration of walking ($p < .001$) at 10 months. Members of the control group ($n = 26$) also increased their walking ($p < .05$), although to a lesser degree. These findings could be interpreted to suggest the possibility that adoption of a cat encouraged the owner to spend additional time at home and thus forego walks.

The two case control studies (Friedmann & Thomas, 1995; Rajack, 1997) and two longitudinal studies (Serpell, 1991; Siegel, 1990) suggest that dog and cat ownership might have different associations with health status. No differences in risk factors for coronary heart disease were found between dog and other pet owners (Anderson et al., 1992). There have been too few people who own only pets other than dogs and cats in each of these studies to begin to explore differences in health among them.

The mechanisms for differences in health status of dog and cat owners as well as which aspects of health might be differentially affected by these animals remain to be evaluated. It does appear that owning a dog encourages people to exercise more. The absence of long-term benefits for cat owners supports this possibility. In Serpell's (1991) study, the physiological benefits associated with acquiring a dog could have been the result of increased physical activity engendered in walking the animal. However, those who adopted dogs already tended to walk more at baseline than those who adopted other animals and the control group. In fact, the absence of long-term benefits for cat owners supports this possibility. The likelihood that there are differences in contribution of dogs and cats to their respective owners' health also raises questions about differences between people who choose to own dogs and those who choose to own cats. Differences are generally limited to the amount of exercise the individuals take (Anderson *et al.,* 1992; Dembicki & Anderson, 1996). However, Serpell's (1991) and Serpell and Jackson's (1994) studies demonstrate that these differences may be determinants of which people choose to keep a dog rather than the result of acquiring a dog. Differences in the health experience of those who adopted dogs and cats also may be confounded by differences in stressful life events preceding the adoption of the pet (Serpell & Jackson, 1994).

III. SHORT-TERM HEALTH EFFECTS

In an attempt to understand how pets provide the health benefits derived from animals as just detailed, a number of researchers have investigated the short-term effects of companion animals on people. These short-term effects, measured on the timescale of minutes to weeks rather than months to lifetimes, may be the basis for the long-term effects demonstrated in epidemiologic studies as well as for other more subtle effects. It is, of course, possible that different mechanisms are responsible for the long- and short-term effects.

The vast majority of the studies of the effect of animals on human health utilize experimental techniques in which the health effect of an image of an animal or an animal stimulus is measured. Although the epidemiologic studies cited earlier include pets of all types, a majority of the studies of the short-term impact of animals on human health are limited to the effects of dogs. This is largely a matter of convenience because dogs are kept as pets so frequently and they are easy to handle. In the research investigating the short-term effects of animals, two types of potential health benefits were investigated: direct effects on indicators of stress or health and stress-moderating or -buffering effects. The experimental and quasi-experimental studies investigate whether explicitly and/or implicitly observing animals is associated with direct effects on people's physiology or associated with moderating people's stress responses. Most of the research about direct health effects investigates the effects of animals on physical aspects of health. However, social and psychological aspects of health also are addressed. The evidence for the effects of animals on social aspects of health is included in Chapter 4 and thus is not discussed here.

Researchers have evaluated people's responses to three different types of exposure to animals: (1) people explicitly looking at or observing animals or pictures of animals (Öhman *et al.*, 1978; Lockwood, 1983; Katcher *et al.*, 1983; Rossbach & Wilson, 1992; Eddy, 1995, 1996), (2) people implicitly observing or being in the presence of animals (Sebkova, 1977; Friedmann *et al.*, 1983b, 1986, 1993; Grossberg *et al.*, 1988; Allen *et al.*, 1991; Holcomb *et al.*, 1997; Nagergost *et al.*, 1997; Rajack, 1997), and (3) people touching or interacting with animals (Katcher, 1981; Baun *et al.*, 1984; Wilson, 1987, 1991; Vormbrock & Grossberg, 1988; Allen *et al.*, 1991; Harris *et al.*, 1993; Folse *et al.*, 1994; Straatman *et al.*, 1997).

A. Effects of Explicitly Looking at or Observing Animals or Pictures of Animals

Studies of the impact of looking at or observing animals document the direct impact of animals on people's responses to scenes and the people in them (Lockwood, 1983; Rossbach & Wilson, 1992) and examine the physiologic indicators of parasympathetic nervous system arousal while and/or immediately after watching animals (i.e., Öhman *et al.*, 1978; Katcher *et al.*, 1983; Eddy, 1995, 1996). Only one research group (Katcher *et al.*, 1983) addressed the effect of explicitly looking at or observing animals on people's responses to stressors.

People have long thought that animals can influence perceptions of situations and the people in them. Friendly domestic animals have been used effectively in the advertising and publicity industries to impute safety, credibility, and trustworthiness to people who accompany them (Lockwood, 1983). Evidence from two studies supports the positive influence of looking at animals on some people's moods and perceptions. Young adults ($n = 68$) rated pictorial scenes and the people depicted therein as significantly more friendly, less threatening, and happier when animals were included in these scenes than when animals were not included (Lockwood, 1983). Pictures of people with dogs were rated more highly than pictures of people with flowers by 34 young adults; and the people in the photos were perceived as more relaxed and happy when the dog was present (Rossbach & Wilson, 1992).

Looking at or observing domestic animals is associated with relaxation based on evidence of lowered levels of physiologic indicators of parasympathetic nervous system arousal. Blood pressures of normotensive ($n = 20$) and hypertensive ($n = 15$) subjects decreased progressively while watching fish swim in an aquarium (Katcher *et al.*, 1983). The duration of the decreases was greater when observing an aquarium with fish than when looking at an aquarium with plants and moving water but without fish and than when looking at a wall.

Watching or looking at pictures of nondomesticated animals directly affects people's stress levels (Öhman et al., 1978; Eddy, 1995, 1996). The blood pressures and heart rates of a chimpanzee's caretaker and research assistants who assisted with the chimpanzee ($n = 9$) tended to be lower while watching the chimps than during a relaxation period (Eddy, 1995). In a single case report, the blood pressure and heart rate of a 26-year-old male snake owner were lower during a 6-minute period of watching his pet than during the preceding 6 minutes when he sat alone and relaxed (Eddy, 1996). Research examining the ease of conditioning to potentially phobic stimuli provides a different perspective on people's perceptions of some nondomesticated animals. Öhman et al. (1978) found that pictures of animals culturally associated with fear did not elicit positive feelings or physiologic responses. The three studies of responses to nondomesticated animals provide some insight into the variability of people's physiologic responses to animals.

The stress response-moderating effects of watching animals were evaluated in the study of the physiologic impact of watching fish swim in an aquarium (Katcher et al., 1983). The subjects' blood pressure responses to the stressor of reading aloud at the conclusion of the experimental observation period were less pronounced after watching fish than after watching the other stimuli. On the basis of this comparison, the researchers concluded that watching the fish swim in the aquarium reduced the magnitude of the stress response.

The studies of people observing fish and chimpanzees indicate that observing animals from a safe position often encourages people to relax. The constant motion of the animals studied in this context characteristically attracts the observer's attention. The evidence presented through the comparison of the fish in the aquarium with the fishless aquarium and the wall supports the contention that this attraction might be prerequisite for continued relaxation over a longer time span (Katcher, 1981). The data obtained during observation of loud, rambunctious chimpanzees suggest that profound tranquillity and serenity might not be prerequisites for the decreased parasympathetic nervous system arousal experienced while watching animals (Friedmann et al., 1999).

B. EFFECTS OF IMPLICITLY OBSERVING OR BEING IN THE PRESENCE OF AN ANIMAL

This section focuses on the health effects from animals in situations where an animal is present but the subject is not directed to focus on the animal. This circumstance contrasts with the previous section, which included evidence of the health effects of animals when individuals were explicitly directed to focus their attention on the animals. Implicitly observing or being in the presence of animals has direct impact on both physiologic arousal (Friedmann *et al.*, 1983b) and psychological health status (Sebkova, 1977; Holcomb *et al.*, 1997). In addition, implicitly observing an animal moderates people's stress responses (Friedmann *et al.*, 1983b, 1986; Grossberg *et al.*, 1988; Allen *et al.*, 1991; Rajack, 1997).

The presence of a dog accompanying a researcher directly affected cardiovascular and psychological indicators of arousal. In a home setting, children's ($n = 38$) blood pressures during the entire experiment were lower among those who had the dog present for the first half of the experiment than those who had the dog present for the second half of the experiment (Friedmann *et al.*, 1983b). Two studies reported the impact of pet presence on psychological aspects of health. Both dog owners ($n = 10$) and nonowners ($n = 10$) reported significantly lower anxiety ($p < .05$) and behaved significantly less anxiously ($p < .05$) in a high-stress environment when the experimenter was accompanied by her dog than when she was not (Sebkova, 1977). Subjects paid more attention to the investigator's dog in the high- than in the low-stress situation, suggesting that the antiarousal effect of a nonthreatening animal might be particularly important in stressful situations. The presence of an aviary in an adult day care program tended ($p = .10$) to be associated with lower depression among the 38 clients compared with when the aviary was not present (Holcomb *et al.*, 1997). Further the magnitude of the decreases in depression during the time the aviary was present was correlated with the amount of attention the client paid to the aviary.

In addition to directly affecting health, implicitly observing or being in the presence of animals moderates stress responses. The effect of presence of a friendly dog on the stress response to several stressors has been evaluated (Friedmann *et al.*, 1883b, 1986; Grossberg *et al.*, 1988; Allen *et al.*, 1991; Nagergost *et al.*, 1997; Rajack, 1997). The presence of a friendly dog attenuated ($p < .05$) the cardiovascular stress responses of 38, 9- to 15-year-old children to reading aloud (Friedmann *et al.*, 1983b). In a similar study conducted among college students ($n = 193$), the presence of a dog caused significant moderation of heart rate ($p < .05$), but not blood pressure responses (Friedmann *et al.*, 1986). A friendly dog was also associated with lower blood pressures and heart rate as well as fewer behavioral indicators of distress during the stress of simulated physical (medical) examinations on 23 healthy children (Nagergost *et al.*, 1997).

The presence of a dog buffered the responses to cognitive stressors in some situations but not others. Neither blood pressure nor heart rate responses to two cognitive stressors, mental arithmetic and oral interpretation of drawings, differed between dog-owning college students ($n = 16$) accompanied by their dogs during the experimental protocol and those ($n = 16$) who were not accompanied by their dogs (Grossberg et al., 1988). In contrast, the presence of dogs belonging to woman subjects moderated the women's stress responses to mental arithmetic more than the presence of a supportive friend (Allen et al., 1991). This is consistent with other research indicating greater stress responses in the presence of higher status individuals compared with lower status individuals (Long et al., 1982). The nonjudgmental aspect of the support afforded by the pet was credited with decreasing the stress response.

A more recent study of the effects of the presence of an animal on women's cardiovascular responses to a number of everyday stressors in the normal home environment led to different results (Rajack, 1997). There were no differences in the cardiovascular responses of dog owners with their dogs present ($n = 30$) and nonowners ($n = 30$) to running up and down the stairs and reading aloud. Dog owners tended to have greater heart rate responses to hearing the alarm clock sound ($p < .08$) than nonowners. On the basis of the research summarized earlier, the presence of an animal has the potential to influence stress responses but does not do so uniformly.

Recognizing that there is variability in individuals' responses to the presence of animals, researchers addressed the role of attitudes toward animals in the stress-moderating effects of animals of the same type (Friedmann et al., 1993). The blood pressure responses to reading aloud in the presence of a dog were significantly lower for people with a more positive attitude toward dogs than for those with a more negative attitude. This research provides evidence that attitudes toward animals affect the stress-buffering effects of the presence of an animal.

The research design employed in studies is of prime importance for evaluating their results. In studies of the effects of implicitly watching animals conducted to date, those studies utilizing crossover research designs, in which the same individuals are exposed to both the animal present and animal absent conditions, revealed stress-moderating effects from the presence of pets (Allen et al., 1991; Friedmann et al., 1983b, 1986; Nagergost et al., 1997) and those not using crossover designs did not (Grossberg et al., 1988; Rajack, 1997). The ability of crossover designs to evaluate both within-subject and between-subject variability is particularly important for dependent variables such as blood pressure and heart rate, which vary tremendously from minute to minute and from person to person (Friedmann et al., 1999).

The research addressing the effects of implicitly watching or being in the presence of animals suggests that the effects of the presence of an animal on the stress response might be determined by several factors. These include the type and familiarity of the setting, type of stressor, perceptions about the type of animal, and relationship with the animal. For example, the stresses associated with either the setting itself or the nature of the task may overwhelm the stress moderating effects of the presence of the pet.

Based on the data presented, dog ownership is not necessary for individuals to receive stress-moderating benefits from the presence of a friendly dog. Positive perceptions of dogs promote dogs' effectiveness at reducing people's stress responses (Friedmann et al., 1993). Because attitudes toward types of pets are related to choice of pets (Serpell, 1981), particular effort will be required to separate the contributions of attitudes toward pet types and pet ownership itself to the stress-moderating effects of animals.

C. EFFECTS OF INTERACTING WITH ANIMALS

Evidence suggests that interacting with a pet, not necessarily one's own pet, leads to a direct anti-arousal effects (Katcher, 1981; Baun et al., 1984; Wilson, 1987, 1991; Harris et al., 1993) and decreases in depression (Folse et al., 1994), but not necessarily to stress-moderating effects (Straatman et al., 1997). Studies in this section involved explicitly instructing or encouraging participants to interact with the animals.

Initial studies consisted of observing interactions between people and their pets in order to learn more systematically about the ways people interact with their pets and with other friendly animals (for example, Katcher et al., 1983). Touching and talking to the animal were the two most frequent types of interactions with pets.

Interacting with a pet by talking to and touching it is less stress inducing than talking to or reading to other people (Katcher, 1981; Baun et al., 1984; Wilson, 1987, 1991). Blood pressures of dog owners ($n = 35$) recruited from a veterinary clinic waiting room, were measured while they rested without their pets in a private consultation room, interacted with their pets, and read aloud without their pets in the same room (Katcher, 1981). Similarly, blood pressures and heart rate were measured while self-selected undergraduate students ($n = 92$) read aloud, read quietly, and interacted with a friendly but unfamiliar dog (Wilson, 1987). In both studies, none of the cardiovascular levels increased while interacting with a pet; they did increase significantly while reading aloud (p's $< .05$). Further, anxiety levels paralleled the physiologic responses (Wilson, 1991). The physiologic effects of petting one's own pet and someone else's pet were compared (Baun et al., 1984). Blood pressures decreased significantly from the first to the final assessment when dog owners ($n = 24$) petted their own dogs but not when the same individuals petted the unfamiliar dog.

Two reports documented short-term health effects of interacting with animals during animal-assisted therapy. Homebound elderly ($n = 8$) who received routine home visits from a visiting nurse had lower blood pressures after the nurse visited with a dog than after she visited alone (Harris *et al.*, 1993). No decreases in blood pressure occurred between successive weeks or over the 4-week period when the nurse was accompanied by the dog. Depressed college students ($n = 13$) experienced greater decreases ($p < .05$) in depression after 7 weeks of weekly animal-assisted group therapy than students ($n = 24$) who did not participate in these groups (Folse *et al.*, 1994). By contrast, the students ($n = 9$) who participated in directed group therapy with a dog present did not report greater decreases in depression than the control group. While the types of interactions may have been very different from each other and the structured interactions in the experimental and quasi-experimental studies, these studies support the short-term health benefits of interacting with dogs.

The direct physiologic health consequences of touching animals other than dogs also have been reported (Eddy, 1995, 1996). In a case study of one snake owner, blood pressure during 6 minutes of touching his pet was lower than in the periods of relaxing and looking at the snake that preceded it (Eddy, 1996). In contrast, blood pressures and heart rate were higher when the chimpanzee's caretaker and assistants touched/tickled the chimps through a barrier than when they rested or observed the chimps through a barrier (Eddy, 1995). This occurred despite the subject's reported fondness for and lack of fear of the animals.

The stress-moderating effect of touching has been investigated in one study to date (Straatman *et al.*, 1997). After a baseline rest period, an unfamiliar small dog was placed in the laps of the men in the experimental group ($n = 17$) and nothing was placed in the laps of the men in the control group ($n = 19$). The dog remained in the subject's lap for the entire 7-minute speech preparation period and 4-minute televised speech. There were no significant differences in blood pressure and heart rate responses to the stressors between the experimental and control groups. Thus having a dog on the lap did not reduce the arousal associated with the tasks presented in this study.

The differences in physiologic arousal during interaction with animals suggest strongly that the individual's attitude toward an animal is of prime importance in determining whether touching that animal will enhance relaxation. The nonjudgmental aspect of interacting with an animal compared with the demands of interacting with other people is frequently cited as a possible reason for the difference in physiologic arousal during human–human and human–animal interactions (Katcher, 1981; Friedmann *et al.*, 1983b; Friedmann & Thomas, 1985; Allen *et al.*, 1991).

In addition, the variety of ways of physically interacting with animals and the difficulty of standardizing interactions and responses inhibit research in this area. It is difficult to evaluate the relative contributions of the physical movement and exertion that occur during interaction and the contributions of the calming influences of the interaction with animals. In fact, during vigorous interaction the blood pressure and heart rate depressing effects of the animal may be more than counteracted by the effects of the exertion. Further, studies that include interaction often fail to describe the interaction parameters in sufficient detail for the reader to compare them with other studies in a meaningful way. This is especially a problem for studies involving animal-assisted therapy (AAT) (e.g., Harris *et al.*, 1993). Many varied interventions and activities fall within the rubric of AAT. Adding an aviary to a living environment (Holcomb *et al.*, 1997), having an animal present during group therapy sessions (Folse *et al.*, 1994), having a dog accompany a visiting nurse (Harris *et al.*, 1993), and using interaction with an animal as a reward for correct answers (Nathanson *et al.*, 1997) are a few of the activities termed AAT.

Results of the one study addressing the stress-moderating effect of interacting with animals highlight a mechanism that might counteract the stress-moderating effect of interaction with animals. However, since a crossover design was not employed, these results must be interpreted cautiously. A crucial determinant of whether an animal moderates the stress response might well be the type of task the human–animal interaction is expected to moderate. An interaction with an animal can interfere with the successful completion of the stressor task and thus potentiate the stress response rather than moderate it.

IV. SUMMARY

Evidence supports the proposition that animals enhance health. Documentation of the positive impact of animals on human health comes from epidemiologic studies that support long-term health effects of pet ownership (Friedmann *et al.*, 1980; Anderson *et al.*, 1992; Serpell, 1991; Friedmann & Thomas, 1995) and from experimental and quasi-experimental studies that support short-term impact of three categories of human–animal interaction: people explicitly looking at or observing animals or pictures of animals (Lockwood, 1983; Katcher *et al.*, 1983; Rossbach & Wilson, 1992; Eddy, 1995, 1996), people implicitly observing or being in the presence of animals (Sebkova, 1977; Friedmann *et al.*, 1983b, 1986; Grossberg *et al.*, 1988; Allen *et al.*, 1991; Friedmann *et al.*, 1993; Holcomb *et al.*, 1997; Nagergost *et al.*, 1997; Rajack 1997), and people touching or interacting with animals (Katcher, 1981; Wilson, 1987, 1991; Allen *et al.*, 1991; Harris *et al.*, 1993; Folse *et al.*, 1994).

Different types of interaction with animals may have specific health effects. There is consistent evidence that explicitly looking at or observing animals understood as being safe is associated with direct positive impact on health including decreasing physiologic arousal (Katcher *et al.*, 1983; Eddy, 1995, 1996) and making people feel safer (Lockwood, 1983) and happier (Ross-

bach & Wilson, 1992). Observing pictures of animals considered more dangerous resulted in physiologic indicators of stress (Öhman *et al.*, 1978). Looking
at or observing animals also moderates stress responses (Katcher *et al.*, 1983).

The mere presence of an animal without instruction to attend to it was
associated with decreased physiologic arousal (Friedmann *et al.*, 1983b) and
decreased anxiety (Sebkova, 1977) and depression (Holcomb *et al.*, 1997).
There is less consistency in results of studies of the stress-moderating effects
of implicitly observing or being in the presence of animals. Studies in which
the person is exposed to the stressor both with and without an animal present
show stress-moderating effects (Friedmann *et al.*, 1983b, 1986; Allen *et al.*,
1991; Holcomb *et al.*, 1997; Nagergost *et al.*, 1997) and those without crossover
designs do not (Grossberg *et al.*, 1988; Rajack, 1997).

Interacting with a companion animal is associated with direct anti-arousal
effects (Katcher, 1981; Baun *et al.*, 1984; Wilson, 1987, 1991; Harris *et al.*,
1993) and decreases in depression (Folse *et al.*, 1994). There is no evidence
that physically interacting with a companion animal moderates the stress
response (Straatman *et al.*, 1997).

The complex ways in which animals can affect health are illustrative of the
complicated nature of health itself as well as of the multitude of modes of
interactions with animals. The three general categories of interactions described
here are an oversimplification of the range of interactions that occur daily in
the natural setting. While these categories provide a useful structure for exploring issues surrounding the health benefits of animals, many other categorization
schemes also could be useful.

Issues arising in reference to each category of human–animal interaction
are addressed within the section devoted to that topic. Broader questions,
which require further research, include the demographic, cultural, experiential,
and attitudinal bases for differences in the health benefits individuals derive
from pets.

V. DISCUSSION

Until recently, all species kept as pets were expected to have similar physiologic
effects on their owners (Beck & Katcher, 1989). Recent evidence, such as the
epidemiologic studies (Serpell, 1991; Friedmann & Thomas, 1995; Rajack,
1997) reported on here, demonstrate that different types of pets might have
different impact on people's health and its underlying physiology.

The studies conducted to date focus primarily on the effects of pets, and
dogs in particular, on individuals' health. The effects of specific types of animals
on individuals' health are likely based on individuals' previous direct and

indirect experiences with as well as their beliefs, desires, and fears about specific species.

Much of the research addressing the health benefits people derive from companion animals has been devoted to small selected groups of individuals who are expected to benefit or respond uniformly. Evidence does not support this expectation. Variables such as socioeconomic status (Ory & Goldberg, 1983), living alone (Goldmeier, 1986; Zasloff & Kidd, 1994), and ability to continue to participate in customary activities (Lago, 1994) contribute to the benefits individuals derive from their pets. Pet ownership and attachment might not appear to be related to health unless subgroups are stratified according to relevant health-related variables.

Attitudes and attachment play key roles in the effect of animals on human health. We cannot expect all animals to evoke uniform responses from all individuals (Friedmann et al., 1993, 1999). The interpretation of an animal as safe or unsafe may depend on early learning and/or personal experiences. Evidence supports the notion that individuals' responses to AAT with various species are likely to differ according to the individuals' perceptions of different types of animals. Additional research directly addressing perceptions of and responses to a variety of animals would facilitate understanding in this area.

Evidence from studies of other contributors to health indicates that psychosocial variables affect the health of men and women differently. For example, after controlling for physiologic risk factors, a lack of social activity and a lack of emotional support were predictors of myocardial infarction among men, while only a lack of social activities was significant for women (Welin et al., 1996). This issue has not been directly addressed with respect to the health effects of companion animals. Studies of different categories of interaction do tend to report health benefits predominantly for subjects of one sex. The importance of sex and other demographic variables in determining or moderating the effects of animals must be considered (Friedmann et al., 1999).

Epidemiologic evidence links pet ownership with improved health status (Friedmann et al., 1980; Siegel, 1990; Serpell, 1991; Anderson et al., 1992; Friedmann & Thomas, 1995; Dembicki & Anderson, 1996). Most of the research addressing short-term health effects of animals in the three categories of human–animal interaction utilize companion animals not belonging to the research subjects. This research provides evidence that interactions with a companion animal, not necessarily one's own pet, lead to direct health effects.

Studies of the health effects of human–companion animal interaction including those of AAT conducted to date have not addressed many of the issues related to the delimiters of individual health responses to human–animal interactions in a systematic, comparative manner. A concerted effort to evaluate the health effects of animals systematically within a unified theoretical framework would promote understanding of the many interactive components that contribute to health effects of human–animal interactions.

REFERENCES

Allen, K. M., Blascovich, J., Tomaka, J., & Kelsey, R. M. (1991). Presence of human friends and pet dogs as moderators of autonomic responses to stress in women. *Journal of Personality and Social Psychology, 61*, 582–589.

Anderson, W., Reid, P., & Jennings, G. L. (1992). Pet ownership and risk factors for cardiovascular disease. *Medical Journal of Australia, 157*, 298–301.

Baun, M. M., Bergstrom, N., Langston, N. F., & Thoma, L. (1984). Physiological effects of human/companion animal bonding. *Nursing Research, 33*, 126–9.

Beck, A. M., & Katcher, A. H. (1989). Bird–human interaction. *Journal of the Association of Avian Veterinarians, 3*, 152–153.

Centers for Disease Control and Prevention (1997). Dog-bite related fatalities—United States, 1995–1996. *Morbidity and Mortality Weekly Report, 46*(21), 963–967.

Dembicki, D., & Anderson, J. (1996). Pet ownership may be a factor in the improved health of the elderly. *Journal of Nutrition for the Elderly, 15*, 15–31.

Eddy, T. J. (1995). Human cardiac responses to familiar young chimpanzees. *Anthrozoös, 8*, 235–243.

Eddy, T. J. (1996). RM and Beaux: Reductions in cardiac activity in response to a pet snake. *Journal of Nervous and Mental Disease, 184*, 573–575.

Folse, E. B., Minder, C. C., Aycock, M. J., & Santqana, R. T. (1994). Animal assisted therapy and depression in college students. *Anthrozoös, 7*, 188–194.

Friedmann, E., & Thomas, S. A. (1985). Health benefits of pets for families. Special issue: Pets and the family. *Marriage and Family Review, 8*, 191–203.

Friedmann, E., & Thomas, S. A. (1995). Pet ownership, social support, and one-year survival after acute myocardial infarction in the Cardiac arrhythmia Suppression Trial (CAST). *American Journal of Cardiology, 76*, 1213–1217.

Friedmann, E., Katcher, A. H., Lynch, J. J., & Thomas, S.A. (1980). Animal companions and one-year survival of patients after discharge from a coronary unit. *Public Health Reports, 95*, 307–312.

Friedmann, E., Katcher, A. H., Eaton, M., & Berger, B. (1983a). Pet ownership and psychological status. In R. K. Anderson, B. L. Hart, & L. A. Hart (Eds.), *The pet connection: Its influence on our health and quality of life* (pp. 300–308). Minneapolis: University of Minnesota.

Friedmann, E., Katcher, A. H., Thomas, S. A., Lynch, J. J., & Messent, P.R. (1983b). Social interaction and blood pressure: Influence of animal companions. *Journal of Nervous and Mental Disease, 171*, 461–465.

Friedmann, E., Locker, B. Z., & Thomas, S. A. (1986, August). Effect of the presence of a pet on cardiovascular response during communication in coronary prone individuals. Presented at Delta Society International Conference on Living Together: People, Animals and the Environment, Boston, MA.

Friedmann, E., Locker, B. Z., & Lockwood, R. (1993). Perceptions of animals and cardiovascular responses during verbalization with an animal present. *Anthrozoös, 6*, 115–134.

Friedmann, E., Thomas, S. A., & Eddy, T. J. (1999). In A. L. Podberscek, E. Paul, & J. A. Serpell, (Eds.), *Companion animals and us: Exploring the relationships between people and pets.* Cambridge, UK: Cambridge University Press.

Garrity, T. F., Stallones, L., Marx, M. B., & Johnson, T. P. (1989). Pet ownership and attachment as supportive factors in the health of the elderly. *Anthrozoös, 3*, 35–44.

Goldmeier, J. (1986). Pets of people: Another research note. *The Gerontologist,* **26,** 203–206.

Grossberg, J. M., Alf, Jr., E. F., & Vormbrock, J. K. (1988). Does pet dog presence reduce human cardiovascular responses to stress? *Anthrozoös,* **2,** 38–44.

Harris, M. D., Rinehart, J. M., & Gerstman, J. (1993). Animal-assisted therapy for the homebound elderly. *Holistic Nurse Practitioner,* **8,** 27–37.

Holcomb, R., Jendro, C., Weber, B., & Nahan, U. (1997). Use of an aviary to relieve depression in elderly males. *Anthrozoös,* **10,** 32–36.

Jenkins, C. D. (1976). Recent evidence supporting psychologic and social risk factors for coronary disease. *New England Journal of Medicine,* **294,** 1033–1038.

Katcher, A. H. (1981). Interactions between people and their pets: Form and function. In B. Fogle (Ed.), *Interrelationships between people and pets* (pp. 41–67). Springfield, IL: Charles C. Thomas.

Katcher, A. H., Friedmann, E., Beck, A. M., & Lynch, J. J. (1983). Talking, looking, and blood pressure: Physiological consequences of interaction with the living environment. In A. H. Katcher & A. M. Beck (Eds.), *New perspectives on our lives with animal companions* (pp. 351–359). Philadelphia, PA: University of Pennsylvania Press.

Lago, D. (1994). Conceptual frameworks for human animal bond research: A commentary. *Anthrozoös,* **7,** 14–18.

Lierman, T. L. (Ed.). (1987). *Building a healthy America* (pp. 55–59.) New York: Mary Ann Liebert, Inc.

Lockwood, R. (1983). The influence of animals on social perception. In A. H. Katcher, & A. M. Beck, (Eds.), *New perspectives on our lives with animal companions* (pp. 64–71.) Philadelphia, PA: University of Pennsylvania Press.

Long, J. M., Lynch, J. J., Machiran, N. M., Thomas, S. A., & Malinow, K. L. (1982). The effect of status on blood pressure during verbal communication. *Journal of Behavioral Medicine,* **5,** 165–72.

Maslow, A. (1970). *Motivation and personality* (2nd ed.) New York: Harper and Row.

Nagergost, S. L., Baun, M. M., Megel, M., & Leibowitz, J. M. (1997). The effects of the presence of a companion animal on physiologic arousal and behavioral distress in children during physical examination. *Journal of Pediatric Nursing,* **12,** 323–30.

Nathanson, D. E., de Castro, D., Friend, H., & McMahon, M. (1997). Effectiveness of short-term dolphin-assisted therapy for children with severe disabilities. *Anthrozoös,* **10,** 90–100.

Öhman, A., Fredrikson, M., & Hugdahl, K. (1978). Orienting and defensive responding in the electrodermal system: Palmar-dorsal differences and recovery-rate during conditioning to potentially phobic stimuli. *Psychophysiology,* **15,** 93–101.

Ory, M., & Goldberg, E. L. (1983). Pet possession and life satisfaction in elderly women. In A. H. Katcher & A. M., Beck (Eds.), *New perspectives on our lives with companion animals.* eds. (pp. 303–317). Philadelphia, PA: University of Pennsylvania Press.

Plaut, M., Zimmerman, E., & Goldstein, R. (1996). Health hazards to humans associated with domestic pets. *Annual Review of Public Health,* **17,** 221–45.

Rajack, L. S. (1997). Pets and human health: The influence of pets on cardiovascular and other aspects of owners' health. Doctoral dissertation, University of Cambridge, UK.

Rossbach, K. A., & Wilson, J. P. (1992). Does a dog's presence make a person appear more likeable? *Anthrozoös* **5,** 40–51.

Schantz, P. M. (1990). Preventing potential health hazards incidental to the use of pets in therapy. *Anthrozoös* **4,** 14–23.

Sebkova, J. (1977). *Anxiety levels as affected by the presence of a dog.* Unpublished thesis, Department of Psychology, University of Lancaster, UK.

Serpell, J. A. (1981). Childhood pets and their influence on adults' attitudes. *Psychological Reports,* **49,** 651–654.

Serpell, J. A. (1991). Beneficial effects of pet ownership on some aspects of human health. *Journal of the Royal Society of Medicine, 84,* 717–20.

Serpell, J. A., & Jackson, E. (1994, October). Life events and methodological problems in studies of the health benefits of pet ownership. Paper presented at the Sixth Annual Meeting of the International Society for Anthrozoology, New York.

Siegel, J. M. (1990). Stressful life events and use of physician services among the elderly: The moderating role of pet ownership. *Journal of Personality and Social Psychology 58,* 1081–1086.

Straatman, I., Hanson, E. K. S., Endenburg, N., & Mol, J. A. (1997). The influence of a dog on male students during a stressor. *Anthrozoös, 10,* 191–7.

Vormbrock, J. K., & Grossberg, J. M. (1988). Cardiovascular effects of human–pet dog interactions. *Journal of Behavioral Medicine, 11,* 509–517.

Watson, N. L., & Weinstein M. (1993). Pet ownership in relation to depression, anxiety, and anger in working women. *Anthrozoös, 6,* 135–138.

Welin, C. L., Rosengren, A., & Wilhemsen, L. W. (1996). Social relationships and myocardial infarction: A case control study. *Journal of Cardiovascular Risk, 3,* 183–190.

Wilson, C. (1987). Physiological responses of college students to a pet. *Journal of Nervous and Mental Disease, 175,* 606–612.

Wilson, C. (1991). The pet as an anxiolytic intervention. *Journal of Nervous and Mental Disease, 179,* 482–489.

Zasloff, R. L., & Kidd, A. H. (1994). Loneliness and pet ownership among single women. *Psychological Reports, 75,* 747–752.

CHAPTER 4

Psychosocial Benefits of Animal Companionship

Lynette A. Hart

Center for Animals in Society, School of Veterinary Medicine, University of California, Davis, California

I. IMPORTANCE OF PETS IN QUALITY OF LIFE AND FOR SOME VULNERABLE INDIVIDUALS

Companion animals offer one of the most accessible enhancements to a person's quality of life. They are themselves an unconditional support system that can be drawn on at any time of day or night, when family members or friends may be busy with other things or unreachable. Having warm and accepting companionship near at hand provides essential comfort that is available whenever it is especially needed. A source of relaxation and entertainment is always close by. The increased quality of life afforded people by their animals has relatively low cost, in comparison with the efforts involved with human companions. The animal's demands are simple and uncomplicated, and, because the animal does not talk, the conflicts are few as long as the person avoids most behavior problems with the animal through careful selection and management.

Substantial evidence in the research literature on human social support points to the central role of relationships—or the lack of them—as being either stress producing or health promoting. Social networks and support were clearly associated with mortality risk in a classic study of 9-year mortality data; increased mortality rates were associated with each decrease in social connection (Berkman & Breslow, 1983). Adding supportive groups to assist grieving spouses was found in one study to be effective only with those individuals who had inadequate emotional support, because some had already reestablished sufficient emotionally supportive relationships (Barrett, 1978).

Everyone's life brings with it periods of challenge and heartbreak when reliance on friends and family can make a substantial difference in morale and the ability to regain an optimistic view. Yet, regardless of support from family and friends and, in some instances, social programs, medical care, and public outreach assistance, at times people who are at their greatest vulnerability will be without the social relationships they need for a reasonable quality of life. A few examples in which people may be at particular risk are those persons who are facing hearing, visual, or mobility disabilities, living alone in later years, or experiencing the onset of serious medical problems. Although some of these crises are temporary, their initial impact may be almost paralyzing.

Modern living requires coping with rapid changes and complexity, and often brings social isolation that leaves people without the social or family support they need during unexpected crises. Anyone living alone who is socially isolated and possibly experiencing heightened medical problems may begin to feel profoundly alone and lack the will and the ability to move forward. Geographic mobility commonly forces people to relegate their extended family connections to telephone or e-mail connections, rather than interacting in person. Close companionship may no longer be available on a consistent basis. The high costs of loneliness and a lack of social support to human health are well documented (House *et al.*, 1988). Loneliness and depression have been linked with a wide array of diseases, including cancer and cardiovascular disease (Lynch, 1977), and some leading scientists are even suggesting that depression is a central etiologic factor of these diseases (Chrousos & Gold, 1992).

Most animal-assisted activities (AAAs) and animal-assisted therapy (AAT) are directed at individuals who are institutionalized, rather than to precarious individuals who still live at home, but are in jeopardy nonetheless. For those who are struggling to continue living independently, it is reasonable to believe that companion animals can make a difference and perhaps prolong their period of independent living, lessening or delaying their requirements for institutional living or even in-home nursing care. Such a trial has not been conducted. One community program placed animals with elderly individuals, provided some support for their care, and arranged for a longitudinal assessment (Lago *et al.*, 1989); however, participants, most of whom had been given dogs, were challenged with their own health problems. Animals requiring lower effort than dogs, such as cats, may have been more appropriate companions for these elderly persons. The effects of cat ownership have not been studied extensively, but one correlational study in Australia found better scores on psychological health among cat owners than nonowners (Straede & Gates, 1993). A study by Karsh and Burket with few participants observed over a 1-year period reported that long-term cat owners were less lonely, anxious, and depressed than nonowners, and owners also reported some improvements in blood pressure (Karsh & Turner, 1988).

Moving into a state of permanent institutional living involves crossing a great divide that sharply curtails the person's quality of life, reduces contact with the world at large, and generally increases the cost of living (e.g., doubling the cost of in-home care by family members). If companion animals can provide psychosocial health benefits, an investment in providing animal companionship for such individuals could make a significant difference in the person's health, perhaps extending by many months or even a few years the period of carrying on a normal lifestyle.

It is generally recognized that companion animals provide a readily available source of warm support that can be compensatory for human companionship. Certainly the enthusiastic love of the two dogs in Fig. 1 appears convincing to the two owners. Also, cat owners rank their cats higher than their husbands in providing affection and unconditional love (Zasloff & Kidd, 1994a). Although

FIGURE 1   Animals can clearly express their love and affection to their human companions. (Photograph by Bonnie Mader.)

animals in positive relationships enhance the quality of life for people in many situations, the beneficial psychosocial effects of companion animals can most easily be seen and measured with individuals who are psychologically vulnerable; the psychosocial effects are not as obvious in more average situations. As people age, their former social networks generally shrink as they leave the workplace, move into smaller homes, lose friends and family members who have moved away or died, or experience chronic health problems. For such individuals, having companion animals living with them offers a source of reliable and accessible companionship. In one study of elderly dog owners, a majority said their dog was their only friend and believed their relationship with their dog was as strong as with humans (Peretti, 1990).

Individuals with severe physical disabilities who use wheelchairs can be motivated by an animal to perform physical tasks for therapy in the care of the dog, while benefiting socially from a service dog. As a working partner, the dog provides assistance with physical tasks. Children with mental or other disabilities can benefit from the extraordinary experience of therapeutic horseback riding, an occasion affording joyous human social support as well as the unique sensation and physical challenge of riding the horse (Hart, 1992). Empirical research has addressed four areas of psychosocial benefits of companion animals; these effects are reviewed in this section.

A. EFFECTS OF COMPANION ANIMALS ON LONELINESS AND DEPRESSION

Universally, people report that what they value most in their relationships with dogs and cats is the companionship they offer. Although perhaps considered commonplace, animal companionship offers a psychosocial benefit that can provide a meaningful and substantial comfort. Loneliness, lack of companionship, depression, and lack of social support are major risk factors that can impede a person's well-being and even increase the likelihood of suicide or other maladaptive behaviors. Individuals who are experiencing periods of adversity or its onset are at a heightened vulnerability, feeling more needy and subject to feelings of loneliness and depression. Companionship with animals in several studies has been associated with people suffering less depression and loneliness. The animals deeply comfort their human companions and apparently serve as a buffer of protection against adversity, a notion suggested by Siegel (1993). The concept of social support creating both main and buffering effects against stress is well known in discussions of human social support (Thoits, 1982); Siegel extended the buffering effects to include the support companion animals provide.

As set forth in a recent review (Garrity & Stallones, 1998), various methods have been used to assess the effects of contact with companion animals on human well-being. Descriptive, correlational, and experimental research designs are used to test the possibility that animals provide social support. The reviewed correlational studies often were hypothesis based, whether cross-sectional or longitudinal. Studies based on a structural approach to social support assessed simply whether or not a pet was present. The more complex buffering perspective evaluated whether an animal was intervening to soften the impact of stressful life events. Psychological, social, behavioral, and physical types of well-being were examined in these reviewed studies. After expressing some cautions, the authors concluded that the benefits from contacts with pets seem consistent with the benefits supported by research in studies of human social support. Although the benefits appeared to occur on psychological, physical, social, and behavioral levels, the benefits were apparent only in certain situations and under certain circumstances. Pet association frequently appeared beneficial both directly and as a buffering factor during stressful life circumstances, but did not occur in all situations or for everyone. A study of elderly women found that the strength of the relationship with their pets was unrelated to levels of depression (Miller & Lago, 1990). Similarly, an initial study of war veterans found pet ownership associated with improved morale and health (Robb, 1983), but, later, no differences were observed in an analysis of the full sample (Robb & Stegman, 1983).

1. Elderly People

In a study of elderly people, among those who were grieving the loss of their spouses within the previous year and who lacked close friends, a high proportion of individuals without pets described themselves as depressed, whereas low levels of depression were reported by those with pets, even though no differences in health status were found between those with and without pets among elderly people in general (Garrity et al., 1989). Similarly, no differences in health status were found among people 21 to 64 years of age with and without pets (Stallones et al., 1990). Having pets thus seemed to be associated with less depression among these deeply bereaved, elderly individuals, but a similar effect was not found for the general population.

It is essential to bring up a caveat, however: People who seek out animal companionship may be more skilled in making choices that maintain their own well-being. The traits of dependability, intellectual involvement, and self-confidence (comprising the skills of *planful competence*) are strong characteristics that continue throughout life, and individuals who as young people express planful competence seem able to absorb adverse life events in stride and take effective actions to keep their lives on track (Clausen, 1993). A decision to live with an animal could be one aspect of taking effective action in one's life.

We do not really know the mechanism of the correlational protective effect found by Garrity et al. (1989). As already suggested, individuals keeping pets may also have had different social skills and abilities that were reflected in the decision to have a pet. Yet, it may be tempting to ascribe the difference found in this study to the interactions with the pet, reflecting the laughter that a pet invariably brings, the responsibility to nurture another individual, and the loving devotion of a pet.

Living alone, though common in the United States, may itself be inherently stressful for most people. Loneliness occurs often in elderly people and is associated with various diseases. In another correlational study, elderly women living alone were found to be in better psychological health if they resided with an animal. They were less lonely, more optimistic, more interested in planning for the future, and less agitated than those women who lived without a pet (Goldmeier, 1986). Living with a companion animal was not associated with an incremental psychological boost for those women who were living with other relatives. Somewhat surprisingly, a similar protective effect of companion animals was found in a study of women graduate students who lived alone: Those living with a companion animal, or a person, or both, rated themselves as less lonely than the graduate student women living entirely alone, as shown in Fig. 2 (Zasloff & Kidd, 1994b).

2. Depressed People

In the classic budgie-begonia study of depressed community-dwelling elderly, participants were less negative psychologically after prolonged exposure to pet birds (Mugford & M'Comisky, 1975). A recent study, in which the variables were better controlled, examined the depression levels of elderly men who were exposed to an aviary at an adult day health care program (Holcomb et al., 1997). Men were offered the aviary in a repeated treatment design (ABAB) of 2 weeks with no treatment, 2 weeks with treatment, and then a repeat. No difference occurred in depression levels of the men overall with the presence of the aviary, however, a greater reduction in depression was associated with greater utilization of the aviary. The men who sought out the aviary also apparently experienced increased social interaction with family and staff members, while the men who ignored the aviary were unaffected by it.

Using animal-assisted therapy as an intervention for depression in college students has also been used as an experimental approach. The group given AAT subsequently was found to have lower scores on the Beck Depression Inventory than the control group (Folse et al., 1994). Surprisingly, the AAT in conjunction with group psychotherapy was no more effective than the

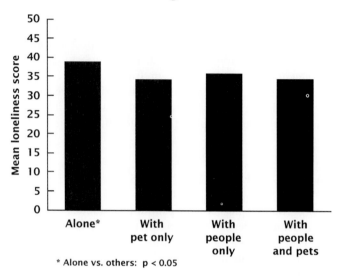

Loneliness Among Single Women: Living Status

(Adapted from Zasloff and Kidd, 1994)

FIGURE 2   Loneliness of women living alone as compared with those having a roommate or pet. (Modified from Zasloff & Kidd, 1994b.)

control, whereas the AAT alone was associated with a reduction in depression. The authors presented several possibilities concerning this result to examine in future studies.

3. People with a Hearing Disability

Providing an assistance dog to someone with a disability is a major intervention with psychosocial effects. Loss of hearing is an invisible disability that limits communication and predisposes people to feeling isolated and lonely. However, a dog serves as a full-time companion. Although an animal cannot participate in a complex conversational interchange, animals can be conversational partners that respond behaviorally to the statements and moods of their human companions. They also facilitate socializing within the neighborhood, more than is anticipated prior to having a hearing dog (Hart et al., 1996). In Hart et al.'s study of people with impaired hearing, those who had a hearing dog rated themselves as less lonely after receiving their dogs and also were less lonely than those who were slated to receive a hearing dog in the near future.

4. Conclusions

The findings that animals alleviate loneliness for women living alone but not those living with others, and that animals seem to offer some psychological protection to people who are deeply grieving and isolated, are consistent with a view that animals may compensate and provide people with basic, daily, essential psychosocial requirements when they are lacking them. Once the basic requirements are met by family or friends, however, it seems that a ceiling is reached such that significant positive effects are more difficult to detect. Evidence also reveals that people differ in the extent to which they draw on the animal companionship that could offer them some comfort.

B. Socializing Effects of Animals

The previous section emphasized the painfulness of loneliness and depression and reviewed some evidence indicating that animals ameliorate this type of isolation. This section reviews the empirical data that point toward the strong socializing impact of animals. Noteworthy in this regard are two studies of institutional environments. Visits with AAAs improved social interactions among residents and staff in a psychiatric facility for elderly women (Haughie et al., 1992) and in a residential home (Francis et al., 1985). Two other studies showed that visits with animals to nursing homes for patients with Alzheimer's disease improved their social interactions (Kongable et al., 1989; Beyersdorfer & Birkenhauer, 1990).

The absence of a supportive network of social companionship is a primary cause leading to depression, stress, suppression of the immune system, and various disease states (Serpell, 1986/1996). Social companionship buffers and reduces the impacts of such stress and anxiety. Viewed in this context, animal companionship offers an accessible compensatory alternative. Animals are consistently available companions especially appreciated by people who have spent much of their lives living with animals. Although animals do not respond verbally to conversation, they convincingly convey their love and affection to their human companions. They respond to conversation sufficiently enough that people almost inevitably speak to their animals. Dogs are particularly avid companions, staying with a person more than cats, and provoking social interactions (Miller & Lago, 1990). They are more interactive when living with a solitary person than with a family, essentially providing compensatory social contact for those who live alone (Smith, 1983).

Animals stimulate people to socialize with other people, often with the animal as a topic of conversation. Even a rabbit or a turtle arouses interest and friendly conversations about the animal from strangers (Hunt et al., 1992).

People may be stimulated to start conversations and to laugh and exchange stories more when a dog is present than when the person is alone (Messent, 1984). This pronounced effect of animals is evident to anyone who takes a friendly animal walking in a neighborhood. The powerful socializing effect is a primary benefit for people using wheelchairs who have a service dog (Eddy *et al.*, 1988; Mader *et al.*, 1989). The dog serves to normalize the social environment for the person with a disability who might otherwise be ignored or treated awkwardly. Figure 3 is a typical example of the interested responses of people to someone with an assistance dog. Similarly, for those with a hearing loss, a hearing dog provides unexpected social benefits, increasing social interactions for the person within the neighborhood and community as shown in Fig. 4 (Hart *et al.*, 1996).

As full-time companions, dogs and cats themselves are conversational partners, even though they do not respond with verbal conversation. Almost everyone talks to their own dog or cat, and virtually all people walking their dogs speak to them (Rogers *et al.*, 1993). People even speak to their birds on a regular basis (Beck & Katcher, 1989). In addition, the animals provoke people to speak to others. Animals of almost any species stimulate conversations, causing people to speak with strangers in a friendly way. A soft furry

FIGURE 3   Neighbors and people in the community approach in a friendly way to meet someone in a wheelchair who has a service dog.

Socializing Effects of Hearing Dogs:
Actual and Prospective Recipients

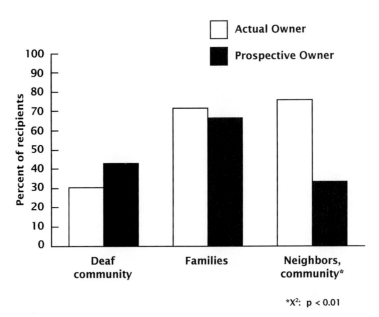

*X²: p < 0.01

(Adapted from Hart, Zasloff, and Benfatto, 1996)

FIGURE 4   Increased socializing as estimated by actual and prospective owners of hearing dogs. (Modified from Hart *et al.*, 1996.)

rabbit appears to be a stronger stimulus for evoking conversations than a turtle (Hunt *et al.*, 1992). In such cases, the animals are a convenient and comfortable topic of conversation. People who regularly walk their dogs talk with acquaintances about their dogs whether or not the dogs are present at the time (Rogers *et al.*, 1993).

Evidence that the social support of a dog enhances health was reported in a recent study of people using assistance dogs, reporting that social facilitation, social support, and an affectionate relationship were all correlated with the person's self-perceived health (Lane *et al.*, 1998). Participants described how the dog created social opportunities with people while also serving as an essential family member and friend, as shown in Fig. 5.

Effects of Service Dogs for Recipients

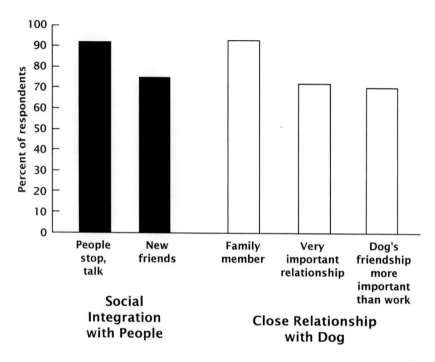

(Adapted from Lane, McNicholas, and Collis, 1998)

FIGURE 5   Reports of recipients of service dogs of effects on socializing with people and the relationship with the dog. (Modified from Lane *et al.*, 1998.)

C. Motivating Effects of Animals

Animals also have the ability to inspire and motivate people to engage in constructive activities that they would not have otherwise. People may sponta-neously decide to arrange to bring an animal into a nursing home, school, or hospital on a regular basis. Often this is done by an individual or a small local group that self-organized for this purpose. As this practice became widespread, it came to be known as offering AAAs, or, if integrated into an overall treatment plan for the patient, AAT. Such volunteers find it rewarding to share their animals with others who enjoy them, to the point that many make commitments to visit facilities on a routine weekly basis. It is important to note that such remarkable motivation probably would not occur if the person were visiting the nursing home alone. The animal partner is the essential participant that makes the effort of the volunteer worthwhile. The main contribution of the animal to AAA may be in inspiring the volunteer, because human visitors alone were found in one study to be as effective as pets alone or human visitors with pets in eliciting smiling and alertness from patients (Hendy, 1987).

As anyone with an active dog knows, dogs can motivate people to take walks. This effect was documented in a study of people before and after adopting a dog (Serpell, 1991). After people adopted a dog, they sharply increased their daily walking for the 10 months of the study. Similarly, elderly people in Southern California who kept dogs reported spending 1.4 hours per day outdoors with the animal (Siegel, 1990, 1993), a much more consistent activity than would be likely even in an organized exercise class.

D. Effects of Animals in Mobilizing Attention and Calming

Even sitting looking at fish in an aquarium relaxes and relieves anxiety for patients in a dental waiting room (Katcher et al., 1984). This calming and comforting effect from animals even applies to individuals with Alzheimer's disease (Fritz et al., 1995). As shown in Fig. 6, Alzheimer's patients still living at home had fewer aggressive and anxious outbursts if they had regular exposure to a companion animal, as compared with patients lacking an animal. The calmer behavior is undoubtedly less distressing and exhausting to the caregiver, who invariably is at risk for burnout in this challenging situation.

Similar calming effects have been reported in therapeutic settings. During group therapy with dissociative patients, a therapy dog was found to offer a calming influence and also alerted the therapist to distressed patients (Arnold, 1995). In another study, a therapy dog's visits to a psychiatric ward were associated with a substantial reduction in noise levels (Walsh et al., 1995).

The calming effects of animals are especially valuable with children exhibiting attention deficit/hyperactive disorder and conduct disorders and have been the basis for therapeutic interventions. An extended series of studies in a learning setting have shown that animals capture and hold children's attention and direct their attention outward (Katcher & Wilkins, 1997). Calming the children was a first essential step. With their attention mobilized and directed outward, agitation and aggression diminish, creating a better teaching environment. The improvements in behavior generalized across to some other teaching situations but did not become universal to all contexts. Another study in a classroom setting involved children with Down's syndrome; a real dog provided a more sustained focus than an imitation dog for positive and cooperative interactions with the dog and the adult (Limond et al., 1997).

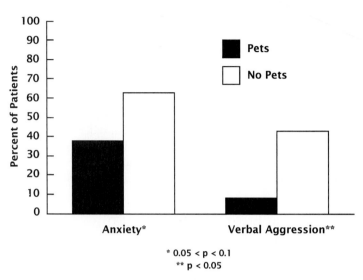

Non-cognitive Symptor
Alzheimer's Patien

* 0.05 < p < 0.1
** p < 0.05

(Adapted from Fritz, Farver, Kass, and Hart, 1995)

FIGURE 6   Reports by caregivers of Alzheimer's patients' symptoms of anxiety and verbal aggression. (Modified from Fritz *et al.*, 1995.)

II. NORMALIZING EFFECTS OF ANIMALS

Most AAT has been directed toward the most vulnerable populations of people, many of whom have little prospect of a full recovery of function and health. What is often not considered is that all people are likely to experience periods in their lives of heightened vulnerability, some temporary and others prolonged. For example, everyone at some time experiences severe illness or disability, suffers through the illness or death of family members, and if they live long enough, sustains the adverse consequences of aging. For anyone, these experiences can create a precarious vulnerable state, particularly if the person lacks a strong network of social support. Whether this precipitating problem represents a new entrenched or a temporary vulnerability, companion animals can normalize a stressful circumstance. They offer engaging and accepting interactions without reflecting back the discomfort, concern, and agitation of the difficult situation. An animal can communicate a message such as "It's not as bad as it seems; everything is fine," and thus help put people more at ease.

ᴀ. Facilitating Normal Development

The effects of dogs in normalizing the social environment were illustrated in a study of schoolchildren who used wheelchairs in classes comprised primarily of able-bodied children. The children using wheelchairs who had service dogs consistently were approached more often on the playground than those without service dogs (Mader *et al.*, 1989). The dogs were able to successfully override the able-bodied children's discomfort with a child's disability and thus promote a more normal psychosocial environment for the developing child. Because the presence of the dog ensured a more welcoming and warm reception, the child with the disability who has a dog was treated more as an able-bodied child. A variant of this effect relates to the fact that older children of siblings nurture and care for younger siblings. However,the youngest siblings or only children give heightened attention to their animals, thus providing themselves with nurturing opportunities they otherwise would miss (Melson, 1988).

B. Ameliorating Emotional Crises and Extenuating Circumstances

Another example of normalizing a social environment comes from a study of patients with Alzheimer's disease who were still living at home with family caregivers. Aggressive outbursts and episodes of anxiety were less common among the patients who had regular contact with companion animals (Fritz *et al.*, 1995). For the caregiver, this calming influence of the animal on the patient would reduce the stress of coping with this difficult disease in a family member and perhaps delay the time when the patient had to be placed in an institutional facility.

Siegel (1993) has proposed that animals play a role as a stress buffer that softens the impact of stressful events. She suggested this theoretical construct after finding that elderly people with companion animals, especially dogs, did not increase their medical visits during times of life stress events; elderly people lacking animals characteristically increased their medical visits following stressful life events.

The stress of going out into the world with a disability or working in a dangerous environment as a police officer can be reduced by the constant companionship of a working dog that also offers assistance with instrumental tasks. The officer in Fig. 7 presumably feels more comfortable in the workplace with his canine companion. It is common for people with a service dog or a police dog to value the dogs' psychosocial contributions above the instrumental assistance; in addition to extraordinary companionship, the dog facilitates social interactions, as shown in Fig. 8 (Paul Knott, personal communication,

FIGURE 7   A canine partner offers great comfort and companionship to an officer.

1999). As shown in Fig. 2 in Chapter 5, people with hearing dogs most frequently mentioned companionship as a pleasure of having the dog, although a statistical comparison with the pleasure of a hearing dog's service was not tested (Hart *et al.*, 1995).

III. INDIVIDUALITY IN HUMAN RESPONSES TO ANIMALS

The psychosocial effects described here should not be taken as evidence to prescribe companion animals generally to individuals who are lonely or depressed. The effects of a particular animal can be positive or negative, varying

FIGURE 8   The enhanced social acceptance facilitated by a service dog may be more significant than the service tasks the dog performs.

with the person and the context. Responses to animals are a highly individual matter, depending on the person's previous life experience with animals, the person's current health and responsibilities, and the species and breeds of animals. Thus, individuals who have had dogs or cats in their early childhood would be more likely to respond to animals in later life than would people with little animal experience. In general, in middle and older age, people are drawn to the species and perhaps even breeds they had previously enjoyed (Kidd & Kidd, 1989). However, medical, economic, and housing situations may limit the practicality of acquiring the most favored species and breed.

A. Personal History with Animals during the Life Cycle

Small children are strongly attracted to their companion dogs and cats (Kidd & Kidd, 1987), as well as to other less familiar, small animals, such as a rabbit or turtle (Hunt et al., 1992). Children are strongly influenced in their feelings for dogs and cats by the attitudes and petkeeping of their parents and grandparents (Kidd & Kidd, 1997). By the time people are adults, they have a wealth of memories of experiences with animals, including positive and negative occasions that may enhance or attenuate their responses to particular animals. There are no naive subjects. Efforts to offer AAA/T or provide enhanced contact with animals generally offer a particular type of experience, one that is not tailored to the specific preexisting attachments that each individual person has had with animals. Many of us have a particular breed that we strongly prefer. A woman who has always kept a German shepherd is likely still to retain that strong preference, even when she is in her eighties and weighs far less than the dog. Offering her a bird or a cat, though safer, may not be desirable or helpful to her. One size does not fit all.

It perhaps seems paradoxical that old age is the period when people are most strongly and deeply attached to their animals, yet this also is the age where the lowest percentage of people keep animals. The people who are most likely to benefit from companion animal ownership are the least likely to have companionship with animals (Poresky & Daniels, 1998).

B. ATTACHMENT AND COMPATIBILITY

The psychosocial benefits of companion animals are strongest when the person is strongly attached to the animal (Garrity et al., 1989). In a recent study, people who were relatively more compatible with their pets reported better mental health overall and fewer physical symptoms; thus, the fit between the animal and the owner on physical, behavioral, and psychological dimensions, as measured by compatibility, also is a key to enjoying psychosocial benefits in companion animal relationships (Budge et al., 1998). Typically, optimal attachment and compatibility are more likely when the animal is of the person's preferred species and breed.

Some preliminary results suggested that dogs were more salient for participants than cats in maintaining morale in the family (Albert & Anderson, 1997). However, other work has presented evidence that cats may elicit attachment as strongly as dogs (Zasloff & Kidd, 1994a). These studies are consistent with the view that psychosocial benefits of pets relate to the companionship they offer, not usually to the instrumental or physical assistance they may provide.

IV. CONCLUSIONS

This chapter has emphasized the role that companion animals play in people's quality of life. Although these contributions can enhance anyone's life, they are especially crucial for persons whose network of social support is limited. Abundant research literature on human social support has documented the essential role of relationships for avoiding early mortality and morbidity. Animals, by offering meaningful love and comfort, provide support that is some-what of a substitute when human companionship is lacking. Animals can play a major positive role in people's lives, particularly if the animal is well suited to the person's living situation, the person is able to easily manage caring for the animal, and behavior problems are avoided.

Health professionals thus have an opportunity to provide leadership in assisting in individualized pet placements with follow-ups to increase the rate of success and anticipate problems before they become serious. Many volunteers who currently bring animal-assisted activities to individuals residing in institutions with guidance could assist precarious individuals still living within the community. Such leadership is also needed to develop new creative solutions for offering more flexible means of having continued contact with animals in later life, but associated with less demanding responsibilities (Peretti, 1990). Community-based councils that include the various constituencies concerned with human and animal health would be well positioned to begin tackling these challenges.

REFERENCES

Albert, A., & Anderson, M. (1997). Dogs, cats, and morale maintenance: Some preliminary data. *Anthrozoos,* 10, 121–124.

Arnold, J. C. (1995). Therapy dogs and the dissociative patient: Preliminary observations. *Dissociation: Progress in the Dissociative Disorders,* 8, 247–252.

Barrett, C. (1978). Effectiveness of widows' groups in facilitating change. *Journal of Consulting and Counseling Psychology,* 46, 20–31.

Beck, A. M., & Katcher, A. H. (1989). Bird human interaction. *Journal of the Association of Avian Veterinarians,* 3, 152–153.

Berkman, L., & Breslow, L. (1983). *Health and ways of living: Findings from the Alameda County study.* New York: Oxford University Press.

Beyersdorfer, P. S., & Birkenhauer, D. M. (1990). The therapeutic use of pets on an Alzheimer's unit. *American Journal of Alzheimer's Care and Related Disorders and Research,* 5, 13–17.

Budge, R. C., Spicer, J., Jones, B., & St. George, R. (1998). Health correlates of compatibility and attachment in human–companion animal relationships. *Society and Animals,* 6, 219–234.

Chrousos, G. P., & Gold, P. W. (1992). The concepts of stress and stress disorders: Overview of physical and behavioral homeostasis. *Journal of the American Medical Association,* 267, 1244–1252.

Clausen, J. A. (1993). *American lives: Looking back at the children of the Great Depression.* New York: Free Press.

Eddy, J., Hart, L. A., & Boltz, R. P. (1988). The effects of service dogs on social acknowledgements of people in wheelchairs. *Journal of Psychology,* 122, 39–45.

Folse, E. B., Minder, C. C., Aycock, M. J., & Santana, R. T. (1994). Animal-assisted therapy and depression in adult college students. *Anthrozoos,* 7, 188–194.

Francis, G., Turner, J. T., & Johnson, S. B. (1985). Domestic animal visitation as therapy with adult home residents. *International Journal of Nursing Studies,* 22, 201–206.

Fritz, C. L., Farver, T. B., Kass, P. H., & Hart, L. A. (1995). Association with companion animals and the expression of noncognitive symptoms in Alzheimer's patients. *Journal of Nervous and Mental Disease,* **183**(8), 359–363.

Garrity, T. F., & Stallones, L. (1998). Effects of pet contact on human well-being. In C. C. Wilson & D. C. Turner (Eds.), *Companion animals in human health* (pp. 3–22). Thousand Oaks, CA: Sage Publications.

Garrity, T. F., Stallones, L., Marx, M. B., & Johnson, T. P. (1989). Pet ownership and attachment as supportive factors in the health of the elderly *Anthrozoos,* **3**, 35–44.

Goldmeier, J. (1986). Pets or people: Another research note. *Gerontologist,* **26**, 203–206.

Hart, L. A. (1992). Therapeutic riding: Assessing human versus horse effects. *Anthrozoos,* **5**, 138–139.

Hart, L. A., Zasloff, R. L., & Benfatto, A. M. (1995). The pleasures and problems of hearing dog ownership. *Psychological Reports,* **77**, 969–970.

Hart, L. A., Zasloff, R. L., & Benfatto, A. M. (1996). The socializing role of hearing dogs. *Applied Animal Behavioural Science,* **47**, 7–15.

Haughie, E., Milne, D., & Elliott, V. (1992). An evaluation of companion pets with elderly psychiatric patients. *Behavioural Psychotherapy,* **20**, 367–372.

Hendy, H. M. (1987). Effects of pet and/or people visits on nursing home residents. *International Journal of Aging and Human Development,* **25**, 279–291.

Holcomb, R., Jendro, C., Weber, B., & Nahan, U. (1997). Use of an aviary to relieve depression in elderly males. *Anthrozoology,* **10**, 32–36.

House, J. S., Landis, K. R., & Umberson, D. (1988). Social relationships and health. *Science,* **241**, 540–545.

Hunt, S. J., Hart, L. A., & Gomulkiewicz, R. (1992). Role of small animals in social interaction between strangers. *Journal of Social Psychology,* **133**, 245–256.

Karsh, E. B., & Turner, D. C. (1988). The human–cat relationship. In D. C. Turner & P. Bateson (Eds.), *The domestic cat: The biology of its behaviour.* Cambridge, UK: Cambridge University Press.

Katcher, A., & Wilkins, G. G. (1997). Animal-assisted therapy in the treatment of disruptive behavior disorders in children. In A. Lundberg (Ed.), *The environment and mental health: A guide for clinicians* (pp. 193–204). Mahwah, NJ: Lawrence Erlbaum Associates.

Katcher, A., Segal, H., & Beck, A. (1984). Comparison of contemplation and hypnosis for the reduction of anxiety and discomfort during dental surgery. *American Journal of Clinical Hypnosis,* **27**, 14–21.

Kidd, A. H., & Kidd, R. M. (1987). Reactions of infants and toddlers to live and toy animals. *Psychological Reports,* **61**, 455–464.

Kidd, A. H., & Kidd, R. M. (1989). Factors in adults' attitudes toward pets. *Psychological Reports,* **65**, 903–910.

Kidd, A. H., & Kidd, R. M. (1997). Changes in the behavior of pet owners across generations. *Psychological Reports,* **80**, 195–202.

Kongable, L. G., Buckwalter, K. C., & Stolley, J. (1989). The effects of pet therapy on the social behavior of institutionalized Alzheimer's clients. *Archives of Psychiatric Nursing,* **3**, 191–198.

Lago, D., Delaney, M., Miller, M., & Grill, C. (1989). Companion animals, attitudes toward pets, and health outcomes among the elderly: A long-term follow-up. *Anthrozoos,* **3**, 25–34.

Lane, D. R., McNicholas, J., & Collis, G. M. (1998). Dogs for the disabled: Benefits to recipients and welfare of the dog. *Applied Animal Behavioural Science,* **59**, 49–60.

Limond, J. A., Bradshaw, J. W. S., & Cormack, K. F. M. (1997). Behavior of children with learning disabilities interacting with a therapy dog. *Anthrozoos,* **10**, 84–89.

Lynch, J. J. (1977). *The broken heart: The medical consequences of loneliness.* New York: Basic Books.

Mader, B., Hart, L. A., & Bergin, B. (1989). Social acknowledgements for children with disabilities: Effects of service dogs. *Child Development,* **60**, 1528–1534.

Melson, G. F. (1988). Availability of and involvement with pets by children: Determinants and correlates. *Anthrozoos,* **2**, 45–52.

Messent, P. R. (1984). Correlates and effects of pet ownership. In E. K. Anderson, B. L. Hart, & L. A. Hart (Eds.), *The pet connection: Its influence on our health and quality of life* (pp. 331–340). Minneapolis, MN: University of Minnesota.

Miller, M., & Lago, D. (1990). The well-being of older women: The importance of pet and human relations. *Anthrozoos,* **3**, 245–251.

Mugford, R., & M'Comisky, J. (1975). Some recent work on the psychotherapeutic value of cage birds with old people. In R. S. Anderson (Ed.), *Pet animals and society: a BSAVA symposium* (pp. 54–65). London: Bailliere Tindall.

Peretti, P. O. (1990). Elderly–animal friendship bonds. *Social Behavior and Personality,* **18**, 151–156.

Poresky, R. H., & Daniels, A. M. (1998). Demographics of pet presence and attachment. *Anthrozoos,* **11**, 236–241.

Robb, S. S. (1983). Health status correlates of pet–human association in a health impaired population. In A. H. Katcher & A. M. Beck (Eds.), *New perspectives on our lives with companion animals* (pp. 318–327). Philadelphia, PA: University of Pennsylvania Press.

Robb, S. S., & Stegman, C. E. (1983). Companion animals and elderly people: A challenge for evaluators of social support. *Gerontologist,* **23**, 277–282.

Rogers, J., Hart, L. A., & Boltz, R. P. (1993). The role of pet dogs in casual conversations of elderly adults. *Journal of Social Psychology,* **133**, 265–277.

Serpell, J. (1986/1996). Health and friendship. In *In the company of animals: A study of human–animal relationships* (pp. 108–126). Cambridge, UK: Cambridge University Press.

Serpell, J. (1991). Beneficial effects of pet ownership on some aspects of human health and behavior. *Journal of the Royal Society of Medicine,* **84**, 717–720.

Siegel, J. (1990). Stressful life events and use of physician services among the elderly: The moderating role of pet ownership. *Journal of Personality and Social Psychology,* **58**, 1081–1086.

Siegel, J. M. (1993). Companion animals: In sickness and in health. *Journal of Social Issues,* **49**, 157–167.

Smith, S. L. (1983). Interactions between pet dog and family members: An ethological study. In A. H. Katcher & A. M. Beck (Eds.), *New perspectives on our lives with companion animals* (pp. 29–36). Philadelphia, PA: University of Pennsylvania Press.

Stallones, L., Marx, M. B., Garrity, T. F., & Johnson, T. P. (1990). Pet ownership and attachment in relation to the health of U. S. adults, 21 to 64 years of age. *Anthrozoos,* **4**, 100–112.

Straede, C. M., & Gates, G. R. (1993). Psychological health in a population of Australian cat owners. *Anthrozoos,* **6**, 30–42.

Thoits, P. (1982). Conceptual, methodological, and theoretical problems in studying social supports as a buffer against life stress. *Journal of Health and Social Behavior,* **23**, 145–159.

Walsh, P. G., Mertin, P. G., Verlander, D. F., & Pollard, C. F. (1995). The effects of a "pets as therapy" dog on persons with dementia in a psychiatric ward. *Australian Occupational Therapy Journal,* **42**(4), 161–166.

Zasloff, R. L., & Kidd, A. H. (1994a). Attachment to feline companions. *Psychological Reports,* **74**, 747–752.

Zasloff, R. L., & Kidd, A. H. (1994b). Loneliness and pet ownership among single women. *Psychological Reports,* **75**, 747–752.

Animal-Assisted Therapy

CONCEPTUAL MODEL AND GUIDELINES FOR QUALITY ASSURANCE

Methods, Standards, Guidelines, and Considerations in Selecting Animals for Animal-Assisted Therapy

Part A: Understanding Animal Behavior, Species, and Temperament as Applied to Interactions with Specific Populations

LYNETTE A. HART

Center for Animals in Society, School of Veterinary Medicine, University of California, Davis, California

I. PROVIDING ANIMAL-ASSISTED ACTIVITIES OR ANIMAL-ASSISTED THERAPY

Animal-assisted therapy (AAT) implies that the person receiving the animal's attention is compromised medically, physically, or mentally, and can benefit from animal companionship. This chapter takes a fresh look at the concepts of animal-assisted activities and therapy (AAA/T) and venues where they are useful, and then deals with selecting appropriate animals. In particular, I suggest broadening the concept and practice of AAA/T to include situations where full-time companionship is provided, rather than offering only periodic visits. When preparing to offer AAA/T, many of the principles are the same as those used when selecting companion animals for normal home environments. The decision to offer someone special activities or therapy through companionship with animals presumes that an animal can provide something that the person needs or that would enhance the person's life in a significant way, or that the animal can add essential motivation to carry out assigned treatments or activities. Psychosocial benefits, motivation for performance of important tasks, and instrumental assistance with tasks may result. Yet one should not expect a one-size-fits-all animal to fulfill everyone's needs or enhance everyone's life. Many individuals dislike certain animals, and most strongly prefer particular types of animals. We are all predisposed by our previous experiences to have specific individualized reactions to particular breeds or species.

A. VOLUNTEERS PROVIDING AAA OR ASSISTING WITH AAT

For the individual who provides it, AAA is a way to provide pleasure and joy to others by sharing an animal. Most providers are volunteers who love their animals and find it rewarding to introduce them to other people. Some receive specialized training to carry out activities that are prescribed as AAT by a physician or other health professional. The practice of volunteers participating in AAA/T swept across the United States during the last 15 years. By now people in every community are aware of the practice of taking animals into nursing homes. Many people have participated in some version of AAA/T, and most know someone who has done it. This significant social movement, though quiet in its effects, has been as broad and impactful in a different way than the animal rights movement, profoundly sensitizing our society to the plight of institutionalized elderly people and underlining the compassionate role of animals in providing companionship. For the providers, although visiting a nursing home alone might be uninteresting and even stressful, offering AAA/T with a companion animal is inherently rewarding and pleasant (Stein, 1993). Many volunteers find AAA/T so motivating that they participate in it regularly over a period of months or even years.

B. HEALTH PROFESSIONALS DIRECTING OR PROVIDING AAT

Specific goals are planned when AAT is designed for a person by an occupational therapist, a physical therapist, a physician, or other health professional who incorporates an animal into the treatment process. The health professional may personally conduct the AAT, such as when a speech therapist utilizes an animal. In other cases, the professional may be assisted by volunteers, which typically occurs with therapeutic horseback riding. Or the health professional may train volunteers in specific procedures that are later prescribed for specific individuals and carried out by supervised volunteers.

II. CONTEXTS FOR PERSONS RECEIVING THERAPY OR ANIMAL COMPANIONSHIP

A. PERIODIC VISITS, OFTEN IN INSTITUTIONAL SETTINGS

When considering people who may benefit from AAA/T, the most common focus has been to bring animals into institutions. Many programs along these lines have been established and are well known to the lay public. Whether in AAA or in structured AAT, periodic visits to institutions are immediately rewarding to volunteers who experience brightening the days of others by sharing their animals, usually dogs. Various studies have reported that residents welcome the special visits and feel uplifted (e.g., Francis *et al.*, 1985). During a dog's visits to institutional geriatric residents, interactions with the dog included grooming and touching (Neer *et al.*, 1987). Elderly psychiatric patients in another study increased their verbal and nonverbal interactions during visits with a dog (Haughie *et al.*, 1992). Most of the individuals in rest homes have little prospect of a substantial return to full health, however, so the prospects of any long-term health benefits are minimal. However, if frequent enough, the visits can add measurably to the quality of life.

Other forms of periodic companionship occur when animals are included in a counseling environment or are used to motivate hospital patients to perform their tasks of physical therapy during rehabilitation. With both institutional visits and counseling the animal remains primarily the responsibility of the volunteer or health professional providing the AAA/T, not the person being served. Concerns for the welfare of the animal are addressed through the individuals providing the AAA/T and there is no need to train the recipient in appropriate animal care. Section III of Part A in this chapter provides an overview of specific selection criteria associated with species of animals. This part of the chapter focuses especially on the challenging goal of providing more full-time or ongoing companionship for AAA/T, especially for the psychosocial benefits such as comfort that is protective against depression or loneliness, motivation for involvement in living, and socialization effects.

B. FULL-TIME COMPANIONSHIP, WITH GUIDANCE AND ASSISTANCE AS REQUIRED

In the conventional parlance, AAA/T consists of a program of periodic visits, usually in an institutional setting. If the person recovers and returns home, the contact with the animal usually ends, though concerned professionals are seeking to continue scheduled visits to patients after they return home, for example, Dr. Judy, Mercy Hospital, Oxnard, California. Compared with periodic visits, more substantial effects may result from developing methods to deliver AAA/T to lonely individuals who still remain self-sufficient, especially the elderly or those with health problems, because it could play a role in improving their health and social involvement (see Chapter 4) and prolonging their period of independent living. Many such individuals would not be able to successfully manage the challenge of acquiring and caring for an animal companion without personalized guidance and assistance. For someone at high risk for loneliness, full-time animal companionship may ameliorate the isolation and play a role in enhancing health and extending the period of normalcy, even when a person is living with cancer or AIDS. With this in mind, some immediate concerns for the volunteer or health professional to consider are the daily tasks of animal care, the acceptability of the animal in the person's housing, the care of the animal during the person's absence or illness, convenient access to veterinary and grooming care (perhaps including house calls), and the affordability of the expenses of food and care. Community programs have the opportunity to pave new ground by facilitating and supporting animal ownership to such motivated individuals who would benefit. For example, one strategy would be including AAA/T as an aspect of in-home supportive services offered through county governments. Whether provided by a public or volunteer organization, the object would be to offer essential support in developing a comprehensive plan for the animal's care while still leaving the central responsibility for the animal with the person. The United States has a growing population of elderly individuals who live alone, especially women, and people with AIDS where loneliness could be ameliorated with companion animals.

A primary challenge when planning full-time companionship that will offer AAA/T to the recipient is ensuring responsible care for the animal. Either alone or assisted by others, the recipient needs to feel that the animal's needs are being fully managed, including assistance as required with some tasks. Some similar economic and caregiving challenges have already been addressed by programs placing guide, service, and hearing dogs, where an assisting dog is the responsibility of the recipient with some guidance and supervision from the issuing agency. As seen in Fig. 1, the love and affection a service dog offers demonstrates the value of full-time animal companionship.

Specifically concerning frail elderly people or those with AIDS, a few programs at humane societies sponsored by pet food companies or others have subsidized the expenses of pet ownership. More ongoing, in-home assistance is needed to provide people with personalized consultation on techniques of basic care, housing issues, pet deposits, pet selection, developing a plan for animal care during absences, and care techniques designed to avoid or lessen

FIGURE 1   Animals offer unconditional acceptance. Even for someone using a wheelchair, the importance of the dog's love often outweighs the specific assistance that the dog provides. (Photograph by Bonnie Mader.)

many behavior problems. Management techniques emphasizing prevention of problems and maintenance of the animal's health are significant strategies that enhance the enjoyment of companionship by curtailing the potential problems that would detract from the relationship (Hart & Hart, 1997).

Some individuals who would desperately prefer living with a companion animal choose not to have one. As the lives of elderly pet owners slow down, they often move into elderly or assisted housing. They may have an animal euthanized, even one that is healthy, sometimes because the animals are not allowed in the new home. When provisions are available to retain or acquire a special animal and the person is able to care for it, the person's quality of life can be greatly enhanced. At other times it is a sorrowful decision made from fear of how the animal will fare when the person dies. This concern can be addressed by developing programs where responsibility for the animal is shared and alternative provisions are in place for excellent care.

Less effortful methods of offering companionship with animals may be appropriate for elderly people who are vulnerable and fragile, while still providing more contact than just a scheduled weekly visit. Many elderly persons may prefer a more passive, yet sustained, involvement with animals to replace the more direct contact they experienced earlier in life (Verderber, 1991); this argues for more flexibility in the available types of involvement. Fostering or "leasing" animals that are affectionate and easy to manage are possibilities that would relieve the person's concerns about the ability to provide a home for the animal's entire lifetime. Sharing responsibility for the animal in this way can curtail a person's fears for the animal's welfare when the person dies. A version of this arrangement is sometimes provided in nursing homes, where the animal officially lives in the facility, either with one person or as a general resident, while the care is provided by the institutional staff. A resident dog stimulates interactions among residents and staff, but over time the effects may shift primarily to staff (Winkler et al., 1989). Providing long-term "loaner" animals, as a kind of AAA/T with fewer demands of ownership, has not been well developed and advocated, although many programs use fostering of animals as a way to increase the housing capacity for animals in humane societies.

One program useful as a model is Pets Are Wonderful Support, PAWS, a volunteer organization in San Francisco and some other cities that provides assistance to people with AIDS in continuing to care for their companion animals, similar to offering attendant care for the animal. Volunteers provide whatever specific help is needed, such as walking a dog, cleaning a cat's litter box, delivering pet food, transporting the animal, or providing care during an absence, and this makes the difference in the person being able to continue having an animal. For more than a decade, PAWS volunteers in the founding San Francisco office have demonstrated a remarkable commitment by sustaining services to about 500 clients. A similar type of effort offering more guidance and consultation tailored to the person's needs could well be targeted to individuals who, though no longer vigorous, continue to manage their lives independently.

C. Ethical Considerations

A strong caution that needs to be emphasized when considering full-time companionship is the extent of effort and ongoing commitment that is required.

The volunteer or health professional has a major role to play in assisting with this decision and assessing whether a full-time responsibility for the animal is appropriate for this situation. If not, other avenues can be explored that provide consistent contact with the animal while still ensuring that the animal is fully cared for and is not a burden to the recipient. One step in the successful placement of an animal with someone who is not robust is to develop a comprehensive plan for all aspects of care and schedule regular follow-up contact to assess where problems are arising that need to be addressed. Facilities placing guide dogs and service dogs typically schedule routine home visits and offer consultation in such problem solving. Almost inevitably, people underestimate the effort an animal requires and perhaps unrealistically expect an animal to be perfectly behaved. Even people who are well informed prior to adoption and have given considerable thought to this decision, such as prospective owners of hearing dogs, greatly underestimate the likelihood of behavioral problems. Frequently, humane societies may provide special obedience training prior to placement with elderly. Here it is useful to build in the person's past experience in caring for animals, placing a species familiar to the person so as to reduce the gap of awareness of what is involved. The process inevitably is challenging and is only worthwhile if the person has a high interest in having an animal.

It cannot be emphasized too strongly that the potential benefits are not without various costs. In particular, acquiring a dog involves assuming responsibility for the numerous daily tasks of care and coping with new complications when arranging for housing and travel. In one longitudinal project that evaluated pet ownership among the elderly where a community organization provided substantial support, the declining health status of participants strongly affected the outcomes. Pets did not exert a strong lasting effect (Lago et al., 1989; Miller & Lago, 1990). Most of the participants had dogs, which perhaps was unrealistic and too challenging given their initial health status.

Also serious may be the shift in a couple's relationship that occurs when a person with a disability forms a close emotional attachment to the dog, and the partner feels excluded (Valentine et al., 1993). The complications arising when dogs are acquired for therapeutic use have not been well studied. A more common problem that is frequently mentioned is that an animal develops behaviors that cause problems for the person. We found in a study of prospective and current hearing dog owners that very few prospective owners anticipated that their well-trained dogs might have behavioral problems; yet half of owners were experiencing some type of behavior problem, as shown in Fig. 2 (Hart et al., 1995). Groups were similar in their estimation of the pleasures of compnionship, the dog providing service for hearing tasks, and security. Both groups mentioned the inevitable complications of traveling with the animal.

Pleasures and Problems of Hearing Dogs:
Actual and Prospective Recipients

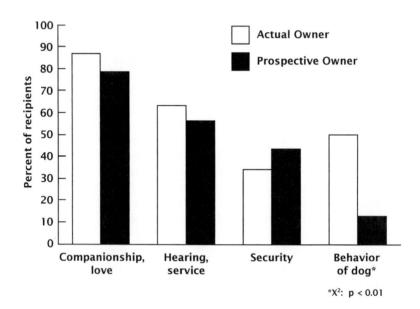

*X^2: p < 0.01

(Adapted from Hart, Zasloff, and Benfatto, 1995)

FIGURE 2   Pleasures and problems of hearing dogs as reported by actual and prospective owners. (Modified from Hart *et al.*, 1995.)

III. SELECTING THE ANIMAL

The circumstance and context are important. Is this animal to be an occasional visitor or a full-time companion? Does the animal's role include providing motivation for the physical exercise of the person? Does the animal add a feeling of security and safety? Is its role that of stimulating social contacts and conversation for someone who is isolated and lonely? Is it the animal's role to assist with a difficult transient circumstance or is the person dealing with an ongoing situation? Will the animal's care be provided by the person receiving the therapy?

An occasional visiting animal to a person in a facility provides entertainment and a pleasant diversion. In such cases, the animal is in the control of someone who is responsible for its care; issues of compatibility with the person's needs and background may not arise in this situation. However, if the person or a family member will be spending substantial amounts of time with the animal and even assuming responsibility for its care, a careful overview of all aspects of the feasibility of caring for and living with this animal is essential.

If it is to be effective and have an optimal outcome, recommending or prescribing an animal requires going beyond a generic recommendation and looking more closely at the entire situation, especially the specifics of the desired outcome. This requires knowing as much as possible about the candidate animals, be they dogs, cats, horses, or species that are more easily confined, as well as the people who will be brought together with the animals. A common mistake is that someone providing AAA/T may especially love cats, or a particular breed of dog, or horses, and may expect others to have similar feelings toward those animals. Volunteers and health professionals providing AAA/T have the obligation to back off from their own strong preferences and instead identify the particular preferences of the people they are serving and the characteristics of the animals they are considering (Zasloff, 1996).

Assessing the background experience of a person with animals is a first start in beginning to understand the person's current feelings regarding animals that have evolved from their experiences and family culture. Preferences for particular species are strongly influenced by the petkeeping practices of parents and grandparents, as shown in Fig. 3, as well as by the person's own petkeeping history. A child given experiences with farm animals, as in Fig. 4, is more likely to also appreciate these animals in adulthood. A second requirement is to be knowledgeable and offer consultation regarding the likely challenges and advantages associated with particular breeds and species in particular situations (Committee on the Human-Animal Bond, undated).

A. Dogs

Dogs account for the overwhelming percentage of animals used for AAA/T, reflecting the strong contribution of enthusiastic volunteers with well-trained dogs who enjoy sharing their charming animals during periodic visits. Delta Society (1995) has produced a home study course and Green Chimneys has prepared a manual of animal-assisted activities (Senter *et al.*, undated) to guide and educate potential volunteers who wish to knowledgeably offer AAA/T. In addition, guidelines for the selection and training of the animals and people involved in the periodic use of dogs in AAA/T have been developed on-site by programs such as Pet Assisted Therapy at Huntington Memorial Hospital in Pasadena, California (Pfau, 1990) and PHUR (Pets Helping Us Recover) at the University of California Davis Medical Center. These guidelines have been

Generational Influences on Pet Ownership

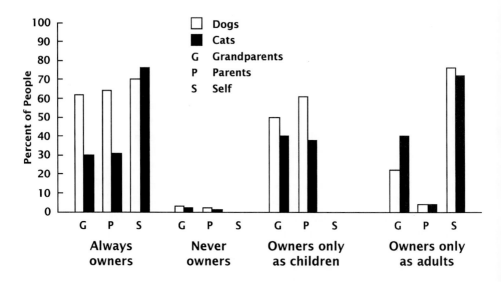

(Adapted from Kidd and Kidd, 1997)

FIGURE 3   Generational influences on pet ownership. (Modified from Kidd & Kidd, 1997.)

adapted for home visits by the SOUL (Source of Unconditional Love) program at Mercy Hospice in Sacramento, California (Levy, undated). Such guidelines include requirements for initial screening of the dogs, maintenance tests, and grooming requirements.

Dogs are the only full-time, around-the-clock companions available to us. They combine this ultimate companionship with the capacity to become working partners. Unlike our human companions, dogs offer themselves as highly interactive, attentive friends who prefer to be with their human caregivers constantly throughout the day. This can be the downside, because many dogs actively insist on and require frequent and extensive interaction. Not surprisingly, dogs are commonly selected as companions for families with growing children; the dogs can tirelessly romp with the children.

Dogs' avid devotion and the high compatibility of human–dog partnerships predisposes them as working companions, and they are now being trained for a burgeoning number of specific tasks (Hart & Hart, 1998). Their tremendous and evident willingness to work with human partners, wanting to please the person, is enhanced by their sensory and muscular capacities that exceed human abilities. Thus, they easily can be trained to work with a person in a

FIGURE 4   Just as family traditions influence adults' preferences for dogs and cats (Kidd & Kidd, 1997), children who have experiences with farm animals such as goats or chickens are likely to retain an interest in those species years later. (Photograph by Joan Borinstein.)

particular rehabilitative task. Certain breeds are trained to extend the human's sensory, kinesthetic, or locomotor abilities by assisting as guide dogs, hearing dogs, police canines, seizure-detecting dogs, termite detecting dogs, service dogs, agriculture sniffing dogs, and so on. In cases where dogs work in government settings, at least within the United States, the dogs often live at home with the handler while off duty, and then move out into the working world with the handler while on duty. As shown in a study of police officers and their canines, a close relationship with the dog at home enhances performance in the targeted working tasks of the partnership; being involved in the selection of the dog also increases success in the relationship (Hart *et al.*, 1996b). Similarly, people with service dogs were found to have a higher quality of relationship when they initiated the idea to acquire a dog (Lane *et al.*, 1998). Considering the wide range of specialized working dogs is useful when thinking about AAA/T; it provides a reminder that dogs can be trained to a required task as needed, even a new, unusual, or unfamiliar task. Often a dog will seemingly learn spontaneously a task that is useful to the person, such as opening a door or providing advance warning of an oncoming seizure.

Although most animals exert a significant socializing effect among people, dogs are truly remarkable in this respect. Serving as 24-hour companions, they also act as social magnets for approaches and topics for conversations, even for people with compromised physical or communication capacities (Eddy *et al.*, 1988; Mader *et al.*, 1989; Hart *et al.*, 1996a). They increase the perceived likability of a person, even more than a cat or bird (Geries-Johnson & Kennedy, 1995). Because they also demand affection, they ensure that the person continues providing nurturance.

Because dogs appear to enjoy working and readily learn extremely specific tasks to perform only on command, they are well suited for other tasks that are less demanding of sensory capacities, but simply require sociability and good manners. Dogs tend to be closely attentive to their primary human companions, but they often express welcoming greetings to other humans, especially their familiar friends. It comes natural to them to serve as social dogs, meeting and greeting new people. This trait can be the basis of a program of AAA/T designed for someone who is lonely or depressed. Dogs can be guided to offer their affection to strangers, and to spend time with new friends, as appropriate. It takes only one person with a well-prepared dog to visit a nursing home facility and enliven it, cheering up the residents who pet and talk to the dog.

Different breeds of dogs differ in their genetic behavioral predispositions to be affectionate, be aggressive, snap at children, or be playful. Of course, dogs within a breed vary across a wide range for each of these behaviors. Several books deal with breed-specific characteristics and may even address specific traits such as excitability, affection demand, and aggressive dominance (Hart & Hart, 1988). For example, golden retrievers generally are less protective than German shepherds or dobermans. Adults have had experience with various breeds of dogs, which leads them to have different expectations of behavior when dealing with specific breeds. Breeds also differ in body size and their size affects the activities that they can readily perform. Larger breeds are usually selected as guide, service, and police dogs, and smaller ones as hearing, termite, and agriculture dogs. A large body size confers additional strength and power for the dog to do work. For police and search-and-rescue work, a strong drive and high trainability are sought for carry through until a sustained job is done. When great strength is not required, the lack of intimidation created by a smaller dog is sometimes an advantage, as with agriculture inspection in large crowds of people when first entering the passport hall of the United States. Thus, certain breeds typically are selected for specific tasks, particularly if instrumental assistance is sought.

Elderly people typically report feeling more comfortable with smaller breeds of dogs that will not be as likely to knock them over, though tripping on them can still be a problem. Smaller dogs also take up less space in a small apartment, yet still can serve as watchdogs. The small breeds usually tend to be reactive and barky, but in a calm, quiet, predictable environment when living with a consistent elderly person, even a small terrier may assume a dignified and calm personality most of the time.

B. Cats

Requiring less effort and being less demanding than dogs, cats are entertaining, beautiful, and offer companionship with calm interactions. Cats have the flexibility to be socially self-sufficient, something that would be stressful to many dogs. In general, cats are known to behave more independently of human expectations than dogs, basically "doing their own thing," whereas dogs may be highly tuned in to the wishes of their human companions.

It is the comforting companionship that accounts for the psychosocial health benefits of animals, such as buffering against loneliness (Zasloff & Kidd, 1994). People especially value affection and playful interactions from their cats; the likelihood of a cat being highly interactive with people is increased if its early life, especially weeks 2 through 7, includes frequent handling by people, while still being cared for by the mother (Karsh & Turner, 1988). Cats give clear messages expressing their wishes to their human companions. Cats establish a strong presence and attract attention to themselves, creating laughter with their funny antics. Yet, their requirements for care are simpler than those of a dog. Thus, they are often preferred by individuals who live alone, partially due to their greater ease of care.

Cats are ideal companions when a low level of interactions, or nonvigorous interaction, is desired. People who already have hectic lives, who are gone during the day, or who are not in vigorous health welcome the limited demands of cats. For anyone with compromised health or strength, a cat poses fewer physical challenges than a dog, does not require outdoor walks, and can be left alone during brief absences or easily cared for at home by a neighbor or friend. Middle-aged women caring for people with Alzheimer's disease felt less burdened and depressed when they had a companion cat (Fritz et al., 1996). Similarly, cats were an ideal companion animal for men with advanced AIDS, whereas the behavioral demands and needs of dogs could be an added stress for some men (Castelli et al., submitted).

Unlike dogs, behavioral problems generally do not arise with cats when left alone during the day. Rather, cats' natural behavioral predispositions, or their interactions with other cats, may lead to problem behaviors that distress the human companions.

C. Horses

Therapeutic horseback riding and hippotherapy are forms of AAA/T that require an extensively managed horse, a professional facility, and expert supervision by a working team. Whether the person is receiving AAA or AAT, it is advisable to provide professional supervision. Volunteers are needed as assistants, and usually are not able to work independently. Generally, the person seeking this form of AAA/T must be transported to the facility to engage in periodic sessions with a horse, assisted by several people. Horses selected must be completely trustworthy. The personal safety of all the people involved necessarily is a more prominent concern than when dealing with a smaller animal that is known to have a good temperament. Thus, with horses it is not possible to give the volunteers a few hours of training and then send individuals out on their own to offer AAA/T with little additional supervision. For the recipient, however, the horse offers a peak experience, perhaps unmatched by any other, with a totally unique physical experience while in a joyous social environment.

D. BIRDS, SMALL MAMMALS, AND FISH

Smaller animals offer the advantage of being more easily confined, and thus may be more acceptable in housing and institutional settings. Yet, they are still companions that respond to nurturing. Many species of birds form a close bond with a particular caregiver and respond to human attention and speech in a way that is rewarding to the person (Kidd & Kidd, 1998). In the Kidd and Kidd study, owners valued their birds' companionship, the bird talking to the owner, and the entertainment. At least three-fourths of these individuals had at least one other animal. These birds were not trouble free: About one-third of owners described their messiness as a problem and one-fifth described them as noisy.

The calm, quiet, and soft traits of guinea pigs make them a consistent favorite species requiring limited effort. Even fish are beautiful and offer relaxation to people, as shown by people's reductions in anxiety while viewing a fish aquarium in a dental waiting room (Katcher et al., 1984).

IV. SPECIAL PROBLEMS AND CONCERNS

Careful planning is required to provide adequate support and assistance to individuals seeking therapeutic full-time contact with a companion animal. One issue that frequently arises concerns the acceptance of companion animals in the person's housing. In one study in California of assisted housing for the elderly, managers experienced very few problems with the introduction of animals into apartments (Hart & Mader, 1986). The managers simply presented the standard pet policy to all residents, and only a low level of enforcement was required. The woman in Fig. 5 found an assisted apartment where her dog was permitted. Many people still have difficulty finding housing where they can keep an animal, even though the legal precedents on the issue have broadened the definition of disability such that animals can be prescribed by physicians for a person's well-being and quality of life, even if the person lacks a very evident disability.

A more basic challenge is that someone who has compromised psychological or physical health is likely to need a specially tailored program of assistance in order to assume responsibility for an animal. Some of these systems have been developed by agencies placing guide or service dogs, but comparable instruction and tutorial support are not currently available for the general population. As an extreme example, people who are homeless would not consider housing where their animals (often their only companions) are not permitted (Kidd & Kidd, 1994). Many, especially women, desire housing, but would require that their animals be accepted. These individuals have great difficulty providing any veterinary care and perhaps adequate food for their animals (Singer et al., 1995), yet the animals unquestionably are providing significant psychosocial support. Volunteers and health professionals can assist

FIGURE 5   If someone has had large dogs as companions throughout life and then must move to a small apartment in later life, finding rental housing where a large dog is allowed becomes especially important. This Afghan hound, Pearl, represents to her human partner several generations of prize-winning Afghans.

in developing plans for how the recipient will manage to care for the animal, including during medical crises of the animal or the person.

REFERENCES

Castelli, P., Hart, L. A., & Zasloff, R. L. Dogs, cats and the social support systems of men with AIDS. Submitted.

Committee on the Human–Animal Bond. (undated). *The veterinarian's way of selecting a proper pet.* Schaumburg, IL: American Veterinary Medical Association.

Delta Society. (1995). *Delta Society Pet Partners program home study course.* Renton, WA: Delta Society.

Eddy, J., Hart, L. A., & Boltz, R. P. (1988). The effects of service dogs on social acknowledgments of people in wheelchairs. *Journal of Psychology, 122*(1), 39–45.

Francis, G., Turner, J. T., & Johnson, S. B. (1985). Domestic animal visitation as therapy with adult home residents. *International Journal of Nursing Studies, 22,* 201–206.

Fritz, C. L., Farver, T. B., Hart, L. A., & Kass, P. H. (1996). Companion animals and the psychological health of Alzheimer patients' caregivers. *Psychological Reports,78,* 467–481.

Geries-Johnson, B., & Kennedy, J. H. (1995). Influence of animals on perceived likability of people. *Perceptual and Motor Skills, 80,* 432–434.

Hart, B. L., & Hart, L. A. (1988). *The perfect puppy: How to choose your dog by its behavior.* New York: W. H. Freeman.

Hart, B. L., & Hart, L. A. (1997). Selecting, raising, and caring for dogs to avoid problem aggression. *Journal of the American Veterinary Medical Association, 210*(8), 1129–1134.

Hart, B. L., & Hart, L. A. (1998). Dogs at work. In *Science year* (pp. 28–41). Chicago, IL: World Book.

Hart, L. A., & Mader, B. (1986). The successful introduction of pets into California public housing for the elderly. *California Veterinarian, 40*(5), 17–21, 27.

Hart, L. A., Zasloff, R. L. & Benfatto, A. M. (1995). The pleasures and problems of hearing dog ownership. *Psychological Reports, 77,* 969–970.

Hart, L. A., Zasloff, R. L., & Benfatto, A. M. (1996a). The socializing role of hearing dogs. *Applied Animal Behaviour Science, 47,* 7–15.

Hart, L. A., Zasloff, R. L., Bryson, S., & Christensen, S. L. (1996b). The role of dogs in police work and as companions. In *Animal Behavior Society abstracts* (p. 34). Flagstaff, AZ: Northern Arizona University.

Haughie, E., Milne, D., & Elliott, V. (1992). An evaluation of companion pets with elderly psychiatric patients. *Behavioural Psychotherapy, 20,* 367–372.

Karsh, E. B., & Turner, D. C. (1988). The human–cat relationship. In D. C. Turner & P. Bateson (Eds.), *The domestic cat: The biology of its behaviour* (pp. 159–177). Cambridge, UK: Cambridge University Press.

Katcher, A., Segal, H., & Beck, A. (1984). Contemplation of an aquarium for the reduction of anxiety. In R. K. Anderson, B. L. Hart, & L. A. Hart (Eds.), *The pet connection: Its influence on our health and quality of life* (pp. 171–178). Minneapolis, MN: University of Minnesota.

Kidd, A. H., & Kidd, R. M. (1994). Benefits and liabilities of pets for the homeless. *Psychological Reports, 74,* 715–722.

Kidd, A. H., & Kidd, R. M. (1997). Changes in the behavior of pet owners across generations. *Psychological Reports, 80,* 195–202.

Kidd, A. H., & Kidd, R. M. (1998). Problems and benefits of bird ownership. *Psychological Reports, 83,* 131–138.

Lago, D., Delaney, M., Miller, M., & Grill, C. (1989). Companion animals, attitudes toward pets, and health outcomes among the elderly: A long-term follow-up. *Anthrozoos, 3*, 25–34.

Lane, D. R., McNicholas, J., & Collis, G. M. (1998). Dogs for the disabled: Benefits to recipients and welfare of the dog. *Applied Animal Behaviour Science, 59*, 49–60.

Levy, M. (undated). *SOUL at Mercy: Source of unconditional love (SOUL). A volunteer program of animal-assisted therapy. Visitation manual.* Sacramento, CA: Mercy Hospice.

Mader, B., Hart, L. A., & Bergin, B. (1989). Social acknowledgements for children with disabilities: Effects of service dogs. *Child Development, 60*(6), 1529–1534.

Miller, M., & Lago, D. (1990). The well-being of older women: The importance of pet and human relations. *Anthrozoos, 3*, 245–251.

Neer, C. B., Dorn, C. R., & Grayson, I. (1987). Dog interaction with persons receiving institutional geriatric care. *Journal of the American Veterinary Medical Association, 191*, 300–304.

Pfau, H. (1990). *PAT at Huntington: A volunteer program of pet-assisted therapy. training manual.* Pasadena, CA: Huntington Memorial Hospital.

Senter, S., Ross, S. B., Jr., & Mallon, G. (undated). *People and animals: A therapeutic animal-assisted activities manual for schools, agencies and recreational centers.* Brewster, NY: Green Chimneys Farm and Wildlife Center.

Singer, R. S., Hart, L. A., & Zasloff, R. L. (1995). Dilemmas associated with rehousing homeless people who have companion animals. *Psychological Reports, 77*, 851–857.

Stein, M. (1993). *The human/companion animal bond enhances motivation for voluntarism.* Unpublished master's thesis, California State University, Sacramento.

Valentine, D. P., Kiddoo, M., & LaFleur, B. (1993). Psychosocial implications of service dog ownership for people who have mobility or hearing impairments. *Social Work in Health Care, 19*(1), 109–125.

Verderber, S. (1991). Elderly persons' appraisal of animals in the residential environment. *Anthrozoos, 4*, 164–173.

Winkler, A., Fairnie, H., Gericevich, F., & Long, M. (1989). The impact of a resident dog on an institution for the elderly: Effects on perceptions and social interactions. *Gerontologist, 29*, 216–223.

Zasloff, R. L. (1996). Measuring attachment to companion animals: A dog is not a cat is not a bird. *Applied Animal Behaviour Science, 47*, 43–48.

Zasloff, R. L., & Kidd, A. H. (1994). Loneliness and pet ownership among single women. *Psychological Reports, 75*, 747–752.

Methods, Standards, Guidelines, and Considerations in Selecting Animals for Animal-Assisted Therapy

Part B: Guidelines and Standards for Animal Selection in Animal-Assisted Activity and Therapy Programs*

MAUREEN FREDRICKSON, MSW AND ANN R. HOWIE, ACSW
Delta Society, Renton, Washington

As the potential benefits to residents and patients from well-planned contacts with animals and the potential liability from unplanned contacts are realized, there is an increasing demand from facility administrators for specialized training and screening procedures for both the people and animals. The benefits of animal-assisted activities and therapy (AAA/T) are influenced by more than the response of a particular person to an animal. The idea that an animal is therapeutic by simply being in an institution is erroneous. While the animal can participate in interactions, the animal's handler must be trained and sensitive to the capacities of that particular animal. This chapter will focus on Standards for the selection of animals working in AAA/T programs and the factors that affect the performance of various animal species.

Incorporation of animals in health care treatment to yield safe and effective outcomes is the result of a dynamic relationship between the client or patient and the animal. Outcomes are affected by a variety of factors. In successful programs the relationship between three components—animal aptitude, facil-

---

* The authors thank Michelle Cobey, Resource Support Coordinator at Delta Society, for her assistance in providing references for this chapter.

ity dynamics, and team skill level—is used to determine the prescription of a particular species and particular animal and handler and health care provider to meet the needs of a client within a specific setting. Each of these variables is highly interdependent.

Selection standards identify those animals that are reliable, controllable, predictable, and suitable to the particular AAA/T task, population, and working environment. Attention is given to species/breed, type, sex, age, size, health, aptitude, suitability, and skills. In addition, consideration is given to the quality of interaction between the handler and the animal.

I. BACKGROUND

A. HISTORICAL SELECTION CRITERIA

In the 1970s many visiting pet programs encouraged volunteers to work with shelter animals. However, by the 1990s all major humane associations and veterinary organizations in the United States recommended against such a practice. The ASPCA reported that "visiting strange settings with unpredictable people and unusual noises stresses the animals, especially young animals that are awaiting adoption" (Shelter Animals, 1992). Animals with unknown health histories and unknown behavior patterns put in contact with vulnerable people increases the risk of zoonotic infection or injury. Also, this practice may reduce the effectiveness of the interaction, because well-trained animals can have skills that enhance interactions with others. In addition, the return of the same animal over time aids in establishing a relationship with clients or patients (New, 1995). In AAT programs, this relationship is often the goal of treatment.

As *resident* pet programs gained acceptance in nursing homes during the 1980s, concern for patient and animal welfare increased. Risk management personnel and insurance providers demanded assurances that the animals placed in the facilities were free from zoonotic disease and were not a physical threat to residents. In 1983, at a conference on the human–animal bond at the University of Minnesota, guidelines for animals in nursing homes were presented, recommending animal placement be preceded by careful evaluation. *Guidelines: Animals in Nursing Homes* (Hines *et al.,* 1983) stated that the evaluation should include interviews with facility administrators, residents, and staff of the institution, consideration of the physical facilities, and assessment of the social needs of the nursing home. In addition, it recommended that the role of the animals in the facility be considered.

These guidelines did not address selection of animals involved in *visiting* AAA/T programs. Visiting animals were most frequently screened through puppy temperament tests and other breed temperament tests. Terry Ryan, dog trainer and developer of testing for animals in the *Guidelines,* noted that the test was specifically written for resident animals with unknown backgrounds. She indicated that "volunteers often lack knowledge on how to screen animals." She suggested that further criteria be developed specific to species.

The Human–Animal Bond in Tennessee (HABIT) program, the San Antonio Chapter of Delta Society, and Pet Pals of Iowa were some of the first programs to develop screening procedures for visiting animals. Evidence indicated that puppy testing was not a valid method of selecting dogs for AAA/T work. An evaluation of the results of puppy temperament tests demonstrated that the test did not predict adult behavior (Young, 1986). These tests also did not evaluate the animal's performance in regard to AAA/T. Health care providers, experienced volunteers, and animal care and welfare professionals recommended that minimum criteria for selection of animals for AAA/T must include medical criteria, temperament/behavioral criteria, and criteria for monitoring animals (New & Strimple, 1988).

In 1991, the Delta Society Task Force on Animal Selection met to develop standard screening protocols for domestic animals involved in AAA/T. Chaired by Mary Burch, Ph.D., the task force surveyed more than 600 evaluators for various programs. The evaluators were asked to rank test items from the most frequently used temperament tests. From this survey the Pet Partners Skills and Aptitude Test® was created. This screening process has gained national and international acceptance as minimum screening requirements for AAA/T animals.

B. Temperament versus Aptitude

Early selection standards called for evaluation of temperament and behavior of animals involved in AAA/T programs. The term *temperament* was most often associated with dogs, whereas *behavior* was used to refer to personality traits of other animals. The separation of these terms caused confusion for volunteers, health care providers, and others. *Temperament* meant one thing to animal behaviorists and another thing to dog breeders. Many dog breeders used the term *temperament* to describe specific breed traits, not as a set of particular responses to stimuli.

Temperament tests did not take into consideration the unique requirements of animals involved in AAA/T. Early practitioners recommended that the criteria for selecting animals consider the following factors: physical characteristics, personality characteristics (particularly predictability of behavior and communicability of the animal's attitudes through its body language), the degree of bonding to humans, and the relationship between the dog and its owner (Holmes, 1988).

The use of temperament as an evaluative tool does not include the fact that many animals exhibit temperament that is suitable as a pet but unsuitable for participation in AAA/T programs. An evaluation of aptitude considers the animal/handler team as a working unit. Aptitude more clearly determines if the team has the ability, capacity, and potential for work in AAA/T.

The Delta Society Pet Partners program specifically separates the skills required of animals and the aptitude needed for successful participation. The test simulates the types of social and physical stresses most frequently encountered in an AAA/T situation. The team is evaluated for its ability to cope with the challenges of each situation and its ability to respond to the situation with calm, nonaggressive communication.

C. DEVELOPMENT OF STANDARDS

With the burgeoning of the AAA/T field and its wide variety of programs, the need for standards became increasingly evident. More than 50 AAA/T practitioners worked for nearly 2 years to identify standards of practice and vocational profiles for AAA/T programs. Delta Society published the results in 1992 in the *Handbook for Animal-Assisted Activities and Animal-Assisted Therapy*. In 1996, the handbook was revised into *Standards of Practice for Animal-Assisted Activities and Therapy*.

Practitioners in the field recognize the importance of involving only carefully selected visiting and resident animals. Minimum screening protocols for animals involved in AAA/T evaluate the animal/handler team as a working unit. Screening procedures must be specifically designed to simulate the unique situations and challenges that the animal and handler most frequently encounter in an AAA/T situation. "Animals that participate in AAA/T are purposefully selected, healthy, safe, and meet risk management criteria. They possess appropriate aptitude, are an appropriate size and age, and demonstrate appropriate skills for their participation to be beneficial to all team members. . . . It is unacceptable to use drugs that may alter the animal's behavior." (Delta Society, 1996, p. 41–42).

II. STANDARDS

Standards are not a new concept. There are standards for people—doctors, engineers, automobile manufacturers, food processors—and professions or industries—medicine, engineering, automotive, food, etc. Standards serve as a model or example against which performance or production can be measured: Needles must be sterile before giving an injection; a bridge must be built with materials strong enough to carry the bridge's intended weight. Standards protect the consumer against inferior goods or services: People can choose an electrical cord that has an underwriter's seal. Properly followed, standards protect the provider from retribution from unhappy consumers: The amount of contaminants in drinking water is at or below what is regulated by law.

Standards for animal selection are no more or less important than standards for provider qualifications or for documentation, for example. However, the *utilization* of standards for animals and their handlers must be emphasized. A great disservice has been done in the field by focusing on the animal to the exclusion of the handler. Whereas it is critical to have an appropriate animal, excluding handlers from the same criteria required of animals increases risk unnecessarily. For example, an inexperienced handler with a veteran animal may place the animal or patient in a compromising—or even dangerous— situation. Thus, the animal and handler work together as a team. As a result, some would argue that criteria for handlers must be even more stringent than that for animals. An additional critical factor to utilizing successful screening procedures is the evaluator's knowledge of AAA/T. To make accurate evaluations about the appropriateness of the handler and animal, evaluators must be familiar with the interplay of the animal's abilities and aptitude within the dynamics of AAA/T.

According to *Standards of Practice,* the primary selection criteria are reliability, predictability, controllability, suitability, and ability to inspire confidence. The contents of *Standards of Practice* will not be repeated here but will be summarized and applied. Readers are encouraged to obtain and consider *Standards of Practice.*

A. RELIABILITY

Reliability means that behavior is dependable or much the same in repeated, similar situations. In order for a therapeutic intervention to be effective, the therapist must feel confident that the animal (and handler) will respond in a basically similar way when placed into similar situations. This is for the safety and well-being of all involved—animal, handler, therapist, patients, staff, and visitors. Reliability can be improved by training.

For example, if a dog is going to be taken into a nursing home, the staff must know that the dog will remain calm, nonaggressive, and happy when (literally) faced constantly with carts, wheelchairs, and walkers. On the other end of the leash, the staff must know that the handler has reliable skills; for example, consistently ensuring that wheelchair wheels are locked and treating the residents with compassion.

A rabbit working in a hospital with severely burned patients must not startle and freeze or flee from swathed hands. On the other end of the leash, the handler must be comfortable with the effects of severe burns and not stare at patients. Further, a horse that will be ridden in an arena by a child with cerebral palsy must have a steady, even gait and the ability to cope with unexpected events, noises, and movements. The handler must accurately observe the horse's body language and level of stress and be able to intervene in a noninvasive, effective manner.

B. PREDICTABILITY

Predictability means that behavior in specific circumstances can be anticipated in advance. Predictability and reliability are closely related. Predictability cannot necessarily be enhanced through training. A study of the interrelationship between various dog behaviors (Goodloe & Borchelt, 1998) found a limited link between obedience training and desirable behaviors. The authors suggested that owners willing to spend more time with their dogs may behave differently with their dogs and therefore reduce the dog's fear in new and unusual situations.

For example, consider a dog that is working with a patient to gain greater extension and flexion in the right arm. The therapist has chosen a game of fetch as the therapeutic intervention for a session. The therapist must have confidence that the dog will fetch the item and participate in the game, rather than become distracted by enticing smells, articles, and people elsewhere in the room.

Further, consider a therapist working with an adult with a mental illness about the effects of the patient's unusual behavior on others. The therapist may choose to work with a horse that will shy away from the adult unless the adult speaks in a softer tone, moves more slowly, and minimizes gesturing. In this example, the handler must take steps to keep the horse safe, but must not interfere with the horse's natural instinct to retreat, or the therapeutic value will be greatly diminished, if not lost.

C. CONTROLLABILITY

Controllability means that behavior can be restrained, guided, or managed. In animals, controllability can often be improved with training. Minimum training requirements should be consistent with the expectations of the animal's performance in the program. For example, a rabbit must be trained to stay in a basket and sit quietly while being carried from bed to bed visiting medically fragile children. It may also be important to train the rabbit how to get safely in and out of the basket. In people, however, controllability is typically a matter of temperament and is not often changed through education.

For example, consider a pony with a group of children. The therapist must be confident that the pony will not nip or kick the children (even if provoked). This is a good example of a situation where the handler's skills are critical. Children can be some of the most unpredictable (and uncontrollable) patients to visit. The pony may be very tolerant and good natured, but every creature has its limits. If the handler allows the children to continue to act in a threatening manner around the pony, the pony will lose patience with the ineffective handler and will take matters into its own hands (or mouth or feet) to defend itself.

Controllability is often an issue with residential animals, where the animal is expected to be controlled by many residents and staff with varying skills and abilities. This is usually an unrealistic expectation, with the unfortunate result that the animal becomes unmanageable or creates problems and must be found another home. (Part of the solution requires one person to be identified with primary responsibility and, thence, control.)

D. SUITABILITY

Suitability means fit or qualified for a purpose. The purpose here is the specific goals the therapist has identified for each session. The animal and handler must be able to help the patient work on those goals in the context of the dynamics of the environment. In addition, neither animal nor handler should pose a health risk to the patient.

For example, adolescent boys in treatment for chemical abuse may be more motivated to learn about reptiles and arachnids than common household pets. Or consider a facility where the hallways are very narrow and crowded with equipment. Staff in this facility usually move rapidly and with task-focused determination. The animal/handler team in this situation must be highly mobile and able to get out of the way quickly. Thus, given these dynamics, which team would be more suited for this environment: a dog on a 6-foot leash, a pot-bellied pig on a wagon, or a rabbit in a basket? (The answer is the rabbit.)

The choice of suitability can also occur between individuals of the same species: consider a vital man in his early sixties recovering from a stroke. He is relearning how to walk, but he forgets that he cannot walk so gets up impulsively, then falls. He also neglects his right side, and loses focus while walking and runs into things on his right side. A therapist wants him to walk supervised with a dog on his right, hoping that will encourage him to attend to the right. Several dogs are available to this therapist. Which would be better: a chihuahua, a sheltie, or a labrador retriever? (The answer is the labrador.)

An often-neglected aspect of suitability is *enjoyment*. Dodging this criterion is not simply unfortunate, it can also be abusive. Does the animal enjoy the interactions, or does it merely tolerate them? Is the handler relaxed and confident with the patient, or is the handler afraid to make eye contact, stiff in posture, and mumbling? Who really wants to make the visits—the animal or the handler? If the handler forces the animal to do things it does not enjoy, it is abuse.

An animal consistently placed in untenable situations will eventually retaliate. Here is another example of how critical the handler's skills are. If a handler is not sensitive to and respectful of the needs of the animal, the handler can inadvertently place his or her needs over those of the animal. This may result in illness for a submissive animal, or aggression in the case of an assertive animal.

E. Ability to Inspire Confidence

Ability to inspire confidence means that people feel comfortable (not threatened) around the team. A person who fears for his or her safety is unable to focus on achieving therapeutic goals. Some examples: A German shepherd, Doberman, or rottweiler is not likely to inspire confidence in a person who has spent time as a prisoner of war. A frail elderly person may feel more confident with a cat on the lap rather than an energetic, bouncy dog on the floor. An immobile person may not want a towering llama to visit, no matter how gentle and house trained it is.

Inspiring confidence does not mean that every animal working in AAA/T must be "perfect" or "brainless" and allow people to do whatever they want to it. On the contrary, sometimes the most therapeutic interactions occur when a troubled patient bonds with an animal with similar characteristics or receives immediate natural consequences (that are not physically harmful). For example, a shy child might gravitate to a shy animal and feel comfortable working with that animal *because* it is shy. A patient that speaks loudly and aggressively can see an animal cringe in response. A person, on the other hand, may hide his or her reaction to the aggressiveness or avoid seeing the patient in the future, both of which are difficult for the patient to connect with the problem behavior.

III. APPLICATION OF STANDARDS TO ANIMAL SELECTION

To have not only safe but also effective AAA/T interactions, people must first know the standards, and then must apply the standards to their situation.

A. Role of the Handler

As mentioned in the previous sections, the animal's handler is integral to the animal's functioning and the therapeutic value of the interaction. Risk is increased without a well-trained, skilled, appropriate handler. The handler may be staff or volunteer.

The most effective handlers are knowledgeable about the following areas:

- Their role and responsibility in AAA/T interactions
- The rationale behind requirements for the animal
- Animal stress
- Animal advocacy
- Techniques for AAA/T interactions with people with various disabilities or illnesses
- Conversation and listening skills
- How to prepare for, conduct, and conclude a visit
- Documentation
- Facility administrative procedures and policies
- Infection control
- Techniques for preventing injuries
- Liability issues

Delta Society's Pet Partners® program provides home study or classroom training in all of these areas, plus more. Some handlers will come to a facility with qualifications that meet or exceed the above list. Others will come with lots of enthusiasm, but few qualifications. A facility must be prepared to check a handler's qualifications and provide needed training before allowing the handler and animal to interact with patients.

In addition to knowledge about AAA/T, an effective handler will demonstrate strong teamwork with his or her animal—the kind of teamwork that inspires confidence in the patient. Teamwork begins with the tone of voice the handler uses with the animal: Is it conversational and unobtrusive or gruff and clipped? Patients can be offended by harsh commands and reassured by a pleasant, relaxed tone. A soft voice coupled with confidence and a strong bond between animal and handler give the impression that the two are working in harmony.

Communication between handler and animal extends beyond verbal into nonverbal, as well. Nonverbal communication with the animal should be constant and not forceful in nature. For example, a patient might not be able to identify that the handler kept a gentle hand on the dog, scratching behind the ears, during most of the AAA/T interaction, but the patient is left with a positive feeling about a strong, respectful relationship between the animal and handler. A handler that must physically place the animal into position and then doesn't touch the animal again except to reposition it leaves an entirely different impression. Both gruff tone of voice and physical pushing/pulling can be distracting and create negative judgments about the relationship between handler and animal.

In summary, key components of the handler's role include these:

- Demonstrate appropriate treatment of people and animals.
- Demonstrate appropriate social skills (eye contact, smiles, confident posture, conversation) needed for interacting with people in AAA/T.
- Demonstrate pleasant, calm, and friendly reaction to and attitude toward animal during various tasks and scenarios.
- Act as animal's advocate in all situations.
- Effectively read the animal's cues (stress, excitement, etc.) and act accordingly.
- Protect and respect the animal's needs.
- Maintain confidentiality.

B. ROLE OF THE EVALUATOR

The evaluator must be familiar with the dynamics of AAA/T interactions. AAA/T is quite different from general household living, and it is quite different from the animal show ring. An evaluator who shows dogs in competition obedience, for example, and is *not* familiar with AAA/T might not pass a dog unless it demonstrated precision obedience skills. However, precision is not needed in most AAA/T interactions.

Each client population responds differently to animals based on behavioral, physical, and environmental dynamics. Evaluators must be familiar with the interplay of the animal's abilities and aptitude and the dynamics of AAA/T settings to make an accurate evaluation. Programs that utilize less stringent screening procedures increase the risk of AAA/T programs to animals, handlers, staff, and clients.

Ideally, the evaluator should be a neutral third party. This minimizes or prevents bias, whether positive or negative. In addition, because AAA/T animals often see strangers, the evaluator needs to see how the animal reacts to strangers. Thus, the evaluator and all assistants should be strangers to the animal. It is extremely useful to have several people participate in the evaluation and in that way simulate crowds, groups, and varying behaviors toward the animal (and handler).

In addition, the evaluator should have experience with the species of animal being evaluated. An evaluator who is not familiar with cats, for example, might not know how to interpret a tail swishing back and forth. A person unfamiliar with llamas might think humming is a sign of pleasure. A person unfamiliar with guinea pigs might think that frozen posture indicates a calm, well-mannered guinea pig. Thus, for the animal's benefit, the evaluator not only needs to know how to interpret behavior, but may also need to direct the handler into training or into an alternate activity with the animal.

The evaluator may need to give the handler feedback about the environment or patient population with whom the team can best fit. The evaluator is in a position of tremendous power when explaining test results, so must have strong "people" or communication skills. Specific, concrete examples from the testing help explain the rationale behind his or her recommendations. For this reason, it is helpful to have standardized, standards-based test exercises based on skills and aptitude needed for visiting situations.

Thus, a good evaluator must possess a unique blend of specialized and general skills, knowledge, and experience.

IV. GUIDELINES FOR ANIMAL SELECTION

The United States has a philosophically, culturally, and ethnically diverse population. As such, people's responses to animals can be equally diverse. Consideration must be given to the diversity of people's experiences and responses to animals when selecting animals for AAA/T programs.

A. CONSIDERATIONS FOR ANIMAL SPECIES AND BREED

While the majority of programs incorporate dogs, other animals can and do provide similar benefits in AAA/T programs. Dogs may be a less-than-suitable species for a particular program for many reasons. Allergies, phobias, and infection risks may make other species such as birds or small animals more appropriate. These animals can be readily screened for appropriate aptitude, behavior, and suitability characteristics to ensure their safety for AAA/T.

When considering whether a species is appropriate for AAA/T, it is critical that the animal be evaluated in terms of the criteria described in earlier sections. The International Association of Human–Animal Interaction Organizations (IAHAIO) Guidelines on AAA and AAT state that only domestic animals will be involved in AAA/T (1998). It is generally recognized that domestic animals tend to possess a higher capacity for coping with people, their behaviors, and their inventions. Prior to incorporating different species into AAA/T programs, the following questions must be answered.

Which is more reliable? In situations where clients are unpredictable or there is minimal staff supervision, caged song birds or fish tanks may be the most effective and safe incorporation of animals. One emergency room program chose to incorporate rabbits rather than dogs because the rabbits were always in a basket. Volunteers and their animals could be quickly and effectively removed from the setting if a patient "crashed."

How do the differences between various species influence AAA/T visits? Behavior patterns are vastly different between carnivorous and noncarnivorous animals. The fact that rabbits and guinea pigs need to eat more frequently than dogs may actually enhance their role in a setting with a goal of increasing patients' nurturing skills. In the same way, these animals require handling and techniques that can accommodate the animal's frequent elimination.

Can the animal be appropriately monitored for signs of stress? This question is perhaps the most important consideration for any species involved in AAA/T programs. Although data are limited with regard to the impact of AAA/T on animals, handlers report a certain degree of changes in animals working in these programs. The handler must be able to monitor the animal's response to *limited* stress in order to avoid overstress. For this reason, most exotic animals or wildlife are not appropriate for AAA/T programs. By the time these species exhibit stress they are usually quite overwhelmed.

In much the same way, dog breeds and breed types must be considered when including them in health care programs. Dog breeds and breed types are a result of selection for specific purposes. This results in a certain amount of predictable behavior patterns or "hard wiring" for specific traits. Not all of these traits are appropriate in the context of AAA/T programs. The general characteristics of breeds and breed types will influence the dog's response to different situations.

Seven different dog breed types are identified by the American Kennel Club: sporting, toy, terrier, working, nonsporting, herding, and hound. There are also some subtypes within these breed types. For example, within the working dog breed type there are protection dogs, drayage dogs, and rescue dogs. Dogs' reactions to various situations would be different depending on the breed, breed type, and subtype.

The general characteristics of breeds and breed types influence suitability, confidence, and safety of the program. Dogs representative of the working, sporting, and herding breeds and breed types respond more actively to events that simulate behaviors or reactions of prey, such as quick movement and high-pitched noises. These types of dogs are more likely to chase and pounce on a ball. Dogs that represent the toy and nonsporting breeds and breed types are more likely to watch the ball. These very separate responses can enhance an AAA/T program or make it less than effective.

B. Environmental Dynamics and Animal Selection

People who work in the field of AAA/T identified the circumstances that make visiting more challenging: greater *distractions* (from the level of staff activity, the environment, etc.), *unpredictable* client behavior, and less *staff* assistance with the interactions. Thus, to help protect AAA/T teams from being placed in situations which may be too difficult for them—or even dangerous—therapists must know how to select appropriate teams to work with. Placing a novice team in a facility with highly unpredictable clients or in a volatile atmosphere with limited staff support will result in increased risk to clients and animals, lowered expectations, and shorter involvement by volunteers.

Consider the Environmental Dynamics Matrix from Standards of Practice shown in Fig. 1. This matrix conceptualizes the key components necessary for safety in applying standards to the therapist's work environment.

It is essential for facility staff to understand the dynamics of human–animal interactions. Staff must first identify the dynamics present in their work environment, and then they must determine whether or not the animal and handler being considered are appropriate and have the necessary skills to be successful visiting in that environment. Facility staff can use these questions to carefully evaluate their environmental dynamics:

- What is the level of staff assistance for and involvement with animal visits?
- What distractions are present?
- How unpredictable is client behavior?
- What is the general activity level in the work environment?

For example, consider a skilled nursing facility with a long-term care unit, a transitional care unit, and an Alzheimer's unit. Each unit probably has distinctly different dynamics, which would affect the visiting animal and handler team. For this purpose we will evaluate just one unit: the long-term care unit. Here the residents are mostly bed bound or use wheelchairs so they are not very active (low resident activity level). Many of the residents are socially and physically withdrawn, having little interaction with others (mostly predictable client behavior). The staff would like the team to visit from room to room, so the team is exposed to lots of "activity"—staff movement, carts wheeling about, food being brought back and forth, etc. (high distractions and staff activity level). In addition, the staff is so overworked that no one is available to be with the team during the visit (low staff assistance).

Where would this unit fit in the matrix of Fig. 1? Lack of staff ability to assist is not as big a risk factor with this population (withdrawn and immobile) as it would be with a more active or unpredictable population. However, low staff assistance, even with this population, means that risk is increased. For example, without specific guidance from a staff member, a well-meaning animal handler could place a little dog on the lap of a person who is afraid of or allergic to dogs. Or the handler could give a drink of water to a thirsty person

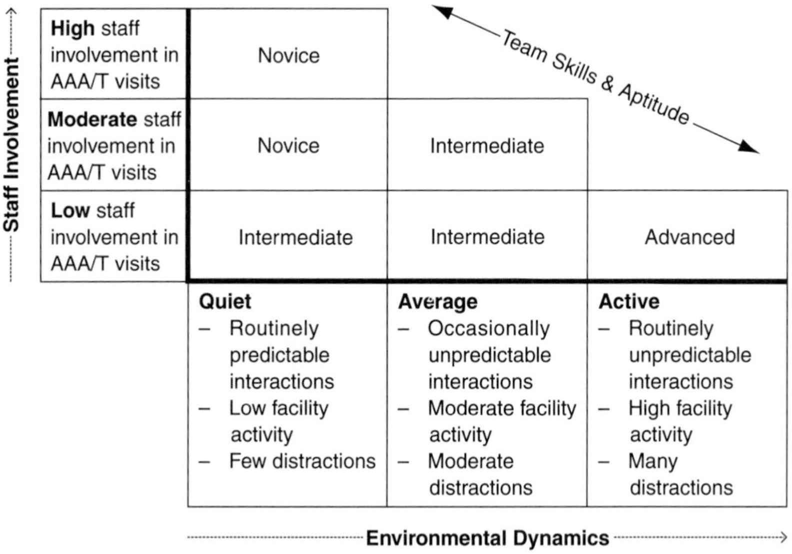

Staff Involvement	Quiet	Average	Active
High staff involvement in AAA/T visits	Novice		
Moderate staff involvement in AAA/T visits	Novice	Intermediate	
Low staff involvement in AAA/T visits	Intermediate	Intermediate	Advanced
	Quiet – Routinely predictable interactions – Low facility activity – Few distractions	**Average** – Occasionally unpredictable interactions – Moderate facility activity – Moderate distractions	**Active** – Routinely unpredictable interactions – High facility activity – Many distractions

Team Skills & Aptitude

---------------------------------- **Environmental Dynamics** ---------------------------------->

Team Skills and Aptitude –

Novice
- Meets or exceeds minimum qualifications
- Basic social skills
- Able to think critically and respond appropriately to unusual situations some of the time
- Close teamwork between animal and handler is evident some of the time

Intermediate
- Exceeds minimum qualifications
- Intermediate social skills
- Able to think critically in many unusual situations and respond appropriately most of the time
- Close teamwork between animal and handler is evident most of the time

Advanced
- Far exceeds minimum qualifications
- High degree of social skills
- Able to think critically in all situations and respond appropriately
- Exceptional teamwork between handler and animal is evident at all times

FIGURE 1   Environmental Dynamics Matrix.

asking for water, not knowing that this resident is someone who must have only thickened liquids. Without staff assistance, the handler is left on his or her own to deal with the residents. This kind of situation requires increased skill and good judgment on the part of the handler.

Another significant dynamic affecting the team is the high activity level. The residents are not active, but activity from residents is only part of the activity on this unit. Staff may take their environmental distractions (i.e., staff movement, carts, food) for granted, but an animal won't! This kind of constant, purposeful, rapid activity is not part of a typical household and can be frightening for many animals (and handlers!). Thus, this unit would do best with an intermediate team or perhaps a confident, experienced novice team.

V. RISK MANAGEMENT

The *Standards of Practice* states "health and management practices help to maintain optimal animal health and well-being through appropriate hygiene, management, specific preventative care and prompt attention to illness" (p. 42). Minimum standards for medical screening require annual vaccinations, internal and external parasite control protocols, appropriate grooming and cleanliness, and additional screening procedures as identified by the facility, local public health law, and immunological status of patients.

Concerns about zoonotic infections and public health and environmental issues involving animals in treatment are the most frequently stated reasons for not incorporating AAA/T programs. Curiously, these concerns have never been substantiated. A handful of studies indicates that properly cared for animals do not pose additional health risks and that the benefits outweigh the small, easily preventable risks involved (Anderson *et al.*, 1992; Kale, 1992; Patient's Best, 1992; Waltner-Toews & Ellis, 1994).

VI. CONCLUSIONS

Most animals involved in AAA/T visit a facility along with the handler who may be a volunteer or a staff person at the facility. Some animals are selected and placed as permanent residents of a facility. Animals placed without thorough planning, selection, and staff commitment can be improperly cared for and even injured. Behavioral problems resulting from poor training or boredom reduce effectiveness in stimulating residents or cause fear or injury. If a facility makes a commitment in terms of resources and trained staff, resident animals can be a successful model (Lee *et al.*, 1987; Thomas 1994). Stated plainly in *Guidelines for the Introduction of Pets in Nursing Homes and Other Institutions,* "The environmental pets need a committed person, or people, to attend to their care, welfare and hygiene regularly and ensure that they do not become just another fixture" (1990, p. 15).

Animal screening protocols must be tested for validity and continually improved. Retrospective analysis of incident reports and pass/fail rates could lead to an understanding of the behavioral and training requirements for safe and reliable animals. At this time the greatest attention has been directed toward screening dogs. In many facilities dogs may be less effective than other species of animals. Screening for these animals, especially nondomestic animals, is still in its infancy.

REFERENCES

Anderson, W. P., Reid, C. M., & Jennings, G. L. (1992). Pet ownership and risk factors for cardiovascular disease. *Medical Journal of Australia, 157,* 298–301.

Delta Society. (1996). *Standards of practice for animal-assisted activities and animal-assisted therapy.* Renton, WA: Delta Society.

Goodloe, L. P., & Borchelt, P. L. (1998). Companion dogs temperament traits. *Journal of Applied Animal Welfare Science,* 1(4), 303–338.

Guidelines for the introduction of pets in nursing homes and other institutions. (1990). Glasgow: The Society for Companion Animal Studies.

Hines, L. M., Lee, R. L., Zeglen, M. E., & Ryan, T. (1983). Guidelines: Placement of animals in nursing homes. Paper presented at the Conference on the Human–Animal Bond, University of Minnesota, Minneapolis, MN, and University of California, Irvine, CA.

Holmes, A. E. (1988). Minimum temperament/behavioral criteria. Paper presented at the seventh annual Delta Society Conference, People, Animals and the Environment: Exploring Our Interdependence, Orlando, FL.

Kale, M. (1992). Kids & animals, a comforting hospital combination. *InterActions,* 10(3), 17–21.

Lee, R. L., Zeglan, M. E., Ryan, T., Gowing, C. B., & Hines, L. M. (1987) *Guidelines: Animals in nursing homes* (rev. ed.). Renton, WA: Delta Society & California Veterinary Medical Association.

New, J. C. (1995). Quality of life of companion animals. Paper presented at the 7th International Conference on Human–Animal Interactions: Animals, Health and Quality of Life, Geneva, Switzerland.

New, J. C., & Strimple, E. (1988). Therapy dog criteria: Minimum medical criteria. Paper presented at the seventh annual Delta Society Conference, People, Animals and the Environment: Exploring Our Interdependence, Orlando, FL.

Patients' best friend? Hospital dogs raise spirits, not infection rates. (1992, December). *Hospital Infection Control,* pp. 162–164.

Shelter animals inappropriate for visiting programs. (1992). *Pet Partners Newsletter,* 2(6).

The IAHAIO Prague guidelines on animal-assisted activities and animal-assisted therapy (1998, September). Guidelines adopted at IAHAIO General Assembly, Prague.

Thomas, W. H. (1994). *The Eden alternative: Nature, hope and nursing homes.* Columbia, MO: University of Missouri.

Waltner-Toews, D., & Ellis, A. (1994). *Good for your animals, good for you, how to live and work with animals in activity and therapy programs and stay healthy.* Ontario, Canada: University of Guelph.

Young, M. S. (1986). The relationship between behavior at six to eight weeks of age and selected adult behavior patterns in dogs: An evaluation of the use and misuse of "Campbell's Behavior Test for Puppy Selection." Paper presented at Delta Society International Conference, Living Together: People, Animals and the Environment, Boston, MA.

CHAPTER 6

Designing and Implementing Animal-Assisted Therapy Programs in Health and Mental Health Organizations

GERALD P. MALLON
Hunter College School of Social Work, City University of New York, New York, New York

SAMUEL B. ROSS, JR., AND LISA ROSS
Green Chimneys Children's Services, Brewster, New York

I. INTRODUCTION

Although health and mental health systems continually examine fresh and original approaches to serve their client constituents, new proposals are seldom greeted with enthusiasm within organizational structures (Bolman & Terrance, 1991; Brager & Holloway, 1978; Dutton, 1992; Ket de Vries & Miller, 1984; Morgan, 1986; Moss-Kanter, 1982, 1988). One relatively new approach that utilizes a variety of animals including companion animals, farm animals, and injured wildlife as adjuncts in the treatment of various populations has been, or soon may be, considered by health or mental health organizations (Mallon, 1994a,b). Utilizing animals in health and mental health organizations is a proposal that has engendered both the regard and the ire of administrators.

The emerging breadth of its applications and the involvement of skilled professionals from diverse disciplines have made animal-assisted therapy (AAT) more than a "therapeutic" intervention. Although AAT is beginning to be recognized as a treatment modality much like dance, music, art, and poetry therapy

Handbook on Animal-Assisted Therapy: Theoretical Foundations and Guidelines for Practice

(Beck & Katcher, 1984), it is also important to note that the main difference between AAT and other adjunctive therapies is that the central "tools" in this intervention are living, breathing, interacting creatures. This is an important element because when animals are introduced into a health or mental health delivery system, unique organizational issues must be considered.

Utilizing a predominantly social work approach to organizational administration, this chapter contains advice to help organizations decide whether or not to utilize AAT and to aid implementation. With Green Chimneys Children's Services as our organizational model of choice, the authors, who are among the principal administrators of this program, focus on rules and principles that guide program development.

II. ANIMAL-ASSISTED THERAPY

Boris M. Levinson (1962) was the first professionally trained clinician to formally introduce and document the way in which companion animals could hasten the development of a rapport between therapist and patient and increase patient motivation (Mallon, 1994c). First termed *pet therapy* by Levinson, this approach is now known as animal-assisted therapy. Originally ridiculed by his colleagues for presenting such a "preposterous" technique, Levinson continued to research, write, and speak about the efficacy of this novel intervention throughout his life.

Levinson initially advocated utilizing animals with children in residential treatment and wrote extensively about it (Levinson, 1968, 1969, 1970, 1971, 1972; Levinson & Mallon, 1996). In an attempt to gather data on the utilization of animals in organizations, Levinson conducted the first survey documenting the use of pets in residential schools (Levinson, 1968). With a sample of 160 residential and day schools identified from the *Directory for Exceptional Children*, a response rate of 75.6% ($N = 121$) was obtained. Levinson found that 40.7% did not permit pets in the schools. State regulations, fear of diseases, the labor-intensive nature of caring for pets, and potential mistreatment by the children were all cited as reasons for barring animals in organizational settings.

In the 1970s the American Humane Education Society commissioned a survey to determine how many institutions in the country were using animals in facilitating the treatment of clients. The survey indicated results (48%) similar to those found earlier by Levinson. Several of the institutions surveyed reported disadvantages as well as advantages. (Arkow, 1982). In many cases, these programs were developed in a surge of enthusiasm, by well-meaning, but overzealous and inexperienced individuals (Daniel *et al.*, 1984). By the 1980s, then, the necessity of careful program design became clear. Although many other AAT programs are rapidly emerging both in this country and abroad, one organization that has thoughtfully and carefully crafted an animal-assisted program for children is Green Chimneys Children's Services, located in Brewster, New York, 60 miles outside of New York City.

III. THE GREEN CHIMNEYS MODEL

The main campus of Green Chimneys Children's Services is a temporary home for the 102 children and adolescents and 30 day students who share its rural environs with barnyard animals, domestic companion animals, and wildlife. But the healing power of human–animal interactions has been an active component in this organizational therapeutic milieu for more than 50 years.

This former dairy farm was purchased in 1947 by the Ross family, and the organization was originally designed as an independent boarding school for very young children. Operating as Green Chimneys School for Little Folk, the educationally based facility incorporated the dairy farm into the children's daily lives. Initially, the staff did not know or appreciate the therapeutic part of this alliance. The staff saw the animals as merely providing companionship, socialization, pleasure, and education for the students. They soon realized, however, that they were providing much more.

In the early 1970s, the school evolved into a residential treatment center that specialized in the care of children with emotional and behavioral needs. Children came with histories of severe neglect; sexual, physical, and emotional abuse; homelessness; family substance abuse; and behavioral and educational difficulties. Many had learning disabilities and had experienced very limited success in school. Most were hospitalized for aggressive behaviors, suicide attempts, or chronic depression. The majority lived in poverty. Most had experienced significant psychosocial stressors at home, in school, and in their communities.

Although many changes occurred as the organization changed its program to meet the needs of a new population, the human–animal interactions component remained intact. The staff realized that these special children, mostly from urban environments, could truly benefit from interactions with animals.

IV. ORGANIZATIONAL ISSUES

The eventual success or failure of a proposed organizational innovation is a consequence of the interplay of power and politics at numerous levels—individual, intraorganizational, interorganizational, and societal (Frost & Egri, 1991). The Continuous Quality Improvement Council of Green Chimneys, which consists of the agency's executive director, the organization's founder, the clinical director, the chief fiscal officer, and the associate executive directors, meets on a weekly basis to monitor review agency practices and procedures and to ensure that all parts of the organization are functioning at optimal efficiency. This council provides leadership and direction, and acts as a sounding board on major organizational issues, including the utilization of animals in our treatment programs.

Other health and mental health organizations that wish to implement an animal-assisted program component must consider the level of support that the innovation can amass on multiple levels. The following questions represent areas that the Green Chimneys' Continuous Quality Improvement Council recommends as important considerations to be discerned by other organizational administrators who wish to implement an AAT program:

- Is there administrative support for the idea?
- Does the idea have board support and will it need board approval?
- Does the innovation have staff who will support the idea?
- Will new staff have to be trained and hired?
- Has anyone asked the clients if they think this is a good idea?
- How will the innovation be funded, and what costs will be incurred throughout the process?
- What are the salient issues with respect to infection control?
- What are the issues with respect to safety and humane treatment of animals?
- What liability issues need to be considered?

And, in the age of managed care:

- Are there measurable outcomes that will enable the organization to document and evaluate the program's effectiveness?
- How can this intervention be monitored for continuous quality improvements?

V. PROGRAM DESIGN ISSUES

A. STAFF ISSUES

Because animals have always been a part of the Green Chimneys approach to working with children and families, we have always enjoyed the support of our organization's board of directors and agency administrators. But as the agency has grown, we have often had to find ways to ensure that our animal focus is maintained.

Knowledgeable, experienced, and enthusiastic personnel greatly influence a program and ensure programmatic longevity. A consistent core staff make management easier. After a great deal of experimentation and trial and error logic, Green Chimneys has found that an animal-assisted program can be staffed by licensed and credentialed personnel (social workers, nurses, psychologists, physicians, occupational therapists, physical therapists, vocational therapists, teachers) and other staff (child care workers, school personnel, recreation workers, nurses aides, therapy aides); and volunteers can provide animal-assisted activities (AAAs). It has been an ongoing challenge for our organization to determine which staff positions or responsibilities should be filled by professionals, which should be staffed by trained personnel, and which are suited for volunteers. Over the years we found that many of the staff currently employed by the agency came forward to fill roles in working with both children and animals. Two key factors were their desire to incorporate animals into their work with people and their commitment to designing innovative approaches to working with people in need. An additional essential element was whether or not they had the support of their supervisors in this endeavor.

Green Chimneys has historically recognized that those helping professionals who work with both people and animals need to be flexible, but there is also a need for structure, consistency, and limits. Many different philosophies are represented by those who are interested in developing approaches to working with animals and humans. Before any new program can be developed, it will need to be approved by the organization's board of directors and administrative staff. The first question that most boards of directors and administrators will want an answer to is this: How does this project relate to the organization's mission, vision, values, goals, and needs? On a secondary level, both bodies will want to know about costs, about maintaining the program, about agency personnel and client support, and about liability. When interviewing for positions, administrative staff must seek out the candidate's specific beliefs and personal stance. For example, will a vegetarian be able to talk to clients about slaughtering animals for meat? Is the person unsure of how the animal will be treated? Know where the candidate stands on issues that may come up in the workplace. Staff surveys may be another important step that can permit their voices to be heard when considering a new intervention.

B. CLIENT ISSUES

Although it has been written that the human–animal bond is universal (Mallon, 1992, Senter, 1993, p. 1), the reality is that not all people like animals. Some clients may be allergic to specific animals, some may have a phobia about a particular animal, others may just not have had positive experiences with animals. At Green Chimneys many of these issues are immediately addressed at intake, when the client first arrives for services. Clients are screened for allergies and asked about fears or dislikes for particular animals. This information is then integrated into the client's initial prospective treatment plan. Although Green Chimneys would like all of its clients to have a positive experience with animals, the organization respects the fact that not all children respond the same way to animal-assisted approaches to treatment.

Another means for assessing patient satisfaction or dissatisfaction is to conduct a survey of the clients' likes and dislikes about their treatment. This is more or less standard practice in most health and mental health organizations in today's managed care environment. A client-focused survey soliciting patient response toward animals is an important place to begin the process.

VI. ANIMAL SELECTION

Choosing animals at Green Chimneys to be part of our AAT program is an exciting endeavor, but animal selection can also be an imposing task. Again, we would caution that those wishing to introduce animals into an existing organization should start small. Zoning and health regulations will undoubtedly affect the location, nature, and size of programs incorporating animals. Geography also plays a large role in the selection of animals. Organizations in urban environments obviously need to consider restricting the program to smaller companion animals (see Senter, 1993, Chapters 4 and 5). Some programs may choose to have a visiting AAA program, rather than having animals in residence. Rural programs, such as our Green Chimneys' program, utilize a wide variety of animals including farm animals and captive wildlife. Our wildlife program is coordinated by an individual who is a licensed wildlife rehabilitator (see Senter, 1993, Chapters 2 and 3). Most of our wild animals have sustained injuries and are only temporarily placed at the farm for rest, medical care, and eventual release. The size of the physical space needed for each animal is determined by the animal's physical size and need for space. An administrative policy should also be in place that ensures that all animals are healthy, have up-to-date vaccinations, and a record kept on file of their health status.

Concern for the physical well-being of the clients is a major priority in health and mental health care-related organizations. Cleanliness, infection control, and risk of illness related to zoonotic conditions claim a central focus in most health and mental health care systems. Organizations interested in adopting an AAT approach must research federal, state, and local regulations early in the planning process to consider possible limitations for such an intervention. It can be very disappointing for those interested in designing an AAT program to discover that rigid local health laws prohibit such techniques.

VII. COST EFFECTIVENESS

Initial start-up and continued financing, in any organization, plays a large role in the decision to develop or not develop a new program. This is particularly true for nonprofit organizations. Regardless of how useful an AAT program is deemed to be for an organization, the bottom line for most agency administrators and boards is how much it is going to cost and how will it be funded? Our Green Chimneys founder, Dr. Sam Ross, and our organization's development staff spend a great deal of time and energy on fund-raising efforts to keep all of our programs fiscally sound. Although this process can be a time-consuming enterprise, the good news is that incorporating animals does not have to be an expensive undertaking. There are many ways to raise money for programs. Innovative thinking and creativity are the keys.

All new programs have start-up costs, dictated by the size and nature of the innovation. "Start small" is a good maxim. Funds for animal upkeep and maintenance refer to the day-to-day expenses of keeping animals. These costs will vary from program to program, but generally include food, shelter, veterinary costs, grooming costs, and staff salary costs.

At Green Chimneys we have found five ways to support an animal-assisted program: (1) use of present funds, (2) foundation or corporate support, (3) fee for service, (4) outright donations, and (5) sale of items. Where costs are minimal and programs are small, using present funds may be a quick-start solution. Many foundations or corporations, especially those with an obvious interest in animals, can provide possible seed money to start a program. Fees for services can be generated through visiting animal programs or by offering specialized training. Donation from the community and sales in the community not only help support the program, but bring the organization's name out into the community. Linking the community to the program's efforts to help its constituents can be useful in many ways.

VIII. LIABILITY

All organizations are concerned about the potential for liability issues. Obviously there are risks inherent in having animals on site in a health or mental health organization. Green Chimneys has developed a documented safety plan for both clients and animals, and we would recommend that such a plan be considered a necessity for every organization. In the sections that follow, we discuss our Green Chimneys protocols for minimizing risk. These should be carefully considered and followed by organizational staff. The first place that organizations should start when considering liability issues is by reviewing their current insurance carrier's policies about animals. If animals are included in the policy coverage and the organization's carrier is clear that the organization is launching a new initiative then there is no need for further coverage. If animals are not included in the current coverage then the organization *must* obtain coverage for staff, clients, and visitors.

IX. OUTCOMES

The widespread ardor about the almost universal efficacy of animal-assisted programs has for many years all but obscured any serious questioning of its possible risks. In the age of managed care, health and mental health organization administrators must evaluate the effectiveness of their interventions. Any program evaluation of a health or mental health organization must also include a review of the effectiveness of an organization's animal-assisted programs (Anspach, 1991). Although organizational administrators must develop stringent criteria used for what constitutes a therapeutic gain, they must also develop criteria for what constitutes an effective programmatic intervention. Some suggested questions that should be assessed include these: Is this intervention cost effective? Are there other interventions that are equally clinically appropriate and useful, but more cost effective? How many clients are utilizing this service in a given cycle? What are the instruments used by program evaluators to determine clinical or program effectiveness with respect to this intervention? Therefore, guidelines for the implementation of an animal-assisted program need to identify conditions necessary to preserve the health and safety of both the animals and clients, and to ensure that the intervention is programmatically effective. Administrators should resist the attempt to rationalize the implementation of such programs solely as a kind of therapy that has universal benefits solely because of its appeal.

X. INFECTION CONTROL ISSUES

Even in the best AAT programs, there is an element of risk. At Green Chimneys we have been aware of and respond to these risk factors on a daily basis. Animals bite, some produce allergic reactions, and some pass on zoonotic diseases. Therefore, an AAT program must develop infection control policies that address the need for some animals to avoid contact with certain people, and to develop surveillance procedures and responses. Every setting where pets or animals of any type are located must have some rules in place (Ross, 1989, p. 5). At Green Chimneys we maintain a health record on each animal and we recommend this task as an essential component of any planned AAA/T program.

XI. RULES THAT GUIDE ANIMAL-ASSISTED THERAPY PROGRAMS

Following Lewis's (1982) advice, rules that guide an intervention to action specify the practice. The Continuous Quality Improvement Council at Green Chimneys has focused a great deal of attention on the development of rules to guide practice in our AAT approaches to treatment. These rules are enumerated for all Green Chimneys staff as a part of the agency's initial formal orientation process and are codified in writing in our organization's literature. We have found the following rules to be useful and we believe they are adaptable for other organizations:

1. House animals are to be approved by the organization's administrator or designee.
2. Appropriate animals include dogs, cats, birds, fish, hamsters, gerbils, guinea pigs, rabbits, and, where appropriate conditions exist, farm animals such as goats, sheep, ducks, chickens, cows, and horses.
3. Wildlife are not permitted in the program unless they are cared for under the supervision of a licensed individual and then only in a rehabilitative circumstance.
4. At the time of admission, a medical record is started on each animal and is kept up to date as long as the animal remains in the organization.
5. Animals are to have up-to-date vaccinations.
6. Animals are to have an annual physical by a qualified veterinarian.
7. Animals who are ill are to be treated by a qualified veterinarian.
8. Aggressive animals will be removed immediately.
9. Dogs or cats are to be altered or spayed.
10. The administrator or designee is responsible for acceptable animal husbandry practices.
11. Animals are to be controlled by leash, command, or cage.
12. Animals are not permitted in the following areas: areas where food is cleaned, stored, or prepared; vehicles used for the transportation of food; patient/staff's toilet, shower, or dressing rooms; and drug preparation areas, nursing stations, and sterile and cleaning supply rooms.
13. All pet utensils, food, and equipment used for maintenance of pets are to be kept in an area separate from clients' food preparation areas.
14. Animals are to be fed according to schedule posted where the animals live and are cared for.
15. Animals are not to be fed human food.

16. Freshwater is to be made available for the animals at all times.
17. Food handlers are not to be involved in animal care, feeding, or cleanup of animal food or waste.
18. Dogs and cats are to be effectively housebroken.
19. Animal waste is to be picked up and disposed of in a trash receptacle made available for this purpose.
20. Any animal that bites a staff member or patient is to be quarantined for 10 days.
21. Animals who die on the premises are to be disposed of in accordance with the established organizational procedure.
22. Animals from outside the agency are permitted to visit the premises through a prearranged agreement under rules for visiting pets.
23. Animals are to be groomed daily.
24. All staff (except for kitchen workers, for sanitary reasons) are encouraged to be involved in actively caring for the animals.
25. Clients are to be involved in caring for the animals.
26. Animals are to be part of weekly sessions with the clients.

XII. PRINCIPLES THAT GUIDE ANIMAL-ASSISTED THERAPY PROGRAMS

If a worker is "lacking a rule," the worker will search his or her own memory for a principle. This practice principle tells the worker what to do. Rules are clear cut and therefore, can be more rapidly recalled from memory. The principle that is more abstract requires a more time-consuming and complex mental undertaking to recover from memory (Lewis, 1982, pp. 57–58). Principles are expressions of goals and permit staff to have leeway regarding the means by which they are carried out.

In identifying principles for the AAT practitioner, we offer the following, which are used at Green Chimneys:

1. All animals will be carefully selected and subject to behavioral assessment to determine their aptitude for working with people.
2. At time of hire, staff will be surveyed to determine allergies, fears, or dislike of animals. Attitudes of workers will be measured to evaluate former relationships with animals.
3. At time of intake, clients will be surveyed to determine allergies, fears, dislike, or past abusive behavior toward animals. Attitudes of clients will be measured to evaluate former relationships with animals.

4. The rights of individuals who do not wish to participate in the program will be considered first and off-limits areas for animals will be maintained for this purpose.

5. Companion animals should not pose a threat or nuisance to the clients, staff, or visitors.

6. Workers should integrate the patient's interactions with animals into their comprehensive treatment plan, with specific and relevant goals.

7. The worker will strive to assure the patient the opportunity to choose his or her own goals in work with the animals and assist him or her in identifying and achieving this end.

8. Sessions that involve animal-assisted therapy must be documented in the weekly progress notes.

9. The worker will document any and all interactions that may be novel behavior as a result of the human–animal bonding.

10. The worker will closely supervise and monitor any patient who has a past history of animal abuse.

11. The worker will closely supervise and monitor the temperament of all animals who are utilized with patients. Animals will be permitted to rest every hour and a half and not be permitted to work more than 5 hours per day.

12. The worker should process animal-assisted activities to assist the patient in exploring new or possibly previously unexplored issues.

13. The worker should encourage the patient to work with her or him in settings other than the offices, that is, conduct a session while taking the dog for a walk.

14. The worker should utilize the animals with the patient to explore areas that can be seen as "dress rehearsal for life," that is, birth, death, pregnancy.

15. The worker should utilize the animal-assisted interaction to aid the patient in mastering developmental tasks.

16. The worker should utilize the animal to promote feelings of self-worth in the patient whenever possible.

17. The worker should utilize the animal to promote responsibility and independence in the patient.

18. The worker should utilize the animal to teach the patient the need to sacrifice or undergo inconvenience for the sake of a loved one.

19. The worker should make every effort to utilize the animal to promote companionship, warmth, and love with the patient.

20. The worker should remember that utilizing an animal is not an "open sesame" or a panacea to working with or uncovering the "inner world" of the troubled patient.

21. The worker should work to maintain the "therapy" component in animal-assisted therapy.
22. The worker should utilize the animal to teach lessons in life, thereby promoting and nurturing appropriate emotional responses from clients.

XIII. CONCLUSIONS

Encouraging well-designed, carefully evaluated interventions is essential to responsible current and future AAT program development. A diverse array of helping professionals are often in search of ways to improve the quality of life of persons who have overwhelming obstacles to overcome. To those clients who could benefit from an animal companion, a health or mental health care professional may be able to facilitate a new or support a long-established relationship by being sensitive to what is occurring in the field and by knowing which resources are available (Netting *et al.,* 1988, pp. 63–64). Our challenge is for health and mental health organizations to look for meaningful ways to incorporate animals into our human services organizations in mutually beneficial partnerships.

While what has been offered here is not, as Levinson pointed out, the panacea to the world's ills, it is a beginning. Animals can fulfill an important role for many people, but organizations that wish to set in motion such interventions must be careful to also initiate rules and principles to guide this practice. Although the labor-intensive nature of integrating animals into a health or mental health system may at first seem a daunting task, the organizational benefits of such an intervention are numerous (Mallon, 1994a,b). The introduction of animals into a human service system will not produce additional competitiveness or alienation, but can, instead, provide that calming, unqualified attention and love that are needed to help some clients flourish, moving away from illness and toward health. As health and mental health organizations struggle to find their niche in an ever expanding network of diverse services, we must be alert to novel and creative approaches to helping our clients, including in some cases where indicated, utilizing an array of diverse animals as adjuncts in the treatment of various populations.

REFERENCES

Anspach, R. R. (1991). Everyday methods for assessing organizational effectiveness. *Social Problems,* 38(1), 1–19.
Arkow, P. (1982). *Pet therapy: A study of the uses of companion animals.* Colorado Springs, CO: Humane Society of the Pikes Peak Region.

Beck, A. M., & Katcher, A. H. (1984). A new look at pet-facilitated therapy. *Journal of American Veterinary Medicine Association,* 184(4), 414–420.

Bolman, L., & Terrance, D. (1991). *Reframing organizations.* San Francisco: Jossey-Bass.

Brager, G., & Holloway, S. (1978). *Changing human service organizations: Politics and practice.* New York: Free Press.

Daniel, S., Burke, J., & Burke, J. (1984). Educational programs for pet-assisted therapy in institutional settings: An interdisciplinary approach. *Veterinary Technician,* 5(2), 394–397.

Dutton, J. E. (1992). The making of organizational opportunities: An interpretive pathway to organizational change. *Research in Organizational Behavior,* 15, 195–226.

Frost, P. J., & Egri, C. P. (1991). The political process of innovation. *Research in Organizational Behavior,* 13, 229–295.

Kets de Vries, M. F. R., & Miller, D. (1984). *The neurotic organization.* New York: Harper Business.

Levinson, B. (1962). The dog as co-therapist. *Mental Hygiene,* 46, 59–65.

Levinson, B. (1968). Household pets in residential schools. *Mental Hygiene,* 52, 411–414.

Levinson, B. (1969). *Pet-oriented child psychotherapy.* Springfield, IL: Charles C. Thomas.

Levinson, B. (1970). Nursing home pets: A psychological adventure for the clients (part I). *National Humane Review,* 58, 14–16.

Levinson, B. (1971). Household pets in training schools serving delinquent children. *Psychological Reports,* 28, 475–481.

Levinson, B. (1972). *Pets and human development.* Springfield, IL: Charles C. Thomas.

Levinson, B., & Mallon, G. P. (1996). *Pet-oriented child psychotherapy* (2nd ed.). Springfield, IL: Charles C. Thomas.

Lewis, H. (1982). *The intellectual base of social work practice.* New York: The Lois and Samuel Silberman Fund and Haworth Press.

Mallon, G. P. (1992). Utilization of animals as therapeutic adjuncts with children and youth: A review of the literature. *Child & Youth Care Forum,* 21(1), 53–65.

Mallon, G. P. (1994a). Some of our best therapists are dogs. *Child and Youth Care Forum,* 23(2), 89–101.

Mallon, G. P. (1994b). Cow as co-therapist: Utilization of farm animals as therapeutic aides with children in residential treatment. *Child and Adolescent Social Work Journal,* 11(6), 455–474.

Mallon, G. P. (1994c). A generous spirit: The work and life of Boris Levinson. *Anthrozoos,* 7(4), 224–231.

Morgan, G. (1986). *Images of organization.* Newbury Park, CA: Sage Publications.

Moss-Kanter, R. (1982). Dilemmas of managing participation. *Organizational Dynamics,* 3, 5–27.

Moss-Kanter, R. (1988). When a thousand flowers bloom: Structural, collective, and social conditions for innovation in organization. *Research in Organizational Behavior,* 10, 169–211.

Netting, F. E., Wilson, C., & New, J. C. (1988). The human–animal bond: Implications for practice. *Social Work,* 39(1), 60–64.

Ross, S. B. (1989). Children and animals: Many benefits—some concerns. *The New York State Outdoor Education Association,* 23(2), 2–13.

Senter, S. (Ed.). (1993). *People and animals: A therapeutic animal-assisted activities manual for schools, agencies and recreational centers.* Brewster, NY: Green Chimneys Press.

CHAPTER 7

Program Evaluation and Quality Assurance in Animal-Assisted Therapy

MARY R. BURCH
Behavior Management Consultants, Inc., Tallahassee, Florida

I. INTRODUCTION

The benefits of using animals in therapy settings have been reported for centuries (Burch, 1995). Animals have been used to help practitioners achieve program goals in every setting imaginable. Individuals in nursing homes, prisons, schools, physical rehabilitation, and a variety of specialty programs have experienced firsthand the powerful healing potential of animals.

The late 1970s and 1980s marked a turning point in the growth of animal-assisted therapy (AAT) as an established field. National programs for animal-assisted therapists registered large numbers of volunteers, training courses were developed, animals were certified, AAT conferences were held at the local, state, national, and international level, and there was a dramatic surge in the literature pertaining to AAT. Having witnessed the positive effects of animals in therapeutic settings, both researchers and practitioners advocated increases in the availability of AAT services. By the 1990s, thousands of animal-assisted therapy volunteers were working in programs around the world.

For most types of educational and habilitation programs, the 1990s could be characterized as a time when taxpayers, program administrators, and govern-

Handbook on Animal-Assisted Therapy: Theoretical Foundations and Guidelines for Practice
Copyright © 2000 by Academic Press. All rights of reproduction in any form reserved.

ment officials began to demand more accountability and documentation of program quality. With this increase in the demand for accountability, by the 1990s, the area of program evaluation was becoming an increasingly essential and important component of AAT programs.

II. PROGRAM EVALUATION

Historically, the field of program evaluation has changed dramatically in the past 40 years. Guba and Lincoln (1985) identified four distinct phases that have occurred during the evolution of program evaluation. In the early development of the field, evaluators were often measurement specialists. These specialists were usually outside consultants who were hired to measure some particular aspect of a program. Statistics was a primary tool in assessing program effectiveness.

In the second phase of the development of program evaluation, evaluators focused on identifying objectives for a particular program, then measuring how closely outcomes reflected the original goals. As program evaluation became a more commonly accepted practice, program evaluators became involved in making value judgments about program goals and initiatives. It was during this third phase in this rapidly evolving field that program evaluation moved beyond educational settings and into social, government, medical, and specialty settings such as animal-assisted therapy.

In most programs using program evaluation strategies, the fourth and final phase of program evaluation is currently in place. According to Guba and Lincoln (1985), this fourth phase can be characterized by evaluators who have gone beyond simply measuring effects to become extremely involved in the dynamics of the program. Sensitive to the political and social climate in a given facility, these evaluators work closely with program staff and administrators and involve them in making decisions about the evaluation process. Administrators should be actively involved in making decisions about program evaluations that involve staff, funding, or other resources from the facility and have implications for the overall facility program.

If the current trends continue, program evaluation might eventually become as integral to an AAT program as the training and interventions already are. Rather than using short pre- and poststatistical evaluations to evaluate program effects, ideally the evaluation process will be ongoing with routine feedback given to the administrators and decision makers (e.g., community boards, human rights committees) who will ultimately be responsible for implementing programs and approving continued evaluations. The administration of a facility generally has a significant interest in whether or not a particular program results in documented client improvement or a substantial cost savings. Robinson and

Robinson (1989) refer to the new role of program evaluators as professionals who form "strategic partnerships with management."

III. PURPOSES OF PROGRAM EVALUATION

In the early years of program evaluation, evaluators focused on outcomes and summative evaluations. Summative evaluations were used to make summary decisions such as to continue or discontinue a program based on the results (Basarab & Root, 1992). In an AAT program, if after an intervention has been in place for several months, a program evaluator gathers postprogram data, a summative evaluation has been used. In more recent years, the use of formative evaluation techniques in program evaluation has increased. Formative evaluations are in place throughout a program and are used to make adjustments in an ongoing process (Basarab & Root, 1992). An example of the use of formative evaluation would be modifying a training program for AAT volunteers during the second week of training when it became apparent volunteers were having trouble mastering the material designed for a 10-week course.

Program evaluation in AAT has several purposes. Program evaluation assists in planning for the future, determining needed interventions and program modifications, and documenting outcomes for justifying funding or the allocation of resources. Program evaluation in AAT settings can be used to assess current program status and whether or not AAT interventions with clients are effective. Animal-assisted therapists can use program evaluation as a diagnostic tool that gives direction for future goals for clients. If a client in an AAT program began to show greater physical strength after walking with a dog, physical therapists might decide to develop new treatment plan goals involving walking (e.g., walk to the dining room, walk to the yard outside where the dog is waiting). Program evaluation can also be used to conduct a cost–benefit analysis of the AAT program. Basically, in AAT settings, the program evaluation process helps decision makers determine, after considering all of the variables, if a particular program or procedure has value and should be continued.

Just as programs can be evaluated, the process of program evaluation can also undergo evaluation. The Joint Commission on Standards for Educational Evaluation (1981) identified four major categories by which a program evaluation can be evaluated. These areas include utility, feasibility, propriety, and accuracy. Utility refers to whether or not an evaluation serves the needs of the audience. Feasibility addresses whether or not a program evaluation is realistic and economically sound. The consideration of propriety ensures that sufficient concern has been shown for the clients who will be affected, and finally, accuracy refers to the process of determining the program evaluation has been implemented in a technically correct, systematic manner.

IV. AREAS OF PROGRAM EVALUATION

Program evaluations for AAT programs can address a variety of areas. Ten main areas can be identified: mission statement, physical plant, clients, animals, volunteers, staff, curriculum, cost–benefit analysis, results, and long-term impact (Table I) (Burch, 1996). Each of these areas includes subcategories and may be referred to by different terminology depending on the program evaluator.

A. MISSION STATEMENT

The mission statement for any program provides a broad description of the intent of the program. The mission statement provides the starting point from which goals and objectives are developed. When evaluating a mission statement and the accompanying goals and objectives, program evaluators would determine if there is a clear relationship between the activities of the program and the mission statement. Program evaluators would also determine if an AAT program's mission statement was practical, attainable, and related to the goals and short-term objectives that had been identified. A mission statement that described the mission of a facility's AAT program as to "use animals so each child in the program can function independently in the community," would not be appropriate or reasonable in a setting for children with severe disabilities. A mission statement that would propose to use animals to teach new skills "so that each child can function as independently as possible" would be more reasonable.

TABLE I   Animal-Assisted Therapy: 10 Areas of
Program Evaluation

1. Mission Statement
2. Physical Plant
3. Clients
4. Animals
5. Volunteers
6. Staff
7. Curriculum
8. Cost Benefit
9. Results
10. Long-term Impact

B. Physical Plant

For AAT programs, the physical plant includes the building where the program will take place. This could be a nursing home, rehabilitation hospital, or any other type of facility with an AAT program. Included in the physical plant portion of the program's evaluation are outside areas such as yards where clients might exercise dogs, hallways where fish tanks are placed, or dayrooms where cages of small animals or birds might be located. The physical plant needs to be adequately arranged so as to facilitate the activities of the AAT program. If AAT programs are related to client goals such as ambulation, adequate space should be designated in the facility where clients can walk with therapy animals. When animals live at facilities, compliance with health codes related to infection control and sanitation are a part of the AAT evaluation. For example, during inclement weather, animals can be brought indoors, but they should not be housed in the closet with clean linens or in food preparation areas.

C. Clients

Other names for clients depending on the particular setting are patients, residents, or students. Basically, the clients are the consumers who will be the recipients of AAT services. The client portion of program evaluation addresses the procedures that are used for selecting clients for AAT, as well as whether or not individuals or groups of clients could benefit from the services. For example, while animals have been used to reduce the pain reported by some clients, an elderly client who was suffering and screaming from the intense pain caused by a broken hip would certainly be better served with a medical intervention than AAT. In a juvenile justice setting where teenage boys have frequent incidents of behavioral acting out, an AAT program built around the use of smaller, more fragile animals would not be recommended until the behavior problems of the teenagers were under control. The role of program evaluation here could be related to the behavioral goals of individual teenagers and the formative evaluations (e.g., daily data) of their behavioral progress.

The AAT client portion of the program evaluation is directly related to the portion of the program evaluation described as "results." Client responses and behavior changes related to AAT are most often measured by the use of questionnaires and surveys, statistical measures, and single-subject design methodology. In some residential facilities such as nursing homes and developmental disabilities settings, family members and staff respond to quality of life questionnaires as part of the overall facility evaluation. Quality of life measures are receiving increased interest in AAT settings. Oftentimes "an improved quality of life" is the justification for the implementation of AAT programs (Keil, 1998).

D. ANIMALS

The selection of animals in an AAT program can make or break a program. Animals should be selected to match client characteristics and program needs. Animal selection relates to species selection, breed selection, and the careful selection of individual animals within a breed in order to fully maximize the benefits of the AAT program. A toy breed of dog, such as a Maltese, would most likely be a better bed companion for a bed-ridden person in a nursing home than a giant breed, such as a Great Dane. A person with allergies might do better with a short-haired cat in AAT sessions than with a Persian. A child who was quiet and fearful would be better placed with a calm, reserved, Welsh Springer Spaniel than a dog of the same breed who was extremely active and full of energy. An adult who had an inability to be gentle with more fragile animals such as hamsters might benefit more from an AAT program involving riding a horse.

The animals in AAT programs can be evaluated in a variety of categories including suitability for the program, health, and behavior. Veterinary assessments and checklists are typically completed for most AAT animals. The behavior of AAT animals is assessed by using checklists of skills related to a basic level of training such as the American Kennel Club's (1996) Canine Good Citizen Test.

The training and behavior of animals in AAT programs is also important. Program evaluators determine if animals are under control and if their presence enhances the habilitation process, or if the animal becomes simply one more thing that needs to be managed. All animals in AAT settings should have passed the necessary health and veterinary screenings. Program evaluation in AAT should ensure that all animals are healthy, clean, and well groomed.

E. VOLUNTEERS

During a complete AAT program evaluation, AAT volunteers will be evaluated. Factors relating to volunteers include the number of contact hours provided to clients, volunteer behaviors related to interacting with clients, volunteer behaviors related to handling therapy animals, and volunteer turnover rates. Most facilities require that AAT volunteers complete general facility orientation and volunteer training. When AAT programs rely heavily on volunteers, the role of competency-based training and feedback in the therapy setting is critical.

Turnover is a particular problem in programs depending on volunteers. In only a few months, Savishinsky (1992) reported a 30% attrition rate among 100 volunteers who visited facilities with their animals. In evaluating this program, it was determined that the most likely reason for the high attrition was that the volunteers were unprepared for the emotional stress involved with working in a nursing home. Studies such as this are valuable because they identify problems that can be addressed in future program evaluations. If the problem was that volunteers were unprepared for the experience in the nursing home, program evaluators could work with AAT decision makers to evaluate interventions that would ensure volunteers were more prepared. Such interventions might include more time in the facility before beginning volunteering, additional training, and developing procedures to carefully match individual volunteers with specific settings.

F. Staff

Staff who might be involved in some aspect of a facility's AAT program most commonly include administrators, medical staff, managers, departmental directors, therapists and other health care professionals, teachers, and direct care staff. Only when an AAT program has the support and cooperation of administrators, managers, and directors will it achieve maximum success. The role of the staff who work directly with clients is also critical. Staff evaluations can be in the form of questionnaires, interviews, checklists, direct observation of staff behavior, and consumer (client and family) evaluations of staff performance. In a quality AAT program, therapists will work with AAT personnel and volunteers to identify the goals and treatment strategies that are the most appropriate for each client.

G. Curriculum

The curriculum is the content of the AAT program. Ideally, the curriculum will be driven by the habilitative goals and objectives for individual clients. The goals of the facility should match the curriculum and goals for individual clients. Specific interventions and activities should match the needs of individual clients. For example, brushing dogs is a worthwhile activity and it can improve dexterity and fine-motor coordination. However, in a group of clients for whom ambulation has been identified as a priority, walking dogs might be an activity more suited to achieving significant therapeutic results. Other program issues, such as scheduling, are tied closely to the curriculum of the

AAT program and these issues can also be considered during a program evaluation.

H. Cost–Benefit Analysis

In the area of program evaluation, cost–benefit analysis is an important consideration. Cost–benefit analysis refers to the portion of the program evaluation that essentially answers the question "Considering the cost of the program, was it worth it?" A cost–benefit analysis can determine the benefits of a particular program and put a dollar value on those benefits, calculate the total costs related to a program, and compare the benefits and the costs (Kee, 1994). One obvious benefit related to AAT programs is the volunteer labor. Even though volunteers are not paid, a dollar amount can be calculated to estimate the value of volunteer services. Using a simple log or sign-in procedure, the number of contact hours with clients in an AAT program should be documented to assess the worth of the contribution made by volunteers.

Some benefits are extremely important even though they may be more difficult to quantify. For example, if a person has made tremendous gains as the result of therapy dog intervention, they might sustain fewer injuries and therefore need less medical care; they might require fewer medications or fewer one-on-one staff hours, and they may have a shorter length of stay in a facility.

In the cost–benefit analysis portion of program evaluation, benefits are compared to costs in order to assess overall program value. Because AAT programs are very often largely staffed by volunteers, there may be limited costs with regard to staffing the program. Costs to facilities for AAT programs could be one-time, fixed costs such as constructing fencing or housing for animals; recurring costs such as transportation costs related to getting clients to a specialty program (e.g., riding horses at a stable); and staff-related costs, such as salaries of facility personnel who will supervise AAT volunteers.

I. Results

The remaining two areas of AAT program evaluation, results and long-term impact, relate to the outcomes of the program. Results encompass client progress and size of effect changes that can be measured with individual client assessments, questionnaires, statistical measures, and single-subject design data.

J. Long-Term Impact

The long-term impact of AAT can be assessed by implementing follow-up measures as a part of the AAT program evaluation. There is a need for more longitudinal studies that show the long-term effects of AAT programs and the lasting role that AAT might have on improving specific skills and quality of life. Longitudinal studies and follow-up measures should document whether or not there are any lasting benefits of AAT once a client leaves the facility or no longer participates in the program. If follow-up data were available for teenage AAT participants that showed they went to get their own pets, live a well-adjusted life, and choose a vocation related to AAT, the funding for AAT programs would be dramatically increased.

V. CLIENT EVALUATIONS: MEASURING AAT RESULTS AND LONG-TERM IMPACT

To measure the results an AAT program has had with regard to increasing client skills or changing behavior, program evaluators can use three broad categories of data: (1) individual client progress data, which may include acquisition data or reduction programming data; (2) group research design data; and (3) single-subject research design data.

A. Individual Client Participation and Progress Data

In many therapeutic settings, data are required to document client participation and progress in activities. Data can be obtained for individual clients by using (1) standardized assessments that are administered on a regular basis, (2) direct observation of specific behaviors, (3) task analysis data from skill acquisition programming data, and (4) reduction program data from programs designed to reduce problem behaviors.

B. Standardized Assessments

Standardized assessments are administered in most therapeutic settings as a routine part of the habilitation process. Standardized assessments are available for every type of specialty area. A comprehensive client assessment would include information such as the client's mental and cognitive functioning, academic abilities, physical abilities, health, leisure, and social skills. Assessments are generally administered at least yearly as a part of a habilitation planning process. The information from annual assessments is used to develop goals and objectives for therapy. Standardized assessments or portions of the assessment tools could be administered periodically to provide therapists with diagnostic information.

C. DIRECT OBSERVATION OF SPECIFIC BEHAVIORS

As part of an AAT program evaluation, evaluators can conduct direct observations of specific client behaviors. For example, if a goal for a particular client was to have the client engage in verbal interaction with others, data could be taken during sessions when the client was with and without the therapy animal. Another important aspect of AAT program evaluation is measuring any lasting effects of the animals. When the therapy cat leaves, is the client still more verbal 1 hour later? What about 2 hours later? To document the effects of animals both before and after sessions, an observation system and data collection system could be developed, and an observer would simply watch the client during the specified times and record the number of verbalizations. If there were consistently more verbalizations with the animal present, there would be some indication that the AAT program was having a positive effect on the client. Kongable et al., (1989) observed clients and recorded eight social behaviors in three conditions that included no dog, a dog temporarily visiting, and a dog permanently placed in the facility. Direct observation was used and the results indicated that the presence of a dog increased the number of social behaviors. Although standard data collection methods would provide a more objective picture of client progress, when direct observations are conducted, some therapists record the results as narrative, anecdotal records, which can be compiled as case studies. Even though anecdotal notes are widely used, as AAT program evaluations become more sophisticated, anecdotes will less often be acceptable as a means of reporting program effectiveness.

D. TASK ANALYSIS TRAINING TO TEACH NEW SKILLS

The task analysis method is used when a skill would be more easily taught if it were broken into smaller units of behavior. A task analysis involves breaking the task down into a sequence of steps that the learner must perform in order to complete the task (Gagne, et al., 1992). If an animal-assisted therapist wanted to teach a child with severe physical disabilities to brush a therapy dog, the task could be broken into steps that would include (1) reach for the brush, (2) pick up the brush, (3) put the brush on top of the dog's head, (4) move the brush from the head to the middle of the back, and (5) move the brush from the middle of the back to the base of the tail. The steps could be listed on a data sheet that the therapist would score during each session. A graph of acquisition data could be developed from the task analysis data that showed the rate at which each of the skills was performed independently.

Burch (1991) used the task analysis approach to document client progress in AAT settings. In a training program designed to teach a 3-year-old substance-exposed child who was refusing to walk to ambulate to a therapy dog, a 10-step task analysis was developed. The task analysis began with the child crawling to the dog, then walking by holding one of the therapist's hands, and finally, walking with no assistance. The child accomplished all 10 steps of the task analysis in 11 sessions; in the 11th session, he walked 5 feet independently.

E. REDUCTION PROGRAM DATA FROM PROGRAMS DESIGNED TO REDUCE PROBLEM BEHAVIORS

In addition to their usefulness at teaching new skills, animals in therapy settings can also be used to reduce client behavior problems. Program evaluators can evaluate one aspect of program effectiveness by reviewing data from AAT programs designed to reduce client behavior problems. Clients with stereotypical behaviors such as rocking, hand-flapping, or making noises may engage in fewer maladaptive behaviors if an animal is present. Because reducing or eliminating behavior problems is an important part of the therapeutic process, the effects of animals on the reduction of unwanted behaviors should be a part of all comprehensive AAT program evaluations. There is a need for more studies that focus on the effects of animals on decreasing unwanted behaviors.

VI. STATISTICAL RESEARCH DESIGN

Formal assessments, direct observations of behavior, task analysis data, and reduction programming data can be used to provide program evaluators with information regarding the progress of individual clients. Although this information is a critical part of the habilitation planning and therapeutic process, at times the AAT program will need to be evaluated according to more rigorous standards. When funding is an issue or when a particular treatment needs to be evaluated as to its effectiveness, there is a need to go beyond independent sets of individual client data and to begin analyzing the entire AAT program.

The most common method of evaluating the effects of AAT programs has been to use group statistical designs. In these designs, participants are most often randomly assigned to groups and different groups receive different treatments. The data are analyzed using statistical procedures. When statistics are used to evaluate programs, most often, a sample is selected from the population with the hopes of being able to generalize the results to the whole population. In statistics, a population is the entire group that has something in common, such as all of the people in nursing homes everywhere who receive animal-assisted therapy services. Statistics can be used in program evaluation to describe sets of numbers, make inferences about groups, compare results, and to test a research hypothesis. When statistics are used to evaluate AAT programs, questions such as these can be answered:

1. Which of several procedures is the most effective in AAT settings?
2. Will conducting an AAT session one way be more effective than doing it another way?
3. What is the probable outcome of an AAT program in a particular place?
4. When clients receiving AAT are compared to clients who have not received the services, what are the differences in specified variables?

When statistics are used, the first step for program evaluators and researchers is to decide which questions should be asked. Then they determine which statistical test is the most appropriate tool for answering the questions. Statistical tests commonly used to evaluate the effects of an AAT program include t-tests, chi-square (χ^2), and regression analysis.

A. t-Tests

The t-test can be used in program evaluation to assess the generalizability of data. The t-test for statistical significance tests the null hypothesis that there is no difference between two groups (Newcomer, 1994). The t-test is one of the most commonly used tests in AAT research. Batson et al. (1998) used a t-test to evaluate the effectiveness of the presence of a therapy dog on socialization and physiologic indicators of stress in adults with Alzheimer's disease. Dependent variables included both social and physiologic variables such as verbalizations, looks, smiles, leaning toward stimulus, praise, heart rate, and blood pressure. The data showed that mean scores for social variables such as smiles, tactile contact, and looks were significantly higher when the pet was present.

B. Chi-Square

Both the chi-square test and the *t*-test can be used to address the issue of generalizability of the data. The chi-square test, also written as χ^2, can also be used to test the relationship or association between two variables. For example, a chi-square test could be used to select companion animals to be trained by juvenile offenders for placement with senior citizens. In a hypothetical study, 125 elderly prospective pet owners could be asked to choose one of three types of dogs they would prefer. The AAT researchers might also want to consider an additional variable and determine if their choices were related to whether or not the individual was an elderly male or female (e.g., would women prefer smaller dogs?).

McNicholas and Collis (1998) used chi-square as one of the measures in a study designed to evaluate the relationship between pet ownership and health in Type A individuals. In this study, the two sexes were equally represented in three pet ownership groups that included owners of cats/dogs, other animals, and no animals. The data showed that there was a tendency for more females to be pet owners than males, that participants who were older (i.e., 56 to 65 years) had a higher than average nonownership, and a lower than average cat/dog ownership.

Friedmann and Thomas (1995) used chi-square analyses to evaluate the relationship between pet ownership and survival status. In a study with 369 participants, data showed a significant relationship between survival of cardiac parents and dog ownership. The study showed that dog owners were more likely to be alive 1 year after the baseline assessment than patients who did not own dogs.

C. Regression Analysis

Regression is an analytical technique that can be used to predict values for a criterion or dependent variable based on historical trends in that criterion or on other factors that are assumed to influence it (Newcomer, 1994). The regression model represents the average change in the criterion across time or in the other factors that are assumed to influence it. When regression is used to evaluate AAT programs, it is frequently used in connection with widescale policy or program evaluations to provide estimates of changes in behaviors that the program is likely to produce. For example, data on recidivism among women inmates might be used to estimate the impact a dog training program in a prison had on specific behaviors. When regression is used to show predicted values, a measure that is often reported is the coefficient of determination, also known as R-square (Newcomer, 1994).

Keil (1998) used a regression procedure in a descriptive study related to the role of human–animal bonding in the quality of life of older adults. A stepwise regression procedure was used to determine the impact of five variables (i.e., gazing, appeal, stress, and two dummy coded animal variables) on the level of human–animal attachment. The data presented as an R-square showed that four variables, including gazing with the animal (looking into the animal's eyes), dog ownership, stress, and appeal of the animal's appearance, explained 31% of the variance in the human–animal interaction.

Triebenbacher (1998) also used a regression analysis in a similar study designed to investigate the developmental differences in the relationship between children's attachment to companion animals and their self-esteem. The results showed that there were developmental differences in children's attachment to their companion animals and their self-esteem ratings. The R-square was used to present data that showed the greatest amount of variance was in the elementary school model and the least amount was with the middle school model.

VII. SINGLE-SUBJECT RESEARCH DESIGN

Single-subject research design is seen far less frequently in AAT research and program evaluation than group statistical designs. This is unfortunate because single-subject methodology lends itself well to providing an ongoing assessment of program progress. Further, single-subject design embraces the goals of the behavior analytic approach that permits one to understand the behavior of individual participants. In a single-subject approach, individual differences are not obscured by the averaging process that is required by statistical design (Sidman, 1960).

Single-subject research designs were first developed in animal operant conditioning (Burch & Bailey, in press). The designs have been adapted and used to evaluate applied problems in educational, health, business, human services, community issues, and a variety of other areas. The goal of single-subject designs is to demonstrate the functional relationship between an event and a target behavior (Bailey, 1979). In single-subject methodology, the term *functional* is used in a cause-and-effect sense and refers to an arrangement where the contingency is "turned on and off repeatedly" (Bailey, 1979). If the behavior occurs each time the contingency is "turned on," then ceases each time it is "turned off," a functional relationship has been established. Using single-subject techniques, researchers and trained practitioners can answer AAT questions such as these:

1. Is the person more likely to cooperate in an ambulation program if the therapy dog is present?
2. Are residents calmer when they have fish tanks in the day room?
3. Which of these two AAT conditions results in the desired behavior change?

Several types of single-subject designs can be used both for research purposes and for program evaluation. The most common of these designs include AB designs and related variations (although these have no experimental control), reversal designs, multiple baseline designs, and multi-element designs.

A. AB Designs

The AB design begins with some quantification of the dependent variable, the variable that is expected to change as a result of the intervention. The "A" represents a baseline condition in which the specified variables are observed and quantified before any treatment takes place. The "B" in the AB design represents the treatment phase and shows the data after the treatment or intervention has been implemented. Figure 1 shows data presented in the AB format. The data in Fig. 1 are from an AAT program implemented with a 24-year-old male with profound mental retardation. A reinforcer sampling assessment showed that animals were a potential reinforcer. In pilot sessions, when animals were present, the participant would sit up in his wheelchair and vocalize. In the baseline phase, observers counted the number of vocalizations during leisure time when no animals were present. In the intervention phase,

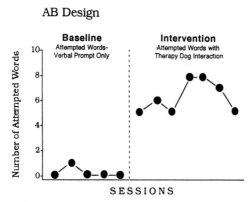

FIGURE 1   AB design showing attempted words in baseline (verbal prompts to talk) and treatment (with therapy dog interaction).

vocalizations were counted when a trained therapy dog stood next to the wheelchair for petting.

B. REVERSAL DESIGNS

In single-subject design, experimental control can be demonstrated by "turning the behavior on and off" (Bailey, 1979). The reversal design shows that a particular treatment or intervention is responsible for the behavior change when the onset of the intervention results in the onset of the specified behavior. Reversal designs are used when it is expected that results are reversible, that is, that behavior will return to baseline levels when the intervention is removed. It is not ethical to use a reversal design when the removal and return to baseline levels will cause negative effects to the participant. For example, if regularly scheduled access to a therapy cat caused a child to stop engaging in self-injury, it would not be ethical to remove the successful intervention simply for the purpose of demonstrating experimental control.

Figure 2 shows a reversal design that was used to evaluate the effects of adding a dog care program to the vocational class of a 39-year-old man with moderate mental retardation. The problem prior to the intervention was that the participant was leaving class about 15 minutes early each day. Despite teacher requests to stay until class had been dismissed, the participant would leave early in order to go and wait for lunch. When the care of the resident beagle was added to the participant's list of jobs, he was sufficiently motivated

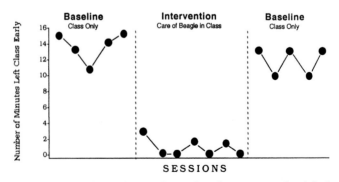

FIGURE 2 Reversal (ABA) design showing the number of minutes a student left class early in baseline (vocational class only) and treatment (allowed to care for dog in class) conditions.

to stay in class for the entire time. When the dog care intervention was removed as a part of the reversal design, leaving class early returned to the baseline rate.

Other variations on the reversal design include BAB formats and conducting more than one reversal (ABABA).

C. Multiple Baseline Designs

The multiple baseline design is one in which some treatment condition is applied successively across two or more baselines that have been established (Bailey, 1979). When it is not possible or ethical to use a reversal design, the multiple baseline can be used to demonstrate experimental control. Multiple baseline designs can be implemented across behaviors, participants, or settings. Figure 3 shows a multiple baseline design that was used to evaluate the effects of a therapy dog in individual therapy sessions for two preschoolers who had been diagnosed as electively mute.

In the baseline condition, the children were prompted and encouraged to say words. During the intervention phase, the therapist removed one of the child's shoes. The trained therapy dog was sent to fetch the shoe and turn and sit with the shoe in his mouth. The child was told, "He's a dog; he doesn't know what to do. If you want your shoe, say, 'give shoe.'" The commands for the therapy dog of "go" and "sit" were added after the first intervention session for each child. Through the use of a multiple baseline design, it was shown

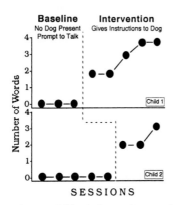

FIGURE 3 Multiple baseline (across children) design showing the number of words said by electively mute children when a therapy dog was used in treatment.

that a therapy dog was an effective intervention for the two children with elective mutism.

D. MULTI-ELEMENT DESIGN

The multi-element design, also known as the multi-element baseline design, operates by bringing the same behavior (of either one or several subjects) under the control of several different experimental procedures (Bailey, 1979). The multi-element design is versatile and can be used across different behaviors of the same participant, across different participants with the same behavior, and across different settings with the same participant and behavior. For example, a multi-element design could be used with one AAT participant to determine if several different behaviors change as a result of AAT interventions. The multi-element design could also be used to measure AAT results with several different participants. Because multi-element and other single-subject designs can be used to evaluate the effects of a program has on more than one individual, the term *single subject* can be misleading. *Single subject* does not refer to only one client; it means that data for each individual client can be evaluated independently and that data are not presented as an average. The multi-element design can also be used to evaluate the same target behaviors across settings. For example, if the participant is more vocal around therapy animals, can this effect be seen outside as well as in the dayroom?

Figure 4 shows the multi-element data for an AAT program related to ambulation. The participant was a 30-year-old woman with severe mental retardation.

Multi-Element Design

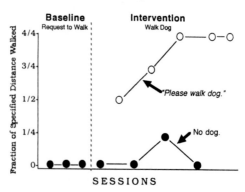

FIGURE 4   Multi-element design showing the distance walked when instructions alone were given, and when the client was asked to walk the therapy dog.

She was nonverbal and noncompliant with staff requests. Medical staff had identified walking a specified distance each day as a priority goal. The participant would smile and vocalize when she saw the facility's resident dog. Much of the day she sat in a chair refusing to walk and holding a stuffed dog. Every other day, when the staff attempted to take the participant for a walk, they brought the dog and said, "The dog needs to go for a walk. Can you take her?" The data show that in the dog condition, there was far greater compliance with the ambulation program. On the nondog days, the prompt, "Would you like to go for a walk?" resulted in almost no compliance.

When a multi-element design is used to evaluate a program, the different experimental conditions may occur within the same session or day, or, in some cases, within the same week. Multi-element designs might be used in AAT to evaluate the effects of animals/no animals, verbal praise/no praise, instructions/no instructions.

VIII. CONCLUSIONS

Program evaluation has become a critical area for AAT. In the late 1980s and 1990s the field of animal-assisted therapy began to experience a dramatic shift from case studies, anecdotes, and heartwarming stories to systematic evaluation and research as the bottom-line criteria for justifying programs and procedures. AAT programs can be evaluated in a number of areas, including the overall mission statement, physical plant for the program, clients, animals, volunteers, staff, curriculum and other program specifics such as scheduling, and cost benefits of the AAT services. In addition, the results and long-term impact of AAT can be evaluated using traditional research methods such as statistical and single-subject research designs.

Even though single-subject designs have much to offer in terms of providing clear pictures of client behavior change and a methodology that trained professionals can use, they have not yet been widely used in AAT research and program evaluation. Effective, comprehensive program evaluation models can use single-subject techniques for the ongoing formative evaluation of the AAT program. Using single-subject designs, program evaluators can answer questions pertaining to the procedures and specifics of a program. For example, if an AAT program were developed to put small animals around a nursing home, single-subject methods could be used to determine where cages and fish tanks should be placed, how many animals should be provided, and what kinds of training or prompting clients should receiving regarding the animals. Once the program was in place, summative evaluations involving the use of statistical designs could be used to evaluate the pre- and postintervention effects.

Group statistical designs demonstrate statistical significance; single-subject designs are tools that can be used by program evaluators to demonstrate clinical significance. As AAT continues to evolve, program evaluation should encompass both full-scale, traditional statistical studies as well as the ongoing measurement of individual client behavior change.

REFERENCES

American Kennel Club (1996). *The Canine Good Citizen program.* New York: American Kennel Club.

Bailey, J. S. (1979). *Research methods in applied behavior analysis.* Tallahassee, FL: Copy Grafix Publishing.

Basarab, D. J., & Root, D. K. (1992). *The training evaluation process.* Norwell, MA: Kluwer Academic Publishers.

Batson, K., McCabe, B., Baun, M. M., & Wilson, C. (1998). The effect of a therapy dog on socialization and physiological indicators of stress in person diagnosed with Alzheimer's disease. In C. Wilson and D. Turner (Eds.), *Companion animals in human health.* Thousand Oaks, CA: Sage Publications.

Burch, M. R. (1991). Animal-assisted therapy and crack babies: A new frontier. *Pet Partners Newsletter,* 1, 2. Renton, WA: Delta Society.

Burch, M. R. (1995). *Volunteering with your pet: How to get started in AAT with any kind of pet.* New York: Howell Book House.

Burch, M. R. (1996). *Evaluating animal-assisted therapy programs: Documenting and measuring effectiveness.* Tallahassee, FL: Behavior Management Consultants, Inc.

Burch, M. R., & Bailey, J. S. (1999). *How dogs learn: The science of operant conditioning.* New York: Howell Book House.

Friedmann, E., & Thomas, S. A. (1995). Pet ownership, social support, and one-year survival after acute myocardial infarction in the cardiac arrhythmia suppression trial (CAST). *American Journal of Cardiology,* 76, 1213–1277.

Gagne, R. M., Briggs, L. J., & Wager, W. W. (1992). *Principles of instructional design.* Fort Worth, TX: Harcourt Brace & Company.

Guba, E. G., & Lincoln, Y. S. (1985). The countenances of fourth-generation evaluation: Description, judgment, and negotiation. In D. J. Palumbo (Ed.), *The politics of program evaluation.* Newbury Park, CA: Sage Publications.

Joint Commission on Standards for Educational Evaluation. (1981). *Standards for the evaluation of education programs, projects, and materials.* New York: McGraw-Hill.

Kee, J. E. (1994). Benefit–cost analysis in program evaluation. In J. S. Wholey, H. P. Hatry, and K. E. Newcomer (Eds.), *Handbook of practical program evaluation.* San Francisco: Jossey-Bass Publishers.

Keil, C. P. (1998). Loneliness, stress, and human–animal attachment among older adults. In C. Wilson and D. Turner (Eds.), *Companion animals in human health.* Thousand Oaks, CA: Sage Publications.

Kongable, L. G., Buckwalter, K. C., & Stolley, J. M. (1989). The effects of pet therapy on the social behavior of institutionalized clients. *Archives of Psychiatric Nursing,* 3(4), 191–198.

McNicholas, J., & Collis, G. (1998). Could Type A (coronary prone) personality explain the association between pet ownership and health? In C. Wilson and D. Turner (Eds.), *Companion animals in human health.* Thousand Oaks, CA: Sage Publications.

Newcomer, K. (1994). Using statistics appropriately. In J. S. Wholey, H. P. Hatry, and K. E. Newcomer (Eds.), *Handbook of practical program evaluation*. San Francisco: Jossey-Bass Publishers.

Robinson, D. G., & Robinson, J. C. (1989). *Training for impact: How to link training to business needs and measure results*. San Francisco: Jossey-Bass Publishers.

Savishinsky, J. S. (1992). Intimacy, domesticity, and pet therapy with the elderly: Expectation and experience among nursing home volunteers. *Social Science and Medicine, 34*, 1325–1334.

Sidman, M. (1960). *Tactics of scientific research*. New York: Basic Books.

Triebenbacher, S. L. (1998). The relationship between attachment to companion animals and self-esteem: A developmental perspective. In C. Wilson and D. Turner (eds.), *Companion animals in human health*. Thousand Oaks, CA: Sage Publications.

Best Practices in Animal-Assisted Therapy

GUIDELINES FOR USE OF AAT WITH SPECIAL POPULATIONS

The Centaur's Lessons: Therapeutic Education through Care of Animals and Nature Study

AARON HONORI KATCHER
The Devereux Foundation, Villanova, PA 19085 and University of Pennsylvania, Philadelphia, PA 19103

GREGORY G. WILKINS
William Penn School District, Lansdowne, PA 19050-1699

I. THEORETICAL RATIONALIZATION FOR USING ANIMAL-ASSISTED THERAPY WITH ATTENTION DEFICIT/ HYPERACTIVITY DISORDER

A hypothesis explaining the efficacy of treatment centered on contact with animals and nature is described using Barkley's conceptualization of attention deficit/hyperactivity disorder (ADHD). In brief, Barkley suggests that the cardinal features of ADHD (i.e., poor sustained attention, impulsivity, and hyperactivity) can be reduced "to a single core impairment in delayed responding or response inhibition" (Barkley, 1994, p. 18). We will suggest that the evolutionary development of the human brain was shaped by the necessity to forage and hunt. As a by-product of this necessity, humans have an innate tendency to pay attention to animals and the natural surroundings. The tendency to pay attention to animals is in turn associated with an increased capacity for response inhibition, which is particularly enabling for children with ADHD or those who have difficulty learning from lecture or textual materials.

Handbook on Animal-Assisted Therapy: Theoretical Foundations and Guidelines for Practice

ADHD (American Psychiatric Association [APA], 1994) is a biologically handicapping condition that is characterized by developmentally inappropriate degrees of inattention, impulsivity, and hyperactivity (Barkley, 1990). As described, the central impairment of ADHD is one of behavioral dysregulation in response inhibition to an event or stimulus. ADHD has a definite neurologic substratum in which the orbitofrontal cortex and its rich interconnections to the limbic system are implicated. This substratum adversely affects the capacity for delayed responding, particularly as required by diverse contextual demands. ADHD is also a relatively stable behavioral condition that emerges in early childhood and persists with tenacity into adolescence and early adulthood (Barkley et al., 1990; Hallowell & Ratey, 1994). Fluctuating attention, impulsivity, and hyperactivity are typically transsituational in nature and accordingly are manifest across academic, occupational, home, community, and interpersonal contexts.

Individuals with ADHD often tend to have more spontaneity than normals. Their thinking is at times unrestrained and creative, but at other moments is quite disorganized and tangential. Their speech patterns are compromised in that they exhibit inarticulateness, dysfluencies, and psycholinguistic impairments. They act unpredictably and lack the intermediate reflection between impulse and action that is required for goal-directed or context-regulated behavior. The central focus of disinhibition and the inadequacies of accommodating responses to situational demands result in a panoply of symptoms associated with ADHD, including behavioral impulsivity, disruptiveness, variability in attention and performance, disorganization, interpersonal tactlessness, impatience, mood changes, and sensation seeking typically in the form of risk-taking behaviors.

Most relevant to the conceptualization of animal-assisted therapy and education (AAT/E) and the deficiencies of ADHD is the deficit in the modulation of behavior in response to contextual demands. For example, when confronted with situations in which a delay of gratification and work toward more distal goals with larger rewards are required, ADHD children select the immediate, smaller rewards that require less persistence of effort to achieve. Games with peers that require sharing, cooperation, and frequent behavioral restraint constitute a nemesis for these impulsive children. The disinhibited behaviors of ADHD children have deleterious effects on almost every aspect of their daily lives. While in school, such children are frequently out of their seats, talking to and disrupting classmates, making atypical vocal noises, roaming about the classroom without permission, playing with objects not related to the assigned task, restlessly moving their limbs while working, and engaging in task-unrelated commentaries on any topic of ephemeral appeal.

It is important to emphasize that the primary deficit with ADHD is not just excessive movement, but the failure to regulate activity level to setting or task demands that is so socially problematic in this condition. Another characteristic that has been found in empirical studies of ADHD children pertains to excessive variability of task or work performance over time. Kupperman (1988, as cited in Barkley, 1990) noted the fact that these children have performed well on a few occasions will be held against them the rest of their academic careers. From a diagnostic perspective, it is essential that occasional observations of adequate, or even good, attention or behavioral controls not be used to rule out a potentially disabling condition such as ADHD. Instead, such observations may be used to consolidate an enriched understanding of the specific aspects, tasks, and contextual demands that either facilitate or diminish an ADHD child's performance.

The problems of ADHD children are seldom limited to the core ADHD symptoms themselves. ADHD children and adolescents frequently exhibit an interrelated cluster of psychosocial problems including aggression, oppositional defiant behavior, conduct disturbance, academic underachievement, diminished self-esteem, depression, and peer rejection. The oppositional defiant or noncompliant behavior of ADHD children is a particularly relevant psychosocial objective for treatment. In combination with ADHD, noncompliant behavior with respect to developmentally appropriate tasks is a significant predictor of later conduct maladjustment during adolescence and adulthood.

ADHD is a disorder that has been the object of rigorous scientific investigation during the last several decades. In conceptualizing this disorder, a number of theoretical formulations have been proposed regarding its deficits and primary characteristics. Despite the consensus on many dimensions of ADHD, considerable controversy has arisen concerning its central and causative deficits. A comprehensive review of previous theories of ADHD is beyond the focus of this paper. Instead, a recently proposed unified theory of ADHD (Barkley, 1994), which has impressive empirical support, will be discussed because it offers an advantageous framework for understanding its symptoms and permits an optimal assimilation of associated research findings. Relying heavily on the seminal essays of Jacob Bronowski (1977) regarding the distinctive capacities that arose during the evolution of human language, Barkley suggested that the cardinal impairment of ADHD is impaired response inhibition or insufficient delayed responding to a stimulus or event. This implies that such persons experience less success in accommodating themselves to the demands of academic, social, and occupational tasks that place a premium on delayed responding, specifically when the consequences associated with performance in the context are weak, delayed, or virtually nonexistent. It is essential to note that Barkley's theory of ADHD stresses that this disorder is a dysregulation of ongoing behavior, not a deficit in knowledge or skills (Barkley, 1994; Kinsbourne, 1989).

In delineating the formative features that resulted from the evolution of human language and thought, Bronowski elaborated four uniquely human capabilities—separation of affect, prolongation, internalization of language, and reconstitution—which are a direct product of man's enhanced capacity for delayed responding (Barkley, 1994, pp. 26-45). The cognitive capacities that are derived from delayed responding include first separation of affect. Through the imposition of a delay between the presentation of an event and its response, the human brain is afforded sufficient time to separate the informational content of an event from its emotional counterpart. Such a capacity structures logical and rational appraisals of events, which enables flexibility in dealing with the content or facts of an event without interposing an emotional bias. In this way, one can formulate a response that is more adaptive than would have occurred had one reacted more passionately and without necessary delays.

Prolongation is a second consequence of the capacity to protract the delay in responding to an event and is comparable in many ways to the neuropsychologic concept of working memory. Humans have an innate capacity to hold an event that has just transpired in memory and to sustain this mental representation of the event for long intervals. Such a capacity accentuates the salience of an event in working memory and enables the extraction and comparison of this information with equivalent events that were previously stored in memory. Barkley's theory holds that, because those with ADHD cannot inhibit and postpone their initial response to a situation, "they will be less likely to engage in these mental activities or, if they do, these actions will not be very effective" (Barkley, 1994, p.2). Thus, individuals with an attenuated capacity for prolongation have a limited sense of time, are susceptible to the negative effects of immediate gratification, are less goal directed and organized, and give less consideration to the probable consequences of intended actions.

Internalization of language is a third consequence of an increased capacity in response inhibition and simply means the ability to talk to ourselves. Deficits in the delay of responding interfere with the internalization of language and the effective deployment of self-directed speech, rules, and instructions as guiding, regulating, and controlling influences on current adaptive behavior. Bronowski defined the critical nature of internalized language in terms of its effects of freeing the individual from his immediate and encircling context by bringing ongoing behavior under the control of directions, goals, plans, and anticipated future events. Barkley then clarifies the ways in which ADHD children differ from normal children with respect to these effects. Importantly, ADHD children demonstrate more variability in their responses to tasks because their behavior is more contingency shaped and less rule governed; they are more susceptible to the effects exerted by immediate contingencies and momentary changes in the environment; they perform less capably in contexts in which extreme delays in consequences exist; and they are developmentally delayed in the growth trajectory of rule-governed behavior. Not only does language enable efficacious self-control, but it permits us to construct new rules to use when we are confronting a problem.

Reconstitution refers to the capacities of analysis and synthesis that are permitted by the delay or inhibition of responses. Analysis is a vital skill that involves the decomposition of a stimulus or event into its constituent parts, and synthesis is a process whereby dissembled parts are examined, manipulated, and reconstructed into new messages or events. This capacity enables novel constructions and meanings to be derived from distributed parts. The process of reconstruction endows humans with unparalleled skills of problem solving, imagination, and creativity. Those with ADHD are accordingly poorer than normals in dissembling messages and events into parallel units of analysis, as well as in employing recombinative processes in assembling these units into new responses or constructions. This deficiency limits the extent to which one can select from new reconstructions of prior ideas and events and simultaneously constrains effective actions.

ADHD children also have greater problems with aggressive behavior and interpersonal conflicts than do normal children. More than half of our subjects were aggressive, argumentative, noncompliant, socially rejected, and resistant to control of their behavioral excesses. These subjects also were ascribed frequently as significant violators of age-appropriate social norms and the rights of others. In other words, these subjects meet the diagnostic criteria of the *Diagnostic and Statistical Manual for Mental Disorders* (DSM-IV, APA, 1994) for conduct disorder (CD) and oppositional defiant disorder (ODD). The superimposition or comorbidity of CD on ADHD occurs with a moderate frequency (Barkley, 1990, 1994) and usually within families and social milieus characterized by interpersonal disequilibrium, chaotic familial situations, and conflicts and in which behavior is controlled by violence and coercive interaction patterns (Kadzin, 1987a,b, 1989; Patterson, 1979, 1986, 1991). With such brutalizing and traumatic experiences, children become suspicious and mistrustful and project their own angry and retaliatory impulses onto others. Research concerning the treatment of CD is crucial at the present time because no treatment has been demonstrated to ameliorate its symptoms or controvert its negative prognosis. Moreover both CD and ADHD conditions present many serious risk factors such as school failure and underachievement, psychiatric hospitalization, occupational difficulties, marital distress, and criminal behavior later in life (Kadzin, 1987b, 1985).

Of central relevance to our work on animal-assisted therapy, conduct-disordered children and adolescents often exhibit deficits in social competence with corresponding difficulties in peer relationships. Empirical studies demonstrate that in comparison with peers, those with conduct disorders are frequently more aggressive, less empathic, and more deficient in interpersonal problem-solving skills, and they tend to misperceive their environment, often incorrectly attributing hostile and malevolent intentions to others (Dodge, 1985).

In choosing to set up an intervention structured around observant contact with animals, we made a number of assumptions based on the theoretical concepts and data just reviewed.

1. The presence of the animals would have the ability to capture and hold the children's attention. This assumption is based on the most limited interpretation of the biophilia hypothesis (Wilson, 1984; Kellert & Wilson, 1993), that is, that the human brain has been shaped to pay selective attention to animals.

2. The attention directed at animals is associated with behavioral inhibition because the child does not know what the animal is going to do. The animal is a stimulus that continues to have novelty. The behavioral inhibition creates the time for the child to formulate questions about the animal. The animal creates a "need to know" or a curiosity that can be satisfied only if the child frames the appropriate questions.

3. The child can become familiar with the animal's behavior, but must still pay close attention to the animal because the details of the creature's actions cannot be predicted. This sustained attention is associated with the prolongation of the idea or image of the animal in the child's mind that would facilitate the generation of more questions.

4. Because the child's anxiety about handling the animal can be rapidly desensitized while the curiosity about the animal is prolonged by the animal's continuing behavior, or the need to know information about the animal, the child experiences the separation of affect and information and can better compartmentalize those two aspects of apprehension.

5. The presence of the animal, because it directs the child's attention outward, lowers the level of arousal, and permits the child to more accurately perceive the behavior of the therapists, and other children, thus inhibiting the use of preformed negative attributions about the therapist's intention. This tendency would favor the development of a web of positive attributions toward the animal, the staff associated with the animals, and the other children.

6. The play of children with conduct disorder is almost always aggressive (Wilkins & Sholevar, 1995). The animals give the children an opportunity for elaborating affectionate nurturing play.

7. Children with ADHD and conduct disorder tend to make negative attributions about their peers, parents, and adults, projecting hostility and justifying their own aggressive behavior. People paired with animals are per-

ceived positively and when animals are introduced into therapy, there is more positive interaction between patient and therapist.

8. The competency obtained through mastery of fear, learning the behaviors necessary to care for the animals, and the increased ability to experience rewarding social interaction from animals, from staff, and from other children would increase self-esteem and increase the probability that the child would be willing to learn in other contexts.

9. By breaking down the learning process into units that are spoken as well as performed, the child is helped to develop a capacity for the monitory speech that guides moral and problem-solving behavior in normal children (Vygotsky, 1986). As noted this monitory speech is less well developed in children with ADHD.

II. THE COMPANIONABLE ZOO METHOD

Many children learn actively and creatively from only books or images on a screen. However, many other children who do not have that capacity for abstract learning are shut away from their own potential by the nature of modern teaching. Perhaps as much as one-third of all children are doomed to spend years in school feeling that they are failing at simple tasks that others do well (Sennett & Cobb, 1972). They are excluded from feeling successful and competent. Some of these will be rescued by the praise and success they attain in sports and a much smaller minority will have their musical or artistic talents awakened in school, but for the large majority of that bottom third of the class, school will be an exercise in failure. These children will leave school too soon, and will be unable to apply for the jobs created by the communication revolution. Worse, they will be angered by years of failure and sometimes, because their own anger developed early, they will live a life at the margins, encountering unemployment, substance abuse, and crime.

We have been treating children with severe ADHD, conduct disorder, developmental disorders including autism, and a variety of functional disorders through use of education structured around the care of animals and nature study. Our experience also extends to special education classes in public schools with children diagnosed as having serious emotional problems or learning disorders. We now have 8 years of experience and the method is being used in five of Devereux's campuses, two public schools, and a residential campus of the Wordsworth Academy. We have conducted one controlled clinical trial of the method lasting for 9 months and have used correlational methods to evaluate the effectiveness of the programs when we could no longer use a control group. The locus of treatment is always a collection of animals maintained in a classroom or a small building. The children help care for the animals, learn about the animals, interact with them as pets displaying touch-talk dialogue and affection, play with them, and, when they are competent, demonstrate them to children in other classes or to adults in senior centers or hospitals. The children also have learning structured around nature study, and trips to diverse locations such as zoos, nature centers, state parks, and animal fairs. The method has been described in detail in a manual title *The Centaur's Lessons* (Katcher & Wilkins, 1999).

The composition of a zoo varies with the location and the needs of the patient population. In almost all zoos there is a basic population of caged birds, lizards, rabbits, chinchillas, guinea pigs, hamsters, and aquarium fish. Where there is outdoor space and room for paddocks there are pot-bellied pigs, goats, sheep, and miniature horses. The zoo at the Devereux campus where children with autism and developmental delays are treated has many birds and fish tanks because the visual environment is important in entraining the attention of these children. The list of animals at any zoo is never static and depends on what is purchased by the zoo instructors, bred in the zoo, or donated. All zoos except those in the public schools have gardens and the children participate in gardening as they do in the care of animals. At these zoos animal waste is composted for the garden, and some of the garden produce is fed to the animals. Just as the opportunities for nature study vary with weather and season, the zoos and gardens are never static.

Within each campus or school the zoo is a place apart and acts as a frame or boundary (see the section on evaluation). The frame is literally territorial, and the change in demeanor experienced by the children in the zoo can be seen to alter at the boundaries. When the animals are about outside, the boundary extends as far as the animals, as far as direct eye contact can be maintained with zoo staff. When the weather is bad and people and animals are shut inside, the boundary is at the threshold of the zoo. The space inside the boundary is a space with new rules for behavior, these rules are dependent on the presence of the animals, but the presence of the animals is only a necessary, not a sufficient, condition for the new way of behaving. To understand the workings of the zoo, it is necessary to understand how it is set apart from a regular classroom.

Animals are out of place in a regular schoolroom, much like Mary's little lamb, perhaps because they make children laugh and play, both actions being defined as incompatible with learning. Classrooms are usually, except for kindergarten and perhaps first grade, designed to be sterile so that they do not induce the eye to wander. Classrooms are designed to give the teacher complete control over the children's attention. When animals are present, the possibility of unplanned agendas is always present. The children have more to attract their eyes, and can find relief from the teacher without retreating into their own private world of fantasy. Animals join children in a common world out of the teacher's control. They continually offer testimony that the world is more than words and definitions, and that the power of the teacher is limited. Because animals so fundamentally change the balance of power in the classroom, they create a discontinuity—a break—between the classroom and the child's expectations about school. The animals tell the child that things will be different here.

In our Companionable Zoo, the difference was also marked by a ceremony at the door. The children were expected to greet the instructors and the other children in the zoo. When they entered the zoo, they entered a community of people and animals, and the existence of that society and its members had to be recognized. To greet a person or an animal implied that the individual was not an object but someone who was owed the obligation of recognition and polite discourse. The children in Devereux are there because they failed at home and failed at school and failed in their community. We wanted the zoo to be a place where dialogue would be rewarding and where interaction could be a source of comfort, pleasure, and validation.

Once within the boundary of the zoo, the children were given only two general rules: (1) Be gentle with the animals and talk to them softly! (2) Respect the animals and the people in the zoo and avoid speech that devalues them! These two rules were not learned nor obeyed immediately and consistently by all students. The children needed repeated gentle reminders session after session, but these precepts were critical to the educational dialogue in the zoo. The first of these rules was designed to reinforce the impact of the zoo animals on the children's behavior. By selectively commanding the attention of the children, the animals improved behavioral inhibition and decreased the tendency to interact aggressively and chaotically with each other. However, this innate response to the animals' presence needs reinforcement—needs to be incorporated into a "rule of the place" to gain consistent and enduring control over the behavior of these volatile children. The insistence of the teachers that the animals must be handled gently at all times reinforces the innate response to animal contact. Asking the students to speak gently has the same consequences. Speech is a kind of action, and gentle speech calms the speakers as well as the animals they handle. The animals' behavior also reinforces these rules. When the student slows down, uses less muscle tension, and less grasping behavior when handling the animals, the animals respond with less fear, less escape behavior, and more exploration and interaction. One of the most hyperactive children in the program was bitten by almost every animal in the zoo during his first days in the program—including a most phlegmatic turtle—because he grasped too tightly and moved too quickly. He went on to be one of the most successful students in the program, but it was the animals, not the teachers or medication, that slowed him down in the zoo.

The second general rule, "Respect the animals and the people in the zoo and avoid speech that devalues them!," defines the social relationships in the Companionable Zoo. It states that everyone in the zoo has obligations toward the animals, staff, and students thus defining relationships in the zoo as moral relationships—relationships of mutual obligation. In the school outside of the zoo, all relationships are material. Behavior is good when it earns points for privileges such as access to video games, opportunities for more independence, purchases at the school store, and trips to stores and films, and bad when it leads to loss of points or privileges, restraints, and isolation in "focus" groups, or being bound to a counselor in one-to-one supervision. In the zoo behavior is good when it contributes to the welfare of others or enlarges your own knowledge and skill, that is, when it contributes to your own welfare, and bad when it violates the rights of others. Careful attention is paid to speech, because speech is always action—it is always directed at others and sets a precedence for other actions. The practice of asking students to be "respectful of the animals" reflects, of course, a kind of anthropomorphic thinking, since respect is a human concept, with no obvious equivalent in animal behavior. It is a kind of anthropomorphic thinking that is appropriate if you believe that animals have "rights," however, a commitment to animal rights is not the motive for using terms like *respect* to designate the children's obligation to the animals. We use those terms for two reasons. First, because we wish the children to adopt a set of values toward animals that include the moral demands for responsibility and care. Second, we wish the children to reason back and forth from a consideration of the animals needs and the needs of people including their own. We want them to compare their obligations toward the animals with their obligations toward other people, and learn to anticipate other people's needs and feelings in the way they anticipate the needs and feelings of animals. We want them to gain the same good feelings from looking out for the welfare of other people as they get from looking out for their animals' welfare. This precept to respect animals and people supports the reflexive nature of the curriculum.

The zoo because it is a place for animals first and then a place for people, exists in strong contrast to the rest of the institution. The rest of the institution is focused only about the children serving to keep them out of reality, and provide them with a "special" education. This is the primary and only mission of the institution. In the zoo, the animals are the primary mission, and their care is a priority that is given the same salience as the zoo's teaching mission. This gives the zoo a connection with a wider reality beyond the institution and beyond the other schools the children have experienced as well. It is critical to the method of the Companionable Zoo that the students know that the zoo exists for the animals as well as for teaching and therapy. The Companionable Zoo is more than a classroom. It is a part of the world, not unlike the way a farm is part of the world. The zoo instructors are teachers, but they have a primary responsibility to care for the animals in the zoo and its garden. The students are there to be educated but must share those obligations and responsibilities toward the animals. When the children go to the local nature center, they come to learn, but also to aid in the maintenance of that nature center. They come to learn and do real work. To understand the zoo curriculum, both its assets and deficiencies, it is necessary to understand how responsibility and work are interdigitated with learning and discovery.

The first task given the new students was learning the general requirements for care of animals and the proper means of holding them. They were shown how to hold each kind of animal, how to support the hind legs and backs of the rabbits to prevent them from jumping and falling, how to use gloves to hold unfamiliar "bitey" animals like gerbils, how to hold a chinchilla up by its thick short tail, and how to hold an iguana by its body, never by its tail. They were shown how to clean cages and that included taking the waste out to the garden to provide fertilizer for the vegetables being grown to feed the animals. The children were given reasons for each rule of animal care. There were always three elements to learning:

1. They had learn the rule well enough so that they could articulate it for others.
2. They had to learn the reasons justifying the rule. If the rule being learned was "When you pick up a rabbit you must support its hind legs," the justification was "The rabbit could injure its back by kicking out in the absence of a resistant surface."
3. They had to demonstrate mastery of the skill inherent in the rule.

With this kind of learning, the child learns that the rules are rational, not arbitrary, he achieves a mastery of a skill, and he has all of the requisite knowledge to articulate the rule and its justification to others. The zoo experience provided the child with seven immediate gains:

1. He earned the approval of the instructors for responsible behavior.
2. He formed a working alliance with the instructors through sharing their "real" work.
3. He had the self-satisfaction of mastering a rewarding skill.
4. He had the sensual satisfaction of petting the animal.
5. He was defined as a caregiver instead of a care receiver and had the innate satisfaction of nurturing another being.
6. Perhaps for the first time, he was able to engage in a learning dialogue in calming, pleasurable circumstances.
7. He learned information that could be valuable "social currency" and shared with other children and adults thus increasing his social competence.

We borrowed the idea of the skill card from Green Chimneys where they had been using them successfully for years. A skill card is very much like the list of requirements for a Boy or Girl Scout merit badge. It specifies what skills the student must master and what knowledge she must have at her command to be permitted to proceed independently. Learning the skills and knowledge on an animal skill card was the prerequisite to being trusted to care for that animal. In initially designing the skill cards, the information was kept to the minimum necessary to rationalize the requirements for the animal's welfare. Children who were learning to care for a chinchilla had to learn that the wild animal lived in the high Andean deserts. That "fact" rationalized two requirements for the chinchilla's welfare: (1) They could not tolerate temperatures above 85°F, and (2) they had to be provided with access to a tray of sand from time to time so that they could take "dust baths." Children could learn the skill card one step at a time if necessary. Because of the low levels of reading skills in many children, the instructor would read the statement aloud, and then ask the child to read it aloud or to repeat it. Then the rule would be discussed, and if any skill, such as holding the animal, cleaning its cage, or changing food and water, was involved, the student would practice that skill. At the same time the instructor would encourage free discussion about the animal and some of the implications of its requirements for care. When a step was mastered it would be joined to another step. When a new step was to be learned, previous items were first reviewed. Finally, when the student could repeat all of the statements in the card and demonstrate the skills on several successive days, she was deemed ready to handle the animal independently.

With the exception of the public schools, all zoos were located in situations where the children had access to the natural history of open meadow, woodlot, wetlands, and streams. We could also take them off campus to state parks and could organize field trips to public zoos and aquaria. On outdoor excursions we built the skill work around four complementary themes: (1) preservation of the integrity of the environment, (2) respect for the concerns of other people who are responsible for the environment or who are also enjoying it, (3) personal safety, and (4) Recognition of those features that make any environment a distinct place.

For example, on visiting a state park the children learn that the rule about walking on paths is designed to preserve the unique plant life of the place and to prevent needless destruction of nesting sites. They learn that they must sign in at the ranger station before going on a hike both to acquaint the ranger about how many people are in the park that day and to protect themselves in case they become lost and fail to return. At the same time the instructors will keep the noise and exuberance to a reasonable level by telling the children that people come to state parks to be away from the kinds of noise and confusion people create—that people have a need for tranquillity motivating them to be out in nature is not a self-evident concept to most children. If the children have been working on their "dangerous plants" skill cards, the instructors might review poison ivy recognition or, in season, illustrate the difficulty of distinguishing between safe and dangerous fungi. If there is going to be a campfire, fire safety is reviewed.

All during the walk the children will be asked to identify trees or to recognize gross features of the geology of the place such as the way in which a stream might cut its valley. A stream will evoke talk about the water cycle or the animals that inhabit streams. Each bird that rests in sight will contribute its name and the way it gains a living. Insects also contribute their lessons, some as simple as the difference between the number of legs on grasshoppers and spiders or as complex as the metamorphosis of caterpillars into butterflies.

To let the children learn from nature, we had to begin as guides not teachers. Our first duty was to bring about an encounter between the child and the natural world, the world that all of evolution has designed him to inhabit. From this encounter and free interaction, the learning could proceed. The encounter had to be active, sensuous, and spontaneous. The child had to spend some time moving through those spaces, unbounded by buildings or objects made by people, at his own speed and at a variety of speeds. He had to touch, hold, smell, plunge into, fall on, and sometimes listen to. Rocks had to be picked up or turned over, rotten logs kicked at, insects chased, and tree limbs jumped for. When the child had thus grasped the place to him, the dialogue could begin. Questions pushed their way up from ground to voice. Nature was theirs to talk about, and being carried by the spoken word it could exist between the child and the instructor, between one child and another. Answers to questions were designed to encourage the child to turn away from this dialogue with people, back to the inquiry with nature. Experience and dialogue were the foundations of learning. In this sense, all learning came from nature, but it came into a dialogue between people. Learning was a social skill and was designed to equip a child to enter into conversation with others (Vygotsky, 1986).

Knowledge is usually not perceived as valuable unless it has value for others. Identification between pupil and teacher cannot flourish unless the student can imitate the teacher. One reason why students like, respect, and want to be like their athletic coaches so much more than they wish to emulate their teachers is that the coach permits the student athlete to demonstrate and even excel at the skills the coach teaches. Athletic skills and knowledge are also more valuable than book knowledge because other children value athletic skills and knowledge. In the Companionable Zoo we knew that the children valued the skills and information they learned, yet we knew that unless they could actively give those skills and knowledge to others, their knowledge and their ability would be incompletely validated and incompletely valued. For this reason we set up a visitation program in which the students could bring their animals to other Devereux campuses and permit other children to handle them, while telling them a little about the animals. We thought that the capacity to help others handle animals safely—for the person and the animal—and offer information about animals should be acknowledged as a skill. The student trainer skill card reviewed basic knowledge about the student's animal, the procedure for holding and positioning an animal so that someone could pet it, the use of gloves to prevent bites and drop cloths to prevent soiling, and safety procedures for transporting the animal and controlling the animal at the site of the visit.

Once they completed the student trainer skill card, they were permitted to go on trips with their animal or a house animal, and with the aid of the zoo instructors conduct a demonstration for another group of students or adults. The students have made trips to other campuses at Devereux, working some- times with children that they perceived to have disabilities, and sometimes with students who were like themselves. They also traveled to two other treatment centers, one day school for children with emotional and physical handicaps, and another that was a residence for children and adults with mental retardation. They visited public schools demonstrating the animals and animal care to regular and special education classes. They even visited one private school that catered to gifted students. In addition to visiting children they also brought their animals to a recovery center for adults with head trauma and to several homes for the aged.

On some of these visits they worked very hard, making presentations to five or six classes in a morning or afternoon. The visits were another—and perhaps the most convincing—affirmation of their status as "experts" about animals. They were best at the interactive process of demonstrating the animal, and were very patient even with seriously compromised children or adults. During these visits, for the first and only times in their careers as patients, they shared the task of therapy with the instructors.

III. AN EMPIRICAL STUDY OF PROGRAM EFFECTIVENESS

Evaluating the effectiveness of an educational program is achieved the same way that you judge a stew or a pasta sauce—you taste it. You sit back and watch the children and the teachers and see what happens. After a few hours, or at most several visits, you know if the class feels good, tastes good. You judge from the children's faces, their eyes, the body language of teachers and students. You hardly need attend to the words said. You watch the amount of activity that is generated by the students, how well they stay on task and what kind of questions they ask. If possible, you ask them about what's going on and judge their responsiveness to you and the quality of bringing you into the picture. Sometimes it is a matter of sheer comfort. Are you comfortable? Is the classroom a good place to be? Is it a place you would like to bring your own children?

The first problem for the evaluator is distinguishing between the increased hopes and expectations created by a new and manifestly attractive method and the real effect of the teaching mechanism. Many new teaching methods appear to work because the teacher is encouraged, that is, pumped up by the expectation of better results, and that enthusiasm is communicated to the students. Unless carefully controlled studies are performed, you may have to wait for years until the novelty has worn off sufficiently to obtain a legitimate estimate of the power of the method itself. New curricula are similar to new diets. When everybody is talking about them, they always work. When the publicity stops, the pounds do not seem to come off so miraculously and the children do not seem to learn so wondrously. To evaluate the Companionable Zoo (CZ) program, we chose to compare it to an Outward Bound (OB) program. The OB curricula are highly attractive to the kind of behavioral disturbances and physically oriented clients that are referred to Devereux Brandywine. It was novel. No outdoor skills program was in place at the time. Moreover, there have been empirical studies attesting to OB's training and therapeutic effects including increasing self-esteem and promoting responsible behaviors. OB, as a therapeutic intervention, enabled a fair comparison with the CZ activities, evoking comparable enthusiasm, especially because an experienced specialist who believed wholeheartedly in the method taught it.

The experiment used a rigorous methodology to compare the two treatment interventions (OB and CZ) for treatment effectiveness. The empirical focus was not merely the extent of behavioral change associated with the influence of the CZ program, but also the extent of behavioral change that occurred in different situational contexts (i.e., the regular school, residential program, and the CZ program). To achieve these objectives, measures of client behavioral change in the regular school program were compared to the client behavior ratings obtained from teachers who neither taught nor interacted with their pupils in the CZ program.

Prior to starting the study, clients were selected and randomly assigned to either the CZ or OB program. Not entirely trusting the randomness of client assignments with small sample groups (i.e., $n < 100$), demographic variables including age, full scale IQ, DSM-III-R or DSM-IV diagnoses, and educational attainment were compared across the two groups. There were no significant differences between the demographic variables of the two groups at pretest, which ensures somewhat initial comparability of the OB and CZ groups. The total age distribution of the clients was slightly skewed in a negative direction. The age range of the clients was 7 to 16 inclusively. The total mean age of the clients was 12.58, and the standard deviation was 1.53. Letters of consent for client participation were sent to parents or guardians for approval for their children to participate in this study. These letters described both the CZ and OB programs, delineated potential gains for program participation, described potential risks, and theoretical rationale and supporting research for conducting this study. After parental consent was obtained for client participation, the study was described to potential clients so that informed assent to participate in the study was obtained.

A partial crossover experimental design was used with 55 children. Participation in the CZ and OB programs was voluntary so that a measure of the children's preferences, as well as responses, could be obtained. Children participated in the two groups for approximately 5 hours per school week. After 6 months, the clients in the OB group were assigned to the CZ or the animal and nature education program, and the clients in the CZ group were returned to their regular school program. They were, however, permitted to visit their animals in their free time. The reason for the partial crossover design was the strong belief that it was unethical to separate the children from their pets.

Attendance provided the first evidence that the CZ program was effective. The children would race through their morning chores and breakfast to make time to come to the zoo before their regular classes. The CZ was the most attractive activity that was measured in the regular school program. The average group attendance during the summer for the CZ and OB groups was 93% and 71%, respectively. This difference was significant ($t = 3.43$, 52 df, $p < .001$). In the fall term, the average attendance for the CZ and OB programs was 89% and 64%, respectively, which was also significantly different ($t = 2.81$, 48 df, $p < .01$).

When the OB group shifted after 6 months to the CZ program, there was a significant increase in attendance. The same children, who had a 67% voluntary attendance rate in OB group, now attended the CZ program 87% of the time ($t = 2.94$, 28 df, $p < .01$). The clients from both groups also visited the zoo in their own free time in the afternoon and weekend, performing comparable work in educational learning and application tasks as they performed during the regular school program. The attractiveness of the zoo was one of the best measures of successful involvement in the CZ program. Of importance, the clients who visited the zoo most often during their free time were also the clients who demonstrated higher performance levels in the CZ program ($r = .55$, 54 df, $p < .01$).

As discussed in greater detail earlier, the CZ curriculum was flexible in design and content so that experiential learning tasks were incorporated into the curriculum and formalized to an extent. Learning tasks, even when acquired through spontaneous exploration such as calculating a tree's age, were delineated into component and informational parts. Later these tasks were formalized into skill cards for the instructional purposes of other clients. In this way, children learned actively through their experiences in the zoo. In one term, the clients progressed through an average of eight skill areas completely, and partially through three or four more Some students who had made minimal progress in the regular school program for as long as 4 years rapidly accomplished learning tasks in the zoo. Using a variety of criteria such as the number of skill areas mastered, scores on objective knowledge tests, and results of weekly progress reviews, it was observed that 80% of the clients made a good clinical response to the CZ curriculum.

Impulse control and aggressive behaviors were consistently modulated better in the CZ program than in the regular school program and residential settings. For their protection, children often were restrained as a result of uncontrolled behavior or explosive outbursts in both the residences and the classroom. No child, on the other hand, was ever restrained in the Companionable Zoo, although estimating from the frequency of restraints during the regular school day, 35 incidents of restraints were predicted ($p < .001$). Teachers used a visit to the zoo as a therapeutic intervention to calm children who otherwise might have been restrained or medicated. In the 6 years since the conclusion of the controlled study, there have been no restraints in any of the three Devereux zoos in the Philadelphia area.

The Child Behavior Checklist (CBCL) and Teacher Report Form (TRF) are empirically derived behavior rating scales, which, with latest completed revisions, yield standardized scores on narrowband and broadband scales (Achenbach, 1991.) The CBCL and TRF were developed with the intent of contrasting the behavior ratings of children and adolescents with conduct disturbances to be compared to the normative or original standardization data established by content or rating informant across different informants (teachers versus parents) and contexts of performance (CZ versus the regular school program and the residential program). The CBCL and TRF were used to assess the severity of the children's behavioral problem in the zoo, the regular school program, and the residences. We used the significant change in symptom pattern with respect to the externalizing and total behavior scores in the regular school program as the critical measure of success.

If 5 hours a week in the zoo could improve behavior in the regular school classes, then the zoo method could equip children to succeed where they had to succeed, if they were to succeed in our society. The special education teachers completed a TRF on the clients prior to the beginning of the study, at 3 months, at 6 months, at the end of the fall term when the groups "crossed over," and again before the spring term, 5 months later. There were no differences between the two groups before the start of the study. The randomization procedure that was employed to assign the children to the two groups was effective.

At the end of 3 months, the CZ and OB groups were not different with respect to level of behavioral pathology in the regular school setting. At 6 months, however, the clients in the CZ group had significantly lower levels of behavior symptoms than the OB group (i.e., externalizing and total problem scores) in the regular school program. The difference in levels of externalizing and total behavior problems was significant and clinically meaningful. That is, an inspection of the average CZ externalizing and total problem scores demonstrates that client functioning was substantially closer to normative levels than was the OB group. Subsequent to the partial crossover, the children assigned first to the CZ were permitted now to visit the zoo and their animals in the afternoon and evenings, but not during the school day. At this point, their performance in regular school classes worsened again. The TRF provides measures of narrowband and broadband scales. Significant changes were observed in the total problem score and externalizing score, the second of which is composed of items measuring behaviors characterized by aggression, social disruption, interpersonal coercion, property destruction, and impulsivity (Figs. 1 and 2). Given their debilitating effects on adaptive functioning, these behaviors were those of particular interest to the study.

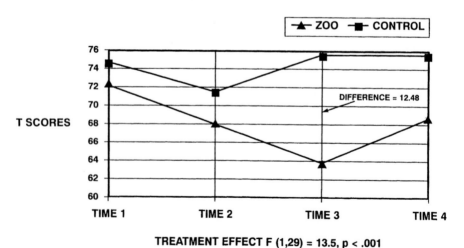

FIGURE 1   Controlled clinical trial: total problem score (school) and TRF.

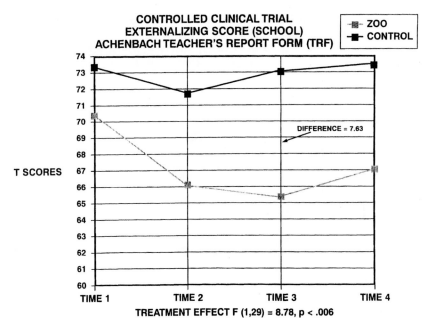

FIGURE 2   Controlled clinical trial: externalizing score (school) and Achenback TRF.

We concluded that AAT/E has large and broadly distributed therapeutic effects on children and adolescents with significant emotional and behavioral disturbances. Positive effects include decreases such as in undercontrolled and aggressive behavior. There were also positive effects in terms of improving client cooperation with instructors, the extent of engagement with learning, and the appropriateness of behavioral control in regular school classes. These changes were demonstrated with valid measures of behavior in this controlled clinical trial.

As salient as these treatment effects were, they were also strongly influenced by context. Immediate behavioral changes were seen in the zoo. In the CZ, the clients displayed their best behavior and worked closest to their capacity. In the zoo, there was little that distinguished these children in residential placement from the children one would see in any public school. These obvious behavior changes were reflected in the behavior ratings of the CZ instructors. Their ratings of problem behaviors were invariably lower than the ratings of either the teachers in the regular school program or the counselors in the residences. The externalizing score and total symptom level in the schools were, in turn, always lower than those obtained through the behavior ratings of the residential counselors (Fig. 3).

INFLUENCE OF CONTEXT ON SYMPTOMS
TOTAL PROBLEM AND EXTERNALIZING SCORES RATED
IN ZOO,SCHOOL AND RESIDENCES
ACHENBACH TRF AND CBCL

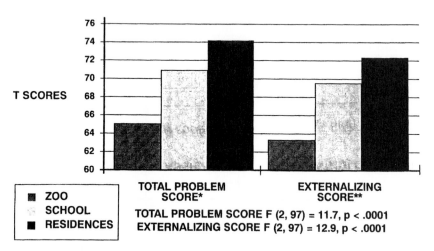

FIGURE 3   Influence of context on symptoms: total problem and externalizing scores rated in zoo, school, and residences. Achenbach TRF and CBCL.

We can also illustrate the power of context on assessment by the results that were obtained in measuring client self-esteem with the Piers-Harris Children's Self Concept Scale (Fig. 4). Initially, we attempted to document improvement in the self-esteem of clients following their entrance into the CZ, but unfortunately the children had already completed the Piers-Harris measures in their regular classrooms, prior to the end of the first 6 months. At this measurement, there were no differences in self-esteem ratings between CZ and OB groups. To test this hypothesis, all clients were randomized further into two groups, one of which was administered the self-esteem measure in the zoo setting, and the other in context of their regular school program. At this point, there was a significant difference between context and self-esteem scores, indicating that clients tested in the zoo had higher self-esteem scores than an equivalent group of clients who were tested in their regular school program ($t = 2.82$, 23 df, $p < .01$). These results point to the importance of a type of contextual effect.

We obtained these results while comparing the CZ (same as AAT/E) program against the OB control group. After the study was concluded in May 1991,

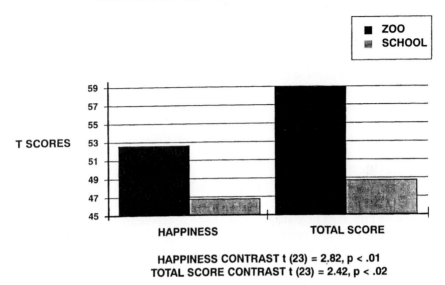

FIGURE 4   Influence of context on self-esteem. Piers-Harris Children's Self-Concept Scale.

we enlisted all of the children in the middle school program into the zoo. We felt that our evidence was strong enough to suggest we had no right to withhold such treatment from any child any longer. The Brandywine admissions office began to bring all prospective students and their parents to the zoo as part of the recruitment procedures. The children were given the explicit promise that the zoo and its nature activities would be part of their treatment program.

Even though we no longer had a control group we still wished to see if the program continued to be an effective treatment intervention. We monitored attendance, which always remained as high as it was in the first months of the study. We continued for 4 more years without the necessity of using a single restraint in the zoo. Children learned their skill cards at the same rate year after year, and became excellent teachers when taken on the now regular visitations to other schools, hospitals, and residences for the aged.

All of this information did not tell us if the children and adolescents were continuing to improve external to the zoo experience. We wanted to know if the improved behavior seen in the zoo generalized to their regular school classrooms and other residential activities. To test for the sustained effects of the zoo program, we contrasted the progress in the regular school of two groups of children: One group was formed from the better performers in the zoo, and the other from the those clients who did not succeed in zoo and nature activities. Performance ranks were made by the zoo teachers, and the total group was divided in half by a median split: those above the median rank and those below. We then compared their Achenbach ratings made by the regular school teachers, at the beginning and ending of the school year (Figs. 5 and 6). We observed that there was no significant difference in symptom level at the start of the school year, but nine months latter the children in the high zoo performance group had lower symptom scores and the children in the low zoo performance group had increased symptom scores. These findings gave us firm evidence that the program was still having the same beneficial effects on behavioral symptoms as it did during the clinical trial.

IV. SUMMARY AND CONCLUSIONS

The data presented here suggest that children, especially children who find it difficult to learn in a regular school setting, are more responsive to learning tasks as well as less symptomatic when they are participating in the care of animals and engaged in nature study. As suggested here and elsewhere in this volume, the concept of biophilia is useful in partially explaining these results.

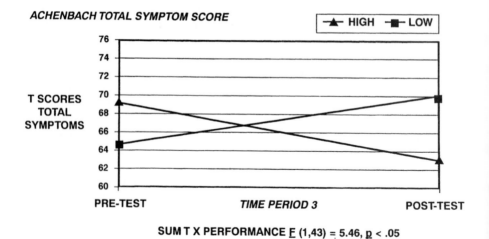

FIGURE 5   Effects of performance in the companionable zoo on classroom behavioral pathology: Achenbach total symptom score.

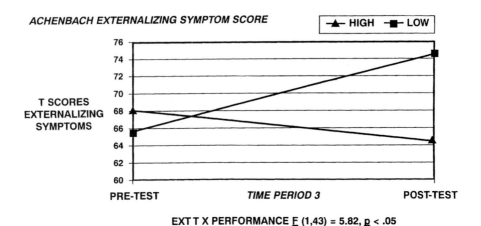

FIGURE 6   Effects of performance in the companionable zoo on classroom behavioral pathology: Achenbach externalizing symptom score.

However, it is important to recognize that the children form social relationships with the animals and that these social processes may be just as important in the therapy. These social processes occur with the animals but are guided by general moral and procedural guidelines set by the zoo instructors. It is also important to realize that there are many processes taking place in the zoo experience, including these:

- The opportunity to reduce arousal by paying attention to animals and natural settings
- Loss of fear engendered by contact with unfamiliar animals
- Social interaction with animals (It is important to recognize that children almost always perceive animals as social others.)
- Care of animals and gardens
- Display of affection toward animals with touch-talk dialogue
- Play with animals
- Mastery experiences through training animals
- Tracking animals (Tracking animals is one of the most ancient of human skills. Fortunately, through the use of cameras to capture prey, our children can hunt humanely. The only animals they actually hunt in the traditional fashion are fish and the worms that they use for bait or as food for the iguanas.)

- Gathering (Just as the children garden, they gather nuts, fruit, and a variety of edible plants. It gives them almost the same thrill of the hunt as does fishing.)
- Orienting (The ability to find their way in wilderness using the sun, stars, and compass makes use of the capacity for spatial orientation.)
- Wilderness experience (The fear mastery, risk exercise, and competence-building facets of a wilderness experience, from 2- or 3-day hikes in forest or simply a night out camping by the pond, can rapidly build a sense of competence and generate pleasurable memories.)
- Species identification and species classification (The building of animal categories may be the best way to train children in categorical classification.)

Because of the nature of the program we have no idea how much each of these activities contributes to the overall effectiveness of the program. The role of all of these processes can be explained, in part, by two broad theoretical constructs that should guide and inform the use of AAT/E in the treatment and the education of children: evolutionary biology and particularly the biophilia hypothesis, and object relationships, specifically, the idea of the transitional relationship (see Chapter 19, Part A).

REFERENCES

Achenbach, T. M. (1991). *Manual for the Child Behavior Checklist 14—16 and 1991 scoring profile.* Burlington, VT: University of Vermont, Department of Psychiatry.

American Psychiatric Association. (1994). *Diagnostic and statistical manual of mental disorders* (4th ed.). Washington, DC: American Psychiatric Association.

Barkley, R. A. (1990). *Attention deficit hyperactivity disorder: A handbook for diagnosis and treatment.* New York: Guilford.

Barkley, R. A. (1994). Impaired delayed responding: A unified theory of attention-deficit hyperactivity disorder. In D. K. Routh (Ed.), *Disruptive behavior disorders, in childhood* (pp. 11–57). Plenum: New York.

Barkley, R. A., Fischer, M., Edelbrock, C. S., & Smallish, L. (1990). The adolescent outcome of hyperactive children diagnosed by research criteria, I: An 8 year prospective follow-up study. *Journal of the American Academy of Child and Adolescent Psychiatry* 29, 546–557.

Bronowski, J. (1977). *Human and animal languages. A sense of the future* (pp. 104–131). Cambridge, MA: The MIT Press.

Dodge, K. (1985). Social cognition and children's aggressive behavior. *Child Development,* 51, 162–170.

Halloway, E. M., & Ratey, J. J. (1994). *Answers to distraction.* New York: Pantheon.

Katcher, A., & Wilkins G. G. (1993). Dialogue with animals—Its nature and culture. In S. R. Killer & E. O. Wilson (Eds.), *The biophilia hypothesis: A theoretical and empirical inquiry* (pp. 173–203). Washington, DC: Island Press.

Katcher A. and Wilkins, G.G., (1998) Animal assisted therapy in the treatment of disruptive behavior disorders in children. In Ante Lundberg (Ed.), *The Environment and Mental Health.* Mahwah, NJ: Lawrence Erlbaum Associates.

Katcher, A., and Wilkins, G. G., (1999). *The Centaur's Lessons*. Unpublished manuscript.

Kazdin, A. E. (1985). *Treatment of antisocial behavior, in children and adolescents*. Homewood, IL: Dorsey Press.

Kazdin, A. E. (1987a). Treatment of antisocial behavior in children: Current status and future directions. *Psychological Bullentin* **102**, 187–203.

Kazdin, A. E. (1987b). *Conduct disorders in childhood and adolescence*. Newbury Park, NJ: Sage Publications.

Kazdin, A. E. (1989). Developmental psychopathology: Current research, issues, and directions. *American Psychologist* **44**, 180–187.

Kellert, S., & Wilson, E. O. (1993). *The biophilia hypothesis*. Washington, DC: Island Press.

Kinsbourne, M. (1989). Control system instability in hyperactive children. In L. M. Bloomingdale (Ed.), *Attention deficit disorder* (Vol. 3, pp. 104–106). New York: Pergamon.

Patterson, G. R. (1979). Treatment for children with conduct problems: A review of outcome studies. In S. Feshbach & A. Fracek (Eds.), *Aggression and behavior change: Biological and social process* (pp. 83–132). New York: Praeger.

Patterson, G. R. (1986). Performance models for antisocial boys. *American Psychologist* **41**, 432–444.

Patterson, G. R. (1991). Parenting skills for what? Meditational models work better. Paper presented at the annual meeting of the Society for Research in Child Development, Seattle, WA.

Sennett, R., and Cobb, J. (1972). *The hidden injuries of class*. New York: W. W. Norton.

Vygotsky, L. (1986). *Thought and language*. Cambridge, MA: The MIT Press

Wilkins, G. G., & Sholevar, G. P. (1995). Manual-based psychotherapy. In G. P. Sholevar (Ed.), *Conduct disorders in children and adolescents*. Washington, DC: American Psychiatric Press.

Wilson, E. O. (1984). Biophilia, Cambridge, MA: Harvard University Press

CHAPTER 9

Animals and Therapists: Incorporating Animals in Outpatient Psychotherapy

AUBREY H. FINE

School of Education and Integrative Studies, California State Polytechnic University, Pomona, California

I. INTRODUCTION

The troubled boy would not speak at all at preschool and barely spoke to his parents. But the boy broke his silence for a conure named Tilly who squawked a greeting in his doctor's office. Tilly squawked: "Pretty baby, hello, pretty baby, hello," and the 4.5-year-old answered the bird with a shy hello. The boy talked to the bird, he explained "because the bird talked to me first."

This true story was reported in the *Los Angeles Times* by Sandra Ferrell Bazrod. She described in her story how a local psychologist in California utilized animals to connect therapeutically to his clients. "Dr. Dolittle may have talked to the animals, but Fine uses the animals to talk to children,

Handbook on Animal-Assisted Therapy: Theoretical Foundations and Guidelines for Practice

helping them relax, gain confidence and express themselves" (Bazrod, 1993, p. J-4).

The example given is only one of many showing how clinicians have incorporated a variety of multidimensional approaches to enhance therapeutic outcomes with their clients. In particular, the integration of animals as therapeutic change agents provides therapists with an effective alternative for connecting with their clients. The animals appear to act as a viable ancillary in developing a more nurturing and safer environment for clients.

As has been articulated throughout this book, the value of the human–animal bond has been seriously investigated for many decades. Furthermore, the bond between humans and animals has also been paid homage to by the popular press and the film industry. Recently, various films in our pop culture have portrayed the importance of the human–animal bond (films such as *Homeward Bound, The Return of the Yellow Dog, Andre,* and *Free Willy*) and its impact. There has also been a proliferation of books focusing on the importance of wildlife to humans as a recognition of the positive impact that animals have on the lives of people: *Animals as Teachers and Healers* (Chernak-McElroy, 1996), *Chicken Soup for the Pet Lover's* Soul (Canfield *et al.,* 1998), and *The Compassion of Animals* (Von Kreisler, 1997). It seems a logical next step for mental health professionals to try to incorporate the human–animal bond connections into their practices where applicable. As Bern Williams once stated: "There is no psychiatrist in the world like a puppy licking your face."

A. OBJECTIVE OF THE CHAPTER

The objective of this chapter is to provide the reader with practical insight on how animals may be incorporated into a therapeutic practice. Within this context, the author will also provide suggested guidelines to ensure quality control for the client's and animal's safety. Case studies are incorporated to illustrate various situations in which the human–animal bond seemed to enhance the therapeutic outcome.

However, the reader is cautioned not to view this approach as a panacea. McCulloch (1984) strongly points out that there is limited research demonstrating the therapeutic utility of employing the human–animal bond. Fine, in an interview with Kale (1992), pointed out that animals could have a therapeutic impact on children when the approach was integrated with other strategies. "To say that the therapeutic changes occur solely in isolation would perhaps be quite misleading" (p. 14). Despite positive anecdotal examples, the reader needs to recognize that there is limited empirical support and limited research validating the overall effectiveness of this approach. Siegel (1993) as well as Beck and Katcher (1984) point out that although the utilization of animals may be highly appealing, the evidence that a patient has enjoyed an interaction with an animal does not imply that the procedure is therapeutic. Additionally an article by Serpell (1993) concurs with this sentiment. Serpell (1983) reported at a meeting of the Society for Companion Animal Studies that animal-facilitated therapy needs to be based on sound theory before it gains any widespread acceptance. Voelker (1995) also noted that the biggest challenge facing advocates of animal-assisted therapy who claim that it improves outcomes can be summed in two words: "Prove it" (p. 1898). Voelker points out that the major difficulty in obtaining outcome data in animal-assisted therapy is that many of the professionals applying these strategies do not see the necessity of conducting outcome research or, possibly, they do not take the time to validate outcomes. This lack of documentation and thorough investigation leaves a large void on the efficacy of this approach. It seems that most clinicians persevere and incorporate the modality primarily on qualitative impressions that have been observed or heard about.

Therefore, I strongly emphasize the importance of empirically investigating the therapeutic utility of animals in clinical practices, serving clients of all ages, in order to demonstrate the efficacy of this modality. The findings from quality-designed studies will help clinicians and researchers answer a variety of questions, including these: Under what conditions are animal-assisted activities the most beneficial? With what populations does it appear to work the best? Under which theoretical orientation (e.g., humanistic, cognitive, behavioral) does the incorporation of animals seem the most effective therapeutically?

Having considered the limitations cited, let us now go on to my template of suggestions of what clinicians might consider when incorporating animals within their therapeutic practice in an effective way.

II. CONSIDERATION 1: WHY CLINICIANS MAY FIND ANIMALS THERAPEUTICALLY BENEFICIAL

A. ANIMALS AS A SOCIAL LUBRICANT FOR THERAPY

Early research investigating the incorporation of animals within outpatient psychotherapy was somewhat limited. Nevertheless, Rice *et al.* (1973) conducted a study to evaluate the extent to which animals were used by psychotherapists in the United States as a whole. Their study also attempted to classify the ways in which animals served psychotherapeutic roles. One hundred and ninety members (64% of the sample) of the APA's Division of Psychotherapy responded to the survey. The findings of their study suggested that 40 clinicians

(21%) indicated that they used animals or animal content in conjunction with their psychotherapy.

The most powerful finding from this study pertained to the specific uses of the animal within the therapeutic setting. The researchers reported that some therapists found some utility in actually having animals present in therapy, whereas others utilized animals in a conceptual manner. Common commentaries about the utilization of real animals pertained to employing an animal as a vehicle for cultivating or modeling the positive nature of interpersonal relationships. Most of the responders pointed out that animals were used to ease the stress of the initial phases of therapy to establish rapport. The researchers also reported isolated uses of animals such as suggesting that a patient obtain a pet as a means of introducing practical caretaking responsibilities. The conceptual use of animals by most reporting clinicians was most frequently symbolic. Therapists often incorporated animal content to formulate interpretations of patient's fantasies or underlying themes in their discussions.

Mallon (1992) points out that the animals should not be considered as substitutes for human relationships but as a complement to them. It has been noted that animals appear to decrease the initial reservations that may develop from initially entering therapy. Arkow (1982) suggested that the animal may act as a link in the conversation between the therapist and the client. He called this process a rippling effect. Others such as Corson and Corson (1980) describe this process as a social lubricant. It appears that the presence of the animal allows the client a sense of comfort, which then promotes rapport in the therapeutic relationship.

Case Study

Linda (not her real name) was referred to Dr. Fine for suspected selected mutism. Linda was 7 years of age and only spoke in her own home. She appeared to be very shy and uncomfortable in public settings. Naturally, her selective mutism impacted her school performance, where she interacted very little in class.

When her parents initially met to explain Linda's symptoms, they were quite certain that she would not speak in the office. Ironically, at our first meeting, Linda was greeted at the door by a loving, warm-hearted golden retriever named Puppy. It was amazing to watch Linda immediately become attracted to Puppy. Puppy, not being bashful, went full barrel into Linda. She wouldn't let Linda alone. She expected Linda to keep up the petting and constant attention. In observing Linda's reaction, I decided to take clinical advantage of the immediate bond between the child and Puppy. I called the golden retriever over to me and asked her to go to the back room. I alluded to Linda that if she wanted Puppy to continue to play with her, all she had to do was call her over. To Linda's parents' surprise, they watched and listened to their daughter call Puppy over. Tears rolled from the parents' eyes as they watched in shock as Puppy returned to interact with their daughter. From that day forward, Linda made remarkable progress. It appeared that Puppy had reached within her and made it easier for her to speak. Our interactions were made easier. Through an approach that included successive desensitization, Linda began to speak very clearly in my office and outside. Goals were established and Linda soon began to speak more outside her home.

To help Linda speak at school, Puppy visited her class. Linda was responsible for introducing Puppy to her classmates (this was practiced in earlier therapy sessions). Although she spoke quietly, she amazed her classmates by speaking. After the class, Puppy, her teacher, Linda, and myself had a short meeting to discuss how we could make it more comfortable for her to participate in various class meetings. Although Linda seemed apprehensive in our discussions, she did speak briefly. During the next few months, Linda spoke more descriptively. She appeared more willing to open up and interact. Her grades also improved.

One cannot only attribute Linda's growth to her contact with Puppy. However, it appears that her relationship with Puppy acted as an early catalyst for change. It seems the elderly golden retriever made Linda more comfortable in engaging.

Beck *et al.* (1986) suggested that a therapist who conducts therapy with an animal present may appear less threatening and, consequently, the client may be more willing to reveal him- or herself. This perception was also found by Peacock (1986), who reported that in interviews in the presence of her dog, children appeared more relaxed and seemed more cooperative during their visit. She concluded that the dog served to reduce the initial tension and assisted in developing an atmosphere of warmth. Numerous studies have elicited similar findings. Baun *et al.* (1984) suggested that animals appear to have a calming effect on humans and reduce arousal. In their study, the data linked tactile contact with a dog with experimentally induced low blood pressures.

B. Benefits of Animals as an Extension to a Therapist: A Method for Rapport Building

Animals are often known for the zealous greetings they provide to visiting clients they encounter. Levinson (1965), in a pioneer article on the use of pets (in the treatment of children with behavior disorders), implied that bringing in the animal at the beginning of therapy frequently assisted in helping a reserved client overcome anxiety about therapy. Many therapy dogs are more than willing to receive a client in a warm and affectionate manner.

For example, in most cases animals can become an extension of the therapist. Personally, the animals that work with me are very responsive to greeting visitors. Children look forward to seeing Puppy (a golden retriever), Hart (a black Labrador), Boomer (a dusky conure), or Snowflake (an umbrella cockatoo). The dogs eagerly walk over to the children, encouraging attention. These initial encounters ease the tension at the beginning of every meeting. As an initial icebreaker, the therapeutic environment seems to be enriched. The animals seem to regulate the emotional climate.

Levinson (1964), a pioneer of utilizing animals in therapeutic relationships, suggested that the animals may represent a catalyst in helping a child make more progress in a clinician's setting. It seems evident that the animals' presence may make the initial resistance easier to overcome.

Case Study

Several years ago, a 15-year-old boy, who was diagnosed as being depressed, was referred to my office. When he entered the waiting room he became very intrigued with the fish tanks. It seemed that over the years he had developed a strong interest in tropical fish. This common interest appeared to enhance our therapeutic rapport quickly. During the next 6 months, our common interest went beyond talking about and observing the fish to a higher level of involvement. After careful consideration and planning, we both believed that putting together a 60-gallon saltwater tank would be therapeutically beneficial for him. Indirectly and directly, his involvement and efforts in helping select the fish, plants, scenery, and rocks not only enhanced our bond but definitely appeared to diminish his sense of demoralization. Jeff had something to look forward to. His drive to fight off his lethargy and helpless thoughts seemed to be impacted by the sight of a new environment that he helped design and build. He would frequently stop at the office to check on the fish, taking pride in his accomplishments. Although Jeff continued to battle with his depression, he also continued to find refuge and support in the tank he established. The partnership we established in developing the tank was a definite asset to our working relationship.

C. THERAPEUTIC BENEFIT OF ANIMALS IN THERAPY: A CATALYST FOR EMOTION

Brody (1988) reported in the *New York Times* that a growing number of mental health and health professionals had applied the human expression of laughter and joy therapeutically to reduce stress and foster recovery in patients with various illnesses. Animals within therapeutic settings can also elicit a range of emotions from laughter to sorrow. Often in the literature on animal-assisted therapy more attention has been given to the softer emotions, which the human–animal bond instills. Nevertheless, recognition that animals can exhibit humorous behaviors is relevant. Norman Cousins (1989), in his premier writing of *Head First: The Biology of Hope,* has emphasized for decades that humor is not only beneficial in improving an individual's mental state, but also his or her physical constraints. Laughter and joy are two ingredients that positively impact a person's quality of life. It seems apparent that not only do animals promote warmth within a relationship, they may also bring joy and a smile.

Numerous examples can be applied to illustrate this phenomenon. For example, a playful cockatoo or a puppy getting itself into mischief can always garner a smile. There have been numerous occasions where the animals incorporated therapeutically get themselves in comical/playful situations. It seems that when this occurs, the laughter generated has therapeutic value.

Selectively, animals are in a unique situation to display emotions and behaviors that may not be deemed professionally appropriate for a human service provider. For example, in difficult periods within therapy, a client may be in need of comforting and reassurance. The presence of an animal may become that catharsis. The holding of an animal or the petting of an animal (whether a cat, dog, or a bunny) may act as a physical comforter and soothe many patients. The touching of the animal and the proximity to the animal may also represent an external degree of safety within many clients.

Moreover, an additional benefit of the animals may be their contribution in helping clients gauge excessive emotion and reactive behavior. On numerous occasions, the author has witnessed that when a dispute would take place, the animal's presence seemed to lend some comfort and stability to the environment. The adults seemed to regulate their reactiveness, possibly because they were aware of the animal's presence. Furthermore, in working with children who are quite active and impulsive, it is amazing to observe how large birds (cockatoos and macaws) seemed to help promote a decorum for what is or is not considered acceptable behavior. It seems that most children gave tremendous respect to the birds' presence (possibly some unconscious intimidation), and the reduction in their disruptive behavior was evident. Most children seemed to realize that their escalated behaviors would cause an uneasiness in the birds, which they did not want to cause. In addition to this one benefit, as a followup to the child's outbursts and the bird's ability to help reduce the tension, discussions on self-control and behavioral regulation were introduced.

D. ANIMALS ACTING AS ADJUNCTS TO CLINICIANS

Mallon (1992) emphasizes that the animals must be considered as adjuncts in the establishment of a therapeutic relationship and bond. Hoelscher and

Garat (1993) suggest that when relating to a therapist with an animal, people with difficulties sometimes find the animals to be a catalyst for discussion. For example, several years ago, an 8-year-old girl visited the office. She was very intrigued about the birds she saw and wanted to hold a few of the small lovebirds. Without asking if she could hold the bird, she eagerly put her hand toward the animal. To her dissatisfaction, the bird hissed at her. Shortly after this experience, I explained to the girl that she needed to ask the bird's permission (and mine) to touch the animal. Ironically, this was followed by a powerless response of "I know what you mean." Her response to my statement piqued my attention, since she was referred for depressive symptoms. I picked up the lovebird and began to scratch her head. I told the girl that the bird was very sensitive to touch, and there were certain spots that she didn't like to be touched. At this point, the girl became very teary eyed and responded by saying once again (very sadly this time) "I know what you mean." Shortly after, she began to reveal a history of sexual abuses by one of her grandparents. It was apparent the serendipitous use of the bird acted as a catalyst to promote a discussion on feelings that she had buried. During the course of her treatment, we used the example of the bird to help her gain insight on the importance of giving people permission to embrace you, and how you have the right to tell people that your body is private.

E. Vicarious Use of the Relationship with Animals: Role Modeling

A valued benefit of incorporating animals clinically is the vicarious outcomes that a client may develop as a consequence of the interaction between the clinician and the animals. For example, the loving relationship between the animal and the therapist may explain by example to the client some of the caring traits of the clinician. This outcome may enhance the development of the therapeutic relationship and alliance. Personally, over the years, this writer has been amazed by the comments he has received from clients observing his interaction with the animals. The most common response pertains to the interaction with the animals and how some clients compare these interactions with their own child– parent relationships (since most of his clients are children and their parents). Other clients comment on how well the animals are treated, including the elements of compassion, consistency, firmness, and love. These scenarios can be used to demonstrate to the client appropriate interactions and responses to behaviors.

Experienced clinicians will attest to the numerous occasions (during sessions) on which boundaries need to be placed on the animals. This demonstration of limit setting should be a valuable teaching tool for the clients. The therapist can use these episodes as opportunities to model specific discipline or problem-solving strategies. For example, within my office, one of the many therapy birds that I use is a sulfur-crested cockatoo. She periodically has a tremendous need for attention, and one approach that she uses is to screech. Parents are always amazed with my approach and the explanation that I give to them. The most common approach applied is extinction, and the eventual reinforcement of the appropriate behavior when it is demonstrated (verbal praise and petting the bird). The outcome to this interaction eventually leads to an informal discussion on behavior management, which may have implications to their own child-rearing practices.

As can be seen, numerous episodes occur on which a clinician could draw. It is of utmost importance that the therapist take advantage of teachable moments and learning opportunities. Discussions with adults on boundary setting, the need to be loved and admired, and appropriate ways of interacting are all relevant.

III. CONSIDERATION 2: THE THERAPEUTIC ENVIRONMENT—ANIMALS AS AN ASPECT OF MILIEU THERAPY

Modifications to the work environment may also be considered a valuable contribution that animals can influence. The perceived environment appears to be more friendly and comfortable to incoming clients. Barnard (1954) pointed out that it was Ernst Simmel's pioneer work that gave serious thought to the manipulation of the environment to meet the unconscious needs of clients. In her paper, Barnard (1954) reported that in ancient times, even pagan temples (which promoted healing) provided an atmosphere of encouragement and hope. She noted that in an ancient institution in Cairo, patients were entertained daily with musical concerts as one source of their therapy. The underlying force within milieu therapy is a recognition of the "climate" within the environment and its impact on the client. Sklar (1988) points out that there is a constant interaction between the client and the therapist that is impacted by the physical and emotional environment that is created in the clinician's office. Sklar's writings as well as Langs' (1979) suggest that the development of an effective therapeutic alliance may actually begin with the creation of a proper therapeutic environment. Sklar reports that many outpatient clinics neglect attention given to the physical plant in which the therapeutic process unfolds. Goldensohn and Haan (1974) report that client's readiness for psychotherapy could be disturbed by the simplicity of a clinic's decor and perhaps by its disorder.

Sklar (1988) also reported that many facilities that provide mental health services appear to be proud of the happy, affectionate family atmosphere that the clinic attempts to create. He suggested that one must not only focus on the client's internal dynamics for treatment to become successful, but in addition the therapists must address the clinical space within which treatment is ongoing.

As the research suggests, little attention appears to be given by most therapists to the elements that enhance their therapeutic environment. Light music, lighting, and climate control have always been intuitively associated with a more comfortable environment. These ingredients seem to promote a sense of security and comfort. It seems obvious that living beings could also be utilized to complement the work environment by making it more appealing and relaxing. Of utmost value is that the animals appear to bring a certain sense of security and warmth into the environment. For example, Katcher, *et al.* (1984) reported, in their study on anxiety and discomfort before and during dental surgery, that subjects viewing the aquarium appeared more comfortable and less anxious than those subjects in a control group not viewing an aquarium. Watching a school of fish swim harmoniously can be quite relaxing for some. With proper lighting and an attractively designed tank, clients might feel more at ease when they enter an office or while undergoing a therapy session. Over the years, I have found fish tanks to be extremely enticing. The gentleness of the fish and the ambiance developed can be truly beneficial to a therapy session.

Unfortunately, when schools in a fish tank are not properly selected, the outcome can make people feel uncomfortable, especially if the fish incorporated are aggressive and hyperactive. For example, early in my own personal utilization of fish tanks for the ambiance they promote, my selection of fish was not appropriate. Two fish in the school were quite active and aggressive. They would often be observed fighting and chasing each other. Rather than finding the fish tank to be relaxing and comforting, many of the clients noted that they felt uneasy watching the fish. One adult was overheard saying that the activity level of the fish reminded her of the chaos that she witnesses within her own home, especially with her children. Although this event serendipitously led to a discussion about her concerns with her children, it didn't put her at ease.

With the importance of a therapeutic environment now established, it is notable to appreciate how animals can be viewed within this dimension. Beck *et al.* (1986) suggests that animals have the capacity to modify a person's environment. Friedmann *et al.* (1983) have demonstrated that people appear to exhibit lower blood pressure and verbally express feelings of relaxation in the presence of a dog, while Katcher *et al.* (1983) have been able to correlate a similar phenomenon in people viewing a tank of fish. Lockwood (1983) hypothesizes that this outcome may occur because people perceive most situations with animals as safer and perhaps more benign than situations involving humans.

Very few studies have been implemented investigating the impact that animals have in altering the therapeutic effects of an environment. Beck *et al.* (1986) initiated a study in Haverford, Pennsylvania, where their initial hypothesis speculated that the animals would alter the therapeutic environment and make it less threatening to patients with various mental illnesses. These patients (who met in a room containing birds) attended sessions more faithfully and became more active participants in comparison to a control group. The researchers' findings reported that the experimental group (who had their therapy in the presence of the birds) had a greater rate of attendance and demonstrated more frequent participation than did the nonbird group. In addition, their findings from the Brief Psychiatric Rating Scale identified a reduction in hostility scores in clients within the experimental milieu. The researchers believed that this outcome was enhanced due to the impression the clients had about the birds (that the animals were perceived by the patients as less hostile, and therefore the clients felt more at ease in the presence of the animals).

Not only can animals be used to perhaps enhance the milieu as well as the relationship between the client and the therapist, but in addition the therapist can also observe how the client relates and interacts with the animal. The client may unconsciously be overbearing and controlling to the animal or for that manner may act coldly and unresponsively. These experiences may provide a therapist with an alternate diagnostic window through which to view a client.

IV. CONSIDERATION 3: INCORPORATING THEORY IN PRACTICE: ANIMAL-ASSISTED THERAPY FROM A LIFE STAGE PERSPECTIVE

A clinician's theoretical orientation will have a strong bearing on the incorporation of animals within his or her therapeutic approach. An explanation that seems to naturally align itself is Erikson's theoretical orientation. Erikson views development as a passage through a series of psychosocial stages, each with its particular goals, concerns, and needs. Although the themes may repeat during a life cycle, Erikson noted that certain life concerns were more relevant during specific eras. For example, as people age and experience new situations, they confront a series of psychosocial challenges. This author recommends that clinicians should consider the various eight stages of psychosocial development and reflect on how the application of animals may be appropriate. Table I (adapted from the findings of Hall and Lindzey, 1978) illustrates the major

TABLE I   Erik Erikson's Eight Stages of Development

Stage 1: Basic Trust vs. Basic Mistrust (First Year)
   Virtue—Hope
   Estrangement, Separation, and Abandonment

Stage 2: Autonomy vs. Shame and Doubt (Second Year)
   Virtue—Will

Stage 3: Initiative vs. Guilt (3–5 Years Old)
   Virtue—Purpose

Stage 4: Industry vs. Inferiority (Sixth Year to Puberty)
   Virtue—Competence (Workmanship)

Stage 5: Identity vs. Identity Confusion (Adolescence)
   Virtue—Fidelity

Stage 6: Intimacy vs. Isolation (Young Adulthood)
   Virtue—Love
   Elitism

Stage 7: Generativity vs. Stagnation (Middle Adulthood)
   Virtue—Care
   Generational (Parental Responsibilities toward Youth)

Stage 8: Integrity vs. Despair (Older Adulthood)
   Virtue—Wisdom—Integration of life experiences
   Ritual—Integration
   Perverted Ritual—Sapientism (Pretense of Being Wise)

---

elements found within each stage. The following subsections provide an interpretation of how Erikson's theory can be applied to animal-assisted therapy.

A. Suggested Developmental Goals and Treatment Purposes for Children

Within the first series of life stages, the primary goals that need to be achieved pertain to a child's needs to feel loved and to develop a sense of industry and competence. In a practical sense, animals can assist the clinician in promoting unconditional acceptance. The animal's presence in therapy (as discussed previously) may assist a child in learning to trust. Furthermore, the animal may also help the clinician demonstrate to the child that he is worth loving. Unfortunately, for some children, their reservoirs of life successes are limited and they feel incompetent. This sense of incompetence may be acted out aggressively toward others or internally against oneself. A therapist may utilize an animal to help a child see value in life.

Animal-assisted therapy can eventually go beyond the office visits. A clinician may suggest to a family the value of having a pet within the home. The animal may help a child develop a sense of responsibility as well as importance in life.

For instance, the case study of Scott comes to mind when considering this position. Scott was 12 years old when I first met him. He could be described as functioning in the borderline range of intelligence as well as demonstrating a severe learning disability. Perhaps Scott's greatest barrier to successful integration was his inability to relate with peers. Scott lacked social savoir faire. He was constantly bullied by others and was the brunt of their vicious jokes. He was friendless. I had worked with Scott over a 2-year period. Our visits were interrupted for a short while because he moved away. When he was 15 he returned to my practice, still demonstrating many of the same undeveloped social behaviors.

Throughout our visits, our major treatment goal was to help Scott develop social insight. Unfortunately, he had difficulty generalizing the skills and continued to suffer. During the course of the treatment, Scott became very intrigued with the birds that I had in my practice. He seemed attentive to their behaviors, especially their speech. Because all the birds were hand raised, they were receptive to Scott picking them up and gently stroking their heads. Eventually, Scott asked if he could take one of the birds home for a few weeks. The bird was great company for Scott. They were inseparable. Scott accepted his role graciously and took great care of the bird. After a month, Scott wanted his own pet. Through the gracious assistance of a bird breeder, I was able to secure a bird for Scott. During the next year, Scott started to come out of his shell. He joined an aviary club, and also began breeding birds on his own. Although he still didn't possess effective social skills, the birds allowed Scott to get out on his own. Through the birds, Scott was able to have some substance to talk about. He also had purpose in his life. The birds became Scott's counterparts. They gave him attention and made him feel worthwhile. As noted earlier, the primary goal of Erikson's stage for childhood is developing a sense of industry versus a sense of inferiority. The birds in Scott's life helped him feel more competent and capable. Utilizing Erikson's terminology, the birds seemed to impact his sense of industry.

Therapists may use the experience of the interaction between the child and the therapy animal as an opportunity to observe and assess if a child may psychologically benefit from having a pet within the home. Levinson (1965) reported that a pet within the home may be an excellent extension to therapy. The pet could provide the child with constant solace and unconditional joy and warmth.

Bryant (1990) reports that animal companions have been cited as providing important social support for children. Bryant reports that animals within a home may assist children in developing a greater sense of empathy for others. Further studies such as those of Poresky and Hendrix (1990) and Covert *et al.* (1985) have documented similar outcomes. These researchers suggest that pet ownership may be extremely valuable in enhancing a child's self-esteem and social skills, as well as a sense of empathy. Although Paul and Serpell (1996) are in agreement with these findings qualitatively, they indicated that most of the research conducted has not demonstrated any firm causal relationship between childhood pet ownership and alterations in the psychological well-being of children. It is interesting to note that many researchers seem to agree that there appears to be qualitative support for the value of the human–animal bond but that there are difficulties in quantifying this value. Perhaps some of the challenges that researchers are being confronted with pertain not only to quality research protocols presently under investigation, but also a possible measurement problem.

However, some studies such as Bryant's (1990) do demonstrate some promise in promoting the therapeutic benefit of pets for children. In her study, Bryant studied the potential social-emotional benefits and liabilities of children having pets. Although the study and its implications were based on children, it is important for clinicians to consider some of the findings as being pertinent for adolescents and adults. Two hundred and thirteen children were surveyed as part of the sample under investigation. Furman's (1989) "My Pet" inventory was utilized to assess the subjects' interests. A factor analysis of Furman's inventory indicated that from a child's perspective, there are four factors in which the child–pet relationship can be viewed as potentially beneficial. The factor of *mutuality* was defined by Bryant (1990) as having to do with the experience of both giving and receiving care and support for the animal. Furman (1989) originally identified these variables as companionship and nurturance. The *enduring affection* factor identifies the child's perception of the lasting quality of the relationship with his or her pet. This factor focuses on the child's perception of the permanence of the emotional bond between the child and the animal. The third factor, titled *enhanced affection,* identifies the perception from the child that the child–pet relationship makes him or her feel good, as well as important. This factor is a crucial element that clusters the admiration and affection between the animal and the child. Finally, the factor of *exclusivity* focuses on the child's internal confidence in the pet as a confidant. This factor appears to be extremely crucial for therapists to underscore. It is within this factor that a child may rely on the pet companion to share private feelings and secrets. This may be an important outlet, especially when there are limited friends and supports within the community or the home. Mallon (1994b) also points out that there is evidence that a child may use an animal as a confidant. In his study on the effects of a dog in a therapeutic setting treating children with behavior disorders, the staff observed that the children would often utilize the dog as a sounding board or a safe haven to discuss their problems and troubles.

Bryant (1990) suggests that the viewing of the child–pet relationship may be extremely valuable in understanding the dynamics within the family. Negative relationships may also be indicative of existing or impeding crises within the family.

On the other hand, within the study, Bryant (1990) also pointed out some of the limitations to the child–pet relationship. Some of the constraints included distress associated with taking care of the pet, the unfair grief of a pet acting mean, or the rejection of the child by the pet. These data are in agreement with other researchers such as Kidd and Kidd (1980, 1985) who point out that the choice of animal for a child has to be a proper match. Different breeds of animals (dogs, cats, and birds) may offer unsuitable physical and psychosocial benefits to their owners. Unfortunately, if the wrong animal or breed is selected as a pet for the child, the effective bond described earlier may not develop.

B. Suggested Developmental Goals and Treatment Purposes for Adolescents

Erikson views the period of adolescence as a time where the teenager must achieve a sense of identity. The teen goes through many physical and mental changes in his or her quest to secure an adult-like status. The developmental period appears to be the first time that a conscious effort is made to define a sense of self. During this period, the teen begins to organize drives, beliefs, and ambitions toward a consistent and clear image of self. It is during this time frame that the emotional stability of the youth may be extremely fragile. Some teens may be unable to cope with the many physical, social, and developmental expectations that come with this passage. Their strong need for affiliation and the need to be wanted and able to fit in may become primary goals within therapy. A clinician may find an animal's presence valuable in making the teen feel more at ease during a visit. The teen may be more willing to take down some of the barriers, if she or he feels more comfortable. Furthermore, although a teen may project the need to be adult-like, the teen may appreciate the free spirit of an animal. The comfort the youth may receive may allow him or her to feel more appreciated.

The value identified earlier with regard to the psychosocial benefits of having a pet as a child may also be pertinent to a teenager. A therapist may strongly suggest to a family the consideration of having a pet with teens that appear to be experiencing some social isolation. Kidd and Kidd (1990), in their study on high school students and pets, suggested that pet ownership

may be beneficial both to adolescents who are having challenges in personal
independence as well as mature interfamilial relationships.

C. Suggested Developmental Goals and Treatment Purposes for Adults

Therapists who focus more on adults may also find Erikson's insight beneficial.
With young adults, their need to recognize that they can also take care of
others may become a great starting point for discussion. A therapist may use
a therapy animal as a starting point to discuss decisions about having children
or, for that matter, child-rearing practices. It is not uncommon for some
therapists to suggest to young couples that they try to rear a pet as a precursor
to deciding if they are ready for children. The animal's presence may be an
ideal introduction to this topic. Furthermore, adults experiencing parenting
challenges and couples who are experiencing marital dysfunction may find
the metaphors and the stories related to bringing up children and learning to
share one's life with another person to be appropriate topics. The presence of
animals, and examples incorporating animals, may give some clarity to the
subject of generativity versus self-absorption.

D. Suggested Developmental Goals and Treatment Purposes for the Elderly

Finally, animals may tremendously impact a clinician's ability to interact with
elderly clients. Similar to the role that an animal may have in treating a
child, a therapist may find an animal extremely useful in securing a positive
relationship with an elderly client. Clients who have had a history of animals
within their lives may find the animal's presence extremely advantageous in
reminiscing past life events. It is amazing how a lifetime growing up with an
animal may make it easier for some people to reflect major milestones in their
lives. Reflections of the past may become more crystallized as a consequence
of compartmentalizing specific events, which may have revolved around or
included pets. A clinician may ascertain that the presence of the animal may
act as a catalyst for reliving past events.

Furthermore, the clinician may also recommend to an elderly patient that
they consider purchasing a pet. Research such as that by Ory and Goldberg
(1983), Friedman et al. (1980), Kidd and Feldman (1981), Jenkins (1986),
and Garrity et al. (1989), as well as the information noted in the chapter on
aging, all suggest the inherent value of seniors having pets. A client's sense of

value could be tremendously enhanced as a consequence of feeling needed once again. In addition, many individuals will thrive from the positive attention they will receive from their companion animal. In some cases, the human–animal relationship may become the necessary ingredient, which alleviates a perceived sense of loneliness and isolation. Findings from research by Hunt *et al.* (1992) suggested that unobtrusive animals evoked social approaches and conversations from unfamiliar adults and children. It is apparent that the presence of an animal may become a social lubricant for spontaneous discussions with passing strangers. Furthermore, the walking of pets would also possibly enhance an individual's physical health and stamina. Kidd and Fellowman (1981) point out that since dogs require considerable energy in care, their survival rate might be associated with the greater physical activity on behalf of their owners.

V. CONSIDERATION 4: THE EXTENSION OF LIVE ANIMALS—UTILIZING SYMBOLISM AND METAPHORS OF ANIMALS

Mallon (1994a) discovered that animals have been symbols of power and nurturance. The metaphors of flight with birds and strength of horses can be used therapeutically by therapists to help their clients uncover internal concerns. McMullen and Conway (1996) and Angus (1996) point out that metaphors are extensively utilized by clients in their conversations with therapists. Their research suggests that the incorporation of metaphor themes throughout the course of therapy may actually represent a productive indicator of the therapeutic relationship. Kopp (1995) pointed out that metaphors are similar to mirrors in their ability to reflect inner images within people. Metaphor therapy resides on the position that people in general structure their reality metaphorically. Both the client and the clinician can apply metaphors as a method of discovering and understanding client's concerns. The imagery generated from the metaphors can be used to help the client uncover how she or he is coping or feeling. For example, a client could be talking to a therapist about feeling overwhelmed about her daily life. When asked what she plans to do about it, the client responds quickly by stating " I really don't want to open that can of worms right now." The metaphor of the "opening of the can of worms" may represent the client's unwillingness to scramble and try to clean up the mess that she is in right now (rushing around trying to prevent the mess that would be made when the worms squirm out). She doesn't want to face the formidable task of putting her life in order. The metaphor helps to accentuate that position.

Angus and Lawrence (1993) point out that in positive therapeutic outcomes, both the client and the therapist are able to draw on a primary set of metaphoric scenarios in which the ongoing events within the client's life can be truly understood and integrated. For example, a mother of a child with a serious behavior disorder utilized the metaphor of feeling caged as an expression of the restrictions she felt as a consequence of her son's disruptive behavior. Throughout the course of her treatment, we embellished the metaphor with not only problem-solving strategies but also with stories, which edified similar scenarios. The stories were incorporated to lend some support or alternatives to strengthen the therapeutic discovery.

A poignant story of Eli Wiesel, the 1986 Nobel Peace Prize recipient, comes to mind when discussing the mother's metaphor of being caged. Wiesel was a keynote speaker in January 1987 at an annual dinner of 600 survivors of the Holocaust. At the reception, he shared his insightful perceptions on the struggles of humanity to provide equal access to all its citizens. The audience was moved by an anecdote, which captured his feelings. When Wiesel was a student, he once came across a man carrying a bird in a cage. The man was taking a birthday gift to a friend. "Does your friend like birds?" Wiesel asked. "I don't know," replied the man, "but come with me and see what happens." As the man was about to present the gift to his friend, the friend asked him to open the cage and set the bird free. The wish was granted and the man immediately beamed with internal joy. That was his gift. Wiesel went on to explain that there was no greater joy, no greater reward, or act of faith than setting another creature free or at least promoting its salvation or welfare. This was the woman's major goal. She wanted to feel free of her restraining emotional cage and more effective as a mother.

Throughout my years of utilizing birds therapeutically, I have also used birds metaphorically. None of my birds is ever caged, but with the clients we talk about cages as boundaries. Probably the most effective metaphors and stories about birds pertain to their grace in flight. Therapeutic discussions range from the majestic eagle soaring freely to the beauty in the flight of a flock of birds. Equally as beneficial are the sad metaphors that can be applied to a clipped (wings) or grounded bird.

Additional metaphors may include feeling chained or leashed, smothered, or being in a cocoon. Clients may develop therapeutic gains when the metaphors applied also suggest a resolution. For example, the entire process of metamorphosis is an excellent metaphor that illustrates a transformation. The caterpillar goes through the arduous task of spinning its cocoon that initiates the metamorphosis from its present state to the magnificent butterfly. For months the caterpillar leads its sheltered existence as its body is transformed. Therapeutically, the process of metamorphosis can be valuable in explaining two challenges. Numerous insightful dialogues can be developed on either of these two themes. Some clients will benefit from a discussion of the process of transformation, whereas others may gain some insight into themselves while discussing the sheltering of a being in a protective environment. Furthermore, the short-lived life of a butterfly can also be related to the price that some will take for the outcome.

A. STORYTELLING

De Shazer (1994) and Combs and Freedman (1990) imply that embellishing a client's thoughts through storytelling stems from the narrative psychotherapy tradition. The insights from this approach suggest that meaning is given to our lives and movement occurs in therapy when we have transformational stories that help put our lives in a new context. The narrative approach to therapy suggests that some clients appear to be stuck in their lives and the new stories generated help them gain a better understanding of their life conditions. Furthermore, the various stories may also lend credible approaches and provide insight for possible resolution. It seems that for some clients, the previous stories they rehearse in their heads to cope with their challenges aren't effective any longer or lose their meaning. Therapeutic storytelling that takes advantage of thematic concerns can integrate narratives that pertain directly to the client's concerns.

Experientially, since the author's practice incorporates animals, he also applies metaphors and uses stories with animals to help clarify certain positions to his clients. Freeman (1991) points out that stories are appropriate in different manners at all stages of life. A clinician's ability to care for and maintain effective communication between his or her patients can be augmented and enhanced by the stories we hear and share. The use of tales can be utilized as a source of support and expression as a child or an adult works through a specific concern. The story may reflect a specific dilemma that the individual is attempting to confront and provide some insight on methods for resolution. Fine (1999) suggests that stories help us see the world from the inside perspective of other people. Through stories, outcomes and consequences of decisions are illustrated. Stories of events concerning people or animals can be an inspiring approach to apply with our clients. The stories can therapeutically illustrate and uncover specific concerns and issues, and also help our clients unravel their concerns from other perspectives.

The incorporation of metaphors, storytelling, and puppetry is a definite extension to traditional usage of animals. Nevertheless, it seems logical for therapists with training in storytelling as well as AAT to combine both procedures. When a carefully selected story is matched with a child's or an adult's needs, the process can be tremendously cathartic. Stories that incorporate animals may be easier for the child client to identify with.

B. PUPPETRY

In addition to simple storytelling, the use of puppets to act out the stories seems to strengthen this process. For example, Haworth (1968) suggested that animal puppet characters appear to provide a basis for identification but, at the same time, allow a disguise so that a child has less of a need to be guarded. Linn *et al.* (1986) and Linn (1977) identify several attributes of puppetry that may contribute to its efficacy. The articles both advocate that the process of puppetry is immediately involving, active, and quite intimate. Puppets may serve as a catalyst for a child's interaction as she or he manipulates the puppet. Secondly, puppets can be used to talk directly with the child, and the child doesn't assume any other character. Therapists who have therapy animals within their practice could use puppets of the same breed as the animals. These puppets could act as "a talking extension" for the animal with which the child has bonded. The author has found this approach very valuable with his younger primary school-aged clients.

Irwin and Shapiro (1975) point out that although there is a wealth of qualitative writing with regard to the diagnostic and therapeutic value of puppetry with children, there is little research on how it can be effectively applied in clinical settings. He does suggest that puppetry, because of its stimulating qualities and manipulative material, readily stimulates children in revealing both private symbols and thoughts. The scenarios applied and the fantasies acted out may provide the clinician with a clearer picture of the child's inner world and she or he copes. The process may also be therapeutic in its release of expression and emotion, without the child having to take personal responsibility for what has been said. As stated earlier, the animated animals could be viewed as an extension of the live animals and could make discussing hard subjects an easier option.

The content of the puppet therapy sessions could be loosely focused on the recurring themes identified in previous therapy sessions. Themes for the puppetry should relate to the client's goals but could include scenarios that act out behavioral control, anger, fear, rejection, social skills, as well as abandonment. The therapist should be observant of the types of animals the child selects in the puppet sessions. Diagnostically, this can shed a great deal of insight; that is, does the child select timid or aggressive animals? Furthermore, the therapist can observe the child's interaction with the puppets and assess how the child is reacting. For example, if the puppet scenario were open ended, the child would have a choice of developing a fantasy that either demonstrated a nurturing, caring personality versus an aggressive style. The style in which the child interacts with the puppets may shed tremendous clinical insight. Finally, a clinician could use the puppetry sessions as an opportunity to help the child develop problem-solving alternatives for various challenges.

VI. CONSIDERATION 5: THERAPEUTIC ALTERNATIVES UTILIZING ANIMALS—EXPANDING OUR CLIENTS' TRADITIONAL THERAPY

A. WALKING THERAPY

Serendipitously, I discovered what I have called "walking therapy." Clinicians may find many pleasant routes where they can walk with their clients and find privacy. As discussed in Chapters 2, 8 and 16, biophilia is a fundamental human need to affiliate with other living organisms (Kahn, 1997). The Kahn research reveals that children have an abiding affiliation with nature. Combining the therapeutic usage of animals along with nature exploration could be a powerful approach with some clients. A natural outcome of having a therapy animal is to walk the animal. While walking, not only does one have the opportunity to engage in discussion, but also to experience the surroundings. At times, the serendipitous observations may enhance or stimulate the ongoing conversation between the clinician and the client. The writer has found walking to be a productive part of therapy in some cases. When working with clients whose concerns are nonthreatening, the walk may put the client at ease. While working with children, most do not appear to become distracted while on a walk, but rather engage in discussions freely. While taking a walk, many life examples can be illustrated. For example, if the dog needs to relieve him- or herself, the client must learn to be patient and understanding. Furthermore, the clinician can model responsible behavior and bring materials to clean up the mess.

The two types of animals that I utilize the most frequently on these sojourns are birds and dogs. While walking, children seem to display a great sense of pride in leading the animal. In fact, on numerous occasions I stop the walk and make a point out of how important the child appears leading the animal. This redirection emphasizes the importance of the special bond. They are periodically stopped by a pedestrian who may ask them a question about the animal and, in most cases, the interactions are quite pleasant.

Over the years, I have experimented with different variations of walking with the animals. Sometimes, it is just a casual stroll through the community, eventually returning to the office after a period of time. Sometimes our walks bring us to a schoolyard or a park, where we sit at a park bench or table and continue our therapeutic discussions. This alternative complements the therapeutic option by continuing the therapy and by taking advantage of the outdoors. Personal experience has found that some children begin to reveal their thoughts while our walk has started, but the discussion is enhanced when concentrated attention is given to the dialogue while sitting at the park. Sitting at the bench or around the table gives both the client and the clinician a chance to elaborate on the specific topics as well as to problem solve the concerns. Practically, therapists will find it valuable to have a pad of paper and a pen to document discussions and appropriate goals for follow-up. The natural environment, along with the animals, seems to be an added benefit in strengthening the rapport with the child. This approach need not be applied often and could be used on special occasions or with clients who appear to gain the most through it.

B. Clinical Applications

Over the years, walking therapy has been applied with many of my clients. A population that seems to have had the greatest gains is children with selective mutism and those with separation anxiety. By using the walk as an excuse to leave the office, children who experience separation anxiety begin to practice leaving their parents. The ventures beyond the office can be used as true experiences for separation. The client can be instructed to develop alternative cognitive structures that promote optimal thinking.

In the several cases of treating children with selective mutism, the walks with the dogs or birds are initially utilized as an opportunity to get the child to talk louder. While walking, there may be many competing sounds, which may impede our ability to hear each other. Requesting that the child speak louder is simply a reality of the environment. Amazingly, as the children become more comfortable with the animals, and begin to enjoy our walks, their comfort and confidence seem to increase.

A natural occurrence during the walk is the occasional interruption from another pedestrian walking by. The animal seems to stimulate greetings from passers-by. This outcome may eventually be a planned goal for the walk. Early in treatment, a clinician may select a route where there likely will not be any people on the road. However, as the client's confidence seems to build, a clinician may plan to take a route where interaction will be generated. A clinician may use some time prior to the walk to prepare the client with strategies in the event that a civilian may try to start up a conversation. The walk then could represent a true test to assess progress. The client then can return to the office and, with the clinician's support, evaluate the outcome.

Some clinicians may live in communities where there are established dog parks. It is now quite common in various cities to find parks where dogs interact. The clinician is advised to investigate and visit these parks (to learn about the protocol of entering the park as well as to observe the various dogs attending) prior to incorporating this procedure as part of his or her practice. This initial step could help avert unexpected pitfalls. The clinician could develop an action plan prior to therapeutically instituting this component. Vicariously, so much can be observed and learned in the dog park. The animals represent a small microcosm of the real world. There will be large and small dogs, hefty and lean dogs, playful and docile dogs, and finally aggressive and passive species. The observation of all of these animals can be applied to discuss the importance of understanding individual differences. Specific behaviors observed in any given dog may become valuable lessons for clarification with the clients. For example, when observing an aggressive encounter between two dogs, a generalization can be formulated by comparing this clash with human examples. A client may be more willing to initiate a personal exploration on the topic when it is initially disguised in discussing the observed battle. The framework of the discussion could eventually be modified to focus more directly on humans, and then more specifically on the client. One of the most teachable lessons from the interactions at the dog park pertains to the compatibility of most of the dogs. In most cases, all the dogs get along. This outcome easily translates to a major lesson underlying the visit: That if all the dogs can learn to get along, so can children who may presently have social challenges.

The most pertinent discussions pertain to the dogs that are overactive. Clinicians who primarily serve children will find the vicarious observations illuminating, especially when they are watching dogs that are hyperactive. The clinician can help the child observe how the impulsive and intrusive behavior of the dogs may agitate others. These observations may eventually be a catalyst for further personal discussion and problem solving.

The walks through the community or in the park may be useful for some clinicians. This option will not only help clients feel more relaxed, but the milieu may enhance their willingness to talk and reflect.

C. PETS ARE LOVING PROGRAM

The Pets Are Loving (PAL) project (Fine, 1992) was established to enhance the sense of responsibility and self-esteem of children with learning disabilities and an attention deficit (Fig. 1). The purpose of the program was to prepare and supervise children to become mentors with their animals for the elderly. The program was cosponsored by a local retirement community. Selected candidates for the program (the children) were screened with their animals to assess their compatibility and suitability. All animals (in this case primarily dogs and cats) were evaluated to assess their efficacy in being viable companion animals. Those animals that did not meet the requirements were not incorporated. Their owners were encouraged to continue in the program but were paired with one of the project's animals.

After careful consideration, a training protocol was established for all participating mentors. The ratio of supervision within this program was five mentors to two staff members. Table II identifies the highlights of the mentors' training:

The PAL program was designed to be 10 weeks long. At any given time, five children were enrolled with two group leaders supervising. The two staff leaders were selected due to their background in both working with children as well as understanding animal behavior. The compatibility of the children as well as their animals was also taken into consideration. Each child was given a manual and a binder (Fine, 1993) to help them collate their materials as well as a writing space for their reflective thoughts. Qualitative evaluations

FIGURE 1   The PAL project.

TABLE II   Major Components of the PAL Training Program

1. The elements of being a mentor:
   A. An overview of the PAL project. What should the mentors expect? (e.g., when the program would meet, where the program would be held, the behavioral expectations, an explanation of their role, and duration of each visit).
   B. An interactive discussion on how one interacts with the elderly. What should the mentor expect when interacting with the seniors? What should a typical visit be like?
   C. Skills of communication.
   D. The code of expected behavior: Guidelines for expected behaviors.

2. An explanation of aging:
   A. An interactive discussion on the myths and stereotypes of the elderly. How to positively understand and respect seniors (reducing stereotypical fears and anxieties).
   B. Methods of interacting with the seniors (e.g., learning how to talk quietly and move a little slower, how to help a senior with mobility).

3. Expected behaviors of the companion animals:
   A. Guidelines for how to introduce your pet to a senior.
   B. Guidelines for behavioral compliance.

4. Preparation for the session:
   A. Guidelines for grooming the animal as well as yourself.
   B. A discussion of reflective journal writing and weekly compulsory entries documenting the experience.
   C. Being an active member of discussion group (reflection discussions held after every session).

suggested the program was effective for both the mentors and the elderly. Most children found the experience valuable. The experience seemed to alter their stereotypes about the aging process. The mentors also appeared to have experienced an enhancement of their behavioral control in public settings. The small group discussions appeared helpful in aiding the children in reflecting on the benefits and purposes of the experience.

VII. CONSIDERATION 6: PRACTICAL SUGGESTIONS FOR CLINICIANS' USE OF ANIMALS

A. TRAINING AND LIABILITY

Therapists considering incorporating animals within their practice must seriously consider the factors of liability, training, and the safety and welfare of both the animal and the client. Hines and Fredrickson (1998) and the Delta Society's Pet Partners program strongly advocate that health care professionals must have training on techniques of AAT. Clinicians also need to be aware of best practice procedures ensuring quality, as well as safety, for all parties. Those clinicians living in North America should register through the Delta Society for a 1-day workshop or a home study course. In an effort to achieve the best possible qualitative results, Hines and Frederickson strongly suggest that health care staff receive training. They point out that without adequate training on how to apply AAT, therapists may inappropriately incorporate animals and get poor results. The Pet Partners program developed by the Delta Society includes in-service training on a variety of areas, including an awareness of health and skill aptitude of the animals, as well as strategies to incorporate the animals with the clients. The Pet Partners program should be considered a valuable introductory course. All of the training will aid practitioners in gaining appropriate guidelines for quality practice (Hines and Fredrickson, 1998).

After successfully completing the course (which also includes a written test and an aptitude of the animal) one can become registered by the Delta Society. All those who are registered will receive continued education through bimonthly newsletters as well as an opportunity to attend various seminars and workshops. A valuable benefit of being registered is the liability insurance program that is incorporated.

B. Office Management and Decor

Not a lot of attention needs to be given to the dimension of office management and decor, but it must be discussed. Having animals within one's therapeutic practice will have an impact on the office's decor. One must make sure that the work environment still maintains a clean and orderly presence. This is not only a provision for ambiance, but also for health requirements. Those who may want to use birds in their practice should make sure that the cages are cleaned daily and that any food on the floor is cleaned up as quickly as possible. Other animals in cages or using litter boxes should also be monitored for cleanliness. Finally, dogs and cats should be able to access a fresh bowl of clean water whenever they have the need.

C. Animal Welfare

It is evident that the safety of one's patient would be the highest priority. Nevertheless, the therapist must also consider the safety and welfare of the animals used in therapeutic practice. In Chapter 5, Hart, Frederickson, and Howie discuss numerous concerns that should be addressed when selecting animals. Their discussions also highlight the various symptoms that identify whether an animal is becoming stressed. In lieu of repeating a similar commentary, the writer will primarily identify cardinal rules that should be adhered to by all clinicians planning to incorporate animals. However, the clinician is strongly encouraged to review the content of Chapter 5, as well as manuals such as the Pet Partners program for further information.

To assist in identifying guidelines for animal safety and welfare, the author has elected to incorporate some of the guidelines that Hubrecht and Turner (1998) highlighted when evaluating an animal's welfare in all living environments. The conditions noted were originally established by the United Kingdom Farm Animal Welfare Council. All of the categories emphasized by Hubrecht and Turner seem very applicable when evaluating the welfare and the safety of animals utilized in therapy. All clinicians must make a conscious effort to persevere and safeguard their animals' quality of life. Hubrecht and Turner adamantly argue that if an animal is not properly cared for or, for that matter, if the animal appears stressed while working, the human–animal relationship will not develop effectively. Furthermore, the outcomes from the misuse of an animal will most likely jeopardize any therapeutic benefit or gain.

As clinicians our concerns must be with both the clients we serve and the animals that work with us. We must certify that the physical, mental, and emotional care of our animals is irreproachable. This tenet must be followed at all times! Our animals' rights (for quality of life and safety) as an active member of the therapeutic team must be addressed and protected.

All animals need to be safe from any abuse or danger from any client at all times. Furthermore, the therapist must be aware of the animal's need for some quiet time and relaxation during any given therapeutic day. The animal must be able to find a safe refuge within the office that he or she can go to if exhausted or stressed. Throughout the day, the animal needs to have a break from actual patient contact and be able to express normal animal behavior. The clients (especially children) need to learn to respect this decision and allow the animal a rest period. In cases of older animals, the animal may need the time to recoup energy. When the animal is ready to return to the therapeutic area, she or he should be allowed to do so. The therapist may need to inform some of the clients (especially children) that they have to respect the animal's need for privacy and rest. Some children may want to smother the animal with love and physical attention. When this occurs, instruct the client in the best manner to hug an animal without being confining.

Numerous other concerns may be thought of in relation to Hubrecht and Turner's (1998) third identified provision. Specifically, our therapy animals must be free from pain, injury, or disease. The therapist must practice good health procedures for all the animals being utilized. All animals should be up to date on all inoculations and visually appear in good health. If the animal seems ill, stressed, or exhausted, medical attention must be given.

Care needs to be given to the animal's physical appearance. The animal should be properly groomed and look presentable. This can set a good example for all clients. The animals should be under the supervision of a veterinarian who is aware of the therapeutic dimension of the animals' life. The animals should be seen on an intermittent basis to ensure that they are in good health. The veterinarian may also act as a medical adviser, guiding the clinician on any medical concerns that may pertain to the animals' welfare. There are so many variables that must be taken into consideration. For example, if an animal hasn't been well, how do you determine when he or she is ready to return to assisting with therapy?

Additionally, as an animal ages, his or her schedule for therapeutic involvement will have to be curtailed. This may cause some disruption and adjustment to a therapist's method of practice. You may find this alteration a difficult transition for you and your clients to accept. However, this transition may also be emotionally difficult for the animal as well. A dog that is used to an active schedule may initially appear demoralized at the adjustment to the amount of involvement. For example, Puppy (an aging golden retriever), who has worked clinically in my outpatient program for about 8 years, is now about 13 years of age. She tires quickly and naps throughout the day. When she gets tired, she wanders to my office and sleeps under my desk. When she is ready to resume her duties, she wanders back to the treatment rooms. Although she is aging, the response she receives from all her visitors is still strong and affectionate.

D. Precautions for the Clients

Therapists must make wise choices when selecting animals for their practice. Not all pets make good adjunct therapists. Many suggestions given in Chapter 4 should be reconsidered in this chapter. Additionally, certain species of animals may be more appropriate for children than adults. A clinician who is considering incorporating animals within his or her psychotherapy must strongly consider what animals will serve the best purpose. This may mean further studying and purchasing of animals that best suit the needs. Unfortunately, a good home pet may not be suitable for therapy.

Wishon (1989) points out that an underestimated problem that may occur in the animal–human bond are the pathogens that can be transmitted from animals to human beings. This process is now known as *zoonoses*. Wishon (1989) reports that most cats and dogs carry human pathogens, which along with those carried by other animals, have been associated with more than 150 zoonotic diseases. However, Hines and Fredrickson (1998) point out that the data regarding the transmission of zoonotic diseases in any AAT programs have been minimal. Practitioners are advised to work closely with veterinarians and other public health specialists to ensure the safety of the animals as well as the clients involved.

The clinician should be aware of any fears of animals or allergies before utilizing animals adjunctively with specific clients. This will ensure that the addition of the animal will not complicate the therapy.

E. ADDITIONAL CONCERNS

Numerous other concerns must be considered by a clinician prior to introducing animals into a practice. Although some of the concerns cannot be completely planned for, the therapist must be aware of them. For example, a clinician should consider how to handle explaining an illness of the animal to his or her clients and how to explain the death of a beloved animal. Both of these variables are realistic concerns that must be considered seriously. Over the years, concerned attached clients have had difficulties accepting these inevitable problems. Furthermore, the introduction of new animals into a practice will also need attention. A suggestion is to transition gradually all new animals, so that you are comfortable with the behavior. At times, young animals (specifically rambunctious young puppies) will need significant attention until they are capable of being more actively involved.

VIII. CONCLUSIONS

With thought and planning, animals can make a major contribution to a therapist's arsenal in treating clients. Animals can enhance the therapeutic environment by making the milieu more emotionally and physically accessible to clients. Some clinicians may still be skeptical of the therapeutic value of the human–animal bond, and may initially underestimate the clinical utility of animals as an adjunct to therapy. It is understood, as discussed at the outset of this chapter, that the lack of documentation and thorough investigation of outcome research leaves a large void on the efficacy of this approach. Interested clinicians may initially incorporate animals solely to develop rapport with clients. Nevertheless, after reading this chapter, a skilled and well-informed clinician should be able to recognize a multitude of benefits that animals can fulfill. A therapist may have to make some adjustments to his or her practicing philosophy to ease the incorporation of animals into one's professional repertoire.

Those clinicians who craft a place for animals in their therapeutic regime will not be disappointed with their efforts. Their therapeutic milieu and approach will be richer as a consequence. As George Eliot writes in Mr. Gilfil's Love Story, "Animals are such agreeable friends. They ask no questions and they pass no criticism." The unconditional love and devotion that an animal will bring to a therapeutic practice will be an asset that may never be thoroughly understood but should be appreciated and harnessed.

REFERENCES

Angus, L. (1996). An intensive analysis of metaphor themes in psychotherapy. In J. Mio & A. Katz (Eds.), *Metaphor: Implications of applications* (pp. 73–85). Mahwah, NJ: Lawrence Erlbaum Associates.

Angus, L., & Lawrence, H. (1993). An intensive analysis of metaphor themes in brief dynamic therapy. In J. Mio (Ed.), *Metaphor: Cognition & application.* Symposium of the first annual meeting of the American Psychology Association, Toronto, Canada.

Arkow, P. (1982). *Pet therapy: A study of the use of companion animals in selected therapies.* Colorado Springs, CO: Humane Society of Pikes Peak Region.

Barnard, R. (1954). Milieu therapy. *Menninger Quarterly,* 8(2), 21–24.

Baun, M., Bargstrom, N., & Langston, N. (1984). Physiological affects of human/companion animal bonding. *Nursing Research,* 50, 126–129.

Bazrod, S. (1993, June 6). Helping kids' confidence take off. *Los Angeles Times,* p. J-4.

Beck, A., & Katcher, A. H. (1983). *Between pets and people: The importance of animal companionship.* New York: G. P. Putnam's Sons.

Beck, A., & Katcher, A. (1984). A new look at pet-facilitated therapy. *Journal of the American Veterinary Medical Association,* 184, 414–421.

Beck, A., Hunter, K., & Seraydarian, L. (1986). Use of animals in the rehabilitation of psychiatric inpatients. *Psychological Reports,* 58, 63–66.

Blue, G. F. (1986, December). The value of pets in children's lives. *Childhood Education,* pp. 85–90.

Brody, J. (1988, April 7). Personal health: Increasingly, laughter as potential therapy for patients is being taken seriously. *The New York Times,* p. B8.

Bryant, B. (1990). The richness of the child–pet relationship: A consideration of both benefits and costs of pets to children. *Anthrozoos,* 3, 253–261.

Canfield, J., Hansen, M., Becker, M., & Kline, C. (1998). *Chicken Soup for the Pet Lover's Soul.* Deerfield Beach, FL: Health Communications, Inc.

Chernak-McElroy, S. (1996). *Animals as Teachers and Healers.* New York: Ballantine Books.

Combs, G., & Freedman, J. (1990). *Symbol story and ceremony using metaphor in individual and family therapy.* New York: Norton.

Corson, S. A., & Corson, E. O. (1980). Pet animals as nonverbal communication mediators in psychotherapy in institutional settings. In S. A. Corson & E. O. Corson (Eds.), *Ethology and nonverbal communication in mental health* (pp. 83–110). Oxford: Pergamon Press.

Cousins, N. (1989). *Head first: The biology of hope.* New York: E. P. Dutton.

Covert, A. M., Nelson, C., & Whiren, A. P. (1985). Pets, early adolescents and families. *Marriage and Family Review,* 8, 95–108.

De Shazer, S. (1994). *Words were originally magic.* New York: Norton.

Fine, A. (1992, July). *The flight to inner freedom: Utilizing domestic animals and exotic birds in the psychological treatment of children with unhealthy self-esteem.* Paper presented at the Sixth International Conference on Human–Animal Interactions, Montreal, Canada.

Fine, A. (1993). *Pets are loving project. A manual and resource guide for supporting children.* Pomona, CA: California State Polytechnic University Graphics.

Fine, A. (1999). *Fathers and sons; Bridging the generation.* South Bend, IN: Diamond Communications.

Freeman, M. (1991). Therapeutic use of storytelling for older children who are critically ill. *CHC,* 20(4), 208–213.

Friedmann, E., Katcher, A. H., Lynch, J. J., & Thomas, S. A. (1980). Animal companions and one-year survival of patients after discharge from a coronary care unit. *Public Health Reports,* 95, 301–312.

Friedmann, E., Katcher, A., Thomas, S., Lynch, J., & Messant, P. (1983). Social interaction and blood pressure: influence of animal companions. *Journal of Nervous and Mental Disease,* 171, 461–465.

Furman, W. (1989). The development of children's social networks. In D. Belle (Ed.), *Children's social networks and social supports* (pp. 151–172). New York: Wiley.

Garrity, T. F., Johnson, T. P., Marx, M. B., & Stallones, L. (1989). Pet ownership and attachment as supportive factors in the health of the elderly. *Anthrozoos,* 3, 35–44.

George, M. H. (1992). Child therapy and animals. In C. E. Schaefer (Ed.), *Innovative interventions in child and adolescent therapy* (pp. 401–418). New York: John Wiley & Sons.

Goldensohn, S., & Haan, E. (1974). Transference and countertransference in a third party payment system (HMO). *American Journal of Psychiatry,* 83, 255–260.

Gonski, Y. (1985). The therapeutic utilization of canines in a child welfare setting. *Child & Adolescent Social Work Journal,* 2(2), 93–105.

Gunby, P. (1978). Pets for cardiac therapeutics. *Journal of the American Medical Association,* 241, 438.

Hall, C., & Lindzey, G. (1978). *Theory of personality* (3rd ed.). New York: Wiley.

Hines, L., & Fredrickson, M. (1998). Perspective on animal-assisted activities and therapy. In B. C. Turner & C. C. Wilson (Eds.), *Companion animals in human health* (pp. 23–39). Thousand Oaks, CA: Sage Publications.

Hoelscher, K., & Garfat, T. (1993). Talking to the animals. *Journal of Child and Youth Care,* 8(2), 87–92.

Hubrecht, R., & Turner, D. C. (1998). Companion animal welfare in private and institutional settings. In B. C. Turner & C. C. Wilson (Eds.), *Companion animals in human health* (pp. 267–289). Thousand Oaks, CA: Sage Publications.

Hunt, S., Hart, L., & Gomulkiewicz, R. (1992). Role of small animals in social interactions between strangers. *The Journal of Social Psychology,* 132,#2, 245–256.

Irwin, E. C., & Shapiro, M. I. (1975). Puppetry as a diagnostic and therapeutic technique. *Transcultural Aspects of Psychiatric Art,* 4, 86–94.

Jenkins, J. L. (1986). Physiological effects of petting a companion animal. *Psychological Reports,* 58, 21–22.

Kahn, P. H. (1997). Developmental psychology and the biophilia hypothesis: Children's affiliation with nature. *Developmental Review,* 17, 1–61.

Kale, M. (1992). How some kids gain success, self-esteem with animals. *InterActions,* 10(2), 13–17.

Katcher, A., Friedmann, E., & Beck, A. (1983). Talking, looking, and blood pressure: Physiological consequences of interaction with the living environment. In A. Katcher and A. Beck (Eds.), *New perspective on our lives with companion animals* (pp. 351–359). Philadelphia: University of Pennsylvania Press.

Katcher, A., Segal, H., & Beck, A. (1984). Contemplation of an aquarium for the reduction of anxiety. In R. K. Anderson, B. L. Hart and L. Hart, *The pet connection: Its influence on our health and quality of life* (pp. 171–178). Minneapolis: University of Minnesota Press.

Kidd, A. H., & Kidd, R. M. (1980). Personality characteristics and preferences in pet ownership. *Psychological Reports*, 46, 939–934.

Kidd, A., & Feldman, B. (1981). Pet ownership and self-perceptions of older people. *Psychological Reports*, 48, 867–875.

Kidd, A. H., & Kidd, R. M. (1985). Children's attitudes toward their pets. *Psychological Reports*, 57, 15–31.

Kidd, A. H., & Kidd, R. M. (1990). High school students and their pets. *Psychological Reports*, 66, 1391–1394.

Kopp, R. R. (1995). *Metaphor therapy*. New York: Brunner/Mazel.

Langs, R. (1979). *The therapeutic environment*. New York: Jason Aronson.

Langs R. (1981). *Classics in psychoanalytic technique*. New York: Jason Aronson.

Levinson, B. M. (1965). Pet psychotherapy: Use of household pets in the treatment of behavior disorder in childhood. *Psychological Reports*, 17, 695–698.

Linn, S. (1977). Puppets and hospitalized children: Talking about feelings. *Journal of the Association for the Care of Children in Hospitals*, 5(4), 5–11.

Linn, S., Beardslee, W., & Farkas Patenaude, A. (1986). Puppet therapy with pediatric bone marrow transplant patients. *Journal of Pediatric Psychology*, 11,#1, 37–46.

Lockwood, R. (1983). The influence of animals on social perception. In A. K. Katcher and A. M. Beck (Eds). *New perspectives on our lives with companion animals*, (pp. 351–362). Philadelphia, PA: University of Pennsylvania Press.

Mallon, G. P. (1992). Utilization of animals as therapeutic adjuncts with children and youth: A review of the literature. *Child and Youth Care Forum*, 21(1), 53–67.

Mallon, G. P. (1994a). Cow as co-therapist: Utilization of farm animals as therapeutic aides with children in residential treatment. *Child and Adolescent Social Work Journal*, 11, 455–474.

Mallon, G. P. (1994b). Some of our best therapists are dogs. *Child & Youth Care Forum*, 23(2), 89–101.

McCulloch, M. J. (1984). Pets in therapeutic programs for the aged. In R. K. Anderson, B. L. Hart, & L. A. Hart (Eds.), *The pet connection* (pp. 387–398).

Minneapolis: Center to Study Human-Animal Relationships and Environment.

McMullen, L., & Conway, J. (1996). Conceptualizing the figurative expressions of psychotherapy clients. In J. Mio & A. Katz (Eds.), *Metaphor: Implications and applications* (pp. 59–73). Mahwah, NJ: Lawrence Erlbaum Associates.

Netting, F. E., Wilson, C., & New, J. C. (1987, January–February). The human–animal bond: Implications for practice. *National Association of Social Workers*, 60–64.

Ory, M. G., & Goldberg, E. L. (1983). Pet possession and life satisfaction in elderly women. In A. H. Katcher & A. M. Beck (Eds.), *New perspectives on our lives with companion animals*. Philadelphia, PA: University of Pennsylvania Press.

Paul, E. S., & Serpell, J. A. (1996). Obtaining a new dog: Effects on middle childhood children and their families. *Applied Animal Behavior Science*, 47, 17–29.

Peacock, C. (1986, August). *The role of the therapeutic pet in initial psychotherapy sessions with adolescents*. Paper presented to Delta Society International Conference, Boston.

Poresky, R., & Hendrix, C. (1990). Differential effects of pet presence and pet bonding in young children. *Psychological Reports*, 67, 51–54.

Rice, S., Brown L., & Caldwell H. (1973). Animals and psychotherapy: A survey. *Journal of Community Psychology*, 1, 323–326.

Ross, S. B. (1983 March). The therapeutic use of animals with the handicapped. *International Child Welfare Review*, 56, 26–39.

Serpell, J. A. (1981). Childhood pets and their influence on adults' attitudes. *Psychological Reports*, 49, 651–654.

Serpell, J. A. (1983, Spring). Pet psychotherapy. *People–Animal–Environment*, pp. 7–8.

Siegel, J. M. (1993). Companion animals: In sickness and in health. *Journal of Social Issues,* **49**, 157–167.

Sklar, H. (1988). The impact of the therapeutic environment. *Human Sciences Press,* **18**(2), 107–123.

Voelker, R. (1995). Puppy love can be therapeutic, too. *The Journal of the American Medical Association,* **274**, 1897–1899.

Von Kreisler, K. (1997). *The compassion of animals.* Rocklin, CA: Prima Publishing Co.

Wishon, P. M. (1989). Disease and injury from companion animals. *Early Child Development and Care,* **46**, 31–38.

CHAPTER 10

Animal-Assisted Therapy in Specialized Settings

BEN P. GRANGER
Department of Social Work, Colorado State University, Fort Collins, Colorado

LORI KOGAN
Department of Psychology, Colorado State University, Fort Collins, Colorado

We need another and wiser and perhaps more mystical concept of animals. For the animal shall not be measured by man. In a world older and more complete than ours they move finished, and complete, gifted with extensions of the senses we have lost or never attained, living by voices we shall never hear. They are not brethren, they are not underlings; they are other nations, caught with ourselves in the net of life and time, fellow prisoners of the splendor and travail of the earth.
—from *The Outermost House* by Henry Beston, 1928

I. INTRODUCTION

This chapter describes and discusses the variety of animal-assisted therapy (AAT) programs and approaches that are being used in a number of settings with different client populations. Illustrations include schools, nursing homes, hospitals, rehabilitation centers, and prisons. Reasons for the variation of AAT are presented.

Although the number of AAT programs throughout the country is increasing, the generic use of the term *AAT* is still nebulous. The Delta Society has worked at addressing this issue by creating a broad general definition (Delta Society, 1996). They define AAT as a goal-directed intervention that utilizes the human–animal bond as an integral part of the treatment process. The animals and handlers/owners are screened and trained to meet specific criteria and work with professionals who help set therapeutic goals, guide the AAT

Handbook on Animal-Assisted Therapy: Theoretical Foundations and Guidelines for Practice
Copyright © 2000 by Academic Press. All rights of reproduction in any form reserved.

sessions, and evaluate the progress (Gammonley *et al.*, 1996). Using this definition, animal-assisted therapy can be differentiated from animal-assisted activities (AAA) and other interactions with animals. To further clarify the difference between AAT and AAA, the Delta Society defines AAA as goal-directed activities that improve a client's quality of life through the use of the human–animal bond. These sessions are not, however, guided by a professional or necessarily evaluated (Gammonley *et al.*, 1996). Even when these general definitions are used as guides, there is no consensus on exactly what AAA and AAT entail. Although the multidisciplinary aspect of AAT adds many positive factors, it also creates additional challenges in creating general guidelines and definitions.

A contributing factor to the current status of AAT is the lack of research and references in the literature that detail AAT protocol or how it is actually conducted. AAT, as delivered in a number of specialized settings, can still be regarded as being in its early professional development, especially when compared to other therapies such as music, occupational, speech, hearing, and physical therapies. It is perhaps more akin to an adjunctive therapeutic intervention that is used by a number of professionals (i.e., psychiatrists, psychologists, social workers), as well as other therapists and trained volunteers.

Although a number of critical questions regarding the validity of AAT remain, support from those who have experienced the positive effects of AAT is increasing. It is both a challenging and encouraging time for increasing the understanding and appreciation of the human–animal bond, the therapeutic use of companion animals, and more specifically AAT.

II. VARIATION OF AAT IN SPECIALIZED SETTINGS

There are numerous reasons for the variation in AAT, including the species, breed, and training level of the animals involved in AAT programs; the level of training and characteristics of the human partner and/or professional; the nature and purpose of the setting and client population; and knowledge level of AAT by individual programs or facilities. Each of these reasons is discussed next.

A. VARIETY OF ANIMALS

1. Dogs

These companion animals are the most common species used in AAT. The type of dog selected depends on its temperament, level of training, and setting in which it will work. Small and large dogs work well with different populations, as do both pure and mixed breeds. An important aspect of choosing a dog for AAT is careful screening and training. Screening should involve three main components: veterinary screening, temperament testing, and skills or training testing. Veterinary screening involves a complete physical examination, necessary vaccinations, and a check for internal and external parasites. Usually this is performed by the owner's veterinarian. Documentation of a clean bill of health should be presented before beginning any program. Temperament testing is designed to indicate how a dog will react in new situations or during startling events. Although some dogs are simply not suited for therapy work, other dogs will respond positively with practice and exposure to situations in which they first appear nervous or stressed. Temperament testing should include several situations that have the potential to be stressful or novel to a dog. Examples include exuberant or clumsy petting, restraining hugs, staggering people, angry yelling, being bumped from behind, petting from several people at one time, and being held by or left alone with a stranger. Other factors that should be tested include overall sociability and reactions to various new situations (Burch, 1996).

The skills test used by many AAT organizations is the American Kennel Club's Canine Good Citizen (CGC) test. Most aspects of the test involve learned behaviors and not actual personality traits. The 10 parts included in the CGC test include accepting the approach of a friendly stranger, allowing a stranger to pet them, allowing a stranger to groom and examine them, walking on a loose leash, walking through a crowd of people, sitting on command as well as staying in place, coming when called, behaving politely when exposed to other dogs, not panicking when faced with distractions, and maintaining training skills when handled by someone other than their owner. All three components of testing are equally important and mandatory to adequately screen and certify a dog for AAT. Furthermore, periodic checks in each area should be done to monitor any changes that might occur over time.

2. Cats

Felines work especially well with people that are afraid of or are allergic to dogs and can also become certified as animal partners. The ideal cat for this purpose is one that enjoys being petted and seeks out human attention. Any cat must be able to be petted in the numerous ways that may arise during an AAT session. They must also accept being touched all over their body and being held upside down. Cats are held by several strangers during certification testing, both with the owner present and absent. The animal must also get along with other cats and dogs and be able to accept new environments. Additionally, they must not get stressed while being transported, nor get scared of loud noises or unexpected behaviors. AAT with cats can provide clients an opportunity to learn more about breeds of cats and how to care for them. In addition, they can help improve gross and fine-motor skills through playing with toys, as well as brushing, petting, and feeding activities. Most cats, however, due to their level of trainability, are used for AAA rather than AAT.

3. Rabbits

These furry creatures are sometimes used in AAT when a dog or cat may not be appropriate, and many can become certified animal partners after going through a careful screening process. To pass certification testing, a rabbit must be easily transported and enjoy different types of handling. The evaluation includes particular items such as easily being passed from the owner to strangers, being placed on a table (in a carrier) for 30 seconds, and having a stranger hold the animal for 2 minutes. The rabbit must also allow basic petting, clumsy petting, and petting by numerous people at once. It must also tolerate being touched on all parts of the body, including the mouth, teeth, ears, and paws. Rabbits must be tolerant of individuals with disabilities and the equipment they might utilize including walkers, crutches, and wheelchairs. They must also be able to handle loud noises, being in crowds, and people yelling. Rabbits that pass these requirements can be used with a variety of populations and have been found to be a favorite among small children (Mallon, 1994). They provide variation to the usual AAT animals and can be used to work on fine-motor skills through holding and petting. Responsibility can be taught through learning to care for a small vulnerable animal.

4. Birds

A variety of birds have been used in wide-ranging settings to alleviate depression and provide an impetus for social interaction (Mugford & M'Comisky, 1975; Holcomb et al., 1997). The most common birds used are parakeets, finches, and canaries (Bernard, 1995). Birds in long-term care facilities can be used to enhance self-esteem and a sense of responsibility by encouraging residents to help in the daily care and maintenance tasks. Larger birds can be used outside of cages within a safe setting. When selecting a large bird, it is important to obtain one that was bred in the United States (identified by a closed band on their foot) as opposed to one that was captured from wild populations. Although some birds are used in AAT, most birds are used as visual stimulation similar to fish tanks. They can, however, serve in an AAT capacity with the proper supervision, goals, and implementation.

5. Horses

AAT with horses offers many unique aspects that are not available with smaller animals. The use of horses within a therapeutic setting falls under four broad categories: hippotherapy, riding therapy, riding for rehabilitation, and vaulting (Biery, 1985). Hippotherapy literally means "therapy with the help of a horse." It refers to a passive type of riding, in which the horse moves the rider. The gait of a horse has been shown to closely resemble that of the human walk, so by sitting on a walking horse, a rider's body can go through the physical motions of walking without having any weight placed on the legs (Engel, 1992). Hippotherapy has been used successfully with one-sided paralysis and other problems with asymmetry (Biery, 1985). It has also shown positive results for people with cerebral palsy: a relaxation of spastic and rigid muscles; increased coordination, balance, and posture; and reinforcement of normal movement patterns (McCowan, 1984).

Although similar to hippotherapy, which is classified as a passive therapy, riding therapy can be either passive or active. Therefore, riding therapy can include times when the rider allows the horse to lead, as well as times when the rider takes an active role in the exercises. Benefits of riding therapy are many, including increased flexibility, walking balance, gross motor coordination, and cardiorespiratory function (Biery, 1985). When the rider takes active control over the horse, he or she is then said to be riding for rehabilitation. Areas that can be targeted include coordination and psychological or social problems. In addition, riders work on sequential tasks by practicing the activities that must take place prior to riding, thereby enhancing long-term memory skills. Learning to control one's behavior is naturally taught during riding for rehabilitation as the rider learns what behaviors result in positive responses from the horse.

Vaulting, defined as "gymnastic exercises on horseback," is one variation of riding therapy. It provides a unique opportunity for the development of communication and trust between the rider and the horse. Only when they cooperate with each other will vaulting activities be performed correctly. Most riding programs combine different types of horse therapy, thereby offering a wide range of benefits including improved balance and arm and leg coordination; and increased muscle strength, mobility, self-esteem, attention span, and self-control (Biery, 1985; Brock, 1988; McCowan, 1984; Fox et al., 1984).

Because the goals for each type of riding therapy differ, the selection of the proper horse or each activity is paramount. Because hippotherapy is designed to improve a rider's posture, balance, mobility, and function (Sayler, 1992), the movements of the horse are extremely important. The horse must move with a symmetrical, balanced, rhythmic gait. As with all types of AAT, the personality of the horse is a key component to successful therapy. Care should be taken to select a therapy horse who is patient and gentle to help ensure positive experiences for all involved.

6. Farm Animals

Other large animals that have been used as therapeutic interventions in addition to horses include cattle, poultry, and pigs. These animals have been used with a variety of different populations including people with mental impairment and emotional problems (Diesch, 1984). Positive results of interactions with farm animals include improved communication, an increased feeling of worth, and a sense of being needed. Several therapeutic communities have been built around the idea of AAT with farm animals. Bittersweet Farms is one example of a successful program that serves autistic adults. Together with horticulture, carpentry, and special projects, animal care is an important therapeutic component in the program (Kay, 1990). Farm animals are also used at Green Chimneys residential treatment center. This center serves children with behavioral, emotional, and academic problems. Children at Green Chimneys report that they feel happy when they visit the farm, and choose to visit when they want to feel better. The farm is seen by the children as a place to go when they are upset or angry. The animals also allow children to explore nurturing behaviors and provide an opportunity for confidential communication that can make discussing difficult items easier (Mallon, 1994).

Through working with farm animals, numerous skills can be taught or enhanced. Examples of cognitive skills include species care and information, measuring abilities practiced when feeding, and time management used for feeding and exercising schedules. There are many possibilities for the enhancement of gross and fine-motor skills including sweeping, feeding, shoveling, brushing, and milking. While caring for the animals, clients work on responsibility, the ability to be consistent and punctual, and following a set schedule.

7. Dolphins

Although many people do not get the opportunity to work with dolphins, these animals can provide a unique AAT experience. Dolphins in therapy are seen as useful for two primary reasons: their intelligence level and the stress-reducing capabilities of water. Dolphins seem to be closer to humans in their multimodal learning style and cognitive abilities than most other animals (Nathanson, 1989). It is therefore probable that dolphins have a greater capacity to sustain interest in a task, and provide a powerful reinforcement for therapeutic interventions (Nathanson & de Faria, 1993). Because water has been shown to a useful tool for many areas (i.e., increasing motor skills, providing greater flexibility in movement, and alleviating anxiety and depression), dolphin AAT provides a fresh alternative to traditional therapies and has been shown to increase motivation, attention span, gross and fine-motor skills, and speech and language (Nathanson, *et al.*, 1997). Short-term dolphin-assisted therapy can be used to help children with severe disabilities move up to a new level of functioning in a short period of time. These improvements are favorably comparable to conventional speech or physical therapy alone, with the addition of dolphin-assisted therapy creating more cost-efficient and expedient results (Nathanson, 1998). Because dolphin-assisted therapy can help reduce the amount of time needed in multiple conventional long-term therapies and special resources within the school system, the cost of this type of therapy is well worth the initial investment (Nathanson *et al.*, 1997).

The characteristics, level of training, and care of any type of animal obviously impact the delivery and form of AAT. The important point made is that the very nature of AAT, with the use of a variety of species and breeds, their temperaments, and personalities, complicates the understanding of this form of therapeutic intervention. To some extent, this explains the variation as well as the difficulty in evaluating the effectiveness of AAT with various client populations.

B. LEVEL OF TRAINING AND CHARACTERISTICS OF THE HUMAN PARTNER AND/OR PROFESSIONAL

Of equal importance are the humans engaged in AAT; the persons who are frequently regarded as "on the other end of the leash." These persons can include the owner/handler or trained volunteer, professional, staff member of an agency, or a combination of these persons in a team arrangement. The knowledge and skill base, the training and understanding level in AAT, and the personal characteristics of these persons all present important factors that bring about variation.

1. Volunteers

Persons volunteering from varying "walks of life" with different levels of education, training, and work experience tend to have one chief characteristic in common. They are all believers in the importance of the human–animal bond and the therapeutic use of companion animals. Whereas each volunteer is unique, which challenges training requirements, in many ways the human–animal bond factor provides a central point of departure for such aspects as training, suitability for volunteering, maintaining commitment, and the level of enjoyment/satisfaction of participating in AAT in partnership with a companion animal.

At the same time, AAT requires professional guidance and direction. When volunteers are not human service professionals (i.e., social workers, psychologists, psychiatrists, teachers, therapists) ongoing training and supervisory requirements are essential for effective AAT services. Delta Society's Pet Partners program is one example of addressing this issue; however, the extensiveness and ongoing continuity of the training is not in sufficient depth for delivering AAT. The Delta Society and others are considering additional approaches, such as developing certificate-type programs, that may further help in preparing and supervising persons, whether volunteers or professionals.

2. Professionals

Similarly, although the commitment to the human–animal bond exists, for the most part professionals have not had formal preparation for conducting AAT. Most disciplines do not have content in this area in their curriculum. While professionals are competent in their chosen field of practice, there is the need for both training and supervision in AAT. To date this issue has not been adequately addressed.

3. Staff Members

Whether a volunteer or professional, staff members in agencies or programs where there is the support for and use of animals in therapeutic situations frequently seek opportunities to participate in AAT. Although this should be encouraged, there is the issue of how to provide in-service training and credentialing to ensure quality and evaluation of AAT intervention outcomes.

Whether the animal is a horse, cat, or dog, and regardless of what role the human plays, she or he must be qualified and trained to work with that animal. This involves in-depth training for both the human and animal. When working as an AAT team, the human must feel comfortable and confident with the animal partner. In addition, the human partner should feel confident working with the population or client group receiving the therapy. Training should be provided in order to ensure the human partner is qualified to work with the client.

C. NATURE AND PURPOSE OF THE SETTING AND CLIENT POPULATION

There are numerous specialized settings with a variety of populations that can benefit from AAT. These include the elderly in long-term care facilities, homebound elderly, patients with terminal illnesses, patients in hospitals, children in various settings, and inmates in prisons and correctional facilities.

1. Long-Term Care Facilities

The use of AAT with the elderly has expanded rapidly in long-term care facilities, adult day care centers, and private homes. For those that reside in long-term care facilities, therapies that enhance social, psychological, and physical well-being are necessary to combat the negative effects that often accompany relocating to a facility. AAT offers the opportunity for uncritical, nonjudgmental social interaction as well as providing an avenue for sensory stimulation (Struckus, 1991). Weekly AAT sessions help some nursing home residents keep track of the days of the week because they have something to look forward to. By leaving a picture of the animal, residents can have a visual cue to help remind them during the week of their sessions. Many residents enjoy having a picture of "their" animal and like to show it to visitors and other residents.

Studies investigating the effects of AAT with institutionalized elderly have shown positive results in increased attention, improved psychological well-being, appropriate interpersonal interaction and social awareness, an increase in life satisfaction, socialization, communication, concentration, and a decrease in depression (Andrysco, 1982; Francis et al., 1985; McQuillen, 1985; Rowell, 1990; Fick, 1993; Lapp, 1991; Kongable et al., 1989; Haughie et al., 1992).

Characteristics of animals that appear useful in promoting positive changes with the elderly include their ability to stimulate a number of senses, positive responses to clients, nonjudgmental nature, encouraging caregiving behaviors, and their need for exercise and activity (Struckus, 1991). Positive results of AAT have also been found for homebound elderly who have shown a decrease in blood pressure and pulse rate after exposure to AAT sessions (Harris et al., 1993).

2. People with Terminal Illnesses

Patients with terminal illnesses can also benefit from AAT. People with a terminal illness work through the five stages described by Kubler-Ross (denial, anger, bargaining, depression, and acceptance) most smoothly when others around them are seen as supportive and are able to remain emotionally and physically close (Kubler-Ross, 1969). Because death makes many people uncomfortable, even caretakers can unconsciously give signals that increase patients' anxiety and fear levels. Animals, with their unconditional acceptance, have been found to be useful in helping people work through their feelings. Additionally, Muschel (1984) found that patients with terminal cancer felt more in control when they were able to care for an animal. When patients have another living creature to care for, they are able to shift some of the focus from their own illness. They are able to hold and caress an animal, often in ways they would like to be held and touched. AAT provides one avenue of tactile stimulation that is often lacking in the terminally ill. Especially when someone has a misunderstood illness or one that brings up fear in others, the unconditional acceptance of the animal seems to help people cope. These animals can lessen patients' fears, despair, loneliness, stress levels, and isolation for people with numerous types of terminal illnesses including AIDS (Haladay, 1989).

3. Hospitals

Medical centers offer other specialized settings in which the presence of AAT is growing with a wide variety of patients showing benefits. Difficulties that have shown improvement include impaired communication, ineffective coping, impaired physical mobility, self-concept problems, sensoriperceptual alteration, impaired social interactions, and altered thought processes (Barba, 1995). Other hospitals report that AAT sessions have helped patients with verbal abilities, memory skills, and motor skills. Stress reduction is often a benefit seen in hospital settings since animals provide a distraction for the patients. This is especially beneficial for patients with pain, anxiety, hyperactivity, or high blood pressure (Arkow, 1982; Bernard, 1995). Because animals make people appear less sick to others (Rossbach & Wilson, 1992), animals can also improve social interactions with visitors. By giving families and friends something else to focus on, communication can become less strained and forced. AAT is also useful for patients that are self-conscious.

Because animals are nonjudgmental, a person's self confidence and self-esteem can improve with animal contact. People are often self-conscious about physical differences during (or after) an illness or accident. These differences could range from speech problems to a lack of muscle coordination or movement. Patients can quickly sense when their changes make other people uncomfortable. Animals provide a wonderful resource for much needed unconditional acceptance. Animals do not care if someone slurs words or drools. They allow people to relax and just enjoy the direct physical contact of holding and petting a living creature. Cole and Gawlinski (1995) found that patients described their feelings after AAT sessions as happier, calmer, and less lonely. Furthermore, almost half of the patients in one survey indicated that the opportunity to participate in AAT sessions would help determine their choice of hospitals (Voelker, 1995). When dealing with physically weak or sick individuals, appropriate screening and precautions need to be followed carefully to guard against zoonoses (diseases that can be transmitted from animals to humans) and accidents. Although the risks of zoonoses are always present, they tend to be overestimated, and are actually low even for immunosuppressed patients with cancer or HIV (Barba, 1995).

4. Schools

AAT in school settings, working with emotionally disturbed, is another developing area. Levinson (1964) was one of the first pioneers to report the benefits of AAT for children with various disabilities including those who are nonverbal, inhibited, autistic, withdrawn, or schizophrenic. Although one of the first to actually document his use of animals, Levinson found that 33% of practitioners surveyed utilized animals at some point in their practice (Beck & Katcher, 1984). The use of AAT has shown success with autistic children particularly in increasing self-esteem, socialization, and development of language skills (Law & Scott, 1995). Additionally, problem-solving skills can be improved through implementing planning and strategy techniques when working with the animal. AAT has also shown success with children who have emotional or physical problems, as well as children who have been abused or neglected. One way in which this is accomplished is to introduce the animal as a topic of conversation and mutual interest point. Whereas many children are reluctant to talk about what is going on at home, for instance, they are usually open to talking about how an animal looks or feels. Some AAT sessions begin with the human partner talking to the animal instead of directly to the child. In this way, the child does not feel threatened and oftentimes will join in the conversation.

AAT also allows children an outlet for the tender, loving part of themselves and helps them control and regulate their own behavior while developing empathy toward other living creatures (Ross, 1992; Gonski, 1985). Through successes with the animal, many children are able to increase their self-esteem and thereby have more confidence when approaching new tasks.

5. Institutional Settings

AAT is used with inpatient psychiatric patients to help with assessment and diagnosis as well as create social interaction for isolated patients (Holcomb & Meacham, 1989). Furthermore, increased self-esteem and sense of dignity for these patients can be facilitated through AAT (Hundley, 1991). The AAT program at Lima State Hospital for the Criminally Insane provides an excellent example. During a yearlong study, patients on wards with animals present needed only half the medication of other wards. Furthermore, they demonstrated reduced violence and made significantly fewer suicide attempts than patients on wards with no animals present (Lee, 1984). After the steady success of the initial program, Lima has since branched out to include caring for disadvantaged animals. This element of the program has shown success in inducing patients' empathy toward other living creatures. Since 1996, the facility has also begun training puppies for the Pilot Dog program, which provides free guide dogs for people who are blind. This provides patients the opportunity to learn a marketable skill and develop pride in their accomplishments.

Several other institutions have implemented dog training programs that benefit everyone involved. The Pets as Therapy program, at Purdy Treatment Center for Women, trains dogs for people with various disabilities. Women in the program feel they are doing something of value and show a decrease in depression levels. Similar programs exist at Washington State Correctional Center for Women and Gainesville Work Camp (Bustad, 1996).

The Wild Mustang program, although terminated in 1992, demonstrated success in a multitude of areas. This program initially involved taming and training wild horses that were in danger of dying from starvation or thirst. The horse problem began when the New Mexico Bureau of Land Management (NMBLM) began removing wild horses from public rangelands because of overcrowding. Since the Wild and Free-Roaming Horse and Burro Act of 1971 required humane care and treatment for these horses, the NMBLM created a partnership with the New Mexico Department of Corrections in which inmates would halter break the mustangs and prepare them for sale to the general public (NMBLM, 1989). Handling the horses allowed inmates the opportunity to do meaningful work with tangible rewards. This program was a win–win situation. The horses were handled humanely, the NMBLM was able to improve its public image, and the correctional facility was able to offer work to its inmates that did not threaten any private industry. The Wild Mustang program helped the inmates in several ways. The opportunity to work with the wild mustangs allowed the inmates to assume a nurturing role, practice autonomy, and gain a sense of responsibility. Inmates that participated in the program had fewer disciplinary reports (when substance abuse issues were addressed) and an increased ability to handle stress. The recidivism rate for inmates in the program was significantly lower than the rate for New Mexico State correctional facilities (Cushing & Williams, 1995).

These different populations and their use of AAT demonstrate the wide range in which AAT is appropriate and useful. Each setting has its own unique needs and residents, therefore, each type of AAT will focus on different goals and strategies. The wide arena in which AAT can be beneficial provides unending opportunities to see AAT at work. It also, however, makes it that much more of a challenge to define exact criteria and definitions.

D. PROGRAM LEVEL OF UNDERSTANDING OF AAT

Related to the preceding discussion is the variation in AAT that is based on the level of understanding that the agency or program has relative to this intervention. Efforts at providing in-service training for staff in facilities have proven to be useful. However, factors such as staff turnover and the difficulty of including all staff members in training opportunities (including the director or administrative staff) challenge agencies' ability to understanding what AAT is and how it can be an important part of their therapeutic program.

To a large extent AAT is viewed as, and is, a volunteer activity. While volunteers are important to any social service and healthy organization, frequently this impacts how and to what extent AAT is incorporated into the professional therapeutic services provided by an agency. For example, frequently the volunteer coordinator is assigned as the agency contact person for AAT. The more traditional professional staff members (i.e., social workers, psychologists, special education teachers, other therapists) are not. When an agency or program has a more coherent understanding of AAT as an effective therapeutic intervention, then there is a greater level of cooperation, communication, and appreciation.

Payment or fees for AAT services often depend on whether agencies acknowledge AAT as an effective intervention and part of the treatment plan. Currently, the majority of AAT is not third-party reimbursable. Like many other worthwhile programs, many AAT programs suffer from insufficient funding with too much time and energy used to locate the funds necessary to operate. Each agency's perception of AAT impacts education and training issues, as well as the variety/level of AAT being conducted. There is the broad conception that AAT is more of a supportive activity that fits with other volunteer services. This does not necessarily reflect on the support for AAT from programs, but it does indicate the present status and level of understanding of this intervention.

III. DESCRIPTION OF THE STRUCTURES AND APPROACHES OF AAT

Other considerations relative to AAT are the structures through which AAT programs are provided and the particular approach(s) used. Structures can include the following: a university affiliated program, an autonomous nonprofit organization, an agency-based program, an individual volunteer, and the independent practitioner. AAT approaches include the human–animal team, volunteer and companion animal, professional and companion animal, and staff member and companion animal. A brief description of these structures and approaches is presented. It is important to recognize that the context in which AAT is delivered impacts quality and accountability issues.

A. UNIVERSITY-AFFILIATED PROGRAM

Some universities have been successful in developing human–animal bond interdisciplinary centers where AAT programs are developed and delivered, along with other research, training, and service components. A university-affiliated program is a well-established structure for responding to unique practice areas. However, there are only a few such centers around the country that focus on the human–animal bond (i.e., Colorado State University, University of Tennessee, Purdue University, University of California–Davis). There are significant merits to this approach, including having available the interdisciplinary resources of a university. The program at Colorado State University is described later in this chapter as illustrative.

B. NONPROFIT ORGANIZATIONS

AAT programs are more frequently related to organizations that obtain non-profit status and have varying degrees of organizational structure, including a board of directors, paid and volunteer staff, and a budget. An advantage of this approach is that AAT is conducted under an auspice that provides guidance and some level of ongoing supervision and interaction. These organizations usually have the capacity to compete for foundation funding, and maintain volunteer commitment through training, and ongoing team-building experiences.

C. AGENCY-BASED PROGRAMS

Some direct service organizations, such as long-term care facilities, develop their own AAT programs through staff who have some expertise in the human–animal bond field. Frequently it is the activities coordinator, or another professional staff member, who initiates an AAT program as part of her or his responsibilities or from an understanding of the significance of AAT with clients.

D. INDIVIDUAL VOLUNTEER AND INDEPENDENT PRACTITIONER

Another delivery mode of AAT is a person who wants to use the human–animal bond experience as a vital part of her or his volunteer or professional responsibilities. The level and quality of AAT can vary considerably based on such factors as the degree of training of the animal and human partner and ongoing supervision. Issues can also arise relating to liability and quality control.

Related to the structure through which AAT is provided are the approaches in AAT that are presently being used. These include the human–animal team, professional with companion animal, staff member with companion animal, and volunteer with companion animal.

E. HUMAN–ANIMAL INTERVENTION TEAM

When using this modality, there is a conscious effort to create a team consisting of the animal, owner/handler, and agency professional that can work together with a specific client or resident. The intent is to have an ongoing connection between the expertise or contributions of all team members as AAT is conducted in a facility. There is significant merit to this approach based on treatment goals and objectives being developed and carried out by team members who have specialized knowledge and skill essential for effective intervention. In a school setting, for example, the special education teacher can be the designated professional working with the companion animal and owner in each AAT session. In this situation, the teacher is the expert on the social, psychological, and learning dynamics of the child, and the owner/handler is the expert on how the human–animal team can interact with the child. With this approach there is greater opportunity to specify treatment objectives, to more effectively carry these out, and to evaluate progress—all vital components of AAT.

F. PROFESSIONAL WITH COMPANION ANIMAL

This approach is used most frequently in private practice, where the therapist and her or his companion work together. The therapist determines when and under what conditions the animal could facilitate treatment. Under these circumstances, AAT can vary considerably based on knowledge and skill of the therapist and training/temperament of the animal. It is less likely to be reported in the literature or systematically evaluated. It is more of an adjunctive intervention that is determined by the therapist as potentially beneficial to the client.

G. STAFF MEMBER WITH COMPANION ANIMAL

This approach is similar to professional with companion animal, except that AAT is conducted within the auspices of the specified agency of the staff member. Based on the interest and expertise of the staff member she or he is either directly involved in AAT or is responsible for developing an AAT program within the agency. With interest and commitment generated from the agency, frequently the human–animal intervention team approach is developed.

H. VOLUNTEER WITH COMPANION ANIMAL

This approach is the most prominent within AAT with volunteers showing a wide range of expertise. They, for example, can be professionals who want to engage in the therapeutic use of companion animals, or can be so-called "laypersons" who have acquired a knowledge and skill base (along with their companion animals) and want to engage in AAT. These persons seek out agencies where they can be part of AAT, or join a program where they and their companion animal can become a human–animal team.

IV. HUMAN–ANIMAL INTERVENTION TEAM: AN EXAMPLE OF ONE AAT APPROACH

The human–animal intervention (HAI) team is presented as illustrative of one approach that has developed a specific protocol and has had its potential effectiveness in AAT protocol evaluated (Granger et al., 1998). The intervention team consists of a trained owner/volunteer; her or his medically, behaviorally screened, and trained companion animal (usually a dog); and a designated professional staff member from an approved school (or social service/health agency). This intervention team works within the supervised structure and policies/procedures of the human–animal bond organization to which the team is responsible, as well as the school or social welfare/health agency in which the therapy is performed.

In this particular organizational arrangement the human–animal bond program is university centered at Colorado State University. HABIC (Human–Animal Bond in Colorado) is an interdisciplinary program between the College of Applied Human Sciences (specifically the Department of Social Work, in cooperation with the Department of Occupational Therapy, and the School of Education) and the College of Veterinary Medicine and Biomedical Sciences. HABIC is a nonprofit entity that receives all funding through external grants and contracts, foundation support, program fees, and individual donors and memberships. In addition to direct service, HABIC provides training and internship opportunities for students and also research/evaluation of AAT.

The protocol for the HAI team is described in Fig. 1. This figure focuses on school settings; however, the steps in the protocol are essentially the same for other settings (i.e., residential treatment, long-term care, rehabilitation, health, and corrections). This protocol is focused on providing a consistent pattern of operation that can be evaluated in determining validity, reliability, and the merits for replication. From a practice perspective the purposes of this protocol include initial and ongoing training/supervision of the human–animal team(s), careful planning and carrying out of treatment objectives (including evaluation of outcomes) through a designated team, close and continuous relationships with the facility, and an effective administrative structure. Related to the protocol is the selection of goals and strategies that are determined by the intervention team. An example of this is provided in Table I.

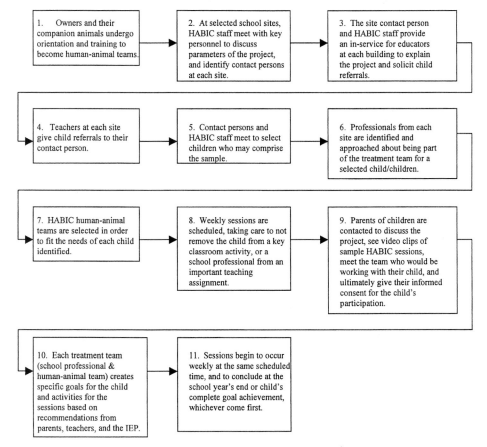

FIGURE 1   Human intervention team protocol.

TABLE I   Goals and Selected Strategies

Goal Setting

Goals to be addressed for each participant were selected by the students' special education teacher. Once goals were identified, specific strategies used by human–animal teams to work on each goal were implemented. Goals and selected strategies for each participant were as follows:

Participant A

Identified goal area	Selected session strategies
Decrease negative comments. Increase use of praise and positive comments.	a. Work with the human–animal team to learn appropriate praising techniques. b. Process session events to confront this issue directly and transfer it to other situations.
Decrease self-talk relating to the fantasy world.	a. Work with the human–animal team to emphasize the importance of staying focused on the "here and now" with the animal when giving commands. b. Process session events to confront this issue directly and transfer to other situations.
Decrease distractibility.	a. Work with the human–animal team to help maintain concentration on the work with the animal when giving commands. b. Process session events to confront this issue directly and transfer to other situations.
Improve relationships with peers. Improve relationship with the other participant.	a. Work with the human–animal team to use the participant's relationship with the animal as a metaphor for human relationships. b. Create and deliver a presentation with the other participant about HABIC experiences.
Increase amount of eye contact with people.	a. Work with the human–animal team to develop appropriate eye contact. b. Work at transferring that skill to other relationships.
Improve appropriateness of voice tone with people.	a. Work with the human–animal team to develop appropriate tone of voice when training the animal. b. Work at transferring that skill to other relationships.

Participant B

Identified goal area	Selected session strategies
Decrease learned helplessness. Increase sense of control over self and environment.	a. Work with the human–animal team to effectively command the animal and problem solve. b. Process session events to confront this issue directly and transfer to other situations.

(continues)

TABLE I   (*Continued*)

Participant B	
Identified goal area	Selected session strategies
Decrease pouting and tantrumming. Increase age appropriate behavior.	a. When situations of frustration or nonsuccess arise while working with the human–animal team, process session events to confront this issue directly and transfer to other situations. b. Reinforce age-appropriate responses to frustration and nonsuccess.
Improve relationships with peers. Improve relationship with the other participant.	a. Work with the human–animal team to use the participant's relationship with the animal as a metaphor for human relationships. b. Create and deliver a presentation with the other participant about HABIC experiences.
Increase amount of eye contact with people.	a. Work with the animal–human team to develop appropriate eye contact. b. Work at transferring that skill to other relationships.
Improve appropriateness of voice tone with people.	a. Work with the human–animal team to develop appropriate tone of voice when training the animal. b. Work at transferring that skill to other relationships.

V. SELECTED ISSUES

A number of current issues relate to implementing a successful AAT program. Some of these include attention to animal needs, volunteer and professional training, matching human–animal teams and clients, evaluation, and funding issues.

A. ANIMAL NEEDS

In addition to the training and screening that need to occur for any type of animal, care should be taken to ensure that all animals involved in AAT enjoy the activity. Only animals that receive satisfaction from engaging in AAT sessions should be included as therapy animals. Limiting the time an animal is "on duty" and keeping the animal safe from accidents or aggressive client behavior are major responsibilities of the human team member. The quality of AAT declines when the experience ceases to be a positive experience for all involved.

B. Training and Supervision of Volunteers

Ongoing training and support of volunteers are important issues relating to the quality of AAT. All new human–animal teams should go through extensive training prior to beginning AAT. Only after a team has successfully completed all requirements should it visit a facility. In this way, potential recipients are not disappointed if the volunteer does not meet the necessary requirements. After pertinent background information has been received concerning the human–animal team, many programs offer different levels of training for the team. The volunteers should be trained in what to actually do in AAT sessions and well as have some experience or education concerning the type of clients they will be assisting. Most volunteers find it useful to observe several sessions before doing one themselves. Supervision should be available to help with any problems or questions. Feedback on supervised sessions provides a wonderful resource for volunteers to continue to develop their skills.

To help keep things running smoothly, support meetings for each facility's volunteers should be offered. In this way, volunteers visiting the same facility can get acquainted with one another, share experiences, and discuss concerns. One important topic that often bears addressing in support meetings is the level of involvement for volunteers. Volunteers need to understand the boundaries within the facilities in which they work. While volunteers are oftentimes professional people, it is imperative they understand agency policies and procedures. The role of a volunteer should, therefore, be clearly defined. All volunteers should be clear about who to contact for advice, suggestions, or concerns.

C. Training and Supervision of Professionals

There is the related issue concerning the training of professionals who engage in AAT, and the supervision and accountability of these professionals. As noted, most disciplines do not include content on AAT in their curriculum. A few universities are offering a course or two, and a trend is beginning of developing certificate-type programs. However, for the most part these are quite superficial, lacking in depth, and do not require experiential learning opportunities. Once a professional has completed a course or continuing education-type of training, there is no ongoing supervision. In addition to this standard of training, the specific content needs to be determined.

D. Matching Human–Animal Teams and Clients

During initial assessments, careful consideration should to be given to matching the needs of the resident with the characteristics and availability of the human–

animal team. To best facilitate an appropriate match between a team and a client, the contact person and the human–animal team should walk through the facility and meet the potential clients. Since oftentimes clients are not able to accurately indicate their preferences when queried, a walk-through can help determine what factors are desired and/or needed.

E. EVALUATION AND DETERMINING AAT EFFECTIVENESS

Evaluation is an important defining characteristic of AAT. Many people and programs refer to what they do with animals as AAT, but are not evaluating the effectiveness of their program. In addition, most studies to date are descriptive and do not make use of qualitative or quantitative measures. Crucial elements of AAT include goal setting, evaluation, and the willingness to alter AAT sessions to best meet clients' goals. Goals that can be obtained through the use of AAT are as diverse as the population served, but all must be monitored and tracked. Often this monitoring is achieved through predesignated meetings with all those involved to reflect on the progress seen and implement new ideas. One example, to illustrate, is the verbal ability of a stroke patient. The first aspect involved is some type of verbal ability base rate before therapy begins. The next step includes creating a treatment plan with input from all involved participants. The treatment plan should specifically state the activities for each session, expected goals, and a time frame for reaching each goal. Additionally, how each goal will be measured should be decided before starting AAT sessions. In this example, it would be imperative to involve the speech therapist in the goal-setting stage. The words and phrases practiced in AAT sessions should also be practiced during speech therapy. In this way, AAT works as an adjunct therapy, helping the speech therapist achieve greater results with a patient.

This is a significant issue impacting the validity of AAT as a therapeutic intervention. Based on this chapter's presented material there is difficulty in evaluating AAT due to numerous variable factors. Until AAT can more clearly be defined as to its parameters and protocol, this will continue to be an issue hindering its professional development and recognition.

F. FUNDING

All of the preceding issues have impact on financial considerations such as third-party reimbursement, funding of AAT by agencies and programs, and the degree to which AAT is regarded as a "volunteer" activity. Competing for grants and foundation funds is a challenge for most anyone. Without solid data that demonstrate to funding bodies that AAT makes a difference in responding to the health, social, and psychological needs of specific clients, we will continue to struggle with the issue of adequate funding.

VI. CONCLUSIONS

We have described the current status of AAT in specialized settings. It is a picture of considerable variation and levels of quality. Much of this is related to the very nature of AAT and the complexity of the human–animal bond. Other factors influencing AAT include the variety of animals involved, their temperament and level of training, and the human team member and her or his level of training and personal characteristics. The setting or agency where AAT takes place and the variety of clients also influences how AAT is conducted.

The interdisciplinary nature of AAT in many respects enriches its content, but also contributes to different ways of conducting or implementing this therapeutic intervention. Professionals, trained staff, and volunteers all engage in various levels of AAT based primarily on their understanding of and personal commitment to the human–animal bond. Some efforts have been made to establish guidelines for AAT; however, this falls short of addressing the wide variation that presently exists.

AAT protocol or how one conducts this type of intervention is noticeably absent from the literature. This is another factor that contributes to the difficulty of evaluating the effectiveness of AAT, and thus to its credibility as a legitimate and significant intervention. In spite of these factors, the therapeutic use of companion animals, and specifically AAT, is continuing to expand into multiple areas of social and health services. Contributions in the literature are also increasing to help define the parameters of AAT and the standards through which AAT should be conducted.

REFERENCES

Andrysco, R. M. (1982). A study of ethnologic and therapeutic factors of pet-facilitated therapy in a retirement-nursing community. *Dissertation Abstracts International,* 43(1-B), 290.

Arkow, P. (1982). *How to start a pet therapy program.* Alameda, CA: Latham Foundation.

Barba, B. E. (1995). The positive influence of animals: Animal-assisted therapy in acute care [see comments]. *Clinical Nurse Specialist,* 9(4), 199–202.

Beck, A. M., & Katcher, A. H. (1984). A new look at pet-facilitated therapy. *Journal of the American Veterinary Medical Association,* 184(4), 414–421.

Bernard, S. (1995). *Animal assisted therapy: A guide for health care professionals and volunteers.* Whitehouse, TX (P.O. Box 1696, Whitehouse, TX 75791): Therapet.

Biery, M. J. (1985). Riding and the handicapped. *Veterinary Clinics of North America Small Animal Practice, 15*(2), 345–354.

Brock, B. (1988). Effect of therapeutic riding on physically disabled adults. Doctoral dissertation, University of Indiana.

Burch, M. R. (1996). *Volunteering with your pet: How to get involved in animal-assisted therapy with any kind of pet.* New York: Howell Book House.

Bustad, L. K. (1996). Reflections on the human–animal bond. *Journal of the American Veterinary Medical Association, 208*(2), 203–205.

Cole, K. M., & Gawlinski, A. (1995). Animal-assisted therapy in the intensive care unit. A staff nurse's dream comes true. *Nursing Clinics of North America, 30*(3), 529–537.

Cushing, J. L., & Williams, J. D. (1995). The Wild Mustang program: A case study in facilitated inmate therapy. *Journal of Offender Rehabilitation, 22*(3–4), 95–115.

Delta Society. (1996). *Standards of practice for animal-assisted activities and animal-assisted therapy.* Renton, WA: Delta Society.

Diesch, S. L. (1984). Companion animals on the farm. In P. Arkow (Ed.), *Dynamic relationships in practice: Animals in the helping professions* (pp. 257–270). Alameda, CA: Latham Foundation.

Engel, B. T. (1992). Therapeutic riding programs Instruction and Rehabilitation. In *A Handbook for Instructors and Therapists.* Durango, CO: Barbara Engel Therapy Services.

Fick, K. M. (1993). The influence of an animal on social interactions of nursing home residents in a group setting. *American Journal of Occupational Therapy, 47*(6), 529–534.

Fox, V. M., Lawlor, V. A., & Luttges, M. W. (1984). Pilot study of novel test instrumentation to evaluate therapeutic horseback riding. *Adapted Physical Activity Quarterly, 1*(1), 30–36.

Francis, G., Turner, J. T., & Johnson, S. B. (1985). Domestic animal visitation as therapy with adult home residents. *International Journal of Nursing Studies, 22*(3), 201–206.

Gammonley, J., Howie, A., Kirwin, S., Zapf, S., Frye, J., Freeman, G., & Stuart-Russell, R. (1996). *Animal-assisted therapy therapeutic interventions.* Renton, WA: Delta Society.

Gonski, Y. A. (1985). The therapeutic utilization of canines in a child welfare setting. *Child & Adolescent Social Work Journal, 2*(2), 93–105.

Granger, B., Kogan, L., Fitchett, J., & Helmer, K. (1998). The human–animal team approach to animal assisted therapy. *Anthrozoos, 11*(3).

Haladay, J. (1989). Animal assisted therapy for PWA's: Bringing a sense of connection. *AIDS Patient Care, 3*(1), 38–39.

Harris, M. D., Rinehart, J. M., & Gerstman, J. (1993). Animal-assisted therapy for the homebound elderly. *Holistic Nursing Practice, 8*(1), 27–37.

Haughie, E., Milne, D., & Elliott, V. (1992). An evaluation of companion pets with elderly psychiatric patients. *Behavioural Psychotherapy, 20*(4), 367–372.

Holcomb, R., & Meacham, M. (1989). Effectiveness of an animal-assisted therapy program in an inpatient psychiatric unit. *Anthrozoos, 2*(4), 259–264.

Holcomb, R., Jendro, C., Weber, B., & Nahan, U. (1997). Use of an aviary to relieve depression in elderly males. *Anthrozoos, 10*(1), 32–36.

Hundley, J. (1991). Pet project. The use of pet facilitated therapy among the chronically mentally ill. *Journal of Psychosocial Nursing & Mental Health Services, 29*(6), 23–26.

Kay, B. R. (1990). Bittersweet Farms. Special issue: Residential services. *Journal of Autism & Developmental Disorders, 20*(3), 309–321.

Kongable, L. G., Buckwalter, K. C., & Stolley, J. M. (1989). The effects of pet therapy on the social behavior of institutionalized Alzheimer's clients. *Archives of Psychiatric Nursing, 3*(4), 191–198.

Kubler-Ross, E. (1969). *On death and dying.* New York: Macmillan.

Lapp, C. A. (1991). Nursing students and the elderly: Enhancing intergenerational communication through human–animal interaction. *Holistic Nursing Practice, 5*(2), 72–79.

Law, S., & Scott, S. (1995). Tips for practitioners: Pet care: A vehicle for learning. *Focus on Autistic Behavior*, 10(2), 17–18.

Lee, D. (1984). Companion animals in institutions. In P. Arkow (Ed.), *Dynamic relationships in practice: Animals in the helping professions* (pp. 229–236). Alameda, CA: Latham Foundation.

Levinson, B. (1964). Pets: A special technique in child psychotherapy. *Mental Health*, 48, 243–248.

Mallon, G. P. (1994). Cow as co-therapist: Utilization of farm animals as therapeutic aides with children in residential treatment. *Child & Adolescent Social Work Journal*, 11(6), 455–474.

McCowan, L. L. (1984). Equestrian therapy. In P. Arkow (Ed.), *Dynamic relationships in practice: Animals in the helping professions* (pp. 237–256). Alameda, CA: Latham Foundation.

McQuillen, D. (1985). Pet therapy: Initiating a program. *Canadian Journal of Occupational Therapy*, 52(2), 73–76.

Mugford, R. & M'Comisky, J. (1975). Some recent work on the psychotherapeutic value of cage birds with old people. In *Pet Animals and Society: A BSAVA Symposium*, pp. 54–65.

Muschel, I. J. (1984). Pet therapy with terminal cancer patients. *Social Casework*, 65(8), 451–458.

Nathanson, D. E. (1989). Using Atlantic bottlenose dolphins to increase cognition of mentally retarded children. In P. Lovibond & P. Wilson (Eds.), *Clinical and Abnormal Psychology* (pp. 233–242). North Holland: Elsevier.

Nathanson, D. E., (1998). Long-term effectiveness of dolphin-assisted therapy for children with severe disabilities. *Anthrozoos*, 11(1), 22–32, 1998.

Nathanson, D. E., & de Faria (1993). Cognitive improvement of children in water with and without dolphins. *Anthrozoos*, 6(1), 17–29.

Nathanson, D. E., de Castro, D., Friend, H., & McMahon, M. (1997). Effectiveness of short term dolphin-assisted therapy for children with severe disabilities. *Anthrozoos*, 10(2/3), 90–100, 1997.

New Mexico Bureau of Land Management, (1989). *A winning combination: Wild horses and prison inmates*. (BLM-NM-GI-89-022-4370). Santa Fe, NM: Bureau of Land Managment.

Ross, S.B. (1992). Building empathy to reduce violence to all living things. *Journal of Society for Companion Animal Studies*, 4(1), 4–5.

Rossbach, K. A., & Wilson, J. P. (1992). Does a dog's presence make a person appear more likable? Two studies. *Anthrozoos*, 5(1), 40–51.

Rowell, M.C. (1990). Creature comfort: Animals as therapists. *California Pharmacist*, 37(10), 37–40.

Sayler, P. (1992). Selecting the hippotherapy horse. In B. T. Engel (Ed.), *Therapeutic riding programs instruction and rehabilitation. A Handbook for Instructors and Therapists* (pp. 86–87). Durango, CO: Barbara Engel Therapy Services.

Struckus, J. E. (1991). Pet-facilitated therapy and the elderly client. In P. A. Wisocki (Ed.), *Handbook of clinical behavior therapy with the elderly client. Applied clinical psychology* (Vol. xviii, pp. 403–419). New York: Plenum Press.

Voelker, R. (1995). Puppy love can be therapeutic, too. *Journal of the American Medical Association*, 274(24), 1897–1899.

The Role Animals Play in Enhancing Quality of Life for the Elderly

Mara M. Baun and Barbara W. McCabe

College of Nursing, University of Nebraska Medical Center, Omaha, Nebraska

I. ELDERLY TRANSITIONS

We live in a world that is witness to a tremendous growth in the population of persons who are 65 and older. It is a well-established fact that the oldest-old (85+) represent the fastest growing segment of our population. Researchers and scientists are beginning to seriously consider the ramifications of these demographic changes in our society. There is increased attention directed to health promotion for persons of all ages. Although the lives of humans and animals have been intertwined for thousands of years, there is still much to be learned about the effects of the human–animal companion bond, particularly as it affects the health and the quality of life of older persons. To capitalize on the benefits of the human–animal companion bond, it is essential that one have some familiarity with the aging process and how this process affects the everyday life of older people. An understanding of age-related changes and transitions that occur in the life of older people can provide the basis for interventions that enhance quality of life.

"Come grow old with me! The best is yet to be." This well-known line from Browning's work may be prophetic as we now look at the remarkable

Handbook on Animal-Assisted Therapy: Theoretical Foundations and Guidelines for Practice
Copyright © 2000 by Academic Press. All rights of reproduction in any form reserved.

237

discoveries that scientists have made and are continuing to make about changes that accompany the aging process. As data mount, dispelling myths once thought to characterize human aging, there is a growing certainty that the best is yet to be. No longer do we automatically accept the fact that old age is an event that occurs at age 65, but a process that begins at birth, a process that is a very individualized, representing the cumulative effects of the person's internal and external environment. That which was once thought of as age-related change is slowly beginning to be revised as researchers are discovering that many of the characteristics of age are influenced by disease or disuse rather than normal life processes. Undoubtedly, there are profound data to indicate that cells have a finite period of life. While Hayflick's (Hayflick, 1994; Hayflick & Moorhead, 1961) well-known experiments about cell division continue to be supported in the literature, there is increased attention to the internal mechanisms that speed up or delay cellular activities that lead to the death of a cell. Because aging is a dynamic interactive process influenced by the internal and external environment, scientists would be remiss if they did not direct their attention to examine the interplay of an individual's external environment on the aging process. One such area is that of the positive effect of the human–animal companion bond on quality of life for older persons.

To ensure that the promise, "the best is yet to be" is realized by the chronologically old, it is important to understand the difference between the natural results of aging and warning signals of disease and to identify specific instances where companion animals might play a role in compensating for losses that occur with age-related changes. While many changes attributed to aging can be recognized easily (visual changes, hearing impairment, alterations in hair growth, decline in short-term memory, loss of bone mass, decrease in height, loss of strength and stamina, and menopause), it is important to remember that these observed changes have their origins at the cellular level. As these exact mechanisms are identified, the mystery of normal aging will be elucidated. Although we have made considerable progress in teasing apart normal consequences of aging from syndromes of disuse and disease, there is much that still must be learned. Despite the current limitations on understanding what aging is and the consequences of aging, it is essential that we continue to raise questions about symptoms and behaviors that present in humans who have reached the socially recognized time of life called old age and to propose interventions that compensate for or delay these changes. Questions to guide future investigations include these: What is the role of companion animals in preserving and enhancing the quality of life of older persons? What are the health benefits of companion animals for older persons? What role can companion animals play in compensating for age-related change in older persons? What are the essential criteria to select an appropriate companion animal for an older person? Is there a place for companion animals in institutional settings?

To propose and explore possible roles of companion animals with older people, it is important to reflect on some of the physiologic changes that occur with aging. Many of the changes that have been attributed to age actually begin in earlier years, but more attention is directed toward these changes when one reaches and surpasses the chronological age of 65 years.

II. SENSORY CHANGES

Sensory changes are among the first age-related changes noted by individuals and by society in general as outward and visible signs that one is growing older. The subtle, uncompensated alterations in sensory structure and function can have a profound effect on the quality of life of the older individual because these changes affect how one receives and responds to stimuli. Often it is these changes that make older persons vulnerable to ageist comments and attributions about their ability to function in our society.

A. VISION

Visual changes begin in the mid-forties but become more pronounced with each passing decade. External and internal structural changes in the eye and surrounding tissue result in decreased visual acuity, decreased tolerance of glare, decreased ability to adapt to dark and light, reduced contrast sensitivity, restricted color recognition, and decreased peripheral vision. In some instances, visual changes that occur with aging can be modified with prescriptive lenses. In addition, attention to environmental modifications will compensate for the needed increase in illumination, color contrasts, and glare reduction and support existing visual acuity. For those persons whose vision cannot be corrected with prescriptive lenses or surgical procedures, animals, especially seeing eye dogs, can compensate for the visual changes that cannot be altered with current opthomological interventions, thus allowing the older person to independently move about the environment. Proper correction of visual deficits will enable the older person to enjoy the soothing experience of watching fish swim about in an aquarium, observe the antics of a young kitten play with a ball of yarn, or watch wild animals scurrying and birds flying about outdoors. Any one of these visually stimulating activities keeps the older person "connected" to his or her environment and serves as an important means of sensory stimulation.

B. HEARING

Hearing loss is the third most frequently reported chronic condition of persons 65 and older. *Presbycusis* is a global term used to describe hearing loss associated with the aging process. There are two forms of presbycusis: sensory presbycusis, which affects the older person's ability to hear high-pitched sounds, and neural presbycusis, which affects speech discrimination. For many hearing-impaired older persons, consonants such as *sh, f, v, t, p,* and *b* are frequently misunderstood, thus leading to communication difficulties that may result in a mislabeling of older persons as cognitively impaired. Hearing loss can indirectly affect self-esteem, producing self-doubt and self-imposed isolation from others. For those persons who have a hearing deficit that can be corrected or improved with hearing aids, it is essential to be properly fitted for such devices and receive the proper training in their use. A person whose hearing has diminished or failed is deprived of not only the joy of sound but may be placed in jeopardy if unable to hear sounds that warn of danger. An older person who has a hearing deficit may not venture outdoors out of fear at not being able to hear sounds of impending danger. A companion animal can serve as an alert system while outdoors but also to draw the older person's attention to guests and intruders. In addition, the companion animal can reinforce the older person's attempts to communicate verbally especially when taking the animal outdoors.

C. Touch

Touch sensitivity is also known to be reduced in older people. The skin has been referred to as the largest organ of the body. While the skin serves many physiologic functions, such as protection of internal organs, regulation of temperature, and synthesis of vitamin D, it is involved in sensory perception and expression of feelings. It is now recognized that changes in the skin (dryness, wrinkling, laxity, uneven pigmentation and proliferative lesions) are not the result of normal aging but represent a response to genetic makeup, lifestyle habits, and/or environmental conditions. Age-related changes in the appearance and texture of the skin, however, continue to be interpreted as outward and visible signs that a person is old. It is this interpretation that often leads to many undesirable comments being made about persons over 65 which could result in isolation. As the circle of significant others that the older person has contact with in later years begins to diminish in numbers, the older person's opportunities to touch and be touched change accordingly. These changes occur at a time when the need for tactile stimulation takes on greater importance because the threshold of tactile stimulation increases as one ages. Pets provide an opportunity to fulfill the need to touch and be touched. The cold wet nose of a faithful canine friend, the velvet feel of a cat's sleek coat, the softness of a bunny's ears, the gentle peck of a budgie can be the stimulus that connects the older person to reality. The short periods of time that one goes outdoors with one's pet can provide the necessary exposure to the sun to absorb vitamin D, which is essential to bone health.

D. SMELL AND TASTE

Changes in the olfactory and gustatory systems are less noticeable, but nonetheless play an important role in the health and well-being of older persons. The olfactory bulbs show significant atrophy with age, thus resulting in a diminished sense of smell. This decline impacts the older person by reducing the pleasurable smells that are associated with cooking, thus indirectly affecting appetite. There is a gradual but significant loss of taste buds resulting in a decreased ability to enjoy the flavor of foods. Food intake is also influenced by the social environment. The importance of good nutrition to the overall health of older persons cannot be denied. For an older person living alone, having a pet to prepare food for may serve as a stimulus to prepare food for one's self. Also, the presence of pets during meals can be a substitute for other social contact. In addition, the reduced sense of smell places the older person at risk for injury related to undetected smoke from fire and as well as toxic odors. Pets often alert their owners to undesired or dangerous changes in the environment.

III. CARDIOVASCULAR SYSTEM

Many changes associated with the aging process are now recognized to be related to genetics and lifestyle choices rather than to disease processes per se. While researchers continue to struggle with the challenge of separating normal age-related changes from pathologic conditions, cardiovascular disease continues as a leading cause of death among persons over 65 (Lakatta, 1993). Progress has been made in separating risk factors into two categories, nonmodifiable and modifiable. It is in the area of modifiable risk factors that companion animals can make an important difference in promoting quality of life for older persons. Petting a companion animal has been associated with a reduction in blood pressure and an increase in relaxation. Walking a pet or playing catch with a pet may be just the stimulus that is needed for the older person to engage in activity. Having to walk and/or care for the pet gives the older person a reason to get up in the morning.

IV. MUSCULOSKELETAL SYSTEM

The changes that occur in the musculoskeletal system have a direct effect on the manner and ability of older persons to move about in their environment.

Although disease processes, such as arthritis or osteoporosis, do affect a large number of older people, many of the observed impairments in musculoskeletal functioning are related to disuse. The adage "use it or lose it," takes on particular importance in relation to flexibility, strength, endurance, and bone mass. Getting fit and staying fit should be a top priority. It is in the area of musculo-skeletal fitness that companion animals take on particular importance. Brisk walking is the simplest form of weight-bearing exercise and can easily be done with a pet dog. Throwing a ball or holding up an object for a cat to paw at provides an opportunity to exercise arm and shoulder joints.

V. IMPORTANCE OF PETS TO THE ELDERLY

The most common thread in literature about the elderly is loss. Generally, the more advanced the age the greater the losses experienced. These losses encompass physical losses, such as mobility, vision, and hearing; psychological losses, such as memory and problem-solving abilities; and social losses, such as support, institutionalization, and deaths of loved ones. Once a loss occurs, what is lost usually does not return, at least not to the same level previously experienced. How an elderly person deals with loss may be the single greatest factor affecting the quality of the remaining years. The presence of a companion animal to whom one is attached may be a moderator in helping the elderly person deal with some of the losses.

A number of studies have found that pet ownership enhances the lives of elderly persons living in the community. Dog owners in mobile home parks are twice as likely to go for walks, talk more often about activities occurring in the present, and report less dissatisfaction with their social, physical, and emotional states that non-dog owners (Rogers *et al.,* 1993). Dog owners may also be more sociable and thus have dogs.

The most famous study of the therapeutic value of pets for the elderly was conducted in England by Mugford and M'Comisky (1975) in which either a budgerigar or a begonia was placed in the homes of free-living elderly. A control group had no intervention. At the end of 5 months, only the group who had received the budgie had improved social attitudes, mental health, and happiness. Not only had the elderly subjects formed attachments to the birds, they had become powerful topics for conversation that could displace discussions of the past and medical ailments.

One of the most difficult losses for the elderly occurs during the loss of a spouse. Dog owners who form bonds with their dogs report fewer health problems (Bolin, 1987) and less depression (Garrity *et al.,* 1989) after loss of a spouse than non-dog owners. All studies of the elderly during bereavement have not demonstrated beneficial outcomes, however. A slightly negative impact of pet ownership on coping levels during stressful times was reported in one study (Lund et al., 1984). Another area needing study is the effect of loss of a pet for the elderly person who already may have lost friends and family. The loss of a beloved pet may represent the last significant other.

The well-being of the elderly may or may not be related to their attachment to pets. An Australian study (Crowley-Robinson & Blackshaw, 1998) found that more than one-third of the elderly studied spend more than 8 hours per day with their pets, and that dogs were the preferred species. Dog ownership, however, did not affect either their owners' happiness or their incidence of depression. A study conducted in the United States had similar findings in that no relationship was found between pet attachment and feelings of depression, and pet variables had relatively little impact on psychological or physical well-being (Miller & Lago, 1989). The relationship between pet ownership and happiness for the elderly may be more related to socioeconomic status than to pets alone (Ory & Goldberg, 1983).

It is possible that pet attachment positively affects the health of the elderly, thereby helping to alleviate one of the common losses experienced in the later years, that of health. Siegel (1990) studied 938 Medicare enrollees in a health maintenance organization and found that respondents who owned pets reported fewer doctor contacts than those who did not own pets. Dogs appeared to buffer their owners from the impact of a stressful life. Dog owners in comparison to owners of other pets spend more time with their pets and feel that their pets are more important to them. Pet attitudes and ownership also are significant predictors of higher levels of both health and morale (Lago et al., 1989).

Pets have lessened the impact of the loss of personal freedom for persons confined to residential centers such as nursing homes. The presence of a pet enhances the treatment milieu (Brickel,1979; Thomas,1994). Cats stimulate patient responsiveness, give patients pleasure, and act as forms of reality therapy (Brickel, 1979). Dogs increase interactive behaviors among nursing home residents, although the effects are somewhat short term (Buelt et al., 1985; Fick, 1993; McArthur et al., 1986; Winkler et al., 1989). Birds can decrease depression among elderly in rehabilitation settings (Jessen et al., 1996) and adult day care centers (Holcomb et al., 1997).

Among Alzheimer's patients in the home, the presence of companion animals has resulted in fewer episodes of verbal aggression and anxiety and fewer mood disorders (Fritz et al., 1995). Among institutionalized persons with Alzheimer's, socialization is increased in the presence of a companion animal (Batson et al., 1998; Kongable et al., 1989) and behavioral distress is decreased (Churchill et al., 1999).

In summary, considerable research has been done on the effects of companion animals in alleviating the losses common among the elderly. Nevertheless, there still is a need to conduct studies on the long term effects of human–animal interactions. Such studies could lead to modification of some of the regulations governing institutions for the elderly that separate them from their animals.

VI. PET SELECTION

A. FREE-LIVING ELDERLY

Recommending a pet for an elderly person is a challenging opportunity. Even though a number of studies have demonstrated that pets can be beneficial to the elderly, for example in alleviating depression and increasing socialization, finding the right pet for a particular person can be difficult. The primary consideration is the health and safety of the person.

Many elderly have mobility difficulties. It is not uncommon for elderly persons to walk with canes or walkers and to be somewhat unsteady on their feet. While a young dog can provide much affection and entertainment, it may be too strong for the elderly person to walk on a leash or it might be able to cause a fall by jumping against the legs or tripping the person. The elderly may not be able to move quickly enough to get a puppy house broken. Thus, an older dog, particularly one who has been obedience trained, socialized, and housebroken, may be a good alternative. Often dog breeders, especially those who show their dogs, have adult dogs who are still young but are no longer going to be shown and whom they would like to place in loving homes. These purebred dogs usually are excellent examples of the breed, have been bred for good temperament, have been socialized to dog shows where they had to perform in front of hundreds of people and dogs, and thus make excellent pets.

Other sources of well-trained dogs are the agencies who train dogs as service dogs, for example, seeing eye, hearing, and assistant dogs for people with handicaps. At present, there is a 75% dropout rate for these dogs, that is, three-quarters of the dogs who have been specially reared do not succeed in their formal training program. Generally, they make excellent pets because they have had systematic socialization and obedience training since they were young puppies. There are, however, long lists of people waiting to adopt these dogs, and the puppy raisers generally have the first option to adopt the dog if it is rejected during the formal training program.

Many humane societies have adopt-a-pet programs, some designed specifically for the elderly. While there are many animals at Humane Society shelters who can become excellent pets, careful consideration needs to be given to the elderly person's abilities and the pet's needs. If the animal was brought to the shelter for behavior problems, an elderly person may not be able to provide the appropriate behavior modification. On the other hand, sometimes wonderful pet animals are available for adoption.

Elderly persons seeking to acquire a dog will have individual needs and likes and dislikes. Sometimes as individuals age their self-concept does not change as their bodies become more limited, and they may be unrealistic in assessing what they can and cannot do. Their memories of a loved dog may not include the difficulties encountered during puppyhood, and they may only remember the docile, well-behaved older dog in the last years of its life. Thus, seeking advice on the type of dog to be acquired from an experienced dog person and health care provider may be very useful in matching the individual with the right dog.

Most major cities have one or more kennel clubs and dog training clubs. Often these clubs provide public service through maintaining a telephone to assist persons with dog-related questions. Some purebred dog clubs participate in rescue programs where they take unwanted dogs of their breed, rehabilitate them if necessary, and place them in good homes. Some of these rescued dogs might make excellent pets for the elderly. Also, veterinarians can provide advice about the care requirements of various breeds. Another avenue of information on purebred dogs is the American Kennel Club, which has an excellent web site (http:/www.akc.org) and can refer inquiries to the national breed clubs. In addition, there are numerous home pages on various breeds of dogs and other dog-related activities that can be accessed through one of the search engines on the Internet. Most libraries have sections on dogs.

It is a good idea for anyone, particularly the elderly, not to be impulse driven in the acquisition of a pet. Besides the monetary investment, there may be a 10- to 15-year commitment involved in the acquisition of a pet. A few weeks of investigation and planning can be a good investment in making sure that the acquisition of the pet is a positive experience. Sometimes, it is useful if an adult child partners with the elderly person in the process of pet adoption. The adult child then hopefully will have some commitment to assisting the elderly person throughout the process. The elderly need to recognize their current and potential limitations that could occur during the life of the pet. If there is a strong potential that the person will not be able to care for the pet throughout its entire life, an arrangement might be made with a family member or other responsible person to take the pet if the elderly person becomes unable to provide care either temporarily or permanently.

A few retirement homes allow elderly residents to bring their pets with them, but the elderly have to be able to care for the pet, and there may be restrictions on the size and species of the pets allowed. Hopefully, the number of institutions allowing personal pets will increase in the future. Most nursing homes do not have facilities for personal pets. One of the greatest sources of distress for the institutionalized elderly can be the loss of their beloved pets.

Many nursing homes do have regular pet visitation programs and allow individuals' pets to visit on a regular basis. Family members or friends can keep the pet and bring it to see its owner. A particularly sad occurrence is for the pet to be taken to the local Humane Society when its owner is institutionalized and then euthanized or placed with strangers so that the elderly person experiences not only the loss of personal independence, but also the loss of a real significant other.

Sometimes, the choice of a pet other than a dog is ideal for an elderly person. Cats, for example, require less personal care than dogs. Nonetheless, the elderly person needs to be mobile enough to change the litter box and responsible enough to feed and care for the cat. Eyesight needs to be good enough to avoid tripping over any pet who has access to the floor.

Sometimes, a caged animal, such as a bird, might be a better choice if the elderly person has difficulty with mobilization. Birds can be excellent companions. Most domestic birds can be hand trained thus providing physical contact but also can be kept in cages. The elderly person needs to be able to provide food and water and clean the cage regularly.

Many other small animals could provide touch and affection for elderly persons. Gerbils, Guinea pigs, mice, rats, rabbits, hamsters, turtles, and snakes are but a few of the potential small animals that could be wonderful pets. Sometimes it is not possible to predict to which animals strong bonds can develop. Physical contact with the animal is extremely important in the choice of a pet for some people but is not a strong consideration for others, for example, who may find that watching fish in a tank can provide many hours of intense enjoyment.

A major consideration in the acquisition of pets by the elderly is access to veterinarian care. Frequently, elderly persons are no longer able to drive. Finding someone to take the pet to the veterinarian's office may be problematic. Even though there are many ways for the elderly to get transportation for their own health care appointments, there are no similar services for animal health care. In addition, many elderly are living on fixed incomes and may not be able to afford the additional costs of health care for pets. A few cities provide low-cost clinics for animal health care, some particularly for animals belonging to the elderly, but again the elderly have to find transportation to the clinics. Some veterinarians practice in mobile vans. The availability of such a veterinarian for pets of the elderly would be of great assistance in allowing the elderly to maintain pets in their homes. Provision for the animal's health care needs to be a critical part of the planning that takes place prior to the acquisition of a pet. Sometimes, if it is not feasible for the elderly to have personal pets, wild animals, such as birds and squirrels, can fill the gap. The elderly can get many hours of enjoyment from watching birds and squirrels at feeders.

B. INSTITUTIONALIZED ELDERLY

A variety of animals can be used in institutions either as residents or as regular visitors. The most common are dogs, cats, rabbits, small rodents, birds, and fish. Dogs, cats, and rabbits generally visit on a regular basis, although some institutions have acquired them as residents.

The success of a resident animal in an institution for the elderly depends on a number of factors. Probably the most important is careful planning prior to the acquisition of the animal. The first step is to review the regulations of review boards and accrediting organizations about resident or visiting animals. If there is no contradiction to the acquisition of an animal, the next step is to decide which animal is best for that institution.

Staff need to consider who will be responsible for the animal. It is generally overly optimistic to assume that the elderly will care for resident animals. Responsibility needs to be assigned to staff members. If some aspects of care can occasionally be done by elderly residents, that care needs to be accomplished under the supervision of staff members. Thus, staff need to be willing to assume additional duties in relation to a resident animal. The nature of the animal to be acquired, therefore, has implications for staff workload. A dog, for example, needs food, toileting, and exercise on a regular schedule 24 hours a day 7 days a week. Thus, all shifts will need to make provisions for its care. It is possible for the day shift to be excited about the acquisition of a resident animal and the night shift to resent the added responsibilities. In such an institution, a caged bird which requires less care that can be given on only one shift might be a better choice.

Part of the planning for the acquisition of an institutional pet is to consider potential allergies among residents and staff. It may be necessary to specially treat the animal to reduce the disbursement of allergens, for example, dander, that trigger allergic reactions. Also, toenails need to be kept well trimmed and blunt to prevent injury to frail skin. Likewise, a plan needs to be in place for flea and other parasite prevention.

The potential for zoonotic infections, that is, infections that can be transmitted between species, needs careful consideration. Any animal brought into an institution should be given a complete examination by a licensed veterinarian prior to introduction. There should be a plan for regular examinations to ensure that it remains free of parasites and infections, that immunizations are current, and that preventatives, such as heart worm pills, are administered appropriately.

There may be some residents who should not interact with the pet such as those who are immunocompromised or allergic. The plan for the resident animal needs to include provisions for protecting these residents.

Another consideration in acquiring a resident animal is the location of the nursing home. Residents coming primarily from rural settings often have very different views of animals than those who have been city dwellers all their lives. Even animals traditionally regarded as companions, such as dogs and cats, may be considered as appropriately living outside and performing some instrumental function. Retired farmers may prefer interactions with farm animals, such as sheep and chickens, to dogs and cats. They can get a great deal of satisfaction watching these animals through the window as opposed to petting or cuddling companion animals.

The age of the animal also is a significant factor to be considered in planning. Puppies, although cute and appealing, need housebreaking and training. Older animals have the potential to have training completed before placement. One important consideration is that the animal needs to be temperament tested to ensure that it is suitable for interaction with the residents. Most cities have animal trainers who can perform this function.

Another consideration is that the animal needs time alone away from constant interaction with humans. While staff are not expected to work 24 hours a day, neither should such "work" be expected from the resident animal. Planning for a place where the animal can be away from people for part of each day and get its proper rest is essential. Such planning requires an understanding of the behavior of the species. Dogs, for example, generally are most active in the morning and evening and sleep a great deal in between. Planning for a resident dog might include an enclosure with a shelter on the grounds where the dog can be placed in the middle of the day as well as for the night.

Some institutions have found that a more satisfactory arrangement for having a therapy animal, particularly animals such as dogs and cats, is to have the animal reside with one of the staff. Then, the animal comes to "work" with the staff member and goes home at the end of the shift to a more normal living arrangement where it can get its own needs met. Such an arrangement also negates the need for staff to provide 24-hour, 7-days-a-week care for the animal.

The need for careful planning prior to the acquisition of an animal for an institution for the elderly cannot be emphasized too much. It would be well to have a committee of stakeholders formed to consider aspects of acquisition of the animal and to generate a written set of guidelines that would become part of the institution's policies and a budget for care of the animal. Such careful planning should result in a happy and therapeutic relationship between the animal, staff, and residents.

VII. GUIDELINES FOR ANIMAL-ASSISTED THERAPY WITH THE ELDERLY

Many institutions for the elderly have resident pets, and many have regular pet visitation programs. While many studies have demonstrated the beneficial effects of contact with pets for a variety of persons, including the elderly, the long-term effects of resident pets and pet visitation programs have not been examined. Nonetheless, the idea of bringing pets into contact with institutionalized elderly has become quite popular in the United States and elsewhere.

There is no doubt that the presence of pets in a setting such as a nursing home where one ordinarily does not expect to see them provides a source of distraction and novelty. All one has to do is witness the attention a dog gets as it walks into a unit. Residents, staff, and visitors descend on the dog almost like it is a magnet. Yet, the question of what the long-term effects of contact with a companion animal for the institutionalized elderly are has yet to be answered.

Distraction from one's ordinary daily life in a nursing home is not without merit. Also, pets provide a source of affectionate physical contact that often is lacking in an institutional setting. Perhaps these effects are enough to justify the cost of maintaining these programs. There are important areas to consider in instituting an animal-assisted therapy program.

1. *Choice of animal.* Most pet visitation programs utilize companion animals such as dogs, cats, rabbits, and Vietnamese pot-bellied pigs. These animals can be transported easily to the institution and walked or carried to interested residents. One criterion for animals' being included as regular visitors is that they be tested for their suitability to interact with strangers. Many pet therapy groups have established their own testing programs. National organizations, such as the Delta Society (*http://www.petsforum/delta*), have standardized testing that can be done by a local person who is certified. Once the animal has passed the test, it receives a certificate that it can be an institutional visitor. Often, it is eligible to wear some sort of symbol of this certification so that persons who see it in the institution know that it has been tested.

2. *Orientation of pet handlers.* The persons bringing the animals to the institution need to have an orientation to that institution. They need to know in which sections of the building, generally eating areas, animals are not allowed. Also, they should be informed about the types of persons they will encounter and how to deal with problems if they should arise. The safety both of the residents and of the persons and animals visiting is of utmost importance. It is possible for cognitively impaired elders to behave in strange ways and to attempt to injure animals and their handlers. Staff members need to be aware of animals visiting an institution and to provide information on residents who might benefit from such visitation as well as those who should not be approached. Animals visiting an institution should be under the direct physical control of the handler at all times.

Many persons who participate in animal visitation programs continue to do so for many years because it is so personally rewarding for them to be part of the human–animal team. One has only to see the delight and interest on so many otherwise sad or blank elderly faces when allowed to interact with a companion animal to be "hooked" forever and convinced that animals truly are good for the elderly!

REFERENCES

Batson, K., McCabe, B., & Baun, M. M. (1998). The effect of a therapy dog on socialization and physiologic indicators of stress in persons diagnosed with Alzheimer's disease. In C. C. Wilson & D. C. Turner (Eds.), *Companion animals in human health* (pp. 203–215). Thousand Oaks, CA: Sage Publications.

Bolin, S. E. (1987) The effects of companion animals during conjugal bereavement. *Anthrozoos*, 1(1), 26–35.

Brickel, C. M. (1979). The therapeutic roles of cat mascots with a hospital-based geriatric population: A staff survey. *The Gerontologist*, 19, 368–372.

Buelt, M. C., Bergstrom, N., Baun, M. M., & Langston, N. (1985). Facilitating social interaction among institutionalized elderly through use of companion dog. *The Journal of the Delta Society*, 2(1), 62–63.

Churchill, M., Safaoui, J., McCabe, B., & Baun, M. M. (1999). Effects of a therapy dog in alleviating the agitation behavior of sundown syndrome and in increasing socialization for persons with Alzheimer's disease. *Journal of Psychosocial Nursing and Mental Health Services*, 37(4), 16–22.

Crowley-Robinson, P., & Blackshaw, J. K. (1998). Pet ownership and health status of elderly in the community. *Anthrozoos*, 11(3), 168–171.

Fick, K. M. (1993). The influence of an animal on social interactions of nursing home residents in a group setting. *The American Journal of Occupational Therapy*, 47(6), 529–534.

Fritz, C. L., Farver, T. B., Kass, P. H., & Hart, L. A. (1995). Association with companion animals and the expression of noncognitive symptoms in Alzheimer's patients. *The Journal of Nervous and Mental Disease*, 183(7), 459–463.

Garrity, T. F., Stallones, L., Marx, M. B., & Johnson, T. P. (1989). Pet ownership and attachment as supportive factors in the health of the elderly. *Anthrozoos*, 3(1), 35–44.

Hayflick, L. (1994). *How and why we age*. New York: Ballantine.

Hayflick, L., & Moorhead, P. S. (1961). The serial cultivation of human diploid cell strains. *Experimental Cell Research*, 25, 585–621.

Holcomb, R., Jendro, C., Weber, B., & Nahan, U. (1997). Use of an aviary to relieve depression in elderly males. *Anthrozoos*, 10(1), 32–36.

Jessen, J., Cardiello, F., & Baun, M. M. (1996). Avian companionship in alleviation of depression, loneliness, and low morale of older adults in skilled rehabilitation units. *Psychological Reports*, 78, 339–348.

Kongable, L. G., Buckwalter, K. C., & Stolley, J. M. (1989). The effects of pet therapy on the social behavior of institutionalized Alzheimer's clients. *Archives of Psychiatric Nursing*, 3(4), 191–198.

Lago, D., Delaney, M., Miller, M., & Grill, C. (1989). Companion animals, attitudes toward pets, and health outcomes among the elderly: A long-term follow-up. *Anthrozoos*, 3(1), 25–34.

Lakatta, E. (1993). Cardiovascular regulatory mechanisms in advanced age. *Physiological Review*, 73, 413–467.

Lund, D. A., Johnson, R. J., Baraki, H. N., & Dimond, M. R. (1984). Can pets help the bereaved? *Journal of Gerontological Nursing*, 10(6), 8–12.

McArthur, M., Brunmeier, C., Bergstrom, N., & Baun, M. (1986). The effect of a pet dog on the social interaction of mentally impaired institutionalized elderly. *People, Animals, and Environment*, 4(2), 25.

Miller, M., & Lago, D. (1989). The well-being of older women: The importance of pet and human relations. *Anthrozoos, 3*(4), 245–251.

Mugford, R. A., & M'Comisky, J. G. (1975). Some recent work on the psychotherapeutic value of cage birds with old people. In R. S. Anderson, (Ed.), *Pet animals and society* (pp. 54–65). London: Bailliere-Tindall.

Ory, M. G., & Goldberg, E. L. (1983). Pet possession and well-being in elderly women. *Research on Aging, 5*(3), 389–409.

Rogers, J., Hart, L. A., & Boltz, R. P. (1993). The role of pet dogs in casual conversations of elderly adults. *The Journal of Social Psychology, 13*(3), 265–277.

Siegel, J. M. (1990). Stressful life events and use of physician services among the elderly: The moderating role of pet ownership. *Journal of Personality and Social Psychology, 58*(6), 1081–1086.

Thomas, W. H. (1994). *The Eden alternative: Nature, hope, and nursing homes.* Sherburne, NY: The Eden Alternative Foundation.

Winkler A., Fairnie, H. Gericevich, F., & Long, M. (1989). The impact of a resident dog on an institution for the elderly: Effects on perceptions and social interactions. *The Gerontologist, 29*(2), 216–223.

CHAPTER 12

History, Theory, and Development of Human–Animal Support Services for People with AIDS and Other Chronic/ Terminal Illnesses

KENNETH GORCZYCA
Pets Are Wonderful Support, San Francisco, California

AUBREY H. FINE
School of Education and Integrative Studies, California State Polytechnic Institute, Pomona, California

C. VICTOR SPAIN
College of Veterinary Medicine, Cornell University, Ithaca, New York

---

People come to visit but they can only stay on hour and then they have to go; my cat, she's always there.
                              —Bob, pet owner with AIDS

Afraid of infection, I fear the birds (Tuberculosis), the cats (Toxoplasmosis), my dog, my horse (Mycobacterium avium), and people. For weeks I was reluctant to leave the house. I didn't ride my horse for several months. Walking in the park or at the beach was unpleasant because of the birds. My doctors gave contradictory advice—Dr. (A) said to get rid of all animals. Dr. (B) said it didn't matter and enjoy what life I had left. My cousin asked if I couldn't get a bubble like the bubble boy.
    —Stephen Yarnell, M.D., *When Doctors Get Sick*, 1987

I. INTRODUCTION

Terminal or chronic illness may have a tremendous impact on daily living as well as quality of life for those who suffer the illness. For some, these health impairments may restrict social opportunities as well as cause them to disengage from social relationships.

In this chapter, we briefly review the prevalence of AIDS and other chronic illnesses and key issues facing people with these diseases. We then explain how animals can enhance the quality of life for people with chronic and terminal illnesses, drawing on an ecosystem model of how animals contribute to a quality home life for patients who are still able to live at home. [Note that traditional animal-assisted therapy (AAT) programs and the benefits of animals in hospital-based programs are discussed elsewhere in this book.] The ecosystem model delineates the multiple sources of support an individual may draw on and the role a companion animal can play as a source of support. The second part of this chapter focuses on more practical aspects of such programs by reviewing how guidelines were developed for human–animal support services (HASS) for persons with acquired immunodeficiency syndrome (see Table I). It then deals with specific concerns health care providers may want to consider when investigating the impact of companion animals on persons with AIDS and individuals with other chronic or fatal illnesses. Finally, it describes the Pets Are Wonderful Support (PAWS) program in San Francisco and how similar programs can be implemented elsewhere.

TABLE I   Definitions of HASS, AAA, and AAT

Human–animal support services (HASS) are programs that help keep persons with chronic/terminal illnesses or disabilities together for as long as possible with their current animal companions in a mutually beneficial relationship. HASS provides financial, emotional, and practical assistance to the disabled pet owner. HASS programs can be independent, volunteer-run, nonprofit organizations or can be programs under the umbrella of other organizations such as humane associations or societies, veterinary hospitals, schools or associations, AIDS organizations, or other similar human or animal community service organizations.

Animal-assisted activities (AAA) are goal-directed activities designed to improve the patients' quality of life through the utilization of the human–animal bond. Animals and their handlers must be screened and trained, but are not guided by a credentialed therapist.

Animal-assisted therapy (AAT) utilizes the human–animal bond in goal-directed interventions as an integral part of the treatment process. Working animals and their handlers must be screened, trained, and meet specific criteria. A credentialed therapist working within the scope of practice of his or her profession sets therapeutic goals, guides the interaction between patient and animal, measures progress toward meeting therapy goals, and evaluates the process.

II. CHRONIC AND TERMINAL ILLNESS

A. AN OVERVIEW

Chronic and terminal conditions affect people's physical and mental health, social life, and employment status. While terminal conditions by definition, lead to death, chronic conditions persist over a long period of time (see Table II). Some chronic conditions are highly disabling, others less so. Some chronic

TABLE II   Chronic Illnesses and Leading Causes of Death in 1994

Prevalence of selected chronic conditions in the United States, 1994[a] (covers civilian noninstitutionalized population in millions of people)	
Chronic sinusitis	34.9
Arthritis	33.4
Deformities or orthopedic impairments	31.0
High blood pressure	28.2
Hearing impairments	22.4
Heart conditions	22.2
Asthma	14.6
Chronic bronchitis	14.0
Visual impairments	8.6
Diabetes	7.8
Cataracts	6.5

Death rates by leading cause, 1994[b] (death rates per 100,000 resident population in United States)	
Total deaths	875.6
Heart disease	281.3
Cancer	205.2
Cerebrovascular disease	58.9
Chronic obstructive pulmonary disease	37.0
Accidents and adverse effects	35.1
Diabetes mellitus	21.8
Motor vehicle accidents	16.3
HIV	16.2
Suicide	12.0
Homocide	9.6

[a]Source: U.S. National Center of Health Statistics, Vital and Health Statistic Series 10, No. 193, 1998.
[b]Source: U.S. National Center for Health Statistics, Monthly Vital Statistics Report, 1998.

conditions, especially diabetes, may not disable a person currently, but may lead to severely disabling effects if not treated early and effectively. Some terminal conditions such as AIDS have become more chronic in nature as new and more effective treatments have become available. Some people return to former levels of daily activity after recovering from a heart attack, stroke, trauma or other acute episode; some do not. Some individuals with chronic conditions live full, productive, and rewarding lives; for others, isolation, depression, and physical pain are the consequences of severe chronic illness (Hoffman, 1995).

Chronic conditions affect people of all ages and all strata of society. Contrary to popular misconceptions, the elderly are not the only ones with chronic and debilitating conditions (see Table III). Almost 100 million people in the United States have some form of chronic condition, from minor ailments such as sinusitis to severely disabling illnesses such as stroke (Hoffman, 1995). In 1995, one in six people in the United States (41 million) had a chronic condition that inhibited their lives to some degree. In 1993, 8 million working-age adults in the United States were prevented from working due to a disability caused by a chronic condition. At least 9 million people with disabilities in the United States need help with either personal care or home management. Of these, 40% are under 65 years of age. In addition, approximately 10–15% of children in the United States have chronic health impairments (Gortmaker, 1985). Furthermore, approximately 1 million children in the United States have a condition severe enough to affect their daily living (Perrin and MacLean, 1988). Approximately 10 million children have less severe chronic illnesses such as asthma (Thompson and Gustafson, 1996). Animal companions can provide many benefits to people with chronic/terminal illness (see Table IV).

TABLE III Percentage of Noninstitutionalized Persons with Chronic Conditions, By Age Group, 1987

0–17 years	14%
18–44 years	31%
45–64 years	29%
65+ years	26%
88.5 million people	

Source: Hoffman, C., and Rice, D. Estimates based on the 1987 National Medical Expenditure Survey. University of California, San Francisco, Institute for Health and Aging, 1995.

TABLE IV   Benefits That Animal Companions Can Give for People with Chronic Illnesses

---

Provide companionship

Decrease feelings of loneliness

Act as a surrogate for other relationships

Decrease stress

Provide a reason to exercise

Give the human caregiver a sense of purpose

Ease social interactions in public

Provide security to children and adults

B. AIDS: An Overview

Acquired immunodeficiency syndrome (AIDS) is one of the most serious health problems the U.S. public has ever faced. AIDS is caused by the human immuno-deficiency virus (HIV). HIV attacks the immune system and eventually reduces an infected person's ability to resist other infections and diseases. An estimated three-quarters of a million people in the United States are infected with HIV, with as many as 40,000 new infections each year in the United States (United Nations AIDS/WHO, 1998). Worldwide, the epidemic is out of control with 5.8 million new infections in 1998 (Table V). HIV is transmitted sexually, through contact with infected blood or infected needles, from mother to child

TABLE V   Global Summary of the HIV/AIDS Epidemic, December 1998

People newly infected with HIV in 1998	5.8 million
North America	44,000
Western Europe	30,000
Sub-Saharan Africa	4.0 million
Number of people living with HIV/AIDS	33.4 million
North America	890,000
Western Europe	500,000
Sub-Saharan Africa	22.5 million
AIDS deaths in 1998	2.5 million
Cumulative AIDS deaths as of 1998	13.9 million

Source: United Nations AIDS Statistics and World Health Organization estimate.

during pregnancy or by breastfeeding. The progression from HIV to AIDS is usually a slow process and it may be 10 years or longer from the time of initial infection with HIV until symptoms of AIDS appear. Once immunosuppression has occurred, people with AIDS (PWAs) become susceptible to opportunistic infections. These opportunistic infections may typically cause minimal disease in healthy persons, but can lead to death in PWAs. As more effective and less toxic treatments become available, AIDS is becoming a chronic condition. Unfortunately, the expensive therapies are not generally available to populations in the developing world or to the uninsured in the developed world, leading to the evolution of two distinct epidemics. An estimated 45% of Americans infected with HIV own pets (Spencer, 1992) (Figures 1 and 2). Many other PWAs have contact with animals through traditional AAT programs while hospitalized or in a hospice.

FIGURE 1   PAWS San Francisco client Robert Welch (died in 1998) and Minnie (adopted by PAWS President, Ilana Strubel, DVM). (Photograph by Pali Boucher, 1997. Reprinted courtesy of PAWS.)

FIGURE 2 PAWS San Francisco client Emilio (died January, 1999) and L'amour (adopted by his sister). (Photograph Pali Boucher, 1997. Reprinted courtesy of PAWS.)

C. Psychosocial Impact of Illness: the AIDS Virus

The psychological burden produced by AIDS and HIV infection can exceed that produced by any other medical condition (Maj, 1991). PWAs face not only the disease process but also its psychological ramifications. Primary to these obstacles are HIV's incurability and the associated public hysteria and misunderstanding (Cherry and Smith, 1993). A wealth of information suggests that PWAs are targets of stigmatization (Bennett, 1990). Individuals with AIDS often describe feelings of isolation, alienation, estrangement, and loneliness (Carmack, 1991). Two categories of loneliness have been described: emotional isolation and social isolation (Weiss, 1973). Emotional isolation appears to develop as a direct result of absence of an attachment figure. Social isolation, on the other hand, occurs when an individual lacks (or perceives a lack of) an effective social network. Research reported by Christ *et al.* (1986) suggests that PWAs may be especially susceptible to the experience of loneliness. They reported 75% of patients with AIDS have diminished social support from friends, family, and significant others.

III. HOW ANIMALS HELP CHILDREN AND ADULTS ADAPT TO THEIR ILLNESSES

A. A Theoretical Model

It is apparent that the quality of life for children and adults with chronic or terminal illnesses depends on the support mechanisms available. Quality of life is defined as an overall well-being that encompasses physical, material, social, and emotional well-being (Felce and Perry, 1993). It is believed that perceived quality of life for persons with various illnesses depends, in part, on how an individual attempts to cope with his or her medical challenges. When one feels supported and perceives fewer challenges, his or her quality of life may be enhanced.

For this chapter, the authors have selected a definition of social support that includes meaningful social contact, availability of confidants, and companionship (Dean and Lin, 1977). One cannot enhance any individual's quality of life in a vacuum or in isolation. Schalock (1996) suggests that the use of social supports is an efficient and effective way to maximize someone's independence, productivity, and life satisfaction. These social supports can include family members, other people, technology, in-home living assistance, and for that matter, even pets. Wilson (1991) suggests that more scientific investigation is needed to study the interaction between animals and humans. This research may be valuable in discovering the role animals can play in social support. Nebbe (1991) points out various studies that suggest that families with pets appeared to be more emotionally secure. Another study conducted by Levine and Bohn (1986) found that children in families with pets appeared to show greater empathy for other human beings.

The authors have considered many models in an attempt to describe how companion animals and animal-assisted activities can be understood as an important dimension of support. A theoretical "ecosystem" model, developed by Bronfenbrenner (1979), seems applicable in describing the support mechanisms that people use for overcoming the stresses of having a chronic and/or terminal illness (Fig. 3). This model consists of a series of nested contexts called a *microsystem, exosystem,* and *macrosystem.* The original model has been utilized to describe many significant challenges confronting families, including divorce and child abuse (Belsky, 1980a). This model views a person's life as

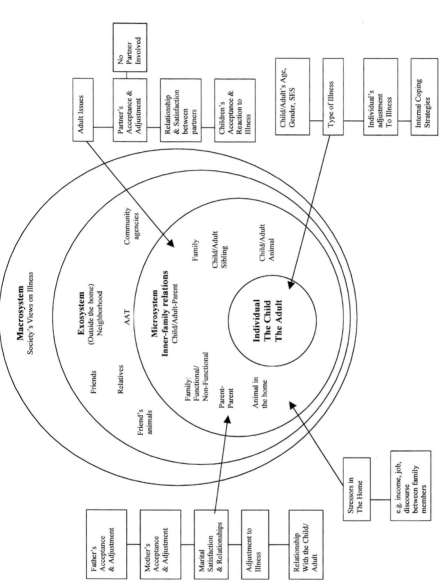

FIGURE 3 The ecosystem model displaying the various layers within the ecosystem and how they are all interrelated.

a social unit embedded within various formal and informal social units (Shea & Bauer, 1991).

Bronfenbrenner's model explains behavior similarly to the way a naturalist would view nature. An individual's ecosystem may be visualized as a series of layers that are all connected. The most central layer is what he called the *microsystem*. This system incorporates all the variables within his or her home that either can support or contaminate the growth of an individual. A child or adult who has a functioning support system at home may adapt more effectively to his or her illness. The impact of the medical challenge on any family appears dependent on the number of factors imposed by the condition. These factors may include the family resources (e.g., financial, job), the relationships within the family, and the social support system both within the family and the community. The *exosystem* consists of all other support systems found outside the home. Financial, medical, and emotional supports found in formal and informal neighborhood opportunities can make the life of a person with a chronic illness more livable or more of an ordeal. These options may be found formally at a work site, clinics, various religious institutions, and numerous community social service agencies. Informally, a person's sense of well-being may be lifted as a direct result of the contributions made by extended family members and close friends. Having good neighbors and family members who will frequently visit or call can tremendously impact one's perceived quality of life. Finally, the *macrosystem* is the outermost layer of a human being's ecosystem and incorporates the larger culture of the world in which we all live. This macrosystem may represent the culture's bias and reaction to various illnesses and conditions. Unfortunately, it may be within the cultural macrosystem that the stigma of an illness is developed. According to the tenets of an ecosystem model, there is a positive correlation between the resources secured and an individual's ability to function and adapt more effectively.

Bronfenbrenner urges mental health professionals to view the psychological health of any individual as a direct result of the forces operating within the systems that he or she lives within. The model permits simultaneous consideration of numerous factors within the microsystem, the exosystem, and the macrosystem that can help an individual adapt to illness.

As discussed earlier, the strength within a microsystem is directly related to the relationships that have been cultivated within one's immediate family and household. The microsystems for individuals differ from one to another. Persons with various illnesses may find themselves being responded to differently as a consequence of their specific illness, age, gender, and sexual orientation. Specifically, PWAs may face losing the support network they hold most dear—their family and friends (Cherry and Smith, 1993). Many PWAs find that their families or significant others do not understand or do not want to deal with the challenges of AIDS. Maj (1991) reports numerous incidents in which families refused to talk to their children with AIDS, denied financial assistance, and even returned correspondence unopened. Conversely, there are many PWAs who have supportive microsystems in which their families and significant others have been heroic in helping the PWA live and die with dignity. When individuals live in a supportive and harmonious environment, they are better at handling the stresses related to their illness.

B. ROLE OF PETS

It is within the microsystem that an animal may play the most crucial role. It is not uncommon for a child or an adult to perceive an animal as a peer (Nebbe, 1991). Pets also provide a valuable source of comfort and companionship for many individuals, including children (Wilson, 1991). According to Veevers (1985), animals may act as surrogates when they take the place of people. He suggests that "almost all interaction with companion animals involves some anthropomorphism and can in some way be construed as a surrogate for human relationships" (p. 11). Serpell (1983) further suggests that animals can supply compassion in cases where humans are unable to or are unavailable.

In an article on companion animals for PWAs, Carmack (1991) notes that the animals decrease the person's feelings of isolation and provide a perceived reduction of stress. Stress reduction can, in turn, improve immune system function. Because animals require affection and companionship, they can enhance feelings of being needed and valued. ("I care for them, and it lets me forget about things.") Persons with AIDS may perceive a companion animal as a family member and a direct source of emotional support that is particularly important for someone who may feel isolated and perhaps neglected.

Companion animals in the home may improve quality of life by increasing the amount of exercise in which chronically ill people may engage (Meer, 1984). Pet ownership also improves cardiovascular health by reducing anxiety, loneliness, and depression (Freidman et al., 1983; Katcher, 1981; Wilson, 1984). We think it is reasonable to assume that animals could be used to support more healthy living patterns.

Humans develop a strong attachment bond to animals (Volth, 1985). It is not uncommon to see many companion animals that, for example, sleep in their owners' rooms and accompany them on short trips and holidays. Many companion animals are recipients of special treats and gifts, just like other family members. Volth's research points out that both dog and cat owners can become equally attached to their animals.

According to Siegel (1993), companion animals within the home appear to acquire the ability to elicit positive emotional responses from their owners. Positive responses are initially elicited from the good feelings that are derived from tactile contact with the animal, and this continued pairing usually leads the owner to view the animal as a source of comfort. Interestingly, a social worker in England points out that companion animals appear to demonstrate some of the same attributes that are seen as being favorable in social workers (Hutton, 1982). Companion animals, for example, tend to help people use their own strengths to help themselves; animals tend to have the ability to form and establish relationships quickly; and animals are sensitive to people's feelings and emotions, thus recognizing those occasions when they are needed or wanted. Cusak (1988) suggests that animals can function as human surrogates in a number of roles including friends and confidants. Persons who are secluded within their homes may find the companionship of animals more meaningful. They can act as true friends, not only to pass time with, but to engage in true relationships. Pets can bring laughter and tenderness into a home. They can bring comfort at times when loneliness may be overbearing.

A good illustration of how pets support patients resulted from a study by Muschel (1985) who looked at the effects of animals on enhancing the quality of life of patients with cancer. Animals visited 15 hospitalized patients. Twelve of the 15 patients seemed very concerned about the "visiting" animals' welfare and would go out of their way to reassure the pets. They also seemed more content and outgoing in the presence of the animals and were observed to sing to and play with the animals. Interestingly, Muschel also alluded to how the animals seemed to be valuable as companions while the patients were struggling with facing death: "The animal's quiet, accepting and nurturing presence strengthens, and frees the patient to resolve his or her final experience successfully" (p. 452). Having a companion animal in a patient's home would seem to elicit the same responses.

C. ROLE OF COMMUNITY SERVICES

While we recognize the important role that companion and therapy animals can play for people with chronic illnesses, these people may need assistance in caring for their companion animals from within their exosystem. In most cases research has been done addressing the importance of contemporaries and their relationship to enhance quality of life. Shea and Bauer (1991) point out that relatives, neighbors, friends, and community organizations may provide tremendous support to the individual. An effective exosystem can provide wonderful support and opportunities for an individual. People outside one's immediate microsystem may make life more meaningful and easier. Friends and relatives may make it possible for some people to continue living on their own, by providing intermittent help with the cooking, shopping, and cleaning. The isolation from active society may also be diminished as a consequence of this external support system. Programs such as PAWS (Pets Are Wonderful Support, described later in this chapter) or friends within the community can be a viable resource for helping an individual keep a pet companion at home. Although a person with a chronic/terminal illness may not have the support within his or her microsystem to help take care of a companion animal, there may be people within the exosystem who can fill this void. Close relationships outside the home may provide ongoing support, as well as a sense of stability, in the lives of PWAs (Jue, 1994). Supportive relationships with friends or visiting animals can contribute to the individual's quality of life. These connecting experiences indirectly and directly contribute to offsetting isolation and perhaps enhance a sense of worth. These findings support the role of companion animals and visiting animal programs in decreasing a person's sense of social isolation. Those caring for PWAs and others with compromised immune systems, however, need to understand some of the risks of animal companionship.

IV. HISTORICAL SIGNIFICANCE OF ZOONOSES AND AIDS

Several million people in the United States have compromised immune systems, including an estimated 1 million people living with HIV (Angulo & Glasser, 1994). Other immunosuppressive illnesses and treatments include chemotherapy, some cancers, dialysis, congenital diseases, and others (Table VI). Immunosuppressed persons are susceptible to a number of opportunistic infections

TABLE VI   Immunocompromising Diseases/Conditions

- Alcoholism/liver cirrhosis
- Cancer (some)
- Chronic renal failure
- Congenital immunodeficiencies
- Diabetes mellitus
- HIV/AIDS
- Immunosuppressive treatments for autoimmune diseases, cancer, transplant recipients
- Long-term hemodialysis
- Old age
- Malnutrition
- Pregnancy
- Splenectomy

including zoonoses. Zoonoses are diseases that can be transmitted to humans by other vertebrate animals or shared by humans and other vertebrate animals. Angulo and Glasser reported that about 45% of immunosuppressed individuals may own pets and few immunosuppressed individuals are offered information about zoonoses prevention by health care providers. Although AIDS brought zoonoses out of the closet, the information is important for all immunosuppressed populations.

AIDS was first identified in 1981, when a cluster of case reports in New York City emerged describing a rare pneumonia in young, previously healthy homosexual males. This specific infection, caused by an opportunistic parasite known as *Pneumocystis carinii,* had previously been seen only in patients with immune system dysfunction, cancer, or undergoing chemotherapy treatments. Suddenly, because of AIDS, a large number of people were developing previously rare opportunistic infections. The swiftness of the spread of the virus and the large number of deaths in previously healthy individuals were unprecedented in modern medicine.

Although we knew that companion animals could not carry or transmit AIDS, at the time, many questions about the risks of other infections remained unanswered. The medical community in general was not prepared to answer esoteric questions about catching diseases from "Fluffy," the cat. Veterinarians knew about animal-borne diseases, but little about the degree of increased risk to immunosuppressed humans. Many physicians, unfamiliar with the details of zoonotic transmission, often chose to err on the side of caution, and simply advised their immunosuppressed patients to get rid of their pets to minimize any risks.

Was there a real risk or was there an overreaction by overzealous physicians? In the mid-1980s there was very little in the veterinary or medical literature about the increased risk of zoonoses to immunosuppressed individual pet owners. What made this situation so controversial and complicated was that there was a concurrent cerebral toxoplasmosis epidemic in PWAs. Toxoplasmosis is a parasitic disease seen mostly in cats, but humans and other mammals can acquire it. PWAs were developing symptoms from this infection at previously unknown rates. In addition, infected cat feces were known to be one source of transmission of this infection to people. Because most physicians were unfamiliar with zoonoses (Gorczyca *et al.,* 1989), a real crisis of misinformation about AIDS and zoonoses developed within the health care system. Actually, the toxoplasmosis epidemic was mostly from previous infections that recurred as the person's immune system deteriorated. Toxoplasmosis is more likely to be acquired from eating undercooked meat or from contact with the organism in the environment rather than directly from pet cats. This was not, however, generally known at first.

The recommendation for PWAs to find their pets a new home created a dilemma. People with HIV typically face many losses—of employment, friends, and family. They often feel isolated, rejected, and stigmatized. Their pets provide them with constancy and affection, yet these people were being separated from their pets, sometimes on medical advice. Ironically, they were often the very people who most needed the emotional and psychological benefits their animal companions gave them.

Soon, veterinarians began taking the lead in educating the public and health care fields about zoonotic risk for PWAs. These veterinarians questioned the value of separating animal companions from the people who seemed to need the companionship the most. Veterinarian Malcolm Kram, for example, got the New York State Veterinary Medical Association to develop the first recommendations in 1986 on how to minimize the risks of transmitting zoonoses from animals to people. But not all veterinary organizations were willing to take responsibility for educating the public. In some cases, it was the AIDS support organizations, such as the Shanti Project in San Francisco, that were willing to help (Gorczyca, 1991). These efforts eventually led to the publication of the PAWS' *Safe Pet Guidelines* in 1988. These were the first published guidelines to explain how to minimize zoonotic risks and support the importance of the human–animal bond for PWAs.

Today, there is still little evidence in the literature to support the thinking that people are contracting diseases from their companion animals, except for reptiles (Wong, 1998). In fact, for many physicians who treat PWAs, zoonoses have become a nonissue relative to other concerns about treatment and survival (D. Abrams, personal communication, 1998). Information about zoonoses in immunosuppressed populations is now more readily available. For example, the Healthy Pets, Healthy People Project has brought many resources together (see Appendix 3).

V. HOW PAWS DEVELOPED TO PROVIDE SUPPORT FOR PWAS WITH PETS

Around the same time that zoonoses emerged as an issue for PWAs, these individuals were finding that the ravages of AIDS made it increasingly difficult for them to feed and care for their pets. PWAs who chose to keep their pets often faced, for example, financial burdens and physical constraints (Table VII). Many of these people lacked family support. As with Bronfenbrenner's model, their microsystem was no longer functioning in ways to help them with pet care. Thus, community programs evolved in the exosystem to fill this void and help keep people and pets together.

TABLE VII   Problems PWAs Face in Caring for Their Pets

PWAs may have limited ability to care for their companion animals because of:
  Limited financial resources
  Limited family and/or social support
  Impaired physical ability
  Depression
  AIDS-related dementia
  Risk of zoonotic disease

Intially, other existing animal-oriented or AIDS support organizations were not set up to provide the kind of in-home services PWAs needed to care for their pets. No single group was prepared to cope with this particular dilemma. Clients of the San Francisco AIDS Foundation (SFAF) Food Bank began to request pet food, but because pet food was not initially available, some clients were forced to use their human rations to feed their animal companions. In response, the food bank began carrying pet food in 1985. While the financial needs associated with veterinary care and pet food were obvious, it soon became apparent that pet owners required other services, including assistance with dog walking, boarding services if the person became hospitalized, and adoption services if the person died. Except for carrying pet food at the food bank, the SFAF and other AIDS organizations in San Francisco were not equipped to put resources into the care of companion animals, because the AIDS epidemic quickly overwhelmed social services in San Francisco.

In 1986, a group of people banded together to do whatever was necessary to help their friends with AIDS keep their pets for as long as possible. In recognition of the importance of the human–animal bond, they called their group "Pets Are Wonderful Support," nicknamed "PAWS." Since its founding, the organization has sought to fill in the gaps between other AIDS service and animal-related organizations to address the particular problems and questions faced by immunosuppressed pet owners. Put in terms of Bronfenbenner's ecosystem of support, PAWS is an example of how the exosystem helped keep the companion animal and person together. In comparison to traditional AAT programs in which animals are brought into the hospital or home for short periods, the PAWS services allowed, in essence, 24-hour therapy from an individual's own companion animal.

PAWS became an independent volunteer-operated nonprofit organization in 1987. The main client services have evolved to include financial, emotional, and practical assistance. These include veterinary care and zoonoses education, a pet food bank, foster care and adoption planning, in-home pet care, and pet transportation (Table VIII). PAWS's purpose has been to deliver support services to keep PWAs and their animal companions together for as long as

TABLE VIII   HASS Services Provided by PAWS

- Veterinary care (preventive health and emergency care)
- Pet food bank
- Foster care
- Adoption planning
- Grooming and flea control
- In-home pet care (dog walking; aquarium, bird cage, and cat litter box cleaning)
- Pet transportation
- Administration of medication
- Zoonoses education (brochures, talks, education booths, hotline)
- Veterinary externship program
- Information and referral

possible in mutually healthy environments. During the past two decades, similar organizations and programs in other communities have developed worldwide to fill the niche (see Appendix 2). The authors will use PAWS as a model to describe the various services offered by HASS. Each community is different, and the services offered vary among the different programs, depending on the local funding, volunteer base, AIDS prevalence, and macrosystem/exosystem support. Some HASS organizations assist not only PWAs, but other disabled or elderly populations in need.

VI. SERVICES PROVIDED BY PAWS

A. VETERINARY CARE

The Veterinary Care Program is one of the most important functions of PAWS because keeping a pet healthy is important in keeping the human companion healthy. The program provides an annual physical examination and vaccinations to each client's animal. The visit with a veterinarian also allows for the client to ask questions about zoonoses. To help defray the costs of emergency or other essential medical treatments, PAWS offers annual grants to each client. In addition to grants, PAWS has expanded the exosystem by developing relationships with local veterinarians to offer discounted services to PAWS clients. Volunteers are available to take the pet to the veterinarian if the client is unable. In addition, PAWS encourages and helps to pay for spay/neuter surgeries.

B. Pet Food Bank

The PAWS Food Bank provides monthly allotments of pet food, litter, flea treatments, and pet accessories. The pet food bank is open every weekend and may be accessed once a month by PAWS clients, with delivery provided for homebound clients. Most of the products are donated by pet food manufacturers and distributors, local supermarkets, or by individual donors. Veterinary clinics also donate prescription foods for pets with special needs. Additional food is purchased with funds raised by PAWS development staff and volunteers.

C. Foster Care

Many times, a family member or friend will take care of the person's companion animals if a PWA goes into the hospital or is unable to care for the animal. However, early in the epidemic several pets were found in people's homes unattended when the pet owner was unexpectedly hospitalized. Through the years, there have been many instances in which individuals refused necessary hospital care until they were absolutely sure that their animal would receive proper care. PAWS Foster Care Program was created to provide temporary foster care for PWA's companion animals. If no volunteer foster home is available, PAWS makes arrangements with local kennels, veterinary clinics, or shelters to board the pet. PAWs also temporarily fosters animals that are in a transition to adoption or when the family is making funeral arrangements.

D. Adoption

When clients register with PAWS, they are encouraged to make an adoption plan, including a living will. This step helps provide planning for their pet's future care in the event that they should die before the animal. Individuals are asked to notify PAWS of the future adopting "parent" to ensure the pet will be transferred to the appropriate person in the event of the pet owner's death. If an individual is isolated and has no family or friends willing to adopt their companion animal, PAWS helps to identify possible alternative sources for adoption of their pets. PAWS will screen potential adopters and help find orphaned pets a home by networking throughout the community. Many clients are fearful of what will happen with their pet if they die. The living will addresses clients' fears by developing a plan to secure their pet a good home if and when the person cannot provide it themselves. Because animal welfare is a community problem, PAWS networks with other local animal adoption programs to insure client pets do not become part of the community of unwanted animals.

E. In-Home Services

PAWS volunteers offer litter box cleaning, dog walking, aquarium and aviary cleaning, administration of a pet's medications, pet grooming, pet food delivery, and flea control. Volunteers help bathe animals and trim their nails. Local groomers have also been generous in donating their services to PAWS clients. Veterinary pharmaceutical companies donate flea control products for use by PAWS clients on their pets or in their homes.

F. Zoonoses Education: Safe Pet Guidelines

From the inception of PAWS, zoonoses education has been a priority. In response to the lack of information on the risk of contracting zoonoses for PWAs, PAWS developed the *Safe Pet Guidelines* (see Appendix 1), which were first presented at a meeting of humane educators in 1988. The first hurdle was to educate physicians treating PWAs about the benefits of animal companionship, the small risk of zoonoses, and how to make pets even safer for their patients with AIDS. In the 1990s, many other veterinary organizations and schools, humane societies and the Centers for Disease Control and Prevention (CDC) published guidelines modeled after those published by PAWS (see Appendixes 5 and 6). The Healthy Pets, Healthy People Project brings all of these resources together in one place (see Appendix 3).

Current evidence supports the fact that most therapy or companion animals pose a minimal risk for transmitting zoonotic diseases (PAWS, 1998c). Following preventive measures will reduce the risk that an animal will carry or transmit zoonotic diseases (see Appendix 1). A healthy animal is less likely to pick up diseases and transmit them to humans.

All PAWS clients receive a copy of the *Safe Pet Guidelines* brochures. These guidelines help to educate individuals about which animal-handling behaviors are risky and how to reduce those risks. Consultations with veterinarians also allow for questions about zoonoses to be answered.

A primary goal of PAWS is preventive education including continued outreach to physicians, veterinarians, and other health care workers about the benefits and risks of animal companionship for PWAs and other immunocompromised populations. The organization provides community education at local and national medical and veterinary conferences. This includes information booths, posters, zoonoses talks, a web site and a hotline (see Figures 4 and 5).

G. The Healthy Pets, Healthy People Project

The development of the PAWS veterinary externship program has allowed interested veterinary students the opportunity to gain experience in public

FIGURE 4   An example of a PAWS's educational billboard used in a subway station in San Francisco (Reprinted courtesy of PAWS.)

health, the human–animal bond, and nonprofit organization work. Additionally, the extern helps the PAWS education program evolve. Through the PAWS externship, Stephanie Wong attended the National AIDS Conference, and the World AIDS Conference, and she became aware of the need to bring all current resources on zoonoses prevention into one place. Wong helped establish the Healthy Pets, Healthy People (HPHP) Project in 1998. The HPHP Project has continued to evolve, allowing more veterinary students the opportunity to work with PAWS and other HASS organizations. The HPHP continues to publish booklets and a web site, and staffs educational booths at veterinary, medical, and other professional conferences (see Appendix 3). The student externs answer questions about the benefits of the human–animal bond and the risks of zoonoses. HASS organizations can also offer externship opportunities for students of other disciplines. HPHP is working to bring together the

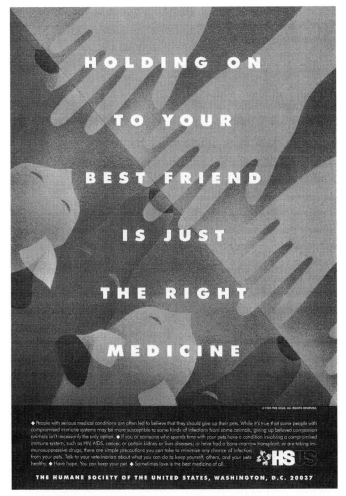

FIGURE 5   An example of a poster developed by the Humane Society of the United States for medical and veterinary waiting rooms. (Reprinted courtesy of The Humane Society of the United States.)

medical and veterinary communities in a common effort to improve animal and human health.

VII. THE AIDS EPIDEMIC: AN UPDATE

Nearly two decades after the AIDS epidemic was first documented in the United States, it continues out of control in most places. Although the epidemic has appeared to slow somewhat in the developed world, explosive AIDS epidemics are occurring in developing countries such as South Africa and India. Ninety-five percent of all HIV-infected people now live in the developing world (UN AIDS/WHO, 1998). New, more effective treatments are helping to make AIDS a chronic disease. However, there still is no cure. Opportunistic infections in PWAs have decreased by 80–90% in developed countries, reportedly due to new highly active antiretroviral therapies and new therapies for opportunistic infections (Wong, 1998). This has led to more long-term survivors in developed countries where these expensive drugs are available. Unfortunately, these new treatments are out of reach for most PWAs in the developing world or the uninsured in the developed world. The new therapies are also causing serious disabling side effects and increasing resistance to the therapy drugs in many people. Wong reports that these side effects are leading to continued isolation and depression, which increases the importance of animal companionship. She also reported that many PWAs are still told to give up their animal companions due to false fears and misinformation about zoonoses in both developed and developing countries.

VIII. EXAMPLES OF HUMAN–ANIMAL SUPPORT SERVICE PROGRAMS

PAWS in San Francisco is just one of dozens of programs worldwide that developed a HASS program for pet owners with chronic/terminal illnesses. HASS programs keep persons with chronic/terminal illness or disability together for as long as possible with their companion animals. Many models have evolved to fill the niche in a particular community (see Appendix 2). Urban areas such as San Francisco (PAWS), Washington, DC (PETS, DC), and New York City (POWARS), with a high population of PWAs, developed independent nonprofit agencies. This model works best where there are large funding and volunteer pools. In areas with more limited resources, the PAWS project typically evolves into a program of the local AIDS support service organization or of the local humane association. This minimizes the duplication of resources and services provided in the community. PAWS, Orange County (at the AIDS Services Foundation) and the Pet Project (at the Monterey County AIDS Foundation) are both examples of projects of AIDS organizations. The SHARE Program (at the Marin Humane Society), the PALS Program (at the Hawaiian Humane Society), and more recently the Phinney's Friends program (at the MSPCA in Boston) are models of programs of humane associations. In some communities, veterinary hospitals have taken on the responsibility of working directly with their local AIDS organizations to provide support services to PWAs. Each organization or program is unique and unaffiliated, although they may be considered loosely connected by similar names and services. In 1993 (St. Louis) and 1994 (New York City) at the Delta Society (a national human–animal bond organization) annual meetings, a PAWS Summit was held for representatives of these organizations nationwide. These meetings fostered the sharing of ideas and experience. Ongoing PAWS Summits are helpful for new and developing programs and organizations.

With the changing nature of the AIDS epidemic, some of these pet care projects have started to help other populations in need. One example is the Marin County Humane Society's SHARE Program, which has offered help to many pet owners with disabilities since the late 1980s. However, this is a unique situation and in most urban communities the resources are insufficient to help everyone suffering through the AIDS epidemic. Hopefully, the future will allow for expansion of pet care support services to all needy populations. The PAWS model is a good start and it would be prudent to incorporate what has been learned by these organizations when expanding these services into present and future HASS programs that will serve the needs of people with other disabilities and the elderly.

IX. GETTING STARTED

If an individual or group feels they want to start a PAWS program in their community, much planning needs to be undertaken. After a local community is assessed for needs and resources, the program planning can start. It is important to find other individuals and organizations to help support this effort. In many cases, the project may start out under the umbrella of an existing AIDS or animal welfare organization. It is much easier to start as a project of an existing organization than to start one from scratch, and this helps pool resources. Careful planning and follow-through are essential, because several PAWS projects have folded in the past. In localities that have a large need for services, a large funding base, and a large volunteer network, an independent volunteer-operated nonprofit organization with a working board of directors can usually be created. As the organization expands, hiring paid staff may also become a necessity. Salaried staff may include an executive dirctor, a volunteer director, a client services director, and others. Some organizations, however, are able to be 100% volunteer run, such as PhillyPAWS.

Community collaboration has been an important aspect in the evolution of HASS organizations. Many resources are available in communities that can help keep pets and people together, including local veterinary medical associations, humane associations, animal care and control agencies, veterinary hospitals, and AIDS service organizations. These organizations can sponsor educational talks, place articles in their newsletters, and help with fund-raising and public relations efforts. In addition, board members or volunteers may be located through networking with these resources. Other organizations and businesses can also be helpful in public relations and in locating other resources.

Specific guidelines must be developed to determine client eligibility (see Appendix 4) and services that will be provided. The program will need to screen clients by diagnosis and financial need. It is best to start out with limited services and expand slowly to avoid overextending the project. The services provided will depend on the resources and volunteer base available in your community.

Volunteerism is essential to a community-based organization. Volunteers can participate in activities ranging from animal care to fund-raising. People volunteer at PAWS for a variety of reasons. Some, for example, have an interest in the human–animal bond and AIDS. Others cannot have their own pets, but want to interact with animals. Volunteering can also be a way to help terminally ill people maintain a better quality of life. Volunteer training is essential. There can be many difficulties working with people that have terminal illnesses, and this can lead to "burnout." However, good training and support can help avoid or minimize burnout. Universal precautions must be taught since AIDS is an infectious disease (see Appendix 7). It is also important for regular communication with the volunteers through meetings, newsletter, e-mail, web sites, phone calls, and appreciation parties.

The board of directors is an essential volunteer role. This body is in charge of setting personnel policies, client service policies, hiring, firing, setting budget, making sure the organization meets legal requirements and more. The board must work with the staff and volunteers to make sure services are provided. The board must also ensure that the organization's insurance needs are met.

The major expenditures of PAWS are staffing, veterinary care, rent for office space and the pet food bank, and insurance. Fund-raising becomes a major focus of the organization or project and can come from a variety of sources. These include donations from individuals, organizations, businesses; grants; in-kind donations of services and pet food; bequests; events; veterinary service donations; and vaccination clinics. Examples of major events include fashion shows, fun runs, bikeathons, dog walkathons, raffles, silent auctions, black tie events and beer busts. Some of the easiest fund-raising results when an organization becomes a beneficiary for an event sponsored by other businesses or organizations.

Each community has many resources available to help nonprofit organizations get started and grow. Also, the Delta Society publishes guidelines for developing AAT programs that are also useful for HASS organizations. PAWS also publishes a "start-up packet" for people wishing to start a PAWS program in their community.

X. CONCLUSIONS

Keeping people with chronic or terminal illnesses together with their animal companions for as long as possible can enhance the person's quality of life. The process also seems to increase longevity and reduce the sense of isolation and loneliness. The HASS models presented in this chapter represent guidelines and "blueprints" for organizational development designed to assist persons with chronic/terminal illnesses while they live within their homes (or the homes of others). Clinicians, veterinarians, and community members interested in enhancing the quality of life for persons with chronic/terminal illnesses may consider using the HASS model as a starting point.

Pets Are Wonderful Support!

APPENDIX 1. GUIDELINES FOR ANIMALS USED IN AAT WITH IMMUNOCOMPROMISED PERSONS*

Current evidence supports the fact that most therapy or companion animals pose a minimal risk for transmitting zoonotic diseases. Pets provide many physical and psychological benefits that outweigh the risks of zoonoses. A healthy animal is less likely to pick up diseases and transmit them to humans. The Centers for Disease Control and Prevention states that companion animals cannot acquire or transmit the human immunodeficiency virus. The following guidelines help explain how to make pets as safe as possible. These preventive measures will help reduce the risk that an animal used in AAT or those living in a home will carry or transmit diseases.

GENERAL GUIDELINES

Diet

- Feed a high-quality commercial diet that is designed for the animal and for his or her stage of life.
- Do not feed the animal raw or undercooked meats or unpasteurized milk. Keep in mind that microwaving may not heat meat sufficiently to kill organisms in it.

*Source: Adapted with permission from Pets Are Wonderful Support's *Safe Pet Guidelines, Questions You May Have About Your Cat and Your Health*, *Questions You May Have About Your Bird and Your Health*, San Francisco, 1998.

- Prevent coprophagy (stool eating). Never let the animal eat his or her own or another animal's feces.
- Provide plenty of clean, fresh water. Do not let the animal drink from the toilet.
- Prevent the animal from raiding the trash.
- Prevent the animal from hunting or eating other animals. Cats can be exposed to toxoplasmosis from eating rodents. Ideally, a cat used for AAT should be kept indoors. If a cat goes outdoors, consider keeping him or her under your direct supervision.

Veterinary Care

- Have all new animals examined by a veterinarian.
- Take the animal to the veterinarian for a checkup at least once each year.
- Keep vaccinations current.
- Have the animal's feces checked by a veterinarian periodically for parasites. New animals should probably also be tested for *Salmonella, Campylobacter,* and *Cryptosporidium.*
- Have cats (particularly a new cat or an outdoor cat) checked for the feline leukemia virus and feline immunodeficiency virus.

Grooming and Flea Control

- Have the animal bathed, brushed, and combed as needed to keep the skin and coat healthy.
- Keep the animal's toenails trimmed to minimize the risk of scratching people. If necessary, ask your veterinarian about rubber caps that can be placed on a cat's nails.
- Use good flea control. Consult with your veterinarian about the best available methods.
- Keep the animal's living and feeding areas clean.
- Wash or change the animal's bedding regularly.

Human Health Measures

Administer first-aid for bites and scratches. Rinse a bite wound or scratch immediately with plenty of cool running water and wash the area with a mild soap or with a "tamed iodine" solution such as Betadine® solution that has been diluted with water. Always consult a physician if someone is injured by an animal bite.

Hygiene

Anyone handling animals should wash his or her hands frequently, especially before eating or smoking. Avoid contact with the animal's bodily fluids such as vomit, feces, urine, or saliva. Do not allow animals to lick a wound on a person's face or body.

Animals to Avoid for Individuals at Higher Risk

Several animals should be avoided when working with individuals at higher risk for zoonoses. These include reptiles (turtles, lizards, and snakes) and amphibians; wild animals and birds, including pigeons; farm animals (particularly cattle, goats, and sheep); nonhuman primates (monkeys); stray animals; and animals with diarrhea. *Salmonella* infection can be transmitted by almost any reptile, many of which are carriers of *Salmonella* without showing any signs of illness. Because reptiles are housed in an environment where they are exposed to their own feces, the bacteria can be found anywhere (and everywhere) on the animal's body. Nonhuman primates carry the greatest risk because of their close genetic relationship to humans. Young farm animals can carry *Cryptosporidium* and other infections.

SPECIFIC CONCERNS ABOUT ZOONOTIC INFECTIONS FROM PARTICULAR ANIMALS

Dogs

Though they pose a minimal risk for transmitting infectious diseases to humans, dogs, particularly puppies, do carry some diseases that could be harmful to someone at higher risk. Parasites that dogs can transmit to people include roundworms, hookworms, whipworms, *Cryptosporidia,* and *Giardia.* In rare instances, dogs can also transmit bacteria such as *Salmonella* and *Campylobacter.* These parasites and bacteria are most often associated with puppies or with adult dogs who are in unsanitary environments. Any new dog or any dog having diarrhea may need to have his or her stool tested for these infections by a veterinarian.

When working with people at higher risk, we recommend using only dogs that are more than 9 months old. Puppies are more likely to harbor infections than healthy adult dogs.

Cats

Conditions Associated with Bartonella henselae *Infections.*

Cat scratch disease (CSD) is a *Bartonella* infection in humans that usually causes fever, fatigue, and swollen lymph nodes. Bacillary angiomatosis (BA) is a rare condition associated with *Bartonella* infection that usually occurs only in people with HIV/AIDS. Patients with BA may have skin lesions that sometimes resemble Kaposi's sarcoma. BA can also affect internal organs such as the liver or spleen. Most cat scratches do not develop into CSD or bacillary angiomatosis.

Cats that carry the agent are generally not ill and show no signs of infection. Recent research shows that cats acquire the organism from fleas. Cats may transmit *Bartonella* to people by scratches or possibly bites. Fleas may also be involved with transmission to people. Cats less than 1 year of age are more likely to be associated with transmission of CSD or BA than are adult cats.

Although tests are available to determine if a cat has been exposed to *Bartonella,* testing is usually not necessary and interpretation of test results can be controversial. The following are guidelines for minimizing the chances that a cat could transmit this disease:

- Avoid rough play. Discourage cats from scratching or biting.
- Keep the cat's nails trimmed short. If the cat tends to scratch frequently, talk with your veterinarian about behavior modification or nail caps for cats to help minimize scratches.
- Wash all bites or scratches immediately with soap and water.
- Don't allow cats to lick open wounds.
- When working with people at higher risk, use only cats that are older than 9 months.
- Use good flea control on cats.

Ringworm

Ringworm is the common name for a group of fungal infections that affect the skin of a large variety of animals, including cats and people. Most cats with ringworm will lose hair and have crusty skin at the infection site. This can look very similar to many other skin conditions, so people should contact their veterinarian if they think their cat may have ringworm. Some cats, particularly certain purebred cats, can carry ringworm without showing any symptoms. Anyone, including someone with a healthy immune system, can potentially contract ringworm from a cat (or other animal) that is carrying the disease. Ringworm is treatable and there is no evidence that it is more severe or more common in people with compromised immune systems.

Toxoplasmosis

Toxoplasmosis is an infection caused by the single-celled parasite *Toxoplasma gondii.* It can infect most mammals (including humans) and some birds. Cats are the only species of animal to pass the infectious stage in their feces. Other animals, however, can disseminate *Toxoplasma* if their infected meat is eaten without being properly cooked.

Cats acquire toxoplasmosis by eating rodents, undercooked meat, the feces of other cats, or contaminated soil. Cats can acquire the infection easily if they are allowed to hunt or are fed raw or undercooked meat. As many as 90% of cats are exposed to *Toxoplasma* in their lives. Most infected cats show no symptoms of the disease. Sometimes there is a short episode of diarrhea, pneumonia, or ongoing neurologic or eye problems. Healthy cats can pass the infection only during the first 2 weeks after they are exposed. After that time, the cat's immune system will usually prevent passing of the organism.

Although a test is available to measure a cat's antibody response to toxoplasmosis, testing cats is usually not necessary because the test results would not change the preventive recommendations. To minimize a cat's chance of infection:

- Do not feed the cat undercooked meat.
- Feed commercial cat foods.
- Prevent the cat from hunting.
- Keep the cat indoors.

Humans will only rarely acquire toxoplasmosis from an infected cat. More commonly, people are exposed through ingestion of undercooked meat, unwashed fruits, or vegetables; congenitally (from an infected mother to her fetus through the placenta); or by accidental ingestion of soil when gardening. About 15–50% of the U.S. population (depending on geographic location) has already been exposed.

A healthy adult human is unlikely to show symptoms when exposed to *Toxoplasma*. If someone is pregnant, however, and only if it is her first exposure, infection can lead to birth defects and possible miscarriage. If someone has a compromised immune system due to conditions such as AIDS/HIV or chemotherapy, toxoplasmosis can be life threatening, often leading to central nervous system disorders. Most cases of toxoplasmosis in immunocompromised people are due to a reactivation of a previous infection rather than a new infection.

Other Zoonotic Diseases of Cats

Cats can occasionally be the source for a variety of intestinal ailments including some bacterial infections (*Salmonella* and *Campylobacter*) and some intestinal parasites (*Giardia, Cryptosporidium,* and roundworms.) These diseases can be spread to people by direct contact with the feces of an infected cat or by contact with soil that has been contaminated by the feces of an infected cat. Many animals other than cats can also carry these infections.

Salmonella and *Campylobacter* are most often spread through undercooked meat or improperly prepared food.

Cats that are carrying one of these infections will sometimes, but not always, have diarrhea. Cats at highest risk for one of these infections are stray cats, young kittens, cats recently adopted from an animal shelter, or cats that are immunosuppressed themselves.

Feline Leukemia Virus (FeLV) and Feline Immunodeficiency Virus (FIV)

Both of these viruses are different from the human AIDS virus (HIV). Both FeLV and FIV are contagious between cats, but neither of them can infect humans, nor can the human virus infect cats. These diseases do, however, suppress the cat's immune system, making the cat more susceptible to diseases that could be passed on to humans. For this reason, it is probably best not to use a cat with FeLV or FIV when working with people at higher risk for zoonoses.

Birds

Infections such as *Mycobacterium avium* complex (MAC), psittacosis (parrot fever), and salmonellosis are the primary diseases associated with pet birds that can potentially be transmitted to humans. Newly adopted birds and birds undergoing other stresses are more likely to carry one of these infectious organisms. There are no specific symptoms characteristic of each disease. If a bird stops eating, loses weight, has vomiting or diarrhea appears fluffed up and chilled, or shows other symptoms, then he or she should be seen by a veterinarian immediately.

These diseases can be transmitted by direct contact with droppings and nasal discharges or by breathing dried, powdered droppings. Birds are not the only source for these infections. It is much more common to acquire them from the environment, undercooked or contaminated foods, or in some cases, from other people. Complete avoidance is impossible. The likelihood of acquiring any of these infections from a pet bird is quite low.

MAC, also known as atypical *Mycobacterium* (a disease similar to tuberculosis), is most commonly acquired from the environment, can cause a variety of symptoms in people, and is suspected to be involved with AIDS wasting syndrome. MAC is a lifelong infection, which can be reactivated as the immune system deteriorates. Drugs are now available that can help control MAC infections in humans.

Psittacosis, an infection with *Mycoplasma psittaci,* produces flulike symptoms and is usually accompanied by a dry cough and fever. Psittacosis can be acquired multiple times. To date, there are no reported cases of psittacosis in people with HIV/AIDS.

Salmonellosis causes fever and gastrointestinal symptoms including stomach cramps and diarrhea. *Salmonella* infections can occur repeatedly and an infected person can become a chronic carrier without showing any symptoms.

Allergic alveolitis is a noninfectious allergic respiratory condition that can develop in people who are sensitive to birds. This condition produces coughing and difficulty breathing. It can be alleviated by total avoidance of bird dander, feathers, and, in some cases, poultry products.

Guidelines to minimize the chance that a bird used for AAT can contract one of these infections or transmit an infection to humans include these:

- Never expose a bird to other birds that have not been tested for psittacosis and quarantined for 45 days. It is especially important to avoid contact with pigeons and other wild birds.
- Avoid situations in which a bird will have casual contact with other birds (such as going to the pet store for wing clips and nail trims). Ideally, birds should be cared for at home rather than in boarding facilities.
- All sick birds should be seen by a veterinarian as soon as possible.
- Clean the bird's cage liner regularly, and particularly before taking the bird to an AAT setting.
- Anyone having physical contact with birds should wash his or hands regularly.
- Do not use wild birds including pigeons in an AAT setting.
- Follow the general *Safe Pet Guidelines* given earlier.

The following guidelines will minimize the chance that a new bird used for AAT has one of these infections:

- Only buy from a reputable source and only buy domestically bred birds—no imports or wild-caught birds.
- Do not buy birds that have been housed with imported birds.
- Avoid pet store birds and any bird that appears sick.
- Always set up a postadoption veterinary visit to have the bird examined.

Testing New Birds for Diseases

Because each situation is different, a veterinarian will be better able to make recommendations for a particular situation. In general, we do not recommend routine screening for MAC or *Salmonella* because even some birds carrying these diseases will have a negative test result. In general, all newly acquired birds in the parrot family should be tested for psittacosis. Veterinarians who have experience with birds can be located by contacting, state or local veterinary medical associations, or the Association for Avian Veterinarians (AAV) at P.O. Box 811720, Boca Raton, FL 33481, telephone: (561)393-8901. The AAV also publishes a useful brochure on psittacosis.

Rabbits and Rodents

Zoonoses transmitted by pet rabbits and rodents (rats, mice, guinea pigs, hamsters, or gerbils) are quite rare. The most common problems usually stem from reactions to rabbit scratches or infections from rabbit or rodent bites. The *Pasteurella* bacteria carried by most rabbits may infect scratches or bite wounds. Scratches and bite wounds should be immediately washed and disinfected. Some external parasites of the rabbit, including fur mites and ringworm (a type of fungal infection), may be transmitted to humans.

Guinea pigs, mice, and rats can occasionally be the source for a variety of human intestinal ailments including some bacterial infections (*Salmonella* and *Campylobacter*), and some intestinal parasites (*Giardia* and *Cryptosporidium*). These diseases can be spread to people by direct contact with the feces of an infected animal or by contact with soil that has been contaminated by the feces of an infected animal.

Horses

Zoonoses transmitted by horses are quite rare. Intestinal parasites and infections such as *Salmonella* can potentially be spread to people. People at higher risk should not come in contact with an immature horse or areas where horses are raised. Adult horses kept in a clean environment pose a minimal risk for transmitting a disease.

APPENDIX 2. HUMAN–ANIMAL SUPPORT SERVICE ORGANIZATIONS FOR PEOPLE WITH AIDS

AUSTRALIA

Pets Are Wonderful Support (PAWS, NSW)
Box 437
Kensington NSW 1465
phone: 61 2 9361 4449
fax: 6 12 9360 7770

CANADA

Pet Program
(Toronto PWA Foundation)
399 Church St, 2nd Floor
Toronto, Ontorio M5B2J6
phone: (416)506-1400

Pet Pal Program
(Pacific AIDS Resource Center)
1107 Seymoure St.
Vancouver, British Columbia V6B558
phone: (604)681-2122

UNITED STATES OF AMERICA

ARIZONA

PAWS, Phoenix
(Affiliate of Phoenix Body Positive)
4021 N. 30th, St., Suite 102
Phoenix, AZ 85016
phone: (602)381-7767
web:*http://www.swlink.net/~bodypos/programs.htm*

CALIFORNIA

Pets Are Loving Support (PALS)
P.O. Box 1539
Guerneville, CA 95446
phone: (707)887-2729
fax: (707)869-9610
web: *http://www.sonic.net/~pals/*

PAWS, Los Angeles
7327 Santa Monica Blvd
West Hollywood, CA 90046
phone: (213)876-7297
fax: (213)876-0511
e-mail: pawsla7327@aol.com
web: *http://www.lexiweb.com/lexiweb/paws/*

PAWS, Orange County
(Affiliate of AIDS Services Foundation)
17982 Skypark Circle, Suite J
Irvine, CA 92714
phone: (949)253-1500

PAWS, San Diego
3022 Cedar St.
San Diego, CA 92103
phone: (619)234-7297
web: *http://www.realsolutions.org/animavol.htm*

Pets Are Wonderful Support (PAWS, SF)
P.O. Box 460487
San Francisco, CA 94146
phone: (415)241-1460
fax: (415)252-9471
e-mail: pawssf@dnai.com
web: *http://www.pawssf.org*

Pet Project
(Monterey County AIDS Foundation)
780 Hamilton St
Seaside, CA 93955
phone: (831)394-4747

SHARE Program
(Marin Humane Society)
171 Bel Marin Keys Blvd.
Novato, CA 94949
phone: (415)883-4621, ext. 255
fax: (415)382-1349

DISTRICT OF COLUMBIA

PETS, DC
2001 "O" Street, N.W.
Washington, D.C. 20036
phone: (202)234-7387
web: *http://www.petsdc.org/*

FLORIDA

Lower Keys Friends of Animals
P.O. Box 1043
Key West, FL 33041
phone: (305)292-5070

GEORGIA

PALS—Pets Are Loving Support
1058 Northside Drive, Suite C
Atlanta, GA 30318
phone: (404)876-7257
fax: (404)249-7387

HAWAII

Maui PAWS
(MAUI AIDS Foundation)
P.O. Box 111
Kula, HI 96790
phone/fax: (808)878-2528

PALS Program
(Hawaiian Humane Society)
2700 Waialae Avenue
Honolulu, HI 96826
phone: (808)946-2187, ext. 217

INDIANA

PAWS Indiana
1350 N. Pennsylvania
Indianapolis, IN 46402
phone: (317)632-0123, ext. 250

ILLINOIS

Windy City PAWS
1508 W. Hollywood Ave.
Chicago, Ill 60660
phone: (773)784-3803
e-mail: wcpaws@wxpaws.com
web: *http://www.wcpaws.com*

MASSACHUSETTS

Phinney's Friends
(MSPCA)
350 South Huntington Avenue
Boston, MA 02130
phone: (617)522-7400

MICHIGAN

WAGS (Wonderful Animals Giving Support)
(Midwest AIDS Prevention Project)
429 Livernois
Ferndale, MI 48220
phone: (888)226-6366
e-mail: MAPP@wwnet.net
web: http://www.wwnet.net/~mapp

MISSOURI

PAWS St. Louis
1425 Hampton Avenue
St Louis, MO 63139
phone: (314) 781-7976
fax (314) 781-7378
e-mail: paws@freewweb.com
web: http://www.paws-stl.org

NEW JERSEY

PetPals of Southern New Jersey
100 Essex Rd, Suite 30
Belmar NJ 80831
phone: (609) 931-4399

NEW MEXICO

PAWS, Albuquerque
(New Mexico AIDS Services)
4200 Silver Avenue SE
Albuquerque, NM 87108
phone: (505)266-0911
fax: (505)266-5104

NORTH CAROLINA

Pets Are Loving Support (PALS)
P.O. BOX 32141
Charlotte, NC 28232
phone: (704)561-5179
fax: (704)375-1628

PENNSYLVANIA

PhillyPAWS
P.O. Box 30262
Philadelphia, PA 19103
phone: (215)985-0206
fax: (215)985-0205
e-mail: philpaws@critpath.org
web: *http://www.hillary.net/paws.html/*

TENNESEE

PAWS Program
(Nashville CARES)
209 10th Ave., N., Suite 160
Nashville, TN 37203
phone: (615)259-4866 ext 157
fax: (615)259-4849
web: http://home.earthlink.net/~nashcare/paws.html

TEXAS

Pet Pals
(AIDS Resource Center)
P.O. Box 190869
Dallas, TX 75219
phone: (214)521-5444
fax: (214)522-4604

WASHINGTON

King County's Pet Project
(The Washington Humane Society for Seattle/Kings County)
13212 S.E. Eastgate Way
Bellvue, WA 98005
phone: (425)649-7566
fax: (425)747-2985
web: http://www.seattlehumane.org

Pet Support Network
(Broadway Veterinary Hospital)
1824 12th Avenue
Seattle, WA 98122
phone: (206)322-5444
fax: (206)328-8780

Current listing of HASS organizations can be found at the following websites: *http://www.pawssf.org* and *http://www.lgvma.org*

APPENDIX 3. HEALTHY PETS, HEALTHY PEOPLE RESOURCE GUIDE*

Pets provide unconditional support and love for many people. However, pets can also carry zoonoses, diseases that can be transmitted from animals to humans. During the past 10 years, much has been researched about the benefits and risks of pet ownership to immunocompromised persons.

Initially, little was known about pet-related zoonoses, and many health professionals were recommending that people with immunocompromising

*Source: Adapted with permission from Healthy Pets, Healthy People Project, 1998.

conditions give up their pets. Today, we know that pets are a minimal risk to immunocompromised persons and that the benefits of animal companionship most outweigh the danger of zoonoses.

The Healthy Pets, Healthy People Project was created to help answer some of the most common questions about pet ownership by immunocompromised persons. This resource guide includes information on disease that compromise the human immune system, the pet-related zoonoses of concern, safe pet guidelines, and an extensive list of current resources on the health risks and benefits of pets to immunocompromised persons.

Health Benefits of Animals to Humans

Although the U.S. Health Service states that pets present only a minimal health risk to immunocompromised persons, 60% of HIV-infected pet owners were told by their physicians that they should not own pets.

Current research has demonstrated that pets provide many physical and psychological benefits that outweigh the small risks of zoonoses. Caring for a pet results in many physical health benefits. Pets decrease blood pressure, cholesterol, and triglyceride levels. They reduce morbidity and mortality related to heart disease. Pet ownership can lead to fewer office visits and a reduction in minor health problems.

Pets provide emotional support at a time when it is most needed. People with immunocompromising diseases can feel isolated and alone. Pets decrease feelings of loneliness and increase feelings of intimacy and constancy.

It is crucial for health professionals to consider the many health benefits that pets provide to immunocompromised persons before making any recommendation about pet ownership. The following resources may be helpful to you and your patients.

Brochures, Pamphlets, and Booklets

Safe Pet Guidelines
Questions You May Have About Your Cat and Your Health
Questions You May Have About Your Bird and Your Health
Pets Are Wonderful Support (PAWS)
P.O. Box 460487
San Francisco, CA 94146
phone: (415)241-1460

HIV/AIDS & Pet Ownership
Tuskegee University School of Veterinary Medicine
Tuskegee, AL 36088
phone: (334)727-8174

Opportunistic Infections and Your Pets
You Can Prevent Taxoplasmosis
You Can Prevent Cryptosporidiosis
Centers for Disease Control and Prevention
CDC National Clearinghouse
phone: (800)458-5231

Safe Reptile Handling Guidelines
Association of Reptile and Amphibian Veterinarians.
PIJAC
1220 19th St., N.W., Suite 400
Washington, DC 20036
phone: (202)452-1525

Psitticosis
Association of Avian Veterinians
P.O. Box 811720
Boca Raton, FL 33481
phone: (561)393-8901

What Every Cat Owner Should Know about FIV
American Animal Hospital Association
12575 West Bayaud Avenue
Lakewood, CO 80228
phone: (303)986-2800

Good For Your Animals, Good For You; How to Live and Work with Animals in Activity and Therapy Programs and Stay Healthy. Walthner-Toews, D., and Ellis, A.; published by University of Guelph

Health Benefits of Animals Packet
DELTA Society
P.O. box 1080
Renton WA 98057
phone: (800)869-6898

Zoonoses Updates (2nd ed.)
American Veterinary Medical Association
1931 N. Meacham Rd St 100
Schaumburg, IL 60178
phone: (800)248-2862

Zoonotic Diseases: The Veterinary Clinics of North America: Small Animal Practice.
January 1987, Vol. 17, No. 1
W.B. Saunders Company

Posters for Veterinary and Medical Offices

Holding on to Your Best Friend Is Just the Right Medicine
Humane Association of the United States
2100 L Street, N.W.
Washington, DC 20250
phone: (202)452-1100

Practice Safe RHEX: Reptile Handling Excellence
Pet Industry Joint Advisory Council
1220 19th Street, N.W., Suite 400
Washington, DC 20036
phone: (202)452-1525

Hotlines

Centers for Disease Control and Prevention
(800)458-5231

Project Inform (AIDS)
(800)822-7422

National AIDS Hotline
(800) 342-2437

Pets Are Wonderful Support
(415)241-1460

Lesbian and Gay Veterinary Medical Association
e-mail only: LGVMA@lgvma.org

Videos

Living with HIV and Pets
Latham Foundation
Clement & Schiller
Alameda, Ca 94501
phone: (510)521-0920

Zoonosis
Latham Foundation

Our Pets, Our Health
DELTA Society
phone: (800)869-6898

Summary Journal Articles

American Veterinary Medical Association
"World AIDS Day 1992—how veterinarians are helping," *Journal of American Veterinary Medical Association,* **201**(1), 1992, 1663–1684.
"Caring for pets of immunocompromised persons," Angulo, F. J. *et al., Journal of American Veterinary Medical Association,* **205**(12), 1994, pp. 1711–1718.

American Humane Association
Operational Guide for Animal Care and Control Agencies: Zoonoses, 1998.

Humane Society of the United States
"HIV/AIDS and Animal Sheltering: What every shelter should know," *Shelter Sense,* **18**(2), 1995, pp. 2–12.

Clinical Infectious Diseases Journal
"Animal-associated opportunistic infections among persons infected with the human immunodeficiency virus," Glaser, C. *et al., Clinical Infectious Diseases,* **18**, 1994, pp. 14–24.
"USPHS/IDSA guidelines for the prevention of opportunistic infections," *Clinical Infectious Diseases,* **21**(suppl. 1), 1995, pp. S21–S43.

WEB SITES

Pets Are Wonderful Support
http://www.pawssf.org

Healthy Pets, Healthy People Project
http://www.lgvma.org

HIV InSite (of the University of California, San Francisco)
http://hivinsite.ucsf.edu

APPENDIX 4. PAWS CLIENT SERVICES POLICIES*

PAWS is dedicated to doing whatever we can to help people with AIDS and their companions. However, due to limited resources and the ever-growing need for our services, it is necessary that we follow these policies.

*Source: Pets Are Wonderful Support, San Francisco, 1998. Reprinted with permission.

Eligibility

1. *Clients*: Any resident of San Francisco who is able to present a letter confirming AIDS diagnosis and proof of low-income status (SSI, SSD, State Disability, General Assistance) is eligible to be a client of PAWS.

Any clients previously accepted into our program shall remain clients, even if they do not currently fit our eligibility requirements for AIDS diagnosis. We will continue to service existing clients who already live outside of SF. We cannot provide services to existing San Francisco clients if they should move.

Once a client no longer has the animal companions he/she registered with PAWS at intake, that person will no longer be considered a PAWS client. If new animals are acquired, that person must ask to be put on the waiting list for consideration as a client.

2. *Animals*: Each client will receive assistance for up to two animals only. Ongoing assistance will be provided for these animals for as long as possible. PAWS will not cover any additional animals who may be added to a client's household. Our mission is to help people with AIDS keep their animals—not to assist people in getting new animals or in replacing animals who die or are lost. Except for rare cases in which the animal's health prohibits surgery, all PAWS animals must be spayed/neutered. If an animal is intact at the time of client intake, the client must agree to have his companion animal spayed/neutered within six months. Due to potential health hazards for our clients, and because of our concern for the animals, PAWS will not cover any animals who are under nine months of age. Reptiles, wildlife, amphibians, primates, ferrets or other animals who pose significant health risk will also be exempt from coverage.

3. *Annual Certification*: If possible, an annual recertification will take place to ensure that all clients are still eligible to receive services.

4. *Special Note*: Although we are concerned about the health and well-being of both human and animal clients, if a human client passes away, his/her animals do not automatically remain PAWS clients. Animals may still receive benefits if their new guardian is eligible to become a client. This new caretaker can and will bypass whatever waiting list exists in order to immediately become a client. However, the new guardian must go through an official intake process and will not receive services without proof of eligibility.

Intake Process

All clients must have an intake interview and complete all required paperwork. The Client Services Director or designated PAWS staff member will complete this interview and ensure the eligibility requirements are met.

Services: Payments and Procedures

PAWS will provide all services (except veterinary care) to clients free of charge. These services may include monthly allotments of food and litter; volunteer assistance with dog walking, kitty litter maintenance and aquarium cleaning; animal bathing and nail clipping; transportation to veterinary or grooming appointments; foster care; adoption services and educational materials. We cannot guarantee any of our services.

1. *Food*: Due to financial constraints, PAWS will not be able to cover all necessary dietary needs for our client animals. The monthly food allotments are meant to be supplemental only. As much as possible we will strive to provide a consistent diet for client animals in our auspices, however specific brands may vary depending on donations received. If animals require special diets we will make sure these diets are available, provided we have a veterinarian-approved special diet form on file.

Clients may visit the Food Bank once every four weeks. If a client is not able to attend in person, he/she may send someone else as long as the PAWS office is notified in advance. Clients must show their Client ID card when picking up food. If a client is homebound, special arrangements will be made for food delivery. Any special arrangements will be made at the discretion of the Client Services Director.

2. *Veterinary care*: Due to financial constraints, PAWS will not be able to cover all necessary veterinary care for client animals. Each client will receive $100 per year (beginning every January) to use towards veterinary expenses. The veterinary allotment cannot be carried over from one year to the next. In addition, through a cooperative program with local veterinarians, clients receive average discounts of 25% on their veterinary care. PAWS will also cover the cost for annual vaccinations (up to $25) and for spay/neuter (up to $65). Except for extreme emergencies, clients must notify PAWS prior to veterinary visits in order to receive financial assistance. At this time, clients will be advised of available funding and directed to the vet clinic that has been treating the animal or that is best suited to the animal's needs. Vouchers will be issued only after this discussion has taken place. In special emergency cases, we will try to assist in whatever ways we can.

3. *Volunteer assistance*: As much as possible we will try to fulfill all requests for volunteer assistance with in-home care, transportation, foster care, etc. Volunteers will not be available for any services not directly related to animal care.

4. *Client ID cards*: All clients will be issued an identification card. This card must be presented whenever a client receives services.

Responsibilities

Clients are responsible for notifying PAWS of any changes in phone number, address, animals status, or income within 10 days of the change.

Loss of Status

PAWS clients will lose their status under these conditions:

- They no longer have the animal(s) whom they had at intake.
- They move out of San Francisco.
- They are abusive to staff, board or volunteers. A client will receive a verbal caution if his/her behavior is considered abusive. This caution will be followed by a letter explaining our policies and an invitation to meet with our Client Services Director to discuss the situation. If a second abusive incident occurs, the client will receive a letter explaining that he/she will no longer be considered a client.

APPENDIX 5

Infections Associated with Animals That Are of Special Concern for Immunosuppressed People: Sources and Symptoms

Infectious agent	Frequency in HIV-infected persons	Likelihood of domestic animals as direct source	Possible domestic animal sources of infections	Other potential sources of infection	Common symptoms
Toxoplasma gondii	Common	Low	Cats	Undercooked meat, soil, unwashed produce	Inflammation of the brain
Mycobacterium avium complex	Common	Very low	Pet birds	Soil and water	Lung, stomach, and intestinal infections
Cryptosporidium	Moderate	Unknown, probably low	Cats, dogs, other domestic pets, farm animals	Water, humans, environment	Severe diarrhea
Cryptococcus neoformans	Moderate	Very low	Pet birds	Bird droppings (esp. pigeons), soil	Headaches and stiff neck
Salmonella	Low	Unknown, probably low	Dogs, cats, reptiles, and farm animals	Foods of animal origin (esp. poultry and eggs)	Severe bloodstream infection, diarrhea
Campylobacter jejuni	Low	Unknown, probably low	Dogs, cats, hamsters, and other domestic animals	Foods of animal origin (esp. poultry, milk), water	Diarrhea
Bartonella henselae	Low	High	Cats	Unknown	Skin lesions, severe bloodstream infection
Giardia lamblia	Low	Low	Dogs? Cats? Farm animals	Person-to-person	Diarrhea
Microsporidia	Rare	Unknown	Unknown	Person-to-person	Diarrhea
Rhodococcus equi	Rare	Low	Farm animals	Soil (esp. with high content of horse manure)	Pnemonia
Mycobacterium marinum	Rare	High	Fish	Aquatic (swimming pools, saltwater, or freshwater)	Skin infections
Listeria monocytogenes	Rare	Low	Farm animals	Raw milk, soil, water	Severe bloodstream infections
Bordetella bronchiseptica	Rare	High	Dogs, pigs	Unknown	Respiratory infections

Source: C. Glasser, F. Angulo, & J. Rooney, *Clinical Infectious Diseases*, 1994: 18: 14–24, The University of Chicago Press. Reprinted with permission.

APPENDIX 6

Infections Associated with Animals That Are of Special Concern for Immunosuppressed People: Reducing the Risks

Animal	Disease	Recommendations
Cats	Toxoplasmosis	Litter box hygiene; have someone else change litter or remove feces daily; wash hands afterward for prevention of infection (only of concern to Toxo-neg persons).
	B. henselae infection, bacillary angiomatosis	Immediately wash cat scratches. Declawing is not warranted; flea control may be helpful.
Dogs	Bordetella bronchiseptica	Persons who are severely immunocompromised may wish to reduce their exposure to large concentrations of dogs.
Cats and dogs	Salmonellosis, camplyobacteriosis	Avoid direct contact with pet feces; wash hands after handling pets, especially before eating; have pets with prolonged diarrhea examined by veterinarian.
Pet birds	M. avium complex infection	No specific recommendations (except isolation and treatment of birds with clinical M. avium complex infections).
	Cryptococcosis	No specific recommendations.
Other birds	Cryptococcosis	Avoid pigeon coops, bird roosts, and other bird-inhabited places where heavy aeorosols of bird feces may occur.
Farm animals	Cryptosporidiosis	Prevent fecal–oral spread; wash hands after contact.
	R. equi infection	No practical guidelines.
Horses	R. equi infection	No practical guidelines.
Fish	M. marinum infection	Aquarium hygiene, have someone else clean the aquarium or wear gloves to clean.
Animals used as food	Toxoplasmosis, salmonellosis	Follow safe food guidelines; eat only well-cooked meat, poultry, eggs or seafood, and pasteurized dairy products.

Source: C. Glasser, F. Angulo, J. Rooney, Clinical Infectious Diseases, 1994: 18:14–24, The University of Chicago Press. Reprinted with permission.
(See Appendix 1 for more detailed guidelines)

APPENDIX 7

Universal Precautions to Prevent HIV Transmission Established by the CDC

1. Treat all human blood and body fluids as potentially infective.

2. Wear gloves before touching blood and body fluids, mucous membranes, or nonintact skin of all humans, and for handling items or surfaces soiled with blood or body fluids. Gloves should be changed and disposed of after contact with the above.

3. Wash hands and other skin surfaces immediately and thoroughly if contaminated with human blood or other body fluids. Hands should also be washed after removing gloves.

4. If there are any accidents or questions, see a physician and have them call PEPline at (888) 737-4448.

Source: Centers for Disease Control and Prevention.

REFERENCES

Angulo, F., & Glasser, C. (1994). Caring for pets of immunocompromised persons. *Journal of American Veterinary Medical Association, 205*(12), 1711–1718.

Belsky, J. (1980a). Child maltreatment: An ecological integration. *American Psychologist, 35*, 320–335.

Belsky, J. (1980b). Early human experience: A family experience. *Developmental Psychology, 17*, 3–24.

Bennet, M. J. (1990). Stigmatization: Experiences of persons with acquired immune deficiency syndrome. *Issues in Mental Health Nursing, 11*, 141–154.

Bronfenbrenner, U. (1977). Toward an experimental ecology of human development. *American Psychologist, 32*, 513–31.

Bronfenbrenner, U. (1979). *The ecology of human development*. Cambridge, MA: Harvard University Press.

Carmack, B. J. (1991). The role of companion animals for persons with AIDS/HIV. *Holistic Nursing, Practice, 5*(2), 24–31.

Cherry, K., & Smith, D. (1993). Sometimes I cry: The experience of loneliness for men with AIDS. *Health Communications, 5*(3), 181–208.

Christ, G., Wiener, L., & Moynihan, R. (1986). Psychosocial issues in AIDS. *Psychiatric Annals, 16*, 173–179.

Cusack, O. (1988). *Pets and mental health*. New York: The Haworth Press.

Dean, A., & Lin, N. (1977). The stress buffering role of social support; Problems and prospects for systematic investigation. *Journal of Nervous and Mental Diseases, 165*, 408–417.

Felce, D., & Perry, J. (1993). *Quality of life: A contribution to its definition and measurement*. Cardiff, Wales, UK: Mental Handicap in Wales Applied Research Unit.

Fine, A. H., & N. M. Fine. (1996). *Let me in, I want to play*. Springfield, IL: Charles C. Thomas Publisher.

Friedman, E., Katcher, A. H., Thomas, S. A., Lynch, J. J., & Messent, P. R. (1983). Social interactions and blood pressure: Influence of animal companions. *Journal of Nervous and Mental Disease, 171*, 461–465.

Glasser, C., & Angulo, F. (1994). Animal-associated opportunistic infections among persons infected with human immunodeficiency virus, *Clinical Infectious Diseases, 18*, 14–24.

Gorczyca, K. (1991). Special needs for the pet owner with AIDS/HIV. In Latham Foundation Staff (Eds.), *The bond between all living things* (pp. 13–20). Saratoga, CA: R & E Publishers.

Gorczyca, K, Abrams, D., & Carmack, B. (1989). Pets and HIV disease: A survey of provider's knowledge and attitudes. In *Fifth International Conference on AIDS Proceedings,* International Development Research Centre, Ottawa, Canada.

Gortmaker, S. L. (1985). Demography of chronic childhood diseases: Prevalence and impact. *Pediatric Clinics of North America,* 31, 3–18.

Healthy Pets, Healthy People, Wong, S. (Ed.). (1998). *Healthy pets, healthy people resource guide.* San Francisco: Healthy Pets, Healthy People.

Hoffman, C., & Rice, D. (1995). *1997 national medical expenditure survey.* San Francisco: Institute for Health and Aging, University of California, San Francisco.

Hutton, J. S. (1982, November). Social workers act like animals in their casework relations. *Society for Companion Animal Studies Newsheet,* 3, 30.

Jue, S. (1994). Psychosocial issues of AIDS long-term survivors. *Families in Society: The Journal of Contemporary Human Services,* 43, 324–332.

Katcher, A. H. (1981). Interaction between people and their pets: Form and function. In B. Fogle (Ed.), *Interactions between people and pets* (pp. 46–47). Springfield, IL: Thomas.

Levine, M. M., & Bohn, S. (1986). Development of social skills as a function of being reared with pets. *Proceedings of living together: People, animals, and the environment,* Boston, p. 27. Renton, WA: Delta Society.

Maj, M. (1991). Psychological problems of families and health workers dealing with people infected with human immunodeficiency virus. *Acta Psychiatrica Scandinavica,* 83, 161–168.

Meer, J. (1984). Pet theories. *Psychology Today,* 18, 60–67.

Muschel, U. (1985, October). Pet therapy with terminal cancer patients. *Social Casework: The Journal of Contemporary Social Work,* pp. 451–458.

Nebbe, L. L. (1991). The human–animal bond and the elementary school counselor. *The School Counselor,* 38, 362–371.

Perrin, J. M., & MacLean, W. E., Jr. (1988). Children with chronic illness: The prevention of dysfunction. *Pediatrics of North America,* 35, 1325–1337.

Pets Are Wonderful Support. K. Blount & C. V. Spain (Eds.), (1998a). *Questions You May Have About Your Bird and Your Health.* San Francisco: PAWS.

Pets Are Wonderful Support. K. Blount & C. V. Spain (Eds.), (1998b). *Questions You May Have About Your Cat and Your Health.* San Francisco: PAWS.

Pets Are Wonderful Support. K. Blount & C. V. Spain (Eds.), (1998c). *Safe Pet Guidelines,* 2nd ed. San Francisco: PAWS.

Serpell, J. A. (1983, Spring). Pet psychotherapy. *People-Animals-Environment,* pp. 7–8.

Shalock, R. L. (1996). The quality of children's lives. In A. H. Fine & N. M. Fine (Eds.), *Let me in, I want to play* (pp. 84–94). Springfield, IL: Charles C. Thomas Publisher.

Siegel, J. M. (1993). Companion animals: In sickness and in health. *Journal of Social Issues,* 49, 157–167.

Siegel, L. J. (1993). Psychotherapy with medically at-risk children. In T. R. Kratochwill, R. J. Moriss (Eds.), *Handbook of psychotherapy with children and adolescents* (pp. 472–501). Boston: Allyn and Bacon.

Shea, T. M, & Bauer, A. M. (1991). *Parents and teachers of children with exceptionalities: A handbook for collaboration.* Needham Heights, MA: Allyn and Bacon.

Spencer, L. (1992). Study explores health risks and the human/animal bond. *Journal of American Veterinary Medical Association,* 201(11), 1669.

Thompson, R. J., Jr., & Gustafson, K. E. (1996). *Adaptation to chronic childhood illness.* Washington, DC: American Psychological Association.

United Nations AIDS/World Health Organization. (1998). *Report on the Global HIV/AIDS Epidemic.* New York: United Nations.

Veevers, J. E. (1985). The social meaning of pets: Alternate roles for companion animals. In M. B. Sussman (Ed.), *Pets and the family* (pp. 11–30). New York: The Haworth Press.

Volth, V. L. (1985). Attachment of people to companion animals. *Veterinary Clinics of North America, 15,* 289–295.

Weiss, R. S. (1973). *Loneliness: The experience of social and emotional isolation.* Cambridge, MA: MIT Press.

Wilson, C. C. (1991). The pet as an anxiolytic intervention. *Journal of Nervous and Mental Diseases,* 179, 482–489.

Wong, S. (1998). Report from World AIDS conference in Geneva. *Lesbian and Gay Veterinary Medical Association's Good News,* 6(3), 5.

(Special thanks to Erin Farrell, Ilana Strubel and Casimir Gorczyca.)

CHAPTER 13

Service Animals and Their Roles in Enhancing Independence, Quality of Life, and Employment for People with Disabilities

SUSAN L. DUNCAN
Delta Society National Service Dog Center, Renton, Washington

KAREN ALLEN
School of Medicine, State University of New York at Buffalo, Buffalo, New York

I. INTRODUCTION

During the past decade service animals for people with disabilities have become increasingly visible in our communities. It is not uncommon, for example, to see a dog accompanying a person using a wheelchair in theaters, parks, stores, on public transportation, and in a wide variety of employment settings. But questions often arise about these dogs, such as what do these dogs actually *do* for their owners? How necessary are they? How many individuals with disabilities require the type of assistance such animals can provide? What influence do service animals have on quality of life and opportunities for increased independence and employment? In this chapter we address these questions in a variety of ways. First we provide an overview of legal and historical issues related to service animals, followed by a discussion of the demographics of disability in the United States. To highlight the advantages of having a service animal we include case study reports about the lives of three people and their service dogs. We also include comments about areas of consideration for employers and employees. Finally, we consider research

Handbook on Animal-Assisted Therapy: Theoretical Foundations and Guidelines for Practice
Copyright © 2000 by Susan Duncan, Karen Allen, and the Delta Society.

evidence about the potential psychosocial and economic value of service dogs. Our aim in this multifaceted approach is to provide essential information for people with disabilities, educators, and public policy makers.

II. SERVICE ANIMAL AND DISABILITY LEGALLY DEFINED

Although guide dogs are commonly recognized as helpers for people who have visual impairments, many individuals are still unaware that select animals, especially dogs, can be trained to help people who have other types of disabilities. In the United States, all of these specially trained animals are legally categorized as *service animals*. The term *service animal* is defined in the U.S. civil rights law, the Americans with Disabilities Act (ADA, 1990), as "any animal individually trained to do work or perform tasks for the benefit of a person with a disability." The ADA defines disability as "any physical, mental or emotional impairment that substantially limits one or more major life activities" including but not limited to walking, breathing, seeing, hearing, or caring for one's self. The ADA generally protects the rights of individuals with disabilities to be accompanied by their service animals in public places and employment provided the presence or behavior of the animal does not create a direct threat to others or a fundamental alteration to the nature of the business. Other federal laws, such as the Rehabilitation Act, have similar provisions for federal employers who do not have obligations under the ADA.

III. HISTORY AND OVERVIEW OF SERVICE ANIMAL APPLICATIONS

The use of dogs formally trained to help people with physical disabilities began in Germany during World War I, when guide dogs were trained to lead people who had impaired vision. Following the war, the first U.S. training school opened to supply guide dogs to blind applicants. Through the 1950s, guide dogs were the only formally trained service animals with wide public recognition and acceptance as "legitimate." In the 1960s, dogs were trained to alert people who were deaf or hard of hearing to important sounds in the environment, like an alarm, a baby crying, or a knock at the door. The 1970s expanded the role of service animals even further, when dogs were trained to help people with mobility impairments by pulling wheelchairs, retrieving dropped items, opening doors, and other tasks.

Today, those applications for service dogs have been expanded even more. Service animals can help people who have seizure disorders by alerting the person prior to a seizure so the person can assume a safe position before seizure onset, and can help the person reorient after the seizure. Service animals help people with mental or emotional impairments by making themselves available when needed for as long as is needed; anecdotal reports suggest that some of these animals are also able to alert their owners to early signs of decompensation (rising anxiety, for example), which enables them to take measures to avoid a crisis. Service animals that alert people to high or low blood glucose before the person becomes symptomatic have also been reported. Increasingly, service animals are being trained to help people who have multiple disabilities, such as concurrent mobility and hearing impairments.

There are now more than 135 sources for trained service animals worldwide. In the United States, service animals may be trained by organizations, private trainers, or by the individuals with disabilities who will rely on the animals. Prolonged waiting lists (several months to many years due to inadequate supply of well-trained service animals) and expenses (direct costs and/or lost work time) associated with obtaining already-trained service animals often lead people to train their own service animals, or seek assistance from private trainers (Duncan, 1997a). The ADA recognizes all disabilities and all service animals as equally legitimate. There are no uniform, enforceable standards that all trainers, service animals, and handlers (the people with disabilities who rely on the service animals) must meet.

IV. CULTURAL TRENDS AFFECTING THE CHOICE OF SERVICE ANIMALS AS HEALTH CARE OPTIONS

The percent of the population with disabilities increases annually in many countries. Longer life expectancies, improved medical treatments, improved awareness, and greater social acceptance of disability issues all contribute to an international need to accommodate citizens who have disabilities. Greater emphasis on human rights demands that communities become integrated and accessible. Limited economic and social support systems force governments to seek options that help people with disabilities to be as functionally independent as possible, and selfsupporting whenever possible. Service animals trained to meet people's disability-related needs are viable and logical choices to help achieve these goals.

Fifty-four million individuals in the United States have a wide range of disabilities (U.S. Department of Commerce, Bureau of the Census, 1997), but fewer than 0.03% are estimated to have service animals (Duncan, 1997a). Half of those perform only guide work. Many cultural trends and factors that

influence those trends affect whether people choose service animals as a means
to mitigate the limitations created by disabilities. Among them are:

- Awareness about the roles of service animals
- Knowledge of the legal rights of individuals with disabilities
- Acceptance of service animals in the community
- Lifestyle, religious and cultural beliefs and practices
- Availability of service animals, training support
- Availability of funding to acquire and maintain a service animal
- Suitability of needs and skills compared to reasonable expectations for
  service animal performance
- Availability and range of alternative methods to cope with disability
- Family dynamics and attitudes of significant others

V. ANIMAL WELFARE AND ETHICS

Although dogs are still the species most often trained as service animals, other
species (e.g., cats and capuchin monkeys) are sometimes trained. The use of
wild or exotic animals, such as monkeys, is controversial (Kauffman, 1996).
Even though an animal may be able to learn to perform the task, the appropriateness of the individual animal for that work must be considered. The risks
of zoonotic disease transmission (infections that can be transmitted between
humans and animals), safety risks associated with the animal's natural behaviors (such as a propensity to bite, as is the case with capuchin monkeys and
other simians), the durability of its training, and the bioethical concerns for
the animal's welfare during training and when performing as a service animal
are all elements that should be examined before any animal becomes a service
animal. This scrutiny must include the environments and conditions in which
the animal is expected to work and the scheduling of that work.

Service animals can help a person with a disabilty to accomplish activities
of daily living (ADLs) and instrumental activities of daily living (IADLs). ADLs
include getting around inside the home, getting in or out of a bed or a chair,
bathing, dressing, eating, and toileting. IADLs include going outside the home,
getting to and from work, administering money and bills, doing housework,
preparing meals, and keeping appointments. Many ADLs and IADLs are associated with maintaining employment—getting up on time, toileting, dressing,
eating, getting to work, performing the duties of the job, and getting back
home. Seemingly simple tasks can create daunting barriers: the inability to
open the refrigerator or carry supplies necessary to prepare breakfast, exhaus-
tion caused by picking up items that are dropped, constant anxiety from not
being able to see obstacles or to hear the approach of coworkers. Difficulties

with ADLs and IADLs can negatively affect job attendance and job performance. By helping a person complete these activities, the service animal can be the critical link that enables a person with a disability to be connected to the community and to the workplace.

The benefits of service animals vary from person to person, depending on individual needs. The following case studies demonstrate variability of experiences of people who have service animals in the workplace.

VI. DEMOGRAPHICS OF DISABILITY IN THE UNITED STATES

Using data collected by the Survey of Income and Program Participation (SIPP) regarding the number and characteristics of noninstitutionalized people with disabilities from October 1994 to January 1995, McNeil indicates in his report (U.S. Department of Commerce, Bureau of the Census, 1997) some statistics that have implications for employers today and in the future. He determined that 12.7% of the 35 million children in the United States age 6 to 14 had some type of disability, and that the likelihood of having a disability generally increases with age. Disabilities were present in:

- 12.1% of the 25.1 million people aged 15 to 21
- 14.9% of the 95 million people age 22 to 44
- 24.5% of the 30.3 million people age 45 to 54
- 36.3% of the 20.6 million people age 55 to 64
- 47.3% of the 24.5 million people age 65 to 79
- 71.5% of the 6.8 million people age 80 and above

These numbers represent a significant portion of workers and potential workers, many of whom will benefit from assistance with ADLs and IADLs and who may choose a service animal as a way to meet those needs. As health care providers, vocational rehabilitation specialists, and consumers become better educated about the scope of service animal function, and as more well-trained service animals become available, it is likely that the rate of workers accompanied by service animals in the workplace will increase.

VII. CASE STUDIES OF INDIVIDUALS WHO HAVE SERVICE ANIMALS

Although disabilities and work experiences vary from person to person, there are also some similarities that demonstrate the benefits of service animals in the workplace. The following cases provide the workers' perspectives as individuals who have had service animals for different purposes, in different work environments.

A. CASE 1

K. W. is a 28-year-old married female who began having complex partial seizures at age 8, and later developed grand mal seizures. Her seizures did not respond to medication. During graduate school, Ms. W. obtained a service dog to help her manage the interference in her life that the seizures caused. Her service dog warns her approximately 5–10 minutes before a seizure begins, stays with her during the seizures, and can help her after the seizures, and has helped her avoid injury on many occasions. She works as an occupational therapist (OT) with patients who are on ventilators in an acute care rehabilitation hospital. Her employer worked with Ms. W. to identify on-the-job accommodations (a place to lie down after seizures) that help her to maintain a high level of job performance, including having a backup health care provider to monitor the patient on the ventilator should Ms. W. experience a seizure while providing direct patient care. Note that the service dog's alert to an impending seizure provides Ms. W. with an adequate window of opportunity to ensure her own safety and the safety of her clients.

Any concerns about the presence of the animal have been abated because of the positive reception the service dog receives from coworkers and patients. There have been no accidents, injuries to others, or infections associated with the service dog. "When I talked about my disability to my employer, she wanted to know how it was going to affect my job. I told her that my service dog was part of my solution to keep my disability from adversely affecting my work. I just want to be as normal as possible."

B. CASE 2

J. E. is a 46-year-old woman with a deteriorating neuromuscular condition that causes generalized weakness and muscle wasting and arthritis. She uses a motorized cart (scooter) or wheelchair for mobility and wears a leg brace. Prior to her disability which began at age 40, Ms. E. led an active and independent lifestyle that included full-time employment as a speech therapist, hiking, travel, running, and other physical activities. After the onset of her disability, she found she was going out less, "partly because it was physically harder, and partly because it was uncomfortable. People would ignore me, or speak to the person pushing my wheelchair even though it was me they were transacting business with."

Ms. E. obtained a service dog that helps her in many ways, including lifting her legs over the edge of the tub so she can shower, brings her clothes and leg brace, opens the refrigerator, carries her teaching supplies, opens doors, and retrieves items that she drops. She observes that his help allows her to complete tasks and to conserve energy that she can apply instead to her job. The service dog has functioned without incident in an elementary school for 5 years. Ms. E. states that the only objection to the presence of the dog was by a student's parent who stated her child was afraid of dogs, and that she herself was allergic. Introduced gently to the dog, the child on his own initiative began interacting with the dog within 3 weeks and overcame his fear. The mother liked the dog so much that she interacted frequently with it and stated that her allergy was "not really a problem."

When her service dog was at the veterinarian's, Ms. E. had occasion to be without her service dog at work. "Without my service dog, I got a lot more tired a lot faster, just from having to go find people who could help me open doors or carry things. One memorable experience was getting stuck in the stall in the ladies room. I couldn't open the door. My service dog usually helped open the door—he at least could have barked for help and someone would have come. But I called and called until finally someone came to let me out. Most people don't mind being asked to help once in a while as long as they know they are not going to be asked all the time but I don't like having to depend on help from other people all the time. It makes it hard for them to stay on task, and it slows me down, too." She continued, "I only work part time now. If I didn't have my service dog, I'd have to have someone come to help me in the morning and the evening. A lot of people don't realize how expensive it is to hire someone to help, especially on a part-time income."

Ms. E. described the reactions of her coworkers and students to her service dog: "Most of them treat him like one of the faculty. They recognize how much he helps me. It's more disruptive when he's not here, because then I have to ask other people to help me."

C. Case 3

G. R. is a 54-year-old male who became blind before the age of 1. He obtained his first service dog at age 19. Mr. G. was a manager until elective early retirement at age 50. He now works as a systems analyst through a temporary employment agency.

"So far I've had five guide dogs. My dog has always come to work with me. In fact, most of the time my dog is the reason I can get to work, because I take public transportation. The longest I was without a dog was for eleven months. I had to use a white cane, which I've never been very good using, and I hired someone to travel with me. Actually, I hired several someones, because it was difficult to find people who could work the hours I needed, and were willing to travel with me. When I was at work, when I was working full time, a couple coworkers were 'assigned' to help me. We were buddies, but it was not a good situation for any of us. Sometimes they'd try to help me navigate and they'd walk me right into a post or the edge of a sign. Half the time they weren't available when I needed them, so I'd waste time wandering around by myself, trying to find whatever it was I was looking for. One time I fell down the stairs because the fellow helping me steered me too close to the stairwell."

"None of my service dogs have ever done things like that. They just get me places, no big deal. I can trust these dogs to know how to move me safely. My coworkers shouldn't have to learn how to do that, it's not part of their job descriptions and frankly its not part of my job description that I should have to teach them what it's like to be blind. If I can turn over the guide work to my dog, then my coworkers and I can be peers or even friends, but they don't become my caretakers."

Employers may not be aware of the significance of service animals for their employees, or are poorly informed about their ADA obligations toward their employees. Mr. R. said that he has had some difficulties in employment because of his service dog. "My dogs have never caused any disruption or gotten anyone sick or broken anything. But when I worked full time my employer at first wanted me to leave my dog in the office if I was going to be out on the floor. I asked what good that would do, if I left my eyes in the office. Every time he had a reason for me to leave my dog behind, I had to explain why that wouldn't help me. Finally, he agreed to let me take the dog everywhere, and when there were no incident reports, he relaxed. I told him if he hadn't let me have my dog, he probably would have had incident reports from me getting hurt."

Mr. R. experiences similar attitudes among some of the businesses he works with on a temporary basis. "Sometimes a client will say 'no dogs' and my agency has to explain why it's important that I have my guide dog. Usually they work it out so by the time I get there everything's okay. But sometimes the client is still adamant that I can't bring the dog in. I get really tired of fighting that battle over and over again, especially when it is clear that my service dog contributes to my value as an employee. Being able to function in my environment makes me more efficient and reduces my chance of error."

VIII. CONSIDERATIONS FOR EMPLOYERS AND EMPLOYEES

The ADA and other nondiscrimination laws protect qualified individuals so they may have equal access to job opportunities. The ADA defines a qualified individual as one who has a disability and is able to perform the essential functions of the job, with or without an accommodation. Employers may be required by the ADA to provide reasonable accommodations that enable their qualified employees with disabilities to perform their essential job functions. Examples of accommodations can include widening the space in an aisle so a wheelchair can navigate easily, installing grab bars in the bathroom, providing a TTY device in lieu of a regular telephone, and allowing the use of a service animal by an employee. A service animal may in some cases reduce the number of accommodations required by the employer, by helping the individual to overcome existing barriers in the environment. When an individual is protected by the ADA or other civil rights law, failure to provide reasonable accommodation may result in discrimination against the individual. This may become the basis for a legal complaint or lawsuit. Employers are advised to learn their obligations toward employees with disabilities under federal and state nondiscrimination law. For information about federal laws, contact the Equal Employment Opportunity Commission at (800)669–4000. For information about state laws, contact the applicable state's attorney general's office.

A. RISK MANAGEMENT

Risks associated with the presence or behavior of service animals should be assessed based on factors that are demonstrable, not speculative. Each animal must be considered individually within the context of its work with the employee, to determine whether it poses any direct threat or fundamental alteration. This assessment should include not only the effects of the service animal on its environment, but also the effects of that environment on the service animal. There is currently no validated data to suggest that healthy, vaccinated, well-trained service dogs pose any greater threat to public health and safety than the average person (Duncan, in press).

B. CONFLICT RESOLUTION: ALLERGIES, FEARS, AND COMPLAINTS

Of the more than 23,000 requests for service animal information made each year to Delta Society's National Service Dog Center (NSDC), many come from employers who are unfamiliar with service animals. The most frequently mentioned concerns are allergies and fears among the employee's coworkers or customers.

According to the American Academy of Allergy, Asthma and Immunology (1995), approximately 15% of the population is allergic to cats or dogs. Allergy symptoms can range from mild to severe. Contact with animal dander (not hair), saliva, and urine are the chief causes of reactions in people who are allergic.

A person with a disability who is covered by the ADA belongs to a protected class of citizens. If the person's allergy or fear is so severe as to create a disability for that individual, then both that person's and the handler's disability-related needs must be reasonably accommodated. If that person's allergy does not constitute a disability, and the presence or behavior of the service animal does not create a fundamental alteration or direct threat, then the civil rights of the person with the disability must be upheld.

The same test is applied to incidents of fears or other complaints. Often, the solution is as simple as providing adequate space between the service animal (although not separating the service animal from its handler) and the person affected, and adequate routine housekeeping practices. Good employee management, good customer service, and comprehensive knowledge of the rights of the employer and the handler are all necessary skills for conflict resolution involving service animal issues (Duncan, 1997b).

C. PUBLIC AND INTERNAL POLICY

The ADA specifies that the handler is responsible for the service animal's care and behavior at all times; the employer is not responsible to provide stewardship (care and behavior management) for the service animal, nor is the employer required to tolerate a service animal that poses a direct threat or fundamental alteration. Animal welfare laws are mandated at the state or local level and must be observed unless they conflict with the provisions of federal laws. When two federal laws conflict, guidance should be sought from the U.S. Department of Justice, (800)514-0301 to determine which law takes precedence for the employer.

Internal policies should reflect the provisions of current prevailing law, and provide guidance to the employees who are expected to follow and enforce those rules. Information about policy development and employee education can be obtained from Delta Society National Service Dog Center, (800)869-6898.

D. HUMAN RELATIONS AND SOCIAL WELFARE

Analysis of census information (Kraus *et al.*, 1996) concludes that the long-term trend is for people with disabilities to have higher rates of participation in the workforce. Integration and diversity in the workplace are valuable assets to employers. The employment of qualified people with disabilities who have service animals allows the employer to access a reservoir of competent employees who can contribute to the success of the business and to provide community representation of the customer base among the workforce.

Employment of qualified individuals with disabilities who have service animals has both financial and economic implications. Good employees can help businesses increase their profit margins. Employers may be able to receive tax credits for some ADA-related worksite modifications. People who are adequately employed have less need for tax-funded government subsidies and have more disposable income to support local businesses.

Employment of individuals with disabilities who have service animals and compliance with civil rights laws reflect positively on employers. Such practices build community strength and business success.

IX. RESEARCH ABOUT SERVICE ANIMALS

Although there are many anecdotal reports documenting the instrumental and emotional support provided by service animals, little research has systematically addressed the degree to which such animals can actually change the lives of people with disabilities. To date, most existing studies about service animals have used a retrospective survey design, have reported a variety of benefits described by the self-reports of the participants, and have been limited to the dog species. For example, Valentine *et al.* (1993) asked service dog owners with mobility or hearing disabilities to indicate the ways in which they felt their experiences or abilities changed after acquiring their dogs. Trainers of the dogs involved were also asked for their observations about changes in the lives of the people with disabilities. In this study service dog ownership was associated with diminished levels of depression, loneliness, irritability, and other similar constructs. In addition, respondents said that after acquiring dogs they had higher self-esteem, as well as more trust, tolerance, and independence. Overall, the participants in this investigation reported overwhelming satisfaction with their service dogs and described extensive psychosocial benefits. This study is especially interesting because it documents the emotional importance of service dogs, while people with mobility disabilities viewed the practical aspects of dog ownership as very important, and they rated the *emotional* aspects as *extremely* important.

Another retrospective study (Hart *et al.,* 1987) addressed the social facilitation role of service dogs for adults and reported that, relative to a control group without dogs, people with service dogs reported a significantly higher number of social greetings and approaches in public places. Other studies have used short-term, direct observation of adults (Eddy *et al.,* 1988) and children (Mader & Hart, 1989) and have found that service dogs can assist in expanding social interaction for people with physical disabilities.

A. Randomized Controlled Trial about Service Dog Owners

The findings in the retrospective and observational studies cited previously are intriguing, and they contributed to the development of a more recent investigation (Allen & Blascovich, 1996) involving individuals with ambulatory disabilities (i.e., spinal cord injury, muscular dystrophy, multiple sclerosis, or traumatic brain injury) who participated in a randomized controlled trial. The main objective of this study was to increase understanding of the potential value of service dogs by comparing people before and after acquiring such dogs.

1. Methods

a. Participants

Participants in this investigation all had interest in having a service dog and they all required substantial daily personal assistance from family, friends, and paid aides. All individuals had ambulatory motor impairment and had used a wheelchair for mobility for at least 2 years. Many of the participants also had additional cognitive impairments resulting in problems with attention span and memory. Individuals were matched on characteristics, such as age, sex, race, and the nature and severity of disability, to create 24 pairs. Within each pair, individuals were randomly assigned to either the experimental group or the wait-list control group. Table I provides demographic and disability characteristics of the two groups.

b. Procedure

One month after the study began in 1990 individuals in the experimental group received service dogs that had been especially trained for their personal needs. Participants in the control group received their dogs a year later (in month 13 of the study). Data collection occurred every 6 months over a 2-year period, resulting in five data collection points for each participant (months 0, 6, 12, 18, and 24). At each data collection point, several questionnaires were completed and returned by mail.

c. Questionnaires

The questionnaires included in the study elicited self-reports about participants' (1) self-esteem (Rosenberg, 1965), (2) internal versus external locus of control (Paulus, 1983), (3) psychological well-being (Bradburn, 1969), (4) integration into their local communities (Willer et al., 1994), and (5) number of paid and unpaid (family) hours of assistance provided per week. Partici-

TABLE I   Summary Demographic and Disability Data on Matched Groups

	Group			
	Experimental		Wait-list control	
Characteristic	Men	Women	Men	Women
Sample size	12	12	12	12
Race				
White	8	9	8	9
African-American	4	3	4	3
Mean (SD) age, years	25 (1.5)	25 (1.2)	25 (1.3)	25 (1.2)
Marital status				
Married	1	3	2	2
Divorced/separated	7	3	8	4
Never married	4	6	2	6
Disability				
Spinal cord injury	7	4	7	4
Muscular dystrophy	1	1	1	1
Multiple sclerosis	2	6	2	6
Traumatic brain injury	2	1	2	1

pants also completed a specialized demographic questionnaire that included questions about current marital status, educational achievements, work status, living arrangements, and number of paid and unpaid (family members) personal assistance hours they received weekly. In addition, one family member for each participant also completed these questionnaires, providing his or her own perspective about the self-esteem, community involvement, etc., of the family member with the disability.

The constructs measured in the first four dependent variables are frequently considered in research about people with disabilities, and in this study they were measured with well-established, reliable, and valid instruments. The psychological variables (self-esteem, locus of control, and psychological well-being) were chosen because of considerable evidence in the health psychology literature linking these constructs to positive health outcomes. The measure of community integration was included because the degree to which a person with a disability is involved in activities outside his or her own home is an important indicator of successful rehabilitation. Finally, the number of personal assistance hours was assessed to increase knowledge of how much assistance people with severe disabilities were actually receiving in activities of daily living (specifically in the Northeastern United States).

2. Data Analysis

To compare the experimental and wait-list control groups, parametric (analysis of variance, ANOVA) and nonparametric (χ^2) statistical analyses using a dual analytic approach were performed as appropriate on dependent variables. First, experimental and wait-list control groups were compared at the first three data collection points (months 0, 6, and 12), that is, *before* the service dogs were assigned to the control group. Next, the same relative points in time were compared for the two groups, that is, months 0, 6, and 12 for the experimental group were compared with months 12, 18, and 24 for the control group.

3. Results

a. Psychosocial Variables

As indicated in Table II, the analyses just described revealed significant main effects for group and month ($p < .001$ for all comparisons) and significant interactions for group by month ($p < .001$ for all comparisons) for all psychosocial status variables. The top graph in Fig. 1 illustrates mean self-esteem scores of experimental and control group by month, and demonstrates clear differences between groups before the control group received their dogs. As shown in the bottom graph in Fig. 1, however, when compared at the same relative points in time (number of months since receiving the dog), there were no significant differences between the groups. That is, by the end of the study the wait-list control group demonstrated effects of their dogs similar to those of the experimental group. Table II shows that the patterns of means for psychological well-being, internal locus of control, community integration, school status, and part-time work status were all similar to the pattern for self-esteem.

b. Assistance Hours

As shown in Table II, after 12 months the presence of a service dog was associated with a decrease of approximately 60 (68%) biweekly paid assistance hours in the experimental group. The pattern for biweekly unpaid assistance hours provided by family members was similar to that for the paid hours (i.e., a decrease of approximately 25 (64%) hours. The top panel of Fig. 2 depicts the pattern of paid assistance hours and demonstrates that the number of paid hours diminished as months with a dog progressed. Finally, the bottom graph in Fig. 2 illustrates that when duration of time since receiving a dog was considered, the experimental and control groups were nearly identical.

B. POTENTIAL SAVINGS ASSOCIATED WITH SERVICE DOGS

The finding that the presence of a service dog was associated with dramatic reductions in hours of paid and unpaid assistance was unexpected and partici-

TABLE II Frequency of Significant Dependent Variables by Month[a]

Variable	Month				
	0	6	12	18	24
Self-esteem score					
Experimental group	13.0 (2.1)	25.8 (1.6)	35.3 (0.6)	36.2 (0.8)	36.6 (0.7)
Control group	14.1 (1.2)	14.0 (1.2)	14.3 (1.0)	25.3 (1.2)	35.3 (0.5)
Internal locus of control score					
Experimental group	64.4 (4.3)	135.0 (5.2)	179.4 (3.7)	187.6 (3.9)	189.8 (1.8)
Control group	61.5 (2.3)	60.9 (1.9)	61.0 (1.9)	135.2 (3.8)	178.8 (3.7)
Psychological well-being score					
Experimental group	1.6 (0.5)	6.2 (0.5)	8.0 (0.3)	8.1 (0.4)	8.8 (0.4)
Control group	1.8 (0.4)	1.8 (0.4)	1.7 (0.5)	6.3 (0.5)	8.1 (0.3)
Community integration score					
Experimental group	2.3 (0.6)	15.3 (1.0)	25.3 (0.9)	26.7 (0.7)	27.2 (0.5)
Control group	2.2 (0.5)	2.3 (0.4)	2.3 (0.4)	15.7 (0.5)	25.3 (0.5)
School attendance, no. of subjects					
Experimental group	0	15	18	15	11
Control group	0	0	0	10	7
Part-time employment, no. of subjects					
Experimental group	0	9	14	21	23
Control group	0	0	0	15	17
Biweekly paid assistance hours					
Experimental group	87.9 (9.4)	47.4 (5.0)	28.0 (4.8)	20.6 (1.7)	19.6 (1.9)
Control group	83.5 (4.0)	83.5 (4.0)	84.2 (4.0)	42.1 (4.1)	21.3 (1.6)
Biweekly unpaid assistance hours					
Experimental group	38.4 (4.1)	24.5 (6.2)	14.8 (4.3)	12.8 (4.2)	12.0 (5.0)
Control group	39.8 (2.3)	39.8 (2.3)	39.8 (2.3)	22.5 (3.5)	13.4 (2.1)

[a]The values given are mean (SD) unless otherwise indicated. The comparisons made were performed at the same relative data points, i.e., months 0, 6, and 12 for the experimental group and months 12, 18, and 24 for the wait-list control group, and are significant at $p < .001$.

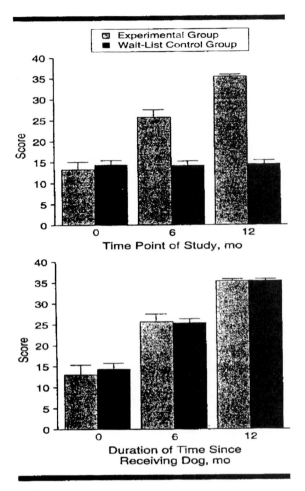

FIGURE 1   Mean self-esteem scores by assignment group and selected month. The experimental group received their dogs 1 month after study initiation, and the wait-list control group received their dogs 13 months after the study began.

pants were subsequently queried about the reasons for diminished assistance. Uniformly, the participants and their family members cited that assistance hours were reduced because they were no longer needed, that is, the dog took the place of many weekly hours of paid and unpaid human assistants. Study participants described how they were able to increase their independence because of their dogs, and said that they developed relationships and bonds with their dogs that were unlike those they had with people who were paid

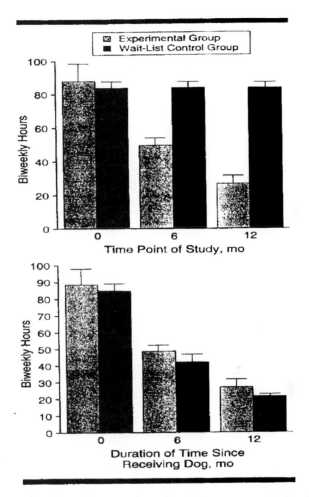

FIGURE 2   Mean biweekly paid assistance hours by assignment group and selected month. The experimental group received their dogs 1 month after study initiation, and the wait-list control group received their dogs 13 months after the study began.

to come to their homes. Although service dogs can do many things, they cannot, of course, totally replace the assistance of people. Interestingly, although all of the participants still needed the assistance of other people, they noted an added benefit was that the presence of the dogs had improved their interactions with paid assistants. A reduced need for paid assistance associated with the presence of a service dog suggests potential economic benefits of service dogs. Figure 3 illustrates savings associated with service dogs at several levels of

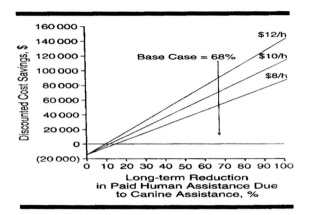

FIGURE 3   Cost savings of service dogs by reduction in paid assistance at several levels of hourly wage and based on a discount rate of 5%.

hourly wage that are commonly paid to personal aides. (For a more detailed projection of long-term reduction in paid assistance due to service dogs, see Allen & Blascovich, 1996.)

C. COMMENT AND RECOMMENDATIONS FOR FUTURE RESEARCH

The results of this study confirm earlier reports about the psychological benefits of service dogs. In addition, however, this study also demonstrates that service dogs are associated with increased levels of social interaction, employment, and use of public transportation. Although only five participants moved to more independent living arrangements after receiving a service dog, several others tried to increase their independence but failed because of policies prohibiting dogs. In the years that have passed since the data for this study were collected, it is hoped a more enlightened view of the role of service dogs has evolved, and a greater degree of independence is possible for people with such dogs.

According to the World Institute on Disability, fewer than 1 million of the 4 million people in the United States who need personal assistance services actually receive them. Because many economic and social policy barriers prevent people with disabilities from receiving the assistance they require, an increased use of service dogs as substitutes for such assistance appears to be a sensible strategy. Whether service dogs would be useful for *all* people with disabilities cannot be determined from the results of this study, in which participants were all chosen because they expressed interest in having a dog. In addition, all participants were selected from support groups, and it is not known if people with good support systems may benefit more from having a dog than those with few friends and family members in their lives. The results of this study, however, demonstrate quite clearly that for a person who *likes and wants a dog,* a service dog can have a positive effect on quality of life and level of independence.

The study described here included only individuals with severe physical disabilities who used wheelchairs for mobility. Clearly there are people with many other types of disabilities who currently have and benefit from service dogs, and future studies should consider people with a wide range of physical and emotional disabilities. It is especially important to learn more about the needs of people with emotional and mental disabilities because such individuals currently experience a great deal of discrimination when they attempt to rent apartments or take their service dogs into public places and work environments. Although the study described here demonstrates that service dogs are excellent sources of psychosocial support, future work needs to expand the focus to explore *specific* ways such support may influence participation in community activities and employment.

A shortcoming of the study described here is that it does not include an objective assessment of the frequency and manner in which people were assisted by their dogs. That is, participants with dogs required fewer hours of daily (human) assistance, but it is not possible to quantify exactly what each dog did or if an individual's type or severity of disability was related to specific tasks performed by dogs. A recent comment about this paper (Coppinger, 1998) observes that since there was no test of what the dogs contributed to the benefits, it is possible to conclude that the benefits of having a service dog could be entirely psychological. Consequently, future investigations should be careful to include a specific assessment of the activities of the dogs involved. Such additional information would increase understanding of the number and range of tasks that service dogs need to able to perform.

To influence social policy and health insurance reimbursement practices, many additional topics about service animals need to be addressed in scientifically rigorous research. For example, studies specifically about the economic impact of service dogs, comparing their capabilities with tasks typically done by personal assistants (or family members) need to be carried out. In addition, community integration needs to be examined in a design that compares the social acceptance of a person with a dog versus a person with a personal assistant. Issues surrounding supply and demand of service dogs as well as questions about need for certification are also topics to be addressed. In addition, several interesting studies could be designed with a focus on qualities, selection, and training of service animals. Such studies would add to knowledge about the relative benefits of specific breeds versus mixed breeds, as well as answer questions about who should train dogs, professional trainers or the people with disabilities who will share their lives with the dogs.

Although a focus on the dog's training and abilities is important, there is still much to be learned about the effects of service dogs on quality of life. As an extension of the controlled trial described, it would be valuable to design a study to evaluate the effectiveness and acceptance of service dogs in work environments. The special role of service dogs in helping children in school, both in instrumental and emotional ways, is also an important topic for research. Finally, most research has focused on dogs and little is known about the influence and public impact of other types of service animals. We hope researchers will consider some of these topics in the near future, and an increased number of people with disabilities will be able to benefit from the special and unique companionship and assistance of animals.

REFERENCES

Allen, K., & Blascovich, J. (1996). The value of service dogs for people with severe ambulatory disabilities: A controlled randomized trial. *Journal of the American Medical Association*, 275(13), 1001–1006.

American Academy of Allergy, Asthma and Immunology. (1995). *Allergies to Animals.* Milwaukee, WI.

Americans with Disabilities Act. (1990). 42 USC § 12101 *et seq.*

Bradburn, N. (1969). *The structure of psychological well-being.* Chicago, IL: Aldine Publishing Company.

Coppinger, R. (1998). Breeding, training and use of service/assistance dogs: A positive critique. Paper presented as a plenary address at the 8th International Conference on Human–Animal Interactions, The Changing Roles of Animals in Society, Prague, Czech Republic, September 10–12, 1998.

Duncan, S. L. (in press). *The implications of service animals in healthcare facilities: A state of the art report.* Washington, DC: Association for Professionals in Infection Control and Epidemiology and Renton, WA: Delta Society.

Duncan, S. L. (1997a). The importance of training standards and policy for service animals. In C. C. Wilson & D. C. Turner (Eds.), *Companion animals in human health* (pp. 251–266). Thousand Oaks, CA: Sage Publications.

Duncan, S. L. (1997b). Service dogs in the workplace: A win–win deal for employer and employee. *Alert 8:1.* Renton, WA: Delta Society.

Eddy, J., Hart, L. A., & Boltz, R. (1987). The effects of service dogs on social acknowledgments for children with disabilities: Effects of service dogs. *Child Development, 122,* 39–45.

Hart, L. A., Hart, B. L., & Bergin, B. (1988). Socializing effects of service dogs for people with disabilities. *Anthrozoos, 1,* 41–44.

Kauffman, M. (1996). The controversy over exotic service animals. *Alert 7:3.* Renton, WA: Delta Society.

Kraus, L. E., Stoddard, S., & Gilmartin, D. (1996). *Chartbook on disability in the United States, 1996.* An InfoUse report. Washington, DC: U.S. National Institute on Disability and Rehabilitation Research, 39.

Mader, B. & Hart, L. A. (1989). Social acknowledgements for children with disabilities: effects of service dogs. *Child Development,* **60**, 1529–1534.

Paulus, D. (1983). Sphere-specific measures of personal control. *Journal of Personality and Social Psychology,* **44**, 1253–1265.

Rosenberg, M. (1965). Society and the adolescent self-image. Princeton, NJ: Princeton University Press.

U.S. Department of Commerce, Bureau of the Census. (1997). Americans with disabilities: 1994–5. *Current Population Reports, Household Economic Studies.* Washington, DC: Mc Neil, J. M.

Valentine, D. P., Kiddoo, M., & LaFleur, B. (1993). Psychosocial implications of service dogs for people who have mobility or hearing impairments. *Social Work and Health Care,* **19**, 109–125.

Willer, B., Ottenbacher, K. J., and Coad, M. L. (1994). The community integration questionnaire: A comparative examination. *American Journal of Physical Medicine and Rehabilitation,* **73**, 103–111.

World Institute on Disability. (1988). A report to the National Council on the Handicapped on measures of promoting personal assistance services for people with disabilities. Berkeley, CA: World Institute on Disability.

CHAPTER 14

Animal Abuse and Developmental Psychopathology: Recent Research, Programmatic, and Therapeutic Issues and Challenges for the Future

FRANK R. ASCIONE
Department of Psychology, Utah State University, Logan, Utah

MICHAEL E. KAUFMANN
American Humane Association, Englewood, Colorado

SUSAN M. BROOKS
Green Chimneys, Brewster, New York

I. OVERVIEW

As animals become a more significant component of therapeutic interventions with children and adolescents, greater attention is being paid both to the benevolent and the problematic relations that exist between animals and young people. The field of animal welfare has a long history of attempts to enhance children's attitudes toward and treatment of animals (see Ascione, 1997, for an overview). But as society focuses on the persistent challenge of violence in human relationships, renewed attention is being given to animal abuse as a correlate of and potential precursor to human mental health problems. The role of animals in preventing and treating psychological dysfunction in children and adolescents is also receiving increased scrutiny.

This chapter provides (1) an overview of research on the relation between animal abuse and interpersonal violence (Ascione), (2) a discussion of efforts by animal welfare organizations to use this information to expand their scope to human welfare concerns (Kaufmann), and (3) an illustration of the unique role animals may play in assessment and therapeutic intervention with young

Handbook on Animal-Assisted Therapy: Theoretical Foundations and Guidelines for Practice
325

people who are psychologically at risk (Brooks). Each of us approached this project from our own varying perspectives of developmental psychology, humane education, and child clinical intervention. Yet a common thread in all of our work is the belief that collaboration among professionals is the most fruitful avenue to solving complex human (and animal!) problems.

II. CONFLUENCE OF ANIMAL MALTREATMENT AND INTERPERSONAL VIOLENCE

A. How Do We Define Animal Abuse?

Throughout this chapter, we will refer to nonhuman animals as "animals" for simplicity. Defining animal abuse is a challenging endeavor due to the variety of statuses that animals acquire in different human cultures (Kaufmann, 1999). When we define animal abuse, are we referring to farm animals who provide food for humans, animals used in research (in human and veterinary medicine), wildlife, animals maintained in zoological parks, assistance animals, or companion animals? As cultures, we condone or condemn various practices depending on which status an animal occupies. Clearly, we are faced at the outset with a task more difficult than defining human abuse and one in which international comparisons must be approached with caution.

Agnew (1998) has suggested that attempts to define animal abuse share a number of features: ". . . the harm inflicted on animals should be (1) socially unacceptable, (2) intentional or deliberate, and/or (3) unnecessary (see Kellert & Felthous, 1985; Baenninger, 1991; Ascione, 1993; Vermuelen & Odendaal, 1993)." Animal abuse may include acts of commission or omission, paralleling types of child maltreatment such as child physical abuse and neglect of a child's nutritional needs. In fact, we can easily borrow classifications of child maltreatment and apply them to animals—physical and sexual abuse, neglect, and emotional abuse.

In judging the significance of animal abuse by young people, we must always determine whether the youth's behavior violates community and cultural standards and whether sufficient cognitive maturity is present to indicate that the behavior was intentionally harmful. Both of these factors are relevant for clinical assessment and may also be related to legal statutes pertaining to the treatment of animals.

B. How Do We Measure Animal Abuse?

In some jurisdictions, especially those where animal abuse may be a felony offense, one could examine official records to determine the incidence of animal abuse reported to authorities. However, animal abuse is most often a misdemeanor offense that may not be recorded separately or cannot be extracted from official criminal records. Animal welfare organizations also vary widely in their tracking of animal abuse cases. The current situation is similar to our inability to track the incidence of child maltreatment before mandatory reporting became law.

In cases where official records are available, checklists of different types of maltreatment can be used for categorization, a method employed in South Africa by Vermuelen and Odendaal (1993). A similar process can be applied to the clinical case records of children and adolescents. However, as will be noted later, it is only in the past decade that animal abuse has been highlighted as a symptom of certain psychiatric disorders in young people. Prior to this, clinicians may not have asked about the presence of animal abuse in a child's history. A clinical history that does not contain animal abuse may reflect that no one asked about this symptom as distinct from its actual absence.

Structured interviews about animal abuse have also been used with respondents old enough for verbal questioning. This method has most often used retrospective reporting and been applied to adult clinical and criminal samples (e.g., Felthous & Kellert, 1987; Schiff, et al., in review). As with all self-report methods but especially with sensitive topics, issues of social desirability, reluctance to disclose, or false disclosure to enhance one's reputation for violence must be considered in evaluating such reports. These cautions also apply to the use of a structured interview protocol for children and adolescents developed by Ascione et al., (1997a)—the Cruelty to Animals Assessment Instrument (CAAI).

The CAAI is designed to elicit reports of abusive and kind treatment of pet, farm, wild, and stray animals either observed or performed by children at least 5 years of age. A rating system based on CAAI responses attempts to quantify a child's animal abuse in terms of frequency, severity, chronicity, and level of empathy. However, it has yet to be applied to large samples of young people at risk for psychological disorders.

Unstructured interviews and ethnographic methods (Arluke, 1997) have also been applied to assessing animal abuse. Examples include a police interview of a pedophile who admitted to repeatedly trying to suffocate and then revive a cat by sealing it a plastic garbage bag, and the recent Herbeck case in which the convicted perpetrator said he used animal abuse to soothe himself (*Milwaukee Journal Sentinel Online*, July 6, 1998).

The most commonly used clinical checklist that contains information, albeit meager, on animal abuse is the Child Behavior Checklist (CBCL) developed by Achenbach and Edelbrock (1981). One form of this assessment is administered to parents/guardians and asks about a number of symptoms, including "physical cruelty to animals" during the past 6 months. Respondents rate children on whether each symptom is never, sometimes, or often true of their child. Unfortunately, a youth self-report and a teacher report form of the CBCL do not ask about cruelty to animals. This makes assessment of correspondence between parent and child reports problematic. Offord *et al.,* (1991) found poor correspondence using a variation of the CBCL. One factor that may account for the lack of correspondence is that animal abuse may occur covertly, especially for older children, and parents may be unaware of such acts. In addition, since "cruelty" is not defined for respondents, we do not know the standards they use in making their judgments. Teachers may not see animal abuse but may hear reports of it from their students.

A cruelty to animals item is also included in Kazdin and Esveldt-Dawson's (1986) Interview for Antisocial Behavior and responses to this item differentiate conduct-disordered (see description below) from non-conduct-disordered children.

Two other instruments have been developed specifically for assessing animal abuse in domestic violence situations. The Battered Partner Shelter Survey (Ascione & Weber, 1997a) and the Children's Observation and Experience with Pets (Ascione & Weber, 1997b) assessment were designed for use with women and children who have entered a shelter for women who are battered. These structured interviews allow assessment of threatened and actual animal abuse as well as other information about pet care.

C. How Prevalent Is Animal Abuse in Adults?

Because national records on animal abuse are not available, we must rely on clinical case control studies to estimate its prevalence (i.e., any incidents of abuse within a particular time frame) in adult samples. Felthous and Kellert's (1987) review suggests that in psychiatric and criminal samples, animal abuse is reported by up to 57% of respondents in contrast to near zero rates for respondents in normative comparison groups. In a study of serial sexual homicide perpetrators, prevalence rates approached 70% for men who said they themselves had been sexual abuse victims (Ressler *et al.,* 1988). These estimates must be viewed with caution since definitional and measurement variations between studies may affect self-reports. The MMPI also contains some items related to the treatment of animals but we are not aware of any investigations on animal abuse using this instrument.

D. How Prevalent Is Animal Abuse in Children and Adolescents?

Ascione (1993) reported that between 14 and 22% of adolescent delinquents at facilities in Utah admitted to torturing or hurting animals in the past year. Using norming data from the CBCL (Achenbach & Edelbrock, 1981), children and adolescents seen at mental health clinics display rates of animal cruelty between

10 and 25%, depending on sex of the child. Comparable rates for nonclinic children are under 5%. Recall that animal abuse is not measured on the self-report form of the CBCL. That these percentages may be underestimates is suggested by data from Offord *et al.*, (1991) in which maternal reports of cruelty to animals in a nonclinic sample of 12- to 14-year-olds was 2% but the children's self-reports yielded a prevalence rate of 10%. Again, definitional issues, reduced parental surveillance as children get older, and parental reluctance to admit their children's animal abuse may all contribute to such discrepancies.

E. Do Children and Adolescents "Outgrow" Abusing Animals?

Behaviors that emerge and then "disappear" with increasing age are usually the result of complex interactions between maturational and experiential processes. Animal "abuse" by an older infant or toddler may be a matter of poor motor and impulse control that can easily be dealt with by parental monitoring and intervention. More recalcitrant animal abuse by a child may require more intensive assessment and treatment. A recent theoretical analysis of adolescent antisocial behavior may be applicable here. Moffit (1993) suggested that adolescents who engage in antisocial behavior likely fall into one of at least two groups—adolescence-limited and life-course persistent. In the former group, acting out only becomes prominent during the adolescent period and might even be considered normative. When adolescents leave this period of development, they also leave their antisocial behavior behind. In the latter group, antisocial behavior emerges early in childhood and, if untreated, may persist into adolescence and adulthood. This categorization may also be true for animal abuse as a specific form of antisocial behavior. Note that abusive behavior could shift from an animal to a human victim and/or may become more covert as a child gets older.

When a young child abuses animals, it may allow for early intervention but may also be an indicator that a child may be on a life-course persistent path for antisocial behavior. Therefore, early detection is critical both for separating normative from pathognomic animal abuse and for targeting scarce intervention resources.

F. What Is the Significance of Animal Abuse as a Symptom of the Childhood and Adolescent Psychological Disturbance Known as Conduct Disorder?

Although animal abuse has been considered potentially symptomatic of psychiatric disturbance for centuries (Pinel, 1809), it is only within the past 12 years that animal abuse has been included in standard psychiatric classification manuals. "Cruelty to animals" made its first appearance in the revised third edition of the *Diagnostic and Statistical Manual of the American Psychiatric Association* (DSM-IIIR) in 1987 and has been found to be one of the earliest symptoms of conduct disorder to appear in childhood (Frick *et al.*, 1993). At that time, it was unclear whether animal abuse, as a symptom of conduct disorder, was more similar to property destruction or interpersonal violence. This confusion was resolved in DSM-IV (American Psychiatric Association, 1994) in which physical cruelty to animals is listed among the symptoms in the heading "Aggression toward People and Animals." This change makes intuitive sense since animal abuse involves harm to sentient creatures capable of experiencing pain, distress, and death and speaks to potentially impaired capacity for empathy in the perpetrator. Animal abuse is also listed as a correlate of antisocial behavior in the International Classification of Diseases (World Health Organization, 1996).

These developments now make it more likely that clinicians and other mental health professionals will attend to this symptom during assessment and diagnostic work. Although research has not specifically addressed how often animal abuse is one of the symptoms present in diagnoses of conduct disorder, one estimate suggests that animal abuse may be present in 25% of conduct disorder cases (Arluke *et al.*, 1999).

G. What Biological Factors Appear Related to Animal Abuse?

Although no research, to our knowledge, has been specifically addressed to physiological and biochemical processes that may underlie animal abuse, the importance of such research should not be overlooked. As noted by Lockwood and Ascione (1998), ". . .we will need to attend to brain-behavior relations as we seek a better understanding of the phenomenon of cruelty to animals" (p.151). This information will be valuable for both diagnosis and intervention and would also help identify circumstances when engaging in animal abuse causes significant biochemical change in the perpetrator.

Pharmacologic interventions for violent behavior in general should also be examined for their effectiveness in reducing animal abuse.

H. How Is Animal Abuse Specifically Related to the Physical and Sexual Abuse of Young People?

Although attention to the overlap between animal abuse and child maltreatment is increasing, few existing studies have addressed this issue. DeViney *et al.*,

(1983) found a 60% pet abuse and neglect prevalence rate in a sample of families with substantiated child maltreatment. Friedrich (cited in Ascione, 1993) found that 27–35% of female and male child sexual abuse victims displayed cruelty to animals (the rate was less than 5% in the nonabused samples). These data support anecdotal reports of the overlap and case study examples (see Tapia, 1971, and Section IV, this chapter).

I. What Might Motivate a Young Person to Abuse Animals?

Understanding the motivations underlying animal abuse is essential for designing effective prevention and intervention programs. Ascione, et al., (1997a) discovered a variety of motivations in a sample of at-risk children. These included identification with the aggressor and imitation, modifying one's mood (animal abuse creating excitement), peer-facilitated and forced animal abuse, and sexually reactive animal abuse. The question "Why is the child doing this?" cannot be answered using behavioral checklists. More in-depth assessment will be required as illustrated in the case study in Section IV.

J. What Role Does Empathy Play in Preventing Animal Abuse?

We are only just beginning to explore human capacity for empathizing with other species. The development of empathy between humans is believed to have its roots in early infancy (Eisenberg, 1992; Goleman, 1995) and be dependent on the quality of relationships a child experiences. It is believed that empathy enables humans to help each other and that its absence makes harming others easier. We must explore these phenomena and their applicability to human–animal relations. For example, Magid and McKelvey (1987) note that children with distortions in their attachments may lack empathy and be likely to abuse animals. Empathy to people and empathy to animals are not identical but are sufficiently correlated to command our attention (Weber & Ascione, 1992).

K. Is There a Relation between Domestic, or Family, Violence and Animal Abuse?

Research on the overlap between violence between intimate partners and animal maltreatment is still in its infancy. Despite numerous anecdotal references to this overlap, Renzetti's (1992) research was the first to document the overlap in a study of violent lesbian relationships. In this study, 38% of abused respondents reported that their pets had been hurt by their partners. Ascione (1998) studied this phenomenon in 38 women seeking safety at a shelter for women who are battered. Nearly three-quarters of the women had pets (currently or in the past year) and more than half of these women reported that their pets had been hurt or killed by their partner (similar results were reported in studies from Wisconsin and Colorado [Arkow, 1996]). A recent replication with 101 women who were battered (Ascione, 1999) found similar results. In the replication study, more than 60% of the children in these homes had witnessed animal abuse suggesting one mechanism by which some children might acquire and imitate animal abuse. However, it is also important to note that many children tried to intervene on behalf of their pets when violence erupted in their homes.

L. WHY IS INFORMATION ABOUT ANIMAL ABUSE IMPORTANT?

The studies just described suggest that women, children, and animals are at risk in families experiencing domestic violence. In fact, Ascione (1999) found that nearly one-quarter of the women reported that concern for their pets' welfare had kept them from seeking shelter sooner. In some cases, women may be forced to endanger themselves and their children because they do not know how to ensure their pets' safety if they decide to leave a violent partner. This issue is reinforced by the inclusion of pet abuse on a number of instruments used to assess risk of danger from a violent partner.

M. IS THE INFORMATION ABOUT DOMESTIC VIOLENCE AND ANIMAL ABUSE BEING APPLIED?

The results cited in preceding sections have prompted a number of animal welfare agencies to collaborate with domestic violence programs to provide free or low-cost pet sheltering (either at the shelter facility or with foster caretakers) when a woman decides to leave an abusive partner. The degree of need for such programs is still difficult to determine because only a minority of domestic violence shelters may ask women clients about pet abuse (Ascione *et al.*, 1997).

As these sheltering programs emerge, a number of practical, programmatic, and ethical issues arise (Ascione *et al.*, 1997). For example, funding such programs may become problematic if pets are left for significant periods of time (e.g., months), designating personnel to direct these programs may divert animal shelters from other missions, and animal welfare/human welfare conflicts may arise such as these: How long should sheltering last before adoption or euthanasia is considered? What if a woman is reclaiming her pet but is returning to her abusive partner who had harmed the pet? How does the animal shelter deal with reports that the children in these homes have abused pets?

Other animal-related issues have yet to be addressed. Although we know that children growing up in violent homes may display behavior disorders, how are the pets affected by such an environment? Are these pets less adoptable if given up by their owners? Will domestic violence shelters accept an assistance animal if a client has a handicap such as blindness? Because many battered women return to their partners, can we assist them in developing a safety plan that will keep the women and their children's welfare paramount but also consider pet safety? Davidson (1998) noted that an animal abuse history was used in a parental rights termination case. Is such information relevant for a woman if she is considering a permanent break? Should she have on file a detailed complaint against her partner that could be used at a later time? Are there ways of easing the pain of separation from their pets when women and children must enter a shelter? A strategy developed by the Baltimore Police Department was to take photos of the pets as a reminder that the pets will be well cared for. Can animal welfare programs assist women to find transitional housing that allows pets? To what extent should training about domestic violence issues such as confidentiality and safety factors be provided to animal shelter personnel and foster caretakers?

N. WHEN CHILDREN AND ADOLESCENTS ABUSE ANIMALS, WHAT STEPS SHOULD BE TAKEN TO ADDRESS THIS BEHAVIOR?

We recommend that animal abuse by young people be addressed like any of the other serious symptoms of conduct disorder. Comprehensive and developmentally sensitive assessment will help determine the context of the abuse and its seriousness as well as the child's level of culpability (Hindman, 1992). One could model animal abuse interventions on programs for dealing with childhood fire setting. Curiosity fire setters will likely respond to educational interventions, and humane education can be effective with some children who maltreat animals. Pathological fire setters require more intensive therapy similar to the therapy for animal abuse illustrated by the case study described at the end of this chapter (see Section IV). Interventions will need to consider exposure to family and community violence as well as a child's possible victimization (physical, sexual, emotional) by parents, other caretakers, and siblings.

O. In What Ways Can Child Welfare, Domestic Violence, Animal Welfare, and Law Enforcement Professionals Collaborate in Dealing with Animal Abuse?

Each of these organizations includes among their goals the prevention and reduction of violence to vulnerable victims. Either directly or indirectly, they share interests in both human and animal welfare and safety. Given these shared agendas, areas of collaboration have emerged and are flourishing. Cross-training of child and animal welfare professionals and law enforcement officers (addressed in more detail in Section III of this chapter) is becoming common and should be extended to include domestic violence professionals. When animal welfare organizations seek to strengthen animal abuse laws, coordination with human welfare programs is critical. It would be counterproductive to propose stiffer penalties for abusing an animal than for abusing a child, so animal welfare agencies must be familiar with legislation on all forms of abuse, human and animal.

California and Colorado have now passed legislation incorporating evaluation and counseling, either mandated or recommended, for individuals convicted of animal abuse. Hopefully, these efforts will help reduce recidivism. Both prosecutors and judges need training about these programs especially if the programs' effectiveness can be documented through outcome studies that indicate benefits such as reduced reoffending in states having such programs.

These organizations may also collaborate when developing public service posters and announcements (PSAs). The Baltimore Police Department has developed an ad campaign depicting a woman, child, *and* pet cowering in the shadow of a batterer. The American Humane Association has produced a series of PSAs highlighting the link between animal and human abuse.

Other examples include the case study described by Brooks later in this chapter in which animal-facilitated therapy was used with a disturbed child. Would a similar animal-facilitated component be effective in certain forms of intervention for batterers? Clearly, there are a number of unexplored areas of collaboration between agencies involved with human and animal welfare.

P. What Are the Continuing Needs for the Assessment and Tracking of the Problem of Animal Abuse?

In the United States, the child welfare movement benefited dramatically from public acknowledgment of child maltreatment and legislative attention. We can now obtain documentation of the number of child maltreatment cases reported each year and the percent that are substantiated. Similar data are unavailable, on a national basis, for animal abuse cases. Without such data, we will never know if animal abuse is becoming more or less prevalent and we will lack a baseline against which to measure the effectiveness of prevention and intervention programs.

Congressional legislation resulted in a national system for reporting child maltreatment including designation of mandated reporters. This model is currently absent for animal abuse. Likewise, the Uniform Crime Report tracks incidents of juvenile-perpetrated crimes, such as vandalism, but does not track animal abuse. Thus, those interested in animal welfare cannot use these reporting systems to assess animal maltreatment.

It would be an advantage if animal welfare professionals such as veterinarians and organizations such as animal shelters, at a minimum, were required to keep nationally comparable records on animal abuse reports and investigations. Other sentinels who may note animal abuse include groomers, postal workers, meter readers, and other neighborhood workers. Their watchfulness could also be used to document cases of animals at risk. The standard inclusion of questions about animal abuse on all risk-of-danger assessments for domestic violence cases would also be valuable.

In the area of research, the need for longitudinal analysis of animal abuse especially in childhood and adolescence is critical. We need to be able to differentiate transient from chronic animal abuse since animal abuse may only predict serious mental health disturbance when observations are aggregated over time (Loeber *et al.*, 1993).

III. PROGRAMMATIC RESPONSES TO THE "LINK" BETWEEN VIOLENCE TO PEOPLE AND ANIMALS FROM THE ANIMAL CARE AND CONTROL FIELD

Although research efforts continue to validate the connection between animal cruelty, child abuse, domestic violence, and other forms of interpersonal violence (Ascione & Arkow, 1999; Lockwood & Ascione, 1998), much of the evidence still stems from anecdotal sources, including these:

- Human victims of interpersonal violence recount how animal abuse was a part of their own background.
- Animal care and control agencies encounter incidents where investigation of animal abuse cases leads to the discovery of human abuses such as domestic violence, child abuse, or abuse of the elderly.

- Other professional disciplines, such as social work, psychology, veterinary medicine, and law enforcement provide further evidence that malicious animal abuse often is closely related to abuse and violence between people.

In response to this information, the national animal welfare movement has actively publicized these correlations and drawn attention to the "link" between animal abuse and violence to people. As a national organization dedicated to the protection of children and animals from abuse, neglect, and exploitation, the American Humane Association (AHA), in its "Campaign Against Violence," has been publicizing the link between violence to people and animals since 1991. Other national animal welfare groups such as the American Society for the Prevention of Cruelty to Animals (ASPCA) (Adams, 1992), The Humane Society of the United States (HSUS) (Dowling, 1998), and the Latham Foundation (Child and Animal Abuse Prevention Project) have addressed this issue through publications, conferences, and media campaigns. Although there is a growing response to the "link" from various professionals in law enforcement, social work, and domestic violence prevention, the field of animal care and control has been especially responsive to this issue.

A. Local Animal Care and Control Agencies

Animal care and control is a collective term that includes private humane societies, SPCAs, governmental agencies, and any groups concerned about the treatment of animals at the community level. It is these organizations that

- publicize the link locally and regionally
- have created various programmatic responses on the community level
- continue to be one of the strongest advocates of the issue in the media

Why has the issue of the link between animal abuse and human violence motivated so many animal care and control agencies to act? Have these efforts been successful? Are there any concerns associated with this advocacy? This section informally examines how the animal care and control profession has responded to this issue and continues to define the link between animal abuse and human violence.

B. What Have Been the Primary Motivators for Animal Care and Control Organizations to Become Active in the Area of the Link?

1. Raising Community Awareness and Concern about Animal Abuse

Most animal care and control agencies are overwhelmed by the needs of suffering animals in their community. Services provided to the community primarily consist of sheltering unwanted pets and the adoption of such animals into the community. Additionally, some agencies provide veterinary services and maintain cruelty investigation departments to provide humane law enforcement services. Lobbying on behalf of animal welfare, public education, and adjunct programming such as animal-assisted therapy and humane education further enhance the work of many agencies. Animal care and control agencies, whether nonprofit or municipal, always depend on publicity and public support for their work. By connecting animal cruelty to human abuses, animal care and control organizations are able to reposition traditional animal welfare issues via the link (Wisconsin Humane Society, 1997). For example, before information on the link was available, it was difficult to interest the media in local animal cruelty cases. Studies and statistics that have linked serious interpersonal violence to early childhood cruelty and other link information have helped to make animal cruelty cases more newsworthy.

2. Building Relationships with Related Professionals and Community Groups

Animal care and control agencies are often isolated in their communities. Many agencies have great difficulty establishing cooperation with other community service groups. Social services, law enforcement, schools, and other public services often do not perceive animal care and control providers as relevant to their work. The link between animal cruelty and interpersonal violence greatly enhances the status of animal protection groups. In response to the link, creative programmatic relationships have been formed between animal sheltering groups, domestic violence advocates, social service agencies, schools, and other human service providers. For example, the Michigan Humane Society in Detroit is one of many animal care agencies that has undertaken efforts at community relation building. In 1997, that organization hosted a conference titled "Protect our Future" on the link between animal abuse and human violence. As a result, collaboration is occurring within an informal network of social workers, prosecutors, domestic violence advocates, and other professionals who have been educated on the issue. This type of coalition building continues to take place on the community level in many states and leads to an integration of animal care and control into a broader professional network.

3. Providing Diversified Community Services

The link has prompted the development of new services among animal care and control agencies. Some animal shelters that traditionally housed stray animals and placed these pets up for adoption now house pets short term for victims of domestic violence. Humane education programs are being developed by these agencies that focus on animal-based violence prevention programs for children at-risk. Animal control field officers (ACOs) at many organizations now receive training in recognizing child abuse to better assess family dynamics while investigating suspected cases of animal abuse. The Toledo Humane Society was one of the first groups to offer child abuse recognition training to animal cruelty investigators (Toledo Humane Society, 1994).

Although some domestic violence shelters and social service organizations have adapted programs to the link, the expansion of community services has been most noticeable in animal care and control agencies. Traditionally the animal was the main focus of interventions, now the human component in animal abuse cases (pet abuse in domestic violence, animal hoarding, animal abuse by a child) is approached with increasing sophistication. For example, to more effectively address the human component in the animal abuse scenario and develop intervention programs for perpetrators of animal cruelty, the ASPCA now employs a clinical psychologist.

4. Raising the Profile of an Organization and Its Mission

Many animal sheltering organizations are burdened with the image of "the dog pound" at the edge of town that "kills" unwanted pets. Involvement with the link counters the pervasive image that animal shelters are staffed by people who hate animals or, on the other hand, by "extremists" who care more for animals than they do for people. The link allows animal shelters to retain their primary mission to protect pets, while showing the community that they care about violence to all victims, human and animal (Humane Society of Southern Arizona, 1998).

5. Generating Income

Nonprofit animal organizations (most private humane societies) rely on financial donations from the public. For decades, the key message of protecting animals from suffering has been used to appeal to donors who fund the work of the animal protection group. Although this animal protection message has been effective with a segment of the general public, there are other potential donors who are more likely to be motivated by the correlation between animal abuse and human violence. Therefore, publicizing a program to house the pets of domestic violence victims temporarily at the shelter can create a more "human-focused" image for an animal agency. This repositioning raises an animal organization's profile and can enhance fund-raising by appealing to a broader constituency.

C. What Are the Different Types of Programmatic Responses by the Animal Care and Control Field to the Violence "Link"?

1. Education/Information—Internal

For most animal care and control agencies, the first contact with the link comes via a conference, training, or in the media. Often it is one staff member who shows interest in the issue. If this individual is in a leadership position, the next step frequently is further staff and board education. In larger organizations, this internal education process often consists of sending staff members to national training or hosting a regional training session with knowledgeable speakers who address the subject of the link.

2. Community Education/Coalition Building

Although community education is the initial goal of animal care and control organizations when addressing the link, the notion of community coalition building quickly becomes an important objective. Because of the correlation between animal abuse, child abuse, domestic violence, and other more complex social issues, the animal organization proposes to the community to build a coalition to approach these interconnected issues as a team. It is an "animal" group that most often starts the coalition. Supported by a grant from the Scott Trust (a Keybank Trust), the American Humane Association assisted the Stark County Humane Society, the Toledo Humane Society, and the Humane Society of Hancock County in Ohio in launching a major coalition building effort in the fall of 1998. Audiences will consist of veterinarians, social workers, law enforcement, and various other human and animal protection service professionals. The goal of the project is to establish an ongoing relationship from which further programmatic changes can emerge.

3. Stronger Prosecution of High-Profile Cruelty Cases and Strengthening of Anticruelty Laws

Animal protection can be difficult in the United States because anticruelty laws are poorly defined. Cruelty, such as setting a cat on fire, is a mere misdemeanor in many states and even in states where the act is a felony, judges often underestimate the importance of the crime. Because the victim is seen as "merely" being an animal, it can be very difficult for animal care and control agencies to make the case that the perpetrator of the violence is in need of strong sanctions and interventions. The correlation between animal abuse and human violence repositions the focus from the animal victim to the perpetrator who commits the violence. By supporting the argument that such an individual poses a threat not only to animals but the whole community, stronger prosecution of animal abuse cases can take place. The malicious killing of a petting zoo donkey named Pasado in Washington led to the eventual strengthening of the anticruelty laws of that state.

Even in states where animal cruelty is a felony, a high-profile case of one abused animal, supported by public outrage and link information, can convince a judge to deal more decisively with perpetrators who maliciously abuse animals. Based on link information, Colorado passed a law in 1997 requiring mental health evaluation and counseling for perpetrators of animal cruelty and the Animal Legal Defense Fund (ALDF) offers to help any prosecutor working on an animal abuse case.

4. Short-Term Holding of Animal Victims of Domestic Violence

Increasing numbers of animal care and control agencies are housing animals short term for victims of domestic violence. Animal shelters in Rochester, New York, Toledo, Ohio, San Diego, California, Detroit, Michigan, and many other states now provide this kind of service. Rather than have a human victim of violence remain in the abusive relationship because they cannot take their pets to a human shelter, the animal organization offers refuge for the pet. Most of these programs tend to be informally structured and frequently are conducted as a low-profile service that is advertised to domestic violence shelters and not the general public. This reluctance to publicize the service stems from a fear that demand may overwhelm an agency financially and that the shelter staff and facility could not cope with a large number of animals at one time (American Humane Association, 1998).

5. Programs to Prevent Violence to Animals and People

A notable response to the link by animal care and control agencies has been a renewed interest in how to prevent violence to animals and people from occurring in the first place. Although humane education has long been part of the programming of most animal care and control agencies, new types of outreach programs have been developed. For example, several humane societies in Minneapolis/Saint Paul, have launched "Caring Connections." This joint project introduces at-risk children to shelter dogs in a closely supervised dog training program. Mental health professionals, dog trainers, humane educators, and volunteers from several animal and human service organizations are working together with the children and dogs. Through a formal evaluation process, "Caring Connections" is attempting to demonstrate program benefits for the young people and the dogs. Though academic research has not yet validated the efficacy of such programs, organizations in several parts of the United States are nevertheless starting similar efforts. Other programs to prevent violence to animals and people include efforts to have prison populations train service dogs or to have mandatory humane education classes at animal shelters for individuals cited for nonviolent offenses such as animal neglect.

D. What Types of Programmatic Responses by Animal Care and Control to the Violence "Link" Appear to Be Successful?

1. Programs that Are Sensitive to the Limitations of the "Link"

Although research verifies the correlation between animal abuse and other forms of human violence, evidence linking animal cruelty to different types of perpetrators must be viewed critically. Although Felthous and Kellert (1987) published a study on "Childhood Cruelty to Animals and Later Aggression Against People," the study does not imply that all children who are cruel to animals will grow up to be serial killers. Yet it is tempting to overlook such details when advocating for an emotional topic such as children who are violent to animals. Unfortunately animal care and control spokespeople occasionally overstate the extent of the link in the media or in written materials, thus undermining the agency's credibility.

2. Programs with Realistic Goals and Expectations

Animal care and control agencies commonly are overextended in terms of staff, time, and budgets. Therefore, the most effective approach to the link has been to set realistic expectations and short-term goals. For example, a single training session on the link for all of the shelter staff is a realistic goal for almost any agency. However, starting a program to house the pets of domestic violence victims may be unrealistic for a shelter whose facility already is overcrowded with stray animals.

3. Funded Projects

Without financial support it can be challenging to operate any program. Some of the most successful projects are those with financial backing. The Colorado Springs Domestic Violence Emergency Response Team (DVERT) received a federal grant to focus on high-risk cases of domestic violence. The Humane Society of the Pikes Peak Region is a founding member of the group. A further way to strengthen a coalition is to profit from the experience of each partner. For example, a shelter housing animals for victims of domestic violence should do so only under supervision of and input from a domestic violence agency. Preferably, clients will come to the humane society as referrals from the domestic violence shelter. That way the human victims are screened and advised properly by the human service agency, while the animal agency can focus on taking care of the animal component of the case.

At the start, many coalitions plan training opportunities for interdisciplinary audiences on the link. In the fall of 1997, the William Snyder Foundation for Animals in Baltimore hosted a gathering of more than 100 professionals from various human service and animal protection groups. A second follow-up conference was planned by that group for the fall of 1998 to facilitate a formal emergence of a coalition approach.

E. WHAT KEY CHALLENGES ARISE FOR ANIMAL CARE AND CONTROL AGENCIES CONSIDERING PROGRAMMATIC RESPONSES TO THE VIOLENCE "LINK"?

When animal care and control agencies become involved with the link, they must discuss and consider issues that traditionally may not be part of their organizational mission. Most animal shelter staff do not have to consider substance abuse in the community, teen pregnancy, or child abuse legislation as a central component of their daily work. Yet if they become involved with the link, and especially if they start to work in a coalition with human service workers, they will need to participate in strategizing about these subjects that (on the surface) are far afield from animal protection.

Some animal care and control agencies are isolated from the community network of professional organizations. As a result they are not seen as a vibrant part of the community network and often are not known at all. The "humane society at the edge of town" syndrome is widespread, especially among small to medium shelters in small towns. In such agencies, creating effective community link-related coalitions or projects can be an insurmountable challenge without addressing the underlying issues of isolation first. A further challenge that prevents communication is a lack of knowledge regarding the work of other community services.

Many animal care and control agencies show an initial interest in the link, but cannot muster the needed staff, time, energy, and funding to implement any programs or activities. Even if one person on staff is very committed, without the support from the rest of the agency it can be impossible to generate any momentum on the link. It can be extremely difficult to convince resistant boards or staff members to consider programmatic involvement with the link. The area of human violence sometimes is seen as a "negative" subject that doesn't suit the "image" of a humane society or fit with the main mission of preventing animal cruelty. Often the link simply is not a priority for certain key decision makers, such as a board president who is most interested in spay/neuter or other animal welfare issues.

Although the creation of programmatic change based on the violence link (housing animals for domestic violence victims, humane education to prevent violence, legislative activities to prevent cruelty) can be effective, an animal care and control agency must first assess agency and community readiness for such change. If agencies or communities are not ready for change or encounter other obstacles, it may be more realistic to address these obstacles and introduce link programs following further preparation.

Programs based on the violence link can be labor intensive, time consuming, and require commitment. They also need a sustained momentum. In the past, some animal care and control agencies have shown great enthusiasm initially for the violence link, but after a few start-up efforts (such as a symposium on the topic), nothing much happens and the issue fades. Turnover in staff, reassessment of priorities, or simply being overwhelmed by the everyday challenges of animal care and control work can be the cause for such loss of momentum. A more organized approach to link-related efforts that involve strategic planning, realistic goals, and periodic evaluation can be one way to ensure success.

F. Conclusion

Only time will show how significant the current interest in the "link" between animal abuse and human violence is within the context of the greater society. However, it is apparent that many animal care and control agencies view this correlation as an opportunity. Further programmatic efforts by that professional group are to be expected. The exact impact of this advocacy—on people, animals, animal care and control agencies, human service professionals and society—calls for further study and critical evaluation.

IV. CLINICAL CASE STUDY

This section of the chapter looks at one way to intervene when a child is found to be aggressive or cruel toward animals. The child I will discuss is one who resided at Green Chimneys, a long-term residential treatment center for children. Children who first come to a residential treatment center bring the effects of their short painful lives and, until shown differently, can act out their unresolved distress on all living beings around them.

Green Chimneys has 250 rare breed farm animals and is a wildlife rehabilitation center. The animals are coworkers in the healing of traumatized children. Animals are also integrated into several of the classrooms and dormitories. These animals are the targets for some children's intense feelings when they first come to this residential treatment center.

As a clinical psychologist, I work therapeutically with the children. I include animals in most of my sessions at Green Chimneys' farm and wildlife center. I will present an overview of one case in which working clinically with animals helped a child to stop hurting animals and aided in resolving other issues in his life. Thus far, all the children I have worked with who have been cruel to animals have been male. I will, therefore, use the pronoun *he* as I describe the clinical work I do.

Green Chimneys has a format to target and work with aggression toward animals (see Appendix). I will address this as I discuss the case.

A. History of Prior Contact with Animals

I interview every child within the first week of admittance to the treatment facility. I administer a brief mental status exam to the child as we walk around the farm looking at and talking about all the enjoyable activities the child will be able to do with the animals. I ask specific questions regarding the child's history with animals.

I ascertain whether he likes animals, what type of pets he has had, if any, the animals he likes, whether he has observed someone hurting an animal or if he himself has, whether he has seen an animal die, and whether he thinks it's all right to hurt an animal.

As we traverse the farmyard, I observe the quality of touch the child has with different sized animals. Watching how a child interacts with an animal while holding it gives important information about how he will treat animals and other children, and also gives a window into how the child has been treated. I observe whether or not the child is frightened of very small animals or large ones. Does he exhibit good boundaries in holding an animal? Is he gentle? Does he move too fast around animals? Does he hold them like objects? I observe whether the child attempts to build a relationship with the animal and how the child attempts to do that.

The information from this interview is sent to the first case conference on the child to inform teachers and childcare workers of my findings.

B. FORMAT FOR TRACKING ANIMAL ABUSE

As the farm psychologist, I interview any child who has abused an animal. In conducting an assessment, I try to discover whether the child knew that what he was doing was hurtful to the animal, whether the child had feelings of remorse, the child's level of moral and cognitive functioning, and what additional avenues need to be created in the child's environment for him to learn how to be with animals. The information gathered helps me design responses to the child's cruel actions. The consequences I assign are aimed at providing restitution for the cruelty (see the checklist in the Appendix).

Restitution helps the child know his action of hurting an animal has been dealt with and is finished. Feelings of guilt are avoided by restitution, and the child has a chance to give something back to the animal or to the child's peers who were upset by the cruel behavior. A variety of interventions can be utilized depending on the psychological needs of the child, and whether some form of remorse is evident. Examples include asking the child to write a paragraph about what it feels like to abuse an animal, or asking him to ask the animal's forgiveness or say he's sorry. Depending on the age of the child and the level of cognitive impairment, drawing a picture of the animal and keeping it on his desk has worked to remind the child of what not to do. Cleaning the area where the animal lives, picking up stones in the horse pasture (a necessary but difficult task), or being talked to by a state police officer are examples of short-term interventions.

Many children do not need therapeutic help to stop hurting animals. Some are not mature enough to know what hurts animals and they stop their behavior as they get older and gain knowledge. Others are very curious and invent experiments using animals. Their behavior stops as a result of the culture of Green Chimneys and peer pressure. Principles of humane education are imbedded in this culture, where respect for all living beings is part of the organizational mission.

If a child has more than one incident of cruelty to animals without remorse, and with rageful intent to hurt, he is referred to me for longer term work.

For the purpose of this case study, I will define cruelty as any purposely aggressive behavior aimed at trying to hurt an animal. Aggressive behavior will be defined as any verbal or physical action that is unnecessarily harsh or threatening.

C. CASE STUDY

Calvin (not his real name) came to Green Chimneys when he was 9 years old and was discharged at the age of 13. He was in treatment with me 1 hour per week for 2.5 years. When we were terminating, he came for half hour sessions twice a month for another year.

Calvin's mother had a history of drug abuse and he was removed from her care on a neglect charge. His father was in prison. Calvin lived on and off with his maternal grandmother, his great aunt, and his 24-year-old cousin. Calvin's behavior was always described as problematic and seemed to worsen when he was living with his cousin. This behavior included early excessive crying, tantrums, head banging, rocking, and hyperactivity. He was admitted to a diagnostic center. Here, he fought, bit, and threw objects at peers. He urinated in bottles and threw these at peers. He was then referred to Green Chimneys where these behaviors continued for a time.

His admitting diagnosis, using the DSM-IIIR (*Diagnostic and Statistical Manual of Mental Disorders,* third edition, Revised) was "Axis I—Dysthymia and Conduct Disorder, undifferentiated." Aggression to animals was not noted anywhere in his chart.

The initial clinical formulation, documented by our admitting treatment team, centered around his suffering from early deprivation and neglect. It was felt that his capacity for meaningful relationships had been impaired. His mother's addiction and, hence, the loss of her emotionally and the loss of his father created emotional fragility and deep feelings of rejection, loss, and abandonment. Testing by the psychologist on Calvin's team using the WISC-RIII showed him to be a concrete thinker with a full scale IQ of 97, in the average range.

I found him to have a significant lack of trust in relationships, to be very angry, and to be acting out this anger most of the time. Deep feelings of rejection and loss were underscored by Calvin having three different social workers while at Green Chimneys. He personalized the departure of these therapists and felt no one wanted to work with him. He had a large extended family but no one was able to take care of him. The family rejected adoption.

Calvin was referred to me because, while working at the farm, he hit a baby calf so hard that it had a seizure. To observe how he behaved around animals, and to understand what was occurring for him emotionally that might be acted out on animals, I increased his work time at the farm from a 0.5 hour per week to 1.5 hours per week spread over a week's time. He worked alongside a farm intern doing barn maintenance chores.

When our clinical work together began, our therapy sessions involved walking around the farm as he verbally provoked every living creature he saw in a hyperactive manner. He would curse and talk about how he would kill or mutilate the animals. He would say things like "If no one was here, I'd kill all the animals except Duke and Doc." He was unable to say why he would save these draft horses. Calvin was a bundle of rage. He could not sit down or focus on anything but spewing his rage like a volcano. During this time, I would have to prepare myself emotionally to be with Calvin because his rage was so intense. I would name his feeling and, more importantly, tolerate it.

As Calvin began to trust the continuity of our relationship, he began to see that I was able to accept his rage and that I liked him. After some months of work, we were able to engage in other activities besides walking around the farm. He continued to be verbally aggressive against the animals during most of our early sessions.

Calvin and I began working with a 2-week-old rooster, Sebastian, who lived in a fish tank on my desk since he would be killed immediately in the chicken coop. Sebastian's abandonment by his mother and his vulnerability were fodder for displacement work with Calvin. I told the rooster things I wanted Calvin to hear and found out about Calvin through his interactions with the rooster. Calvin personalized Sebastian's pecking. When the chicken pecked him, Calvin misunderstood and thought Sebastian was purposely trying to hurt him. Much information was gathered about Calvin's own projection of his rage through his interactions with the rooster. He did not understand why something he loved was trying to hurt him. Working with Sebastian allowed many parallels to be drawn with Calvin's feelings about his family. Calvin became so attached to Sebastian that he was allowed to leave his classroom every day for a few minutes to "check" on how he was faring.

As Calvin continued to be calm enough to sit and work with the animals, we interacted with a variety of animal and bird "therapists" in the therapy hut. Two important colleagues at this time were Erika the guinea pig and Tinkerbell the cockatiel. During the many months of our therapy work in the hut, both of these animals were quite sensitive to how Calvin was feeling. As Calvin held Erika on his lap, he would focus on what he felt holding this soft, cuddly, guinea pig. I asked him to locate this feeling in his body and to get an image of the feeling in his heart region, his head, his neck, or his whole body. The feeling could be tension, affection, or anger. I then asked him to let the feeling travel down his arm and into the animal or bird. He would pay attention to how the animal experienced his feelings. Erika and Tinkerbell would move away, tense up, snuggle, or in Tinkerbell's case, allow Calvin to rub the back of her head, depending on what was experienced from his energy.

I used this clinical work to discuss the responses people and animals might have to his behavior and feelings. Calvin began to see that what he did or how he said something had great impact on another being and how he was then treated. Calvin loved birds and particularly wanted Tinkerbell to come to him and stay with him. He saw he had a lot of control over whether this happened or not. He began to see that the tension he carried actually made animals move away from him, the very thing he did not want to happen. We discussed how this also applied to his relationships with peers in his dormitory.

Episodes of hurting animals decreased significantly at Green Chimneys. However, at a visit to a potential foster mother's home, she reported that Calvin had "stomped a kitten to death" because it had been "bothering" him. This incident occurred 1 week before his first social worker was to leave. Calvin did not understand the connections between his angry feelings and his actions when this primitive rage overcame him. This intense feeling of loss, brought on by the imminent departure of his social worker, triggered his feelings of abandonment by his family, and these feelings catapulted him onto a yo-yo of angry behavior that was aggressively acted out in the classroom and the dormitory. Despite his need to discharge his anger, Calvin was also observed to be quiet and gentle with the animals at times, during his job and farm class time. This was seen as hopeful. He was integrating some of the clinical work he was doing.

Calvin escalated his anger toward staff and peers alike. At this time, he put hand lotion in the dormitory dog's bowl. The dog ate it and became sick. His senior worker, his new social worker, and I discussed this incident and decided that Calvin needed a potent consequence for his behavior. Added to this recent cruel act was his disintegrating behavior in the dormitory with the other children.

Calvin did not exhibit any remorse for hurting the dog or for his aggressive behavior toward his peers. He was barred from his farm jobs and therapeutic riding classes for 2 weeks. We took away the privilege of coming to the farm because it was the only activity he cared about at the time. We discussed his anger and pain at not being able to come to the farm. He was not bothered that the dog became sick. We discussed how the dog might feel, paralleling his feelings about not coming to the farm.

Working at the farm was a way for Calvin to begin integrating the work he was doing in therapy. The animals were helping him to change himself in the therapy sessions. His job at the farm was helping him to try on these new ways of being with himself and the animals. He could receive immediate feedback from me or his farm intern as to how he was progressing with dealing with his anger. He would walk into the cow pen and while pushing the cow would say, "I'm in control here." He would obsess about which animal could hurt which animal, what animals could hurt him, and which animal would attack a human being. Each of these episodes could be addressed in the context of what he was learning about himself.

As Calvin slowly began to master his own aggressive drives and to integrate what he learned working with the animals, he was more able to tolerate his painful emotional states. Calvin was practicing in a concrete way, the new learning and awareness he was having in his treatment. This led to an important understanding about himself. He said, "I feel better when I hurt an animal."

This marked a major turning point for Calvin. He now had a more differentiated sense of himself. This enabled Calvin to internalize, or hold inside himself, some of his painful feelings rather than to act them out. Hurting animals allowed him to externalize a painful feeling by acting it out or by projecting a painful feeling onto an animal, feeling that it was the animal who was angry at him. This thought process allowed him to feel justified in hurting animals. He was hurting the animal before it hurt him. Up until this time, he was unable to experience his own anger, and now he understood that as long as he was hurting animals, he did not feel pain.

I gave Calvin 5 weeks advance notice that I would be away for 6 weeks on vacation. At this time, he killed another cat at his potential foster mother's home. He spent the next 5 weeks refusing to meet with me directly in a session. However, we had a lot of contact as Calvin was actively engaged in the relationship. He was very angry that I was going away and was letting me know. He would yell at me across campus, he would address everyone in a group but me, he would swear and follow me, at times yelling at me. I continued to attempt to meet with him at our therapy time, allowing him to express his rage as needed. During this time of focused, more direct expression of rage, he had no other incidents of hurting animals. He was dealing directly with the anger he felt.

When I returned, Calvin came to sessions and angrily spoke of wanting to hurt animals again. I said he killed the cat (prior to my vacation) because he wanted to kill me for going away so long and leaving him. He was not able to say he was angry that I had gone away. His mood and behavior appeared quite labile. He appeared to expect the animals to become aggressive with him, to retaliate against him for his rage. This expectation was sometimes fulfilled since Calvin's behavior toward the animals elicited hurtful behavior. Around this time, Calvin also began to acknowledge his part in scaring animals.

We were working with a parrot named Peaches. He would make angry and aggressive movements toward the bird who would then move away from him. He would laugh as he was being aggressive enjoying his sense of power over another. Rather than automatically acting out toward the animal, he began to have more control over his feelings. We began discussing what he would like to say to human beings as opposed to hurting or scaring this bird. He often responded with "I'm angry."

At this time, parental rights were terminated. Calvin also found out that he had siblings from his biological mother who were all living with his maternal grandmother. He was feeling completely rejected by his family who existed, but not for him. Most of his rage at adults was coming out toward female staff in the dormitory and at his teacher.

Later, another social worker left. In our session on the social worker's last day, Calvin asked to hold Erika, the guinea pig, which he snuggled. He asked me to read a story to him, but with the door to the therapy hut closed so no one could see I was reading him a story. As we read the story, the cockateil he had been working with came to sit on his shoulder and listen also. We discussed the connection between sharing feelings and feeling feelings. He felt "his" animals knew he was sad. He understood that this friend was reaching out to comfort him and felt cared for by the cockateil who did not move away from him. We discussed trust and what trust felt like.

Calvin's paternal grandfather came to visit him. Calvin was very happy about this and walked around the farm showing him all the animals, telling him their names as well as something special about them.

As Calvin was coming to sessions during this time, we continued to work with boundary issues and his projections. We would walk Joe, a ferret, on a leash and Calvin's job was to keep Joe safe as he explored his world. As we walked the ferret, Calvin would have to see what it was about Joe's actions and curious explorations that were putting him in an unsafe place. He had to watch Joe very carefully because Joe was quick. Gauging Joe's actions, Calvin had to respond, lest Joe crawl under the barn or get attacked by a goose. He had to respond to the ferret's actions rather than his own wishes.

Calvin was beginning to say, "I'm angry." He did not know why he was angry, but he began to acknowledge the feeling while working with the animals. He could now come to the session angry, but leave calm.

We began to feed the coyotes together. He was impressed because they were wild and aggressive yet they trusted him to come into their home and did not try to hurt him when we cleaned their pen. We drew parallels to his accepting his own aggressiveness, that he, too, could have a feeling and not have to act it out. He said he could trust our relationship "a little."

Peaches, the parrot, seemed to be helping Calvin. She had many human-like ways. Though she could not talk, she was very keyed into Calvin's energy around her. He could not objectify her, and thus he had to build a relationship with her. He did not try to bait her as he had other animals. He seemed to be trying to find a way to relate to her. He found he had to earn her trust like the coyotes had done with him.

We had begun to talk about the time when he used to hurt or kill animals. Although he continued to be verbally aggressive to the animals, he was not hurting them.

For the second time, I told him I was leaving on a 6-week vacation. "So long this time like last time?" He was able to speak his anger and he refused to come to therapy our next time. Instead I went to his classroom and we looked at a globe and found the country I was going to visit. I gave him extra work time at the farm and a picture of Tinkerbell (the cockateil), him, and me to keep while I was away. I sent him a postcard, telling him I would be back to work with him.

While I was gone, Calvin had episodes of being verbally aggressive to animals when he was angry at someone. He did not hurt animals. Upon my return from vacation, he initially refused to meet with me and said he was angry. I acknowledged his angry feelings. I opened my arms and he allowed himself to be hugged by me.

In the spring of that year, I wrote: "Calvin was referred to me for work around his animal abuse. He has worked hard in this relationship having also to face, harness and redirect how he expresses his rage. Calvin has moved from lying and denial of hurting animals to being able to express how good it felt to hurt animals, to finally managing his own anger and building relationships with the animals who have taught him how to relate. We are working on saying goodbye. Although he is no longer hurting animals, I will see him through until his discharge in June."

As we were terminating, we worked with another new parrot named Lorita, who bit Calvin one day. Calvin began to cry and did not in any way attempt to hurt her. We discussed this, how much it had hurt and how far he had come in not trying to hurt her. He understood she was "just afraid."

Calvin began to share his fears and his desires for discharge as we focused less on his hurting animals and more on saying good-bye and all the different feelings that go with that.

ACKNOWLEDGMENTS

The authors thank Stephanie LaFarge and Barbara Boat for their suggestions and thoughtful comments on an earlier draft of this chapter. Susan Brooks notes that birthing this beginning seed could not have occurred without the care, softball games, fine editorial skills, and excellent typing at different points from Barbara Dubitsky, Lori Capeci-Buccieri and Cindy Diaz—thank you. Thanks to C.B., and to Bruce Barrett for sustaining me with soul nourishing food.

APPENDIX: FORMAT FOR TRACKING ANIMAL CRUELTY

    A. Reporting Cruel, Abusive, or Aggressive Behavior
        1. An incident report is filled out on all children who are cruel to an animal.
        2. Verbal aggression or threats to hurt an animal are given to the farm psychologist verbally.
        3. The farm psychologist processes all incidents and fills out an animal aggression review form.

B. Immediate Short-Term Intervention
   1. The child's level of emotional, cognitive, and moral development is assessed.
   2. Attempts are made to process the incident with the observer.
   3. Repercussions to the child's actions.
   4. Restitution
   5. Humane education
C. Considerations in Long-Term Intervention
   1. Referral for treatment
      a. Acceptance of the child's feelings and level of functioning.
      b. Humane education in the form of hands-on work
      c. Learning about feelings through working with animals; what is a feeling, location of feelings in the body
      d. Anger work
      e. Empathy work, boundary work, projections, and the reciprocity of a relationship.
      f. Termination

REFERENCES

Achenbach, T. M., & Edelbrock, C. S. (1981). Behavioral problems and competencies reported by parents of normal and disturbed children aged four through sixteen. *Monographs of the Society for Research in Child Development, 46*, Serial No. 188.

Adams, C. A. (Ed.) (1992). America's abuse problem. *Animal Watch*, Fall/Winter, 9–16.

Agnew, R. (1998). The causes of animal abuse: A social-psychological analysis. *Theoretical Criminology, 2*, 177–209.

American Humane Association. (1998). *Operational guide for animal care and control agencies—handling the pets of domestic violence victims.* Englewood, CO: Author.

American Psychiatric Association. (1994). *Diagnostic and statistical manual of mental disorders* (4th ed.). Washington, DC: Author.

Arkow, P. (1996). The relationship between animal abuse and other forms of family violence. *Family Violence and Sexual Assault Bulletin, 12*, 29–34.

Arluke, A. (1997, September). Cruelty to animals and human violence: The evidence for the connection. Presentation at the HSUS "First Strike" Symposium, Washington, DC.

Arluke, A., Levin, J., Luke, C., & Ascione, F. (1999). The relationship of animal abuse to violence and other forms of antisocial behavior. *Journal of Interpersonal Violence, 14*, 963–975.

Ascione, F. R. (1993). Children who are cruel to animals: A review of research and implications for developmental psychopathology. *Anthrozoös, 6*, 226–247.

Ascione, F. R. (1997). Humane education research: Evaluating efforts to encourage children's kindness and caring toward animals. *Genetic, Social, and General Psychology Monographs, 123* (1), 57–77.

Ascione, F. R. (1998). Battered women's reports of their partners' and their children's cruelty to animals. *Journal of Emotional Abuse, 1*, 119–133.

Ascione, F. R. (1999). The abuse of animals and human interpersonal violence: Making the connection. In F. R. Ascione and P. Arkow (Eds.), *Child abuse, domestic violence, and animal abuse: Linking the circles of compassion for prevention and intervention* (pp. 50–61). West Lafayette, IN: Purdue University Press.

Ascione, F. R., & Arkow, P. (Eds.) (1999). *Child abuse, domestic violence, and animal abuse: Linking the circles of compassion for prevention and intervention.* West Lafayette, IN: Purdue University Press.

Ascione, F. R., & Weber, C. V. (1997a). *Battered Partner Shelter Survey (BPSS).* Logan, UT: Utah State University.

Ascione, F. R., & Weber, C. V. (1997b). *Children's observation and experience with pets (COEP).* Logan, UT: Utah State University.

Ascione, F. R., Thompson, T. M., & Black, T. (1997a). Childhood cruelty to animals: Assessing cruelty dimensions and motivations. *Anthrozoös, 10,* 170–177.

Ascione, F. R., Weber, C. V., & Wood, D. S. (1997b). The abuse of animals and domestic violence: A national survey of shelters for women who are battered. *Society and Animals, 5,* 205–218.

Baenninger, R. (1991). Violence toward other species. In R. Baenninger (Ed.), *Targets of violence and aggression* (pp. 5–43). Amsterdam: North-Holland.

Davidson, H. (1998). On the horizon: What lawyers and judges should know about the link between child abuse and animal cruelty. *ABA Child Law Practice, 17*(4), 60–63.

DeViney, E., Dickert, J., & Lockwood, R. (1983). The care of pets within child abusing families. *International Journal for the Study of Animal Problems, 4,* 321–329.

Dowling, J. M. (1998). Animal cruelty and human violence: Making the connection. *Animal Sheltering, 21*(1), 5–19.

Eisenberg, N. (1992). *The caring child.* Cambridge: Harvard University Press.

Felthous, A. R., & Kellert, S. R. (1987) Childhood cruelty to animals and later aggression against people: A review. *American Journal of Psychiatry, 144,* 710–717.

Frick, P. J., Van Horn, Y., Lahey, B. B., Christ, M. A. G., Loeber, R., Hart, E. A., Tannenbaum, L., & Hanson, K. (1993). Oppositional defiant disorder and conduct disorder: A meta-analytic review of factor analyses and cross-validation in a clinical sample. *Clinical Psychology Review, 13,* 319–340.

Goleman, D. (1995). *Emotional intelligence.* New York: Bantam Books.

Hindman, J. L. (1992). *Juvenile culpability assessment (2nd rev.).* Ontario, OR: Alexandria Associates.

Humane Society of Southern Arizona. (1998). *Cruelty in common: Animals, people, and a holistic approach to understanding violence.* Tucson, Arizona: Author.

Kaufmann, M. E. (1999). The relevance of cultural competence to the link between violence to animals and people. In F.R. Ascione and P. Arkow (Eds.), *Child abuse, domestic violence, and animal abuse: Linking the circles of compassion for prevention and intervention* (pp. 260–270). West Lafayette, IN: Purdue University Press.

Kazdin, A. E., & Esveldt-Dawson, K. (1986). The interview for antisocial behavior: Psychometric characteristics and concurrent validity with child psychiatric inpatients. *Journal of Psychopathology and Behavioral Assessment, 8,* 289–303.

Kellert, S. R., & Felthous, A. R. (1985). Childhood cruelty toward animals among criminals and noncriminals. *Human Relations, 38,* 1113–1129.

Lockwood, R., & Ascione, F. (Eds.) (1998). *Cruelty to animals and interpersonal violence: Readings in research and application.* West Lafayette, IN: Purdue University Press.

Loeber, R., Keenan, K., Lahey, B., Green, S., & Thomas, C. (1993). Evidence for developmentally based diagnoses of oppositional defiant disorder and conduct disorder. *Journal of Abnormal Child Psychology, 21,* 377–410.

Magid, K., & McKelvey, C. A. (1987). *High risk: Children without a conscience.* New York: Bantam Books.

Moffit, T. E. (1993). "Life-course persistent" and "adolescence-limited" antisocial behavior: A developmental taxonomy. *Psychological Review, 100,* 674–701.

Offord, D. R., Boyle, M. H., & Racine, Y. A. (1991). The epidemiology of antisocial behavior in childhood and adolescence. In D. J. Pepler and K.H. Rubin (Eds.), *The development and treatment of childhood aggression.* (pp. 31–54). Hillsdale, NJ: Lawrence Erlbaum Associates.

Pinel, P. (1809). *Traite medico-philosophique de la alientation mentale* (2nd ed.). Paris: Brosson.

Renzetti, C. M. (1992). *Violent betrayal: Partner abuse in lesbian relationships.* Newbury Park, CA: Sage Publications.

Ressler, R. K., Burgess, A. W., & Douglas, J. E. (1988). *Sexual homicide: Patterns and motives.* Lexington, MA: Lexington Books.

Schiff, K., Louw, D., & Ascione, F. R. (in review). Childhood cruelty to animals in a sample of aggressive and non-aggressive South African criminals.

Tapia, F. (1971). Children who are cruel to animals. *Child Psychiatry and Human Development, 2,* 70–77.

Toledo Humane Society. (1994). *Animal advocates for children: Training manual for cruelty investigative agents.* Toledo, OH: Author.

Vermuelen, H., & Odendaal, J. S. J. (1993). Proposed typology of companion animal abuse. *Anthrozoös, 6,* 248–257.

Weber, C. V., & Ascione, F. R. (1992, July). Humane attitudes and human empathy: Relations in adulthood. Keynote address at the Sixth International Conference on Human Animal Interactions, Montreal, Canada.

Wisconsin Humane Society. (1997). *The critter chronicles: Programs designed to end violence toward animals.* Milwaukee, Wisconsin: Author.

World Health Organization. (1996). *International classification of mental and behavioral disorders (ICD-10).* Cambridge, UK: Cambridge University Press.

SECTION IV

Special Topics and Concerns in Animal-Assisted Therapy

The Companion Animal within the Family System: The Manner in Which Animals Enhance Life within the Home

SANDRA LOOKABAUGH TRIEBENBACHER

Department of Child Development and Family Relations, East Carolina University, Greenville, North Carolina

I. COMPANION ANIMALS IN THE FAMILY

Think back to a time with Darla, Spanky, Buckwheat, Alfalfa, and Petey . . . or what about Lassie and Timmy? Images of humans and their companion animals come vividly to our minds. In more recent years, Eddie on the popular evening sitcom "Frazier," Cathy and Electra in the cartoon strips, and Carl the Rottweiler in a series of children's books are examples of companion animals portrayed as vital family members. The "prototype" of an all-American family often includes the presence of a companion animal. One does not have to search hard in books, television series, or movies to repeatedly find companion animals and humans living, learning, and loving side by side.

The purpose of this chapter is to educate clinicians about the variety of roles companion animals can serve within the family system. While the overall focus is not direct delivery of animal-assisted therapy, much of the information included is intended to assist clinicians as they deliver "animal-informed therapy" for human family members. This chapter specifically addresses the following: prevalence of companion animals within the family; roles, functions, and contributions of companion animals to the family; companion animals within the context of family systems; companion animals across the family life cycle; challenges associated with companion animals in the family; pet loss and bereavement; and contributions of companion animals to children's development. Anecdotes from personal and professional experiences have been incorporated to illustrate specific issues related to human–animal relationships.

A. DEMOGRAPHICS OF COMPANION ANIMALS IN U.S. FAMILIES

Current demographics published by the American Veterinary Medical Association (AVMA, 1997) provide powerful evidence that companion animals are common in U.S. households. Companion animals are part of more than 58.9% (58.2 million) of U.S. households (98.9 million). In 1996, dogs were the most popular companion animal in terms of percentage of households (31.6%), while cats were the most popular companion animal in terms of total population (54.6 million). Households with one dog represented 62.2% of households, and households with one cat represented 48% of the pet-owning households in the United States. Multiple pet households are also a common phenomena with 42% of dog-owning households (dogs were designated as the primary pet) also owning cats. A variety of other animal species, such as birds, rodents, and reptiles, are also considered companion animals in U.S. households. Their presence is often documented but often less likely to be researched.

B. PETS AS FAMILY MEMBERS

Given the obvious visibility of companion animals in families, it seems odd that considerable research has focused on the psychological, social, and physical benefits of dyadic human–animal interactions, but limited attention has focused on the roles and functions of companion animals within the family unit (Albert & Bulcroft, 1988; Cain, 1983; Soares, 1985). "The lack of sociological data on pet–human bonds indicates that family scientists have little insight into an aspect of family life that is shared by millions" (Albert & Bulcroft, 1988, p. 544). Albert and Bulcroft surmise that perhaps pets have been overlooked in family studies because some social scientists have difficulty considering these companion animals as members of the family system (p. 544).

Research has demonstrated (Albert & Bulcroft, 1988; Cain, 1983; Cantanzaro, 1984) that humans consider their companion animals to be "family members." While there is no generally agreed on definition of "family" among family scientists, there are a variety of ways to "define" what constitutes a family.

Some definitions are limiting, focusing on blood relatives and relatives by marriage, other definitions "include not only persons from the immediate nuclear family but also kin of various sorts, friends and pets" (Trost, 1990, p. 431). Viewing families from a framework of "units" such as spousal/cohabitating units, parent–child units, owner-dog units, etc., may be helpful when considering the broad-based notion of families (Trost, 1990).

Within the family unit, one of the most important changes in family function during the last century has been a shift from the expectation of fulfilling societal needs/expectations to fulfilling personal needs for emotional security and companionship (Mancini & Orthner, 1988; Scanzoni, 1987). Interestingly enough, emotional security and companionship are roles that companion animals are often most adept to fulfill! Similarly, the family emotional system "at times . . . may include members of the extended family network and even nonrelatives and pets" (Bowen, 1978, p. 123). Sable (1995) reminds mental health providers that "if pets are seen as family members and attachment figures, there are implications for intervention, prevention, and social policies" (p. 338).

It is important to remember that families come in all varieties with no variety being more important or appropriate than another. Cain (1985) reminds family scientists of the importance of considering the significance of pets as family members in order to conceptualize the family as a whole unit.

C. SYSTEMS THEORY

Based on the assumption that families are composed of a variety of units, systems theory offers an appropriate theoretical foundation on which therapists, psychologists, social workers, and other mental health professionals can incorporate companion animals into treatment plans. Examination of the basic tenets of systems theory allows the mental health provider to view the companion animal as a vital member of the family system (Broderick & Smith, 1979):

1. The family is viewed as a structure of interrelated parts and subsystems within the total family unit.
2. Each part or subsystem carries out certain functions with the family unit.
3. Interdependence among family members is emphasized.
4. Family members do not live in isolation. What affects one member may directly or indirectly affect other members.
5. Family structure can be seen only in the family's interactions.
6. The family is a purposeful system seeking homeostasis.
7. Patterns of interactions among family members are important to consider. These patterns may center around communication, roles,

beliefs, and values. It is the patterns of interactions among family members, including companion animals, that may provide the most meaningful insight to providers.

D. ROLES, FUNCTIONS, AND CONTRIBUTIONS OF COMPANION ANIMALS IN THE FAMILY

Any discussion of roles, functions, and contributions of companion animals in the context of the family system must address several key issues. First, every relationship involving humans and animals is as unique as the individuals involved and is often influenced by such things as age, gender, and personality characteristics. Second, humans and animals do form significant dyadic and even triadic relationships within the family system. Third, we must consider the reciprocal nature of human–animal relationships within the family. All members of the family system impact, either directly or indirectly, the other members of the family.

Of all the roles that companion animals may play within the context of a family, those of friend, confidant, and source of support and affection are probably the most notable and valued of all. Both theoretical and empirical evidence support what we as the human side of the human–animal bond know to be true (Albert & Bulcroft, 1988; Beck & Katcher, 1983; Levinson, 1972). Animal companions typically make few demands of us, relative to our human counterparts, do not hold grudges, are usually always happy to see us even after the briefest of separations, and may reward us with a vocalization, rub, stroke, or tail wag for even the smallest bit of positive attention.

Another significant role that companion animals can serve is that of substitutes for other family members (Albert & Bulcroft, 1988). The animal may fill a void in the family of a member that has physically or emotionally left the family, a family member that has died, or even a family member that has not been born yet.

> For a couple experiencing temporary infertility, the beloved Sheltie, Sadie, was in many ways their "child." Sadie was always at their side; she usually slept in their bed; she received presents during celebrations, and fulfilled many of their needs and desires as "parents." The role as "child" seemed to be cherished by Sadie . . . the constant center of attention in the household.

An interesting footnote to this case is that on the very day that Sadie's parents brought home their first "human child," Alex, from the hospital, Sadie suffered a life-threatening attack of pancreatitis. After careful examination and a series of tests, the veterinarian concluded that the entire episode appeared to be triggered by the stress that Sadie felt with the arrival of a new family member.

And while anthropomorphism, the act of projecting human emotions on animals, is criticized among some in the scientific community, this example certainly leads one to believe that Sadie might have felt threatened by the many changes that resulted from the birth of a human child. The most common shift of family roles in this type of situation is that the animal "child" has been usurped or replaced by the human "child."

Companion animals may also facilitate communication and interactions among human family members. Open and ongoing communication, not only within the family but also with individuals outside the system, is essential and necessary for healthy development. Every individual needs and enjoys varying levels of interaction and as social creatures, communication promotes these interactions. For every parent who has asked their school-age child, "What happened at school today?" and gotten the standard reply of, "Nothing," this next example may provide some insight.

> A mother of a 10-year-old girl, Jessie, decided that communication with her daughter left much to be desired. Jessie's independence and the shift in communication from telling her mother everything to now confiding in her girlfriends was difficult for her mother. Quite by accident one evening, Jessie's mother said to the family dog, Laverne, "I sure wish you could talk. You seem to spend more time with Jessie than anyone in this house. . . . I bet you could give me some pretty juicy information." What Jessie's mother did not realize was that Jessie was standing on the stairs listening to this entire conversation with Laverne. Jessie casually strolled into the kitchen and said, "Mom, Laverne is sworn to secrecy but . . . if you want to know about things you could just ask me." Jessie's mother replied, "Every time I ask you 'What happened at school today?,' you just say, 'Nothing.' " "Well mom, when you say it like that, it sounds like you are questioning me rather than just asking me."

This example provides helpful information in several ways. While attempting to facilitate communication, Jessie's mother was really blocking communication with her daughter. The mother's choice of words was very powerful in creating a distance between mother and daughter. Another interesting point is that both mother and daughter felt as though they could confide in the family dog. Possibly both openly communicated with the dog because the dog was perceived to be a objective, nonthreatening listener—a "sounding board" of sorts. Companion animals do not voice judgments, make critical remarks, or even force us to consider alternative viewpoints.

Companion animals have also described as "barometers" of family atmosphere (Cain, 1991). Family members have described situations where the companion animal was acting very spunky during times of joyous celebration, depressed when a family member was sad or upset, and fighting with other companion animals in the household when there was great tension in the household (Cain, 1983). It would be very easy to once again say that humans are projecting their emotions onto the animals when animals really cannot "feel" as we do. The following example, however, provides compelling evidence that companion animals can and do "read" situations and act accordingly.

> Barbara is 35 years old, married, and the human companion to six dogs. Barbara had major reconstructive surgery on her nose and was confined to quiet bedrest for several weeks following surgery. Barbara's dogs were normally allowed on the bed to nap and snuggle with her and her husband. However, due to the seriousness of the surgery, both Barbara and her husband decided that it was too much of a risk to have the large dogs on the bed for a while. Scruffy, a 20-pound terrier mix, was the exception to this rule. Scruffy was typically a ball of energy who bounded onto the bed then onto Barbara's chest, followed by lots of face licks, as part of their daily routine. The first day that Scruffy was allowed onto the bed with Barbara after her surgery, he quietly crept onto the bed, carefully positioned himself and snuggled on her left side. He was making body contact but never once attempted to leap onto her chest and lick her face. He sniffed the badges on her face from a distance but then repositioned himself at her side. Barbara shared this radical change of behavior with her husband and they decided to do a little research experiment. Under close supervision, they allowed the other five dogs into the bedroom one by one to see their reaction to Barbara. Remarkably all five of the dogs walked up to the side of the bed where Barbara was, wagged their tails, extended their heads for her to pet, sniffed the face bandages at a distance then lay down on the floor beside the bed.

One may ask, "Did these dogs 'read' this situation and determine that it was not appropriate to jump onto the bed and snuggle as usual?" Obviously there is no way to know for sure, but what was fascinating was the fact that in this situation, the dogs appeared to be very perceptive to the tone of the environment during this time of recuperation and acted accordingly.

In some instances, companion animals can provide information to mental health providers about how a family is organized. An interesting role for companion animals within the family system is that of being part of a triangle. "A triangle is formed when the tension within a two person emotional system exceeds a certain level" (Cain, 1985, p. 61). The triangle is a patterned way of handling intense feeling states and can consist of both human and animal family members. Like humans, animals can be triangled into a family system to relieve an uncomfortable situation or divert attention away from salient family issues (Cain, 1985).

Research has provided specific examples where companion animals have been triangled in situations where there was tension between two family members (Cain, 1985). For example, companion animals have been described as doing something "cute" and thereby diffusing a situation and the humans forgot they were angry (p. 61). In other instances, companion animals would approach the people in the tense situation and seek out affection possibly as a way to release frustration and cool down the argument (p. 61). All of these examples again demonstrate that animals may be far more "in tune" with human emotions and reading intimate family situations than we have ever imagined.

E. COMPANION ANIMALS AT DIFFERENT STAGES OF THE FAMILY LIFE CYCLE

Pets appear to serve different roles in families at different points across the family life cycle and these roles undoubtedly vary within each unique family system. Similarly, humans probably serve different roles in the lives of their companion animals at different points across the life cycle. The family development perspective, as described by Duvall (1977), offers a helpful framework for examining the unique contributions of companion animals to families at different developmental stages. This framework offers reference points for examining changes in the family's roles and structure. The stages of the family life cycle are as follows (Duvall, 1977):

Stage 1: Establishment stage (newlyweds)
Stage 2: Families with infants
Stage 3: Families with preschool-age children
Stage 4: Families with school-age children
Stage 5: Families with adolescents
Stage 6: Families with young adults
Stage 7: Middle-aged parents
Stage 8: Aging family members

It is important to note that many families are in overlapping stages, many families do not fit "neatly" into these typologies, and some families do not fit into the prescribed timetable (Duvall, 1985). Additionally, mental health providers will undoubtedly interact with other family forms that are not represented in this framework such as single-parent, blended, homosexual, and other family forms that may face unique challenges and have different family expectations and experiences. This perspective is intended to be used as a "guide" when working with families rather than a rigid framework.

Examination of the companion animal's life cycle within the context of the family life cycle may also provide clinicians with insightful information about the family. Stages of the companion animal's life cycle overlap with stages of the family life cycle. Roles and contributions of both humans and animals continue to evolve and change as both progress through various stages. For example, the young, spunky companion animal in a family with preschool-age children may have a very different role 4 to 5 years in the future. At that time, the family has probably moved on to another stage in the family life cycle, a family with school-age children, as the companion animal has progressed on in his or her life cycle and may be considered to be in the "senior years."

Another issue to consider is multiple companion animals within the family across the family life cycle. For example, a family may currently have or acquire a "family pet" early in the family life cycle and additional companion animals may be added to the family unit as the children reach adolescence and young adulthood. This example illustrates the idea that humans and animals in numerous combinations can form dyads and even triads within the family system.

When considering roles of companion animals within the family, one must make a clear distinction between mere ownership of a companion animal and attachment to that animal. For example, a family may own an animal but not necessarily be highly attached to the animals. This point is illustrated by the high rate of ownership among families with school-age and adolescent children (AVMA, 1997) but a low degree of attachment to their companion animals (Albert and Bulcroft, 1988).

A variety of factors may provide insight into this phenomena. Parents may acquire companion animals because they believe that children should "grow up" with animals and want to promote responsibility in their children. Kidd et al., (1992) found that parents with high expectations of pets teaching responsibility and keeping children busy actually had a high incidence of rejecting/returning companion animals to shelters within 6 months. Parents reported that when challenging behaviors occurred, for example, a kitten clawing the stereo speakers, they responded by getting rid of the animal rather than modifying the environment or seeking training. This point illustrates the fact that the average family in the middle stages of the family life cycle may be experiencing a multitude of activities and there may be limited quality time to invest in the human–animal relationship. During this stage of the family life cycle there may be two working parents and children involved in a variety of school and extracurricular activities, thus leaving barely enough time and energy to provide for the animal's most basic needs.

While pet ownership peaks in the middle stages of the life cycle, pet owner-ship is next highest among young couples, roommates, and older parents (AVMA, 1997). Not surprisingly, pet attachment is high during the following stages: newlyweds, empty-nest, never-married, and widowed (Albert & Bul-croft, 1988). During these family stages, there is a "match" or convergence between ownership and attachment to companion animals.

Among newlyweds, companion animals may serve as anticipatory socializa-tion, or a "dress rehearsal" for possible parenthood later in life because of the many parallels between nurturing and caring for an animal and nurturing and caring for a child. In both instances, there is a need for consistency in guidance; there is a reciprocal display of affection; the adults serve as role models and stimulate development in all domains; there are "experts" to which one can turn for assistance and advice during difficult/troubling times; and there are tremendous rewards for nurturing, caring, protecting, and loving another being (Albert & Bulcroft, 1988; Dosser et al., 1986).

Among divorced, never-marrieds, childless couples, empty-nesters, and widowed people, companion animals may serve as significant emotional substitutes for children or spouses. Companion animals are both givers and receivers of affection and positively contribute to the morale maintenance of those who live alone or have few significant others (Albert & Bulcroft, 1988). Among the divorced, widowed, and empty-nesters, a companion animal may be one element of continuity in a sea of changes in their life. For childless couples and never-marrieds, a companion animal may fulfill their need and desire to "parent." Similar to characteristics of couples that utilize companion animals as a dress rehearsal for parenthood, childless and never-marrieds may continue to portray their companion animals as their children, thus evidenced by high rates of anthropomorphism among childless couples and never-marrieds (Albert and Bulcroft, 1988).

Within the family unit, pet ownership may be a source of social support because the pet provides a sense of continuity over the family life cycle (Levinson, 1972). Companion animals may serve especially important functions during major life events and critical life course transitions. Individuals and family members may have an increased desire and need to be close to their companion animal in situations of divorce, remarriage, widowhood, or transition to the empty nest. "The stress related to the loss and/or addition of new life course transitions may make the affection provided by a pet invaluable" (Albert & Bulcroft, 1988, p. 551). Similarly, it is important to consider the companion animal's stress during times of loss and/or new life course transitions. As humans and animals operate interdependently, life changes can potentially impact both in dramatic ways.

As mental health providers work with families at different stages of the family life cycle, important consideration should be given to possible roles, functions, and contributions of companion animals. Early in the modern-day study of the human–animal bond, Levinson (1968) stated: "The role of the pet in the family will depend upon family structure, the emotional and physical strengths and weaknesses of each of its members, the emotional undercurrents, and the social climate" (p. 511).

F. CHALLENGES ASSOCIATED WITH COMPANION ANIMALS

Up to this point, much of the discussion has focused on the benefits and strengths associated with companion animals. There are, however, challenges associated with companion animals. One challenge associated with companion animals is the financial costs to the family. According to the AVMA (1997), the average dog-owning U.S. household visited their veterinarian twice a year at an average of $73.60 per visit for an average annual expenditure of $186.80. In 1996, total veterinary medical expenditures for dogowners in the United States was $7.008 billion (AVMA, 1997). Medical expenses are one of many financial costs associated with companion animals. Other common expenditures include food, toys, licensing, grooming, and boarding. When you sum all of these factors, it is often a staggering realization just how much it costs to have a companion animal.

Other challenges of companion animals include time commitments and competing demands. As previously discussed, the fast-paced and complex lives characteristic of many American families are often not conducive to ownership of companion animals. Beyond their basic custodial care, most companion animals want and need attention, affection, and social interactions with their human companions. Unfortunately, when many families are forced to prioritize, the companion animal may not rank very high on the list. The decision to adopt a companion animal is only the first of many commitments we make to an animal companion. To reduce the number of abandoned, rejected, and even abused animals, careful consideration must be given to past and present pet ownership experience; time, space, and financial constraints/limitations; and expectations related to human–animal relationships (Kidd *et al.*, 1992). In sum, not every family should include a companion animal. The needs of the family and the animal must be fully examined.

G. THE LOSS OF A COMPANION ANIMAL AND THE IMPACT ON THE FAMILY

Yet another challenge associated with the companion animal is the loss of that animal and the subsequent impact on the family system. Because almost all companion animals have shorter life spans than humans, they are natural born teachers about love and loss as they join us for a decade or so and then leave us (Antinori, 1998). Grief is a natural response to loss. Grieving, however, is a complex emotional experience. Grief reactions vary tremendously because of the unique relationships the companion animal had with different family members. Likewise, the grief reactions and acceptance of the loss will vary from family to family. For many people, the first death experience of childhood is the loss of a companion animal (Levinson, 1984). This event may in many ways have a profound impact on our feelings, thoughts, and perceptions of death and "set the tone" for attitudes that continue into adulthood.

A host of factors may influence grief reactions: (1) age of companion animal, (2) health status of companion animal, (3) circumstances surrounding the death of the companion animal (old age, illness, euthanasia, companion animal disappears), and (4) age and stage of development of each family member.

For example, the loss of a beloved companion animal for a widowed person may be compounded by the loss of a spouse. In many ways, the animal may represent a very happy time in his or her life that was shared with a spouse. If the widow is elderly, the loss of both spouse and companion animal may illuminate the inevitable death of every living creature, including themselves.

Some people do not have a support system (or perceive that they do not have a support system) that can openly facilitate grieving about the loss of a companion animal. This is unfortunate because everyone needs emotional, psychological, and social support when they experience different types of losses. For some people, grief of any sort, especially prolonged grief over the loss of companion animal, seems silly and very childish. It is important for people to find support during this process and if significant others cannot or will not provide this support, then outside support groups may be a choice. Many local humane societies and veterinary practices are involved in pet loss support along with national organizations and hotlines. In some instances, an empathetic yet objective listener may be more helpful and supportive than a loved one who is also grieving the loss.

The death of a companion animal can be especially difficult for children for a variety of reasons. Adults understand, at a cognitive level at least, that companion animals do not live as long as humans. Children, on the other hand, often do not know or understand this. Children are at different stages of both emotional and cognitive development, and thus have different perceptions of death than adults. Until children are approximately 5–7 years of age, they do not understand the three components of death (Speece & Brent, 1984). The concepts include (1) irreversibility, the understanding that once a living thing dies, its physical body cannot be made alive again, and death is irrevocable and permanent; (2) nonfunctionality, the understanding that all life-defining functions cease at death; and (3) universality, the understanding that all living things die. Children during the preschool period may believe that the animal will come back if they wish for it, they may think the animal died because they were "bad" and this is a form of punishment, or they may fear that they too will die soon, along with a variety of other misconceptions often rooted in ideas that are characterized by their somewhat egocentric and "magical" thought.

> Sarah, a 3-year-old, came to day care and announced to the group that her cat, Bagel, had been hit by a car and died. Sarah went on to tell the group that she was sure Bagel was living with God where there are a lot of birds and squirrels. Later in the day, Sarah's teacher asked her how she was feeling since Bagel was gone. Sarah replied, "I feel sad (pause) . . . you know she was three years old. I hope that I don't die too."

Some parents are tempted not to tell their children that the companion animal has died. With good intentions, parents want to "protect" their children from the pain associated with such a loss (Levinson, 1984). Parents often create stories of companion animals simply disappearing or visiting friends or relatives in the country. Unfortunately, children are more perceptive than adults think and children usually do learn the truth surrounding the death.

> Eight-year-old Jonah was very attached to the family's black cat, Sparky. Jonah's family lived on a fairly busy highway and early one morning Sparky was hit and killed by a garbage collection truck. After a quick consultation between his parents, Jonah's father quickly buried the cat. The parents told the three older children in the family what had happened but told them that Jonah would be too upset by the truth . . . so the family "story" would be that Sparky simply must have run off into the woods behind the house. Jonah was very upset by the news of Sparky's disappearance and spent the next several days searching in the woods behind the house for Sparky. By the end of the week, he had stopped searching. Several weeks went by with little discussion about Sparky. Jonah's parents had decided that he was probably "over Sparky." To their dismay and astonishment one morning at breakfast about 3 weeks after Sparky's death, Jonah announced, "I just want you to know that I am not stupid! I now know that Sparky got run over by the trash truck! And just *when* were you going to tell me the truth?"

Children may come to mistrust their parents, believe that open communication within the family is not valued, and see parents as role models for telling lies to avoid painful situations. As difficult as death is for both children and adults, honesty and developmentally appropriate explanations and grief rituals are essential in grieving the loss of a beloved companion animal.

Another common idea for adults is to "replace" the companion animal. However well intentioned this action may be, it is not appropriate for several reasons. First, children need time and support to grieve the loss of the animal. The relationship between the child and beloved animal was unique and should be treated respectfully. Second, adults can be sending the wrong message to children that animals are "disposable" and can be quickly replaced by a new one. Third, the child may choose not to get a new companion animal immediately. The decision to adopt a new companion animal into the family should not be rushed but rather carefully thought out. Allowing oneself to grieve and supporting loved ones who are experiencing grief is a necessary and healthy emotional process.

There are a variety of common grief reactions. Not everyone experiences all of them and the intensity with which we experience them is unique to each individual. There may be shock, denial, sadness, guilt, depression, anger, bodily distress, and protest over the loss of a companion animal. As we let ourselves experience the range of emotions and/or support those around us as they experience these feelings, we really are beginning the healing process.

Healing comes as we reflect on the times we shared with the animal. Rituals are often a healthy tool for healing. By reminiscing we are paying tribute to the animals, to their life in our family, and to our relationship with them. Some suggestions for memorializing include (Antinori, 1998) the following:

Journal writing: free flow of thoughts, feelings, dreams, and memories of the animal

Storytelling: when you first got the animal, the animal's antics and personality, holiday and special occasion remembrances, special shared activities

Album making: photographs with captions and drawings by children

Video viewing: viewing and editing both still and moving clips of your companion animal's life

Poetry/prose writing: what the animal meant to you, special times together

Ceremonies, eulogies, commemorative events: planting a tree in the backyard at the burial site, including a donation to a local animal organization in memory of your companion animal

Any of these "healing tools" can be done at a personal level and kept to oneself, or family members may choose to share selected pieces with one another as they aid each other with the grief associated with loss. A crucial element is to respect each family member's thoughts, ideas, and feelings. People heal in different ways as different rates, and sensitivity to these differences is vital. Part of the healing process for all family members is to openly grieve and support one another as each experiences the loss in his or her own personal way.

While much attention often focuses on humans grieving the loss of a beloved companion animal, it is important to remember that companion animals also grieve the loss of their human companions and other animal companions. Many of the reactions and characteristics associated with human grief parallel animal reactions. Similar to humans, animals may display sadness, depression, lethargy, a host of physical symptoms, and behavioral changes. The animal may be experiencing the "individual" loss of a loved one as well as be reacting to the "family" loss.

H. Summary

There are variations in the roles and functions of companion animals among family members in the same family and certainly from family to family. Despite the differences that may exist, there are probably far more similarities than previously hypothesized. Companion animals serve as sources of love and affection and objects of human attachment, they may function as a substitute for another family member, they appear to facilitate communication and interactions in some instances, and may operate as a gauge or barometer of tension, conflict, or anxiety within a family unit. Given these roles and responsibilities within the family unit, it becomes quite obvious why so many humans consider their companion animal to be a vital family member.

Mental health providers may open up a previously untapped tool and therapeutic strategy by considering the significance and importance of companion animals within the family. Open-mindedness, sensitivity, and respect for the unique relationships between humans and animals may have far-reaching implications for clinical practice. Clinicians should routinely ask about a family's animal companions and their relationships with each family member. As professionals that guide and assist individuals and families, we must emphasize the connectedness and closeness that humans and animals share. Perhaps the simplest, most important, yet overlooked strategy to utilize is to *listen* to the meaning of human–animal relationships.

II. COMPANION ANIMALS AND CHILDREN

Because the relationship between children and companion animals is addressed elsewhere in this handbook, this section only briefly highlights the roles of companion animals during the different stages of children's development and summarizes the potential benefits of companion animals for children. Our understanding of children's, and possibly adults', relationships with animals needs to be viewed as unique and distinct from human–human relationships. While parallels exist between human–human and human–animal relationships, the true essence of human–animal relationships could be overlooked if we solely draw on our knowledge of human relationships as the basis for understanding human–animal relationships (Myers, 1998).

A. EARLY CHILDHOOD

The presence of a companion animal during early childhood (infancy through the preschool years) can provide a variety of meaningful interactions (Swift, 1996). The supervised affection and physical contact between children and companion animals can be mutually reinforcing (Blue, 1986). Because most companion animals present in our homes are social creatures similar to ourselves, there is a biologically and psychologically based need for physical contact and affection. A word of caution must be emphasized at this point in the discussion however. Because young children are often physically clumsy, have difficulty delaying emotional or social gratification, or have experienced few interactions with animals, children and animals must be supervised at all times. Even the most seemingly mild-mannered animal can be unintentionally frightened or hurt by a young child. Toddlers in particular are perhaps the most likely to have inappropriate interactions with animals. During this period of development, toddlers must learn appropriate physical interactions with not only humans but animals as well. It is all too common for a toddler to grab a dog's tail in a playful manner. Unfortunately, most dogs do not understand this type of behavior as playful but perceive it as hurtful or threatening.

Adults must protect the needs and interests of both child and companion animal. It is important for adults to "model" appropriate behavior and interactions with animals and supervise interactions between children and animals.

Companion animals also provide many opportunities for hands-on learning. Young children learn best by being actively engaged in the learning process. Consider this example:

> Suzy, an 8-year-old border collie, is a frequent visitor in preschool classrooms. On one occasion her fur coat was used in a classification activity. The children had to determine if her fur was smooth or rough, how many colors were present, and length of her fur (short or long). With Suzy present in the preschool classroom, the children rubbed and stroked her fur, they viewed her fur from every angle (sitting, standing, laying down), then charted their findings. The activity allowed the children to "learn by doing" with a real, live creature. In turn, Suzy was the recipient of positive, appropriate attention from the children. She was spoken to with calm voices, rubbed in a gentle manner, and treated with kindness and respect.

In terms of social development, companion animals can serve as playmates and social companions. Play can take the form of imaginative play (although it is not always advisable to dress the family cat in doll clothes) or a repetitive game of frisbee in the backyard.

B. Middle Childhood

As previously discussed, pet ownership is common during middle childhood. Children in middle childhood are often considered more mature and responsible for caring duties than children in the preschool years. When children are involved in the feeding, grooming, bathing, and cleaning up the companion animal, it is hoped that they are learning important skills and developing positive attitudes related to caring for another living creature. However, even the most responsible and mature child should not have sole responsibility for the companion animal's total well-being. Although the child may be an active participant in the care of the animal, it is ultimately the responsibility of an adult within the family to ensure that all the animal's needs are being met.

Middle childhood is also a time when children are more involved in home and neighborhood activities as compared to adolescents. As with preschoolers, companion animals may serve as playmates and sources of social interaction for children in middle childhood. Companion animals may also serve to facilitate friendships between children. A child without a companion animal may derive some of the benefits vicariously by playing with a neighbor's companion animal. Because middle childhood children are typically more advanced socially, cognitively, and emotionally than preschoolers, this developmental period offers an excellent opportunity to have the child be an active participant in training the companion animal. Great pride and satisfaction can be derived from teaching the family dog a new trick or completing an obedience class. Adult supervision and modeling of appropriate human-animal interactions provide a valuable learning experience for all involved.

C. Adolescence

During this period of development, adolescents are often very busy and involved with school and extracurricular activities. In many instances, the adolescent and family companion animal have "grown up" together and have a strong attachment relationship. However, due to time and activity commitments, the actual amount of time and interaction between adolescent and animal may be minimal and somewhat sporadic. On the other hand, the unconditional love and nonjudgmental attitudes of companion animals make them perfect candidates for an adolescent to test out new clothes, hairstyles, or hypothetical conversations with the latest heartthrob.

> Emily, a 15-year-old in high school, was torn between going to the homecoming dance with a family friend or going with a 16-year-old "blonde-haired hunk." She had previously committed to the family friend before she was asked out by the hunk. She confided in her girlfriends (who unanimously voted against the family friend), her parents (who unanimously voted in favor of the family friend), and finally in her calico cat, Magic. Emily described her inner turmoil to Magic: She did not want to hurt the feelings of the family friend or the feelings of her family . . . at the same time, she had her reputation at school to consider. After many hours over the course of several nights, Emily reached her decision. She would go to the dance with the family friend . . . but then meet with the hunk at an after-dance party! (No one is sure if the ingenious solution was generated by Magic or not, but everyone seems to have been satisfied!)

D. Summary

Throughout children's development, companion animals can make significant contributions to their overall development. Companion animals can foster mutual respect among living beings (Nebbe, 1995). Teaching children respect for themselves and respect for others is a vital life lesson that often seems to be overlooked in our present-day society. Kindness and humane treatment are both inherently part of the respect we must model and teach children. Development of empathy and nurturance toward others can also be facilitated through human–animal interactions.

Companion animals offer seemingly unlimited opportunities for affection and unconditional love, both of which are key elements in the development of attachment relationships. The attachments children form in childhood, whether to parents, siblings, or even a companion animal, lay the foundation on which all other social relationships are built. An outgrowth of healthy attachment relationships is positive self-esteem. When children feel good about themselves, they are more likely to seek other social relationships and emotionally invest themselves in others.

Companion animals offer children opportunities for developing caretaking skills that in many instances lead to a sense of competence. Children often take great pride in setting a goal and working to accomplish it. And finally, a companion animal is a very natural mechanism letting children experience the life cycle of growth, life, and death. First-hand learning experiences, even though painful, can be sometimes be the most invaluable ones for children. Companion animals afford children opportunities for living, loving, and learning in ways that no other person or tool can.

The relationship between children and animals is potentially beneficial to the animal as well. Children, concrete and literal beings, usually accept people and things "as they are." Children and animals often have relatively few expectations of each other and in many instances simply enjoy the company of one another.

III. CONCLUSIONS

Companion animals appear to enhance the lives of their human companions in many ways. Within the family, they love and accept their human companions unconditionally, they can facilitate communication and social interaction, they can provide an appropriate outlet for stress by serving as a diversion from the trials and tribulations of our busy lives, and they fulfill emotional and social support needs. Companion animals are however, not without some limitations. The presence of a companion animal results in additional responsibilities including financial, caretaking, time, and energy. Nonetheless, humans that share their lives with a companion animal will agree that the benefits far outweigh the costs.

REFERENCES

Albert, A., & Bulcroft, K. (1988). Pets, families, and the life course. *Journal of Marriage and the Family*, 50 (May), 543–552.

American Veterinary Medical Association. (1997). *U.S. pet ownership & demographics sourcebook,* Schaumburg, IL: Center for Information Management, American Veterinary Medical Association.

Antinori, D. (1998). Phoenix rising: Gifts from pet loss. *Proceedings from Delta Society's 17th Annual conference* (pp. 124–127). Seattle, WA: Delta Society.

Beck, A. & Katcher, A. H. (1983). *Between pets and people: The importance of animal companionship.* New York: G. P. Putnam & Sons.

Blue, G. (1986). The value of pets in children's lives. *Childhood Education, 63,* 84–90.

Bowen, M. (1978). *Family therapy in clinical practice.* New York: Jason Aronson.

Broderick, C., & Smith, J. (1979). The general systems approach to the family. In W. R. Burr, R. Hill, F. I. Nye, & I. L. Reiss (Eds.), *Contemporary theories about the family* (pp. 112–129). New York: The Free Press.

Cain, A. O. (1983). A study of pets in the family system. In A. Katcher & A. Beck (Eds.), *Newer perspectives on our lives with companion animals* (pp. 73–811). Philadelphia, PA: University of Pennsylvania Press.

Cain, A. O. (1985). Pets as family members. In M. Sussman (Ed.), *Pets and the family* (pp. 5–10). New York: The Haworth Press.

Cain, A. O. (1991). Pets and the family. *Holistic Nursing Practitioner, 5*(2), 58–63.

Cantanzaro, T. (1984). The human–animal bond in military communities. In R. Anderson, B. Hart, & L. Hart (Eds.), *The Pet Connection* (pp. 341–347). Minneapolis: CENSHARE, University of Minnesota.

Dosser, D. A., Mullis, A. K., Mullis, R. L., & Dosser, K. B. (1986). The decision to parent: Using a pet as a consultant. *Wellness Perspectives, III*(3), 3–8.

Duvall, E. M. (1977). *Family Development* (5th ed.). Philadelphia, PA: Lippincott.

Duvall, E. M. (1985). *Marriage and family development.* New York: Harper & Row.

Kidd, A. H., Kidd, R. M., & George, C. C. (1992). Successful pet adoptions. *The Latham Letter, 13*(2), 4–5.

Levinson, B. M. (1968). Interpersonal relationships between pet and human being. In M. W. Fox (Ed.), *Abnormal behavior in animals.* Philadelphia, PA: W. B. Saunders.

Levinson, B. M. (1972). *Pets and human development.* Springfield, IL: Charles C. Thomas.

Levinson, B. M. (1984). Grief at the loss of a pet. In W. J. Kay, H. A. Nieburg, A. H. Kutscher, R. M. Grey, & C. E. Fudin (Eds.), *Pet loss and human bereavement* (51–64). Ames, IA: The Iowa State University Press.

Mancini, J. A., & Orthner, D. K. (1988). The context and consequences of family change. *Family Relations, 37,* 363–366.

Myers, G. (1998). *Children and animals.* Boulder, CO: Westview Press.

Nebbe, L. L. (1995). *Nature as a guide: Nature in counseling, therapy, and Education.* Minneapolis MN: Educational Media Corporation.

Sable, P. (1995). Pets, attachment, and well-being across the life cycle. *Social Work, 40*(3), 334–341.

Scanzoni, J. (1987). Families in the 1980's. *Journal of Family Issues, 8,* 394–421.

Soares, C. J. (1985). The companion animal in the context of the family system. In M. B. Sussman (Ed.), *Pets and the family* (pp. 49–62). New York: The Haworth Press.

Speece, M. W., & Brent, S. B. (1984). Children's understanding of death: A review of three components of a death concept. *Child Development, 55,* 1671–1686.

Swift, W. B. (1996, May/June). What pets teach kids. *Animals,* pp. 10–13.

Trost, J. (1990). Family from a dyadic perspective. *Journal of Family Issues, 14,* 92–104.

CHAPTER 16

Companion Animals and the Development of Children: Implications of the Biophilia Hypothesis

GAIL F. MELSON

Purdue University, West Lafayette, Indiana

In 1984, E. O. Wilson, the Harvard biologist who earlier had created the field of sociobiology, advanced another intriguing hypothesis. He termed it *biophilia,* an innate interest in life. As a result of co-evolution with other animal species, humans have a biologically based attraction for nature and all its life forms, a tendency to "impute worth and importance to the natural world" (Kellert, 1997, p. 3). Biophilia evolved because of the adaptive advantages it conferred. Animals and the natural environments in which they live were the information-drenched milieus within which humans evolved. As a result, humans tend to attune selectively to animal presence and behavior. Animals serve as sentinels, conveying information about the environment. Moreover, animals are of direct, surpassing interest as food, materials for clothing, and other uses. The biophilia hypothesis suggests that the presence of animals at rest or in a nonagitated state signals well-being and reassurance to humans.

The innate dispositions described by biophilia are considered to be weak in comparison with basic human drives. Like other aspects of "nature," in the nature–nurture sense, behaviors indicative of biophilia are always expressed within specific environments and are culturally malleable. Kellert (1997) describes biophilia as a product of *biocultural* evolution; it is an inborn tendency shaped by learning, culture, and experience. Biophilia does not suggest a love of, or even positive regard for, animals, only intrinsic interest.

In this chapter introduction, I explore the implications of the biophilia hypothesis for understanding the role of animals in children's development. This is timely for several reasons. First, discussions of biophilia to date have largely been applied only to adults, and second, developmentalists, with a few notable exceptions, have ignored animals as important components of children's environments. In part, this "blind spot" may be due to the difficulty of applying existing developmental frameworks, formulated to account for important human–human bonds, to aspects of children's interactions with animals. (For example, attachment theory imperfectly and inadequately maps onto children's bonds with their pets.) The biophilia hypothesis, if given a developmental twist, provides a theoretical framework for identifying aspects of children's development where animals might be particularly important. Biophilia, furthermore, suggests specific propositions concerning *how* animals influence children.

To delineate how the biophilia hypothesis helps integrate existing knowledge about animals in children's lives and also helps generate new areas of inquiry, I consider three important developmental questions: (1) Do animals contribute to a child's perceived security? (2) Are animals significant categories of early perceptual, cognitive, and language development? (3) Do animals play a role in the development of children's emotional intelligence (Goleman, 1995)? For each question, I first suggest hypotheses based on biophilia. Then, I review existing evidence and draw implications for animal-assisted therapy (AAT) with children.

I. DO ANIMALS CONTRIBUTE TO PERCEIVED SECURITY?

Erik Erikson called it "basic trust." John Bowlby called it "felt security." Maslow spoke of survival needs as the most basic in a needs hierarchy. Developmentalists from a variety of perspectives concur that for the helpless infant and dependent child reassurance of one's security and safety are paramount early needs that are typically met within initial caregiving bonds. These first relationships become templates, or internal working models, for subsequent human relationships. Thus, babies assured of their security welcome new ties as likely to be positive.

The biophilia hypothesis posits that because humans co-evolved with animals in their natural settings, the survival of *Homo sapiens* fundamentally depended on alert and careful monitoring of animal and plant life. Animals became sentinels, their behavior the coinage of safety and danger. Hawks drawing lazy circles in the sunlit air signaled that all was well; the squawking melee of birds in sudden flight in a dark, lowering sky spelled looming peril. In this way, calm, friendly animal presence became associated with safety and induced relaxation in humans (Katcher & Wilkins, 1993).

If there is an innate predisposition to associate friendly animal presence with safety, children should derive reassurance from such animal presence, particularly in the absence of human attachment figures. Interacting with companion animals, even just observing them, should produce relaxation effects in children independent of their history with pets. There is convergent evidence that many children with pets turn to them when the children feel negative emotions, such as sadness, anger, or fear. For example, 79% of German fourth graders said they sought out their pets when feeling sad (Rost & Hartmann, 1994). In interviews with Michigan youngsters ages 10 to 14, 75% indicated that when they were upset, they turned to their pets (Covert et al., 1985). When 5-year-olds were asked about who they turned to when feeling sad, angry, afraid, or needing to tell a secret, 42% mentioned their pet (Melson et al., 1998). If one assumes that heightened negative emotions like anger and fear activate the child's need for reassurance (Bowlby, 1969), some children derive security from their pets.

Also consistent with biophilia are findings that the inclusion of a nonthreatening dog or cat in drawings or color photographs of unfamiliar people causes these images to be rated as more friendly, approachable, and safe (Budge et al., 1996; Lockwood, 1983; Rossbach & Wilson, 1992). Similarly, children who are wheelchair bound (Mader et al., 1989) as well as adults out walking (McNicolas & Collis, 1998) are approached more often by friendly passersby when with a dog.

These results should stimulate more research on the security-enhancing properties of animals for children. For example, during times when children are experiencing heightened stress because of major life transitions, such as a new sibling, family move, or divorce, do pet owners more frequently use contact with their companion animals to reestablish the equilibrium of safety? Which children derive greater and which children derive less security from their pets? To what extent, if at all, can animals compensate for the absence or ineffectiveness of human efforts to reassure children? Are the security-enhancing roles of animals limited to dogs and cats? By what process—physical presence, holding, stroking, confiding, etc.—do animals restore perceived security?

II. ARE ANIMALS SIGNIFICANT CATEGORIES OF EARLY PERCEPTUAL, COGNITIVE, AND LANGUAGE DEVELOPMENT?

The biophilia hypothesis suggests that animals will be among the earliest categories that children acquire. This is likely for several reasons. First, if children, like their elders of the human species, are predisposed to attune to the natural world and to animals within it, children's attention will be drawn to the many examples of living things in their environments, and they will begin to abstract common features from these examples. Thus, toddlers repeatedly exposed to four-legged, furry, tail-wagging creatures, and provided with an appropriate label, will soon apply the category "doggie." Second, animals embody the key perceptual characteristics—movement, aliveness, and contrast—that attract and hold infant attention. These characteristics are themselves "hard-wired" in the human brain, predicting differential attentiveness in the first few months of life. As Shepard (1996) noted, "Animals are the primordial ground for this endeavor [of category making] because they are the most nearly perfect set of distinct but related entities, and perhaps because they are alive like us" (p. 58). Finally, biophilia suggests an *emotional* attraction to animals and their natural settings. Such emotional energy should motivate children's drive to extract meaning from the world around them. Stephen Kellert, who, with Wilson, co-edited *The Biophilia Hypothesis* (1993) observed: "Living diversity provides a magic well of emotionally compelling images for applying the art of ordering and labeling so integral to language development" (Kellert, 1997, p. 75).

Is there evidence in early perceptual, cognitive, and language development consistent with these biophilia-inspired generalizations? One strand of research support derives from infant perception studies. Soon after birth, infants are differentially attentive to movement. Quite early, although precisely when is debated, infants perceive a distinction between the movement of living things and the movement of inanimate objects. For example, 7-month-olds register a surprised expression when they see inanimate objects moving without any force being applied to them, but not when people do (Spelke *et al.*, 1995). Cognitive psychologists have interpreted these differential reactions as evidence that a "naive theory of biology"—what living beings are like—and a distinct "naive theory of physics"—what objects are like—have begun to take shape before the first birthday (Siegler, 1998).

A second strand of research comes from observations of children encountering both live animals and moving, inanimate animal toys. Kidd and Kidd (1987) recorded how young children, from 6 to 30 months of age, behaved toward their own pet dogs or cats as compared with a "lifelike" battery-operated toy dog and toy cat. Except for the 6-month-old infants, the children smiled, held, followed, and made sounds to the live animals, especially to the dogs, more than to the toys. These findings, unfortunately, confounded familiarity with animateness of the stimulus—the pet animals were alive, but also familiar to the child, while the toys were novel. To address this, Ricard and Allard (1992) videotaped 9-month-olds and their mothers as each baby encountered one of three equally novel events: a live dwarf rabbit; an attractive wooden turtle that moved, made noises, and flashed lights; or a young, unfamiliar woman. The live rabbit had more drawing power than person or toy; on seeing the animal, the babies were least interested in their mothers and most drawn to explore. Allard and Ricard's interpretation of their findings echoes the claims of biophilia: "the animal was more attractive than an inanimate object . . . also it was seen as an active, living creature, which therefore required some kind of monitoring" (p. 14).

A third strand comes from studies of early semantic development. Words for different animals—*dog, cat, duck, horse, bear, bird,* and *cow*—appear among the first 50 words that most toddlers in the United States say. In one study, more children included the words *dog* and *cat* in their initial productive (i.e., spoken) vocabularies than *juice, milk,* and *ball.* Indeed, more children said these animal category names than any other words except for *mama* and *daddy* or their equivalents (Nelson, 1973). Children learning other languages, including sign language, as well as children without pets, show the same precocious appearance of animal words (Casselli *et al.,* 1995).

Each of these three strands of research is quite thin, consisting only of a few studies. Together, however, they provide some convergent evidence that animals, together with other living beings, are compelling categories for organizing early experience. This preference is undoubtedly shaped by environmental influences. Parents typically direct children's attention to animals by naming them: "Look, it's a cow!" Picture books teaching numbers and alphabet letters disproportionately use animal examples: "D is for Dog." At the same time, infant perception studies support a very early, perhaps innate, perceptual preference for living beings over inanimate objects. The overall pattern of findings is consistent with the description of biophilia as a "weak predisposition shaped by culture, learning, and experience." As biophilia suggests, a core category for organizing understanding of experience is the living/nonliving distinction. It is the living aspects of our experience that capture our interest and are most essential for our survival.

III. DO ANIMALS PLAY A ROLE IN EMOTIONAL INTELLIGENCE?

Goleman (1995) describes emotional intelligence as a complex of social and self-awareness skills that includes recognizing and managing one's own and others' feelings and mental states. Like other humanocentric theorists of development, Goleman uses "people skills" as a synonym for emotional intelligence (p. 43) and attributes its growth only to experiences with other humans. However, the biophilia hypothesis suggests ways in which observation and interaction with animals and other living nonhumans may impact emotional intelligence. I will illustrate the usefulness of a biophilia perspective for exploring the development of two aspects of emotional intelligence: (1) the development of "theory of mind" ideas and (2) the development of nonverbal understanding.

A. THEORY OF MIND

Theory of mind encompasses ideas about mental states and their relations to feelings and actions. For example, by age 3 most children know that mental "objects" like dreams and ideas, unlike physical objects, can't be touched, seen, or picked up, and that actions are motivated by unseen intentions (Meltzoff, 1995; Wellman, 1990). By age 4, more sophisticated theory of mind ideas emerge; actions motivated by false beliefs will be consistent with those beliefs, "real" feelings may be masked by pretense, other minds are essentially unknowable (Whiten, 1991). Developing an accurate theory of mind is key to living in an ordered social universe in which our own behavior and that of others become transparent to us. Biophilia suggests that children (like other humans) readily view animals as minded actors, individuals with intentions and desires whose actions are, at least potentially, intelligible from their mental states. Furthermore, biophilia posits that humans are intrinsically motivated to decode the meaning of animal behavior. In so doing, humans gain insight into their own minds.

Animals have certain qualities that may make them especially effective teachers of theory of mind ideas. Compared to human behaviors, animal behaviors present authentic, pure data about mental states unmuddied by pretense, metaphor, deception, or irony. As Myers (1998) noted, "an animal does not provoke a divided or 'double-bind' situation . . . since it does not present verbal messages that clash with nonverbal ones" (p. 111). In this respect, "reading" the thoughts and feelings of animals may be easier for children than reading those of other humans. But, in other ways, animal minds are more challenging to decode than human ones. Generalizing from their own feelings, children often make inaccurate guesses, treating animal minds anthropomorphically as if disguised human consciousness. For example, in Myers's (1998) observations of preschoolers encountering small animals in their classroom, he notes the following "interpretation" of a turtle sliding into its shell: "She's shy; she wants everybody to go away!" The very differentness of animal species brings young children sharply up against the limits of egocentric thinking, precisely at a time when they are struggling to grasp other minds whose desires or ideas conflict with their own (Astington & Gopnik, 1991). Unfortunately, developmentalists have not designed studies to explore children's understanding of "animal minds" and how such understanding might be related to theory of [human] mind ideas.

B. NONVERBAL SKILLS

The development of nonverbal skills is a central component of emotional intelligence. Goleman (1995), speaking of human–human communication, stresses that "the mode of emotion is nonverbal" (p. 67). An estimated 10% of all U. S. children suffer from "nonverbal illiteracy"; they can't read nonverbal cues in others and use inappropriate or indecipherable behaviors themselves (Rourke, 1989). The biophilia hypothesis suggests that human attunement to animal behavior consists largely of observing and decoding nonverbal behaviors. One implication for development is that interactions with animals, such as pets, may sharpen a child's ability to decode verbal cues. Whether such an ability might generalize to better understanding of human nonverbal behaviors is a question worthy of investigation.

There is some evidence that young children who own pets, or who are more involved with them, show more emotional understanding than comparison children without pets or uninvolved pet owners. For example, 5-year-olds more attached to their pets expressed greater empathy toward other people and animals than less attached youngsters (Melson *et al.,* 1992). Preschoolers with dogs or cats at home were more skilled at predicting the feelings of other people in hypothetical situations than were same-age children without pets (Bailey, 1987). Bryant (1986) found that 7- and 10-year-olds who reported often having "intimate talks" with their pets expressed greater empathy toward peers than same-age children who did not turn to pets in this way.

These findings are consistent with a biophilia hypothesis that, because animal life teems with nonverbal "messages" that humans seek to decode, animals are master teachers of nonverbal understanding. However, the link between pets in children's lives and aspects of emotional intelligence is not consistent or strong enough to do more than raise possibilities for future research. The correlational results themselves are open to multiple interpretations. Young children's abilities to discover and appreciate the feelings and thoughts of other minds *may* be sharpened by deciphering animal communication. On the other hand, young children who are already empathic may be drawn to the challenge of understanding a different being. Research is needed to establish (1) whether and how children are acquiring nonverbal skills from animal contact and (2) the link between nonverbal understanding of animals and of humans.

IV. IMPLICATIONS FOR AAT WITH CHILDREN

As we develop better documentation and evaluation of AAT and AAA with children, the biophilia hypothesis can help guide these efforts. It draws our attention to important *processes* by which guided interactions with animals may benefit troubled children. First, biophilia suggests that animal contact has the potential, if not the power, to promote a child's feelings of safety and security. Second, biophilia calls attention to animals as perceptually and cognitively salient categories. This implies that animals may be effective stimuli for many children in drawing and sustaining their attention, encoding memories, and linguistically organizing thoughts. Third, biophilia hypothesizes that interest in animals leads children to speculate about animal minds as well as human minds as they develop theory of mind ideas. Such speculation draws children into the challenge of decoding distinctive (from human) repertoires of behaviors and may make children more nonverbally literate.

An important implication of biophilia is that children are intrinsically interested in animals, but not intrinsically attracted or attached to them. Thus, in this view, children bring heightened affect to encounters with animals, but this affect is readily channelled into either positive or negative directions. Katcher noted that many of the same boys who benefited from animal contact through his Companionable Zoo intervention had been previously cruel to animals (Katcher & Wilkins, 1993). Biophilia's joint emphasis on innate interest and environmental shaping suggests that AAT and AAA may capitalize on the former and direct it in positive ways to improve both children's functioning and their treatment of other living beings. Because AAT may help channel children's interest in animals in more humane directions, AAT may benefit not only troubled children but animals as well.

REFERENCES

Astington, J., & Gopnik, A. (1991). Developing understanding of desire and intention. In A. Whiten (Ed.), *Natural theories of mind: Evolution, development, and simulation of everyday mindreading* (pp. 39–50). Oxford: Blackwell.

Bailey, C. (1987). *Exposure of preschool children to companion animals: Impact on role-taking skills.* Unpublished Ph.D dissertation, Oregon State University.

Bowlby, J. (1969). *Attachment.* New York: Basic Books.

Bryant, B. (1986, August). *The relevance of family and neighborhood animals to socioemotional development in middle childhood.* Paper presented at the annual meeting of the Delta Society.

Budge, R. C., Spicer, J., Jones, B. R., & St. George, R. (1996). The influence of companion animals on owner perception: Gender and species effects. *Anthrozoös, 9,* 10–18.

Caselli, M. C., Bates, E., Casadio, P., Fenson, J., Fenson, L., Sanderl, L., & Weir, J. (1995). Cross-linguistic lexical development. *Cognitive Development, 10,* 159–199.

Covert, A., Whirren, A., Keith, J., & Nelson, C. (1985). Pets, early adolescence and families. *Marriage and Family Review, 8,* 95–108.

Goleman, D. (1995). *Emotional intelligence.* New York: Bantam Books.

Katcher, A. H., & Wilkins, G. (1993). Dialogue with animals: Its nature and culture. In E. O. Wilson & S. Kellert (Eds.), *The biophilia hypothesis.* Washington, DC: Island Press.

Kellert, S. R. (1997). *Kinship to mastery: Biophilia in human evolution and development.* Washington, DC: Island Press.

Kellert, S. R., & Wilson, E. O. (Eds.). (1993). *The biophilia hypothesis.* Washington, DC: Island Press.

Kidd, A. H., & Kidd, R. M. (1987). Reactions of infants and toddlers to live and toy animals. *Psychological Reports, 61,* 455–464.

Lockwood, R. (1983). The influence of animals on social perception. In A. Katcher & A. Beck (Eds.), *New perspectives on our lives with companion animals* (pp. 64–71). Philadelphia, PA: University of Pennsylvania Press.

Mader, B., Hart, L., & Bergin, B. (1989). Social acknowledgements for children with disabilities: Effects of service dogs. *Child Development, 60,* 1529–1534.

McNicholas, J., & Collis, G. M. (1998). *Dogs as social facilitators: A test of robustness of the social catalysis effect.* Paper presented at the Eighth International Conference on Human–Animal Interactions, Prague, Czech Republic.

Melson, G. F., Peet, S., & Sparks, C. (1992). Children's attachment to their pets: Links to socio-emotional development. *Children's Environments Quarterly, 8,* 55–65.

Melson, G. F., Schwarz, R., & Beck, A. (1998). *Pets as sources of support for mothers, fathers, and young children.* Paper presented at the Eighth International Conference on Human–Animal Interactions. Prague, Czech Republic.

Meltzoff, A. N. (1995). Understanding the intentions of others: Re-enactment of intended acts by 18-month-old children. *Developmental Psychology, 31,* 838–850.

Myers, G. (1998). *Children and animals: Social development and our connections to other species.* Boulder, CO: Westview Press.

Nelson, K. (1973). Structure and strategy in learning to talk. *Monographs of the Society for Research in Child Development, 38,* No. 149.

Ricard, M., & Allard, L. (1992). The reaction of 9- to 10-month-old infants to an unfamiliar animal. *Journal of Genetic Psychology, 154.*

Rossbach, K. A., & Wilson, J. P. (1992). Does a dog's presence make a person appear more likeable? Two studies. *Anthrozoös, 5,* 40–51.

Rost, D. H., & Hartmann, A. (1994). Children and their pets. *Anthrozoös, 7,* 242–254.

Rourke, B. (1989). *Nonverbal learning disabilities.* New York: Guilford Press.

Shepard, P. (1996). *The others: How animals made us human.* Washington, DC: Island Press.

Siegler, R. S. (1998). *Children's thinking.* Upper Saddle River, NJ: Prentice Hall.

Spelke, E. S., Phillips, A., & Woodward, A. L. (1995). Infant's knowledge of object motion and human action. In D. Premack, J. Premack, & D. Sperber (Eds.), *Causal cognition: A multidisciplinary debate.* Oxford: Clarendon.

Wellman, H. (1990). *Children's theory of mind.* Cambridge, MA: MIT Press.

Whiten, A. (1991). *Natural theories of mind: Evolution, development, and simulation of everyday mindreading.* Oxford: Blackwell.

CHAPTER 17

Nature Therapy

LINDA NEBBE

Department of Education: Counselor Education, Drake University, Des Moines, Iowa

There seems to have been a universal need and affection for pets, which took different forms in different cultures and ages. Nevertheless, man in every generation found reaffirmation of his unity with nature and with the elemental forces of nature which may be symbolized by God. It appears that the possession of pets symbolizes this unity with nature and thus satisfies some deep human needs.

Boris M. Levinson, Ph.D. (1972)

I. WHAT IS NATURE THERAPY?

This book is about animal-assisted therapy, a dramatic, fun, joyful, and intriguing method of healing and helping. Animal-assisted therapy, though, may be considered a part of a greater system, all of nature. This chapter expands into that greater system, surveying other dimensions of what might be termed "nature therapy," "ecotherapy," or "environmental therapies." Since this is not a defined field, but a variety of entities, the content of this chapter will reflect the author's concept of the field of nature therapy.

Therapy is defined as:

> a process involving a special kind of relationship between a person who asks for help with a psychological problem and a person trained to provide that help. . . .
> To help individuals thwart overcoming obstacles to their personal growth, wherever these may be encountered, and toward achieving optimum development of their personal resources (Patterson, 1980). (By the Committee on Definition, Division of Counseling Psychology of the American Psychological Association)

Handbook on Animal-Assisted Therapy: Theoretical Foundations and Guidelines for Practice

Nature is more than an intimate part of each individual, and we are part of nature. Upon examination, nature therapy can exist as part of every biophilic value (see Chapter 2). It is human interaction with all facets of nature as well as the human's part in and connection to the entire biosphere. The connection can be as simple as food to eat or a complex philosophical or spiritual, guiding connection.

Although working with nature or elements of nature may not be a counselor or therapist's chosen adjunct therapeutic mode, it is essential for every counselor and therapist to be aware of the intimate connection between humans and the natural environment. Whether an overt part of therapy, or simply a subtle influence, humans are impacted in many ways by their environment. Nature therapy can be viewed as an adjunct therapy or an awareness of the human condition.

Within a professional context, nature therapy can be defined by borrowing from the Delta Society's definition for animal-assisted activities/therapy (Delta Society, 1992) by substituting the term *nature* for *animal:*

> Nature-assisted therapy is a goal directed intervention in which some facet of nature is an integral part of the treatment process. Nature-assisted therapy is delivered and/or directed by a health/human service provider working within the scope of her/his profession. Nature-assisted therapy is designed to promote improvement in human physical, social, emotional, and/or cognitive functioning. Nature-assisted therapy is provided in a variety of settings, and may be group or individual in nature. The process is documented and evaluated.
>
> The professional who delivers and/or directs nature-assisted therapy is a health/human service provider with expertise in incorporating some facet of nature as a treatment modality, and is knowledgeable about that facet of nature. The nature-assisted therapist is licensed and/or recognized by a separate professional discipline. This individual complies with the legal and ethical requirements of his/her profession; as well as local, state and federal laws relating to this work.
>
> Nature-assisted activities provide opportunities for motivational, educational, and/or recreational, benefits to enhance the quality of life. Nature-assisted activities are delivered in a variety of environments by a specially trained professional, paraprofessional, and/or volunteers who possesses specialized knowledge of all facets of the natural environment incorporated into the activity. Some individuals delivering nature-assisted activities include activity directors, camp counselors, educators, and 4-H leaders.

In other words, nature-assisted therapy is delivered or directed by professional therapists or health care professionals; it is goal directed, part of the treatment plan, and documented. Similar activities can also be therapeutic, although they are not delivered by a therapist; they can be referred to as nature-assisted activities. Nature activities can occur in settings that provide education and experiences not specifically designed to be therapeutic. Settings of this type might include a nature camp, scouts, and school environmental education programs. Although nature-assisted therapy may occur in settings other than a therapist's office, it is always directed by the therapist and is part of the therapeutic process.

Upon examination of counseling and therapy theories, nature therapy as an adjunct therapy can be applied to most counseling theories employing many diverse methods and techniques of application. A plant or work of art chosen to enhance the therapeutic environment is one application. Within a behavioral context, the nature encounter may be offered as the reward for another desired behavior outcome. Family systems might consider the pet as part of the family. Individual and family assessment can be augmented by including assessment of behaviors involving the family with a pet or in various environments as well as noting interests and hobbies. The book *The Four Footed Therapist* by Ruckert (1987) focuses on talk therapy, including "homework" assignments talking with pets. *The Healing Earth* by Chard (1994) has a variety of therapeutic interventions designed around experiences with nature and the earth, including growing a garden and meditation under a tree. Knapp and Goodman (1981), in *Humanizing Environmental Education: A Guide for Leading Nature and Human Activities,* have designed values clarification experiences that involve the natural environment. *Nature as a Guide: Nature in Counseling, Therapy, and Education* (Nebbe, 1995) includes many resources as well as case studies and examples of "how to" incorporate nature into the therapeutic experience.

II. ORGANIZED PROFESSIONAL APPLICATION

Three fields of organized professional application of nature therapy have been identified: animal-assisted therapy, horticultural therapy, and natural environmental therapies (Nebbe, 1995). Animal-assisted therapy is covered in depth elsewhere in this book, therefore it will not be reiterated here. It is difficult, however, to differentiate entirely between animal-assisted therapy and nature therapy. Because animal-assisted therapy is part of nature therapy, the definitions are often not exclusive. Different applications may involve different entities. Animal experiences may unfold in a natural environment. Also confusing situations exist; for example, is work with a wild animal considered animal-assisted therapy or nature therapy? In addition, although these are three separate organizational entities, professionals working within these areas experience overlap. Ulrich (1992) suggests that research specifically targeted on the impact of pets on stress level may also be reporting the influence of the natural setting in which the interaction is taking place. He strongly urges practitioners working in all three of these areas to share information and work together.

An overview of horticultural therapy and environmental therapies follows. These fields are broad. The reader is encouraged to go to the resources suggested if more depth is desired.

III. HORTICULTURAL THERAPY

Plants are the base of the food chain. Humans evolved depending on plants for basic food needs. Originally gatherers, humans, as they evolved, discovered they could select, grow, and nurture the plants that were needed and, thus, provide their own food. In addition, plants were used for medicine, housing, tools, clothing, weapons, and pleasure.

A. HISTORY

Early prehistoric references can be found regarding the healing effects of working with and being with plants (Copus, 1980). Documents from Egyptian history tell of physicians prescribing walks in the gardens for disturbed patients and early 19th-century hospitals in Europe involved patients in growing and harvesting crops on institutional farms. In 1879, the Pennsylvania's Friends Asylum for the insane (later the Friends Hospital) had a greenhouse for use with patients with mental illnesses. In Michigan, the Pontiac State Hospital involved its patients with farming activities in the late 19th century.

The beginning of the recent developments in horticultural therapy began at the conclusion of World War II (Copus, 1980). Members of the National Federation of Garden Clubs volunteered at veterans hospitals all over the country, introducing the veterans to growing plants and gardening. In 1950, Dr. Karl Menninger supported patients' involvement in greenhouse operations at the Winter V. A. Hospital in Topeka, Kansas. Later Dr. Menninger established horticultural therapy programs as part of patient treatment at the Menninger Clinic.

During the 1950s, workshops on horticultural therapy were presented around the country. The 1960s and 1970s represented growth and stabilization for horticulture therapy (Copus, 1980). Federal agencies funded a growing number of horticultural demonstration and program expansion projects. The National Council for Therapy and Rehabilitation through Horticulture was founded in 1973. College programs in horticulture therapy were developed. Today the American Horticulture Therapy Association, located in Gaithersburg, Maryland, sponsors annual conferences, publishes a monthly newsletter, networks horticulture therapy efforts, and provides members with other creative horticulture-related benefits.

Informally, horticulture plays a significant role in many of our cultural traditions. Plants as gifts are a symbol of positive thoughts and good wishes. Plants or flowers are given to express friendship, to express get well wishes, to offer apologies, and to wish well for grand openings. Plants, as well, are incorporated into important celebrations and life's special occasions, for example, weddings, funerals, Mother's Day, birthdays, and proms.

B. Research

An emphasis on research has been identified as an essential component of the future of horticulture therapy. The People-Plant Council was formed in 1990 to promote such research. They publish a newsletter and sponsor conferences.

C. How Horticultural Therapy Works

Programs in horticulture therapy can be found in many settings including correctional facilities, alcohol and drug rehabilitation centers, training centers, work co-ops for people with physical and mental handicaps, special education programs for exceptional students, and programs for the blind. People with other disabilities and other groups of people have tailored horticulture therapy programs to fit their needs.

Horticulture therapy programs may include farm, greenhouse, and garden programs. Programs can also be found in hospital rooms, classrooms, and kitchens. Kitchens are included here in reference to an interesting activity involving planting what one would normally consider garbage: avocado pits, carrot tops, citrus seeds, potato eyes, or pineapple tops (Olszowy, 1978).

In one hospital, each child admitted is assigned a plant which the therapist feels best fits that child's situation. The plant receives treatment from the child parallel to the treatment that the child will receive from the hospital staff. Fertilizer is injected into the soil with a needle like the one used to give shots to the child. Broken limbs can be removed from the plant and the plant can continue to grow and be healthy. Often shoots are taken from the plant, rooted, and planted in another pot to signify that the child will be safe and sound away from his family (Rae & Stieber, 1976). In addition, horticultural therapy can aid individuals in gaining new skills; provide opportunities to improve communication skills; stimulate curiosity, questioning, and sensory awareness; provide social interaction; help improve confidence and self-esteem; help relieve stress and tension; create opportunities for self-expression and creativity; aid in teaching about life and life processes; and teach patience and delayed gratification among many other client or patients goals (Olszowy, 1978).

Therapy using horticulture can take place without directly working with plants. A comfortable tone or atmosphere can be set in an office or building by having plants in the environment. Ian McHarg, the architect, believed plants enhance the health of any atmosphere (McHarg, 1969). Taking a walk in a garden, visiting a flower shop, observing plant displays, and sending flowers can be part of horticultural therapy.

D. Problems

A few potential problems must be considered before initiating a project or program of horticulture therapy. Although the term *horticulture therapy* suggests that garden space or greenhouses are desirable, many simple activities can be done with very limited space indoors. At times, special equipment is necessary and expenses must be considered. For some horticulture activities, like growing a plant, time is an issue. Failure of the project or death of the plant may not necessarily be a problem, but will need to be addressed. Proper conditions may be important. At times allergies may pose a problem. Accidents or injuries can occur and a plan for handling them must exist. Getting dirty may bother some people (Nebbe, 1995).

E. Guidelines

These guidelines need to be considered when undertaking a horticultural therapy project:

1. Undertake projects that you can realistically achieve with your client or group.
2. A successful, small project is better than something elaborate that cannot succeed. Simple and small projects will keep the interest of your clients and ensure success.
3. You do not need to be a horticulture expert, but be sure you know what you are doing. In other words, do your homework or go to an expert for advice. Some excellent resources are listed in Appendixes 1 and 2. Do the activity yourself ahead of time to be sure you understand it.
4. Set attainable goals and objectives when you plan each project: Keep those goals and objectives in sight. Be willing to be flexible if your expectations are too high or different from achievable results.
5. Be prepared for the total project including the cleanup. Ample newspapers under your work area, availability of running water, and rags to clean up spills are important materials to have on hand.
6. With simple projects, accidents and injuries are rare, but be prepared for simple first-aid if necessary.

7. Be prepared to deal with the death of a plant as with any loss. Disposal of the plant in a compost pile is more appropriate than a wastebasket and emphasizes the idea of life giving life.
8. Remember you are a role model teaching about life! How you handle and work with the plants sends important messages to your clients. If you model a passion and reverence for life, you are giving a precious gift!

IV. NATURAL ENVIRONMENT THERAPY

The purpose of natural environment therapy is to aid participants as they seek personal identity and "optimum" development of personal resources. Therapy can occur as a result of the natural healing in nature or with the use of therapeutic activities in natural settings. Natural environment therapy involves a variety of possible experiences ranging from a wilderness survival trip to a walk in the garden.

A. HISTORY

Humans evolved with the earth, with and within the natural environment. With the exception of recent years, people have lived in total contact with and as part of the natural environment. Now separated and protected from the natural contact, humans look for ways to fill the emptiness left by the lack of contact. Dubos (1972) suggested that camping, backyard barbecues, fires in fireplaces, pets, plants, and hunting all bring back flashes of the unity from which humans have separated themselves.

Outward Bound (Wilson, 1981), a successful program that reunites people with their environmental roots, originated as part of a unique school program designed by German schoolmaster Kurt Hahn. Conceived in Germany, the school later moved to Wales as a result of World War II. In Wales, the outdoor training program of Hahn's school evolved into another school, Aberdovey, developed to train "soft" British seaman in survival skills. After World War II, Aberdovey evolved into what is known today as Outward Bound.

Outward Bound programs are found all over the world (Wilson, 1981). The philosophy of Outward Bound is learning through experience. Originally a 2-week wilderness survival experience, Outward Bound has been adapted to fit the needs of many diverse groups. The Outward Bound program effectively builds self-confidence, stretches emotional and physical limits, develops leadership skills, and promotes personal growth and responsibility.

The Colorado Outward Bound School was the first of its kind in the United States (Wilson, 1981). It has been a leader in adapting the Outward Bound concept to a variety of situations and populations. These included adult offenders, classroom teachers, corporate personnel, persons with developmental disabilities, recovering alcoholics, incarcerated criminals, juvenile delinquents, and schoolchildren.

Outward Bound is a total living and learning experience that includes three elements (Wilson, 1981):

1. A natural environment devoid of most of the trappings of modern civilization. This is an environment unfamiliar to most participants.
2. A unique social environment of 9 to 12 people living and learning together. This group must act as a team, developing cooperative efforts and group decision-making abilities in order to succeed.
3. A challenge of learning to cope with the environment and the social group. Challenges include tasks of daily living for both the individual and the group.

Other programs have developed from the original Outward Bound concept (Gillis, 1985). One of these is Project Adventure, founded in 1971 (Coriseneau, 1979). Project Adventure calls itself an "alternate to Outward Bound." Those elements of the Outward Bound experience that made it successful were isolated and then put into a feasible program for school.

A Project Adventure curriculum includes the following elements: (1) a sense of adventure, (2) unpredictability, (3) drama, (4) suspense, (5) a high level of expectation, (6) an orientation toward successful experiences, (7) an atmosphere of mutual support, cooperation, and encouragement, (8) an opportunity for enjoyment, fun, and the ability to laugh at oneself and others, (9) a group problem-solving approach to learning, and (10) a combination of active involvement with person/group reflection and evaluation, always open to the teachable moments (Coriseneau, 1979).

The Project Adventure aspects are presented through activities laid out on a "ropes course" or through "incentive games." These activities include elements of individual risk taking and team cooperation.

New Games, developed by Stewart Brand and George Leonard (Fluegelman, 1976), is another action-oriented program inspired by Outward Bound. This book includes a collection of action-oriented games that are safe and fun for all participants and in which everybody wins. Playfair, created by Matt Weinstein and Pamela Kekich (Weinstein & Goodman, 1980), is another Outward Bound-inspired program. Playfair uses an audience participation comedy show format for noncompetitive games to create a high-spirited feeling of community.

School camping and environmental education are defined as subject matter and are also related directly to the influence of Outward Bound. Environmental education deals with all aspects and parts of the school curriculum. In addition, it "utilizes the outdoors to cultivate a reverence for life through an ecological exploration of the interdependence of all living things, one on the other, and to form a land ethic illustrating man's temporary stewardship for the land" (Ford, 1981).

Although defined as subject matter, cognitive in nature, environmental education programs are moving into the awareness and values realm. Steve van Matre (1974), a pioneer in the awareness movement, said it this way: "I feel that self-awareness follows natural awareness, and that it is most often a by-product of pursuing the latter rather than the result of being sought after as an end in itself" (p. 13). Van Matre (1972) also believed "once he (the student) has felt this unity with Nature, he is more hesitant to destroy her; he realizes that to do so would be to destroy himself. And in the process he has achieved a heightened awareness of and a greater sensitivity for all forms of life, including his fellow man" (p. 17).

Clifford Knapp and Joel Goodman (1981) tied together self-awareness and natural awareness by focusing on a person's identity and values with their book *Humanizing Environmental Education: A Guide for Leading Nature and Human Nature Activities,* which featured values clarification and personal awareness.

B. RESEARCH

The effectiveness of the Outward Bound programs has been noted informally and documented formally. The general goals of such programs are affecting students' or participants' attitudes, sense of self-worth, pride, and belief in themselves; affecting the major components of the students' or participants' environment, the living situation, family, school participation, and job potential; and providing systems of support for a minimum of 1 year of continuing reconnection through a caring relationship both in the day-to-day environment of the participant and the wilderness. These programs appear to be successful as noted in participants' behavior changes toward desired goals (Flood & McCabe, 1979; Mills, 1978; Synobody, 1979).

Evidence from studies done involving Project Adventure participants also indicated affective changes in self-concept, improved physical education skills, more self-confidence, and greater self-esteem (Final Quantitative Evaluation for 1971–71 Project Adventure, 1972). Likewise, the teaching of environmental education has been documented as contributing to an individual's growth in attitude toward the environment and enhancement of self-concept (Childs, 1980; Crompton and Sellar, 1981).

C. HOW ENVIRONMENTAL THERAPY WORKS

According to the Colorado Outward Bound Program, there are three dimensions to the therapeutic process of their program: the physical environment, the social group, and the individual (Chase, 1981). A majority of the following material about Outward Bound is taken from the publication by Chase (1981).

The physical environment for the program is the natural environment. Living in the natural environment fulfills people's basic need for personal connection with the natural environment. People developed or evolved in the natural environment. Their theory presumes that returning to that environment provides a natural transition to awaken latent survival instincts.

Living in the natural environment is also a new and different experience for most people. New skills are necessary; new behaviors are learned. The natural environment is a behavior setting that evokes coping rather than defensive behaviors. Examples of coping behavior are self-sufficiency, risk taking, initiative, and cooperation. Coping behaviors in the wilderness are positively reinforced by survival! Contrast this with the defensive behaviors elicited by our stress-producing modern civilization. People are placed in large social groups with an overabundance of ambiguous, conflicting, and threatening stimuli. People tend to respond to this stress with defensive behaviors such as rationalization, repression, denial, social withdrawal, or flight from reality. Such responses become habitual and are difficult to change within the environment that triggers them.

Outcomes of dysfunctional behavior are clear and easily understood within the simplicity and predictability of the natural environment. In the wilderness, there are clear choices and few rules. You are either clean or dirty, hungry or well fed, miserable or comfortable. The natural environment offers a feedback mechanism that is concrete, immediate, unprejudiced, and impartial. People must interact with it in a responsible, coping way to ensure survival.

The second dimension of the therapeutic process of the Colorado Outward Bound program is the social group. The literature about the therapeutic nature of wilderness experiences emphasizes the social or group interaction therapy which fits easily into traditional therapeutic methods and models of therapy (Chase, 1981). In addition, there are new dimensions to the therapeutic value of the social group, because of the unique nature of the natural environment as discussed above.

People evolved not only within the natural environment, but also within small social groups, as opposed to the larger, more confusing social groups of modern civilization. Returning to the natural setting simplifies the social system and nurtures its participants.

Psychologists agree that through interaction with other individuals, the self is defined, nurtured, and maintained. In modern civilization much of an individual's identity and interaction with others is role bound. The life script is written and it is difficult to diverge from that script. In the wilderness setting and the new, smaller social group, people are on an equal basis. Cultural roles, failures, and cultural crutches are left behind. As the experience develops, the common challenges that face the group demand interdependence. Group members must learn to communicate, cooperate, depend on each other, and trust each other.

Individual growth is the third dimension of the therapeutic process experienced in a wilderness survival experience (Chase, 1981). Because of the nature of the experience, the participants encounter a wide range of human reactions including fear, joy, fatigue, hunger, respect, trust, pain, and love. Participants learn to better understand themselves through self-discovery of feelings and learning to deal with these feelings in an appropriate way.

The individual grows while facing the challenges of the environment and of the social group. Many of the challenges are new, frightening, and involve risk. As challenges are met, new skills are developed and a sense of accomplishment achieved. Out of these come greater self-confidence and high self-esteem. "The physical experiences at Outward Bound are not an end, but a means to an end, as they promote individual growth and encourage new levels of cooperation and human relations" (Chase, 1981, p. 11).

Whether it is the total experience and the elements that compose it which are responsible for the impact on the individual or whether it is purely the environment is in question. There is evidence, however, that the environment does have a strong impact on the individual.

The components of a restorative response include "attention/interest to the natural setting accompanied by liking or increased levels of positive affects, reduced levels of negatively toned feelings such as fear and anger, and reductions in physiological arousal (such as sympathetic nervous system activity) from high levels to moderate ranges" (Kellert & Wilson, 1993, p. 99). These affects occur fairly rapidly. He goes on to say that although the terms *stress recovery* and *restoration* are used interchangeably, restoration is not limited simply "to stress recovery situations or to recovery from excessive physiological arousal and negatively toned emotional 'excitement' (anxiety), but could also refer to recuperation from understimulation or prolonged boredom" (Kellert & Wilson, 1993, p. 100).

A great deal of research exists that suggests there is a universal restoration effect with exposure to settings that have savanna-like properties (scattered trees, grass, open space) or water features (Ulrich, 1993).

A study done by Hartig *et al.,* (1991) reported that people randomly assigned to a nature walk reported more positively toned emotional states than individuals assigned to walking for the same period of time in a safe urban area or reading magazines or listening to music.

Another study (Francis & Cooper-Marcus, 1991) sampled university students who lived in the San Francisco area to name the settings they sought out when they felt stressed or depressed. Seventy-five percent cited outdoor places that were either natural settings or urban settings dominated by natural elements such as wooded urban parks, places offering scenic views of natural landscapes, or locations on the edge of bodies of water.

Physiological measures (heart rate, skin conductance, muscle tension, pulse transit time) and self-rating measures all showed that individuals recuperated from the stress induced by watching a stressful movie faster if they viewed color/sound videotapes of natural settings as opposed to similar videotapes of urban areas lacking the natural environment (Ulrich *et al.,* 1991).

Even wall art and window views of peaceful nature settings promoted positive outcomes for individuals in a variety of settings including prisons and hospitals. In addition, the influence of natural settings has been documented to enhance cognitive functioning and creativity (Ulrich, 1993).

D. Goals of Environmental Therapy

There are many goals or benefits of natural environmental therapies. These can be identified as environmental, social, and individual outcomes. Environmental outcomes are related to the natural healing that occurs when an individual is in the natural situation. Social outcomes include group interaction and development of a sense of "community," social skills, conflict management skills, sense of responsibility, and trust. The individual outcomes include enhanced self-confidence and self-esteem, intellectual stimulation, emotional release, development of interests, enrichment of personal understanding, enhancement of physical fitness, and opportunities for recreation (Nebbe, 1995). As noted previously, the restorative effect of the natural setting influences positive outcomes (Ulrich, 1993).

E. Problems

Some problems might be encountered working with natural environment therapy (Nebbe, 1995). Safety has been an ongoing concern of Outward Bound and Project Adventure. Insects, fleas, ticks, mosquitoes, and bees bother many people. Fears associated with the outdoors are often based on ignorance, but they do exist. Weather can be a problem. Often participants express a fear of wild animals. Occasionally wild animals may be present. One of the biggest problems is the possible destruction of the natural environment such as tramping down habitat, picking wild flowers or fruits, or removing parts of the natural environment. In most states, these activities are illegal. Getting lost is a real concern and can happen in the smallest city park.

F. GUIDELINES

These guidelines are recommended for the coordinator of a wilderness or environmental experience to considering previous to planning the wilderness adventure (Nebbe, 1995).

1. On long wilderness outings, and on outings into unfamiliar places, leadership with experience and expertise in wilderness camping is imperative. Nothing should be undertaken if the leaders do not feel completely comfortable with the situation and the environment.
2. On short sojourns, the leader needs to be familiar with the place.
3. The leaders always must be prepared for emergencies. A person trained in first-aid and CPR should be readily available. Also, plans should be ready for any possible situation.
4. The leaders need to be sure someone at a base office knows where the group is going, who is going, what the group will be doing, and when the group is expected back. If possible plan for continued contact via cell phone or similar communication.
5. The leader must be sure participants have written permission for the trip if it is needed.
6. If a physical examination is necessary, be sure it is included as a prerequisite.
7. The leader needs to know about the participants before the trip.
8. The leaders should have a clear idea of goals and expectations of the trip.
9. The leader is responsible for knowing the state and federal laws that may pertain to the trip and any activities of the group (e.g., fires, picking wild flowers, removal of natural objects, and so forth).
10. The participants need to know the guidelines, laws, rules, and expectations for the journey. A prior training or orientation may be necessary.
11. If the experience is of short duration, the leaders should try to make the experience comfortable for the participants. If wet or very cold weather disrupts, they need to have an alternate plan ready. Weather

and uncomfortable conditions are part of longer adventure trips and participants need to be warned that such conditions will occur. Physical and mental preparation make these times more endurable.

V. NATURE AND HUMAN DEVELOPMENT

Interaction and experiences with nature are an essential part of normal human development. By looking at several different models of development and developmental needs, an assessment of the important areas of interaction, of deficit, and of therapeutic application become evident.

A. ERIKSON

An examination and analysis of Erikson's eight stages of human development illuminates the importance of natural experiences in the development of the individual (Erikson, 1950). In stage one, "trust versus distrust" (birth to 1 year) the very young infant who is carried and held safely and securely by a loving parent while in a natural setting, a thunderstorm, or being greeted by a friendly furry face would be less likely to be frightened by those same events occurring later in that child's life. Research has shown that objects shown to infants while very young, and then shown again at 2 years of age do not illicit fear and crying as do those same objects shown for the first time to the older child (Perris et al., 1990). Likewise, traumatic experience that happens in this early stage of development may have a lasting influence on the individual (Bass & Davis, 1994).

Stages two and three, initiative versus guilt (4–6 years) and industry versus inferiority (6–12 years), both involve exploration and investigation of the natural world (Erikson, 1950). This is the time to play outside, make mud pies, look at the clouds and stars, and interact with people and animals in that environment. Joseph Chilton Pearce (1980) changed Erikson's terminology as he described this phase of development as the "earth matrix" during which time it is important for children to discover and interact with the earth and natural world.

Erikson's fifth stage of development, "identity versus identity diffusion" (teenage years), incorporates all of a young person's experiences and knowledge into a quest for personal identity (Erikson, 1950; Erikson 1969). Erikson referred to the elemental parts of identity as "basic" identity, which include who one is in body (species, sex) and what one's biological inheritance is (genealogically and "nature"ly). Once an individual has resolved the elements of basic identity, the person is ready to build on it with the other identity factors. However, a basic identity is difficult to formulate unless the individual is first aware of the choices. Many individuals growing up in the modern technological world have a poor chance of becoming aware of their natural heritage. Learning about it through one-dimensional sources like television and movies is not effective. Awareness comes from experiences and interactions with the earth (Mander, 1978).

B. PIAGET

An understanding of Piaget's theory of cognition (Piaget, 1950) is a helpful guide to the therapist in discerning how children think and, more specifically, think about the living entities in their environment. Children up to an average of 7 years would tend to view animals as peers or objects, depending on how they are represented within their own environment and the broader scope of the culture. Our culture supports the presentation of animals as peers; in movies, literature, and on television animals are dressed up in clothing, acting and talking like humans. Understanding cognitive development helps to explain research findings that teaching children to be kind to animals and to treat animals with respect carries over to being kind to and respecting humans (Santrock, 1995). This ability to understand also applies to other facets of a child's environment and needs to be considered when the therapy media is plants or other aspects of the earth.

C. MASLOW

An examination of Maslow's hierarchy of needs suggests a variety of ways in which an individual's needs may be met through nature and natural experiences (Maslow, 1970). Looking at each step in the hierarchy a therapist can not only assess what the clients deficits are, but fashion therapeutic interventions to meet those needs drawing from the many tools and experiences offered through nature. Maslow's hierarchy of needs is summed up in Table I. What Maslow referred to as "peak experiences," a spiritual or enlightening experience, are often are reported as occurring in the natural environment (Swan, 1977).

Still to be thoroughly analyzed are the natural innuendoes of nature's influence on human development, the subtle connections, influences, and experiences of the natural environment. The effect of the natural cycles such as phases of the moon and tides, effects of the plants and air, influence of weather and atmospheric changes, and the impact of global warming and pollution have been noted, but the actual impact on the human species both physically and mentally is not known.

TABLE I   Maslow's Hierarchy of Needs

Self-Actualization Needs	To find self-fulfillment and realize one' potential
Asthetic Needs	Symmetry, order, and beauty
Cognitive Needs	To know, understand, and explore
Esteem Needs	To achieve, be competent, and gain approval and recognition
Belongingness and Love Needs	To affiliate with others, be accepted, and belong
Safety Needs:	To feel secure and safe, out of danger
Physiological Needs:	Hunger, thirst, and fatigue

Up until 50 years ago, almost all humans developed as an integral part of the natural earth. Life and self-esteem were based on survival. Daily tasks involved essential duties that supported day-to-day survival. Time was spent outside, not protected by air conditioning. People aged naturally, without artificial manipulations to appear older or younger. In our present society it is possible for an individual to live completely secluded from nature. Research has pointed out that in plant-less environments there are greater instances of poor physical and mental health, one evidence being the lack of smiling faces (McHarg, 1969). Self-esteem and identity today, in our culture, are connected to material possessions—what a person has and what a person looks like. Many life tasks seem meaningless, nonessential. The environment the human being has evolved in has been significantly changed and, thus, the individual has lost contact with the natural environment. When the habitat of other species of animals is destroyed or the individual of that species is displaced, it adversely affects the quality of their life or even brings extinction. *Biophilia* refers to the natural affinity humans have to their natural environment that is necessary for mental and physical well-being. When humans alter that environment or break that connection, one can only speculate about the price.

VI. THERAPEUTIC APPROACHES

The following conceptualization can be used to define the therapeutic approaches of nature therapy. Though each category is developed separately, the categories generally overlap. A single experience, for example, hiking or feeding wild birds, may meet goals in more than one area (Nebbe, 1995).

A. INSTRUMENTAL THERAPY

Instrumental therapy encourages people to move more and to do things they would not normally do without the therapeutic media. Examples of instrumental therapy include a guide dog to aid a person with vision impairment; potting and caring for plants; preparing bird feeders; or walking through a natural area to fill a bird bath. Because of the increased mobility and control, the individual experiences more freedom, improves his or her confidence, and increases his or her self-esteem.

B. Relationship Therapy

When people experience an interpersonal interaction with the therapeutic media, they are involved with relationship therapy. People may experience a sensation of being needed and loved. This provides a sense of worth and a sense of responsibility, thus improving self-confidence and self-worth. A person's pet usually is the therapy mode normally considered in relationship therapy, but relationship therapy can exist with a squirrel, a bird, a plant or a "place." The important factor is what the individual perceives. Sometimes people want so badly to have such a relationship that they will perceive the relationship with the smallest bit of encouragement. The memory of the relationship can last long after the experience is over.

C. Passive or Entertainment Therapy

Passive or entertainment therapy is what the name suggests: watch and enjoy. Studies by Beck and Katcher (1983) showed that watching puppies play or observing an animal is stimulating, fun, and relaxing. Watching an aquarium full of fish has been documented to be as relaxing as meditation (Beck & Katcher, 1983). Stress reduction or restorative experiences occur in the natural environment. The relaxation also occurs when the natural environment is viewed on video or in pictures (Ulrich, 1993).

D. Cognitive Therapy

Cognitive (or cognitive behavioral) approaches to therapy combine behavior-change methods with thought-restructuring methods to produce behavior and feeling changes in clients (Thompson & Rudolph, 1992). As people learn more about an animal, a plant, or the environment, they feel more in control and thus better about themselves. Some children who have fears about a dog, for example, will be more confidant when they learn how to approach, pet, and interact with the dog. Often these are fears are based on a lack of information.

When individuals feel more in control of their lives, there is higher self-esteem and self-respect.

Knowledge about plant care, as well as the development of plant care skills, can also increase confidence and self-worth. The feeling of accomplishment and worth that comes from helping a plant grow can give an individual a purpose for being. Furthermore, knowledge about weather and how to protect oneself in dangerous weather situations can give a person more confidence. Knowing the world is round, not flat, has certainly lowered the stress level of sailors!

E. Spiritual Therapy

For some individuals, natural experiences provide a life-renewing energy—a tie with the oneness of all creation. The sight of a soaring bird, the smell of dirt or fresh air, the immensity of the redwood forest, or the power of the ocean can be therapeutic when such an experience touches an individual with the wonder and miracle of life.

Within these broad categories of nature therapy lie a wide range of potential individual goals, benefits, and objectives. Table II, an adaption and extension of a table originally presented by Dr. James Serpell (1983), identifies the areas discussed and was developed to aid in the visualization of the therapeutic approaches.

VII. APPLICATION OF NATURE THERAPY

The practitioner recognizes numerous goals, benefits, or outcomes of nature therapy. Some of the examples that follow are based on the foundation of research, others are based on case studies. The examples here are only exemplary of the many possibilities and are given as examples to stimulate the reader's own imagination and creativity. Each example can be a catalyst to aid the reader to imagine other possible settings, issues, and applications. The examples are taken from actual cases, the names have been changed to protect confidentiality. Where not cited, cases are personal experiences of the author of this chapter.

A. Acceptance or Belonging

With animals we think of the unconditional acceptance they offer. With plants and places humans experience a sense of connection or an unconditional

TABLE II   Therapeutic Approaches of Nature Therapy

Animal assisted therapy	Horticultural therapy	Natural environment therapy
Instrumental Therapy		
Animal becomes an extension of the person.	Person undertakes additional activities.	Person is involved in activities that use motor skills and senses.
Person has some control of the animal.	Person has control while working with the plants.	Person experiences increased mobility.
Relationship Therapy		
Person perceives a warm, personal relationship with the animal.	Person feels that what is being done is worthwhile.	Person feels an identification or a connection with a place.
There is interpersonal interaction between the person and animal.	Person feels needed.	
Person feels needed.		
Person feels loved.		
Passive Therapy		
Person becomes absorbed in the animal's activities.	Person enjoys, with pleasure, the beauty of plants, flowers, trees, gardens, and so forth.	Person enjoys the environmental surrounds.
Person is entertained.		Person relaxes.
Person relaxes.	Person relaxes.	
Cognitive Therapy		
Information promotes understanding, control of life, and respect for life and environment.	Information promotes understanding, control of life, and respect for life and environment.	Information promotes understanding, control of life, and respect for life and environment.
Information enables self awareness and empathy.	Information enables self awareness and empathy.	Information enables self awareness and empathy.
Information releases memories and fantasies.	Information releases memories and fantasies.	Information releases memories and fantasies.
Spiritual Therapy		
Experience brings life renewing energy, sense of oneness with creation, and a sense of peace and well-being.	Experience brings life renewing energy, sense of oneness with creation, and a sense of peace and well-being.	Experience brings life renewing energy, sense of oneness with creation, and a sense of peace and well-being.

belonging can also occur. Rene Dubos (1972) spoke of the special connection people have with places in his book *A God Within.*

Example: Often in hypnosis, the therapist asks the client to go to a safe place. This place can be real or imagined, but it is a place where the client feels safe, comfortable, and empowered. Natural settings that have special meaning to the client are frequently chosen for the client's safe place. Quick relaxation exercises can also utilize this safe place.

Example: A young man in his early twenties with schizophrenia drew great pleasure from the time he spent in his garden. He described it as "his place, the place where he is complete."

B. SOCIALIZATION

Animals, plants, and the environment can be a catalyst for socialization. Cusack and Smith's studies (1984) have shown that when dogs and cats come to visit a care facility, there are more smiles, laughter, and interresident communication than during other therapy or entertainment times. Chase (1981) points out the important socialization component of Outward Bound experiences. Socialization is stated as a goal for individuals working together in horticultural therapy programs (Anderson, 1999).

Example: An example of enhanced social interaction is articulated in an excerpt from *Bring Me the Ocean* by Rebecca Reynolds (1995, p. xi). Irene was an elderly Greek woman. Able to speak only her native Greek, she had become isolated by her inability to communicate with other hospital residents and over the years had lapsed into silence. Her withdrawal was so deep that her silence extended even to her family, to whom she rarely spoke. On the day the "ocean" program came to the hospital, they brought in sand, shells, and thick piles of seaweed. "When Irene saw the seaweed being lifted up out of the buckets, she wheeled her chair over, her expression shifting profoundly. Picking up handfuls of the kelp, Irene smelled its saltiness and began weeping. Slowly, haltingly, she began to speak." Although she spoke in Greek, "we all understood her joy. Such beauty lit her face as she poured forth descriptions of the ocean and her childhood home!"

C. MOBILITY

Nature therapy provides many opportunities for increased mobility. Although the service dog immediately comes to mind when one considers increased mobility, potting a plant or walking in a park also encourage mobility.

Other activities might include digging in a pot or in the earth (range of motion); handling seeds and opening containers (fine motor control); blowing to clear away spilled dirt (speech and breathing); following instructions (sequencing); pointing to an object (visual focus); taking a self-grown plant home or giving it as a gift (adapted from St. Peter Hospital, 1993).

D. MENTAL STIMULATION

Mental stimulation can occur because of increased communication with other people, recalling memories, planning and setting goals, and learning new ideas. Clients frequently like to recall their own experiences and special places.

Example: The therapist asked the 98-year-old terminally ill patient about her life. She looked at a picture on the office wall and smiled as she told of one event, the day she walked across the field to a nearby farm. The tears flowed as she talked of this accomplishment and her pride in its completion. She said this was the one thing she had done in her life that had given her the will to try anything! On later consultation with the medical doctor the therapist learned the patient had a club foot. For a child with this disability, the trek across the field would have been extremely difficult.

Example: There is Bill, 80 years old, and as he is digging in the dirt he begins to talk about his life before the institution. "I once had a farm. I built all the stone walls on my one hundred acres" (Reynolds, 1995, p. 68).

Example: The following is another story from *Bring Me the Ocean* (Reynolds, 1995, p. 9).

> A young tree is shown around, its roots held in burlap so that it can be seen top to bottom before being replanted. A young girl who is blind strokes the roots and says, "*Now* I see how a tree stands! I've never seen roots before."

E. TOUCH

The physical contact involved in many natural experiences can help fill the human need for touch as well as offering opportunities for expression and release. Human's that are touch deprived often reflect this depravation in decreased immunity, and for infants even death (Montagu, 1986). An animal's touch can help people fill this need in ways that are acceptable personally or culturally, when other human touch is not. Other forms of skin and body stimulation come from working with the soil, plants, and the atmosphere.

Example: A Sensory Hike (Nebbe, 1995, p. 178) encourages participants to close their eyes and:

put your hands on the ground and gently feel the top. What is it like? Is it soft, crunchy, cold, or warm? Push your hands under the top covering of the ground. Is it different here? What does it feel like? Warmer or colder? Pick up a bit of the earth or ground near you. Feel it. Keeping your eyes closed, smell it. How does it smell? How do you feel about that smell?

F. Physiological Benefits

Physiological benefits exist in many forms from the benefit of relaxation as well as a healthy environment. The presence of animals can produce a relaxation or stress reduction response (Katcher *et al.,* 1984) as well as experiences in the natural environment (Kaplan, 1992; Ulrich *et al.,* 1991).

Example: Angie, a physical therapist at Des Moines Methodist Hospital, tells of woman with many emotional issues. When the woman was brought to the therapy room, a large room filled with big windows, lots of plants, soft music, canaries, and a bunny, she would relax and begin talking. She said she just liked being in that place (A. Anderson, personal communication, February 3, 1999).

Example: Research supports that walks in natural areas are more stress reducing than walks in urban areas (Hartig *et al.,* 1991).

G. Fulfillment of Basic Needs

Humans have common, basic needs: love, respect, usefulness, acceptance, trust, and worth (Santrock,1995; Glasser, 1981). There are opportunities for these needs to be met by individuals caring for other living things: plants, animals, and environmental spaces.

Example: Angie Anderson (personal communication, February 3, 1999) tells of an elderly patient being transferred from her home to a care facility. The event was wrought with trauma for the woman. One of her main concerns was leaving her plants behind. When arrangements were made to include many of her plants in her new environment she accepted the move. In the new facility she spent a good deal of her time caring for her plants.

H. Nurturing

Animal abuse is a symptom of conduct disorder (American Psychiatric Association, 1994). Members of abusive families frequently are abusive to animals. Children raised in abusive families are often abusive to animals because it is modeled and because displaced anger is directed toward the animals. A high percentage of aggressive, incarcerated criminals are reported as being abusive to animals as children (Ascione, 1992; Lembke, 1994). Outward Bound also targets this population. When survival is dependent on nature, it is respected and treated with care (Wilson, 1981). Nature-assisted activities/therapy, with strong role models will give children choices and may aid in breaking the cycle of abuse (A. Katcher, personal communication, March 18, 1995; Nebbe, 1997).

Example: The school counselor arranged for a wildlife rehabilitator to give a presentation to a group of special education sixth graders with behavior disorders. In the classroom were two boys on probation for acts of violence and vandalism. One of the boys often bragged about his "hobby" of setting cats on fire. The presentation went well, the children appeared to listen and there were no inappropriate remarks or behaviors. The students followed the request to treat the education owl with respect.

Several weeks later, the rehabilitator was surprised to see the two boys at her door. When she opened it, they entered, one with something under his shirt. With tears in his eyes he explained that they had found a mother squirrel who had been hit by a car. The baby he had with him was clinging to the dead mother. As he gently handed the rehabilitator the baby, he noted that it probably had a broken back, but they hoped that she could help it.

Follow up to this event showed a change of behavior for both of these young men. It was as though they had never experienced or even realized there was an alternate choice of behavior. The role model presented by the rehabilitator gave them this alternate choice.

Example: In *Bring Me the Ocean* (Reynolds, 1995, p. 59), Jake describes the effect of the program on him to one of his teachers.

> I think that it has changed me because now . . . I don't hurt animals anymore and play games with them and use them as target practice. . . . Now I try and help them. Now the animals come to me as if they know I'm not going to hurt them.

Example: The fall project was mulching newly planted trees in a school arboretum. After the initial educational explanation was given to the children, one child was asked by an observer what he was doing. His answer was, "Bundling the trees up so they will stay warm all winter" (Norton, personal communication, November 3, 1988).

I. ASSESSMENT

The information shared by individuals about animals and pets in their lives and homes gives therapists/staff insight. Observing individuals (children especially) with animals is also a valuable assessment tool (Levinson, 1969). A generalization may be made that an individual's attitude and behavior toward any living entity also provide assessment information.

J. SELF-UNDERSTANDING

Animal and nature activities increase self-understanding because they increase understanding of the world in which each individual lives. Fears can be addressed, individuals can be empowered.

Example: The earth speaks to us of life and death and life processes. In *Nature as a Guide* (Nebbe, 1995, p. 181), the client is given the task of "going out and finding something dead." This act and the meaning of the experience is then processed with the therapist.

Example: Chard (1994, p. 134) recounts talking about a tree nursery with a terminally ill woman. The tree nursery was a "place" of great importance to her life and history.

> "I've watched a lot of things grow and a lot of things die," she told me.
> "What do you make of all that growing and dying?" I asked.
> "Death doesn't stop life one bit. Life just keeps coming. There is something in the Earth that just won't quit," she replied.
> "And what about you?"
> "I feel like there's something in me that just won't quit either," she concluded.

Example: Assignment of "earth" based tasks or experience is illustrated by Chard (1994) in his book *The Healing Earth.* He suggests many activities where clients are given a task to interact with the natural environment to renew their roots and enhance their self-concept, work through an issue, or become closer to the earth. An example follows of a way to renew one's bond with Mother Earth through sensory immersion with the wind. Chard points out this ceremony can be done anywhere outdoors that is convenient (p. 31):

- Pause from your thinking and business of everyday life.
- Bring your awareness to the feel of the Earth's breath (the wind) moving around your skin and body. The atmosphere is always moving, even if this motion is barely perceptible.
- Notice how our Mother's breath is touching you. Depending upon the strength and consistency of the wind, its touch may feel gentle, firm, playful, or rough.
- If you feel comfortable doing so in your setting, turn your face to the direction of the wind, open your arms wide, and embrace it in return.

K. NATURE AS A SYMBOL OR METAPHOR

Example: Ask the client to go into the park, or prairie, or to simply select something that reminds them of themselves, something that could be their symbol. Ask them why they choose what they did, how it represents them, and explore what this means (Nebbe, 1995, p. 141).

Example: The support group for domestically abused women was gathering for their first meeting when they became aware of a small sparrow hawk being brought into the wildlife rehabilitation center next door. Curious about the bird, they asked many questions. Later the rehabilitator sent word to the group that the bird had been examined and was found to be badly bruised and very thin. It was weak and unable to fly, but there appeared to be no permanent injuries. She felt that with care, it would recover and be releasable.

The group members continued to inquire about the progress of the sparrow hawk and it continued to improve. Eight weeks later they met for their last session in a nearby prairie area. The sparrow hawk was released and flew into the upper branches of the tallest tree in the area. Then it sang (or shouted) to the whole world. The bird was symbolic of the journey the women had made during the previous 8 weeks and of their new emerging freedom.

L. Self-Esteem

Individuals who are mentally ill or have low self-esteem focus on themselves. Animals draw these individuals out of themselves. Rather than thinking and talking about themselves and their problems, they watch and talk to and about the animals (Katcher, 1992). In classrooms with pets the students spend more time on task (Katcher, 1992).

Example: In one school there were two learning disabilities classrooms, both at the second-through fourth-grade levels and both with exceptional teachers. The difference was that one classroom had a pet cat. Often when the school counselor would visit the classroom without the cat she would be assailed by children wanting to tell her about their problems, the wrongdoings of the other children, and all the things that were unfair. In the classroom with the classroom cat, the children would great her instead with stories of the cat. "Look at Muffy!" "Come see what Muffy did today!"

Example: A group exercise taken from *Nature as a Guide* (Nebbe, 1995, p. 144):

> Sit in a circle under a tree. Each individual takes one leaf. Get to know that leaf, then introduce it to the group. Talk about the importance of each leaf, some leaves provide food, some shelter, and all leaves provide oxygen and purify the air animals breath. When all the leaves are introduced, put them into the center of the circle. Mix them up. Then find your leaf. Each leaf is unique, individual, and identifiable. If your leaf were mixed with all the leaves like it from the beginning to the end of time, your leaf would still be unique, as is each worm, human being . . . and you.

M. Nurturing

Nurturing skills are learned. Many at-risk children have not learned nurturing skills through the traditional channel of being nurtured by their parents. By being taught to nurture an animal (or a plant), a child is learning nurturing skills. Psychologically, when one nurtures, one's need to be nurtured is also fulfilled (A. Katcher, personal communication, March 18, 1995).

Example: Often after a rain the children in a zootherapy program gathered the worms from the driveway and parking lot, gently putting them back into the grass. Any worms already crushed or injured became food for animals, like the iguanas in their program. The children perceived that they were helping the worms, the earth, as well as providing food for their pets (A. Katcher, personal communication, March 18, 1995).

N. SAFETY

An animal can open a channel of emotionally safe, nonthreatening communication between client and therapist. The animal's presence may reduce a client's initial resistance (Gonski *et al.,* 1986). Plants in an office or in an environmental space also communicate a friendly and safe place (McHarg, 1969).

Example: One teacher at a treatment center for boys described to Reynolds (1995, p. 20) that the goal of the center "is to create a safe environment for the kids, for you, and for the creatures that you bring with you. That is a very empowering thing for the kids, to be able to create a safe environment. What you give the boys when you come in is the opportunity to give another creature what they really need for themselves."

Example: When the volunteers arrived at the youth shelter the young people came out individually. Heads were bowed, voices were silent. It was obvious something was different. Usually the young people came tumbling out, noisy and excited. Each child selected an animal and went to a different place on the grounds. Some sat under a tree and quietly petted a dog or rabbit. Some walked their pet, alone or with a volunteer. Gradually interaction began to occur. Finally, it was time to leave. The good-byes were said. After arriving home the program director got a call from the youth shelter director. "You won't believe what happened today," the shelter director said. "We had a major incident, anger, violence and threats. One of the worse since I've been here. I actually called you to tell you not to come, but you had already left. I told the kids, they could still see the pets, but if there were any problems we would ask you to leave immediately. Well, you saw what happened, but the most amazing was afterward. The entire group came back inside calmly and peacefully and we were able to process the problems. Any other time something like this has happened it has taken days to get through. Whatever the magic was, we need more of it."

VIII. CONCLUSIONS

This chapter has explored some of the various possibilities of nature therapy. An effort to define nature therapy recognizes three professional subdivisions: animal-assisted therapy, horticultural therapy, and environmental therapies. Although these subdivisions exist due to subject categorization, research, and organizational structures, they are often are interrelated and their applications overlap.

Reading through this chapter, and this book, should provide a stimulus for developing numerous ideas for application. At the end of this chapter is a list of publications (Appendix 1) and a list of organizational resources (Appendix 2) that include many other ideas and possibilities. Finally, as Chard (1994, p. 113) advises, go to the earth:

> When our creativity runs dry, the Earth offers a wellspring of new inspiration, play, and energetic exploration. By activating our creative energies, we can apply ourselves more effectively to a broad expanse of productive areas, such as music, design, problem solving, writing, parenting, business development, and of course, fun. Our Earth Mother offers a rich venue in which to prime our creative pumps.

APPENDIX 1: RECOMMENDED LIST OF PUBLICATIONS

Adil, J. R. (1994). *Accessible gardening for people with physical disabilities: A guide to methods, tools, and plants*. Rockville, MD: Woodbine House.

Chard, P. S. (1994). *The healing earth: Nature's medicine for the troubled soul*. Minnetonka, MN: NorthWord Press, an imprint of Creative Publishing, Inc.

Kellert, S. R., & Wilson, E. O. (Eds.). (1993). *Biophilia hypothesis*. Washington DC; Covelo, CA: Island Press/Shearwater Books.

Levicoff, J., & Levicoff, L. (1993). *Magical migrating monarchs: A program to enhance awareness of our interactive role in the environment*. Jenkintown, PA: Authors.

Moore, B. (1989). *Growing with gardening: Twelve-month guide for therapy, recreation, and education*. Chapel Hill, North Carolina: North Carolina Press.

Nebbe, L. L. (1995). *Nature as a guide: Nature in counseling, therapy, and education*. Minneapolis, MN: Educational Media Corporation.

Reynolds, R. A. (1995). *Bring me the ocean*. Acton, MA: VanderWyk & Burnham.

Rothert, G. (1994). *The enabling garden: Creating barrier free gardens*. Dallas, TX: Taylor Publishing Company.

Ruckert, J. (1987). *The four-footed therapist*. Berkeley, CA: Ten Speed Press.

APPENDIX 2: ORGANIZATIONAL RESOURCES

American Horticultural Therapy Association (AHTA)
909 York St.
Denver, CO 80206-3799
E-mail: ahta@ahta.org

American Humane Association
63 Inverness Drive East
Englewood, CO 80112
Phone: (303)792-9900

Delta Society
289 Perimeter Road East
Renton, WA 98055-1329
Phone: (206)226-7357

Latham Foundation
Clement and Schiller Streets
Alameda, CA 94501
Phone: (415)521-0920

People-Plant Council
Virginia Polytechnic Institute and State University
Blacksburg, VA 24061

REFERENCES

American Psychiatric Association. (1994). *Diagnostic and statistical manual of mental disorders* (4th ed.). Washington, DC: Author.

Anderson, A. (1999). Horticulture therapy program [brochure], Iowa Methodist Medical Center, Des Moines, IA.

Ascione, F. (1992). A review of research and implications for developmental psychopathology. *Anthrozoos* (**VI**), 226–247.

Bass, E., & Davis, L. (1994). The courage to heal: A guide for women survivors of child sexual abuse (3rd ed.). New York: Harper Collins Publishers, Inc.

Beck, A., & Katcher, A. (1983). *Between pets and people.* New York: Putnum.

Bernard, S. (1995). *A guide for health care professionals and volunteers.* Whitehouse, TX: Therapet, L.L.C.

Chard, P. S. (1994). *The healing earth: Nature's medicine for the troubled soul.* Minnetonka, MN: NorthWord Press, an imprint of Creative Publishing, Inc.

Chase, N. K. (1981). *Outward Bound as an adjunct to therapy.* Denver, CO: Colorado Outward Bound School. (ERIC Document Reproduction Service No. ED 241 204)

Childs, S. (1980). *Adventure depravation, a social disease: Self-concept through school camp.* (ERIC Document Reproduction Service No. ED 197 911)

Copus, E. (1980). *The Melwood manual: A planning and operations manual for horticultural training and work co-op programs.* (ERIC Document Reproduction Service No. Ed 200 793)

Coriseneau, C. (1979). The nature of adventure education. *Journal of Physical Education and Recreation,* **50**(1). (ERIC Document Reproduction Service No. ED 171 474), pp. 2–36.

Crompton, J., & Sellar, C. (1981, Summer). Do outdoor education experiences contribute to positive development in the affective domain? *Journal of Environmental Education,* 12(4), 21–24.

Cusack, O., & Smith, E. (1984). *Pets and the elderly: The therapeutic bond.* New York: Haworth Press.

Delta Society. (1992). *Handbook for animal-assisted activities and animal-assisted therapy.* Renton, WA: Author.

Dubos, R. (1972). *A god within*. New York: Charles Scribner's Sons.

Erikson, E. H. (1950). *Childhood and society*. New York: W. W. Norton.

Erikson, E. H. (1969). *Identity: Youth and crisis*. New York: W. W. Norton.

Final quantitative evaluation for 1971–72 project adventure. (1972). (ERIC Document Reproduction Service No. ED 173 059)

Flood, J., & McCabe, B. (1979). *Wilderness school staff report*. (ERIC Document Reproduction Service No. ED 175 582)

Fluegelman, A. (Ed). (1976). *The new games book*. San Francisco: The Headlands Press.

Fluegelman, A. (Ed). *New games*. (1976). Gardin, NY: Dolphin Books.

Ford P. (1981). *Principles and practices of outdoor/environmental education*. New York: John Wiley and Sons.

Francis, C., & Cooper-Marcus. (1991). "Places People Take Their Problems." In Proceedings of the 22 Annual Conference of the Environmental Design Research Association, edited by J. Urbina-Soria, P. Ortega-Andeane, and R. Bechtel. Oklahoma City: EDRA.

Gillis, H. L. (1985). *An active adventure for groups*. (ERIC Document Reproduction Service No. ED 260 879)

Glasser, W. J. (1981). *Stations of the mind*. New York: Harper & Row.

Gonski, Y. A., Peacock, C. A., & Ruckert, J. (1986). *The role of the therapist's pet in initial psychotherapy sessions with adolescents*. Paper presented at the meeting of the Delta Society, Boston, MA.

Hartig, T., Mang, M., & Evans, G. W. (1991). Restorative effects of natural environment experiences. *Environment and Behavior, 23*, 3–26.

Katcher, A. H. (1992). *Pet Partners instructor training*. Renton, WA: Delta Society.

Katcher, A. H., Segal, H., & Beck, A. (1984). Comparison of contemplation and hypnosis for the reduction of anxiety and discomfort during dental surgery. *American Journal of Clinical Hypnosis, 27*, 14–21.

Kaplan, S. (1992). The restorative environment: Nature and human experience. In D. Relf (Ed.), *The role of horticulture in human well-being and social development*. Portland, OR: Timber Press.

Kellert, S. R., & Wilson, E. O. (Ed.). (1993). *Biophilia hypothesis*. Washington, DC; Covelo, CA: Island Press/Shearwater Books.

Knapp, C., & Goodman, J. (1981). *Humanizing environmental education: A guide for leading nature and human activities*. Martinsville, IN: American Camping Association.

Lembke, L. (1994). Bedwetting, fire setting, and animal cruelty. *The Latham Letter, 15*(2). Alameda, CA: The Latham Foundation.

Levicoff, J., & Levicoff, L. (1993). *Magical migrating monarchs: A program to enhance awareness of our interactive role in the environment*. Jenkintown, PA: Authors.

Levinson, B. (1969). *Pet oriented child psychotherapy*. Springfield, IL: Charles C. Thomas.

Levinson, B. (1972). *Pets and human development*. Springfield, IL: Charles C. Thomas.

Mander, J. (1978). *Four arguments for the elimination of television*. New York: Quill.

Maslow, A. H. (1970). *Motivation and personality* (2nd ed.). New York: Harper & Row.

McDonald, E. (1976). *Plants as therapy*. New York: Praeger Publishers.

McHarg, I. (1969). *Design with nature*. Garden City, NY: Natural History Press.

Mills, J. (1978, April). The value of high adventure activities. *Journal of Physical Education and Recreation, 49*, 29.

Moore, B. (1989). *Growing with gardening: Twelve-month guide for therapy, recreation, and education*. North Carolina: North Carolina Press.

Montagu, A. (1986). *Touching: The human significance of the skin* (3rd ed.). New York: Harper & Row.

Nebbe, L. L. (1995). *Nature as a guide: Nature in counseling, therapy, and education* (2nd ed.). Minneapolis, MN: Educational Media Corporation.

Nebbe, L. L. (1997). *The human–animal bond's role with the abused child.* Ames, IA: Department of Education, Iowa State University.

Olszowy, D. (1978). *Horticulture for the disabled and disadvantaged.* Springfield, IL: Charles C. Thomas.

Patterson, C. (1980). *Theories of counseling and psychotherapy* (3rd ed.). New York: Harper & Row.

Pearce, J. C. (1980). *Magical child.* New York: Bantam.

Perris, E. E., Myers, N. A., & Clifton, R. K. (1990). Long-term memory for a single experience. *Child Development, 61,* 1796–1807.

Piaget, J. (1950). *The psychology of intelligence.* London: Routledge & Kegan Paul.

Rae, W., & Stieber, D. (1976). Plant play therapy: Growth through growth. *Journal of Pediatric Psychology,* 1(4), 18–20.

Reynolds, R. A. (1995). *Bring me the ocean.* Acton, MA: VanderWyk & Burnham.

Ruckert, J. (1987). *The four-footed therapist.* Berkeley, CA: Ten Speed Press.

St. Peter Hospital. (1993). *Animal-assisted activities/therapy program* [brochure]. Olympia, WA: Author.

Santrock, J. W. (1995). *Life-span development* (5th ed.). Dubuque, IA: W. C. Brown & Benchmark.

Serpell, J. (1983, Spring). *People, animals, and the environment [bulletin].* Renton, WA: Delta Society.

Swan, J. (1977, Summer). The psychological significance of the wilderness experience. *Journal of Environmental Education,* 8(4), 4–7.

Synobody, L. (1979, April). *Increasing self-concept through Outward Bound.* Paper presented at the annual international convention, Counsel for Exceptional Children, Dallas, TX. (ERIC Document Reproduction Service No. ED 171 009)

Thompson, C. L., & Rudolph, L. B. (1992). *Counseling Children* (3rd ed). Pacific Grove, CA: Brooks/Cole Publishing Company.

Ulrich, R. S. (1992). The power of natural settings. *InterActions,* 10(1), 21–22. Renton, WA: Delta Society.

Ulrich, R. S. (1993). Biophilia, biophobia, and natural landscapes. In S. R. Kellert & E. O. Wilson (Eds.), *The biophilia hypothesis* (pp. 73–137). Washington DC: Island Press/Shearwater Books.

Ulrich, R. S., Simons, R. F., Losito, B. D., Fiorite, E., Miles, M. A., & Zelson, M. (1991). Stress recovery during exposure to natural and urban environments. *Journal of Environmental Psychology,* 11, 201–230.

Van Matre, S. (1972). *Acclimatization.* Martinsville, IN: American Camping Association.

Van Matre, S. (1974). *Acclimatizing.* Martinsville, IN: American Camping Association.

Weinstein, M., & Goodman, J. (1980). *Playfair: Everybody's guide to noncompetitive play.* San Luis Obispo, CA: Impact Publishers.

Wilson, R. (1981). *Inside Outward Bound.* Charlotte, NC: East Woods Press.

CHAPTER 18

The Welfare of Assistance and Therapy Animals: An Ethical Comment

JAMES SERPELL AND RAYMOND COPPINGER

Department of Clinical Studies, Center for the Interaction of Animals and Society, University of Pennsylvania School of Veterinary Medicine, Philadelphia, Pennsylvania

AUBREY H. FINE

School of Education and Integrative Studies, California State Polytechnic University, Pomona, California

I. INTRODUCTION

Ethical questions about the use of animals as therapeutic aides or for assisting persons with disabilities arise out of a tension between interests. Throughout history, people have used animals—whether for food, fiber, sport, adornment, labor, or companionship—as a means of satisfying human interests. But animals also have interests—in avoiding pain, fear, distress, or physical harm, and in pursuing their own needs, desires, and goals through the performance of species-typical patterns of behavior. Relations between people and animals only become morally problematical where there is a conflict of interests between the two: where the human use either causes pain, fear, or harm to an animal, or it in some way thwarts or prevents the animal from satisfying its own needs and goals.

During the last 10 years, purveyors and proponents of animal-assisted activities and therapy (AAA/T) such as the Delta Society have made concerted efforts to professionalize the "industry," and establish selection and training standards that aim to minimize the risks of harm to all concerned, including the animals (Hines & Fredrickson, 1998). However, AAA/T has experienced explosive growth within the last decade, and in many cases these standards have been set in the absence of any systematic or empirical evaluation of the potential risks to animals imposed by current practices. Indeed, there is a general but unsubstantiated feeling across the industry that these are "good" activities for animals to be engaged in. The fact that a large number of animals fail to respond to the nurturing and training they receive has not generally been taken as evidence that they do not want to, or are unable to, participate. Instead, practitioners tend to respond to failure by changing the selection or the training procedures, as if the animals are theoretically capable of responding positively to any demands made of them.

Much of the rest of this handbook has been devoted to demonstrating how the use of therapy and service (assistance) animals significantly enhances human health and well-being. The question we address in this chapter is whether this end morally justifies the means of achieving it. Specifically, our goal is to reexamine the animal–human partnership from the animal's viewpoint to see what the benefits might be for the animal, or to see if the raising, training, and deployment of assistance and therapy animals is causing significant degradation in their welfare.[1] In doing so, however, we recognize that there is a shortage of reliable scientific evidence to reinforce some of our claims. Additionally, the authors want to make an impression for clinicians to examine their ethical responsibility for the welfare of their therapeutic adjuncts. Clinicians must respect the integrity of the animals and recognize that their involvement must be carefully monitored, so that their rights and safety are safeguarded.

The information that follows pertains more to the authors' concerns about the rearing, training and expected responsibilities of service animals. As was explained in Chapter 13, the term *service animal* is defined in the U.S. civil rights law (Americans with Disabilities Act of 1990), as "any animal individually trained to do work or perform tasks for the benefit of a person with a disability." However, some of the issues covered in this discussion have direct relevance to animals incorporated in AAA/T. When appropriate, the authors will also highlight their specific concerns for clinicians' considerations.

---

[1] The concept of welfare or "poor" welfare has been variously defined by animal welfare scientists. Some definitions stress the presence of unpleasant mental or emotional states such as pain, fear, frustration or suffering (Dawkins, 1980); some place the emphasis on impairments to an animal's biological fitness (McGlone, 1993; Broom & Johnson, 1993), while others refer to the extent to which environmental stresses and strains exceed the animal's ability to cope or adapt (Fraser & Broom, 1990). Rather than lend support to any one of these competing definitions, we will consider welfare as comprising elements of all of them.

II. POSSIBLE SOURCES OF ANIMAL WELFARE PROBLEMS WITH SERVICE ANIMALS AND THOSE INCORPORATED IN AAA/T

A. FAILURE TO PROVIDE FOR ANIMALS' BEHAVIORAL AND SOCIAL NEEDS

In addition to having physical requirements for food, water, protection from the elements, etc., most animals have social and behavioral needs that should be provided for whenever possible (Dawkins, 1988). An understanding of these social and behavioral needs by primary caregivers is part of the ethical obligation attending animal ownership and use. Different species tend to have different social and behavioral needs (Mason & Mendl, 1993). Judging the value of a particular behavior or social interaction to an animal may sometimes be difficult. However, in general, if an animal is strongly internally motivated to perform a particular behavior or social interaction, and if its motivation to perform appears to increase following a period of deprivation, it is an indication that the activity or interaction is probably important to the maintenance of that animal's welfare. Common indications of deprivation include animals performing abnormally high frequencies of displacement activities, stereotypies, or self-mutilation (Broom & Johnson, 1993).

All animals need to be safe from any abuse and danger from any client at all times. The animal must be able to find a safe refuge within the working environment to go to if he or she feels exhausted or stressed. Throughout the day, the animal utilized in AAA/T needs to have a break from actual patient contact. Therapy and service animals must be free from pain, injury, or disease. All animals should be kept up to date on their inoculations. If the animal seems ill, stressed, or exhausted, medical attention must be given.

For assistance and therapy animals, welfare problems are most likely to arise in circumstances where animals are either residential within health care settings or spend large amounts of time in holding facilities such as kennels or stables. In the former context, inadequate advance planning, selection, and staff commitment and oversight can lead to animals being improperly cared for (Hines & Fredrickson, 1998). Small mammals, birds, and reptiles that are caged or confined are probably at greater risk of neglect or improper care, and nondomestic species that tend to have more specialized requirements than domestic ones are also likely to be at risk. "Improperly cared for" in these contexts should have the broadest definition. Most often it is defined as animals that are inadequately fed, watered, or cleaned. However, any failure to attend to individual needs should be regarded as improper care. Overfeeding animals to the point of obesity is just as negligent as underfeeding. Giving an animal the opportunity to exercise is not enough without ensuring that the individual takes advantage of the opportunity.

With regard to AAA/T, an additional challenge may arise when an animal begins to age. Naturally, the animal's schedule for therapeutic involvement will have to be curtailed. This may cause some disruption and adjustment to both the clinician as well as the animal.

To assist in organizing some of our thoughts pertaining to the psychosocial concerns and needs of therapy animals, the Appendix has been formulated to identify specific guidelines for consideration. These guidelines are pertinent to both services provided in large-scale institutionally based programs as well as small clinical practices.

Welfare problems may be particularly severe where animals, such as dogs, have been reared in the enriched environment of a human foster home and then kenneled individually for months as part of their final training (Hubrecht, 1995). Such an abrupt change in social and physical environment appears to be highly stressful for some animals (Coppinger & Zuccotti, in press) and may not only affect their immediate welfare, but also has the potential to foster obnoxious behaviors that might preclude successful training and placement.

Assistance animals may also be at risk because of the changing nature of their relationships with successive human owners and handlers throughout their lives. Most of these animals are picked because they are innately social— that is, they are internally motivated to seek social interactions with others— and because they form strong bonds of attachment for their human partners. Having to endure a whole succession of different handlers with different characteristics, experience, and motivations for "ownership" is likely to be to particularly stressful for these individuals. Conversely, and in contrast to free-living animals, most therapy and assistance animals are trapped in systems where they have little control over their social lives, and where they cannot avoid or escape unwelcome or unpleasant social intrusions. Denying animals control over their physical and social environment can have adverse effects on their physical and mental well-being (Hubrecht *et al.*, 1992).

Unfortunately, AAA/T program planners and practitioners sometimes have little firsthand knowledge of animal needs other than hygienic or veterinary considerations, and with many agencies there is confusion as to who is responsible for the animals' social requirements. Veterinarians who attend to the health and immunization of puppies, attendants who clean, feed, and water, trainers who condition the behavior for 1 hour a day, fund raisers, directors, or whomever—none is assigned specific responsibility for the animal's social well-being.

B. Selecting or Breeding Animals
for Assistance

Most domestic animals have been selected to show a higher degree of tolerance of stressful situations and stimuli compared with nondomestic species, even those reared entirely in captivity (Hemmer, 1990). Nondomestic species are also harder to train, and their entrained responses extinguish more quickly in the absence of appropriate reinforcement. Some species, such as many nonhuman primates, are also highly intelligent and socially manipulative (Cheney & Seyfarth, 1990), and this tends to make them potentially unreliable or unsafe as social companions for people. All of these factors make nondomestic species less suitable for use in AAA/T programs, and more likely to experience welfare problems if used.

This point is well illustrated by recent efforts to train and use capuchin monkeys to assist people with serious disabilities. In most cases, these programs have found it necessary to neuter and surgically extract the canine teeth from the monkeys before they can be used safely with such vulnerable human partners. Monkeys may also be required to wear remotely controlled, electric shock-collars or harnesses in order to provide the user with a means of controlling the animal's potentially aggressive and unreliable behavior. Clearly, the necessity of using of such extreme and invasive measures raises doubts about the practical value of such programs, as well as serious ethical questions concerning the welfare of the animals involved.

It is probably fair to say that all animals adopted for AAA/T service have their behavior modified or curtailed to some degree. At the very least they need to be tamed and taught certain non-natural skills through formal education. This is a different process from that used to train most sporting or working dogs where the performance of the desired behavior generally provides its own reward (Coppinger et al., 1998, and see later discussion).

Not all domestic animal species are practical for becoming service animals. Without belaboring the point it would be difficult to conceive of a guiding cat or a hearing ear donkey. In practice, dogs may be the only domestic species that can be reliably trained to perform a wide variety of household tasks for a person with disabilities, but within the dog population as a whole there is considerable individual variation in the suitability of dogs for this type of work.

Some service dogs, such as the hearing ear dogs, are almost exclusively obtained from shelters. Indeed, some of the motivation for training these and other therapy dogs is to rescue some of these otherwise forsaken animals. For example, a large number of greyhounds are used in therapy work, not because they are necessarily the best breed for the work, but because large numbers are culled from racing and would otherwise be euthanized. The recycling of animals relinquished to shelters clearly has a beneficial welfare impact, although some AAA/T practitioners doubt the reliability of these reconditioned pets. Much of the reluctance to use these animals is based on the fear that latent, unacceptable behavior will emerge and cause injury to the person using the animal.

Currently, about half the assistance animal agencies rely on shelter dogs, although identifying suitable dogs among the 4 to 5 million relinquished each year is a major problem. Hearing ear and therapy dogs are perhaps the easiest to locate since there are no size restrictions. One problem for everyone in this system, however, is to identify the animal before the abandonment and confinement process has a permanent damaging effect on its personality. Agencies using these dogs often have a prescribed test that the dog is required to pass in order to be accepted into a program. However, agency personnel vary widely in their ability to interpret test results, and even experienced selectors have no idea if the test is effective in maximizing acceptance of qualified animals, simply because the controlled experiments have never been done. Given the industry's need for qualified dogs, and the ethical benefits of using shelter animals, there is considerable room for improvement in the identification and distribution of serviceable animals from shelters.

In-house breeding programs are favored by guide dog and wheelchair dog organizations. Both kinds of agencies will also purchase dogs and accept donated dogs. The primary reason for producing and buying dogs is to obtain animals of relatively uniform size. It is not that other breeds are not temperamentally suited, but the task to be performed requires a dog with particular physical characteristics. Within the industry, most of the emphasis is on just three breeds: Labrador retrievers, German shepherds, and golden retrievers. Recently, more interest has also been shown in using cross-bred retrievers.

The history of dog breeding until modern times has been to create superior working animals through hybridization. Although there was some breed maintenance from ancient times, the vast majority of our modern sporting and working dogs were the result of random matings accomplished by the animals themselves accompanied by postzygotic culling of unwanted animals. Just prior to the beginning of this century, breeds were created by hybridizing strains in order to achieve working excellence. In the 19th century, a shift toward prezygotic selection began that has intensified ever since. The assumption behind this process is that excellence of form and behavior can be purified and preserved within a breed. Although such breeding practices do tend to produce uniformity of appearance and behavior within breeds, in the absence of periodic outcrossing, they also promote inbreeding depression, and the expression of various recessively inherited "genetic" diseases.

Unfortunately, the assistance dog industry has been slow to recognize these dangers. Agency breeding programs selectively breed "out" undesirable characters such as hip dysplasia, retinal atrophy, fearfulness, and aggression, but they are not breeding "in" desirable characteristics. As a matter of fact, it is impossible to breed "in" to a closed gene pool, which is what a breed is. Each time individuals are removed from the population, because they don't have the minimum quality hips, say, all of their other genes are removed from the population. The next individual is not bred because it is too fearful, and all of its genes are removed, even the ones for good hips. Each generation gets more inbred because of the shrinking genetic variation, creating highly homozygous strains. In theory, dogs generated in these systems are more vulnerable to infectious disease, as well as being more likely to show phenotypic expression of deleterious mutant alleles.

In some agencies considerable attention is paid to inbreeding depression but it is mostly in terms of how to slow the rate, rather than discussions of how to prevent it. There has been some suggestion that sharing breeding stock between agencies could revitalize inbred stock. Progress made at one agency at eliminating genetic defects could then be helpful to other breeders. So far, however, the tendency is for each of the agencies to solve the problems on their own with small populations of dogs.

There is another ethical issue buried within this production system. Creating large numbers of animals year after year with hip dysplasia or retinal atrophy is ethically questionable in itself, but ethical questions also attend the disposal of animals diagnosed with disease and dropped from assistance programs. Should these animals be euthanized or should they be put up for adoption? Overall, these kinds of issues raise certain doubts about the wisdom of maintaining purebred strains of dogs for assistance work.

C. Failure to Take Account of Developmental Events and Processes

There is confusion among many assistance animal programs concerning the difference between genetic, environmental, and developmental effects. For example, one can find statements in the literature declaring that there are no environmental factors that cause CHD (canine hip dysplasia) (Orthopedic Foundation for Animals, 1998). Such statements are incorrect. The embryologic definition of development is the interaction between a gene and its environment (Serpell, 1987). Therefore, a dog with the condition known as hip dysplasia is the product of in herited (genetic) predisposition interacting with the environment at various stages in its development. The environment is as much a "cause" of the condition as are the genes. Precisely the same is true of behavior.

It is well established from research on canid development that early experiences have more profound and longer lasting effects on behavior than those occurring at later stages of the life cycle (Serpell & Jagoe, 1995). It is not difficult to understand why. When a German shepherd puppy is born, it has a brain volume of about 8 cm^3, and at this stage it has all the brain cells it is ever going to have. By 8 weeks its brain has grown to 80 cm^3, and at 16 weeks the brain is approaching its adult size of 120 cm^3. If the brain increases 15 times in volume during this short period, but maintains the same cell number, where is the growth occurring? The answer is that the increase in size is almost all due to the development of connections between the cells. Most of the cells are arranged in a matrix of connections during the first 16 weeks. The matrix is constructed in response to electrical stimulation and activity patterns. How the animal moves, what it perceives with its senses, and the kinds of stresses it endures all determine the pattern of electrical charges that stimulate the growth of the connective matrix. Human children growing up in orphanages have not only smaller brains (not as many connections) than "normal" children but they don't show the same electrical patterning, even though they presumably have the same number of brain cells. This is what is meant by a developmental effect—a synergism between genes and the environment. It does not mean that there are no genetic effects. It means that genetic and environmental effects cannot be separated.

Now consider where most service puppies spend the first 8 weeks of their lives: in a sterilized kennel being protected from any environmental insult that might challenge their little immune systems. The kennel is the equivalent of an orphanage. Kennel workers are very good at keeping puppies sanitized, and will respond positively if you ask if they have heard of the critical period for socialization. But it would be fair to say that few understand what it means in terms of brain development. Why is it that up to 50% of agency-bred dogs are unable to perform the tasks assigned to them? Is it because of genetic flaws, or is it because of the developmental effects of spending the first 8 weeks in an impoverished environment? If the latter, then the "industry" is predisposing puppies to be ill equipped to cope with the demands made on them later in life.

These dogs are growing up on a fabricated diet, in a contrived and impoverished environment in which the handlers' motivations are primarily to do with health care and cost effectiveness. As a system, it pays practically no attention to neurologic and cognitive development. And yet the behavioral result of what happens to a pup during this period is largely permanent. Once the brain connections are made, there is no changing them. How and what a pup can learn is virtually fixed by 1 year of age. Instructors with experience can look at a 1-year-old dog and make a pretty accurate assessment of whether it can learn to be an assistance dog or not. Depending on how the dog was "wired" in those early sensitive periods predetermines how it will behave as an adult. Indeed, the reason why puppy testing does not work as a predictive tool is that the brains of puppies less than 16 weeks of age are incompletely wired, and how they get wired varies greatly depending on the environment to which the pups are adapting.

Agencies and programs raising animals for service or for use in AAA/T have a moral duty to ensure that the animals they produce are correctly prepared for their adult roles. At every stage of growth and development, dogs could and should be shaped and molded to perform their adult tasks. If particular tasks are required of the assistance adult—that is turning on a light—then the dog's developmental exposure should prepare it for such a task. Food boxes could require similar tasks in such a way that the dog achieves a cognitive awareness of what is being performed. How dogs handle novel situations is another major cause of rejection. A fearful dog cannot be trained to deal with novelty. For example, sidewalk grates common in cities may be an insurmountable problem for a dog. Again the types of problems that cause a high failure rate might be eliminated by paying attention to the early (4 to 16-week) developmental environment. If done properly, a dog might even learn to enjoy performing its work simply because it has developed the cognitive ability to transcend operant conditioning and understand what it is doing and why. On the other hand, the "industry" may also have to face the morally uncomfortable possibility that the only way to raise a "good" assistance dog is to raise it in a deprived environment. It may be that the most successful dogs are products of particular kinds of environmental impoverishment; that the more cognitively developed animals are actually ill suited to perform this kind of repetitive and tedious daily work.

D. Using Inappropriate or Inhumane Training Methods

The underlying assumption of operant conditioning is that any animal can learn any performance by external reward or external punishment. For example, a moving animal is rewarded for going in the correct direction and punished for going in the wrong direction. There is a lengthy and complex literature on when, how much, and how often the animal should be rewarded or punished, and about what is actually reinforced. This is essentially the method used to train many service animals.

But two important keys are often missing from this learning paradigm. First, the reason dogs have been so successful as companions is that they are prepared to work for the reward of social interaction with people. Second, because particular dog breeds innately "like" to search for game, or like to herd sheep, it is not essential to reward such performance. Working dog specialists generally consider it impossible to train an animal that does not show the internal motivation to perform the specific task. Most sporting or traditional working dogs, such as sheep dogs or sled dogs, are not aversively conditioned nor are they given food rewards for proper performance. In fact the problem for trainers is to stop the performance short of exhausting the animal (Coppinger & Schneider, 1995). As a generalization, most traditional working dog trainers do not use aversive conditioning as the primary training strategy. Nor do they need to. Dogs tend to "sour" with aversive conditioning, and because many performances depend on stamina and willingness to work, dog trainers avoid associating performance with any form of punishment. On a sled dog team, severe punishment might be used to stop a dog fight, but no driver would attempt to persuade a dog to run by punishing it.

In contrast, aversive conditioning is the primary method of instruction for many assistance dogs. It may be the only method that is practical because many assistance dog tasks are not discrete, nor is the significance of the task understood by the dog. "Find the bird" is a discrete task, regardless of how long it takes. It has a beginning and an end of which the dog is aware. Even the running sled dog is socially facilitated to run because other dogs are running. Pulling the sled is a by-product, secondary to the performance of running with other dogs.

Pulling a wheel chair is fundamentally different from these tasks because there is no intrinsic reward, nor is it socially facilitated in the manner of a sled dog performing with other dogs. Tasks like these are difficult to reward because performance is an ongoing event. You cannot reward the cessation of activity at the end of the pull, and punishment is equally inappropriate (Coppinger *et al.*, 1998).

The attitude of many assistance dogs in public seems to reflect the aversive training techniques, and the internal confusion as to what is expected (Coppinger, personal observations). This is probably more true of wheelchair than guide dogs. The high failure rate in AAA/T animals may in part be due to inappropriate training procedures. There has recently been some interest in "click and treat" methods using a variation of Pavlovian conditioning. This is a useful approach for "civilizing" assistance dogs and works reasonably well on hearing ear and therapy dogs. As yet it has not been demonstrated to work as a viable system for wheelchair or guide dogs. It may be that there is in fact no appropriate or humane training technique for dogs of this type, which might lead one to the ethical conclusion that animals shouldn't be asked to perform such tasks.

At present, it is unclear once a dog graduates from an agency how long it continues to perform satisfactorily. Clearly, with guide dogs, mistakes are immediately noticeable, and incorrect performance can be continually corrected. However hearing ear dogs could cease performing without the client noticing in time to correct the problem. There is a lack of data for any of the assistance dogs on either the competency of performance, the duration of performance, or the value of the performance to the end-user. Allen and Blascovich (1996) have demonstrated that there is value in owning a trained dog, but they give no evidence that the dog's performance of particular tasks is in any way a contributory factor.

E. UNREALISTIC EXPECTATIONS

Therapy animals are not usually required to perform complex or physically demanding tasks for their users, although the possibility of excessive social stimulation certainly exists. Service animals, in contrast, are expected to obey complex commands and perform relatively challenging physical activities that create a potential for welfare problems. In their recent study, Coppinger et al. (1998) have been critical of the unrealistic expectations that some service dog programs have of their protégés. They argue that superficially simple activities, such as pulling a wheelchair or opening a swing door, may impose excessive physical strains on a dog that could result in physical injury over time. Furthermore, since the tasks themselves are potentially aversive, and because the dogs have not been specifically selected for performing these tasks the way most traditional working dogs have, they lack any internal motivation to perform, and may, as a consequence, have difficulty meeting the goals of conventional reward-based training or of retaining responses once they have been entrained (Coppinger et al., 1998).

F. USE OF BADLY DESIGNED EQUIPMENT
AND FACILITIES

By analyzing the "physics" of some of the tasks that service dogs are asked to perform, Coppinger et al. (1998) have recently drawn attention to inherent design flaws in some of the equipment used by persons with disabilities that may result in discomfort or injury to the dogs. Harnesses, for example, suggested that the designers did not understand the basic principles of harness design. Some had pulling webs crossed moving parts, thus chafing the dog badly as it moved. Trying to get a dog to pull a wheelchair that is designed to be pushed forces the dog into awkward positions, increasing the difficulty of the task. Some of the tasks, such as pulling a wheelchair or pulling open a door with the teeth, reach the limits of what a dog is physically able to perform.

Various studies have also been critical of conventional kennel-housing for dogs, most of which has been designed to reduce labor costs and facilitate hygiene rather than with the welfare of the animals in mind. Kennels used to house service dogs during training are often cell-like in appearance with opaque barriers separating adjacent pens. Dogs are usually housed singly or, less often, in pairs, and often there is little in the way of toys or other forms of enrichment to relieve the tedium of kennel existence. Dogs housed in these sorts of conditions for long periods display a range of abnormal, repetitive, or "stereotypic" behavior, such as circling, pacing, "wall-bouncing," and barking (Fox, 1965; Hite *et al.*, 1977; Hubrecht, 1993; Hubrecht *et al.*, 1992; Hughes *et al.*, 1989; Sales *et al.*, 1997). Noise levels from barking in some facilities may also be sufficiently loud to cause permanent damage to dogs' hearing (Sales *et al.*, 1997).

G. END-USER PROBLEMS

Although there have been no systematic studies of the problem, anecdotal observations suggest that some assistance dog users are insufficiently experienced with handling or training dogs. As a consequence, dogs may be given inappropriate or ill-timed commands, punished for failing to respond to these commands, rewarded at the wrong moments, and so on (Coppinger *et al.*, 1998). Not surprisingly, a dog may become confused and apathetic as a result of such inexpert handling, and such problems are likely to multiply with the use of less trainable and more socially manipulative species such as nonhuman primates. Some agencies provide refresher courses for their clients with disabilities, or can send a trainer to the person's home to correct special problems. However, greater continuing education efforts by agencies would certainly help to ensure improved quality of life for animals used in this way.

The issue of continuing education is also a significant concern for clinicians who are applying AAA/T in their own practices. As stated in earlier chapters, although clinicians may be very cognizant of treatment goals with their clients, they may be in need of further training on how to incorporate animals into their practice (therapeutically and safely). Hines and Frederickson (1998) point out that without training in the methods that animal contacts impact various consumers, therapists may incorporate inappropriate animals and procedures that will not maximize treatment outcomes. The Pet Partners program developed by the Delta Society includes in-service training in a variety of areas, including an awareness of health and skill aptitude of the animals as well as strategies to incorporate the animals with the clients. The Pet Partner program should be considered as a valuable introduction course.

Furthermore, Turner, in Chapter 19, discusses his perceptions of the value of continued education. He suggests that educational programs should be interdisciplinary in nature, and must combine sound theory along with good practical training. Some topics he suggested include training in the area of ethology and human–animal interactions, the psychosocial benefits of animals as support systems, and risk management concerns.

Clinicians will be able to find continuing education opportunities at conferences and workshops sponsored by organizations such as the International Association of Human–Animal Interaction Organizations and the Delta Society. Furthermore, opportunities may also be located at conferences and workshops sponsored by local and regional humane societies, as well as many other professional organizations interested in the therapeutic utility of the human–animal bond.

III. CONCLUSIONS AND RECOMMENDATIONS

The concept of using trained and socialized animals to assist people with disabilities, or as therapeutic adjuncts, has great intrinsic appeal, exemplifying as it does for many people the ultimate in mutually beneficial animal–human partnerships. Nevertheless, while the advantages to the humans in these relationships may be obvious, the benefits to the animals are by no means always self-evident. Indeed, the use of animals for animal-assisted activities and therapy imposes a unique set of stresses and strains on them that the "industry" is only just beginning to acknowledge.

In this commentary we have tried to identify a number of potential sources or causes of animal welfare problems in AAA/T work. In doing so, it is not our intention to criticize particular programs or practitioners. Rather our goal is to focus attention on specific practices that may give rise to ethical concerns, and which ought therefore be subjected to further scrutiny and study. Nonetheless, although much of what can be said at this stage is necessarily speculative, we consider the following preliminary recommendations appropriate:

1. Those involved in preparing animals for service and therapy need to educate themselves regarding the particular social and behavioral needs of assistance and therapy animals, both to avoid the consequences of social and behavioral deprivation, as well as to permit animals a degree of control over the levels of social and environmental stimulation they receive.

2. During the process of rearing and training assistance animals, transitions between successive handlers or owners should be carried out in such a way as to cause minimal distress due to the disruption of preexisting social bonds.

3. Nondomestic species should not be used for AAA/T work except under exceptional circumstances (e.g., wildlife rehabilitation) and where appropriate care can be guaranteed.

4. Efforts and resources should be dedicated to developing methods of accurately identifying and distributing suitable assistance animals from among those relinquished to animal shelters. These efforts should include research into appropriate behavioral screening methods.

5. The present level of assistance dog "failure" is ethically unacceptable and needs to be reduced. The "industry" should be more aware of the problems inherent in the use of closed, purebred populations of service and assistance dogs. The potential benefits of outcrossing to other populations, and of cross-breeding should be explored to reduce the prevalence of deleterious genetic diseases and to improve infectious disease resistance.

6. The industry should pay more attention to ensuring that assistance and service animals are adequately prepared during development for the tasks and roles assigned to them as adults.

7. Alternatives to the use of aversive conditioning in the training of AAA/T animals need to be investigated and developed whereever possible, particularly with respect to the training of wheelchair dogs. If necessary, the industry should consider discontinuing the use of animals for particular purposes, if alternatives to aversive conditioning cannot be found.

8. More attention should be given to the design and construction of animal-friendly equipment and holding facilities for AAA/T animals.

9. Continuing education programs for animal end-users should be available to ensure that animals are correctly handled and cared for while in field service.

APPENDIX: ETHICAL GUIDELINES FOR THE CARE AND SUPERVISION OF ANIMALS WHILE UTILIZED IN AAT OR AAA

Goal: Incorporating animals therapeutically to assist human clients.
Issue: How to balance the needs of human clients with respect for the needs of the animal.

BASIC ETHICS PRINCIPLES FOR USE OF THE THERAPY ANIMAL

1. All animals utilized therapeutically must be kept free from abuse, discomfort, and distress, both physical and mental.
2. Proper health care for the animal must be provided at all times.
3. All animals should be capable of having a quiet place where they can have time away from their work activities. Clinicians must practice preventive health procedures for all animals.

4. Interactions with clients must be structured so as to maintain the animal's capacity to serve as a useful therapeutic agent.
5. A situation of abuse or stress for a therapy animal should never be allowed except in such cases where temporarily permitting such abuse is necessary to avoid a serious injury to or abuse of the human client.

PROCEDURES FOR ETHICAL DECISION MAKING REGARDING THERAPY ANIMALS

1. Identify the human needs:
   What does the client need from the therapy animal?
   How much time does the client need to spend with the animal?
   What is the nature of the contact/time spent with the animal?
2. Identify the animal's most basic needs:
   Proper care
   Affection
   Quiet time
3. Compare the human and animal needs:
   Only the most compelling of human need (e.g., avoiding serious mental or physical injury) should ever be allowed to take priority over the basic needs of the animal.

IMPLICATIONS OF PROCEDURE FOR ETHICAL DECISION MAKING REGARDING THERAPY ANIMALS

1. If the intervention is unduly stressing the animal, the clinician should suspend the session or the interaction.
2. Therapists using therapy animals must provide "downtime" for the animal several times a day.
3. Older animals and those faced with large amounts of stress should have their service scaled back or eliminated entirely. Attention should also be given to transition the animal as retirement begins. This will help with the animals' sense of wellness.
4. In a situation where a client, whether intentionally or unintentionally, subjects a therapy animal to abuse, the basic needs of the animal must be respected, even if this means terminating the animal's relationship with the client. In a case where a therapist suspects that a client may be likely to abuse the animal, a therapist must take precautions to protect the animal's welfare and rights. When any evidence of stress

or abuse becomes evident, the therapist must terminate the animal's relationship with the client.

5. Clients who severely abuse a therapy animal may thereby destroy the animal's capacity to help others. Clients in this situation thus violate Principle 4.

REFERENCES

Allen, K., & Blascovich, J. (1996). The value of service dogs for people with severe ambulatory disabilities. *Journal of American Medical Association, 275,* 1001–1006.

Broom, D. M., & Johson, K. (1993). *Stress and animal welfare.* London: Chapman & Hall.

Cheney, D. L., & Seyfarth, R. M. (1990). *How monkeys see the world.* Chicago: Chicago University Press.

Coppinger, R., & Schneider, R. (1995). Evolution of working dogs. In J. A. Serpell (Ed.), *The domestic dog: Its Evolution, Behaviour, and Interactions with People* (pp. 21–47). Cambridge, UK: Cambridge University Press.

Coppinger, R., & Zuccotti, J. (in press). Kennel enrichment: Exercise and socialization of dogs. *Journal of Applied Animal Welfare Science.*

Coppinger, R., Coppinger, L., & Skillings, E. (1998) Observations on assistance dog training and use. *Journal of Applied Animal Welfare Science, 1,* 133–144.

Dawkins, M. (1980). *Animal suffering: The science of animal welfare.* London: Chapman & Hall.

Dawkins, M. S. (1988). Behavioural deprivation: A central problem in animal welfare. *Applied Animal Behaviour Science, 20,* 209–225.

Fox, M. (1965). Environmental factors influencing stereotyped and allelomimetic behavior in animals. *Laboratory Animal Care, 15,*(5), 363–370.

Hemmer, H. (1990). *Domestication: The decline of environmental appreciation* (trans. Neil Beckhaus). Cambridge, UK: Cambridge University Press.

Hines, L., & Fredrickson, M. (1998). Perspectives on animal-assisted activities and therapy. In C. C. Wilson & D. C. Turner (Eds.), *Companion animals in human health* (pp. 23–39). Thousand Oaks, CA: Sage Publications.

Hite, M., Hanson, H., Bohidar, N., Conti, P., & Mattis, P. (1977). Effect of cage size on patterns of activity and health of beagle dogs. *Laboratory Animal Science, 27,* 60–64.

Hubrecht, R. (1993). A comparison of social and environmental enrichment methods for laboratory housed dogs. *Applied Animal Behaviour Science, 37,* 345–361.

Hubrecht, R. (1995). The welfare of dogs in human care. In J. A. Serpell (Ed.), *The domestic dog: Its evolution, behaviour, and interactions with people* (pp. 179–195). Cambridge, UK: Cambridge University Press.

Hubrecht, R., & Turner, D. C. (1998). Companion animal welfare in private and institutional settings. In C. C. Wilson & D. C. Turner, (Eds.), *Companion Animals in Human Health,* (pp. 267–289). Thousand Oaks, CA: Sage Publications.

Hubrecht, R., Serpell, J., & Poole, T. (1992). Correlates of pen size and housing conditions on the behaviour of kenneled dogs. *Applied Animal Behaviour Science, 34,* 365–383.

Hughes, H. C., Campbell, S., & Kenney, C. (1989). The effects of cage size and pair housing on exercise of beagle dogs. *Laboratory Animal Science, 39*(4), 302–305.

Mason, G., & Mendl, M. (1993). Why is there no simple way of measuring animal welfare? *Animal Welfare, 2,* 301–320.

McGlone, J. (1993). What is animal welfare? *Journal of Agricultural and Environmental Ethics, 6* (Supplement 2), 28.

Orthopedic Foundation for Animals. (1998, Summer). What is canine hip dysplasia? *Komodor Komments*, pp. 14–15.

Sales, G., Hubrecht, R., Peyvandi, A., Milligan, S., & Shield, B. (1997). Noise in dog kenneling: Is barking a welfare problem for dogs? *Applied Animal Behavior Science, 52,* 321–329.

Serpell, J. A. (1987). The influence of inheritance and environment on canine behaviour: Myth and fact. *J. Small Anim. Pract., 28,* 949–956.

Serpell, J., & Jagoe, J. A. (1995). Early experience and the development of behaviour. In J. A. Serpell (Ed.), *The domestic dog: Its evolution, behaviour, and interactions with people* (pp. 80–102). Cambridge, UK: Cambridge University Press.

CHAPTER 19

Synergy and Symbiosis in Animal-Assisted Therapy: Interdisciplinary Collaborations

PHIL ARKOW

Chair, Family Violence Prevention Project The Latham Foundation, Alameda, California

I. INTRODUCTION

It is apparent, from the chapters in this book as well as from practical experiences, that one of the most compelling features about animal-assisted activities and therapy (AAA/T) is its multidisciplinary nature. This feature provides the field with unique challenges as well as opportunities. On the negative side, the specialist seeking a degree, a certificate, a program protocol, or a job in the field is constrained by the lack of an AAA/T vocational track or curriculum in, for example, occupational therapy or psychiatry. This is balanced, however, by the positive aspect that AAT/T can be integrated into such diverse fields as pediatrics and geriatrics, long-term care and acute care, hospitals and hospices, and correctional and convalescent facilities—but only if multidisciplinary perspectives are incorporated into the planning, implementation and evaluation of the program.

From the outset, AAA/T was—and remains—an interdisciplinary adventure. The earliest American programs incorporated animals in rehabilitative therapy for returning servicemen in World War II; later, AAA/T was utilized in

Handbook on Animal-Assisted Therapy: Theoretical Foundations and Guidelines for Practice
Copyright © 2000 by Academic Press. All rights of reproduction in any form reserved.

clinical psychotherapy and children's psychiatric facilities. Equestrian therapy evolved a specialized regimen. Protocols for training hearing dogs, and later service dogs, replicated the successes of an earlier generation of guide dogs for the blind. Today, the simple concept of animals helping people has blossomed into an array of programs in which marriage counselors, speech therapists, nurses, animal health technicians, veterinarians, physical and occupational therapists, gerontologists, grief counselors, animal behaviorists, and a host of other disciplines contribute their expertise and professional perspective (Arkow, 1998).

Meanwhile, early proponents of AAA/T, many of whom came from the humane movement, began providing services in what became extensive, if somewhat unorganized, programs of anecdotally based visitations in facilities for a diverse array of populations. This created a schism between the "activities" and "therapy" perspectives resulting in heated academic debates (Beck & Katcher, 1984; National Animal Control Association, 1984) between those satisfied with anecdotal, subjective, qualitative assessments and those arguing for data-based, objective, quantitative evaluations. The schism was an archetype of an age-old conflict between academia and field practitioners, pitting curmudgeonly nitpicking against unbridled enthusiasm. The rift was partially resolved by the Delta Society's publication (1996) of standardized definitions that distinguish between these two overarching perspectives and that recognize the various disciplines that may be included under AAA/T purviews.

What should be an elegantly simple model—animals helping people—is further complicated by internecine struggles among institutional administrators, staff members, patients/clients/residents, volunteers, and the animal participants. These groups' respective needs may not necessarily be congruent and a successful program must balance the interests of each sector accordingly (Arkow, 1988).

The AAA/T field is growing, maturing, and turbulent. For the field to flourish, it is incumbent for practitioners and researchers alike to recognize that AAA/T transcends disciplines, that the contributions of all are needed and welcomed, and that synergy and symbiosis will enhance the remarkable progress that has already been made.

II. THE PROCESS OF COLLABORATION

The track record of AAA/T to date has largely been one in which programs have been implemented because one or two key individuals in an institution have an enthusiastic appreciation for "pet therapy" that may not be accepted widely by colleagues. When these individuals leave the facility, the program often goes by the wayside and it is difficult to reinstate it. The most enduring programs have been those that became institutionalized through a symbiotic, synergistic, interdepartmental, and multidisciplinary group planning process in which all key stakeholders are recognized and invested with responsibility, authority, and decision-making through consensus.

Symbiosis is the relationship that occurs when two dissimilar organisms live together for mutual benefit. The term generally describes two species that each gain a survival edge in cohabiting an ecosystem. Studies of the therapeutic benefits of companion animals (Arkow, 1985) have described pets and people as symbionts in the contemporary urban environment in which each species gains physiologic and psychological benefits.

Organizations should be considered living, evolving organisms as well, macrocosms of the entities within them. Community caregiving agencies, whether shelters for homeless pets, health care institutions, or facilities for the challenged, cannot exist in isolation. Nor do they fit nature's other biological roles of parasites, predators, or prey. They must function symbiotically in the community to survive. They exist to benefit the societal ecosystem and they, in turn, are improved. And they are most effective when they work in concert with one another.

If we think of organizations as organisms, we may view the health care field as an example of a macro-organism that has evolved into specializations that may be considered an evolutionary adaptation. In mature environments where resources are abundant but there is intense competition, an evolutionary advantage is gained by those organisms that fill specialized niches rather than those that are broad generalists (who survive better in a new, open, expanding environment) (Budiansky, 1992).

Distinct service delivery systems have developed to address specific diagnoses and treatment regimens. The result is a profession of specialized practitioners who may miss opportunities for healing that involve cross-fertilization from other disciplines or a holistic perspective on the individual case. One of the attractions of AAA/T is that by crossing the spectrum of so many disciplines, it brings a diverse symbiosis of practices into the treatment milieu.

Synergy generally describes a situation in which the whole is greater than the sum of its parts, in which the relationship which the parts have to each other is a part in and of itself. Covey (1990, pp. 262–263) further described synergy as not only a relationship and a process, but also as an empowering and unifying catalyst. He saw synergy as a means to combine a win–win strategy with empathic understanding of other participant's perspectives to unleash people's greatest creative powers and generate new alternatives that were not in existence previously.

To achieve symbiosis and synergy within an organization or a community requires strategic introduction of group processes. These may include networking, cooperation, coordination, coalition building, and collaboration. These terms are not synonymous. Examples of these five processes in the AAA/T field are presented in Table I.

Networking is an informal, nonhierarchical process of communication with low-key leadership, little conflict, and minimal decision making. Roles are loosely defined. The network primarily creates dialogue and serves as a clearinghouse for information or to organize action.

Cooperation is characterized by informal relationships that exist without any commonly defined mission, structure, or planning effort. Information is shared as needed. Authority is retained by each participant so there is virtually no risk. Resources are separate, as are the rewards.

Coordination is characterized by a more formal relationship and understanding of compatible missions. Some planning and division of roles are required. Communication relationships are established. Authority still rests with the individual entities, but there is now some increased risk to all participants. Resources are available to participants and rewards are mutually acknowledged.

Coalitions form to share ideas and to pull resources from existing systems. Leadership is shared; decision making is formal and involves all members. Communication is frequent and prioritized. Often, the coalition has a specific

TABLE I   Examples of Group Processes in AAA/T

Network

An ad hoc special interest group comes together at a national conference to exchange ideas and strategies regarding a common issue, such as the use of llamas in therapy programs. The group maintains its structure throughout the year via occasional newsletters, an on-line listserv, or informal gatherings.

Cooperation

A service dog training facility refers a potential client to another agency that can meet the person's needs more effectively. The second agency is expected to reciprocate with similar referrals, when appropriate.

Coordination

A humane society establishes a program to bring animals to visit a nursing home. A regular schedule is worked out that requires scheduling volunteers and visits. Various permissions are secured.

Coalition

A statewide task force is created to research issues involved in proposed legislation that would increase the penalties for animal abuse and include animal protection personnel among those mandated to report suspected child abuse to government agencies.

Collaboration

Multiple departments of a hospital are organized to meet on a regular basis as an interdisciplinary task force. The goal is to research, implement, maintain, and evaluate an AAA/T program that will introduce animals into several clinical units.

life span to accomplish a specific objective. Roles, time frames and linkages may be formalized, and an independent budget may be established.

Collaboration connotes a more durable and pervasive relationship. Collaborations bring entities that were previously separated into a new structure with full commitment to a common mission. These relationships require comprehensive planning and well-defined communication channels that operate on many levels. Authority is determined by a collaborative structure. Risk is now much greater because each entity contributes its own resources and reputation. Resources may be pooled or jointly secured, and the products are shared.

Collaboration in organizational development is a relatively new phenomenon. Prior to 1970, many people thought it was synonymous with cooperation or coordination; others gave it a negative connotation associated with wartime "collaborators." Collaboration today connotes joint efforts by disparate groups or systems that are directed to achieving a common goal, outcome, or objective that is mutually accepted. Collaboration combines a wide variety of skills, resources, knowledge, and ideas to translate goals and dreams into action by bringing together a wide range of people and systems for a common good. Collaboration celebrates the beauty of difference (Schindler-Rainman & Lippitt, 1992).

Organizational effectiveness, particularly in turbulent social fields, is enhanced under a model of collaboration in which even former competitors work together under the rubric of shared values and a negotiated order (Emery & Trist, 1965). The need to become more effective in a field noteworthy for proliferating single-interest groups and limited public awareness and credibility has led many to recognize the potential utility of building collaborations. Bringing individuals, organizations, disciplines, departments, and professions together to initiate an AAA/T program achieves a synergy in which human, animal, and material resources can effect change that the members are unable to bring about independently.

III. RESOLVING ORGANIZATIONAL DIFFERENCES

It is to be expected that individual and organizational differences of opinion will emerge whenever two or more entities are brought together to plan a program. The resolution of organizational conflicts may be achieved through a variety of strategies that have been studied by behavioral scientists and practicing managers for many years (Szilagyi & Wallace, 1990). These include competition, accommodation, avoidance, compromise, and collaboration. A number of factors determine which strategy is most effective. These factors include the importance of the decision at hand, the relative power of the interacting parties, and the degree to which individual assertiveness or coopera-tiveness dominates the negotiations.

Collaboration is an effective technique to resolve conflicts in these situations:

- The goal is to find integrative solutions when all sets of concerns are too important to be compromised.
- The goal is to learn.
- It is advantageous to merge insights from people with diverse perspec-tives.
- Long-term success may be achieved by gaining commitment from vari-ous entities by incorporating their concerns into a consensus.
- It is necessary to work through feelings that have interfered with rela-tionships.

IV. THE STAGES OF COLLABORATION

The stages of developing and implementing a multidisciplinary collaboration can be summarized as follows (Arkow, 1995).

A. PRELIMINARY WORK

- Determine whether a collaboration is appropriate.
- Identify potential members.
- Define necessary skills, attitudes, and discipline representations that are important.
- Understand operating principles, constraints, and policies necessary to achieve success.

Step 1: Identify the need or problem.
Step 2: Identify outcome(s) that are sought.
Step 3: Specify the group's function and purpose.
Step 4: Define the roles of potential members and secure their involvement.
Step 5: Convene the group:

- Identify information needed.
- Develop work structures.
- Conduct inventory of resources and skills.
- Assign roles and responsibilities.
- Set initial time frames.

Step 6: Refine the organizational structure:

- Meet information needs.
- Establish decision-making procedures.
- Develop mission, goal, and objectives.
- Establish policies and procedures.
- Define sources of legitimacy and authority.
- Identify additional resources that are needed.

Step 7: Develop short- and long-term plans.
Step 8: Develop strategies.
Step 9: Build individual and organizational capacity:

- Identify and provide training needs.
- Obtain necessary resources.
- Enhance effectiveness through coordination, cooperation, networking, and communication.

Step 10: Implement plans:

- Provide support.
- Overcome barriers.

Step 11: Monitor progress.
Step 12: Recognize accomplishments.

B. POSTPROCESS WORK

- Conduct evaluations.
- Revise program as appropriate.

V. THE BENEFITS OF COLLABORATION

There are numerous advantages to involving the perspectives of various disciplines, departments, professions, and special interests within an institution or a community to solve overarching problems (Boatfield & Vallongo, 1999). These include the following:

- The chance to significantly improve each participating entity's effectiveness in achieving its primary mission
- Preventing duplication of effort, allowing more efficient utilization of resources
- Encouraging the sharing of resources and ideas

- Extending the service area
- The capability of addressing even larger concerns on many levels simultaneously, thereby increasing the potential of effecting systemic change
- Creating a sense of trust and community among the participants by offering nurturance, encouragement, recognition, and feedback to everyone, and by sharing effective methods
- The opportunity to brainstorm solutions and approaches in a larger context, thereby generating innovation and shared experimentation
- Reducing unnecessary competition
- An increased public attention, which may, in turn, lead to an improved ability to affect public policy
- Improved organizational and communication skills with the potential for more effective problem solving in the future and in other collaborations
- A collaborative model may be more likely to attract outside funding from grantmakers or government agencies that seek examples of community partnerships.

VI. RESISTANCE TO COLLABORATION

Collaborations are not necessarily easy to effect. They require extensive commitments of time, patience, diplomacy, and an understanding of each participant's perspective and communications style. In a health care institution, for example, resistance to implementing an AAA/T program traditionally comes primarily from departments charged with risk management, infectious disease control, and housekeeping. Other stakeholders, such as families of residents or patients, and some residents or patients themselves, may be reluctant to risk exposure to what they perceive to be threats of bites, allergies, or unhygienic conditions. And human nature's fear of the unknown may lead to stasis that stifles innovation (Arkow, 1988).

There are numerous reasons, both real and perceived, why organizations in general, and a health care institution in particular, may be reluctant to implement an AAA/T program:

- Inadequate information
- Inadequate training
- No forum for interdepartmental input
- Unwillingness to be a pioneer
- Inadequate financial or human resources to handle existing priorities
- Lack of sanction from governing authorities
- Absence of organizational or professional protocols

- Bureaucratic impediments
- Health and sanitation concerns
- Liability concerns

Other issues that affect the ability of disparate entities to collaborate include:

- Trust
- Communication
- Accountability
- The ability to share power and establish equality in relationships
- Mutual needs
- Common vision
- Realistic time frames
- Realistic expectations regarding outcomes
- Acknowledging the self-interests of participants
- One's willingness to take responsible risks
- Ability to establish senior, personal leadership
- Clarity regarding the governance and maintenance of the collaboration
- Adequate funding

The potential for successful collaborations is greatly enhanced when the following conditions exist:

- A safe space where participants, who represent diverse groups of stakeholders, may engage in open dialogue about their values, visions, and feelings
- An environment in which hierarchical distinctions are equalized
- A concept of "common ground" in which stakeholders may agree to disagree on some issues, which are put aside, thereby allowing energies to be focused on areas in which their values and visions intersect
- Participants feel interconnected, empowered, challenged, and committed
- An appreciation for the value of planning
- Participants focus on possibilities rather than on limitations
- Participants recognize the realities of the situation
- Participants learn from each other
- Creativity is stimulated and encouraged

Strategies that participants can use to overcome institutional and individual reluctance to implement an innovative idea include (Arkow, 1998):

- Inviting a wide spectrum of representative perspectives to help design the program
- Engaging in frank problem-solving discussion
- Recognizing the interdependence of departments involved

- Engaging consultants from programs in similar institutions
- Obtaining empirical and anecdotal data from colleagues and recognized leaders in similar institutions
- Compiling authoritative summaries of research findings and practice applications in a format that is comprehensible and meaningful to key decision makers
- Obtaining outside funding to pay for program research, design, and/or implementation
- Implementing the program on a pilot, trial or demonstration basis
- Being patient and willing to compromise

VII. COLLABORATIVE IMPLEMENTION OF THE AAA/T PROGRAM

Numerous models have been developed to assist those who are implementing AAA/T programs, representing a variety of venues. Implicit in all of these models is the acknowledgment that multiple disciplines and departments must be included in the process.

As examples, an early pet program at the Veterans Administration Medical Center in Albany, New York (Leonpacher, undated) was created only after extensive research was conducted by an ad hoc committee comprised of representatives from Recreation Service, Nursing Service, Social Service, Research Service, the Veterinary Medical Officer, and other departments.

A community-based AAA/T program (Lago et al., 1985) involved local human services providers, veterinarians, animal care providers, groups of consumers/clients, and law enforcement and other municipal agencies. This program made provisions for referrals to and from other community resources. Interdisciplinary advisory boards were created, and committee structures, roles, responsibilities, and organizational development were detailed.

An early model (Lee et al., 1983) described the collaborative process in a flowchart format (Fig. 1) that noted the importance of including numerous staff departments. "The full participation of the entire staff (nurses, aides, and housekeeping and custodial personnel) will be necessary if any animal placement is to succeed. Without staff involvement, the chances of unsuccessful placement are high. The staff of the institution must possess the knowledge to plan a placement well, the energy and enthusiasm to make the placement work, and the commitment to care for an animal properly" (Lee et al., p. 7). Other elements of the planning process include distributing pet preference survey instruments and conducting interviews among the residents; determining the institutional characteristics; assessing the facility's physical and social

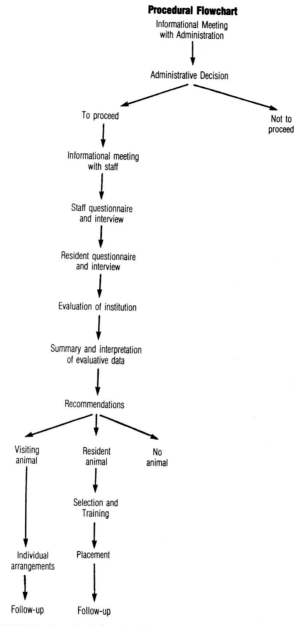

FIGURE 1   Procedural flowchart for placing animals in nursing homes.

spaces; and establishing rules and regulations, and policies and procedures, that will impact the program.

Effective AAA/T program design and implementation requires extensive research and development, components that are particularly critical when introducing a new and unfamiliar concept. Securing consensus among numerous departments is a key part of this process, and several outlines have been published (Abdill & Juppé, 1997; Arkow, 1998) that describe organizational strategies in which interdepartmental and multidisciplinary involvement are implicit if not explicit.

Elements of effective program design include the following:

- Creating an interdisciplinary advisory board, knowledgeable about the patients/clients/residents, animals, departments, and organizations involved, to organize the program
- Determining if the program is feasible for the individuals and the organization and is consonant with the organizational mission
- Ascertaining if time and human and material resources are available for development and implementation
- Establishing costs that are reasonable and compatible with budgetary constraints
- Securing the approval of the organization's governing body
- Gaining input and support from other disciplines to secure their cooperation
- Establishing lines of authority, duties of responsibility, and procedures for quality control
- Providing for backup support and emergency assistance
- Obtaining support from external organizations, such as veterinarians, animal shelters, and community volunteer groups
- Designing evaluation and accountability criteria into the program
- Designing into the program consideration for the welfare of animals, patients/residents/clients, staff, administrators, visitors to the facility, and persons who do not appreciate animals
- Minimizing sanitation, zoonotic, noise, and other environmental impacts that could engender objections to the program
- Minimizing the potential for animal abuse, and understanding potential ethical objections to an AAA/T program (Iannuzzi & Rowan, 1990; Arkow 1998)
- Committing to an organization-wide training effort

Frequently, the veterinary community is overlooked in the AAA/T planning process. This profession's expertise should be invited to monitor the well-being of animal participants and the public health implications of these programs. The American Veterinary Medical Association (1984) published guidelines that encouraged AAA/T practitioners to include veterinarians in animal selection, temperament testing, mitigation of zoonoses, and health care provision.

VIII. EXAMPLES OF COLLABORATION

Some of the most effective models of AAA/T have emerged from the hospital field, an environment accustomed to rigorous programmatic review, outcome-based assessments, and strategic planning processes that often incorporate interdepartmental participation. One such model is the team approach employed by the West Jersey Hospital System in Camden, New Jersey (1997). Planning for the Visiting Animal Program took 26 months. It required conducting national mail and telephone surveys, involved focus groups from numerous support departments, produced a policy and procedures manual, and engaged a team comprised of staff from 14 hospital departments including Infection Control, Volunteer Services, Food Services, Environmental Services, Patient Representative, Plant Engineering, Quality Improvement, Discharge Planning, Community Outreach, Marketing, and several nursing units.

The Visiting Animal Program goal is to provide hospital inpatients with animal-assisted activities that ensure opportunities for motivational, educational, recreational, and/or therapeutic benefits to enhance the quality of life while they are guests of the facility. Volunteers and their animals are coordinated by the Animal Science Technology Program at Camden County College. Each visit includes a hospital staff person who conducts a pre- and post-visit clinical evaluation of the patient's behavior and blood pressure readings. Patients are advised of upcoming visits by announcement cards placed on their dietary trays the day prior to visits: Patients who wish to participate ask their nurse to arrange a visit, and the physician writes an order stating that they may take part.

Collaborative steps that were taken to implement the program included these:

- Presentations to, and approval from, divisional administration, vice president of operations, physicians, president, and board of directors
- Locating certified animal handlers
- Contacting nursing, food services, and housekeeping directors to determine their concerns, obtaining their cooperation, and establishing a commitment for AAA program support
- Conducting a focus group of employees from these departments for the same purpose
- Addressing all concerns identified by the focus groups through a multi-disciplinary quality-improvement team created for the occasion

- Formulating comprehensive policies and procedures covering patient identification, patient protection and contamination, identification of pet and handler, provision of pet toilet facilities, and cleanup of pet accidents
- Providing in-service training to all employees directly involved with the AAA program
- Distributing special editions of in-house publications describing the program to all employees
- Coordinating additional publicity and special events

Needless to say, this degree of interdepartmental and interprofessional cooperation would never have been effected without a significant degree of collaboration.

Other examples of collaboration come from the hospital environment. Hume (1996) described a protocol at Northeast Rehabilitation Hospital in Salem, New Hampshire, that required the disciplines of volunteer training, animal temperament evaluation, and in-service staff education.

One of the oldest and most extensive programs is the Prescription Pet Program at The Children's Hospital (1996) in Denver, Colorado. Animal visits are incorporated into a wide range of treatment milieus including Oncology, the Special Care Nursery, Dialysis Unit, In- and Outpatient Psychology, Medical Day Treatment, and Medical Specialties. Dogs are reevaluated semiannually both medically and behaviorally by two veterinarians, one from the hospital's advisory board and the dog's personal doctor. The hospital's lab conducts tests on throat cultures and fecal samples to test for *Salmonella, Shigella,* and *Campylobacter* pathogens and for parasites. Program guidelines were achieved through a unique collaboration between the hospital's Association of Volunteers and the Denver Area Veterinary Medical Society.

An interdisciplinary model of AAA/T program development in the field of long-term health care comes from the Masonic Home of New Jersey, where Abdill and Juppé (1997) described the introduction of pet programs into a nursing home as a decade-long, evolving process that involved the cooperation and consensus of numerous internal and external constituencies. The growth of this pet therapy program required administrative support, staff recommendations, and the adoption of extensive and practical pet policies and procedures that could not have been accomplished by the Activities Department alone.

> Be realistic and do not try to do it all (something activity professionals are famous for!). Also consider possible turf wars that might occur. What other departments, such as housekeeping, nursing, and/or social services, need to be involved and what might they see as their role in the program? Do not write policies and procedures that concern them without consulting them first. Determine what they are actually willing to do in the implementation of this program. (Abdill & Juppe, 1997, p. 171)

IX. CONCLUSIONS

Engaging a wide range of an organization's stakeholders in a new project promotes synergy. It unleashes the potential for innovative cross-fertilization of ideas, facilitates long-term acceptance and participation, mitigates conflicts, and provides channels of communication to resolve unforeseen problems when they occur. Particularly in the field of AAA/T, in which acceptance of the operating premise is not yet universal and multiple disciplines are drawn, by necessity, into program design, collaborations strengthen the bond not only between people and animals, but also among many organizations, professions, and disciplines in human and animal services.

The relationships between people and animals are complex, multideterminate, and changing; the relationships among people are even more so. The therapeutic applications of the human–animal bond are helping to redefine interspecies interactions as examples of physiologic and psychological symbiosis (Arkow, 1998). Symbiotic relationships among the various disciplines involved with AAA/T can only help the movement to expand into new therapeutic arenas and treatment milieus, develop more professional standards of practice, achieve additional credibility, gather much-needed clinical and research data, qualify for third-party reimbursements, establish career and curriculum tracks, and become recognized as a legitimate, multidisciplinary specialty.

REFERENCES

Abdill, M. N., & Juppé, D. (1997). *Pets in therapy*. Ravensdale, WA: Idyll Arbor.

American Veterinary Medical Association. (1984). AVMA guidelines for veterinarians: Animal-facilitated therapy programs. *Journal of the American Veterinary Medical Association,* 184(2), 146–147.

Arkow, P. (1985). The humane society and the human–companion animal bond: Reflections on the broken bond. *Veterinary Clinics of North America: Small Animal Practice,* 15(2), 455–466.

Arkow, P. (1988). *How to start a pet therapy program*. Alameda, CA: Latham Foundation.

Arkow, P. (1995). *Breaking the cycles of violence: A practical guide*. Alameda, CA: Latham Foundation.

Arkow, P. (1998): *"Pet therapy": A study and resource guide for the use of companion animals in selected therapies* (8th ed.). Stratford, NJ: Author.

Beck, A., & Katcher, A. H. (1984). A new look at pet-facilitated therapy. *Journal of the American Veterinary Medical Association,* 184(4), 414–421.

Boatfield, M. P., & Vallongo, S. (1999). How to build a successful community coalition. In F. R. Ascione & P. Arkow (Eds.), *Child abuse, domestic violence and animal abuse: Linking the circles of compassion for prevention and intervention*. West Lafayette, IN: Purdue University Press.

Budiansky, S. (1992). *The covenant of the wild: Why animals chose domestication*. New York: William Morrow.

Children's Hospital. (1996). *Prescription pet program*. Denver, CO: Author.

Covey, S. R. (1990). *The 7 habits of highly effective people*. New York: Fireside Books.

Delta Society. (1996). *Standards of practice for animal-assisted activities and therapy*. Renton, WA: Author.

Emery, F. E., & Trist, E. L. (1965). The causal texture of organizational environments. *Human Relations, 18*(1), 21–32.

Hume, L. (1996). *Guidelines for developing an animal facilitated therapy program*. Salem, NH: Northeast Rehabilitation Hospital.

Iannuzzi, D., & Rowan, A. (1990). *Ethical issues in animal assisted therapy programs*. North Grafton, MA: Tufts University Center for Animals & Public Policy.

Lago, D., Knight, B., Rohrer-Dann, M., & Friend, G. (1985). *The PACT manual: Promoting bonded relationships between people and animals*. University Park, PA: The Pennsylvania State University.

Lee, R. L., Zeglen, M. E., Ryan, T., & Hines, L. M. (1983). *Guidelines: Animals in nursing homes*. Sacramento, CA: California Veterinary Medical Association.

Leonpacher, R. J. (undated). *A program using pets to enhance the quality of life for VAMC patients*. Albany, NY: Author.

National Animal Control Association. (1984, April/May). Where's the beef? *NACA News*, p. 2.

Schindler-Rainman, E., & Lippitt, R. (1992). Building collaborative communities. In M. R. Weisbord (Ed.), *Discovering common ground*. San Francisco: Berrett-Koehler.

Szilagyi, A. D., & Wallace, M. J. (1990). *Organizational behavior and performance* (5th ed.). New York: HarperCollins.

West Jersey Hospital (1997). *Visiting animal program*. Camden, NJ: Author.

The Future of Education and Research on the Animal–Human Bond and Animal-Assisted Therapy

Part A: The Role of Ethology in the Field of Human–Animal Relations and Animal-Assisted Therapy

DENNIS C. TURNER

Institute for applied Ethology and Animal Psychology, Hirzel, and Zoology Institute, University of Zurich–Irchel, Switzerland

I. INTRODUCTION

As pointed out more than a decade ago (Turner, 1984), the multidisciplinary fields of human–animal relations and animal-assisted therapy (AAT) lacked quantitative, controlled observations on behavior and interactions between owners and their pets and between patients and therapy animals. Without intending to belittle the importance of other disciplines involved or interested in this field, the role that ethology has, and could continue to play, in research and education on the human–animal relationship and AAT should not be underestimated.

Ethology can be defined as the observational, often comparative study of animal and/or human behavior. Whereas in the long run, ethologists are mostly concerned with the biological basis of behavior, their methods and results are not without consequences for the applied fields of human–animal interaction and AAT. As a significant example, one can consider the early studies on dog and cat socialization toward conspecifics and humans (see McCune *et al.*, 1995, for an excellent summary): Both species exhibit a sensitive phase of socialization early in life, during which contacts with members of their own species and/or other species (including humans) influence the social inclinations of individuals for the rest of their lives. In dogs this sensitive phase occurs from 4 to 10 or 12 weeks of age (see Serpell and Jagoe, 1995), depending on the author; in cats, from 2 to 8 (toward humans) or 10 weeks of age (toward conspecifics) (see Karsh, 1984; Karsh & Turner, 1988; Schaer, 1989). Certainly in cats (Hediger, 1988), probably also in dogs (Reichlin, 1994), socialization can take place simultaneously and independently toward members of the same species and toward humans. That dogs and cats involved in visitation and residential therapy programs are socialized toward both is of crucial importance for both risk management and outcomes, not to mention the welfare of the animals themselves (Hubrecht & Turner, 1998).

Animal welfare laws in many countries require that animals be housed and treated in such a way that all of their species-specific needs can be satisfied and that they are not subjected to stress or pain. Therapy animals are no exception. With regard to behavioral and psychosocial needs, ethological studies provide the necessary background information (Turner, 1995a); with regard to stress and pain avoidance, studies from both ethology and veterinary medicine (e.g., Broom & Johnson, 1993) are usually the sources of factual information. Hubrecht and Turner (1998) have provided the most recent review on companion animal welfare in private and institutional settings, but more work is needed in this area. The International Association of Human–Animal Interaction Organizations, IAHAIO, has emphasized the importance of the welfare of therapy animals in its *IAHAIO Prague Guidelines on Animal-Assisted Activities and Animal-Assisted Therapy*.[1]

There have been relatively few ethological studies of the interactions between pets and people, most of these on cats and many from the research team surrounding the author (Goodwin & Bradshaw, 1996; Turner *et al.*, 1986; McCune, 1995; Meier & Turner, 1985; Mertens & Turner, 1988; Mertens, 1991; Turner, 1991, 1995b, in press). These have provided information on the "mechanics" of human–cat interactions; differences between interactions involving men, women, boys, and girls and involving elderly persons versus younger adults; differences in interactions between several breeds of cats; and the influence of housing conditions on such interactions. Cook and Bradshaw (1996) and Goodwin and Bradshaw (1997) have also conducted informative observational studies on human–cat interactions. Many of these results should have consequences for animal visitation and especially psychotherapy programs.

As appropriate in any interdisciplinary field, advances in our knowledge about the human–animal relationship and its therapeutic value can also be

---

[1] Available in various languages from Afirac, 32 rue de Trévise, F-75009 Paris.

secured by combining the methods and results of other disciplines with those of ethology. James Serpell (1983) was the first researcher to consider aspects of a companion animal's behavior in the interpretation results from a nonethological study of the human–dog relationship. He found associations between owner affection toward the dog and such dog behavior and character traits as welcoming behavior, attentiveness, expressiveness, and sensitivity. Over the years, Turner and his research team have borrowed and expanded on the methodology of Serpell's first study to examine the ethology *and* psychology of human–cat relationships (Turner & Stammbach-Geering, 1990; Turner, 1995b; Stammbach & Turner, 1998, in press; Kannchen & Turner, 1998; Rieger & Turner, 1998, in press).

What have ethological studies of human–animal interactions and relationships provided us so far? A few examples, based on the literature just cited, are called for. From the cat research group of Turner, we now know that domestic cats show no spontaneous preference for a particular age/sex class of potential human partners, but indeed *react* to differences in human behavior toward the cats between the different age/sex classes and, therefore, show behavior that would lead us to believe they have preferences. Women and girls tend to interact with cats on the floor, whereas men often do this from a seated position. Children, especially boys, tend to approach a cat quickly and directly and are often first rejected by the animal for this. Adults usually call the cat first and allow the cat to do the approaching. Women speak with their cats more often than men and the cats also vocalize more often with them than with men. Women are also more frequently approached by cats and the animals are generally more willing to cooperate with them than with men. Retired persons show more tolerance or acceptance of the cat's natural behavior and desire less conformity by the cats to their own lifestyles than younger adults. When they interact with their cats, elderly persons do so for longer periods of time, often in closer physical contact with the animals, than younger adults, who nevertheless speak more often with/to their cats from a distance.

Differences in cat behavior related to the animals' sex have been sought but not yet found, although most studies (as well as most cats kept by private persons) were of neutered or spayed animals in past studies. Individual differences in behavior between cats are always statistically significant and these have had to be accounted for in any analysis of other parameters postulated to affect their behavior. Nevertheless, various personality types, for example, cats that prefer playing while others prefer the physical contact of stroking, have been discovered (also statistically) among domestic non-purebred animals. Astonishingly, only one observational study has been published comparing the behavior of just two breeds (Siamese and Persian/longhair) and non-purebred cats in their interactions with humans (Turner, 1995b, in press).

Differences relevant to potential therapy work with cats were found. Nonobservational studies comparing the character traits of many different dog breeds have been conducted with highly significant results for animal-assisted activity/therapy (AAA/T) work (Hart & Hart, 1985, 1988), but ethological studies along the same lines are lacking.

What have studies that combine observational data with indirect, subjective assessments of cat traits and relationship quality by their owners provided? Turner and Stammbach-Geering (1990) and Turner (1991) found correlations that help to explain the widespread popularity of cats, as well as one key to a harmonious relationship between a person and his or her cat: Cats are considered by their owners to be either very independent and unlike humans (who consider themselves, in this case, "dependent") or they are dependent and human-like. Some people appreciate the independent nature of the cat; others, their presumed "dependency" on human care. The authors also discovered that the more willing the owner is to fulfill the cat's interactional wishes, then the more willing the cat is to reciprocate at other times. But the cat also accepts a lower willingness on the part of the owner and adapts its own willingness to interact to that. This "meshing" of interactional goals is one indication of relationship quality.

More recently, Stammbach and Turner (1998, in press) and Kannchen and Turner (1998) combined psychological assessment tools measuring human social support levels, self-perceived emotional support from the cat, and attachment to the cat with direct observations of interactions between women and their cats. Emotional attachment to the cat was negatively correlated with the amount of human social support the owner could count on and positively correlated with the self-estimated amount of emotional support provided by the cat. Attachment to the cat was found to be the more predominant factor governing interactional behavior rather than amount of human support available to the owner.

Most recently, Rieger and Turner (1998, in press) have used psychological tools and ethological observations to assess how momentary moods, in particular, depressiveness, affect the behavior of singly living persons toward their cats. They emphasized that these persons, who had volunteered for the study, were not necessarily clinically depressive. They discovered that the more a person was depressed, the fewer intents to interact were shown. However, the more a person was depressed, the more he or she started an interaction. This means that depressed persons had an initial inhibition to initiate that was compensated by the presence of the cat. People who became less depressed after 2 hours owned cats that were more willing to comply with the humans' intents, than those of people whose "depressiveness" had not changed or became worse. When not interacting, the cat reacted the same way to all moods of the humans. This neutral attitude possibly makes the cat an attractive pacemaker against an inhibition to initiate. Within an interaction the cats were indeed affected by the mood: They showed more head and flank rubbing toward depressive persons. But apparently only the willingness of the cat to comply was responsible for reducing depressiveness. The authors interpreted their results after a model of intraspecific communication between human couples, in which one partner is clinically depressed (Hell, 1994), and found striking similarities. The potential of these findings for AAT sessions involving cats is obvious.

II. UNANSWERED RESEARCH QUESTIONS

Despite the relevant results mentioned from ethological studies and those from investigations combining the methods and interpretations of other disciplines with those from direct observations, we have only begun to "scratch the surface" in the ethological analysis of human–pet relationships. This is true for human–cat, but especially so for human–dog relationships. Given the heavy involvement of dogs in AAA/T programs, it would be prudent to encourage similar studies of dog behavior and human–dog interactions. In particular, the breed differences in behavior and character traits reported in studies using only indirect methods (Hart & Hart, 1985, 1988) are extremely relevant to therapy work and should be substantiated by independent analysis of observational data. Further work on behavioral differences between cat breeds, besides those found between the two character extremes represented by Siamese and Persian cats, is also called for.

Another reason to promote comparative ethological studies of dog–human interactions is the reported difference in general *Gestalt* of the human–dog versus the human–cat relationship (Turner, 1985, 1988): Dog social life is organized around dominance–subordinance relationships, whereas cat sociality (assuming socialization toward humans in the first place) is based on "give and take," mutuality/reciprocity, and respect of their independent nature. This basic difference must be considered especially in psychosocial therapy. Sex differences in dog behavior toward humans have been found (Hart & Hart, 1985, 1988; Sonderegger & Turner, 1996), but these still need to be examined in intact (nonspayed and non-neutered) cats. More detailed work on the communication signals used by dogs and cats in intra- and interspecific interactions is also required, in particular, comparative studies to assess whether the same signals have the same meaning when directed to another species and how that other species interprets them. Mertens and Turner (1988) and Goodwin and Bradshaw (1996, 1997) have made a start, but we have much more to discover in this area.

The study of Rieger and Turner (1998, in press) showed for the first time that moods of cat owners affect their interactional behavior and that the cats can indeed help persons out of a momentary depressive mood. The mechanism through which this probably occurs was postulated, but still needs to be tested; then trials with clinically depressed persons must be conducted. This study also produced the rather surprising (and difficult to defend in front of cat enthusiasts!) result that the cats did not react measurably to the different moods of their owners from the outset, only within an ongoing interaction. However, it is probable that humans and cats send out very fine signals (e.g., gaze, see Goodwin & Bradshaw, 1997) not picked up by the ethogram used in this first study. Again, a finer analysis of communication between cats and their owners using video to record facial mimicry, etc., would be helpful.

Other species than dogs and cats are involved in some AAA/T programs, reportedly with positive outcomes. For example, the effects of watching caged birds or aquarium fish in lowering blood pressure and pulse rate are well documented (Katcher et al., 1983) and their presence can significantly improve the quality of life of residents in institutions (Olbrich, 1995). Nature programs (also involving animals) have reported good results in the treatment of ADHD and CD children (Katcher & Wilkins 1994). Rabbits, guinea pigs, hamsters, etc., are involved in some programs, but also occasionally, improperly housed and/or handled. More ethological studies on proper housing of these species and better education of the AAA/T specialists using them are urgently needed (see later discussion). Again comparative ethological studies of human interactions with these species would be useful: Turner (1992, 1996) has postulated differences in the benefits accrued depending on whether the therapy animal species is interactive and initiative (i.e., establishes contact with the patient of its own volition, such as dogs and many cats do) or simply present during the therapy session as an "ice breaker" (bridge to the therapist) or topic for therapeutic discussion. Presumably many rodent species, caged birds, and fish serve this function.

To summarize, it is clear from the mentioned studies that ethology and ethological methods have much to offer the field of human–companion animal relations and, potentially, animal-assisted therapy, but that much remains to be done. We have, or can expect information on how to ensure the socialization of the animals involved in therapy programs or to assess the degree of socialization in animals up for selection; how to properly house, handle, and care for the animals involved to minimize stress and ensure their health and welfare, thus maximizing potential benefits to the recipients of therapy; differences in interactive behavior between healthy women, men, girls, and boys and between different species and breeds of intact, neutered, or spayed male and female therapy animals, which provide baseline information for therapeutic work with less fortunate human beings; matching the animal and recipient of the therapeutic activities; assessing changes—improvement—in interspecific (human–animal) relationship quality which could (should) parallel changes in interpersonal relationship establishment and quality; and the mechanisms explaining why animals work as cotherapeutic agents.

It is equally clear that the combination of theories, methods, and interpretations from different disciplines can lead to major advances in our understanding of those relations. Therefore, any educational program on human–animal relationships and animal-assisted therapy must, of necessity, be interdisciplinary.

III. A MODEL CURRICULUM FOR CONTINUING EDUCATION IN ANIMAL-ASSISTED COUNSELING/THERAPY AND ANIMAL-ASSISTED ACTIVITIES

An number of universities, mostly in North America, now have faculty positions and/or curricula in human–animal relations (e.g., University of Pennsylvania, Philadelphia; Tufts University, North Grafton; University of California at Davis; Purdue University, West Lafayette; University of Southampton, UK; University of Cambridge, UK) and more will certainly be added to the list as this field expands. IAHAIO has attempted to encourage this with Resolution 5 of its Geneva Declaration[2] of 1995. But few curricula are aimed at the practitioners.

With this in mind, a model 2-year curriculum was developed by an interdisciplinary team representing the fields of ethology, human–animal interactions, animal welfare, psychology, psychiatry, psychotherapy, and social work (Turner et al., 1998). This is being offered for the first time in Europe (Zurich, Switzerland) beginning in April 1999. During development of the curriculum emphasis was placed on the following general points considered to be essential to the outcome: Course work and activities must be scheduled evenings and on weekends to allow participation by persons self-employed elsewhere. A two-tiered level, one for professional counselors (e.g., psychotherapists) and one for persons active in social institutions (e.g., volunteers in animal visitation programs), should be offered, whereas some courses would be attended by persons studying at both levels, and other activities, offered separately for each level. Admission criteria for both levels must be clearly defined. Lecturers and supervisors must be qualified and experienced in the subjects they teach or guide. Theoretical background information as well as practical examples should be covered. Participants at both levels should be given the opportunity to see animal-assisted activities in action during supervised "field trips." For

[2] Available in various languages from Afirac, 32 rue de Trévise, F-75009 Paris.

professional counselors, confidential "suitability evaluations" should take place during the program and the "supervision group" modus must be followed during advanced work. Participants at both levels should complete literature reviews, and a supervised, written final "project report" should be required (to be judged and approved by a joint commission of professionals in the field). An official certificate, specific for each level, should be awarded upon successful completion of all course requirements.

Topics covered and activities foreseen in this 2-year curriculum include the following: introduction to the study of human–animal relationships; review of psychology theory, especially developmental psychology; review of symptoms of frequent psychological disorders; neuroses, and psychopathology; ethology of human–animal interactions; animals as sources of social support; animal welfare; ethical considerations; risk management (safety, zoonoses, animal selection); conversation training; organization of AAAs in institutions; therapeutic riding/hippotherapy; work therapy with farm animals; and special needs and problems of the elderly, children, and juveniles, persons with mental and physical challenges, persons with severe psychological disturbances, and persons in correctional institutions. Visits to institutions offering AAA/Ts, and those providing animals for such, are to be included.

The program offered in Zurich includes some 70 hours of lectures and seminars conducted by a gerontological psychologist, a child psychologist, a psychotherapist, a child and juvenile psychiatrist, a psychiatric nurse, a social worker, a primary school teacher, a special educationist, a physiotherapist/ hippotherapist, the director of a therapy dog visitation program, three veterinarians, the director of a correctional institution, *and* an ethologist. Supervised visits to the following institutions with AAA/Ts cover up to 30 hours: a primary school class, a home for physically and emotionally challenged children, an institution with an animal visitation program in place, an institution offering therapeutic riding, a hippotherapy center, a program offering work therapy with farm animals, a psychiatric clinic, a penal/correctional institution, and a training center for assistance dogs. For the professional counselors (therapists and social workers), 18 hours of supervision group work spread out over the second year of the curriculum are required. Individual, supervised projects at both levels are expected to take between 100 and 200 hours to complete.

Program outcome should be regularly assessed. For the Zurich curriculum this will be undertaken in the third year and measured by (1) critical evaluations by the student participants, (2) reevaluation of the curriculum by the interdisciplinary team of course directors, and (3) assessment of the frequency and quality of practical applications by the former student participants in their own institutions or private practices. The directors of the Zurich curriculum intend to publish the results of this evaluation so that others may profit from their experiences in designing or modifying their own curricula.

In the end, educational programs must be interdisciplinary in another respect, that is, combining theory and practice, offering sound information based on research results of academicians as well as the experience of practitioners in the field.

REFERENCES

Broom, D. M., and Johnson, K. G. (1993). *Stress and animal welfare.* London: Chapman & Hall.

Cook, S. E., & Bradshaw, J. W. S. (1996, July). Reliability and validity of a holding test to measure "friendliness" in cats [abstract]. Presented at ISAZ Conference, Downing College, Cambridge, UK.

Goodwin, D., & Bradshaw, J. W. S. (1996, July). The relationship between dog/dog and dog/human dominance interactions [abstract]. Presented at ISAZ Conference, Downing College, Cambridge, UK.

Goodwin, D., & Bradshaw, J. W. S. (1997, July). Gaze and mutual gaze: Its importance in cat/human and cat/cat interactions [abstract]. Presented at ISAZ Conference, Tufts University School of Veterinary Medicine, North Grafton, MA.

Hart, B. L., & Hart, L. A. (1985). *Canine and feline behavioral therapy.* Philadelphia: Lea & Febiger.

Hart, B. L., & Hart, L. A. (1988). *The perfect puppy: How to choose your dog by its behavior.* New York: W. H. Freeman and Co.

Hediger, A. (1988). Die Freundlichkeit der Katze zum Menschen im Vergleich zur Freundlichkeit der Katze zur Katze. M.Sc. thesis, Zoology Institute, University of Zurich.

Hell, D. (1994). *Welchen Sinn macht Depression? Ein integrativer Ansatz.* Reinbeck bei Hamburg: Rohwolt.

Hubrecht, R., & Turner, D. C. (1998). Companion animal welfare in private and institutional settings. In C. C. Wilson & D. C. Turner (Eds.), *Companion animals in human health.* Thousand Oaks, CA, and London: Sage Publications.

Kannchen, S., & Turner, D. C. (1998). The influence of human social support levels and degree of attachment to the animal on behavioural interactions between owners and cats. In *Abstract Book, 8th International Conference on Human–Animal Interactions, Prague: The Changing Roles of Animals in Society.* Paris: Afirac.

Karsh, E. B. (1984). Factors influencing the socialization of cats to people. In R. K. Anderson, B. L. Hart, & L. A. Hart (Eds.), *The pet connection: Its influence on our health and quality of life,* Minneapolis: University of Minnesota Press.

Karsh, E. B., & Turner, D. C. (1988). The human–cat relationship. In D. C. Turner & P. Bateson (Eds.), *The domestic cat: The biology of its behaviour.* Cambridge: University of Cambridge Press.

Katcher, A. H., and Wilkins, G. G. 1994. Helping children with attention-deficit/hyperactive and conduct disorders through animal assisted therapy and education. *InterActions, 12*(4), 5–9. Renton, WA: Delta Society.

Katcher, A. H., Friedmann, E., Beck, A. M., & Lynch, J. (1983). Looking, talking, and blood pressure: The physiological consequences of interacting with the living environment. In A. H. Katcher & A. M. Beck (Eds.), *New perspectives on our lives with companion animals,* Philadelphia, PA: University of Pennsylvania Press.

McCune, S. (1995). The impact of paternity and early socialisation on the development of cats' behaviour to people and novel objects. *Applied Animal Behaviour Science, 45*(1–2), 111–126.

McCune, S., McPherson, J. A., & Bradshaw, J. W. S. (1995). Avoiding Problems: The importance of socialisation. In I. Robinson (Ed.), *The Waltham book of human–animal interaction: Benefits and responsibilities of pet ownership.* Oxford: Pergamon Press.

Meier, M., & Turner, D. C. (1985). Reactions of house cats during encounters with a strange person: Evidence for two personality types. *J. Delta Soc.* (later *Anthrozoös*), 2(1), 45–53.

Mertens, C. (1991). Human–cat interactions in the home setting. *Anthrozoös* 4(4), 214–231.

Mertens, C., & Turner, D. C. (1988). Experimental analysis of human–cat interactions during first encounters. *Anthrozoös* 2(2), 83–97.

Olbrich, E. (1995). Budgerigars in old people's homes: Influence on behaviour and quality of life. In *Abstract Book, 7th International Conference on Human–Animal Interactions, Geneva: Animals, Health and Quality of Life.* Paris: Afirac.

Reichlin, B. (1994). *Begrüssungsverhalten vor dem Hundeferienheim in Abhängigkeit von früheren Erfahrungen.* Abschlussarbeit, I. E. T. Hirzel, Schweiz: I. E. T.

Rieger, G., & Turner, D. C. (1998). How moods of cat owners, especially depressive moods, affect interspecific interactions and vice versa. In *Abstract Book, 8th International Conference on Human–Animal Interactions, Prague: The Changing Roles of Animals in Society.* Paris: Afirac.

Rieger, G., & Turner, D. C. (in press). How depressive moods affect the behaviour of singly living persons toward their cats. *Anthrozoös* 12(4).

Schaer, R. (1989). *Die Hauskatze.* Stuttgart: Verlag Eugen Ulmer.

Serpell, J. A. (1983). The personality of the dog and its influence on the pet–owner bond. In A. H. Katcher & A. M. Beck (Eds.), *New perspectives on our lives with companion animals,* Philadelphia, PA: University of Pennsylvania Press.

Serpell, J., & Jagoe, J. A. (1995). Early experience and the development of behaviour. In J. A. Serpell (Ed.), *The domestic dog: Its evolution, behaviour and interactions with people.* Cambridge, UK: Cambridge University Press.

Sonderegger, S. M., & Turner, D. C. (1996). Introducing dogs into kennels: Prediction of social tendencies to facilitate integration. *Animal Welfare,* 5(4) , 391–404.

Stammbach, K. B., & Turner, D. C. (1998). Correlations between human social support levels and amount of attachment to cats. In *Abstract Book, 8th International Conference on Human–Animal Interactions, Prague: The Changing Roles of Animals in Society.* Paris: Afirac.

Stammbach, K. B., & Turner, D. C. (in press). Understanding the human–cat relationship: Human social support or attachment. *Anthrozoös* 12(3).

Turner, D. C. (1984). Overview of research on human–animal interaction in Switzerland. *J. Delta Soc.* (later *Anthrozoös*), 1(1), 38–39.

Turner, D. C. (1985). The human–cat relationship: Methods of analysis. In *The human-pet relationship, international symposium on the occasion of the 80th birthday of Nobel Prize winner Prof. Ddr. Konrad Lorenz, October 1983.* Vienna: IEMT and Austrian Academy of Sciences.

Turner, D. C. (1988). Cat behaviour and the human–cat relationship. *animalis familiaris,* 3(2), 16–21.

Turner, D. C. (1991). The ethology of the human–cat relationship. *Swiss Archive for Veterinary Medicine (SAT,* in German), 133(2), 63–70.

Turner, D. C. (1992). Ein Wort zu anderen Tierarten. In M. Gaeng (Ed.), *Mit Tieren leben im Alten- und Pflegeheim.* Munich: Ernst Reinhardt Verlag

Turner, D. C. (1995a). Ethology and companion animal welfare. *Swiss Archive for Veterinary Medicine (SAT,* in German), 137, 45–49.

Turner, D. C. (1995b). *Die Mensch-Katze-Beziehung. Ethologische und psychologische Aspekte.* Stuttgart: Gustav Fischer Verlag (later, Enke Verlag).

Turner, D. C. (1996, June 10–11). Ethological aspects of the human–animal relationship— differences between animal species. Continuing Education Course on Pet Therapy, World Health Organization, WHO Research and Training Centre, Teramo, Italy.

Turner, D. C. (in press). Human–cat interactions: Relationships with, and breed differences between, non-pedigree, Persian and Siamese cats. In A. L. Podberscek, E. Paul, & J. A. Serpell

(Eds.), *Companion animals and us: Exploring the relationships between people and pets*, Cambridge, UK: Cambridge University Press.

Turner, D. C., & Stammbach-Geering, K. (1990). Owner assessment and the ethology of human–cat relationships. In I. Burger (Ed.), *Pets, benefits and practice,* London: British Veterinary Association, BVA Publications.

Turner, D. C., Feaver, J., Mendl, M., & Bateson, P. (1986). Variations in domestic cat behaviour towards humans: A paternal effect. *Animal Behaviour, 34,* 1890–1892.

Turner, D. C., Frick Tanner, E., Tanner-Frick, R., & Kaeser, I. (1998). A curriculum for continuing education in animal-assisted counselling/therapy and animal-assisted activities. In *Abstract Book, 8th International Conference on Human–Animal Interactions, Prague: The Changing Roles of Animals in Society.* Paris: Afirac.

The Future of Education and Research on the Animal–Human Bond and Animal-Assisted Therapy

Part B: Animal-Assisted Therapy and the Study of Human–Animal Relationships: Discipline or Bondage? Context or Transitional Object?

AARON HONORI KATCHER

The Devereux Foundation, Villanova, Pennsylvania 19085, and The University of Pennsylvania, Philadelphia, Pennsylvania 19103

I. INTRODUCTION

This paper will suggest that Wilson's concept of biophilia (Wilson, 1984; Kellert & Wilson, 1993) and Winnicott's (1986) ideas about the transitional relationship can form two poles of theory that could be used to make a series of interesting predictions about animal-assisted therapy (AAT) and its impact on patients. In one sense, the idea of biophilia presents a theoretical perspective that permits study of people's interactions with animals or nature without making any assumptions about the way animals or trees or natural spaces are represented in the mind. However, to study the interactions observed in AAT, or the relationships between people and pets, it is necessary to study how people think and talk about animals. That data, in turn, can be used to make inferences about the kinds of mental constructs that govern the interaction. In brief, pets and people, as Perin suggested (Perin, 1981), have to be examined with the psychoanalytically based constructs of object relationships, especially Winnicott's (1986) concept of the transitional relationship as well as sociobiological theory of biophilia.

Handbook on Animal-Assisted Therapy: Theoretical Foundations and Guidelines for Practice
461

Using both concepts, animal and nature as context (biophilia), and animal as transitional object, this chapter will suggest that the very idea of AAT is probably a misnomer, and that the best interpretation of the evidence we have at hand suggests that there are very few sustained therapeutic effects from contact with animals *that can be demonstrated when the animals are not present.* However, the presence of plants, animals, or natural spaces produces very large and easily observable effects in both normal and compromised populations. These clinical responses are, like the documented health effects of pets, probably dependent on the animals just as the large health effects of human companionship are dependent on the continuing presence of people. It may be more fruitful to think of nature and animals as a context that can optimize health and well-being of the general population and of people with a very wide variety of behavioral problems. In particular, the presence of animals and nature can be thought of as a context that enables people to form more inclusive, more supportive human communities, and permits a broader range of people to achieve a sense of competence and enjoy rewarding social interactions within those communities that incorporate plants, animals, and natural spaces.

The data we have at hand about AAT, the transient physiological changes that occur in the presence of a pet animal, the effects of animals on social interaction, and the effects of pets on human health and behavior all suggest that animals create a context in which very profound changes in human behavior occur. For example, all of the physiological studies detail an effect of context (Baun *et al.,* 1984; DeSchriver & Riddick, 1990; Friedmann *et al.,* 1983; Grossberg & Alf, 1985; Katcher, 1981; Katcher *et al.,* 1983a; Wilson, 1991; Allen *et al.,* 1991) with no evidence of persistence once the animal is no longer present. The same can be said for the studies on the influence of animals on social perceptions: The original observation of Messent (1983) that animals facilitate social interaction; the study of Lockwood (1983), demonstrating that people respond more favorably to human figures drawn with animals; and the study by Hart *et al.* (1987) demonstrating that when children with handicaps go about with their guide or assistance dogs, social interaction is 10 times more frequent than when they travel alone. In all of these situations there is no evidence that the increase in social attractiveness persists once the animal (or the image of the animal) is no longer present.

Where animals are used therapeutically, it is usually the custom to gauge the effectiveness of the therapy by the change of comportment of the patients *while the animal is present.* These effects when measured by anecdotal report (Corson & Corson, 1977) or by some more quantitative technique (Katcher & Wilkins, 1993; Redefer & Goodman, 1989; Beck *et al.,* 1986) are large. What is not easy to discern, at least from reports in the literature, is any effect of the animal's presence after the visiting animals have left the patient's presence (Beck & Katcher, 1984).

In research with children with attention deficit hyperactivity disorder reported in this volume (Katcher & Wilkins, 1983) an immediate strong effect of the presence of animals—largely small animals such as rodents, reptiles, birds, and rabbits—was observed. Yet for the first 3 months of the study there were no significant differences in the children's behavior in their regular school classes. It was only when they had been in the program for 6 months that the behavior change induced by the Companionable Zoo program generalized to the school. However, at no time did it ever affect the children's behavior in the residences where they spent their afternoon and evenings. It was also true that all the positive clinical effects were observed while students had some access to animals.

It would facilitate the exploration of animals as a context or a frame in which certain changes in human behavior occur, if animals were studied as part of a wider context—the presence of plants, animals, and geographic features common to humankind's traditional environment: *the one in which almost all of human evolution occurred.* The time since the inception of agriculture is only 10,000 years; the advent of major cities occurred only 5,000 years ago; and the time in which major portions of the world's population have been encapsulated within man-made structures has been only 150 years—a trivial amount of time in evolutionary scales.

Biophilia is a unifying evolutionary concept coined by E. O. Wilson (Wilson, 1984; Kellert & Wilson, 1993) The concept of biophilia suggests that the human brain is structured to pay selective attention to other kinds of life, and as a result contact with other species, plant and animal, may have important influences on cognition, health, and well-being. Wilson, to rephrase Levi Strauss, believes that animals are not only good to think but necessary to perceive as well. Unfortunately, the idea of biophilia is conflated with moral import, much in the same way as the term *companion animal bond.* It is, however, possible to frame a definition of biophilia independently of any value placed on nature, animals, or biodiversity. For example, a child may kill birds with rocks or nurse a fledgling robin for precisely the same reason: an attraction to animals. An attenuated definition of biophilia that suggests merely that we do pay selective attention to the form and motion of plants, animals, and natural settings permits exploration of the hypothesis without postulating an inherent moral position or a genetic basis for the behavior. We can then explore if exercising this tendency through interacting with nature is beneficial to our well-being and health, leaving open the possibility of cultural rather than genetic transmission.

Recognition of biophilia as a highly general phenomenon suggests that companion animals are only one component of the natural world and they must be examined within a wider array of life. To understand how animals influence human behavior, it is necessary to discern their influence independently of the influence of houseplants, gardens, a view of a tree from a window, and all of the other ways in which people maintain contact with the natural world. The evidence that natural scenery plants, trees, and parks have powerful effects on human behavior, quality of life, and health is as great, or in some areas greater, than equivalent data for the influence of animals (Ulrich, 1979, 1983, 1993). Ulrich (1984) presented data that having a view of a park from a hospital window resulted in being discharged earlier and less use of narcotic analgesic medication. In a wide variety of studies he and his coworkers also demonstrated that looking at nature slides reduced stress in the same way that contact with animals has been shown to reduce stress.

Separation of the effect of the animals in the foreground from the effects of nature in the background would permit investigators to compare processes that are part of interaction with pets to similar activities with other kinds of life. For example, caring for pets could be examined in contrast to caring for gardens or houseplants or enjoying bird feeders or feeding or providing habitat for other kinds of wild animals. Thomas (1994) demonstrated that importing children, animals, and gardens into residences for the aged resulted in decreased medication use and increased longevity. His theoretical orientation was a restoration of a more natural community, less abstract than evocation of the biophilia hypothesis.

The many activities that could influence our health and well-being because they were part of our evolutionary and historical past need not be studied as a unit, but the component parts can be elegantly contrasted with another. For example, in Messent's (1983) study of sociability, the effect of being in the park was additive to the effect of the animals' presence. Unfortunately in the study of Hart *et al.* (1987) on the influence of the presence of an assistance dog on social contacts in public places, no notation was made about any variation in the presence of vegetation. In the Companionable Zoo controlled study of the effects of nurturing animals on children in residential treatment, described earlier, all of the children in both the experimental and control groups were living on the same 300 acres of farmland, and the control group was out of doors in an Outward Bound program, while the experimental group was with the animals in the Companionable Zoo. The results implied that the effect of the animals was additive to any effect of all of those woods, fields, and wetlands.

It is particularly important to consider the biophilia hypothesis when examining the health effects of animal ownership because systematic errors can be introduced by failing to do so. There are strong correlations between dog ownership and single family dwellings and suburban or rural residence (Beck & Katcher, 1996). Thus the effects of gardens, trees, and access to open spaces can be conflated with the effects of pet ownership in surveys. The same problem is present in the longitudinal studies of health and pet ownership. The studies of pets and survival after myocardial infarction, (Friedmann *et al.*, 1980) and the observations of decreased utilization of health services by elderly pet owners (Siegel, 1990), did not take into account the presence of gardens, houseplants, or the activities of gardening or walking amid trees and parks. The studies of facilitation of social interaction or positive social attribution by the presence of animals have not been systematically compared with similar effects that might be produced by the presence of attractive vegetation. Certainly the use of natural settings in advertising suggests that they have the ability to alter human response biases.

More importantly, the failure to incorporate the idea of a general biophilic response tendency into experimental designs has turned our attention away from the effects of plants, animals, and natural spaces on communities. The premature use of the medical model (the widespread use of the term *animal-assisted therapy* directly implies the use of the medical model) and the study of individual patients rather than social contexts have turned attention away from the social effects of inclusion of plants and animals in human families and communities including those in inner cities, schools, hospitals, and residences for the aged or others who cannot live independently. Because one of the most salient effects reported for AAT is social facilitation, and increase in social attractiveness, it would be expected that human communities in which animals and nature were represented could integrate a wider variety of people including those with significant handicaps. It would also be expected that conventional measures of social support, which have been shown to have such a profound influence on health, would also increase.

If the idea of inclusive community is used to reflect back on AAT as it is currently practiced one notes that most AAT is done with volunteers who visit institutions with their pet animals. In the absence of data to the contrary, it is a reasonable hypothesis that the presence of the animal makes the visitation easier for the volunteer, that is, the presence of the animal facilitates the inclusion of the AAT therapist into the hospital or institution. The animal irradiates the entire institution, making patients, staff, and volunteers more attractive to each other.

Thomas (1994) in describing the effects of the inclusion of plants, animals, and children into nursing homes speaks of reconstituting communities. In our work at Devereux, we found that in the presence of the animals and gardens, cooperative, affiliative relationships among the students and between students and instructors were greater than in the rest of the institution. This social attraction and cohesion was noted by visitors who felt that the students' interactions with them had the same welcoming character. Data have shown that, compared to the rest of the institutions in which they are housed, the zoos are characterized by the absence of aggressive and violent behavior. However, that benign, cooperative behavior is dependent on the presence of animals, gardens, and natural settings. When the child leaves the setting, the behavior reverts.

Just as it would be foolish to ignore the contextual effects of animals and nature that are not dependent on any special or particular kind of social relationship with individual animals, it would be equally foolish to ignore the obvious delight that people take in forming both transient and long-lasting social relationships with individual animals. These relationships can be described from an ethological perspective, but to understand them it is necessary to examine the words people use about their animals, how they use those words, and importantly what fantasies about animals' conscious or unconscious do those words imply. Perhaps the best way to explore our ideas about animals and how they influence the ways in which we examine AAT is to explore some of the meanings of the term *human–animal bond:* Although the term *human–animal bond* is consistently evoked by people who do animal-assisted therapy, the therapy is almost never dependent on a persisting bond between patient and animal, instead it is dependent on an *enduring bond between the therapist and his or her animal.* Perhaps the most reliable and well-documented characteristic of AAT as it is currently practiced is the devotion of the volunteer therapists (with the exception of residences for seniors that have adopted the Eden Alternative, or rehabilitation hospitals, there are comparatively few paid positions in AAT) and their faith in the value of contact with their beloved pet for clients or patients. When these therapists are asked to explain the effects of contact with animals on the clients they serve the two most common tropes used are "unconditional love" and "the human–animal bond".

The first question worth exploring is why the term *human–animal bond* is so consistently evoked by people active within the field of AAT. Certainly the growth of research into the nature of human interaction with companion animals was nurtured by people who were deeply concerned with the welfare of animals (Bustad, 1990), and they seized on the term *human–animal bond* because it held the implication that a bond, that is, a sense of mutual obligation, should exist between people and their pets. Unfortunately, in practice, there is no agreed upon definition of what constitutes a bond, nor any way of determining if a bond can be said to exist at all.

Perhaps the best illustration of the highly elastic and almost useless application of the term *bond* can be seen in the work *The Inevitable Bond* (Davis & Balfour, 1992). In this excellent compilation of articles the most diverse kinds of relationships are described, from the evasive and agonistic behaviors of a captive octopus to the prolonged and intricate dialogues that Irene Pepperberg conducted with her African grey parrot, Alex. No apologies are made for this inclusiveness, instead the editors state in the introduction: "The critical reader will note that we have not offered a single or binding definition of key terms in our thesis such as *bond, interaction, and relationship.* Nor have we attempted to restrict our contributors' use of these terms" (italics are the authors) (Davis & Balfour, 1992, P. 4) Unfortunately, none of the authors discusses what circumstances would lead one to assert that a bond does *not* exist between a scientist and the animal object of study. As a result we are left with no reason for the constant assertion that a bond exists—indeed the use of the word *inevitable* forces us to conclude that it will exist in any circumstances in which scientist and animal come together, perhaps even an anesthetized animal and an unconscious researcher. One is left with the suspicion that the editors want to use the term *bond* because of its moral and emotional connotations, not because it defines a particular kind of relationship that can be said to be present or absent. Since scientists who experiment with living animals are under strong attack by the animal rights movement, one wonders if the desire to use the term and make the assertion that the bond is inevitable can be defensive in nature?

If one wishes to assert that bonding is an explanation of the efficacy of AAT one should demonstrate that the subjects show some evidence of mourning or distress if a particular therapy animal is removed and replaced with another. Indeed, were mourning to occur, it would constitute a significant negative side effect of the therapeutic interaction. There is no study where evidence of this sort has been presented. I know of none in which the effect of constant contact with one animal has been contrasted with limited contact with a number of animals. Certainly, in practice, therapists report that subjects do ask after particular dogs, but in the realities of practice volunteers and their animals rotate or are replaced over time. In our work with children (Katcher & Wilkins, 1993, 1997, and this volume), none of the effects we observed were dependent on bonding with or adoption of a single animal, and it was our impression that contact with many animals and introduction of new animals enhanced the therapeutic and educational effect. Children in the program liked raising chicks and ducklings, that were then sold to dealers for animal food. The same children raised mice and rats, playing with them helping in their care, and using the same touch talk dialogue seen with dogs—and later participated in feeding these animals to snakes and hawks with no signs of distress. Snakes, a kind of animal that is feared by many subjects, have been used in our Companionable Zoo programs and described in the literature as having the same therapeutic effects as "furry" animals.

How transient relationships become persistent ones, that is, how a bond develops, is not known, and the problem is beyond the scope of this paper (Katcher & Rosenberg, 1979; Stutts, 1994). It is relevant not to the therapeutic effects of AAT, but to the motivation and comportment of AAT practitioners. To understand AAT, it is necessary to recognize that the process is dependent on relatively transient and relatively stereotyped interactions with unfamiliar (to the patient or client) animals that have the following characteristics:

- It can occur immediately, instantaneously, with a strange (unknown) animal and can be terminated equally abruptly without evident signs of mourning.
- It is characterized by a kind of touch talk dialogue that has the form of intimate dialogue and resembles that occurring between people in the general population and their pets, parents, and children or between lovers.
- The process is characterized by expressed positive affect by patients, staff, and AAT therapist.
- The presence of the animal acts like an adjective, modifying the behavior of the people in the same field with the animal and modifying the social perceptions of those observing the interaction.
- Play and games are important parts of the interaction. The play can be described behaviorally, but it is conceptual as well as evidenced by the common practice of dressing the animal in human clothing.
- The presence of the animal results in increased frequency of social interaction between people and animals and between people.
- The contact with the animal frequently stimulates recall and reminiscences about other animals, and people associated with those animals that were part of the person's history.
- Responses of normal and clinical populations are qualitatively similar.

This kind of rapidly formed, easily terminated relationship can be best understood in the context of Winnicott's (1971, 1986) concept of a transitional relationship and transitional object. The depth and breath of Winnicott's conceptualization of the "transitional object" has been sadly constricted by its automatic equation with a stuffed toy or a fragment of a torn and soiled blanket. Winnicott who, more than any other psychoanalytic theorist knew the value of play in human life, talked of a "transitional relationship", that both created and transcended the play with the stuffed toys and security blankets of early childhood. In a transitional relationship a child or an adult takes the attributes of a purely subjective object, a fantasy object, and projects them onto some real entity in the external world. In the transitional relationship the play is the movement of attributes of fantasy objects from an internal space to real objects in external space.

Animals make good transitional beings because they move and show intentional behavior, behaving more like a person than a stuffed toy who just lies there unless moved by the child. Unlike stuffed toys who provide soft touch, animals are capable of giving active affection and seeking out the child. But most importantly, they can never contradict the attributes projected onto them with words. Throughout our entire lives, our animals are there as transitional objects, being what we imagine them to be, serving as vehicles for projecting those admirable traits that we find so lacking in fellow human beings. They even serve with their coat of shining virtues to redefine by contrast the uncertain and amoral world of human companions.

The importance of fantasy in relationships with animals was first described by Perin (1981) in a sadly neglected theoretical article. Perin noted that our expectations from relationships with dogs were "supersaturated" and described them as "transitional objects." However she also noted a transitivity in the relationship: "They do not reconcile that, however, with their equal certainty that dogs represent surrogate children. Although they do not say so, perhaps what they mean is that babying encompasses being babied in that people are giving what they want to get, or that in the minds of infants they and their mother are felt to be one" (p. 81). She also suggests that we turn to animals for this kind of love because we realize that re-creation of the mother–infant bond is impossible in real life. More importantly, she suggests that the anger at least some feel about giving up the security of being a loved infant, or the anger stemming from bad parenting, can also be projected onto the human–animal relationship. In this she follows Winnicott who noted of the transitional object that "It must survive instinctual loving, and also hating, and, if it be a feature, pure aggression."

The animal is also a split object. This is not to say that many if not most owners cannot observe the reality of the animals' behavior; however, they do tend to talk about their animals as if they had human traits of love, devotion, loyalty, and compassion, which are purely human attributes because they are defined by words used by people and cannot be reduced to behavioral attributes alone. The significance of the anthropomorphic terminology is discussed later, but it is important that part of the verbal and behavioral play with animals in the space defined by the transitional relationship is the creation of a representation of the animal that is impossibly good, and represents a wish rather than a reality. Pet animals and the animals used in therapeutic contexts become "good" split objects, but animals can also be "bad" objects as well. Consider the old reputation of wolves, snakes, sharks, spiders, rats, and many insects.

The degree to which accurate perception of animal behavior and fantasy associated with the transitional relationship can coexist can be seen in the writings of Konrad Lorenz about dogs. For much of his career, Lorenz (1953) contrasted the noble race of dogs who were one "one man dogs" (I think the emphasis was on "man" and one wonders if the ideal dyad was not noble dog and German man) and descended from the equally noble wolf with the indiscriminately affectionate women's dogs assigned a descent from the morally reprehensible jackal. Thus Lorenz, one of the founding fathers of ethology, permitted his need to create a transitional object out of his dogs triumph over his undoubted abilities as a scientific observer. The idea of "one-man" or now "one-woman" dogs is in itself another bit of evidence for the transitional nature of our relationship with pets. Winnicott gives as the first characteristic of the transitional object, "The infant assumes rights over the object" (1986, p. 258).

Training in formation of transitional relationships with pet animals (or even a wider variety of animals) begins with the stuffed animals of the nursery and continues in the stories we read to children in which animals act out human roles, sometimes along with their animal ones, and sometimes without. It continues, as Perin (1981) suggested, in the whole set of expectations for more than human virtue, built up around pets and the human–animal bond. Play with animals in a transitional relationship has an ancient and probably universal history that antedates Western culture or recorded history. If the beliefs of modern hunting and gathering tribes are any clue to ancient belief, animals were always given souls, not much different from, and perhaps interchangeable with, human souls. This kind of anthropomorphic reasoning did not, of course, interfere with highly accurate observations of the realities of animal behavior. Objective "ethological" observations of animal behavior and transitional relationship with animals always ran hand in hand.

If we recognize the transitional character of relationships with pet animals and the kind of conceptual play that exists in that relationship we can make a number of interesting predictions about AAT:

• Because most AAT therapists work with their own pets and are closely bonded to them (For instance, Delta "pet partners" are registered in owner–animal pairs), their own behavior may change significantly in the presence of their animals. We do not know to what extent the client response to the animal is conditioned by the behavior of the owner. This is an academic problem at present when volunteers administer most therapy, but if the field should become professionalized, and health professionals who are not particularly bonded to animals or to the animal used in therapy, this question could assume clinical importance. Would AAT be different if the therapists were not involved in the kind of loving care of animals that builds bonds?

• Parents do not make good observers of their own children's behaviors. It would follow that AAT therapists who are bonded to animals may not be good observers of the process. Indeed, if they were "objective observers," the process might not operate in the same way. For this reason, as Turner (this volume) suggested, good ethological observations of the AAT process are required, and judgments about clinical results are best made from videotapes so that the observer is not subject to the attribution biases produced by the presence of the animal.

• If pet animals were transitional objects, we would expect hostile and destructive responses as well as the social facilitation usually reported. Because of the bonding between therapist and animal, we would expect that these episodes would go underreported because they are usually perceived as therapeutic failures.

• The most remarkable effects of AAT, the social facilitation and positive attribution bias, represent a previously unexamined aspect of object relationships. There is, to my knowledge, no other illustration of so common an event that has the ability to improve the social attractiveness of people. Moreover, there is no good explanation of why pet animals have that ability or what the limits are—cultural, historical or psychological—of that positive change in social attractiveness.

II. CONCLUSION

This chapter has discussed the value of using the very different concepts of biophilia and transitional relationships to study human–animal interaction, particularly those observed in AAT. It suggested that there is value in placing interaction with animals in the wider context of interaction with plants, gardens, open spaces, and wilderness. More importantly, it suggests that use of the medical model inherent in the idea of AAT for describing the effects of interactions between people and animals obscures more than it illuminates. Therapy is an impoverished way of examining the powerful effects of human–animal interaction because it ignores the sustaining function of human–animal interaction and the dependence of the beneficial effects of contact with animals on the animal's continuing presence. Importantly an emphasis on "therapy" distracts us from the very powerful effects that animals and the people who are devoted to them could have on building communities that have the capacity of including a highly diverse range of human beings and helping all to both reach their full potential for health and well-being.

REFERENCES

Allen, K. M., Blascovich, J., Tomaka, J., & Kelsey, R. M. (1991). Presence of human friends and pet dogs as moderators of autonomic responses to stress in women. *Journal of Personality and Social Psychology* **61**, 582–589.

Baun, M., Bergstrom, N., Langston, N., & Thoma,I. (1984) Physiological effects of petting dogs: Effects of attachment. In R. Anderson, B. Hart, & A. Hart (Eds.), *The pet connection: Influence on our Health and Quality of Life*. St. Paul, MN: Grove Publishing

Beck, A. M., & Katcher, A. (1984). A new look at pet facilitated therapy. *Journal of the American Veterinary Association* **184**, 414–421.

Beck, A. M., & Katcher, A. (1996). Between Pets and People: The Importance of Animal Companionship. West Lafayette, Indiana, Purdue University Press.

Beck, A. M., Serarydarian, L., & Hunter, G. F. (1986). Use of animals in the rehabilitation of psychiatric inpatients. *Psychological Reports, 58*, 63–66.

Bustad, L. (1990). *Compassion: Our last great hope*. Renton, WA: Delta Society.

Corson, S. A., & Corson, E. (1977). The socializing role of pet animals in nursing homes: An experiment in non-verbal communication therapy. In L. Lewvi (Ed.), *Society, stress, and disease* (pp. 1–47). London: Oxford University Press.

Davis, H., & Balfour, D. (1992). *The inevitable bond.* Cambridge, UK: Cambridge University Press.

DeSchriver, M., & Riddick, C. (1990). Effects of watching aquariums on elders' stress. *Anthrozoös* 4(1), 44–48.

Friedmann, E., Katcher, A., Lynch, J., & Thomas, S. (1980). Animal companions and one-year survival of patients discharged from a coronary care unit. *Public Health Reports,* 95(4), 307–312.

Friedmann, E., Katcher, A., Thomas, S., Lynch, J. J., & Messent, P. (1983). Social interaction and blood pressure: Influence of animal companions. *Journal of Nervous and Mental Disease,* 171, 461–465.

Grossberg, J., & Alf, E. (1985). Interaction with pet dogs: Effects on human cardiovascular response. *J. Delta Society* 2, 20–27.

Hart, L. A., Hart, B. L., & Bergin, B. (1987). Socializing effects of service dogs for people with disabilities. *Anthrozoös,* 1(1), 41–44.

Hirsh-Pasek, K., & Treiman, R. (1982). Doggerel: Motherese in a new context. *Journal of Children's Language* 9(1), 229–237.

Katcher, A. (1981). Interactions between people and their pets: Form and function. In Bruce Fogle (Ed.), *Interrelations between people and pets.* Springfield, IL: Charles C. Thomas.

Katcher, A. (1983). Man and the living environment: An excursion into cyclical time. In A. Katcher & A. Beck (Eds.), *New perspectives on our lives with companion animals.* Philadelphia, PA: University of Pennsylvania Press.

Katcher, A., & Beck, A. (1989). Human–animal Communication. In E. Barnow (Ed.), *International encyclopedia of communications,* London: Oxford University Press.

Katcher, A., & Beck, A. M. (1991). Animal companions; more companion than animal. In M. Robinson & L. Tiger (Eds.), *Man and Beast Revisited* Washington, DC: Smithsonian Institution.

Katcher, A., & Campbell, C. (1990). Social interaction with animals. Paper presented to the 1990 Meeting of the Pavlovian Society, Philadelphia, PA.

Katcher, A., & Rosenberg, M., (1979). Euthanasia and the management of the client's grief. *Compendium on Continuing Education for the Small Animal Practitioner,* 1, 887.

Katcher, A., & Wilkins, G., (1993). Dialogue with animals: Its nature and culture. In S. Kellert & E. O. Wilson (Eds.), *The biophilia hypothesis.* Washington, DC: Island Press.

Katcher, A., & Wilkins, G. (1997). Animal Assisted Therapy in the Treatment of Disruptive Behavior Disorders. In A. Lundberg (Ed.), *Environment and Mental Health,* pp. 193–204. Mahwah, NJ: Lawrence Erlbaum Associates.

Katcher, A., Friedmann, E., Beck, A., & Lynch, J. (1983a). Looking, talking and blood pressure: The physiological consequences of interaction with the living environment. In A. Katcher & A. Beck (Eds.), *New perspectives on our lives with companion animals.* Philadelphia, PA: University of Pennsylvania Press.

Katcher, A., Segal, H, & Beck, A. (1984). Comparison of contemplation and hypnosis for the reduction of anxiety and discomfort during dental surgery. *American Journal of Clinical Hypnosis,* 27, 14–21.

Kellert, S., & Wilson, E. O. (1993). *The biophilia hypothesis* Washington, DC: Island Press.

Lockwood, R. (1983). The influence of animals on social perception. In A. Katcher & A. Beck (Eds.), *New perspectives on our lives with companion animals.* Philadelphia, PA: University of Pennsylvania Press.

Lorenz, K. Z. (1953). *Man meets dog.* New York: Penguin Books.

Messent, P. (1983). Social facilitation of contact with other people by pet dogs. In A. Katcher and A. Beck (Eds.), *New perspectives on our lives with companion animals.* Philadelphia, PA: University of Pennsylvania Press.

Perin, C., Dogs as symbols in human development. In B. Fogle (Ed.), *Interrelations between People and Pets*. Springfield, IL: Charles C. Thomas.

Redefer, L., & Goodman, J. (1989). Brief report: Pet-facilitated therapy with autistic children. *Journal of Autism and Developmental Disorders*, 19(3), 461–467.

Siegel, J. (1990). Stressful life events and use of physician services among the elderly: The moderating role of pet ownership. *Journal of Personality and Social Psychology*, 58(6), 1081–1086.

Stutts, J. (1994). Pet bereavement counseling: Factors related to pet owner depression in a local veterinary hospital versus a veterinary teaching hospital. Doctoral dissertation, Waldon University, Minneapolis, MN.

Thomas, W. (1994). The Eden Alternative: Nature, Hope and Nursing Home, Sherburne, New York: The Eden Alternative Foundation.

Ulrich, R., (1979). Visual landscapes and psychological well-Being. *Landscape Research*, 4(1), 17.

Ulrich, R., (1983). Aesthetic and affective response to natural environment. In I. Altman & J. Wohlwill, (Eds.) *Behavior and the natural environment*. New York: Plenum.

Ulrich, R. (1984). View through a window may influence recovery from surgery. *Science*, 224, 420.

Ulrich, R. (1993). Biophilia and Biophobia. In S. Kellert & E. O. Wilson (Eds.), *The biophilia hypothesis*. Washington, DC: Island Press.

Wilson, C. (1991). The pet as an anxiolytic intervention. *Journal of Nervous and Mental Disease*, 179, 482–489.

Wilson, E. (1984). *Biophilia*. Cambridge, MA: Harvard University Press.

Winnicott, D. W., (1971). *Playing and reality*. London, Tavistock.

Winnicott, D. W. (1986). Transitional objects and transitional phenomena. In P. Buckley (Ed.), *Essential papers on object relations*. New York: New York University Press.

INDEX